LEARNSMART ADVANTAGE WORKS

LEARNSMART®

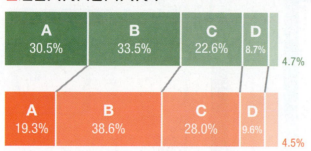

A	B	C	D	
30.5%	33.5%	22.6%	8.7%	4.7%

A	B	C	D	
19.3%	38.6%	28.0%	9.6%	4.5%

Without LearnSmart

More C students earn B's

*Study: 690 students / 6 institutions

Over 20%
more students pass the class with LearnSmart

*A&P Research Study

LEARNSMART® Pass Rate - 70%

Without LearnSmart Pass Rate - 57%

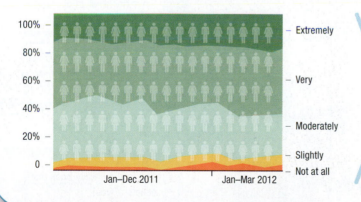

- Extremely
- Very
- Moderately
- Slightly
- Not at all

Jan–Dec 2011   Jan–Mar 2012

More than 60%
of all students agreed LearnSmart was a very or extremely helpful learning tool

*Based on 750,000 student survey responses

> AVAILABLE ON-THE-GO

http://bit.ly/LS4Apple

http://bit.ly/LS4Droid

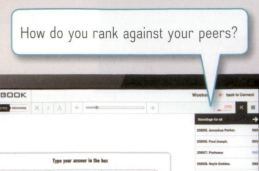

How do you rank against your peers?

Let's see how confident you are on the questions.

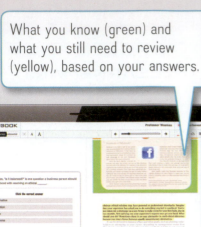

What you know (green) and what you still need to review (yellow), based on your answers.

COMPARE AND CHOOSE WHAT'S RIGHT FOR YOU

	BOOK	LEARNSMART	ASSIGNMENTS	
connect	✓	✓	✓	LearnSmart, assignments, and SmartBook—all in one digital product for maximum savings!
connect Looseleaf	✓	✓	✓	Pop the pages into your own binder or carry just the pages you need.
connect Bound Book	✓	✓	✓	The #1 student choice!
SMARTBOOK™ Access Code	✓	✓		The first and only book that adapts to you!
LEARNSMART ADVANTAGE Access Code		✓		The smartest way to get from a B to an A.
CourseSmart eBook	✓			Save some green and some trees!
create™	✓	✓	✓	Check with your instructor about a custom option for your course.

> Buy directly from the source at http://shop.mheducation.com.

Focus on Personal Finance

An Active Approach to Help You Achieve Financial Literacy

FIFTH EDITION

The McGraw-Hill/Irwin Series in Finance, Insurance, and Real Estate

Stephen A. Ross,
Franco Modigliani Professor of Finance and Economics, Sloan School of Management, Massachusetts Institute of Technology, Consulting Editor

FINANCIAL MANAGEMENT

Block, Hirt, and Danielsen
Foundations of Financial Management
Fifteenth Edition

Brealey, Myers, and Allen
Principles of Corporate Finance
Eleventh Edition

Brealey, Myers, and Allen
Principles of Corporate Finance, Concise
Second Edition

Brealey, Myers, and Marcus
Fundamentals of Corporate Finance
Eighth Edition

Brooks
FinGame Online 5.0

Bruner
Case Studies in Finance: Managing for Corporate Value Creation
Seventh Edition

Cornett, Adair, and Nofsinger
Finance: Applications and Theory
Third Edition

Cornett, Adair, and Nofsinger
M: Finance
Third Edition

DeMello
Cases in Finance
Second Edition

Grinblatt (editor)
Stephen A. Ross, Mentor: Influence through Generations

Grinblatt and Titman
Financial Markets and Corporate Strategy
Second Edition

Higgins
Analysis for Financial Management
Eleventh Edition

Kellison
Theory of Interest
Third Edition

Ross, Westerfield, and Jaffe
Corporate Finance
Tenth Edition

Ross, Westerfield, Jaffe, and Jordan
Corporate Finance: Core Principles and Applications
Fourth Edition

Ross, Westerfield, and Jordan
Essentials of Corporate Finance
Eighth Edition

Ross, Westerfield, and Jordan
Fundamentals of Corporate Finance
Eleventh Edition

Shefrin
Behavioral Corporate Finance: Decisions that Create Value
First Edition

White
Financial Analysis with an Electronic Calculator
Sixth Edition

INVESTMENTS

Bodie, Kane, and Marcus
Essentials of Investments
Ninth Edition

Bodie, Kane, and Marcus
Investments
Tenth Edition

Hirt and Block
Fundamentals of Investment Management
Tenth Edition

Jordan, Miller, and Dolvin
Fundamentals of Investments: Valuation and Management
Seventh Edition

Stewart, Piros, and Heisler
Running Money: Professional Portfolio Management
First Edition

Sundaram and Das
Derivatives: Principles and Practice
Second Edition

FINANCIAL INSTITUTIONS AND MARKETS

Rose and Hudgins
Bank Management and Financial Services
Ninth Edition

Rose and Marquis
Financial Institutions and Markets
Eleventh Edition

Saunders and Cornett
Financial Institutions Management: A Risk Management Approach
Eighth Edition

Saunders and Cornett
Financial Markets and Institutions
Sixth Edition

INTERNATIONAL FINANCE

Eun and Resnick
International Financial Management
Seventh Edition

REAL ESTATE

Brueggeman and Fisher
Real Estate Finance and Investments
Fourteenth Edition

Ling and Archer
Real Estate Principles: A Value Approach
Fourth Edition

FINANCIAL PLANNING AND INSURANCE

Allen, Melone, Rosenbloom, and Mahoney
Retirement Plans: 401(k)s, IRAs, and Other Deferred Compensation Approaches
Eleventh Edition

Altfest
Personal Financial Planning
First Edition

Harrington and Niehaus
Risk Management and Insurance
Second Edition

Kapoor, Dlabay, Hughes, and Hart
Focus on Personal Finance: An Active Approach to Help You Achieve Financial Literacy
Fifth Edition

Kapoor, Dlabay, and Hughes
Personal Finance
Eleventh Edition

Walker and Walker
Personal Finance: Building Your Future
First Edition

Focus on Personal Finance

An Active Approach to Help You Achieve Financial Literacy

FIFTH EDITION

Jack R. Kapoor
COLLEGE OF DUPAGE

Les R. Dlabay
LAKE FOREST COLLEGE

Robert J. Hughes
DALLAS COUNTY COMMUNITY COLLEGES

Melissa M. Hart
NORTH CAROLINA STATE UNIVERSITY

McGraw Hill Education

FOCUS ON PERSONAL FINANCE: AN ACTIVE APPROACH TO HELP YOU ACHIEVE FINANCIAL LITERACY, FIFTH EDITION

Published by McGraw-Hill Education, 2 Penn Plaza, New York, NY 10121. Copyright © 2016 by McGraw-Hill Education. All rights reserved. Printed in the United States of America. Previous editions © 2013, 2010, 2008, and 2006. No part of this publication may be reproduced or distributed in any form or by any means, or stored in a database or retrieval system, without the prior written consent of McGraw-Hill Education, including, but not limited to, in any network or other electronic storage or transmission, or broadcast for distance learning.

Some ancillaries, including electronic and print components, may not be available to customers outside the United States.

This book is printed on acid-free paper.

2 3 4 5 6 7 8 9 0 RMN/RMN 1 0 9 8 7 6 5

ISBN 978-0-07-786174-2
MHID 0-07-786174-4

Senior Vice President, Products & Markets: *Kurt L. Strand*
Vice President, General Manager, Products & Markets: *Marty Lange*
Vice President, Content Design & Delivery: *Kimberly Meriwether David*
Managing Director: *James Heine*
Executive Brand Manager: *Charles Synovec*
Lead Product Developer: *Michele Janicek*
Product Developer: *Jennifer Upton*
Director of Digital Content Development: *Doug Ruby*
Digital Development Editor: *Meg B. Maloney*
Marketing Manager: *Melissa S. Caughlin*
Production Program Manager, Economics and Finance: *Mark Christianson*
Content Project Managers: *Keri Johnson/Kristin Bradley*
Senior Buyer: *Michael McCormick*
Senior Designer: *Debra Kubiak*
Cover Image: *© AJ Wilhelm/Getty*
Lead Content Licensing Specialist, Image: *Keri Johnson*
Lead Content Licensing Specialist, Text: *Beth Thole*
Compositor: *SPi Global*
Printer: *R. R. Donnelley*

All credits appearing on page or at the end of the book are considered to be an extension of the copyright page.

Library of Congress Cataloging-in-Publication Data

Kapoor, Jack R., 1937–
  Focus on personal finance : an active approach to help you achieve
financial literacy/Jack R. Kapoor, Les R. Dlabay, Robert J. Hughes, Melissa M. Hart.—Fifth edition.
    pages cm
  ISBN 978-0-07-786174-2 (alk. paper)
  1. Finance, Personal. 2. Investments. I. Dlabay, Les R. II. Hughes, Robert
James, 1946– III. Hart, Melissa M. IV. Title.
HG179.K368 2016
332.024—dc23
                                                          2014041672

The Internet addresses listed in the text were accurate at the time of publication. The inclusion of a website does not indicate an endorsement by the authors or McGraw-Hill Education, and McGraw-Hill Education does not guarantee the accuracy of the information presented at these sites.

www.mhhe.com

Dedication

To my wife, Theresa, and my children, Karen, Kathryn, and Dave; and in the memory of my parents, Ram and Sheela Kapoor

To my wife, Linda, and my children, Carissa and Kyle; and the memory of my parents, Les and Mary Dlabay

To my mother, Barbara Y. Hughes; and my wife, Peggy

To my husband, David Hart; and my children, Alex and Madelyn

Focus on . . . the Authors

Jack R. Kapoor, EdD, *College of DuPage*

Jack Kapoor is a professor of business and economics in the Business and Technology Division of the College of DuPage, Glen Ellyn, Illinois, where he has taught business and economics since 1969. He received his BA and MS from San Francisco State College and his EdD from Northern Illinois University. He previously taught at Illinois Institute of Technology's Stuart School of Management, San Francisco State University's School of World Business, and other colleges. Professor Kapoor was awarded the Business and Technology Division's Outstanding Professor Award for 1999–2000. He served as an assistant national bank examiner for the U.S. Treasury Department and has been an international trade consultant to Bolting Manufacturing Co., Ltd., Mumbai, India.

Dr. Kapoor is known internationally as a co-author of several textbooks, including *Business: A Practical Approach* (Rand McNally), *Business* (Cengage Learning), *Business and Personal Finance* (Glencoe), and *Personal Finance* (McGraw-Hill). He served as a content consultant for the popular national television series *The Business File: An Introduction to Business* and developed two full-length audio courses in Business and Personal Finance. He has been quoted in many national newspapers and magazines, including *USA Today, U.S. News & World Report,* the *Chicago Sun-Times, Crain's Small Business,* the *Chicago Tribune,* and other publications.

Dr. Kapoor has traveled around the world and has studied business practices in capitalist, socialist, and communist countries.

Les R. Dlabay, EdD, *Lake Forest College*

Teaching about the "Forgotten Majority" (the three billion people living on $2 or less a day) is a priority of Les Dlabay, professor of business at Lake Forest College, Lake Forest, Illinois. He believes our society can improve global business development through volunteer time, knowledge sharing, and financial donations. In addition to writing several textbooks, Dr. Dlabay teaches accounting and various international business courses. His "hobbies" include a collection of cereal packages from over 100 countries and banknotes from 200 countries, which are used to teach about economic, cultural, and political aspects of international business environments.

His research involves informal and alternative financial services, microfinance, and value chain facilitation in base-of-the-pyramid (BoP) market settings. Dlabay has presented more than 300 workshops and seminars for teachers and community organizations. He serves on the boards of Bright Hope International (www.brighthope.org), which emphasizes microenterprise development through microfinance programs, and Andean Aid (www.andeanaid.org), which provides tutoring assistance to school-age children in Colombia and Venezuela. Professor Dlabay has a BS (Accounting) from the University of Illinois, Chicago; an MBA from DePaul University; and an EdD in Business and Economic Education from Northern Illinois University. He has twice received the "Great Teacher" award at Lake Forest College.

Robert J. Hughes, EdD, *Dallas County Community Colleges*

Financial literacy! Only two words, but Bob Hughes, professor of business at Dallas County Community Colleges, believes that these two words can change your life. Whether you want to be rich or just manage the money you have, the ability to analyze financial decisions and gather financial information are skills that can always be improved. Dr. Hughes has taught personal finance, introduction to business, business math, small business management, small business finance, and accounting for over 35 years. In addition to *Focus on Personal Finance* and *Personal Finance,* published by McGraw-Hill/Irwin, he has authored college textbooks for Introduction to Business, Business Mathematics, and Small Business Management. He also served as a content consultant for two popular national television series, *Dollars & Sense: Personal Finance for the 21st Century* and *It's Strictly Business,* and he is the lead author for a business math project utilizing computer-assisted instruction funded by the ALEKS Corporation. He received his BBA from Southern Nazarene University and his MBA and EdD from the University of North Texas. His hobbies include writing, investing, collecting French antiques, art, and travel.

Melissa M. Hart, CPA *North Carolina State University*

Melissa Hart is a permanent lecturer in the Poole College of Management at North Carolina State University. She was inducted into the Academy of Outstanding Teachers in 2012. She teaches courses in personal finance and corporate finance. She has developed multiple ways to use technology to introduce real-life situations into the classroom and the distance education environment. Spreading the word about financial literacy has always been a passion of hers. It doesn't stop at the classroom. Each year she shares her common-sense approach of "No plan is a plan" to various student groups, clubs, high schools, and outside organizations. She is a member of the North Carolina Association of Certified Public Accountants (NCACPA) where she serves on the Accounting Education Committee. She received her BBA from the University of Maryland and an MBA from North Carolina State University. Prior to obtaining an MBA, she worked eight years in public accounting in auditing, tax compliance, and consulting. Her hobbies include keeping up with her family's many extracurricular activities as well as working on various crafts. She travels extensively with her family to enjoy the many cultures and beauty of the state, the country, and the world.

Dear Personal Finance Students and Professors

Question: How important are the financial decisions you make?

Answer: Because financial decisions can change your life, they are very important. Just for a moment think about the decisions you make every day. For example:

- What happens if you run out of money before your next payday?
- Should you pay cash or use a credit card?
- How much insurance do you need?
- Is this a good investment?
- How much should you save for retirement?

For most people, the answers to questions like these affect not only their financial security, but also their quality of life. And while the answers to these questions are based on your unique personal situation, this book and accompanying digital study tools are designed to help you discover the answers to these questions, and many more.

Text (or eBook)

While the new, fifth edition of *Focus on Personal Finance* does not guarantee that you will become a millionaire, it does provide the information you need to develop a plan to achieve financial security. New to this edition is the "3 Steps to Financial Literacy" feature. Each of the three steps is designed to give you a starting point to help master the material in each chapter and includes websites and apps to help you start your personal financial journey. Current content, examples, exhibits, and box features within each chapter also illustrate how to apply important concepts to your life. And at the end of each chapter, a chapter summary, discussion questions, financial problems, and cases help you reinforce important concepts and review for exams. This edition also includes a new continuing case that illustrates the financial challenges a young couple experiences as they journey through the ups and downs of life. Finally "Your Personal Financial Plan" sheets at the end of each chapter help you build a plan that will enable you to achieve your personal and financial goals both now and in the future.

Digital Package

As authors, we recognize the importance of providing quality digital products to enhance learning. We're especially proud of our digital study tools that accompany this edition. For example, both the McGraw-Hill Connect™ and LearnSmart websites contain student learning activities—all designed to help you experience success. For more information about these digital products, visit the McGraw-Hill website at www.mheducation.com.

Thank You

We sincerely thank you for your current and past support of *Focus on Personal Finance*. We invite you to take a look at this new edition to see how *Focus on Personal Finance* can help you create the "right" financial plan to help you achieve your personal and financial goals. Finally, we encourage you to email us if you have comments or suggestions about the text or our digital study tools.

Welcome to the new *Focus on Personal Finance!*

Jack Kapoor

kapoorj@att.net

Les Dlabay

dlabay@lakeforest.edu

Bob Hughes

bhughes@dcccd.edu

Melissa Hart

mmhart@ncsu.edu

New to This Edition

The fifth edition of *Focus on Personal Finance* contains new and updated boxed features, exhibits and tables, articles, and end-of-chapter material. The following grid highlights some of the more significant content revisions made to *Focus*, 5e.

Global Changes for all chapters
- New chapter opener.
- Action items for each learning objective.
- A revised *Your Personal Finance Dashboard* feature at the end of each chapter.
- A new *Continuing Case* feature at the end of each chapter.
- Revised and updated problems.
- Updated websites and apps on all "Your Personal Financial Plan" sheets.

CHAPTER 1 Personal Financial Planning in Action	• Revised Exhibit 1–1 with expanded financial activities for various life situations. • New coverage of the role of the financial system for personal financial decisions. • New Exhibit 1–2 with an overview of the financial intermediaries and markets that facilitate personal financial decisions. • Revised *Figure It Out!* feature on using time value of money for achieving financial goals comparing formula, table, spreadsheet, and financial calculator methods.
CHAPTER 2 Money Management Skills	• Revised Exhibit 2–1 with suggestions for storing and organizing financial documents in various formats. • New content on storing financial documents "in the cloud." • New in-text example for calculating net worth. • Updated content on selecting a savings technique. • New *From the Pages of Kiplinger's Personal Finance* with suggestions for budgeting and tracking your finances. • New end-of-chapter case to evaluate and recommend actions for a household budget.
CHAPTER 3 Taxes in Your Financial Plan	• New *Caution!* feature on IRS scams. • Updated tax rate schedules (for 2014). • Updated section: Calculating your Tax. • Revised *Figure It Out!* feature: Short-Term and Long-Term Capital Gains. • Revised *Personal Finance in Practice:* New tax form exhibits. • Revised Exhibits 3–3 and 3–4 give updated tax forms. • Revised Exhibit 3–5, showing tax tables and tax rate schedules. • Updated electronic filing instructions. • New coverage: 529 plan tax implications. • New *From the Pages of Kiplinger's Personal Finance* feature on taxes to consider when traveling. • Revised content on tax strategies. • Revised *Figure It Out!* feature: Tax Credits vs. Tax Deductions.

CHAPTER 4 Financial Services: Savings Plans and Payment Accounts	• Updated and expanded coverage of online and mobile banking. • New coverage of the expanded use of and many fees associated with prepaid debit cards. • New Exhibit 4–2 provides an overview of mobile banking services. • Updated coverage of "problematic" financial services such as pawnshops, payday loan companies, and rent-to-own centers. • New *From the Pages of Kiplinger's Personal Finance* covering techniques for enhanced saving. • Updated coverage of various types of certificates of deposit. • New coverage of peer-to-peer payments, which allows the transfer of money to another person by e-mail or with a secured website. • New *Digi-Know?* with coverage of chip-embedded credit and debit cards to enhance security and reduce fraud.
CHAPTER 5 Consumer Credit Advantages, Disadvantages Sources, and Costs	• New content in Advantages of Credit section highlighting the benefits that major credit card issuers provide to their customers. • New summary of advantages and disadvantages of credit. • Updated Exhibit 5–2: Volume of Consumer Credit. • Updated *Did You Know?* feature in the Credit Card section. • Updated statistics for stored value cards for 2014. • Updated *Did You Know?* feature in the Applying for Credit section. • New material on credit scores: What is a credit score and what factors are used to calculate it? • New *Did You Know?* feature: What's in Your FICO Score? • New material on FICO and VantageScore: the consequences of not maintaining a sound credit score can be very costly. • New What Can You Do to Improve Your Credit Score? section and information on how you can avoid credit-repair scams. • New *From the Pages of Kiplinger's Personal Finance* feature on how to combat data theft. • New material in Cosigning a Loan section: Private lenders are placing borrowers into default and making balance due all at once when the cosigner dies or files for bankruptcy. • New material on the Consumer Financial Protection Bureau's activities in 2014. • Updated material in the Chapter 7 Bankruptcy section on filing and administrative fees. • Updated Exhibit 5–10: U.S. Consumer Bankruptcy Filings, 1980–2014.
CHAPTER 6 Consumer Purchasing Strategies and Wise Buying of Motor Vehicles	• New *Did You Know?* feature that provides money-saving tips and actions to avoid overspending. • New *Caution!* feature warning shoppers about buying fake and counterfeit products that can waste money and be dangerous. • New *From the Pages of Kiplinger's Personal Finance* comparing various sources of previously-driven vehicles. • New "Upside Down" example warning consumers to avoid a situation in which the loan amount owed may exceed the current value of the vehicle. • Revised text coverage of the consumer complaint process.

CHAPTER 6 (Cont.)	• New Exhibit 6–6 with detailed information for each step of the consumer complaint process. • New *Did You Know?* feature with suggested websites to assist with basic legal documents.
CHAPTER 7 Selecting and Financing Housing	• Revised coverage of standard lease forms when renting. • New *From the Pages of Kiplinger's Personal Finance* covering current advice on renting or buying your housing. • Updated information on the process for financing a home purchase. • Revised content on types of mortgages. • Updated information on common closing costs (Exhibit 7–9). • Expanded information on actions to take when attempting to lower your property taxes.
CHAPTER 8 Home and Automobile Insurance	• Added new material on Superstorm Sandy in the Potential Property Losses section. • Updated *Personal Finance in Practice* feature on flood facts. • New *From the Pages of Kiplinger's Personal Finance* feature: "If my home is damaged by a summer storm, will my insurance cover repairs?" • New *Personal Finance in Practice* feature: Are You Covered?
CHAPTER 9 Health and Disability Income insurance	• New *From the Pages of Kiplinger's Personal Finance* feature on long-term care. • Updated material in the *Personal Finance in Practice* box; HSAs: How They Work in 2014. • New and revised material in the Health Insurance and the Patient Protection and Affordable Care Act of 2010 section. • New section on the Affordable Care Act and the Individual Shared Responsibility provision. • New *Personal Finance in Practice* feature on the Affordable Care Act: Checklist for You and Your Family. • Updated and revised the section on high medical costs. • Updated Exhibit 9–6: U.S. National Health Expenditures, 1960–2022. • New *Did You Know?* feature: The average cost of a 3-day hospital stay. • New *Did You Know?* feature: Victims of medical identity theft.
CHAPTER 10 Financial Planning with Life Insurance	• Updated the How Long Will You Live? section. • Updated Exhibit 10–1: Life Expectancy Tables, All Races, 2009. • Revised the Types of Life Insurance Companies and Policies section. • New *Did You Know?* feature: 75 million American families depend on life insurance products. • Added new material in the Term Life Insurance section. • New *Did You Know?* feature: 146 million individual life insurance policies in force in 2013. • Expanded the discussion on group life insurance. • New *Did You Know?* feature: What to do if you lose your life insurance policy. • New *Did You Know?* feature: Insurance industry payouts.

CHAPTER 10 (Cont.)	• Expanded discussion on annuities. • New discussion on index annuities. • New *Caution!* feature emphasizes that an annuity is a long-term financial contract.
CHAPTER 11 Investing Basics and Evaluating Bonds	• A new *From the Pages of Kiplinger's Personal Finance* feature provides tips for saving money and tactics to improve money management. • A new *Did You Know?* feature provides information about the Motley Fool and Kiplinger websites. • Updated material and new examples are used in the section How the Time Value of Money Affects Your Investments. • New material about the risks of lost income and decrease in value is provided in the section Safety and Risk section. • A new Exhibit 11–3 helps students determine their investment risk profile. • In the Factors That Reduce Investment Risk section, updated statistics for the long-term performance of stocks and bonds are provided. • A new *Digi-Know?* feature provides information about the Treasury Direct website at www.treasurydirect.gov. • A new convertible bond example for Wesco Corporation is included in the Types of Bonds section. • New information about the speculative nature of high-yield (junk) bonds is provided in the Types of Bonds section. • A new example describes how Union Pacific Corporation used a sinking fund to make sure funds were available to repay a corporate bond issue. • An updated *Did You Know?* feature provides information about the yields for 10-year U.S. treasury notes and high-grade corporate bonds. • A new interest calculation for a 4 percent IBM bond is provided in the Interest Income section. • A new example for calculating approximate market value is included in the Dollar Appreciation of Bond Value section. • An updated Exhibit 11–7 provides current information found on the Yahoo! bond website for an AT&T bond. • An updated *Case in Point* provides revised or new investment options that students must evaluate.
CHAPTER 12 Investing in Stocks	• Updated statistics for the long-term performance of stocks and bonds is provided in the Common and Preferred Stock section. • A new Exhibit 12–1 provides information on the record date and ex-dividend date for a Microsoft quarterly dividend. • A new *Did You Know?* feature provides information about how fraudsters use a practice called "pump and dump" to increase the price of a stock before selling the stock at a profit. • The Dollar Appreciation of Value section and a new Exhibit 12–2 illustrate how investors made money by buying and then selling Johnson & Johnson stock at the end of a three-year period. • In the Possibility of Increased Value from Stock Splits section, the effect of a two-for-one stock split by Under Armour is explained.

CHAPTER 12 (Cont.)	• Exhibit 12–3 now provides revised definitions for blue-chip, micro cap, and penny stocks.
	• The information available on the Yahoo! Finance website for Facebook is discussed in the updated The Internet section and a new Exhibit 12–4.
	• A discussion of the information available from Value Line for the Disney Corporation is provided in the Stock Advisory Services section and a new Exhibit 12–5.
	• A new *From the Pages of Kiplinger's Personal Finance* feature presents information about how investors can use the information in a firm's annual report to become better investors.
	• An updated *Did You Know?* feature provides information on the Dow Jones Industrial Average.
	• New and updated examples are included in the Numerical Measures That influence Investment Decisions section.
	• A new example includes information about projected earnings for Starbucks in the Projected Earnings section.
	• New information on beta and an example of a beta calculation for Google is provided in the Other Factors That Influence the Price of a Stock section.
	• A new example describes how Papa Murphy's used an initial public offering (IPO) to obtain financing.
	• A new *Did You Know?* feature describes investor options for holding securities (physical certificates, street name, or direct registration) until they are sold.
	• A new Exhibit 12–6 illustrates typical commissions charged for online, telephone, and broker-assisted stock transactions.
	• In the Sample Stock Transactions section, a new example provides information about a limit order for eBay.
	• In the Sample Stock Transactions section, a new example provides information about a stop-loss order for General Motors.
	• A new *Personal Finance in Practice* feature describes the techniques investors can use to pick a winning stock.
	• Exhibit 12–7 illustrates the dollar cost averaging concept for an investment in Johnson & Johnson over a seven-year period using current stock values.
	• In the Selling Short section, a new example describes how an investor could profit using the selling short technique for a General Motors stock transaction.
	• A new *Case in Point* asks students to evaluate the Disney Corporation using the information in the Value Line report in Exhibit 12–5.
CHAPTER 13 Investing in Mutual Funds	• To illustrate how important funds are for investors, updated statistics are provided in the Why Investors Choose Mutual Funds section.
	• An updated *Did You Know?* feature provides information about who owns mutual funds.
	• A new Exhibit 13–1 provides information about the type of securities contained in the Invesco Dividend Income Fund.
	• New statistics about the number of closed-end, exchange-traded, and open-end funds are included in the Characteristics of Funds section.
	• The fee table in Exhibit 13–2 has been updated to illustrate current fees for the Davis Opportunity Fund.
	• The investment objective for the Vanguard Mid-Cap Fund is now included in the Classification of Mutual Funds section.

CHAPTER 13 (Cont.)	• A new *Did You Know?* feature illustrates the type of funds investors use to obtain their financial goals. • The number of socially responsible funds has been updated in the *Did You Know?* feature. • A new *From the Pages of Kiplinger's Personal Finance* feature describes how employees can lower the fees associated with their retirement accounts. • A new Exhibit 13–4 describes the information about the T. Rowe Price Value Fund available from the Morningstar website. • A detailed Morningstar research report for the Oakmark Global Select I Fund is illustrated in Exhibit 13–5. • A new Exhibit 13–6 describes a portion of the funds included in the "Kiplinger 25" list of funds. • In the Return on Investment section, the example for the Fidelity Stock Selector All-Cap Fund has been updated with current price information. • A new *Did You Know?* feature provides both new and updated information about the characteristics of mutual fund owners. • A new *Case in Point* asks students to evaluate the Oakmark Global Select I Fund using the information in the Morningstar report illustrated in Exhibit 13–5.
CHAPTER 14 Starting Early: Retirement and Estate Planning	• New Saving Smart for Retirement section. • Updated Exhibit 14–2: How an Average Older (65+) Household Spends Its Money. • New *Caution!* box on safeguarding your Social Security card. • Revised *Did You Know?* feature: Estimated average monthly Social Security benefits in 2014. • Revised and updated the section on Individual Retirement Accounts. • New *Did You Know?* feature: Roth IRAs versus traditional IRAs. • New *From the Pages of Kiplinger's Personal Finance* feature: Roth 401(k)s. • New *Did You Know?* feature: IRA assets in 2013. • Updated stated amount will. • Updated credit shelter trust. • Updated estate taxes and gift taxes.
APPENDIX A Education Financing, Loans, and Scholarships	• New Exhibit A–1: Education compared to earnings and unemployment. • Revised information for the 2014–15 academic year for loans and federal grants. • New Exhibit A–3: Student loan default statistics.
APPENDIX B Developing a Career Search Strategy	• New highlighted example on social media résumés through LinkedIn, Twitter, and other online networks. • Revised coverage for a professional presentation of your résumé. • Additional suggestions for a résumé makeover (Exhibit B–1). • Revised Exhibit B–2 with a sample cover letter. • Updated coverage on techniques for submitting a résumé. • New Exhibit B–4 with suggestions for updating career planning activities.

Focus on . . . Learning

Three Steps to Financial Literacy

Getting your finances in order is simpler than you think, and we're here to show you how. These new chapter opening features break down key action items you need to take to address the most important personal finance issues from the chapter, as part of this edition's emphasis on taking action. These steps tie in to the "Your Personal Finance Dashboard" feature at the end of each chapter.

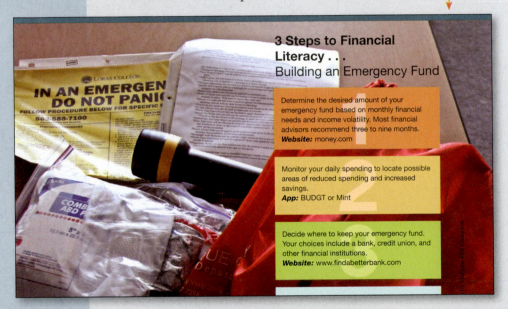

3 Steps to Financial Literacy . . .
Building an Emergency Fund

1. Determine the desired amount of your emergency fund based on monthly financial needs and income volatility. Most financial advisors recommend three to nine months. *Website:* money.com

2. Monitor your daily spending to locate possible areas of reduced spending and increased savings. *App:* BUDGT or Mint

3. Decide where to keep your emergency fund. Your choices include a bank, credit union, and other financial institutions. *Website:* www.findabetterbank.com

---

ancial Decisions

e money available. However, the amount, along with needs and vary from person to person. In this book, you will have the opportu-rent situation, learn about varied financial paths, and move forward security.

o handle their finances so that they get full satisfaction from each al financial goals may include buying a new car or a larger home, er training, contributing to charity, traveling extensively, and ensur-ing working and retirement years. To achieve these and other goals, , and set priorities. Financial and personal satisfaction are the result s that is commonly referred to as *personal money management* or ning.

uation and Financial Planning

nning is the process of managing your money to achieve personal . This planning process allows you to control your financial situation. or household has a unique situation; therefore, financial decisions t specific needs and goals.

nancial plan can enhance the quality of your life and increase your g uncertainty about your future needs and resources. A **financial** port that summarizes your current financial situation, analyzes your

LO1.1

Identify social and economic influences on personal financial goals and decisions.

ACTION ITEM

Do you have an emergency fund for unexpected expenses?

☐ **Yes** ☐ **No**

personal financial planning The process of managing your money to achieve personal economic satisfaction.

financial plan A formalized report that summarizes your current financial situation,

Learning Objective References

Citations in the margins next to the relevant text refer to corresponding chapter objectives listed at the beginning of each chapter.

Action Items

As part of this edition's emphasis on taking action to gain financial skills, *new* Action Items are posted at the start of each main section of a chapter. These are designed to get you thinking about what daily actions you can be taking to achieve financial literacy and independence.

An interactive and engaging chapter opener gets students organized and demonstrates the relevance of the material to their own lives.

Learning Objectives

Learning objectives highlight the goals of each chapter for easy reference. Throughout the book, in the end-of-chapter material, and even in the supplement materials, these objectives provide a valuable foundation for assessment.

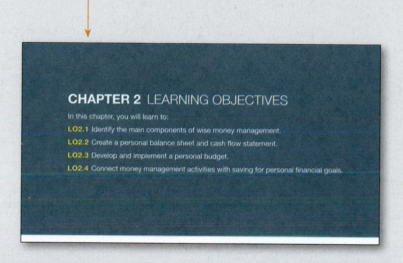

CHAPTER 2 LEARNING OBJECTIVES

In this chapter, you will learn to:

LO2.1 Identify the main components of wise money management.

LO2.2 Create a personal balance sheet and cash flow statement.

LO2.3 Develop and implement a personal budget.

LO2.4 Connect money management activities with saving for personal financial goals.

YOUR PERSONAL FINANCIAL PLAN SHEETS

5. Financial Documents and Records
6. Creating a Personal Balance Sheet
7. Creating a Personal Cash Flow Statement
8. Developing a Personal Budget

A Successful Money Management Plan   **LO2.1**

                                           Identify the main components
                                           of wise money management.

"Each month, I have too many days and not enough money. If the month were only 20 days long, budgeting would be easy."

Your Personal Financial Plan Sheets

A list of the "Your Personal Financial Plan" worksheets for each chapter is presented at the start of each chapter for easy reference.

Examples

Worked-out examples featuring key concepts and calculations appear throughout the text, a valuable feature for students to see how personal finance works in practice.

have not yet repaid. The more often you make payments, the lower the interest you'll pay. Most credit unions use this method.

EXAMPLE: Using the Simple Interest Formula on the Declining Balance

Using simple interest on the declining balance to compute interest charges, the interest on a 5 percent, $1,000 loan repaid in two payments, one at the end of the first half-year and another at the end of the second half-year, would be $37.50, as follows:

First payment:

$$I = P \times r \times T$$
$$= \$1,000 \times 0.05 \times 1/2$$
$$= \$25 \text{ interest plus } \$500, \text{ or } \$525$$

Second payment:

$$I = P \times r \times T$$
$$= \$500 \times 0.05 \times 1/2$$
$$= \$12.50 \text{ interest plus the remaining balance of } \$500, \text{ or } \$512.50$$

Total payment on the loan:

$$\$525 + \$512.50 = \$1,037.50$$

Using the APR formula,

$$\text{APR} = \frac{2 \times n \times I}{P(N+1)} = \frac{2 \times 2 \times \$37.50}{\$1,000(2+1)} = \frac{\$150}{\$3,000} = 0.05, \text{ or } 5 \text{ percent}$$

ADD-ON INTEREST With the add-on interest method, interest is calculated on the full amount of the original principal, no matter how frequently you make payments. When

stores, charging a meal at a restaurant, and using overdraft -end credit. As you will soon see, you do not apply for open-hase, as you do with closed-end credit. Rather, you can use rchases you wish if you do not exceed your **line of credit,** the it the lender has made available to you. You may have to pay ne use of credit, or other finance charges. Usually you have ithin 30 days without interest charges or to make set monthly nt balance plus interest. Some creditors allow you a grace bill in full before you incur any interest charges.

g check credit. Also called a *bank line of credit,* this is a ed amount that you can use by writing a special check. nts over a set period. The finance charges are based on the e month and on the outstanding balance.

pular. The average cardholder has more than nine credit d gasoline cards. Cardholders who pay off their balances in wn as *convenience* users. Cardholders who do not pay off known as *borrowers.*
offer a grace period, a time period during which no finance ccount. A **finance charge** is the total dollar amount you pay

line of credit The dollar amount, which may or may not be borrowed, that a lender makes available to a borrower.

interest A periodic charge for the use of credit.

revolving check credit A prearranged loan from a bank for a specified amount; also called a *bank line of credit.*

finance charge The total dollar amount paid to use credit.

Key Terms

Key terms appear in bold type within the text and are defined in the margins. A list of key terms and page references is located at the end of each chapter.

Your Personal Financial Plan Sheet References

The integrated use of the "Your Personal Financial Plan" sheets is highlighted with an icon. This visual helps integrate this study resource into the learning process and continue to track personal financial habits.

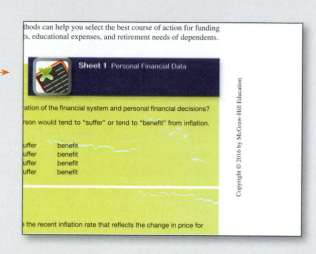

Practice Quizzes

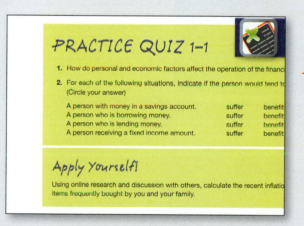

Practice Quizzes at the end of each major section provide questions to help assess knowledge of the main ideas covered in that section. These will determine whether concepts have been mastered or if a need exists to do additional study on certain topics.

Exhibits and Tables

Throughout the text, exhibits and tables visually illustrate important personal finance concepts and processes.

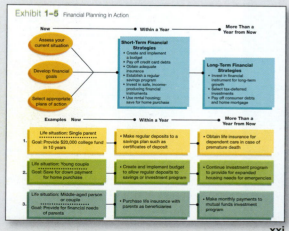

Focus on . . .
Personal Finance in Real Life

Did You Know?

Each chapter contains several *Did You Know?* boxes. The **yellow** notes contain fun facts, information, and financial planning assistance for wise personal financial actions.

    Green *Did You Know?* boxes recommend socially conscious financial activities for students interested in giving back to others.

    Blue *Digi-Know?* boxes share tips and topics on using technology to help manage your finances.

---

did you know?

According to the National Endowment for Financial Education, 70 percent of major lottery winners end up with financial difficulties. These winners often squander the funds awarded them, while others overspend and many end up declaring bankruptcy. Having more money does not automatically mean making better financial planning choices.

STEP 2: Develop Your Financial Goal

You should periodically analyze your financial values and goal The purpose of this analysis is to differentiate your needs fro your wants. Specific financial goals are vital to financial pla ning. Others can suggest financial goals for you; however, y must decide which goals to pursue. Your financial goals c range from spending all of your current income to developing extensive savings and investment program for your future fina cial security.

---

did you know?

Nearly one billion people around the world live on $1 or less a day. Various organizations provide these people with basic need items and future opportuni- ties. Bright Hope International assists the extreme poor by providing food, clothing, shelter, health care, education, orphan support, microloans, job training, and spiritual guidance. You can help to provide assistance to the extreme poor at www.brighthope.org.

CONSEQUENCES OF CHOICES Every decision clos off alternatives. For example, a decision to invest in stock m mean you cannot take a vacation. A decision to go to school fu time may mean you cannot work full-time. Opportunity cost what you give up by making a choice. These trade-offs cann always be measured in dollars. However, the resources you gi up (money or time) have a value that is lost.

EVALUATING RISK Uncertainty is also a part of eve decision. Selecting a college major and choosing a career fie involve risk. What if you don't like working in this field or ca not obtain employment in it? Other decisions involve a ve low degree of risk, such as putting money in an insured sa ings account or purchasing items that cost only a few dollar Your chances of losing something of great value are low in the situations.

    In many financial decisions, identifying and evaluating ri are difficult. Common risks to consider include:

---

digi - know?

The use of mobile apps for personal finan- cial activities continues to expand with instant access to bank accounts, budget amounts, investment information, and time value of money calculations. Some of the most popular are mint, Unsplurge, Easy Money, and Pocket Money, with costs ranging from free to a few dollars.

for six years, starting at the end of the first year, you will ha $357.65 at the end of that time ($50 × 7.153). The near "Figure It Out!" box presents examples of using future value achieve financial goals.

PRESENT VALUE OF A SINGLE AMOUNT Anoth aspect of the time value of money involves determining the cu rent value of an amount desired in the future. **Present value** the current value for a future amount based on a particular inte est rate for a certain period of time. Present value computatio also called *discounting*, allow you to determine how much deposit now to obtain a desired total in the future. For examp using the present value table (Exhibit 1–3C), if you want $1,0 five years from now and you earn 5 percent on your savings, y need to deposit $784 ($1,000 × 0.784).

From the Pages of . . . Kiplinger's Personal Finance

FROM THE PAGES OF . . . Kiplinger's Personal Finance

Which Route Is Best for You?

	CPO	NON-CPO	PRIVATE PARTY
	Certified pre-owned vehicles are as close to a new-car-buying experience as you can get. You'll pay an extra $1,500 to $2,500 com- pared with non-CPO vehicles.	Dealers sell vehicles they acquire at auc- tion or through trade- ins that aren't scooped up by the CPO pro- grams. You'll likely pay at least 10% more to a dealer than to a private party.	The cheapest way to buy a used car. Private sellers can sell a used car for a higher price to you than they could to a dealer, but they can't inflate the price as much.
Condition	Excellent—models are five years old or newer with fewer than 60,000 miles. **Because many CPOs are off- lease, they have had only one owner.**	Mostly cosmetic reconditioning. **Don't expect repairs to be made.** Most dealers offer a vehicle history report from Auto- Check.com or Carfax .com.	It varies. **Ask for maintenance records** and get a vehicle history report on AutoCheck.com or Carfax.com.
Inspection	A 100- to 200-point inspection. Vehicles are repaired and reconditioned. **Worn parts are replaced, saving money on future maintenance.**	A dealer's service department inspects the car, but **get your own mechanic to go over the car** before you buy.	**You're on your own.** If the seller won't agree to let you take it to a mechanic, move on to the next prospect.
Warranty	Usually a year or two extension of new-car comprehensive and power-train warranty, **backed by the man- ufacturer, not the dealer.**	You get **what's left of the new-car war- ranty.** Resist the hard sell on an extended warranty. Some states have laws to protect used-car buyers.	As with a dealer sale, you get **what's left of the new-car warranty.** If you get stuck with a lemon, you have little or no recourse.
Financing	Carmakers' finance companies offer lower rates than you'd pay on non-CPO loans. **You may save hun- dreds of dollars in interest.**	The F&I department will arrange financing, **but dealers may get a commission.** Get prequalified at your bank or credit union and compare offers.	**You'll have to pay cash.** If you need a loan, consider draw- ing on a home-equity line, or get a used- car loan at a bank or credit union.

Jessica L. Anderson

SOURCE: Reprinted by permission from *Kiplinger's Personal Finance*. Copyright © 2014. The Kiplinger Washington Editors, Inc.

1. From your perspective, what are the benefits and drawbacks of each of the three alternatives for buying a motor vehicle?

2. What factors should a person consider before buying an extended warranty?

3. What actions would you suggest when using any of the three alternatives presented in the article?

194

This one-page chapter feature presents a recent article from the well-known *Kiplinger's Personal Finance* magazine related to a chapter topic. Each article covers a personal finance issue to consider, using the questions that accompany the article. This is an excel- lent tool to develop critical thinking and writing skills!

Personal Finance in Practice

These boxes offer information that can assist you when faced with special situations and unique financial planning decisions. They challenge you to apply the concepts you have learned to your life and record personal responses. Many of these boxes have been updated to include exercises and topics on ethics in personal finance.

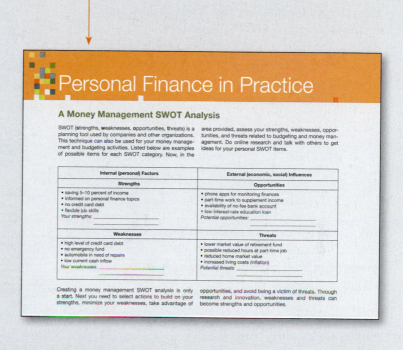

Figure It Out!

This boxed feature presents important mathematical applications relevant to personal finance situations and concepts.

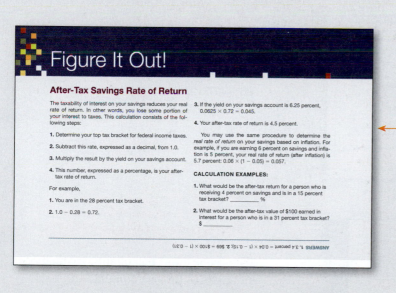

Focus on . . .
Practice and Assessment

Personal Finance Dashboard

Having read the chapter, you now consider your financial progress. The dashboard feature is designed to help you monitor key performance indicators in your personal financial situation. The next step will be to review your habits and take action for better results.

Chapter Summary

Organized by learning objective, this concise content summary is a great study and self-assessment tool, located conveniently at the end of chapters.

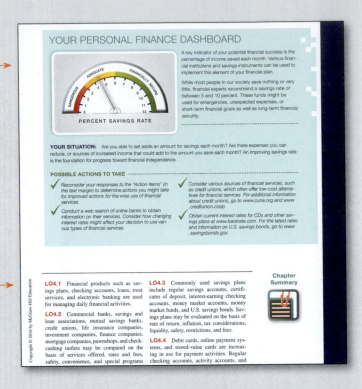

Key Formulas

A list of *Key Formulas* and page references appears at the end of select chapters, grouped for easy reference.

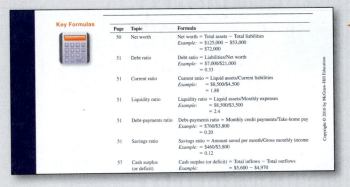

Discussion Questions

These questions test qualitative analysis of personal finance content.

Self-Test Problems

Self-Test Problems are worked out using step-by-step solutions so that students can see how they were solved. This user-friendly feature increases students' comprehension of the material and gives confidence to solve the end-of-chapter problems.

Self-Test Problems

1. The Rule of 72 provides a guideline for determining how long it takes your money to double. This rule can also be used to determine your earning rate. If your money is expected to double in 12 years, what is your rate of return?
2. If you desire to have $10,000 in savings eight years from now, what amount would you need to deposit in an account that earns 5 percent?

Self-Test Solutions

1. Using the Rule of 72, if your money is expected to double in 12 years, you are earning approximately 6 percent (72 ÷ 12 years = 6 percent).
2. To calculate the present value of $10,000 for eight years at 5 percent, use Exhibit 1–3C (or Exhibit 1–C in the appendix to Chapter 1): $10,000 × 0.677 = $6,770

24

Problems

(*Note:* Some of these problems require the use of the time value of money tables in the appendix directly following this chapter, a financial calculator, or spreadsheet software.)

1. Using the Rule of 72, approximate the following amounts: (LO1.1)
   a. If the value of land in an area is increasing 6 percent a year, how long will it take for property values to double?
   b. If you earn 10 percent on your investments, how long will it take for your money to double?
   c. At an annual interest rate of 5 percent, how long will it take for your savings to double?
2. In 2011, selected automobiles had an average cost of $16,000. The average cost of those same automobiles is now $20,000. What was the rate of increase for these automobiles between the two time periods? (LO1.1)
3. A family spends $46,000 a year for living expenses. If prices increase 3 percent a year for the next three years, what amount will the family need for their living expenses after three years? (LO1.1)
4. Ben Collins plans to buy a house for $220,000. If the real estate in his area is expected to increase in value 2 percent each year, what will its approximate value be seven years from now? (LO1.2)
5. What would be the yearly earnings for a person with $6,000 in savings at an annual interest rate of 2.5 percent? (LO1.3)
6. Using time value of money tables (Exhibit 1–3 or chapter appendix tables), calculate the following: (LO1.3)
   a. The future value of $550 six years from now at 7 percent.
   b. The future value of $700 saved each year for 10 years at 8 percent.

Problems

A variety of problems allow students to put their quantitative analysis of personal financial decisions to work. Each problem is tagged with a corresponding learning objective for easy assessment.

ADJUSTING THE BUDGET

In a recent month, the Constantine family had a budget deficit, which is something they want to avoid so they do not have future financial difficulties. Jason and Karen Constantine and their children (ages 10 and 12) plan to discuss the situation after dinner this evening.

While at work, Jason was talking with his friend Ken Lopez. Ken had been a regular saver since he was very young, starting with a small savings account. Those funds were then invested in various stocks and mutual funds. While in college, Ken was able to pay for his education while continuing to save between $50 and $100 a month. He closely monitored his spending. Ken realized that the few dollars here and there for snacks and other minor purchases quickly add up.

Today, Ken works as a customer service manager for the online division of a retailing company. He lives with his wife and their two young children. The family's spending plan allows for all their needs and also includes regularly saving and investing for the children's education and for retirement.

Jason asked Ken, "How come you never seem to have financial stress in your household?"

Ken replied, "Do you know where your money is going each month?"

"Not really," was Jason's response.

"You'd be surprised by how much is spent on little things you might do without," Ken responded.

"I guess so. I just don't want to have to go around with a notebook writing down every amount I spend," Jason said in a troubled voice.

"Well, you have to take some action if you want your financial situation to change," Ken countered.

That evening, the Constantine family met to discuss their budget situation:

Case in Point

67

Case in Point

Students can work through a hypothetical personal finance dilemma in order to apply concepts from the chapter. A series of questions reinforces your successful mastery and application of these chapter topics.

Continuing Case

This feature allows students to apply course concepts in a life situation. It encourages students to evaluate the finances that affect a household and then respond to the resulting shift in needs, resources, and priorities through the questions at the end of each case.

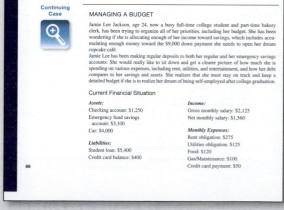

Continuing Case

MANAGING A BUDGET

Jamie Lee Jackson, age 24, now a busy full-time college student and part-time bakery clerk, has been trying to organize all of her priorities, including her budget. She has been wondering if she is allocating enough of her income toward savings, which includes accumulating enough money toward the $9,000 down payment she needs to open her dream cupcake café.

Jamie Lee has been making regular deposits to both her regular and her emergency savings accounts. She would really like to sit down and get a clearer picture of how much she is spending on various expenses, including rent, utilities, and entertainment, and how her debt compares to her savings and assets. She realizes that she must stay on track and keep a detailed budget if she is to realize her dream of being self-employed after college graduation.

Current Financial Situation

Assets:
Checking account: $1,250
Emergency fund savings account: $3,100
Car: $4,000

Liabilities:
Student loan: $5,400
Credit card balance: $400

Income:
Gross monthly salary: $2,125
Net monthly salary: $1,560

Monthly Expenses:
Rent obligation: $275
Utilities obligation: $125
Food: $120
Gas/Maintenance: $100
Credit card payment: $50

68

Daily Spending Diary

Do you buy a latte or a soda every day before class? Do you and your friends meet for a movie once a week? How much do you spend on gas for your car each month? Do you like to donate to your favorite local charity a couple of times a year?

These everyday spending activities might go largely unnoticed, yet they have a significant effect on the overall health of an individual's finances. The Daily Spending Diary sheets offer students a place to keep track of *every cent they spend* in any category. Careful monitoring and assessing of these daily spending habits can lead to better control and understanding of your personal finances.

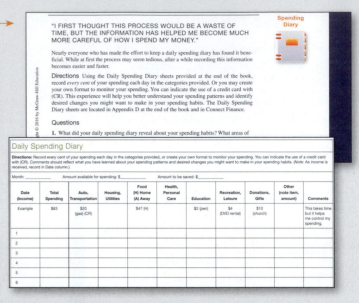

Your Personal Financial Plan

The "Your Personal Financial Plan" sheets that correlate with sections of the text are conveniently located at the end of each chapter. The perforated worksheets ask students to work through the applications and record their own personal financial plan responses. These sheets apply concepts learned to your unique situation and serve as a roadmap to your personal financial future. Students can fill them out, rip them out, submit them for homework, and keep them filed in a safe spot for future reference. Excel spreadsheets for each of the "Your Personal Financial Plan" sheets are available through Connect.

Key websites and apps are provided to help students research and devise their personal financial plan, and the "What's Next for Your Personal Financial Plan?" section at the end of each sheet challenges students to use their responses to plan the next level, as well as foreshadow upcoming concepts.

Look for one or more "Your Personal Financial Plan" icons next to most Practice Quizzes. This graphic directs students to the Personal Financial Plan sheet that corresponds with the preceding section.

Online Support for Students and Instructors

Few textbooks provide such innovative and practical instructional resources for both students and teachers. The comprehensive teaching–learning package for *Focus on Personal Finance* includes the following:

For Instructors

The Instructor's site, delivered through Connect, provides the instructor with one resource for all supplementary material, including:

- *Instructor's Manual:* Created and revised by the authors, this supplement includes a "Course Planning Guide" with instructional strategies, course projects, and supplementary resource lists. The "Chapter Teaching Materials" section of the *Instructor's Manual* provides a chapter overview, the chapter objectives with summaries, introductory activities, and detailed lecture outlines with teaching suggestions. This section also includes concluding activities, ready-to-duplicate quizzes, supplementary lecture materials and activities, and answers to concept checks, end-of-chapter questions, problems, and cases.

- *Test Bank,* revised by Michelle Grant, Bossier Parish Community College consists of true–false, multiple-choice, problem-solving, and essay questions. These test items are organized by the learning objectives for each chapter. This resource also includes answers and an indication of difficulty level.

- *Computerized Testing Software,* McGraw-Hill's EZ Test is a flexible and easy-to-use electronic testing program. The program allows instructors to create tests from book-specific items. It accommodates a wide range of question types, and instructors may add their own questions. Multiple versions of the test can be created, and any test can be exported for use with course management systems such as WebCT or BlackBoard. EZ Test Online gives you a place to easily administer your EZ Test–created exams and quizzes online. The program is available for Windows and Macintosh environments.

- Chapter *PowerPoint Presentations* revised and enhanced by Janet Payne and Vance Lesseig, Texas State University offer more than 300 visual presentations that may be edited and manipulated to fit a particular course format. If you choose to customize the slides, an online digital image library allows you to pick and choose from all of the figures and tables in the book.

Assurance of Learning Ready

Assurance of learning is an important element of many accreditation standards. *Focus on Personal Finance,* 5e is designed specifically to support your assurance of learning initiatives. Each chapter in the book begins with a list of numbered learning objectives which appear throughout the chapter, as well as in the end-of-chapter problems and exercises. Every test bank question is also linked to one of these objectives, in addition to level of difficulty, topic area, Bloom's Taxonomy level, and AACSB skill area. Connect, McGraw-Hill's online homework solution, and EZ Test, McGraw-Hill's easy-to-use test bank software, can search the test bank by these and other categories, providing an engine for targeted Assurance of Learning analysis and assessment.

AACSB Statement

McGraw-Hill Education is a proud corporate member of AACSB International. Understanding the importance and value of AACSB accreditation, *Focus on Personal Finance,* 5e has sought to recognize the curricula guidelines detailed in the AACSB standards for business accreditation by connecting selected questions in the test bank to the general knowledge and skill guidelines found in the AACSB standards.

The statements contained in *Focus on Personal Finance,* 5e are provided only as a guide for the users of this text. The AACSB leaves content coverage and assessment within the purview of individual schools, the mission of the school, and the faculty. While *Focus on Personal Finance,* 5e and the teaching package make no claim of any specific AACSB qualification or evaluation, we have, within the test bank, labeled selected questions according to the six general knowledge and skills areas.

For Students (available through Connect and through your class instructor)

Digital Broadcasts

View chapter-related videos to see how personal finance topics are applied in everyday life.

Narrated Student PowerPoint

Every student learns differently and the *Narrated PowerPoint* was created with that in mind! Revised and expanded by Lynn Kugele, University of Mississippi, they guide students through understanding key topics and principles by presenting real-life examples based on chapter content.

And More!

Looking for more ways to study? Self-grading crossword puzzles will help you learn the material. You can also access Excel templates for the "Your Personal Financial Plan" sheets and the Daily Spending Diary.

McGraw-Hill's

Less Managing. More Teaching. Greater Learning.

McGraw-Hill Connect Finance is an online assignment and assessment solution that connects students with the tools and resources they'll need to achieve success.

Connect helps prepare students for their future by enabling faster learning, more efficient studying, and higher retention of knowledge.

McGraw-Hill Connect Finance Features

Connect Finance offers a number of powerful tools and features to make managing assignments easier, so faculty can spend more time teaching. With Connect Finance, students can engage with their coursework anytime and anywhere, making the learning process more accessible and efficient. Connect Finance offers you the features described below.

Simple assignment management With Connect Finance, creating assignments is easier than ever, so you can spend more time teaching and less time managing. The assignment management function enables you to:

- Create and deliver assignments easily with selectable end-of-chapter questions and test bank items.
- Streamline lesson planning, student progress reporting, and assignment grading to make classroom management more efficient than ever.
- Go paperless with the eBook and online submission and grading of student assignments.

Smart grading When it comes to studying, time is precious. Connect Finance helps students learn more efficiently by providing feedback and practice material when they need it, where they need it. When it comes to

teaching, your time is also precious. The grading function enables you to:

- Have assignments scored automatically, giving students immediate feedback on their work and side-by-side comparisons with correct answers.
- Access and review each response; manually change grades or leave comments for students to review.
- Reinforce classroom concepts with practice tests and instant quizzes.

Instructor Library The Connect Finance Instructor Library is your repository for additional resources to improve student engagement in and out of class. You can select and use any asset that enhances your lecture.

Student Study Center The Connect Finance Student Study Center is the place for students to access additional resources. The Student Study Center:

- Offers students quick access to lectures, practice materials, eBooks, and more.
- Provides instant practice material and study questions, easily accessible on the go.

LearnSmart Students want to make the best use of their study time. The LearnSmart adaptive self-study technology within Connect Finance provides students with a seamless combination of practice, assessment, and remediation for every concept in the textbook. LearnSmart's intelligent software adapts to every student response and automatically delivers concepts that advance the student's understanding while reducing time devoted to the concepts already mastered. The result for every student is the fastest path to mastery of the chapter concepts. LearnSmart:

- Applies an intelligent concept engine to identify the relationships between concepts and to serve new concepts to each student only when he or she is ready.
- Adapts automatically to each student, so students spend less time on the topics they understand and practice more on those they have yet to master.
- Provides continual reinforcement and remediation, but gives only as much guidance as students need.
- Integrates diagnostics as part of the learning experience.
- Enables you to assess which concepts students have efficiently learned on their own, thus freeing class time for more applications and discussion.

SmartBook SmartBook is an extension of LearnSmart—an adaptive eBook that helps students focus their study time more effectively. As students read, SmartBook assesses comprehension and dynamically highlights where they need to study more.

Student progress tracking Connect Finance keeps instructors informed about how each student, section, and class is performing, allowing for more productive use of lecture and office hours. The progress-tracking function enables you to:

- View scored work immediately and track individual or group performance with assignment and grade reports.
- Access an instant view of student or class performance relative to learning objectives.

Lecture Capture through Tegrity Campus—For an additional charge Lecture Capture offers new ways for students to focus on the in-class discussion, knowing they can revisit important topics later. This can be delivered through Connect or separately. See below for more details.

McGraw-Hill Connect Finance McGraw-Hill reinvents the textbook learning experience for the modern student with the new Connect Finance. The new Connect Finance provides all of the Connect Finance features plus the following:

- An integrated eBook, allowing for anytime, anywhere access to the textbook.
- Dynamic links between the problems or questions you assign to your students and the location in the eBook where that problem or question is covered.
- A powerful search function to pinpoint and connect key concepts in a snap.

In short, the new Connect Finance offers you and your students powerful tools and features that optimize your time and energies, enabling you to focus on course content, teaching, and student learning. Connect Finance also offers a wealth of content resources for both instructors and students. This state-of-the-art, thoroughly tested system supports you in preparing students for the world that awaits.

For more information about Connect, go to **connect .mheducation.com** or contact your local McGraw-Hill sales representative.

Tegrity Campus: Lectures 24/7

Tegrity Campus is a service that makes class time available 24/7 by automatically capturing every lecture in a searchable format for students to review when they study and complete assignments. With a simple one-click start-and-stop process, you capture all computer screens and corresponding audio. Students can replay any part of any class with easy-to-use browser-based viewing on a PC or Mac.

Educators know that the more students can see, hear, and experience class resources, the better they learn. In fact, studies prove it. With Tegrity Campus, students quickly recall key moments by using Tegrity Campus's unique search feature. This search helps students efficiently find what they need, when they need it, across an entire semester of class recordings. Help turn all your students' study time into learning moments immediately supported by your lecture.

To learn more about Tegrity watch a two-minute Flash demo at **http://tegritycampus.mhhe.com.**

McGraw-Hill Customer Care Contact Information

At McGraw-Hill, we understand that getting the most from new technology can be challenging. That's why our services don't stop after you purchase our products. You can e-mail our Product Specialists 24 hours a day to get product training online. Or you can search our knowledge bank of Frequently Asked Questions on our support website. For Customer Support, call **800-331-5094** or visit www.mhhe.com/support. One of our Technical Support Analysts will be able to assist you in a timely fashion.

Thank You!

We express our deepest appreciation for the efforts of the colleagues whose extensive feedback over the years has helped to shape and create this text.

Janice Akao, *Butler Community College*

Sophia Anong, *University of Georgia*

Anna Antus, *Normandale Community College*

Eddie Ary, *Ouachita Baptist University*

Chris A. Austin, *Normandale Community College*

Gail H. Austin, *Rose State College*

Kali Bard, *Crowder College*

Judy Bernard, *Bluegrass Community and Technical College*

Tom Bilyeu, *Southwestern Illinois College*

Ross Blankenship, *State Fair Community College*

William F. Blosel, *California University of Pennsylvania*

John Bockino, *Suffolk County Community College*

Karen Bonding, *University of Virginia*

Lyle Bowlin, *Southeastern University*

Michael Brandl, *University of Texas–Austin*

Jerry Braun, *Daytona State College–Daytona Beach*

Darleen Braunshweiger, *Nassau Community College*

Jennifer Brewer, *Butler County Community College*

Bruce Brunson, *Virginia Tech*

Peg Camp, *University of Nebraska–Kearney*

Ron Cereola, *James Madison University*

Stephen Chambers, *Johnson County Community College*

It-Keong Chew, *University of Kentucky*

Mary Emily Cooke, *Surry Community College*

Trung Dang, *Lone Star College North Harris*

Beth Deinert, *Southeast Community College—Milford*

Julie Douthit, *Abilene Christian University*

Bill Dowling, *Savannah State University*

Chip Downing, *Massasoit Community College*

Dorsey Dyer, *Davidson County Community College*

John D. Farlin, *Ohio Dominican University*

Garry Fleming, *Roanoke College*

Paula G. Freston, *Merced College*

Robert Friederichs, *Alexandria Technical College*

Mark Fronke, *Cerritos College*

Caroline S. Fulmer, *University of Alabama*

Dwight Giles, *Jefferson State Community College*

Michael Gordinier, *Washington University*

Shari Gowers, *Dixie State College*

Michelle Grant, *Bossier Parish Community College*

Michael P. Griffin, *University of Massachusetts–Dartmouth*

Monte Hill, *Nova Community College–Annandale*

Ward Hooker, *Orangeburg–Calhoun Tech College*

Ishappa S. Hullur, *Morehead State University*

Samira Hussein, *Johnson County Community College*

Dorothy W. Jones, *Northwestern State University*

Richard "Lee" Kitchen, *Tallahassee Community College*

Jeanette Klosterman, *Hutchinson Community College*

Robert Kozub, *University of Wisconsin–Milwaukee*

Margo Kraft, *Heidelberg College*

John Ledgerwood, *Bethune-Cookman College*

Marc LeFebvre, *Creighton University*

Nolan Lickey, *Utah Valley State College*

Joseph T. Marchese, *Monroe Community College*

Kenneth L. Mark, *Kansas City Kansas Community College*

Paul S. Marshall, *Widener University*

Jennifer Morton, *Ivy Tech Community College of Indiana*

Allan O'Bryan, *Rochester Community & Tech College*

Carl Parker, *Fort Hays State University*

David M. Payne, *Ohio University*

Aaron Phillips, *California State University–Bakersfield*

Padmaja Pillutla, *Western Illinois University*

Barbara Purvis, *Centura College*

Brenda Rice, *Ozarks Technical Community College*

xxx

Carla Rich, *Pensacola Junior College*

John Roberts, *Florida Metropolitan University*

Sammie Root, *Texas State University–San Marcos*

Clarence Rose, *Radford University*

Joan Ryan, *Clackamas Community College*

Martin St. John, *Westmoreland County Community College*

Tim Samolis, *Pittsburgh Technical Institute*

Steven R. Scheff, *Florida Gulf Coast University*

James T. Schiermeyer, *Texas Tech University*

Joseph Simon, *Casper College*

Vernon Stauble, *San Bernardino Valley College*

Lea Timpler, *College of the Canyons*

Michael Trohimczyk, *Henry Ford Community College*

Dick Verrone, *University of North Carolina–Wilmington*

Randall Wade, *Rogue Community College*

Shunda Ware, *Atlanta Technical College*

Kent Weilage, *McCook Community College*

Sally Wells, *Columbia College*

Micheline West, *New Hampshire Tech*

Marilyn Whitney, *University of California–Davis*

Bob Willis, *Rogers State University*

Glen Wood, *Broome Community College*

Russell Woodbridge, *Southeastern College*

Many talented professionals at McGraw-Hill Education have contributed to the development of *Focus on Personal Finance*. We are especially grateful to Chuck Synovec Jennifer Upton, Melissa Caughlin, Keri Johnson, Debra Kubiak, Debra Sylvester, and Kristin Bradley.

In addition, Jack Kapoor expresses special appreciation to Theresa and Dave Kapoor, Kathryn Thumme, and Karen and Joshua Tucker for their typing, proofreading, and research assistance. Les Dlabay would also like to thank Bryna Mollinger for her help reviewing the manuscript. Finally, we thank our spouses and families for their patience, understanding, encouragement, and love throughout this project.

Brief Table of Contents

CHAPTER 1 Personal Financial Planning in Action   2

CHAPTER 2 Money Management Skills   44

CHAPTER 3 Taxes in Your Financial Plan   74

CHAPTER 4 Financial Services: Savings Plans and Payment Accounts   106

CHAPTER 5 Consumer Credit: Advantages, Disadvantages, Sources, and Costs   140

CHAPTER 6 Consumer Purchasing Strategies and Wise Buying of Motor Vehicles   188

CHAPTER 7 Selecting and Financing Housing   218

CHAPTER 8 Home and Automobile Insurance   248

CHAPTER 9 Health and Disability Income Insurance   284

CHAPTER 10 Financial Planning with Life Insurance   320

CHAPTER 11 Investing Basics and Evaluating Bonds   348

CHAPTER 12 Investing in Stocks   386

CHAPTER 13 Investing in Mutual Funds   422

CHAPTER 14 Starting Early: Retirement and Estate Planning   458

APPENDIX A Education Financing, Loans, and Scholarships   492

APPENDIX B Developing a Career Search Strategy   502

APPENDIX C Consumer Agencies and Organizations   514

APPENDIX D Daily Spending Diary   518

PHOTO CREDITS   527

INDEX   528

Focus on . . . the Cover

How do you feel when you look at this cover? We hope the image on the book conveys a feeling of relaxation and overall peace of mind—both achieved, in part, by developing a solid financial plan. From cover to cover, this text's goal is to help you gain the financial literacy and personal finance skills you need to make sound financial decisions for life. Use this book as a tool to help you plan for a successful financial future!

Contents

1 Personal Financial Planning in Action 2

Making Financial Decisions 3

Your Life Situation and Financial Planning 3

Financial Planning in Our Economy 4

Financial Planning Activities 7

Developing and Achieving Financial Goals 9

Types of Financial Goals 9

Goal-Setting Guidelines 9

Opportunity Costs and the Time Value of Money 10

Personal Opportunity Costs 11

Financial Opportunity Costs 11

A Plan for Personal Financial Planning 15

Step 1: Determine Your Current Financial Situation 16

Step 2: Develop Your Financial Goals 16

Step 3: Identify Alternative Courses of Action 17

Step 4: Evaluate Your Alternatives 17

Step 5: Create and Implement Your Financial Action Plan 19

Step 6: Review and Revise Your Plan 20

Career Choice and Financial Planning 22

Appendix: Time Value of Money 32

2 Money Management Skills 44

A Successful Money Management Plan 45

Components of Money Management 45

A System for Personal Financial Records 46

Personal Financial Statements 48

Your Personal Balance Sheet: The Starting Point 48

Your Cash Flow Statement: Inflows and Outflows 51

A Plan for Effective Budgeting 54

Step 1: Set Financial Goals 54

Step 2: Estimate Income 55

Step 3: Budget an Emergency Fund and Savings 55

Step 4: Budget Fixed Expenses 55

Step 5: Budget Variable Expenses 57

Step 6: Record Spending Amounts 57

Step 7: Review Spending and Saving Patterns 58

Money Management and Achieving Financial Goals 60

Selecting a Saving Technique 62

Calculating Savings Amounts 62

3 Taxes in Your Financial Plan 74

Taxes in Your Financial Plan 75

Planning Your Tax Strategy 75

Types of Tax 75

The Basics of Federal Income Tax 78

Step 1: Determining Adjusted Gross Income 78

Step 2: Computing Taxable Income 78

Step 3: Calculating Taxes Owed 81

Step 4: Making Tax Payments 83

Step 5: Deadlines and Penalties 84

Filing Your Federal Income Tax Return 85

Who Must File? 85

Which Tax Form Should You Use? 85

Completing the Federal Income Tax Return 85

How Do I File My State Tax Return? 88

How Do I File My Taxes Online? 88

What Tax Assistance Sources Are Available? 91

Tax Preparation Services 92

What If Your Return Is Audited? 93

Tax Planning Strategies 95

Consumer Purchasing 95

Investment Decisions 95

Retirement and Education Plans 97

Changing Tax Strategies 98

Flat or VAT Tax? 98

4 Financial Services: Savings Plans and Payment Accounts 106

Planning Your Use of Financial Services 107

Managing Daily Money Needs 107

Sources of Quick Cash 108

Types of Financial Services 108

Online and Mobile Banking 109

Prepaid Debit Cards 110

Financial Services and Economic Conditions 110

Sources of Financial Services 111

Comparing Financial Institutions 111

Types of Financial Institutions 112

Problematic Financial Businesses 113

Comparing Savings Plans 115

Regular Savings Accounts 115

Certificates of Deposit 115

Interest-Earning Checking Accounts 118

Money Market Accounts and Funds 118

U.S. Savings Bonds 118

Evaluating Savings Plans 120

Comparing Payment Methods 124

Electronic Payments 124

Checking Accounts 125

Evaluating Checking and Payment Accounts 126

Other Payment Methods 127

Managing Your Checking Account 127

5 Consumer Credit: Advantages, Disadvantages, Sources, and Costs 140

What Is Consumer Credit? 141

The Importance of Consumer Credit in Our Economy 141

Uses and Misuses of Credit 142

Advantages of Credit 142

Disadvantages of Credit 143

Summary: Advantages and Disadvantages of Credit 143

Types of Credit 144

Closed-End Credit 144

Open-End Credit 145

Credit Cards 145

Sources of Consumer Credit 147

Loans 148

Applying for Credit 151

Can You Afford a Loan? 151

General Rules of Credit Capacity 151

The Five Cs of Credit 151

Your Credit Report 153

Credit Scores 155

Other Factors Considered in Determining Creditworthiness 157

What If Your Application Is Denied? 157

What Can You Do to Improve Your Credit Score? 158

The Cost of Credit 160

Finance Charge and Annual Percentage Rate 160

Tackling the Trade-Offs 161

Calculating the Cost of Credit 163

Protecting Your Credit 166

Billing Errors and Disputes 166

Identity Crisis: What to Do If Your Identity Is Stolen 166

Protecting Your Credit from Theft or Loss 167

Protecting Your Credit Information on the Internet 167

Cosigning a Loan 169

Complaining about Consumer Credit 169

Consumer Credit Protection Laws 169

Consumer Financial Protection Bureau 171

Managing Your Debts 171

Warning Signs of Debt Problems 171

Debt Collection Practices 172

Financial Counseling Services 173

Declaring Personal Bankruptcy 173

6 Consumer Purchasing Strategies and Wise Buying of Motor Vehicles 188

Consumer Buying Activities 189

Practical Purchasing Strategies 189

Warranties 191

Research-Based Buying 192

Major Consumer Purchases: Buying Motor Vehicles 195

Phase 1: Preshopping Activities 195

Phase 2: Evaluating Alternatives 196

Phase 3: Determining Purchase Price 198

Phase 4: Postpurchase Activities 201

Resolving Consumer Complaints 203

Step 1: Initial Communication 203

Step 2: Communicate with the Company 204

Step 3: Consumer Agency Assistance 205

Step 4: Legal Action 205

Legal Options for Consumers 205

Small Claims Court 205

Class-Action Suits 206

Using a Lawyer 206

Other Legal Alternatives 206

Personal Consumer Protection 206

7 Selecting and Financing Housing 218

Evaluating Renting and Buying Alternatives 219

Your Lifestyle and Your Choice of Housing 219

Renting versus Buying Housing 219

Rental Activities 220

Home-Buying Activities 225

Step 1: Determine Home Ownership Needs 225

Step 2: Find and Evaluate a Home 226

Step 3: Price the Property 227

The Finances of Home Buying 229

Step 4: Obtain Financing 229

Step 5: Close the Purchase Transaction 234

Home Buying: A Summary 236

A Home-Selling Strategy 236

Preparing Your Home for Selling 236

Determining the Selling Price 237

Sale by Owner 238

Listing with a Real Estate Agent 238

8 Home and Automobile Insurance 248

Insurance and Risk Management 249

What Is Insurance? 249

Types of Risk 250

Risk Management Methods 250

Planning an Insurance Program 251

Property and Liability Insurance in Your Financial Plan 254

Home and Property Insurance 255

Homeowner's Insurance Coverages 255

Renter's Insurance 258

Home Insurance Policy Forms 259

Home Insurance Cost Factors 262

How Much Coverage Do You Need? 262

Factors That Affect Home Insurance Costs 263

Automobile Insurance Coverages 264

Motor Vehicle Bodily Injury Coverages 264

Motor Vehicle Property Damage Coverage 266

No-Fault Insurance 267

Other Automobile Insurance Coverages 267

Automobile Insurance Costs 268

Amount of Coverage 268

Motor Vehicle Insurance Premium Factors 269

Reducing Vehicle Insurance Premiums 269

9 Health and Disability Income
Insurance 284

Health Insurance and Financial Planning 285

What Is Health Insurance? 285

Health Insurance Coverage 288

Types of Health Insurance Coverage 288

Major Provisions in a Health Insurance Policy 291

Health Insurance Trade-Offs 293

Coverage Trade-Offs 293

Which Coverage Should You Choose? 294

Private Health Care Plans and Government
Health Care Programs 295

Private Health Care Plans 295

Government Health Care Programs 298

Health Insurance and the Patient Protection and
Affordable Care Act of 2010 300

The Affordable Care Act and the Individual Shared
Responsibility Provision 303

Disability Income Insurance 305

The Need for Disability Income 305

Sources of Disability Income 306

Disability Income Insurance Trade-Offs 306

Your Disability Income Needs 307

High Medical Costs 308

Why Does Health Care Cost So Much? 310

What Is Being Done about the High Costs of
Health Care? 310

What Can You Do to Reduce Personal
Health Care Costs? 311

10 Financial Planning with Life
Insurance 320

What Is Life Insurance? 321

The Purpose of Life Insurance 321

The Principle and Psychology of Life Insurance 322

How Long Will You Live? 322

Do You Need Life Insurance? 322

Estimating Your Life Insurance Requirements 323

Types of Life Insurance Companies
and Policies 325

Types of Life Insurance Companies 325

Types of Life Insurance Policies 326

Selecting Provisions and Buying Life
Insurance 329

Key Provisions in a Life Insurance Policy 329

Buying Life Insurance 332

Financial Planning with Annuities 336

Why Buy Annuities? 337

Costs of Annuities 337

Tax Considerations 338

11 Investing Basics and Evaluating
Bonds 348

Preparing for an Investment Program 349

Establishing Investment Goals 349

Performing a Financial Checkup 350

Getting the Money Needed to Start an Investment
Program 352

How the Time Value of Money Affects Your
Investments 353

Factors Affecting the Choice of
Investments 355

Safety and Risk 355

Components of the Risk Factor 356

Investment Income 358

Investment Growth 358

Investment Liquidity 358

Factors That Reduce Investment Risk 359

Asset Allocation and Diversification 359

Your Role in the Investment Process 361

Conservative Investment Options: Government Bonds 364

The Psychology of Investing in Bonds 364

Government Bonds and Debt Securities 365

Conservative Investment Options: Corporate Bonds 367

Why Corporations Sell Corporate Bonds 367

Why Investors Purchase Corporate Bonds 369

A Typical Bond Transaction 370

The Decision to Buy or Sell Bonds 371

The Internet 371

Financial Coverage for Bond Transactions 372

Bond Ratings 372

Bond Yield Calculations 373

Other Sources of Information 374

12 Investing in Stocks 386

Common and Preferred Stock 387

Why Corporations Issue Common Stock 388

Why Investors Purchase Common Stock 388

Preferred Stock 391

Evaluating a Stock Issue 392

The Internet 392

Stock Advisory Services 394

Newspaper Coverage and Corporate News 397

Numerical Measures That Influence Investment Decisions 398

Why Corporate Earnings Are Important 398

Dividend Yield and Total Return 400

Other Factors That Influence the Price of a Stock 401

Buying and Selling Stocks 403

Secondary Markets for Stocks 403

Brokerage Firms and Account Executives 404

Should You Use a Full-Service, Discount, or Online Brokerage Firm? 404

Computerized Transactions 405

Sample Stock Transactions 405

Commission Charges 406

Long-Term and Short-Term Investment Strategies 407

Long-Term Techniques 407

Short-Term Techniques 409

13 Investing in Mutual Funds 422

Why Investors Purchase Mutual Funds 423

The Psychology of Investing in Funds 424

Characteristics of Funds 425

Classifications of Mutual Funds 431

Stock Funds 431

Bond Funds 432

Other Funds 432

Choosing the Right Fund for a Retirement Account 433

How to Make a Decision to Buy or Sell Mutual Funds 435

Managed Funds versus Index Funds 436

The Internet 437

Professional Advisory Services 438

The Mutual Fund Prospectus and Annual Report 440

Financial Publications and Newspapers 441

The Mechanics of a Mutual Fund Transaction 442

Return on Investment 443

Taxes and Mutual Funds 444

Purchase Options 445

Withdrawal Options 447

14 Starting Early: Retirement and Estate Planning 458

Planning for Retirement: Start Early 459

Saving Smart for Retirement 460

Conducting a Financial Analysis 460

Estimating Retirement Living Expenses 462

Your Retirement Income 464

Employer Pension Plans 464

Public Pension Plans 466

Personal Retirement Plans 468

Annuities 471

Living on Your Retirement Income 471

Estate Planning 473

The Importance of Estate Planning 473

What Is Estate Planning? 473

Legal Documents 473

Legal Aspects of Estate Planning 474

Wills 474

Types of Wills 474

Formats of Wills 475

Writing Your Will 475

A Living Will 476

Trusts 477

Types of Trusts 478

Taxes and Estate Planning 478

Appendixes

A   Education Financing, Loans, and Scholarships 492

B   Developing a Career Search Strategy 502

C   Consumer Agencies and Organizations 514

D   Daily Spending Diary 518

Photo Credits 527

Index 528

Focus on Personal Finance

1 Personal Financial Planning in Action

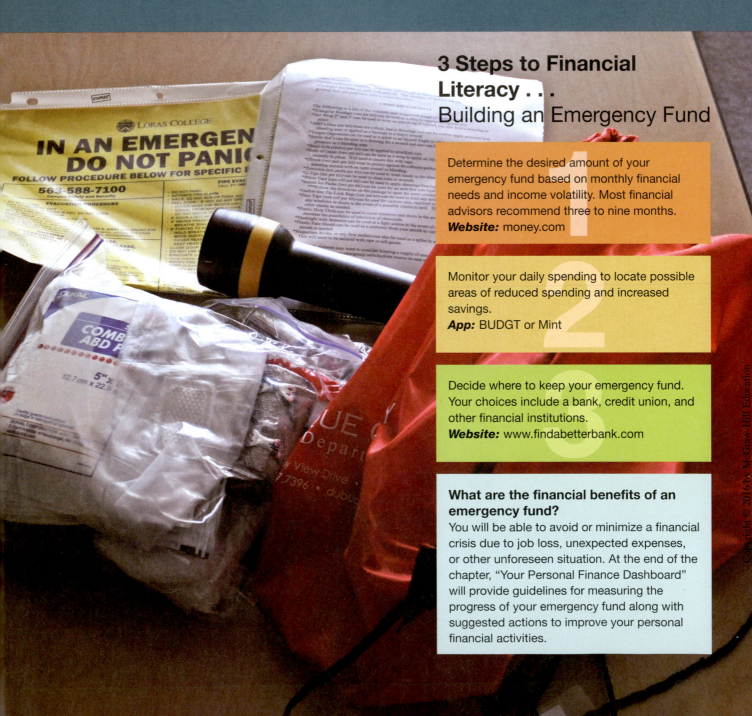

3 Steps to Financial Literacy . . .
Building an Emergency Fund

Determine the desired amount of your emergency fund based on monthly financial needs and income volatility. Most financial advisors recommend three to nine months.
Website: money.com

Monitor your daily spending to locate possible areas of reduced spending and increased savings.
App: BUDGT or Mint

Decide where to keep your emergency fund. Your choices include a bank, credit union, and other financial institutions.
Website: www.findabetterbank.com

What are the financial benefits of an emergency fund?
You will be able to avoid or minimize a financial crisis due to job loss, unexpected expenses, or other unforeseen situation. At the end of the chapter, "Your Personal Finance Dashboard" will provide guidelines for measuring the progress of your emergency fund along with suggested actions to improve your personal financial activities.

CHAPTER 1 LEARNING OBJECTIVES

In this chapter, you will learn to:

LO1.1 Identify social and economic influences on personal financial goals and decisions.

LO1.2 Develop personal financial goals.

LO1.3 Calculate time value of money situations associated with personal financial decisions.

LO1.4 Implement a plan for making personal financial and career decisions.

YOUR PERSONAL FINANCIAL PLAN SHEETS

1. Personal Financial Data
2. Setting Personal Financial Goals
3. Achieving Financial Goals Using Time Value of Money
4. Planning Your Career

Making Financial Decisions

Every person has some money available. However, the amount, along with needs and financial choices, will vary from person to person. In this book, you will have the opportunity to assess your current situation, learn about varied financial paths, and move forward toward future financial security.

Most people want to handle their finances so that they get full satisfaction from each available dollar. Typical financial goals may include buying a new car or a larger home, pursuing advanced career training, contributing to charity, traveling extensively, and ensuring self-sufficiency during working and retirement years. To achieve these and other goals, people need to identify and set priorities. Financial and personal satisfaction are the result of an organized process that is commonly referred to as *personal money management* or *personal financial planning*.

Your Life Situation and Financial Planning

Personal financial planning is the process of managing your money to achieve personal economic satisfaction. This planning process allows you to control your financial situation. Every person, family, or household has a unique situation; therefore, financial decisions must be planned to meet specific needs and goals.

A comprehensive financial plan can enhance the quality of your life and increase your satisfaction by reducing uncertainty about your future needs and resources. A **financial plan** is a formalized report that summarizes your current financial situation, analyzes your financial needs, and recommends future financial activities. You can create this document on your own (by using the sheets at the end of each chapter) or you can seek assistance from a financial planner or use a money management software package.

LO1.1

Identify social and economic influences on personal financial goals and decisions.

ACTION ITEM

Do you have an emergency fund for unexpected expenses?

☐ **Yes** ☐ **No**

personal financial planning The process of managing your money to achieve personal economic satisfaction.

financial plan A formalized report that summarizes your current financial situation, analyzes your financial needs, and recommends future financial activities.

Advantages of effective personal financial planning include

- Increased effectiveness in obtaining, using, and protecting your financial resources throughout your life.
- Increased control of your financial affairs by avoiding excessive debt, bankruptcy, and dependence on others.
- Improved personal relationships resulting from well-planned and effectively communicated financial decisions.
- A sense of freedom from financial worries obtained by looking to the future, anticipating expenses, and achieving personal economic goals.

Many factors influence financial decisions. People in their 20s spend money differently from those in their 50s. Personal factors such as age, income, household size, and personal beliefs influence your spending and saving patterns. Your life situation or lifestyle is created by a combination of factors.

As our society changes, different types of financial needs evolve. Today people tend to get married at a later age, and more households have two incomes. Many households are headed by single parents. More than 2 million women provide care for both dependent children and parents. We are also living longer; over 80 percent of all Americans now living are expected to live past age 65.

adult life cycle The stages in the family situation and financial needs of an adult.

As Exhibit 1–1 shows, the **adult life cycle**—the stages in the family situation and financial needs of an adult—is an important influence on your financial activities and decisions. Your life situation is also affected by events such as graduation, dependent children leaving home, changes in health, engagement and marriage, divorce, birth or adoption of a child, retirement, a career change or a move to a new area, or the death of a spouse, family member, or other dependent.

values Ideas and principles that a person considers correct, desirable, and important.

In addition to being defined by your family situation, you are defined by your **values**—the ideas and principles that you consider correct, desirable, and important. Values have a direct influence on such decisions as spending now versus saving for the future or continuing school versus getting a job.

Financial Planning in Our Economy

Daily economic transactions facilitate financial planning activities. Exhibit 1–2 shows the monetary flows among providers and users of funds that occur in a financial system. These financial activities affect personal finance decisions. Investing in a bond, which is a *debt security,* involves borrowing by a company or government. In contrast, investing in stock, called an *equity security,* represents ownership in a corporation. Other financial market activities include buying and selling mutual funds, certificates of deposit (CDs), and commodity futures.

economics The study of how wealth is created and distributed.

In most societies, the forces of supply and demand set prices for securities, goods, and services. **Economics** is the study of how wealth is created and distributed. The economic environment includes business, labor, and government working together to satisfy needs and wants. As shown in Exhibit 1–2, government agencies regulate financial activities. The Federal Reserve System, the central bank of the United States, has significant economic responsibility. The Fed, as it is often called, attempts to maintain an adequate money supply to encourage consumer spending, business growth, and job creation.

GLOBAL INFLUENCES The global economy can influence financial activities. The U.S. economy is affected by both foreign investors and competition from foreign companies. American businesses compete against foreign companies for the spending dollars of American consumers. When the level of exports of U.S.-made goods is lower than the level of imported goods, more U.S. dollars leave the country than the dollar value of foreign currency coming into the United States. This reduces the funds available for

Exhibit 1–1   Financial Planning Influences, Goals, and Activities

Life Situation Factors Affect Financial Planning Activities

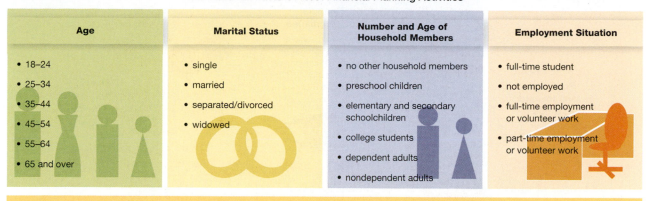

Age	Marital Status	Number and Age of Household Members	Employment Situation
• 18–24 • 25–34 • 35–44 • 45–54 • 55–64 • 65 and over	• single • married • separated/divorced • widowed	• no other household members • preschool children • elementary and secondary schoolchildren • college students • dependent adults • nondependent adults	• full-time student • not employed • full-time employment or volunteer work • part-time employment or volunteer work

TIME TO TAKE ACTION . . . COMMON FINANCIAL GOALS AND ACTIVITIES

- Obtain appropriate career training.
- Create an effective financial recordkeeping system.
- Develop a regular savings and investment program.

- Accumulate an appropriate emergency fund.
- Purchase appropriate types and amounts of insurance coverage.
- Create and implement a flexible budget.

- Evaluate and select appropriate investments.
- Establish and implement a plan for retirement goals.
- Make a will and develop an estate plan.

SPECIALIZED FINANCIAL GOALS AND ACTIVITIES FOR VARIOUS LIFE SITUATIONS

Young, Single (18–35)	Young Couple with Children under 18	Single Parent with Children under 18	Young, Dual-Income Couple, No Children
• Establish financial independence. • Obtain disability insurance to replace income during prolonged illness. • Consider home purchase for tax benefit.	• Carefully manage increased need for the use of credit. • Obtain an appropriate amount of life insurance for the care of dependents. • Use a will to name guardian for children.	• Obtain appropriate health, life, and disability insurance. • Contribute to savings and investment fund for college. • Name a guardian for children and make other estate plans.	• Coordinate insurance coverage and other benefits. • Develop investment program for changes in life situation (larger house, children). • Consider tax-deferred contributions to retirement fund.

Unmarried Couple, No Children	Older Couple (50+), No Dependent Children	Mixed-Generation Elderly Individuals and Children under 18	Older (50+) Single Person, No Dependent Children
• Plan joint and individual bank and credit accounts. • Communicate budgeting attitude differences. • Discuss and share joint and individual financial goals. • Consider a home purchase with a property agreement.	• Review financial assets and estate plans. • Consider household budget changes several years prior to retirement. • Plan retirement housing, living expenses, recreational activities, and part-time work.	• Obtain long-term care, life, and disability insurance coverage. • Use dependent care service. • Provide for handling finances of elderly if they become ill. • Consider splitting investment cost—elderly get income while alive, principal to survivors.	• Make arrangement for long-term health care coverage. • Review will and estate plan. • Plan retirement living facilities, living expenses, and activities. • Monitor investments to consider current financial needs and market conditions.

Exhibit **1–2** The Financial System

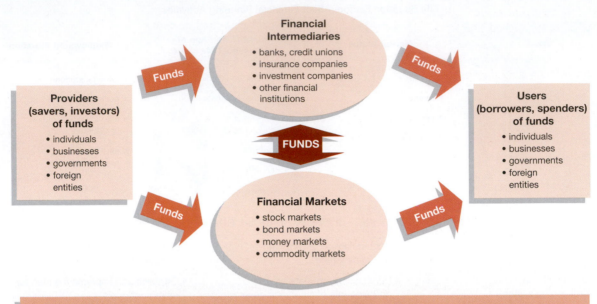

Financial Regulators: Federal Reserve System, Federal Deposit Insurance Corporation, National Credit Union Administration, Office of the Comptroller of the Currency, Consumer Financial Protection Bureau, Securities and Exchange Commission, state banking agencies, state insurance agencies.

domestic spending and investment. Also, if foreign companies decide not to invest in the United States, the domestic money supply is reduced. This reduced money supply can cause higher interest rates.

inflation A rise in the general level of prices.

INFLATION Most people are concerned with the buying power of their money. **Inflation** is a rise in the general level of prices. In times of inflation, the buying power of the dollar decreases. For example, if prices increased 5 percent during the last year, items that previously cost $100 would now cost $105. This means more money is needed to buy the same amount of goods and services.

Inflation is most harmful to people with fixed incomes. Due to inflation, retired people and others whose incomes do not change are able to afford fewer goods and services. Inflation can also adversely affect lenders of money. Unless an adequate interest rate is charged, amounts repaid by borrowers in times of inflation have less buying power than the money they borrowed.

Inflation rates vary. During the late 1950s and early 1960s, the annual inflation rate was in the 1 to 3 percent range. During the late 1970s and early 1980s, the cost of living increased 10 to 12 percent annually. At a 12 percent annual inflation rate, prices double (and the value of the dollar is cut in half) in about six years. To find out how fast prices (or your savings) will double, use the *Rule of 72:* Just divide 72 by the annual inflation (or interest) rate.

EXAMPLE: Rule of 72

An annual inflation rate of 4 percent, for example, means prices will double in 18 years (72 ÷ 4 = 18). Regarding savings, if you earn 6 percent, your money will double in 12 years (72 ÷ 6 = 12).

More recently, the reported annual price increase for goods and services as measured by the consumer price index has been in the 2 to 4 percent range. The *consumer price index (CPI)*, computed and published by the Bureau of Labor Statistics, is a measure of the average change in the prices urban consumers pay for a fixed "basket" of goods and services.

Inflation rates can be deceptive since the index is based on items calculated in a predetermined manner. Many people face *hidden* inflation since the cost of necessities (food, gas, health care), on which they spend the greatest proportion of their money, may rise at a higher rate than nonessential items, which could be dropping in price. This results in a reported inflation rate much lower than the actual cost-of-living increase being experienced by consumers.

Deflation, a decline in prices, can also have damaging economic effects. As prices drop, consumers expect they will go even lower. As a result, consumers cut their spending, which causes damaging economic conditions. While widespread deflation is unlikely, certain items may be affected and their prices will drop.

INTEREST RATES In simple terms, interest rates represent the cost of money. Like everything else, money has a price. The forces of supply and demand influence interest rates. When consumer saving and investing increase the supply of money, interest rates tend to decrease. However, as borrowing by consumers, businesses, and government increases, interest rates are likely to rise.

Interest rates can have a major effect on financial planning. The earnings you receive as a saver or an investor reflect current interest rates as well as a *risk premium* based on such factors as the length of time your funds will be used by others, expected inflation, and the extent of uncertainty about getting your money back. Risk is also a factor in the interest rate you pay as a borrower. People with poor credit ratings pay a higher interest rate than people with good credit ratings. Interest rates influence many financial decisions.

did you know?

U.S. consumer prices between 1970 and 1980 nearly doubled, while between 2000 and 2010 prices rose only about 27 percent. Some countries, such as Bolivia and Zimbabwe, have encountered *hyperinflation* in their history, with consumer prices increasing more than 50,000 percent.

Financial Planning Activities

To achieve a successful financial situation, you must coordinate various components through an organized plan and wise decision making.

OBTAINING (CHAPTER 1) You obtain financial resources from employment, investments, or ownership of a business. Obtaining financial resources is the foundation of financial planning, since these resources are used for all financial activities.

PLANNING (CHAPTERS 2, 3) Planned spending through budgeting is the key to achieving goals and future financial security. Efforts to anticipate expenses along with making certain financial decisions can reduce taxes, increase savings, and result in less financial stress.

SAVING (CHAPTERS 2, 4) Long-term financial security starts with a regular savings plan for emergencies, unexpected bills, replacement of major items, and the purchase of special goods and services, such as a college education, a boat, or a vacation home. Once you have established a basic savings plan, you may use additional money for investments that offer greater financial growth.

BORROWING (CHAPTER 5) Maintaining control over your credit-buying habits will contribute to your financial goals. The overuse and misuse of credit may cause a situation in which a person's debts far exceed the resources available to pay those debts. **Bankruptcy** is a set of federal laws allowing you to either restructure your debts or remove

bankruptcy A set of federal laws allowing you to either restructure your debts or remove certain debts.

certain debts. The people who declare bankruptcy each year may have avoided this trauma with wise spending and borrowing decisions. Chapter 5 discusses bankruptcy in detail.

SPENDING (CHAPTERS 6, 7) Financial planning is designed not to prevent your enjoyment of life but to help you obtain the items you want. Too often, however, people make purchases without considering the financial consequences. Some people shop compulsively, creating financial difficulties. You should detail your living expenses and your other financial obligations in a spending plan. Spending less than you earn is the only way to achieve long-term financial security.

MANAGING RISK (CHAPTERS 8, 9, 10) Adequate insurance coverage is another component of personal financial planning. Certain types of insurance are commonly overlooked in financial plans. For example, the number of people who suffer disabling injuries or diseases at age 50 is greater than the number who die at that age, so people may need disability insurance more than they need life insurance. Yet surveys reveal that most people have adequate life insurance but few have adequate disability insurance.

INVESTING (CHAPTERS 11, 12, 13) Although many types of investments are available, people invest for two primary reasons. Those interested in *current income* select investments that pay regular dividends or interest. In contrast, investors who desire *long-term growth* choose stocks, mutual funds, real estate, and other investments with potential for increased value in the future. You can achieve investment diversification by including a variety of assets in your *portfolio*—these may include stocks, bond mutual funds, real estate, and collectibles such as rare coins.

RETIREMENT AND ESTATE PLANNING (CHAPTER 14) Most people desire financial security upon completion of full-time employment. But retirement planning also involves thinking about your housing situation, your recreational activities, and possible part-time or volunteer work.

Transfers of money or property to others should be timed, if possible, to minimize the tax burden and maximize the benefits for those receiving the financial resources. Knowledge of property transfer methods can help you select the best course of action for funding current and future living costs, educational expenses, and retirement needs of dependents.

 Sheet 1 Personal Financial Data

PRACTICE QUIZ 1–1

1. How do personal and economic factors affect the operation of the financial system and personal financial decisions?

2. For each of the following situations, indicate if the person would tend to "suffer" or tend to "benefit" from inflation. (Circle your answer)

A person with money in a savings account.	suffer	benefit
A person who is borrowing money.	suffer	benefit
A person who is lending money.	suffer	benefit
A person receiving a fixed income amount.	suffer	benefit

Apply Yourself!

Using online research and discussion with others, calculate the recent inflation rate that reflects the change in price for items frequently bought by you and your family.

Developing and Achieving Financial Goals

LO1.2

Develop personal financial goals.

Why do so many Americans—living in one of the richest countries in the world—have money problems? The answer can be found in two main factors. The first is poor planning and weak money management habits in areas such as spending and the use of credit. The other factor is extensive advertising, selling efforts, and product availability that encourage overbuying. Achieving personal financial satisfaction starts with clear financial goals.

ACTION ITEM

Do you have specific financial goals that you hope to achieve in the future?

☐ **Yes** ☐ **No**

Types of Financial Goals

What would you like to do tomorrow? Believe it or not, that question involves goal setting, which may be viewed in three time frames:

- *Short-term goals* will be achieved within the next year or so, such as saving for a vacation or paying off small debts.
- *Intermediate goals* have a time frame of two to five years.
- *Long-term goals* involve financial plans that are more than five years off, such as retirement, money for children's college education, or the purchase of a vacation home.

Long-term goals should be planned in coordination with short-term and intermediate goals. Setting and achieving short-term goals is commonly the basis for moving toward success of long-term goals. For example, saving for a down payment to buy a house is a short-term goal that can be a foundation for a long-term goal: owning your own home.

A goal of obtaining increased career training is different from a goal of saving money to pay a semiannual auto insurance premium. *Consumable-product goals* usually occur on a periodic basis and involve items that are used up relatively quickly, such as food, clothing, and entertainment. *Durable-product goals* usually involve infrequently purchased, expensive items such as appliances, cars, and sporting equipment; these consist of tangible items. In contrast, many people overlook *intangible-purchase goals*. These goals may relate to personal relationships, health, education, community service, and leisure.

Goal-Setting Guidelines

An old saying goes, "If you don't know where you're going, you might end up somewhere else and not even know it." Goal setting is central to financial decision making. Your financial goals are the basis for planning, implementing, and measuring the progress of your spending, saving, and investing activities. Exhibit 1–1 offers typical goals and financial activities for various life situations.

Your financial goals should take a SMART approach, in that they are:

- **S**—*specific*, so you know exactly what your goals are and can create a plan designed to achieve those objectives.
- **M**—*measurable* by a specific amount. For example, "Accumulate $5,000 in an investment fund within three years" is more measurable than "Put money into an investment fund."
- **A**—*action-oriented*, providing the basis for the personal financial activities you will undertake. For example, "Reduce credit card debt" will usually mean actions to pay off amounts owed.
- **R**—*realistic*, involving goals based on your income and life situation. For example, it is probably not realistic to expect to buy a new car each year if you are a full-time student.
- **T**—*time-based*, indicating a time frame for achieving the goal, such as three years. This allows you to measure your progress toward your financial goals.

 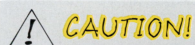

CAUTION!

Most financial planning professionals have a code of ethics, but not all abide by these principles. To avoid financial difficulties and potential fraud, make sure your financial planner strictly applies industry policies regarding confidentiality, integrity, objectivity to prevent a conflict of interest, and a commitment to continuing education.

Personal Finance in Practice

Developing Financial Goals

Based on your current situation or expectations for the future, create one or more financial goals based on this four-step process:

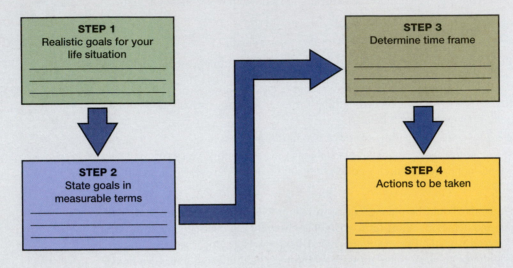

STEP 1
Realistic goals for your
life situation
_____
_____
_____

STEP 2
State goals in
measurable terms
_____
_____
_____

STEP 3
Determine time frame
_____
_____
_____

STEP 4
Actions to be taken
_____
_____
_____

Sheet 2 Setting Personal Financial Goals

PRACTICE QUIZ 1–2

1. What are some examples of long-term goals?

2. What are the main characteristics of useful financial goals?

3. Match the following common goals to the life situation of the people listed.

   a. Pay off student loans   _____ A young couple without children
   b. Start a college savings fund   _____ An older person living alone
   c. Increase retirement contributions   _____ A person who just completed college
   d. Finance long-term care   _____ A single mother with a preschool daughter

Apply Yourself!

Ask friends, relatives, and others about their short-term and long-term financial goals. What are some of the common goals for various personal situations?

LO1.3

Calculate time value of money situations associated with personal financial decisions.

Opportunity Costs and the Time Value of Money

In every financial decision, you sacrifice something to obtain something else that you consider more desirable. For example, you might forgo current buying now to save funds for future purchases or long-term financial security. Or you might gain the use of an expensive item now by making credit payments from future earnings.

Opportunity cost is what you give up by making a choice. This cost, commonly referred to as the *trade-off* of a decision, cannot always be measured in dollars. Opportunity costs should be viewed in terms of both personal and financial resources.

Personal Opportunity Costs

An important personal opportunity cost involves time that when used for one activity cannot be used for other activities. Time used for studying, working, or shopping will not be available for other uses. Other personal opportunity costs relate to health. Poor eating habits, lack of sleep, or avoiding exercise can result in illness, time away from school or work, increased health care costs, and reduced financial security. Like financial resources, your personal resources (time, energy, health, abilities, knowledge) require planning and wise management.

Financial Opportunity Costs

Would you rather have $100 today or $103 a year from now? How about $120 a year from now instead of $100 today? Your choice among these alternatives will depend on several factors including current needs, future uncertainty, and current interest rates. If you wait to receive your money in the future, you want to be rewarded for the risk. The **time value of money** involves the increases in an amount of money as a result of interest earned. Saving or investing a dollar instead of spending it today results in a future amount greater than a dollar. Every time you spend, save, invest, or borrow money, you should consider the time value of that money as an opportunity cost. Spending money from your savings account means lost interest earnings; however, what you buy with that money may have a higher priority than those earnings.

INTEREST CALCULATIONS Three amounts are used to calculate the time value of money for savings in the form of interest earned:

- The amount of the savings (commonly called the *principal*).
- The annual interest rate.
- The length of time the money is on deposit.

These three items are multiplied to obtain the amount of interest. Simple interest is calculated as follows:

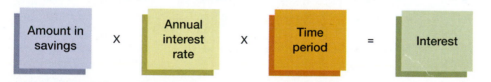

For example, $500 on deposit at 6 percent for six months would earn $15 ($500 × 0.06 × 6/12 or ½ year).

The increased value of money from interest earned involves two types of time value of money calculations, future value and present value. The amount that will be available at a later date is called the *future value*. In contrast, the current value of an amount desired in the future is the *present value*. Five methods are available for calculating time value of money:

1. *Formula calculation.* With this conventional method, math notations are used for computing future value and present value.
2. *Time value of money tables.* Traditionally, before calculators and computers, future value and present value tables were used (see Exhibit 1–3) to provide for easier computations.

ACTION ITEM

Do you set aside an amount of money on a regular basis for various financial goals?

☐ **Yes** ☐ **No**

opportunity cost What a person gives up by making a choice.

time value of money
Increase in an amount of money as a result of interest earned.

Exhibit 1–3

Time Value of Money Tables (condensed)

A. Future Value of $1 (single amount)

	PERCENT				
Year	5%	6%	7%	8%	9%
5	1.276	1.338	1.403	1.469	1.539
6	1.340	1.419	1.501	1.587	1.677
7	1.407	1.504	1.606	1.714	1.828
8	1.477	1.594	1.718	1.851	1.993
9	1.551	1.689	1.838	1.999	2.172
10	1.629	1.791	1.967	2.159	2.367

B. Future Value of a Series of Annual Deposits (annuity)

	PERCENT				
Year	5%	6%	7%	8%	9%
5	5.526	5.637	5.751	5.867	5.985
6	6.802	6.975	7.153	7.336	7.523
7	8.142	8.394	8.654	8.923	9.200
8	9.549	9.897	10.260	10.637	11.028
9	11.027	11.491	11.978	12.488	13.021
10	12.578	13.181	13.816	14.487	15.193

C. Present Value of $1 (single amount)

	PERCENT				
Year	5%	6%	7%	8%	9%
5	0.784	0.747	0.713	0.681	0.650
6	0.746	0.705	0.666	0.630	0.596
7	0.711	0.665	0.623	0.583	0.547
8	0.677	0.627	0.582	0.540	0.502
9	0.645	0.592	0.544	0.500	0.460
10	0.614	0.558	0.508	0.463	0.422

D. Present Value of a Series of Annual Deposits (annuity)

	PERCENT				
Year	5%	6%	7%	8%	9%
5	4.329	4.212	4.100	3.993	3.890
6	5.076	4.917	4.767	4.623	4.486
7	5.786	5.582	5.389	5.206	5.033
8	6.463	6.210	5.971	5.747	5.535
9	7.108	6.802	6.515	6.247	5.995
10	7.722	7.360	7.024	6.710	6.418

NOTE: See the appendix at the end of this chapter for more complete future value and present value tables.

3. *Financial calculator.* A variety of calculators are programmed with financial functions. Both future value and present value calculations are performed using appropriate keystrokes.

4. *Spreadsheet software.* Excel and other spreadsheet programs have built-in formulas for financial computations, including future value and present value.

5. *Websites and apps.* Many time value of money calculators are available online and through mobile devices. These programs may be used to calculate the future value of savings as well as loan payment amounts.

FUTURE VALUE OF A SINGLE AMOUNT Deposited money earns interest that will increase over time. **Future value** is the amount to which current savings will grow based on a certain interest rate and a certain time period. For example, $100 deposited in a 6 percent account for one year will grow to $106. This amount is computed as follows:

future value The amount to which current savings will increase based on a certain interest rate and a certain time period; also referred to as *compounding.*

$$\text{Future value} = \$100 + (\$100 \times 0.06 \times 1 \text{ year}) = \$106$$

The same process could be continued for a second, third, and fourth year; however, the computations would be time-consuming. The previously mentioned calculation methods make the process easier.

An example of the future value of a single amount might involve an investment of $650 earning 8 percent for 10 years. This situation would be calculated as follows:

Formula	Time Value of Money Table	Financial Calculator	Spreadsheet Software
$FV = PV(1 + i)^n$ $FV = 650(1 + 0.08)^{10}$ $FV = \$1,403.30$ *i*—interest rate *n*—number of time periods	Using Exhibit 1–3A, multiply the amount deposited by the factor for the interest rate and time period. $650 \times 2.159 = \$1,403.35$ (The slight difference in this answer is the result of rounding the decimal places.)	PV , I/Y , N , PMT , CPT FV 650 PV , 8 I/Y , 10 N , 0 PMT , CPT FV $1,403.30 (Different financial calculators will require different keystrokes.)	=FV(rate, periods, amount per period, single amount) =FV(0.08,10,0,−650) =$1,403.30

NOTE: Expanded explanations of these time value of money calculation methods are presented in the appendix following this chapter.

Future value computations are often referred to as *compounding,* since interest is earned on previously earned interest. Compounding allows the future value of a deposit to grow faster than it would if interest were paid only on the original deposit. The sooner you make deposits, the greater the future value will be. Depositing $1,000 in a 5 percent account at age 40 will give you $3,387 at age 65. However, making the $1,000 deposit at age 25 would result in an account balance of $7,040 at age 65.

FUTURE VALUE OF A SERIES OF DEPOSITS
Many savers and investors make regular deposits. An *annuity* is a series of equal deposits or payments. To determine the future value of equal yearly savings deposits, time value of money tables can be used (see Exhibit 1–3B). For this table to be used, and for an annuity to exist, the deposits must earn a constant interest rate. For example, if you deposit $50 a year at 7 percent

did you know?

If you invest $2,000 a year (at 9 percent) from ages 31 to 65, these funds will grow to $470,249 by age 65. However, if you save $2,000 a year (at 9 percent) for only 9 years (ages 22 to 30), at age 65 this fund will be worth $579,471! Most important: Start investing something now!

Time Value of Money Calculations for Achieving Financial Goals

Achieving specific financial goals may require making regular savings deposits or determining an amount to be invested. By using time value of money calculations, you can compute the amount needed to achieve a financial goal.

Situation 1: Jonie Emerson has two children who will start college in 10 years. She plans to set aside $1,500 a year for her children's college education during that period and estimates she will earn an annual interest rate of 5 percent on her savings. What amount can Jonie expect to have available for her children's college education when they start college?

Formula	Time Value of Money Table	Financial Calculator	Spreadsheet Software
$FV = Annuity \dfrac{(1 + i)^n - 1}{i}$ $FV = \dfrac{1,500(1 + .05)^{10} - 1}{.05}$ $FV = \$18,866.85$	Using Exhibit 1–3B, multiply the amount deposited by the factor for the interest rate and time period. 1,500 × 12.578 = $18,867	[PV], [I/Y], [N], [PMT], [CPT] [FV] 0 [PV], 5 [I/Y], 10 [N], 1,500 [PMT], [CPT] [FV] $18,866.84 (Different financial calculators will require different keystrokes.)	= FV(rate, periods, amount per period, amount) = FV(0.05,10, −1,500) = $18,866.84

Conclusion: Based these calculations, if Jonie deposits $1,500 a year at an annual interest rate of 5 percent, she would have $18,867 available for her children's college education.

Situation 2: Don Calder wants to have $50,000 available in 10 years as a reserve fund for his parents' retirement living expenses and health care. If he earns an average of 8 percent on his investments, what amount must he invest today to achieve this goal?

Formula	Time Value of Money Table	Financial Calculator	Spreadsheet Software
$PV = \dfrac{FV}{(1 + i)^n}$ $PV = \dfrac{50,000}{(1 + .08)^{10}}$ $FV = \$23,159.94$	Using Exhibit 1–3C, multiply the amount desired by the factor for the interest rate and time period. 50,000 × 0.463 = $23,150	[FV], [N], [I/Y], [PMT], [CPT] [PV] 50,000 [FV], 10 [N], 8 [I/Y], 0 [PMT], [CPT] [PV] $23,159.67 (Different financial calculators will require different keystrokes.)	= PV(rate, periods, payment, future value amount type) = PV(0.08,10,0,−50,000) = $23,159.67

Conclusion: Don needs to invest approximately $23,160 today for 10 years at 8 percent to achieve the desired financial goal.

NOTE: Expanded explanations of these time value of money calculation methods are presented in the appendix following this chapter.

digi – know?

The use of mobile apps for personal financial activities continues to expand with instant access to bank accounts, budget amounts, investment information, and time value of money calculations. Some of the most popular are mint, Unsplurge, Easy Money, and Pocket Money, with costs ranging from free to a few dollars.

for six years, starting at the end of the first year, you will have $357.65 at the end of that time ($50 × 7.153). The nearby "Figure It Out!" box presents examples of using future value to achieve financial goals.

PRESENT VALUE OF A SINGLE AMOUNT Another aspect of the time value of money involves determining the current value of an amount desired in the future. **Present value** is the current value for a future amount based on a particular interest rate for a certain period of time. Present value computations, also called *discounting,* allow you to determine how much to deposit now to obtain a desired total in the future. For example, using the present value table (Exhibit 1–3C), if you want $1,000 five years from now and you earn 5 percent on your savings, you need to deposit $784 ($1,000 × 0.784).

PRESENT VALUE OF A SERIES OF DEPOSITS You may also use present value computations to determine how much you need to deposit now so that you can take a certain amount out of the account for a desired number of years. For example, if you want to take $400 out of an investment account each year for nine years and your money is earning an annual rate of 8 percent, you can see from Exhibit 1–3D that you would need to make a current deposit of $2,498.80 ($400 × 6.247).

Additional details for the formulas, tables, and other methods for calculating time value of money are presented in the appendix at the end of this chapter.

present value The current value for a future amount based on a certain interest rate and a certain time period; also referred to as *discounting*.

Sheet 3 Achieving Financial Goals Using Time Value of Money

PRACTICE QUIZ 1–3

1. What are some examples of personal opportunity costs?

2. What does time value of money measure?

3. Use the time value of money tables in Exhibit 1–3 (or a financial calculator) to calculate the following:

    a. The future value of $100 at 7 percent in 10 years.
    b. The future value of $100 a year for six years earning 6 percent.
    c. The present value of $500 received in eight years with an interest rate of 8 percent.

Apply Yourself!

What is the relationship between current interest rates and financial opportunity costs? Using time value of money calculations, state one or more goals in terms of an annual savings amount and the future value of this savings objective.

A Plan for Personal Financial Planning

We all make hundreds of decisions each day. Most of these decisions are quite simple and have few consequences. However, some are complex and have long-term effects on our personal and financial situations, as shown here:

LO1.4

Implement a plan for making personal financial and career decisions.

ACTION ITEM

Do you consider various types of risks when making personal financial decisions?

☐ Yes   ☐ No

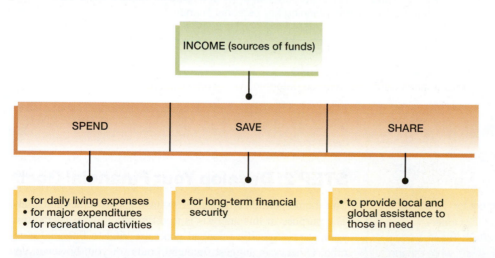

While everyone makes decisions, few people consider how to make better decisions. As Exhibit 1–4 shows, the financial planning process can be viewed as a six-step procedure that can be adapted to any life situation.

Exhibit **1–4** The Financial Planning Process

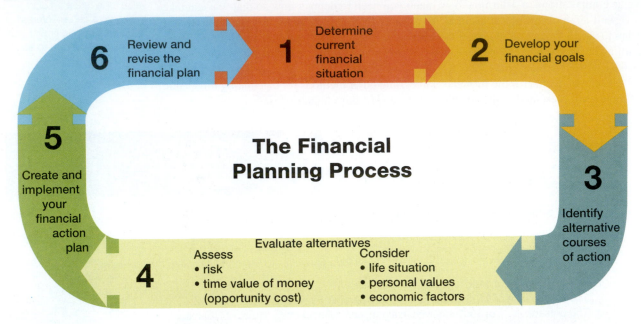

STEP 1: Determine Your Current Financial Situation

In this first step, determine your current financial situation regarding income, savings, living expenses, and debts. Preparing a list of current asset and debt balances and amounts spent for various items gives you a foundation for financial planning activities. The personal financial statements discussed in Chapter 2 will provide the information needed in this phase of financial decision making.

EXAMPLE: Step 1, Determine Your Current Situation

Carla Elliot plans to complete her college degree in the next two years. She works two part-time jobs in an effort to pay her educational expenses. Currently, Carla has $700 in a savings account and existing debt that includes a $640 balance on her credit card and $2,300 in student loans. What additional information should Carla have available when planning her personal finances?

_____

Example from Your Life

What actions have you taken to determine your current financial situation?

_____

did you know?

According to the National Endowment for Financial Education, 70 percent of major lottery winners end up with financial difficulties. These winners often squander the funds awarded them, while others overspend and many end up declaring bankruptcy. Having more money does not automatically mean making better financial planning choices.

STEP 2: Develop Your Financial Goals

You should periodically analyze your financial values and goals. The purpose of this analysis is to differentiate your needs from your wants. Specific financial goals are vital to financial planning. Others can suggest financial goals for you; however, *you* must decide which goals to pursue. Your financial goals can range from spending all of your current income to developing an extensive savings and investment program for your future financial security.

EXAMPLE: Step 2, Develop Financial Goals

Carla Elliot's main financial goals for the next two years are to complete her college degree and to maintain or reduce the amounts owed. What other goals might be appropriate for Carla?

_____

Example from Your Life

Describe some short-term or long-term goals that might be appropriate for your life situation.

_____

STEP 3: Identify Alternative Courses of Action

Developing alternatives is crucial when making decisions. Although many factors will influence the available alternatives, possible courses of action usually fall into these categories:

- *Continue the same course of action.* For example, you may determine that the amount you have saved each month is still appropriate.
- *Expand the current situation.* You may choose to save a larger amount each month.
- *Change the current situation.* You may decide to use a money market account instead of a regular savings account.
- *Take a new course of action.* You may decide to use your monthly saving budget to pay off credit card debts.

Not all of these categories will apply to every decision; however, they do represent possible courses of action. For example, if you want to stop working full-time to go to school, you must generate several alternatives under the category "Take a new course of action." Creativity in decision making is vital to effective choices. Considering all of the possible alternatives will help you make more effective and satisfying decisions. For instance, most people believe they must own a car to get to work or school. However, they should consider other alternatives such as public transportation, carpooling, renting a car, shared ownership of a car, or a company car.

Remember, when you decide not to take action, you elect to "do nothing," which can be a dangerous alternative.

EXAMPLE: Step 3, Identify Alternatives

To achieve her goals, Carla Elliot has several options available. She could reduce her spending, seek a higher-paying part-time job, or use her savings to pay off some of her debt. What additional alternatives might she consider?

_____

Example from Your Life

List various alternatives for achieving the financial goals you identified in the previous step.

_____

STEP 4: Evaluate Your Alternatives

You need to evaluate possible courses of action, taking into consideration your life situation, personal values, and current economic conditions. How will the ages of dependents affect your saving goals? How do you like to spend leisure time? How will changes in interest rates affect your financial situation?

Copyright © 2016 by McGraw-Hill Education

did you know?

Nearly one billion people around the world live on $1 or less a day. Various organizations provide these people with basic need items and future opportunities. Bright Hope International assists the extreme poor by providing food, clothing, shelter, health care, education, orphan support, microloans, job training, and spiritual guidance. You can help to provide assistance to the extreme poor at www.brighthope.org.

CONSEQUENCES OF CHOICES Every decision closes off alternatives. For example, a decision to invest in stock may mean you cannot take a vacation. A decision to go to school full-time may mean you cannot work full-time. Opportunity cost is what you give up by making a choice. These trade-offs cannot always be measured in dollars. However, the resources you give up (money or time) have a value that is lost.

EVALUATING RISK Uncertainty is also a part of every decision. Selecting a college major and choosing a career field involve risk. What if you don't like working in this field or cannot obtain employment in it? Other decisions involve a very low degree of risk, such as putting money in an insured savings account or purchasing items that cost only a few dollars. Your chances of losing something of great value are low in these situations.

In many financial decisions, identifying and evaluating risk are difficult. Common risks to consider include:

- Inflation risk, due to rising or falling (deflation) prices that cause changes in buying power.
- Interest rate risk, resulting from changes in the cost of money, which can affect your costs (when you borrow) and benefits (when you save or invest).
- Income risk may result from loss of a job or encountering illness.
- Personal risk involves tangible and intangible factors that create a less than desirable situation, such as health or safety concerns.
- Liquidity risk occurs when savings and investments that have potential for higher earnings are difficult to convert to cash or to sell without significant loss in value.

The best way to consider risk is to gather information based on your experience and the experiences of others and to use financial planning information sources.

FINANCIAL PLANNING INFORMATION SOURCES Relevant information is required at each stage of the decision-making process. In addition to this book, common sources available to help you with your financial decisions include (1) the Internet; (2) financial institutions, such as banks, credit unions, and investment companies; (3) media sources, such as newspapers, magazines, television, radio, podcasts, and online videos; and (4) financial specialists, such as financial planners, insurance agents, investment advisors, credit counselors, lawyers, and tax preparers.

EXAMPLE: Step 4, Evaluate Alternatives

As Carla Elliot evaluates her alternative courses of action, she should consider both her short-term and long-term situations. What risks and trade-offs should Carla consider?

_____

Example from Your Life

In your life, what types of risks might be encountered when planning and implementing various personal financial activities?

_____

Which Path Will You Choose? Only One Will Result in Financial Security

Do you feel stress when you think about money? Are your financial decisions influenced by emotions rather than valid information? Do you often have disagreements about money?

To address these and other financial concerns, two paths exist for your daily money decisions. The *easy* path involves little thinking, no planning, and minimal effort, usually resulting in wasted money and financial difficulties. In contrast, the *appropriate* path takes some time and effort, but results in lower stress and personal financial security.

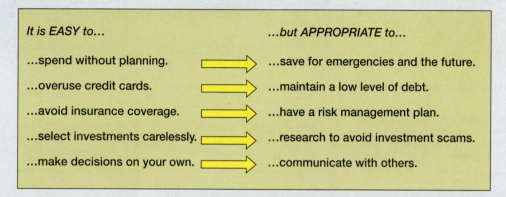

It is EASY to...	*...but APPROPRIATE to...*
...spend without planning.	...save for emergencies and the future.
...overuse credit cards.	...maintain a low level of debt.
...avoid insurance coverage.	...have a risk management plan.
...select investments carelessly.	...research to avoid investment scams.
...make decisions on your own.	...communicate with others.

You can easily start to move yourself from *easy mistakes* to *appropriate actions* with these steps:

1. *Do something.* Start small, such as saving a small amount each month. Or decide to reduce your credit card use.

2. *Avoid excuses.* Do not tell yourself that "I don't have time" or "It's what everyone else is doing."

3. *Rate your current situation.* Indicate on this scale where you are currently in relation to the two available paths:

Spender   Saver

Financial difficulties   Financial security

4. *Set your mission.* Create a *personal finance mission statement* to communicate your personal values, financial goals, and future vision. This paragraph (or list or drawing or other format) will remind you and family members of your desired path for financial security. The wording describes where you want to be, and how you will get there. Develop your financial mission statement by talking with those who can help guide your actions. Your personal finance mission statement may include phrases such as "My financial mission is to change my spending habits for . . . ," ". . . to better understand my insurance needs . . . ," or "to donate (or volunteer) to local community service organizations."

Choosing whether to take *easy* or *difficult* actions can result in reduced emotional stress, improved personal relationships, and expanded financial security.

STEP 5: Create and Implement Your Financial Action Plan

You are now ready to develop an action plan to identify ways to achieve your goals. For example, you can increase your savings by reducing your spending or by increasing your income through extra time on the job. If you are concerned about year-end tax payments, you may increase the amount withheld from each paycheck, file quarterly tax payments, or shelter current income in a tax-deferred retirement program.

To implement your financial action plan, you may need assistance from others. For example, you may use the services of an insurance agent to purchase property insurance or the services of an investment broker to purchase stocks, bonds, or mutual funds. Exhibit 1–5 offers a framework for developing and implementing a financial plan, along with examples for several life situations. Also, Appendix A provides information on financing your education.

Exhibit **1–5**   Financial Planning in Action

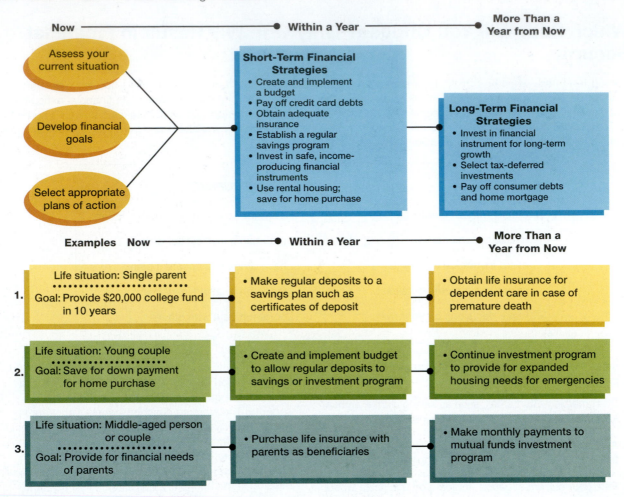

Copyright © 2016 by McGraw-Hill Education

EXAMPLE: Step 5, Create a Financial Plan

Carla has decided to reduce her course load and work longer hours in an effort both to reduce her debt level and to increase the amount she has in savings. What are the benefits and drawbacks of this choice?

Example from Your Life

Describe the benefits and drawbacks of a financial situation you have encountered during the past year.

STEP 6: Review and Revise Your Plan

Financial planning is a dynamic process that does not end when you take a particular action. You need to regularly assess your financial decisions. You should do a complete review of your finances at least once a year. Changing personal, social, and economic factors may require more frequent assessments.

When life events affect your financial needs, this financial planning process will provide a vehicle for adapting to those changes. A regular review of this decision-making

Yours, Mine and Our Accounts

Figuring out how to blend your finances means fewer things to fight about.

Whether you're newlyweds, soon to be wed, or an old married couple, money is at least as important to a balanced, happy marriage as love and sex. Money is a common cause of conflict—and even divorce—among couples. Blend your financial lives successfully, and you are more likely to have a happy marriage.

Because opposites attract, combining money-management styles that conflict is among the greatest challenges married couples face. Early and frequent communication is critical, says Cathy Pareto, a financial advisor in Coral Gables, Fla. That includes discussing your debts, income, credit history, investments and goals. "You've got to meet in the middle," Pareto says. "Otherwise, I promise you there will be fights."

Starting out. The first conversation could be an uncomfortable one. Maybe one of you has a low credit score or a lot of credit card debt. Or perhaps you have significant differences in your approach to spending and saving. Until you've had plenty of honest dialogue, set the ground rules and built the trust you need to put your money together, Pareto recommends keeping accounts mostly separate. "Better to wait

to commingle than to do it too soon and be unpleasantly surprised to learn that you have an irresponsible partner."

You may be able to make do with an informal split of your finances. Alee Papazian, 27, and Brooks Heckner, 31, of Cambridge, Mass., who plan to marry this summer, have been living together since 2006. They have no shared accounts or assets, so they divvy up their mutual expenses. To account for a gap in their earnings, Heckner pays $75 more in rent each month. Papazian pays the utility bills, and Heckner covers the cable and Internet. Then they eyeball most of their other expenses to determine a fair split.

Shannon Hancock, 33, and Scott Knight, 42, who are getting married in September, are more comfortable with the prospect of combining accounts. They chat monthly about their individual budgets, which Hancock expects will help with their transition to budgeting as a couple. They plan to open a joint checking account, from which they could pay their mortgage and other bills, and sign up for a joint credit card.

After the honeymoon. Especially after you buy a house and have kids, it makes sense to merge more of your

finances—although most financial advisors recommend that you each keep at least one credit card in your own name and have access to some money that you can spend without having to consult your spouse (you should check with each other about large purchases). Since Julie Billing, 37, and her husband, Greg, 39, of West Milton, Ohio, got married more than 14 years ago, they have stuck to a strategy of merging their bank accounts. Julie usually handles the bill paying and budgeting. Having such a "family CFO" is a common way for couples to handle expenses, says Pareto.

Talk frequently about your plans, and don't let your emotions become stumbling blocks. Doug Pauley, a financial advisor in Austin, Tex., says sometimes it can help to consult a financial counselor or a financial planner you both trust, who can add perspective and help defuse arguments.

Lisa Gerstner

1. What are reasons for money causing conflicts among couples and with other household members?

2. Which of the actions discussed might be of value to you and others for effective personal financial planning?

3. What additional information is available at www.kiplinger.com to assist you with your financial decisions?

FROM THE PAGES OF . . . Kiplinger's Personal Finance

process will help you make priority adjustments that will bring your financial goals and activities in line with your current life situation.

EXAMPLE: Step 6, Review and Revise the Plan

Over the next 6 to 12 months, Carla Elliot should reassess her financial, personal, and educational situation. What types of circumstances might occur that could require that Carla take a different approach to her personal finances?

_____

Example from Your Life

What factors in your life might affect your personal financial situation and decisions in the future?

_____

Career Choice and Financial Planning

Have you ever wondered why some people find great satisfaction in their work while others only put in their time? As with other personal financial decisions, career selection and professional growth require planning. The lifework you select is a key to your financial well-being and personal satisfaction.

Like other decisions, career choice and professional development alternatives have risks and opportunity costs. In recent years, many people have placed family and personal fulfillment above monetary reward and professional recognition. Career choices require periodic evaluation of trade-offs related to personal, social, and economic factors.

In addition, changing personal and social factors will require you to continually assess your work situation. The steps of the financial planning process can guide your career planning, advancement, and career change. Your career goals will affect how you use this process. If you desire more responsibility on the job, for example, you may decide to obtain advanced training or change career fields. Appendix B provides a plan for obtaining employment and professional advancement.

EXAMPLE: Your Career Planning Decisions

Based on your current or future career situation, describe how you might use the financial planning process (Exhibit 1–4) to plan and implement an employment decision.

_____

_____

Sheet 4 Planning Your Career

PRACTICE QUIZ 1–4

1. What actions might a person take to identify alternatives when making a financial decision?

2. Why are career planning activities considered to be personal financial decisions?

3. For the following situations, identify the type of risk being described.

_____ Not getting proper rest and exercise.

_____ Not being able to obtain cash from a certificate of deposit before the maturity date.

_____ Taking out a variable rate loan when rates are expected to rise.

_____ Training for a career field with low potential demand in the future.

4. For the following main sources of personal finance information, list a specific website, organization, or person whom you might contact in the future.

Type of information	Specific source	Contact information
Website		
Financial institution		
Media source		
Financial specialist		

Apply Yourself!

Talk to friends, relatives, and others about their personal financial activities. Ask about potential risks involved with making financial decisions. What actions might be taken to investigate and reduce these risks?

YOUR PERSONAL FINANCE DASHBOARD

EMERGENCY SAVINGS FUND

A *dashboard* is a tool used by organizations to monitor key performance indicators, such as delivery time, product defects, or customer complaints. As an individual, you can use a *personal finance dashboard* to assess your financial situation.

An often overlooked financial action is the creation of an emergency fund. Financial advisors commonly suggest saving three to six months of living expenses for unexpected situations. More may be needed if you are self-employed.

YOUR SITUATION: Have you started your emergency fund? Do you make progress each month? As with driving, a personal finance dashboard allows you to keep track of your progress to a destination.

POSSIBLE ACTIONS TO TAKE

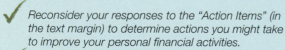 *Reconsider your responses to the "Action Items" (in the text margin) to determine actions you might take to improve your personal financial activities.*

✓ *Obtain information from various sources to reduce spending and increase savings.*

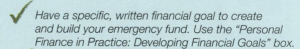 *Have a specific, written financial goal to create and build your emergency fund. Use the "Personal Finance in Practice: Developing Financial Goals" box.*

✓ *Use time value of money computations to help grow your emergency fund. Calculators are available at www.dinkytown.net, www.moneychimp.com/calculator, and www.rbcroyalbank.com/tools.html.*

Chapter Summary

LO1.1 Financial decisions are affected by a person's life situation (income, age, household size, health), personal values, and economic factors (prices, interest rates, and employment opportunities). The major elements of financial planning are obtaining, planning, saving, borrowing, spending, managing risk, investing, and retirement and estate planning.

LO1.2 Financial goals should take a S-M-A-R-T approach with goals that are: Specific, Measurable, Action-oriented, Realistic, and Time-based.

LO1.3 Every decision involves a trade-off with things given up. Personal opportunity costs include time, effort, and health. Financial opportunity costs are based on the time value of money. Future value and present value calculations enable you to measure the increased value (or lost interest) that results from a saving, investing, borrowing, or purchasing decision.

LO1.4 Personal financial planning involves the following process: (1) determine your current financial situation; (2) develop financial goals; (3) identify alternative courses of action; (4) evaluate alternatives; (5) create and implement a financial action plan; and (6) review and revise the financial plan.

Key Terms

adult life cycle 4

bankruptcy 7

economics 4

financial plan 3

future value 13

inflation 5

opportunity cost 11

personal financial
  planning 3

present value 14

time value of money 11

values 4

Discussion Questions

1. In your opinion, what is the main benefit of wise financial planning?   (LO1.1)
2. What factors in an economy might affect the level of interest rates?   (LO1.1)
3. Talk with several people about their financial goals. How have their employment situations affected their financial decisions?   (LO1.2)
4. What are possible drawbacks associated with not considering opportunity costs and time value of money when making financial decisions?   (LO1.3)
5. Describe risks that you might encounter when making financial decisions over the next few years.   (LO1.4)

Self-Test Problems

1. The Rule of 72 provides a guideline for determining how long it takes your money to double. This rule can also be used to determine your earning rate. If your money is expected to double in 12 years, what is your rate of return?
2. If you desire to have $10,000 in savings eight years from now, what amount would you need to deposit in an account that earns 5 percent?

Self-Test Solutions

1. Using the Rule of 72, if your money is expected to double in 12 years, you are earning approximately 6 percent (72 ÷ 12 years = 6 percent).
2. To calculate the present value of $10,000 for eight years at 5 percent, use Exhibit 1–3C (or Exhibit 1–C in the appendix to Chapter 1): $10,000 × 0.677 = $6,770

(*Note:* Some of these problems require the use of the time value of money tables in the appendix directly following this chapter, a financial calculator, or spreadsheet software.)

1. Using the Rule of 72, approximate the following amounts: (LO1.1)

    a. If the value of land in an area is increasing 6 percent a year, how long will it take for property values to double?
    b. If you earn 10 percent on your investments, how long will it take for your money to double?
    c. At an annual interest rate of 5 percent, how long will it take for your savings to double?

2. In 2011, selected automobiles had an average cost of $16,000. The average cost of those same automobiles is now $20,000. What was the rate of increase for these automobiles between the two time periods?   (LO1.1)

3. A family spends $46,000 a year for living expenses. If prices increase 3 percent a year for the next three years, what amount will the family need for their living expenses after three years?   (LO1.1)

4. Ben Collins plans to buy a house for $220,000. If the real estate in his area is expected to increase in value 2 percent each year, what will its approximate value be seven years from now?   (LO1.2)

5. What would be the yearly earnings for a person with $6,000 in savings at an annual interest rate of 2.5 percent?   (LO1.3)

6. Using time value of money tables (Exhibit 1–3 or chapter appendix tables), calculate the following: (LO1.3)

    a. The future value of $550 six years from now at 7 percent.
    b. The future value of $700 saved each year for 10 years at 8 percent.
    c. The amount a person would have to deposit today (present value) at a 5 percent interest rate to have $1,000 five years from now.
    d. The amount a person would have to deposit today to be able to take out $500 a year for 10 years from an account earning 8 percent.

7. If you desire to have $10,000 for a down payment for a house in five years, what amount would you need to deposit today? Assume that your money will earn 4 percent.   (LO1.3)

8. Pete Morton is planning to go to graduate school in a program of study that will take three years. Pete wants to have $8,000 available each year for various school and living expenses. If he earns 4 percent on his money, how much must he deposit at the start of his studies to be able to withdraw $8,000 a year for three years?   (LO1.3)

9. Carla Lopez deposits $3,000 a year into her retirement account. If these funds have average earnings of 8 percent over the 40 years until her retirement, what will be the value of her retirement account?   (LO1.3)

10. If a person spends $10 a week on coffee (assume $500 a year), what would be the future value of that amount over 10 years if the funds were deposited in an account earning 3 percent?   (LO1.3)

11. A financial company that advertises on television will pay you $60,000 now for annual payments of $10,000 that you are expected to receive for a legal settlement over the next 10 years. If you estimate the time value of money at 10 percent, would you accept this offer?   (LO1.3)

12. Tran Lee plans to set aside $2,200 a year for the next seven years, earning 3 percent. What would be the future value of this savings amount?   (LO1.3)

13. If you borrow $8,000 with a 5 percent interest rate to be repaid in five equal payments at the end of the next five years, what would be the amount of each payment? (*Note:* Use the present value of an annuity table in the chapter appendix.)   (LO1.3)

 **To reinforce the content in this chapter, more problems are provided at connect.mheducation.com.**

YOU BE THE FINANCIAL PLANNER

While at some point in your life you may use the services of a financial planner, your personal knowledge should be the foundation for most financial decisions. For each of these situations, determine actions you might recommend.

Situation 1: Fran and Ed Blake, ages 43 and 47, have a daughter who is completing her freshman year of college and a son three years younger. Currently they have $34,000 in various savings and investment funds set aside for their children's education. With the increasing cost of education, they are concerned about whether this amount is adequate. In recent months, Fran's mother has required extensive medical attention and personal care assistance. Unable to live alone, she is now a resident of a long-term care facility. The cost of this service is $4,600 a month, with annual increases of about 5 percent. While a major portion of the cost is covered by her Social Security and pension, Fran's mother is unable to cover the entire cost. In addition, the Blakes are concerned about saving for their own retirement. While they have consistently made annual deposits to a retirement fund, current financial demands may force them to access some of that money.

Situation 2: "While I knew it might happen someday, I didn't expect it right now." This was the reaction of Patrick Hamilton when his company merged with another business and moved its offices to another state, resulting in his losing his job. Patrick does have some flexibility in his short-term finances since he has three months of living expenses in a savings account. However, "three months can go by very quickly," as Patrick noted.

Situation 3: Nina Resendiz, age 23, recently received a $12,000 gift from her aunt. She is considering various uses for these unexpected funds including paying off credit card bills from her last vacation, or setting aside money for a down payment on a house. Or she might invest the money in a tax-deferred retirement account. Another possibility is using the money for technology certification courses to enhance her earning power. Nina also wants to contribute some of the funds to a homeless shelter and a world hunger relief organization. She is overwhelmed by the choices, and comments to herself, "I want to avoid the temptation of wasting the money on impulse items. I want to make sure I use the money on things with lasting value."

Questions

1. In each situation, what are the main financial planning issues that need to be addressed?
2. What additional information would you like to have before recommending actions in each situation?
3. Based on the information provided, along with Exhibit 1–1 and the financial planning process, what actions would you recommend in each situation?

SETTING FINANCIAL GOALS

Jamie Lee Jackson, age 24, has recently decided to switch from attending college part-time to full-time in order to pursue her business degree, and aims to graduate within the next three years. She has 55 credit hours remaining in order to earn her bachelor's degree, and knows that it will be a challenge to complete her course of study while still working part-time in the bakery department of a local grocery store, where she earns $390 a week. Jamie Lee wants to keep her part-time job at the grocery store as she loves baking and creates very decorative cakes. She dreams of opening her own cupcake café within the next five years.

Jamie Lee currently shares a small apartment with a friend, and they split all of the associated living expenses, such as rent and utilities, although she would really like to eventually have a place of her own. Her car is still going strong, even though it is seven years old, and she has no plans to buy a new one any time soon. She is carrying a balance on her credit card and is making regular monthly payments of $50 with hopes of paying it off within a year. Jamie has also recently taken out a student loan to cover her educational costs and expenses. Jamie Lee just started depositing $1,800 a year in a savings account that earns 2 percent interest, in hopes of having the $9,000 down payment needed to start the cupcake café two years after graduation.

Current Financial Situation

Checking account: $1,250

Emergency fund savings account: $3,100

Car: $4,000

Student loan: $5,400

Credit card balance: $400

Gross annual salary: $2,125

Net monthly salary: $1,560

Questions

1. Using "Your Personal Financial Plan" sheet 2, what are Jamie Lee's short-term financial goals? How do they compare to her intermediate financial goals?
2. Browse Jamie Lee's current financial situation. Using the *SMART* approach, what recommendations would you make for her to achieve her long-term goals?
3. Name two opportunity costs that would be considered in Jamie Lee's situation?
4. Jamie Lee needs to save a total of $9,000 in order to get started in her cupcake café venture. She is presently depositing $1,800 a year in a regular savings account earning 2 percent interest. How much will she have accumulated five years from now in this regular savings account, assuming she will be leaving her emergency fund savings account balance untouched and for a rainy day?

"I FIRST THOUGHT THIS PROCESS WOULD BE A WASTE OF TIME, BUT THE INFORMATION HAS HELPED ME BECOME MUCH MORE CAREFUL OF HOW I SPEND MY MONEY."

Nearly everyone who has made the effort to keep a daily spending diary has found it beneficial. While at first the process may seem tedious, after a while recording this information becomes easier and faster.

Directions Using the Daily Spending Diary sheets provided at the end of the book, record *every cent* of your spending each day in the categories provided. Or you may create your own format to monitor your spending. You can indicate the use of a credit card with (CR). This experience will help you better understand your spending patterns and identify desired changes you might want to make in your spending habits. The Daily Spending Diary sheets are located in Appendix D at the end of the book and in Connect Finance.

Questions

1. What did your daily spending diary reveal about your spending habits? What areas of spending might you consider changing?
2. How might your daily spending diary assist you when identifying and achieving financial goals?

Name: _____   Date: _____

Personal Financial Data

Purpose: To create a directory of personal financial information.

Financial Planning Activities: Complete the information request to provide a quick reference for vital household data. This sheet is also available in an Excel spreadsheet format in Connect Finance.

Suggested Websites: www.money.cnn.com   www.kiplinger.com   www.20somethingfinance.com

Name	_____	_____
Birth Date	_____	_____
Marital Status	_____	_____
Address	_____	_____
Phone	_____	_____
E-mail	_____	_____
Social Security No.	_____	_____
Driver's License No.	_____	_____
Place of Employment	_____	_____
Address	_____	_____
Phone	_____	_____
Position	_____	_____
Length of Service	_____	_____
Checking Acct. No.	_____	_____
Financial Inst.	_____	_____
Address	_____	_____
Phone	_____	_____

Dependent Data

Name	Birthdate	Relationship	Social Security No.
_____	_____	_____	_____
_____	_____	_____	_____
_____	_____	_____	_____
_____	_____	_____	_____

What's Next for Your Personal Financial Plan?

- Identify financial planning experts (insurance agent, banker, investment advisor, tax preparer, others) you might contact for financial planning information or assistance.
- Discuss with other household members various financial planning priorities.

Setting Personal Financial Goals

Purpose: To identify personal financial goals and create an action plan.

Financial Planning Activities: Based on personal and household needs and values, identify specific goals that require action. This sheet is also available in an Excel spreadsheet format in Connect Finance.

Suggested Websites: financialplan.about.com   www.planwise.com   www.360financialliteracy.org

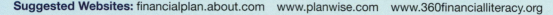

Short-Term Monetary Goals (less than two years)

Description	Amount needed	Months to achieve	Action to be taken	Priority
Example: pay off credit card debt	$850	12	Use money from pay raise	High

Intermediate Monetary Goals (two to five years)

Description	Amount needed	Months to achieve	Action to be taken	Priority

Long-Term Monetary Goals (beyond five years)

Description	Amount needed	Months to achieve	Action to be taken	Priority

Nonmonetary Goals

Description	Time frame	Actions to be taken
Example: set up file for personal financial records and documents	Next 2–3 months	Locate all personal and financial records and documents; set up files for various spending, saving, borrowing categories

Suggested App:
• Urge

What's Next for Your Personal Financial Plan?

- Based on various financial goals, calculate the savings deposits necessary to achieve those goals.
- Identify current economic trends that might influence various saving, spending, investing, and borrowing decisions.

Name: _____   Date: _____

Achieving Financial Goals Using Time Value of Money

Purpose: To calculate future and present value amounts related to financial planning decisions.

Financial Planning Activities: Calculate future and present value amounts related to specific financial goals using time value of money tables, a financial calculator, spreadsheet software, or an online calculator. This sheet is also available in an Excel spreadsheet format in Connect Finance.

Suggested Websites: www.moneychimp.com/calculator   www.grunderware.com   www.investopedia.com/calculator

Future Value of a Single Amount

1. To determine future value of a single amount
2. To determine interest lost when cash purchases are made

(Use Exhibit 1–A in Chapter 1 appendix.)

current amount	times	future value factor	equals	future value amount
$ _____	×	$ _____	=	$ _____

Future Value of a Series of Deposits

1. To determine future values of regular savings deposits
2. To determine future value of regular retirement deposits

(Use Exhibit 1–B in Chapter 1 appendix.)

regular deposit amount	times	future value of annuity factor	equals	future value amount
$ _____	×	$ _____	=	$ _____

Present Value of a Single Amount

1. To determine an amount to be deposited now that will grow to desired amount

(Use Exhibit 1–C in Chapter 1 appendix.)

future amount desired	times	present value factor	equals	present value amount
$ _____	×	$ _____	=	$ _____

Present Value of a Series of Deposits

1. To determine an amount that can be withdrawn on a regular basis

(Use Exhibit 1–D in Chapter 1 appendix.)

regular amount to be withdrawn	times	present value of annuity factor	equals	present value amount
$ _____	×	$ _____	=	$ _____

Suggested App:
• CF Financial Calculator

What's Next for Your Personal Financial Plan?

- Describe some situations in which you could use time value of money calculations for achieving various personal financial goals.
- What specific actions are you taking to achieve various financial goals?

Name: _____ **Date:** _____

Planning Your Career

Purpose: To become familiar with work activities and career requirements for a field of employment.

Financial Planning Activities: Use the *Career Occupational Outlook Handbook* and other information sources (library materials, interviews, websites) to obtain information related to one or more career areas of interest to you. This sheet is also available in an Excel spreadsheet format in Connect Finance.

Suggested Websites: www.monster.com   www.rileyguide.com   careerplanning.about.com

Career area, job titles	
Nature of the work General activities and duties	
Working conditions Physical surroundings, hours, mental and physical demands	
Training and other qualifications	
Earnings Starting and advanced	
Additional information	
Other questions that require further research	
Sources of additional information Publications, trade associations, professional organizations, government agencies	

What's Next for Your Personal Financial Plan?

- Talk with various people who have worked in the career fields of interest to you.
- Outline a plan for long-term professional development and career advancement.

Suggested App:
- Job Search Organizer

Chapter 1 Appendix:
Time Value of Money

- "If I deposit $10,000 today, how much will I have for a down payment on a house in five years?"
- "Will $2,000 saved each year give me enough money when I retire?"
- "How much must I save today to have enough for my children's college education?"

The *time value of money,* more commonly referred to as *interest,* is the cost of money that is borrowed or lent. Interest can be compared to rent, the cost of using an apartment or other item. The time value of money is based on the fact that a dollar received today is worth more than a dollar that will be received one year from today, because the dollar received today can be saved or invested and will be worth more than a dollar a year from today. Similarly, a dollar that will be received one year from today is currently worth less than a dollar today.

The time value of money has two major components: future value and present value. *Future value* computations, which are also referred to as *compounding,* yield the amount to which a current sum will increase based on a certain interest rate and period of time. *Present value,* which is calculated through a process called *discounting,* is the current value of a future sum based on a certain interest rate and period of time.

In future value problems, you are given an amount to save or invest and you calculate the amount that will be available at some future date. With present value problems, you are given the amount that will be available at some future date and you calculate the current value of that amount. Both future value and present value computations are based on basic interest rate calculations.

Interest Rate Basics

Simple interest is the dollar cost of borrowing or earnings from lending money. The interest is based on three elements:

- The dollar amount, called the *principal.*
- The *rate of interest.*
- The amount of *time.*

The formula and financial calculator computations are as follows:

INTEREST RATE BASICS	
Formula	**Financial Calculator***
Interest = Principal × Rate of interest (annual) × Time (years)	Interest = Amount × Rate × Number of (or portion of) years

The interest rate is stated as a percentage for a year. For example, you must convert 12 percent to either 0.12 or 12/100 before doing your calculations. The time element must also be converted to a decimal or fraction. For example, three months would be shown as 0.25, or 1/4 of a year. Interest for 2½ years would involve a time period of 2.5.

Example A: Suppose you borrow $1,000 at 5 percent and will repay it in one payment at the end of one year. Using the simple interest calculation, the interest is $50, computed as follows:

Copyright © 2016 by McGraw-Hill Education

INTEREST RATE BASICS	
Formula	**Financial Calculator***
$50 = $1,000 × 0.05 × 1 (year)	$50 = 1000 × .05 × 1
Example B: If you deposited $750 in a savings account paying 8 percent, how much interest would you earn in nine months? You would compute this amount as follows:	
Interest = $750 × 0.08 × 3/4 (or 0.75 of a year) = $45	−750 $\boxed{PV}$, 8 $\boxed{I/Y}$, 9/12 = .75 $\boxed{N}$, 0 $\boxed{PMT}$, $\boxed{CPT}$ $\boxed{FV}$ 795. 795 − 750 = 45

*NOTE: These financial calculator notations may require slightly different keystrokes when using various brands and models.

Sample Problem 1

How much interest would you earn if you deposited $300 at 6 percent for 27 months? *(Answers to sample problems are later in this appendix.)*

Sample Problem 2

How much interest would you pay to borrow $670 for eight months at 12 percent?

Future Value of a Single Amount

The future value of an amount consists of the original amount plus compound interest. This calculation involves the following elements:

$$FV = \text{Future value}$$
$$PV = \text{Present value}$$
$$i = \text{Interest rate}$$
$$n = \text{Number of time periods}$$

The formula and financial calculator computations are as follows:

FUTURE VALUE OF A SINGLE AMOUNT		
Formula	**Table**	**Financial Calculator**
$FV = PV(1 + i)^n$	FV = PV (Table factor)	$\boxed{PV}$, $\boxed{I/Y}$, $\boxed{N}$, $\boxed{PMT}$, $\boxed{CPT}$ $\boxed{FV}$
Example C: The future value of $1 at 10 percent after three years is $1.33. This amount is calculated as follows:		
$1.33 = $(1.00 + 0.10)^3$	Using Exhibit 1–A: $1.33 = $1.00 (1.33)	1 $\boxed{PV}$, 10 $\boxed{I/Y}$, 3 $\boxed{N}$, 0 $\boxed{PMT}$, $\boxed{CPT}$ $\boxed{FV}$ 1.33

Future value tables are available to help you determine compounded interest amounts (see Exhibit 1–A). Looking at Exhibit 1–A for 10 percent and three years, you can see that $1 would be worth $1.33 at that time. For other amounts, multiply the table factor by the original amount. This process may be viewed as follows:

Future value
(rounded) $1 $1.10 $1.21   FV = $1.33
                    Interest $0.10   Interest $0.11   Interest $0.12

After year   0   1   2   3

FUTURE VALUE OF A SINGLE AMOUNT		
Formula	**Table**	**Financial Calculator**
Example D: If your savings of $400 earns 12 percent, compounded *monthly,* over a year and a half, use the table factor for 1 percent (the monthly rate) for 18 time periods; the future value would be:		
$478.46 = \$400 (1 + 0.01)^{18}$	$478.40 = \$400 (1.196)$	-400 PV, 12/12 = 1 I/Y, 1.5 × 12 = 18 N, 0 PMT, CPT FV 478.46
Excel formula notation for future value of a single amount	=FV(rate, nper, pmt, pv, type)	
	Example D solution =FV(0.01,18, 0, −400) = 478.46	

Sample Problem 3

What is the future value of $800 at 8 percent after six years?

Sample Problem 4

How much would you have in savings if you kept $200 on deposit for eight years at 8 percent, compounded *semiannually?*

Future Value of a Series of Equal Amounts (an Annuity)

Future value may also be calculated for a situation in which regular additions are made to savings. The formula and financial calculator computations are as follows:

FUTURE VALUE OF A SERIES OF PAYMENTS		
Formula	**Table**	**Financial Calculator**
$FV = \text{Annuity} \dfrac{(1 + i)^n - 1}{i}$	Using Exhibit 1–B: Annuity × Table factor	PMT, N, I/Y, PV, CPT FV
This calculation assumes that (1) each deposit is for the same amount, (2) the interest rate is the same for each time period, and (3) the deposits are made at the end of each time period.		
Example E: The future value of three $1 deposits made at the end of the next three years, earning 10 percent interest, is $3.31. This is calculated as follows:		
$3.31 = \$1 \dfrac{(1 + 0.10)^3 - 1}{0.10}$	Using Exhibit 1–B: $3.31 = \$1 × 3.31	-1 PMT, 3 N, 10 I/Y, 0 PV, CPT FV 3.31

This may be viewed as follows:

		$1	$2.10	FV = $3.31
Future value (rounded)		Deposit $1 Interest 0	Deposit $1 Interest $0.10	Deposit $1 Interest $0.21
After year	0	1	2	3

FUTURE VALUE OF A SERIES OF PAYMENTS		
Formula	**Table**	**Financial Calculator**
Example F: If you plan to deposit $40 a year for 10 years, earning 8 percent compounded annually, the future value of this amount is:		
$579.46 = \dfrac{\$40(1 + 0.08)^{10} - 1}{0.08}$	Using Exhibit 1–B $579.48 = \$40(14.487)$	-40 PMT, 10 N, 10 I/Y, 0 PV, CPT FV 579.46
Excel formula notation for future value of a series	=FV(rate, nper, pmt)	
	Example F solution =FV(0.08,10,−40) = 579.46	

Sample Problem 5

What is the future value of an annual deposit of $230 earning 6 percent for 15 years?

Sample Problem 6

What amount would you have in a retirement account if you made annual deposits of $375 for 25 years earning 12 percent, compounded annually?

Present Value of a Single Amount

If you want to know how much you need to deposit now to receive a certain amount in the future, the formula and financial calculator computations are as follows:

PRESENT VALUE OF A SINGLE AMOUNT		
Formula	**Table**	**Financial Calculator**
$PV = \dfrac{FV}{(1 + i)^n}$	Using Exhibit 1–C: $PV = FV$(Table factor)	FV, N, I/Y, PMT, CPT PV
Example G: The present value of $1 to be received three years from now based on a 10 percent interest rate is calculated as follows:		
$\$0.75 = \dfrac{\$1}{(1 + 0.10)^3}$	Using Exhibit 1–C: $0.75 = \$1(0.751)$	1 FV, 3 N, 10 I/Y, 0 PMT, CPT PV − .75131
This may be viewed as follows:		

This may be viewed as follows:

	Present value (rounded)	$0.75		$0.83		$0.91		$1
			Discount (interest) $0.075		Discount (interest) $0.0825		Discount (interest) $0.0905	
After year	0			1		2		3

Present value tables are available to assist you in this process (see Exhibit 1–C). Notice that $1 at 10 percent for three years has a present value of $0.75. For amounts other than $1, multiply the table factor by the amount involved.

Example H: If you want to have $300 seven years from now and your savings earn 10 percent, compounded *semiannually* (which would be 5 percent for 14 time periods), finding how much you would have to deposit today is calculated as follows:

$\$151.52 = \dfrac{\$300}{(1 + 0.05)^{14}}$	Using Exhibit 1–C: $151.50 = \$300(0.505)$	300 FV, 7 × 2 = 14 N, 10/2 = 5 I/Y, 0 PMT, CPT PV − 151.52
Excel formula notation for present value of a single amount	=PV(rate, nper, pmt, fv, type)	
	Example H solution: =PV(0.05,14, 0,−300) = 151.52	

Sample Problem 7

What is the present value of $2,200 earning 15 percent for eight years?

Sample Problem 8

To have $6,000 for a child's education in 10 years, what amount should a parent deposit in a savings account that earns 12 percent, compounded *quarterly?*

Present Value of a Series of Equal Amounts (an Annuity)

The final time value of money situation allows you to receive an amount at the end of each time period for a certain number of periods. The formula and financial calculator computations are as follows:

PRESENT VALUE OF A SERIES OF PAYMENTS		
Formula	**Table**	**Financial Calculator**
$PV = \text{Annuity} \times \dfrac{1 - \dfrac{1}{(1+i)^n}}{i}$	Using Exhibit 1–D: PV = Annuity (Table factor)	PMT , N , I/Y , FV , CPT PV

Example I: The present value of a $1 withdrawal at the end of the next three years would be $2.49, for money earning 10 percent. This would be calculated as follows:

$\$2.49 = \$1\left[\dfrac{1 - \dfrac{1}{(1+0.10)^3}}{0.10}\right]$	Using Exhibit 1–D: $2.49 = $1(2.487)	1 PMT , 3 N , 10 I/Y , 0 FV , CPT PV – 2.48685

This may be viewed as follows:

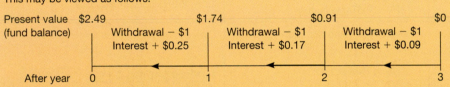

Present value $2.49 $1.74 $0.91 $0
(fund balance)   Withdrawal − $1   Withdrawal − $1   Withdrawal − $1
                      Interest + $0.25   Interest + $0.17   Interest + $0.09

After year   0   1   2   3

This same amount appears in Exhibit 1–D for 10 percent and three time periods. To use the table for other situations, multiply the table factor by the amount to be withdrawn each year.

Example J: If you wish to withdraw $100 at the end of each year for 10 years from an account that earns 14 percent, compounded annually, what amount must you deposit now?

$\$521.61 = \$100\left(\dfrac{1 - \dfrac{1}{(1+0.14)^{10}}}{0.14}\right)$	Using Exhibit 1–D: $521.60 = $100(5.216)	100 PMT , 10 N , 14 I/Y , 0 FV , CPT PV – 521.61

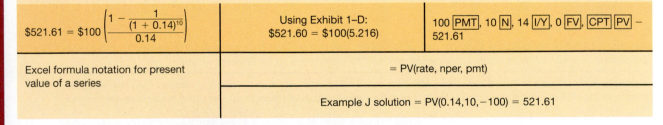

Excel formula notation for present value of a series	= PV(rate, nper, pmt)
	Example J solution = PV(0.14,10,−100) = 521.61

Sample Problem 9

What is the present value of a withdrawal of $200 at the end of each year for 14 years with an interest rate of 7 percent?

Sample Problem 10

How much would you have to deposit now to be able to withdraw $650 at the end of each year for 20 years from an account that earns 11 percent?

Using Present Value to Determine Loan Payments

Present value tables (Exhibit 1–D) can also be used to determine installment payments for a loan as follows:

PRESENT VALUE TO DETERMINE LOAN PAYMENTS	
Table	**Financial Calculator**
$$\frac{\text{Amount borrowed}}{\text{Present value of a series table factor (Exhibit 1–D)}} = \text{Loan payment}$$	$\boxed{PV}$, $\boxed{I/Y}$, $\boxed{N}$, $\boxed{FV}$, $\boxed{CPT}$ $\boxed{PMT}$
Example K: If you borrow $1,000 with a 6 percent interest rate to be repaid in three equal payments at the end of the next three years, the payments will be $374.11. This is calculated as follows:	
$$\frac{\$1,000}{2.673} = \$374.11$$	1000 $\boxed{PV}$, 6 $\boxed{I/Y}$, 3 $\boxed{N}$, 0 $\boxed{FV}$, $\boxed{CPT}$ $\boxed{PMT}$ − 374.10981
Excel formula notation for determining loan payment amount	=PMT(rate, nper, pv)
	Example K solution = PMT(.06, 3,1000) = $374.11

Sample Problem 11

What would be the annual payment amount for a $20,000, 10-year loan at 7 percent?

Answers to Sample Problems (based on TVM tables)

1. $300 × 0.06 × 2.25 years (27 months) = $40.50.
2. $670 × 0.12 × 2/3 (of a year) = $53.60.
3. $800(1.587) = $1,269.60. (Use Exhibit 1–A, 8%, 6 periods.)
4. $200(1.873) = $374.60. (Use Exhibit 1–A, 4%, 16 periods.)
5. $230(23.276) = $5,353.48. (Use Exhibit 1–B, 6%, 15 periods.)
6. $375(133.33) = $49,998.75. (Use Exhibit 1–B, 12%, 25 periods.)
7. $2,200(0.327) = $719.40. (Use Exhibit 1–C, 15%, 8 periods.)
8. $6,000(0.307) = $1,842. (Use Exhibit 1–C, 3%, 40 periods.)
9. $200(8.745) = $1,749. (Use Exhibit 1–D, 7%, 14 periods.)
10. $650(7.963) = $5,175.95. (Use Exhibit 1–D, 11%, 20 periods.)
11. $20,000/7.024 = $2,847.38. (Use Exhibit 1–D, 7%, 10 periods.)

Time Value of Money Application Exercises

1. **(Present value of an annuity)** You wish to borrow $18,000 to buy a new automobile. The rate is 8.6% over four years with monthly payments. Find the monthly payment. (Answer: $444.52)

2. **(Present value of an annuity)** How much money must your rich uncle give you now to finance four years of college, assuming an annual cost of $48,000 and an interest rate of 6% (applied to the principal until disbursed)? (Answer: $166,325.07)

3. **(Present value of a single amount)** How much money must you set aside at age 20 to accumulate retirement funds of $100,000 at age 65, assuming a rate of interest of 7%? (Answer: $4,761.35)

4. **(Future value of a single amount)** If you deposit $2,000 in a 5-year certificate of deposit at 5.2%, how much will it be worth in five years? (Answer: $2,576.97)

5. **(Future value of a single amount)** If you deposit $2,000 in a 5-year certificate of deposit at 5.2% with quarterly compounding, how much will it be worth in five years? (Answer: $2,589.52)

6. **(Future value of an annuity)** You choose to invest $50/month in a 401(k) that invests in an international stock mutual fund. Assuming an annual rate of return of 9%, how much will this fund be worth if you are retiring in 40 years? (Answer: $234,066.01)

7. **(Future value of an annuity)** Instead, you invest $600/year in a 401(k) that invests in an international stock mutual fund. Assuming an annual rate of return of 9%, how much will this fund be worth if you are retiring in 40 years? (Answer: $202,729.47)

Time Value of Money Calculation Methods: A Summary

The time value of money may be calculated using a variety of techniques. When achieving specific financial goals requires regular deposits to a savings or investment account, the computation may occur in one of several ways. For example, Jonie Emerson plans to deposit $10,000 in an account for the next 10 years. She estimates these funds will earn an annual rate of 5 percent. What amount can Jonie expect to have available after 10 years?

Method	Process, Results
Formula Calculation The most basic method of calculating the time value of money involves using a formula.	For this situation, the formula would be: $$PV(1 + i)^n = FV$$ The result should be $$\$10{,}000\,(1 + 0.05)^{10} = \$16{,}288.95$$
Time Value of Money Tables Instead of calculating with a formula, time value of money tables are available. The numeric factors presented ease the computational process.	Using the table in Exhibit 1–A: $10,000 Future value of $1, 5%, 10 years $10,000 1.629 − $16,290
Financial Calculator A variety of financial calculators are programmed with various financial functions. Both future value and present value calculations may be performed using the appropriate keystrokes.	Using a financial calculator, the keystrokes would be: Amount −10,000 PV Time periods 10 N Interest rate 5 I Result FV $16,288.94
Spreadsheet Software Excel and other software programs have built-in formulas for various financial computations, including time value of money.	When using a spreadsheet program, this type of calculation would require this format: = FV(rate, periods, amount per period, single amount) The results of this example would be: = FV(0.05, 10, 0, −10,000) = $16,288.95
Time Value of Money Websites Many time value of money calculators are available online. These web-based programs perform calculations for the future value of savings as well as determining amounts for loan payments.	Some easy-to-use calculators for computing the time value of money and other financial computations are located at • www.investopedia.com/calculator/ • www.dinkytown.net • www.moneychimp.com/calculator • money.cnn.com/tools
Mobile Apps Financial tools on a smartphone or other mobile device are available for time value of money calculations.	• TVM • Time Value of Money Calculator • Time Value of Money Professional

NOTE: The slight differences in answers are the result of rounding.

Exhibit 1–A Future Value (Compounded Sum) of $1 after a Given Number of Time Periods

Period	1%	2%	3%	4%	5%	6%	7%	8%	9%	10%	11%
1	1.010	1.020	1.030	1.040	1.050	1.060	1.070	1.080	1.090	1.100	1.110
2	1.020	1.040	1.061	1.082	1.103	1.124	1.145	1.166	1.188	1.210	1.232
3	1.030	1.061	1.093	1.125	1.158	1.191	1.225	1.260	1.295	1.331	1.368
4	1.041	1.082	1.126	1.170	1.216	1.262	1.311	1.360	1.412	1.464	1.518
5	1.051	1.104	1.159	1.217	1.276	1.338	1.403	1.469	1.539	1.611	1.685
6	1.062	1.126	1.194	1.265	1.340	1.419	1.501	1.587	1.677	1.772	1.870
7	1.072	1.149	1.230	1.316	1.407	1.504	1.606	1.714	1.828	1.949	2.076
8	1.083	1.172	1.267	1.369	1.477	1.594	1.718	1.851	1.993	2.144	2.305
9	1.094	1.195	1.305	1.423	1.551	1.689	1.838	1.999	2.172	2.358	2.558
10	1.105	1.219	1.344	1.480	1.629	1.791	1.967	2.159	2.367	2.594	2.839
11	1.116	1.243	1.384	1.539	1.710	1.898	2.105	2.332	2.580	2.853	3.152
12	1.127	1.268	1.426	1.601	1.796	2.012	2.252	2.518	2.813	3.138	3.498
13	1.138	1.294	1.469	1.665	1.886	2.133	2.410	2.720	3.066	3.452	3.883
14	1.149	1.319	1.513	1.732	1.980	2.261	2.579	2.937	3.342	3.797	4.310
15	1.161	1.346	1.558	1.801	2.079	2.397	2.759	3.172	3.642	4.177	4.785
16	1.173	1.373	1.605	1.873	2.183	2.540	2.952	3.426	3.970	4.595	5.311
17	1.184	1.400	1.653	1.948	2.292	2.693	3.159	3.700	4.328	5.054	5.895
18	1.196	1.428	1.702	2.026	2.407	2.854	3.380	3.996	4.717	5.560	6.544
19	1.208	1.457	1.754	2.107	2.527	3.026	3.617	4.316	5.142	6.116	7.263
20	1.220	1.486	1.806	2.191	2.653	3.207	3.870	4.661	5.604	6.727	8.062
25	1.282	1.641	2.094	2.666	3.386	4.292	5.427	6.848	8.623	10.835	13.585
30	1.348	1.811	2.427	3.243	4.322	5.743	7.612	10.063	13.268	17.449	22.892
40	1.489	2.208	3.262	4.801	7.040	10.286	14.974	21.725	31.409	45.259	65.001
50	1.645	2.692	4.384	7.107	11.467	18.420	29.457	46.902	74.358	117.390	184.570

Period	12%	13%	14%	15%	16%	17%	18%	19%	20%	25%	30%
1	1.120	1.130	1.140	1.150	1.160	1.170	1.180	1.190	1.200	1.250	1.300
2	1.254	1.277	1.300	1.323	1.346	1.369	1.392	1.416	1.440	1.563	1.690
3	1.405	1.443	1.482	1.521	1.561	1.602	1.643	1.685	1.728	1.953	2.197
4	1.574	1.630	1.689	1.749	1.811	1.874	1.939	2.005	2.074	2.441	2.856
5	1.762	1.842	1.925	2.011	2.100	2.192	2.288	2.386	2.488	3.052	3.713
6	1.974	2.082	2.195	2.313	2.436	2.565	2.700	2.840	2.986	3.815	4.827
7	2.211	2.353	2.502	2.660	2.826	3.001	3.185	3.379	3.583	4.768	6.276
8	2.476	2.658	2.853	3.059	3.278	3.511	3.759	4.021	4.300	5.960	8.157
9	2.773	3.004	3.252	3.518	3.803	4.108	4.435	4.785	5.160	7.451	10.604
10	3.106	3.395	3.707	4.046	4.411	4.807	5.234	5.696	6.192	9.313	13.786
11	3.479	3.836	4.226	4.652	5.117	5.624	6.176	6.777	7.430	11.642	17.922
12	3.896	4.335	4.818	5.350	5.936	6.580	7.288	8.064	8.916	14.552	23.298
13	4.363	4.898	5.492	6.153	6.886	7.699	8.599	9.596	10.699	18.190	30.288
14	4.887	5.535	6.261	7.076	7.988	9.007	10.147	11.420	12.839	22.737	39.374
15	5.474	6.254	7.138	8.137	9.266	10.539	11.974	13.590	15.407	28.422	51.186
16	6.130	7.067	8.137	9.358	10.748	12.330	14.129	16.172	18.488	35.527	66.542
17	6.866	7.986	9.276	10.761	12.468	14.426	16.672	19.244	22.186	44.409	86.504
18	7.690	9.024	10.575	12.375	14.463	16.879	19.673	22.091	26.623	55.511	112.460
19	8.613	10.197	12.056	14.232	16.777	19.748	23.214	27.252	31.948	69.389	146.190
20	9.646	11.523	13.743	16.367	19.461	23.106	27.393	32.429	38.338	86.736	190.050
25	17.000	21.231	26.462	32.919	40.874	50.658	62.669	77.388	95.396	264.700	705.640
30	29.960	39.116	50.950	66.212	85.850	111.070	143.370	184.680	237.380	807.790	2,620.000
40	93.051	132.780	188.880	267.860	378.720	533.870	750.380	1,051.700	1,469.800	7,523.200	36,119.000
50	289.000	450.740	700.230	1,083.700	1,670.700	2,566.200	3,927.400	5,998.900	9,100.400	70,065.000	497,929.000

Exhibit 1–B   Future Value (Compounded Sum) of $1 Paid In at the End of Each Period for a Given Number of Time Periods (an Annuity)

Period	1%	2%	3%	4%	5%	6%	7%	8%	9%	10%	11%
1	1.000	1.000	1.000	1.000	1.000	1.000	1.000	1.000	1.000	1.000	1.000
2	2.010	2.020	2.030	2.040	2.050	2.060	2.070	2.080	2.090	2.100	2.110
3	3.030	3.060	3.091	3.122	3.153	3.184	3.215	3.246	3.278	3.310	3.342
4	4.060	4.122	4.184	4.246	4.310	4.375	4.440	4.506	4.573	4.641	4.710
5	5.101	5.204	5.309	5.416	5.526	5.637	5.751	5.867	5.985	6.105	6.228
6	6.152	6.308	6.468	6.633	6.802	6.975	7.153	7.336	7.523	7.716	7.913
7	7.214	7.434	7.662	7.898	8.142	8.394	8.654	8.923	9.200	9.487	9.783
8	8.286	8.583	8.892	9.214	9.549	9.897	10.260	10.637	11.028	11.436	11.859
9	9.369	9.755	10.159	10.583	11.027	11.491	11.978	12.488	13.021	13.579	14.164
10	10.462	10.950	11.464	12.006	12.578	13.181	13.816	14.487	15.193	15.937	16.722
11	11.567	12.169	12.808	13.486	14.207	14.972	15.784	16.645	17.560	18.531	19.561
12	12.683	13.412	14.192	15.026	15.917	16.870	17.888	18.977	20.141	21.384	22.713
13	13.809	14.680	15.618	16.627	17.713	18.882	20.141	21.495	22.953	24.523	26.212
14	14.947	15.974	17.086	18.292	19.599	21.015	22.550	24.215	26.019	27.975	30.095
15	16.097	17.293	18.599	20.024	21.579	23.276	25.129	27.152	29.361	31.772	34.405
16	17.258	18.639	20.157	21.825	23.657	25.673	27.888	30.324	33.003	35.950	39.190
17	18.430	20.012	21.762	23.698	25.840	28.213	30.840	33.750	36.974	40.545	44.501
18	19.615	21.412	23.414	25.645	28.132	30.906	33.999	37.450	41.301	45.599	50.396
19	20.811	22.841	25.117	27.671	30.539	33.760	37.379	41.446	46.018	51.159	56.939
20	22.019	24.297	26.870	29.778	33.066	36.786	40.995	45.762	51.160	57.275	64.203
25	28.243	32.030	36.459	41.646	47.727	54.865	63.249	73.106	84.701	98.347	114.410
30	34.785	40.588	47.575	56.085	66.439	79.058	94.461	113.280	136.310	164.490	199.020
40	48.886	60.402	75.401	95.026	120.800	154.760	199.640	259.060	337.890	442.590	581.830
50	64.463	84.579	112.800	152.670	209.350	290.340	406.530	573.770	815.080	1,163.900	1,668.800

Period	12%	13%	14%	15%	16%	17%	18%	19%	20%	25%	30%
1	1.000	1.000	1.000	1.000	1.000	1.000	1.000	1.000	1.000	1.000	1.000
2	2.120	2.130	2.140	2.150	2.160	2.170	2.180	2.190	2.200	2.250	2.300
3	3.374	3.407	3.440	3.473	3.506	3.539	3.572	3.606	3.640	3.813	3.990
4	4.779	4.850	4.921	4.993	5.066	5.141	5.215	5.291	5.368	5.766	6.187
5	6.353	6.480	6.610	6.742	6.877	7.014	7.154	7.297	7.442	8.207	9.043
6	8.115	8.323	8.536	8.754	8.977	9.207	9.442	9.683	9.930	11.259	12.756
7	10.089	10.405	10.730	11.067	11.414	11.772	12.142	12.523	12.916	15.073	17.583
8	12.300	12.757	13.233	13.727	14.240	14.773	15.327	15.902	16.499	19.842	23.858
9	14.776	15.416	16.085	16.786	17.519	18.285	19.086	19.923	20.799	25.802	32.015
10	17.549	18.420	19.337	20.304	21.321	22.393	23.521	24.701	25.959	33.253	42.619
11	20.655	21.814	23.045	24.349	25.733	27.200	28.755	30.404	32.150	42.566	56.405
12	24.133	25.650	27.271	29.002	30.850	32.824	34.931	37.180	39.581	54.208	74.327
13	28.029	29.985	32.089	34.352	36.786	39.404	42.219	45.244	48.497	68.760	97.625
14	32.393	34.883	37.581	40.505	43.672	47.103	50.818	54.841	59.196	86.949	127.910
15	37.280	40.417	43.842	47.580	51.660	56.110	60.965	66.261	72.035	109.690	167.290
16	42.753	46.672	50.980	55.717	60.925	66.649	72.939	79.850	87.442	138.110	218.470
17	48.884	53.739	59.118	65.075	71.673	78.979	87.068	96.022	105.930	173.640	285.010
18	55.750	61.725	68.394	75.836	84.141	93.406	103.740	115.270	128.120	218.050	371.520
19	63.440	70.749	78.969	88.212	98.603	110.290	123.410	138.170	154.740	273.560	483.970
20	72.052	80.947	91.025	102.440	115.380	130.030	146.630	165.420	186.690	342.950	630.170
25	133.330	155.620	181.870	212.790	249.210	292.110	342.600	402.040	471.980	1,054.800	2,348.800
30	241.330	293.200	356.790	434.750	530.310	647.440	790.950	966.700	1,181.900	3,227.200	8,730.000
40	767.090	1,013.700	1,342.000	1,779.100	2,360.800	3,134.500	4,163.210	5,529.800	7,343.900	30,089.000	120,393.000
50	2,400.000	3,459.500	4,994.500	7,217.700	10,436.000	15,090.000	21,813.000	31,515.000	45,497.000	80,256.000	165,976.000

Exhibit 1-C Present Value of $1 to Be Received at the End of a Given Number of Time Periods

Period	1%	2%	3%	4%	5%	6%	7%	8%	9%	10%	11%	12%
1	0.990	0.980	0.971	0.962	0.952	0.943	0.935	0.926	0.917	0.909	0.901	0.893
2	0.980	0.961	0.943	0.925	0.907	0.890	0.873	0.857	0.842	0.826	0.812	0.797
3	0.971	0.942	0.915	0.889	0.864	0.840	0.816	0.794	0.772	0.751	0.731	0.712
4	0.961	0.924	0.885	0.855	0.823	0.792	0.763	0.735	0.708	0.683	0.659	0.636
5	0.951	0.906	0.863	0.822	0.784	0.747	0.713	0.681	0.650	0.621	0.593	0.567
6	0.942	0.888	0.837	0.790	0.746	0.705	0.666	0.630	0.596	0.564	0.535	0.507
7	0.933	0.871	0.813	0.760	0.711	0.665	0.623	0.583	0.547	0.513	0.482	0.452
8	0.923	0.853	0.789	0.731	0.677	0.627	0.582	0.540	0.502	0.467	0.434	0.404
9	0.914	0.837	0.766	0.703	0.645	0.592	0.544	0.500	0.460	0.424	0.391	0.361
10	0.905	0.820	0.744	0.676	0.614	0.558	0.508	0.463	0.422	0.386	0.352	0.322
11	0.896	0.804	0.722	0.650	0.585	0.527	0.475	0.429	0.388	0.350	0.317	0.287
12	0.887	0.788	0.701	0.625	0.557	0.497	0.444	0.397	0.356	0.319	0.286	0.257
13	0.879	0.773	0.681	0.601	0.530	0.469	0.415	0.368	0.326	0.290	0.258	0.229
14	0.870	0.758	0.661	0.577	0.505	0.442	0.388	0.340	0.299	0.263	0.232	0.205
15	0.861	0.743	0.642	0.555	0.481	0.417	0.362	0.315	0.275	0.239	0.209	0.183
16	0.853	0.728	0.623	0.534	0.458	0.394	0.339	0.292	0.252	0.218	0.188	0.163
17	0.844	0.714	0.605	0.513	0.436	0.371	0.317	0.270	0.231	0.198	0.170	0.146
18	0.836	0.700	0.587	0.494	0.416	0.350	0.296	0.250	0.212	0.180	0.153	0.130
19	0.828	0.686	0.570	0.475	0.396	0.331	0.277	0.232	0.194	0.164	0.138	0.116
20	0.820	0.673	0.554	0.456	0.377	0.312	0.258	0.215	0.178	0.149	0.124	0.104
25	0.780	0.610	0.478	0.375	0.295	0.233	0.184	0.146	0.116	0.092	0.074	0.059
30	0.742	0.552	0.412	0.308	0.231	0.174	0.131	0.099	0.075	0.057	0.044	0.033
40	0.672	0.453	0.307	0.208	0.142	0.097	0.067	0.046	0.032	0.022	0.015	0.011
50	0.608	0.372	0.228	0.141	0.087	0.054	0.034	0.021	0.013	0.009	0.005	0.003

Period	13%	14%	15%	16%	17%	18%	19%	20%	25%	30%	35%	40%	50%
1	0.885	0.877	0.870	0.862	0.855	0.847	0.840	0.833	0.800	0.769	0.741	0.714	0.667
2	0.783	0.769	0.756	0.743	0.731	0.718	0.706	0.694	0.640	0.592	0.549	0.510	0.444
3	0.693	0.675	0.658	0.641	0.624	0.609	0.593	0.579	0.512	0.455	0.406	0.364	0.296
4	0.613	0.592	0.572	0.552	0.534	0.515	0.499	0.482	0.410	0.350	0.301	0.260	0.198
5	0.543	0.519	0.497	0.476	0.456	0.437	0.419	0.402	0.320	0.269	0.223	0.186	0.132
6	0.480	0.456	0.432	0.410	0.390	0.370	0.352	0.335	0.262	0.207	0.165	0.133	0.088
7	0.425	0.400	0.376	0.354	0.333	0.314	0.296	0.279	0.210	0.159	0.122	0.095	0.059
8	0.376	0.351	0.327	0.305	0.285	0.266	0.249	0.233	0.168	0.123	0.091	0.068	0.039
9	0.333	0.300	0.284	0.263	0.243	0.225	0.209	0.194	0.134	0.094	0.067	0.048	0.026
10	0.295	0.270	0.247	0.227	0.208	0.191	0.176	0.162	0.107	0.073	0.050	0.035	0.017
11	0.261	0.237	0.215	0.195	0.178	0.162	0.148	0.135	0.086	0.056	0.037	0.025	0.012
12	0.231	0.208	0.187	0.168	0.152	0.137	0.124	0.112	0.069	0.043	0.027	0.018	0.008
13	0.204	0.182	0.163	0.145	0.130	0.116	0.104	0.093	0.055	0.033	0.020	0.013	0.005
14	0.181	0.160	0.141	0.125	0.111	0.099	0.088	0.078	0.044	0.025	0.015	0.009	0.003
15	0.160	0.140	0.123	0.108	0.095	0.084	0.074	0.065	0.035	0.020	0.011	0.006	0.002
16	0.141	0.123	0.107	0.093	0.081	0.071	0.062	0.054	0.028	0.015	0.008	0.005	0.002
17	0.125	0.108	0.093	0.080	0.069	0.060	0.052	0.045	0.023	0.012	0.006	0.003	0.001
18	0.111	0.095	0.081	0.069	0.059	0.051	0.044	0.038	0.018	0.009	0.005	0.002	0.001
19	0.098	0.083	0.070	0.060	0.051	0.043	0.037	0.031	0.014	0.007	0.003	0.002	0
20	0.087	0.073	0.061	0.051	0.043	0.037	0.031	0.026	0.012	0.005	0.002	0.001	0
25	0.047	0.038	0.030	0.024	0.020	0.016	0.013	0.010	0.004	0.001	0.001	0	0
30	0.026	0.020	0.015	0.012	0.009	0.007	0.005	0.004	0.001	0	0	0	0
40	0.008	0.005	0.004	0.003	0.002	0.001	0.001	0.001	0	0	0	0	0
50	0.002	0.001	0.001	0.001	0	0	0	0	0	0	0	0	0

Exhibit 1–D Present Value of $1 Received at the End of Each Period for a Given Number of Time Periods (an Annuity)

Period	1%	2%	3%	4%	5%	6%	7%	8%	9%	10%	11%	12%
1	0.990	0.980	0.971	0.962	0.952	0.943	0.935	0.926	0.917	0.909	0.901	0.893
2	1.970	1.942	1.913	1.886	1.859	1.833	1.808	1.783	1.759	1.736	1.713	1.690
3	2.941	2.884	2.829	2.775	2.723	2.673	2.624	2.577	2.531	2.487	2.444	2.402
4	3.902	3.808	3.717	3.630	3.546	3.465	3.387	3.312	3.240	3.170	3.102	3.037
5	4.853	4.713	4.580	4.452	4.329	4.212	4.100	3.993	3.890	3.791	3.696	3.605
6	5.795	5.601	5.417	5.242	5.076	4.917	4.767	4.623	4.486	4.355	4.231	4.111
7	6.728	6.472	6.230	6.002	5.786	5.582	5.389	5.206	5.033	4.868	4.712	4.564
8	7.652	7.325	7.020	6.733	6.463	6.210	5.971	5.747	5.535	5.335	5.146	4.968
9	8.566	8.162	7.786	7.435	7.108	6.802	6.515	6.247	5.995	5.759	5.537	5.328
10	9.471	8.983	8.530	8.111	7.722	7.360	7.024	6.710	6.418	6.145	5.889	5.650
11	10.368	9.787	9.253	8.760	8.306	7.887	7.499	7.139	6.805	6.495	6.207	5.938
12	11.255	10.575	9.954	9.385	8.863	8.384	7.943	7.536	7.161	6.814	6.492	6.194
13	12.134	11.348	10.635	9.986	9.394	8.853	8.358	7.904	7.487	7.103	6.750	6.424
14	13.004	12.106	11.296	10.563	9.899	9.295	8.745	8.244	7.786	7.367	6.982	6.628
15	13.865	12.849	11.939	11.118	10.380	9.712	9.108	8.559	8.061	7.606	7.191	6.811
16	14.718	13.578	12.561	11.652	10.838	10.106	9.447	8.851	8.313	7.824	7.379	6.974
17	15.562	14.292	13.166	12.166	11.274	10.477	9.763	9.122	8.544	8.022	7.549	7.102
18	16.398	14.992	13.754	12.659	11.690	10.828	10.059	9.372	8.756	8.201	7.702	7.250
19	17.226	15.678	14.324	13.134	12.085	11.158	10.336	9.604	8.950	8.365	7.839	7.366
20	18.046	16.351	14.877	13.590	12.462	11.470	10.594	9.818	9.129	8.514	7.963	7.469
25	22.023	19.523	17.413	15.622	14.094	12.783	11.654	10.675	9.823	9.077	8.422	7.843
30	25.808	22.396	19.600	17.292	15.372	13.765	12.409	11.258	10.274	9.427	8.694	8.055
40	32.835	27.355	23.115	19.793	17.159	15.046	13.332	11.925	10.757	9.779	8.951	8.244
50	39.196	31.424	25.730	21.482	18.256	15.762	13.801	12.233	10.962	9.915	9.042	8.304

Period	13%	14%	15%	16%	17%	18%	19%	20%	25%	30%	35%	40%	50%
1	0.885	0.877	0.870	0.862	0.855	0.847	0.840	0.833	0.800	0.769	0.741	0.714	0.667
2	1.668	1.647	1.626	1.605	1.585	1.566	1.547	1.528	1.440	1.361	1.289	1.224	1.111
3	2.361	2.322	2.283	2.246	2.210	2.174	2.140	2.106	1.952	1.816	1.696	1.589	1.407
4	2.974	2.914	2.855	2.798	2.743	2.690	2.639	2.589	2.362	2.166	1.997	1.849	1.605
5	3.517	3.433	3.352	3.274	3.199	3.127	3.058	2.991	2.689	2.436	2.220	2.035	1.737
6	3.998	3.889	3.784	3.685	3.589	3.498	3.410	3.326	2.951	2.643	2.385	2.168	1.824
7	4.423	4.288	4.160	4.039	3.922	3.812	3.706	3.605	3.161	2.802	2.508	2.263	1.883
8	4.799	4.639	4.487	4.344	4.207	4.078	3.954	3.837	3.329	2.925	2.598	2.331	1.922
9	5.132	4.946	4.772	4.607	4.451	4.303	4.163	4.031	3.463	3.019	2.665	2.379	1.948
10	5.426	5.216	5.019	4.833	4.659	4.494	4.339	4.192	3.571	3.092	2.715	2.414	1.965
11	5.687	5.453	5.234	5.029	4.836	4.656	4.486	4.327	3.656	3.147	2.752	2.438	1.977
12	5.918	5.660	5.421	5.197	4.988	4.793	4.611	4.439	3.725	3.190	2.779	2.456	1.985
13	6.122	5.842	5.583	5.342	5.118	4.910	4.715	4.533	3.780	3.223	2.799	2.469	1.990
14	6.302	6.002	5.724	5.468	5.229	5.008	4.802	4.611	3.824	3.249	2.814	2.478	1.993
15	6.462	6.142	5.847	5.575	5.324	5.092	4.876	4.675	3.859	3.268	2.825	2.484	1.995
16	6.604	6.265	5.954	5.668	5.405	5.162	4.938	4.730	3.887	3.283	2.834	2.489	1.997
17	6.729	6.373	6.047	5.749	5.475	5.222	4.988	4.775	3.910	3.295	2.840	2.492	1.998
18	6.840	6.467	6.128	5.818	5.534	5.273	5.033	4.812	3.928	3.304	2.844	2.494	1.999
19	6.938	6.550	6.198	5.877	5.584	5.316	5.070	4.843	3.942	3.311	2.848	2.496	1.999
20	7.025	6.623	6.259	5.929	5.628	5.353	5.101	4.870	3.954	3.316	2.850	2.497	1.999
25	7.330	6.873	6.464	6.097	5.766	5.467	5.195	4.948	3.985	3.329	2.856	2.499	2.000
30	7.496	7.003	6.566	6.177	5.829	5.517	5.235	4.979	3.995	3.332	2.857	2.500	2.000
40	7.634	7.105	6.642	6.233	5.871	5.548	5.258	4.997	3.999	3.333	2.857	2.500	2.000
50	7.675	7.133	6.661	6.246	5.880	5.554	5.262	4.999	4.000	3.333	2.857	2.500	2.000

2 Money Management Skills

3 Steps to Financial Literacy . . .
Improved Cash Flow

1 Plan a system to monitor your cash inflows (income) and outflows (spending).
App: Cashflow

2 Identify your fixed expenses. Seek actions to take to control and reduce variable expenses.
Website: budgeting.about.com

3 Spend according to your plan to avoid a negative cash flow and to keep away from debt problems.
App: Spending Tracker

Why is an improved cash flow important for your financial situation?
A positive monthly cash flow will allow you to set aside funds for future financial security and avoid financial difficulties. At the end of the chapter, "Your Personal Finance Dashboard" will provide additional information on measuring your cash flow situation.

CHAPTER 2 LEARNING OBJECTIVES

In this chapter, you will learn to:

LO2.1 Identify the main components of wise money management.

LO2.2 Create a personal balance sheet and cash flow statement.

LO2.3 Develop and implement a personal budget.

LO2.4 Connect money management activities with saving for personal financial goals.

YOUR PERSONAL FINANCIAL PLAN SHEETS

5. Financial Documents and Records

6. Creating a Personal Balance Sheet

7. Creating a Personal Cash Flow Statement

8. Developing a Personal Budget

A Successful Money Management Plan

"Each month, I have too many days and not enough money. If the month were only 20 days long, budgeting would be easy."

Daily spending and saving decisions are at the center of your financial planning activities. You must coordinate these decisions with your needs, goals, and personal situation. Maintaining financial records and planning your spending are essential skills for successful personal financial management. The time and effort you devote to these activities will yield many benefits. **Money management** refers to the day-to-day financial activities necessary to manage current personal economic resources while working toward long-term financial security.

Components of Money Management

As shown here, three major money management activities are interrelated:

3. Creating and implementing a plan for spending and saving (budgeting).

2. Creating personal financial statements (balance sheets and cash flow statements of income and outflows).

1. Storing and maintaining personal financial records and documents.

LO2.1

Identify the main components of wise money management.

ACTION ITEM

My money management strategy involves:

☐ **no spending plan.**

☐ **tracking my spending.**

☐ **using savings to pay current bills.**

money management
Day-to-day financial activities
necessary to manage current
personal economic resources
while working toward long-
term financial security.

First, personal financial records and documents are the foundation of systematic resource use. These provide written evidence of business transactions, ownership of property, and legal matters. Next, personal financial statements enable you to measure and assess your financial position and progress. Finally, your spending plan, or *budget,* is the basis for effective money management.

A System for Personal Financial Records

did you know?

Low-income people in the United States and around the world face a daily financial struggle. Diana lives in Malawi and often has no savings, no food, and poor budgeting skills. However, her money management skills improved through a program of Opportunity International Bank Malawi. Other organizations empowering people in poverty with financial literacy programs include Women's World Banking in Mongolia and Junior Achievement Nigeria.

Invoices, credit card statements, insurance policies, and tax forms are the basis of financial recordkeeping and personal economic choices. An organized system of financial records provides a basis for (1) handling daily business activities, such as bill paying; (2) planning and measuring financial progress; (3) completing required tax reports; (4) making effective investment decisions; and (5) determining available resources for current and future spending.

As Exhibit 2–1 shows, most financial records are kept in one of three places: a home file, a safe deposit box, or a computer. A home file should be used to keep records for current needs and documents with limited value. Your home file may be a series of folders, a cabinet with several drawers, or even a box. Whatever method you use, your home system should be organized to allow quick access to needed documents and information.

safe deposit box A private
storage area at a financial
institution with maximum
security for valuables.

Important financial records and valuable articles should be kept in a location that provides better security than a home file. A **safe deposit box** is a private storage area at a financial institution with maximum security for valuables and difficult-to-replace documents.

The number of financial records and documents may seem overwhelming; however, they can easily be organized into 10 categories (see Exhibit 2–1). These groups correspond to the major topics covered in this book. You may not need to use all of these records and documents at present. As your financial situation changes, you will add others.

How long should you keep personal finance records? Records such as birth certificates, wills, and Social Security data should be kept permanently. Records on property and investments should be kept as long as you own these items. Federal tax laws dictate the length of time you should keep tax-related information. Copies of tax returns and supporting data should be saved for seven years. Normally, an audit will go back only three years; however, under certain circumstances, the Internal Revenue Service may request information from further back. Financial experts also recommend keeping documents related to the purchase and sale of real estate indefinitely.

As more documents are provided electronically and people are storing financial records "in the cloud," consider the following actions:

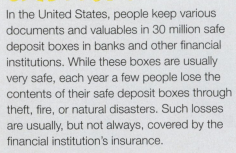

CAUTION!

In the United States, people keep various documents and valuables in 30 million safe deposit boxes in banks and other financial institutions. While these boxes are usually very safe, each year a few people lose the contents of their safe deposit boxes through theft, fire, or natural disasters. Such losses are usually, but not always, covered by the financial institution's insurance.

- Download copies of all statements and forms to your local storage area using a logical system of files and folders.
- Back up files on external media or use an online backup service.
- Secure data with complex passwords and encryption.
- Scan copies of documents so that you no longer need to keep paper versions.
- Take appropriate action to completely erase files when discarding items that are no longer needed.

Hard copies may still be required, such as car titles, birth certificates, property deeds, and life insurance policies. Original receipts may be needed for returns or warranty service.

Exhibit **2–1**   Where to Keep Your Financial Records

Home Files, Home Computer or Online

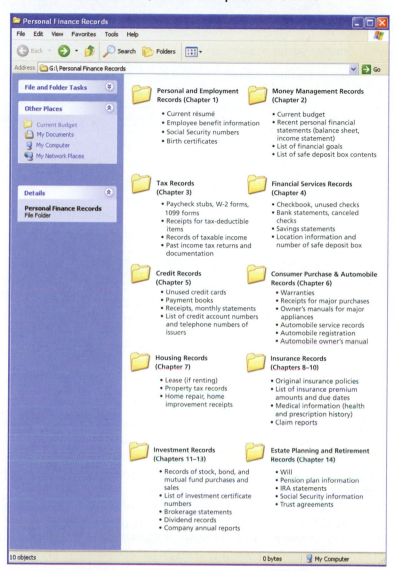

Personal Finance Records

File   Edit   View   Favorites   Tools   Help

Back | Search   Folders

Address   G:\ Personal Finance Records | Go

File and Folder Tasks

Other Places
- Current Budget
- My Documents
- My Computer
- My Network Places

Details

Personal Finance Records
File Folder

Personal and Employment Records (Chapter 1)
- Current résumé
- Employee benefit information
- Social Security numbers
- Birth certificates

Money Management Records (Chapter 2)
- Current budget
- Recent personal financial statements (balance sheet, income statement)
- List of financial goals
- List of safe deposit box contents

Tax Records (Chapter 3)
- Paycheck stubs, W-2 forms, 1099 forms
- Receipts for tax-deductible items
- Records of taxable income
- Past income tax returns and documentation

Financial Services Records (Chapter 4)
- Checkbook, unused checks
- Bank statements, canceled checks
- Savings statements
- Location information and number of safe deposit box

Credit Records (Chapter 5)
- Unused credit cards
- Payment books
- Receipts, monthly statements
- List of credit account numbers and telephone numbers of issuers

Consumer Purchase & Automobile Records (Chapter 6)
- Warranties
- Receipts for major purchases
- Owner's manuals for major appliances
- Automobile service records
- Automobile registration
- Automobile owner's manual

Housing Records (Chapter 7)
- Lease (if renting)
- Property tax records
- Home repair, home improvement receipts

Insurance Records (Chapters 8–10)
- Original insurance policies
- List of insurance premium amounts and due dates
- Medical information (health and prescription history)
- Claim reports

Investment Records (Chapters 11–13)
- Records of stock, bond, and mutual fund purchases and sales
- List of investment certificate numbers
- Brokerage statements
- Dividend records
- Company annual reports

Estate Planning and Retirement Records (Chapter 14)
- Will
- Pension plan information
- IRA statements
- Social Security information
- Trust agreements

10 objects   0 bytes   My Computer

SOURCE: @ Microsoft 2013. Screen capture reprinted with permission.

Safe Deposit Box or Fireproof Home Safe

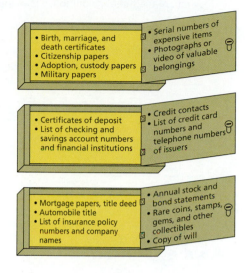

- Birth, marriage, and death certificates
- Citizenship papers
- Adoption, custody papers
- Military papers
- Serial numbers of expensive items
- Photographs or video of valuable belongings

- Certificates of deposit
- List of checking and savings account numbers and financial institutions
- Credit contacts
- List of credit card numbers and telephone numbers of issuers

- Mortgage papers, title deed
- Automobile title
- List of insurance policy numbers and company names
- Annual stock and bond statements
- Rare coins, stamps, gems, and other collectibles
- Copy of will

Computer, Tablet, Phone

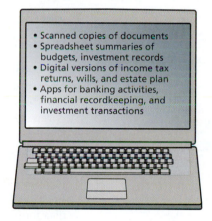

- Scanned copies of documents
- Spreadsheet summaries of budgets, investment records
- Digital versions of income tax returns, wills, and estate plan
- Apps for banking activities, financial recordkeeping, and investment transactions

What Not to Keep . . .

Wastebasket

- Receipts for small, non-tax-deductible purchases
- Expired warranties

Shredder

- Quarterly investment account statements (keep the annual summary statements)
- Documents that you no longer need with personal information such as your Social Security number or account numbers.

Computer Recycle Bin

Empty recycle bin on regular basis. Make sure personal data files are completely erased.

Sheet 5 Financial Documents and Records

PRACTICE QUIZ 2–1

1. What are the three major money management activities?

2. What are the benefits of an organized system of financial records and documents?

3. For each of the following records, check the column to indicate the length of time the item should be kept. "Short time period" refers to less than five years.

Document	Short time period	Longer time period
Credit card statements		
Mortgage documents		
Receipts for furniture, clothing		
Retirement account information		
Will		

Apply Yourself!

Talk to two or three people regarding wise and poor money management actions they have taken in their lives, and about the system they use to keep track of various financial documents and records. Based on this information, what actions might you take now or in the future?

LO2.2

Create a personal balance sheet and cash flow statement.

ACTION ITEM

My cash flow statement details are:

☐ **very simple but useful.**

☐ **very detailed.**

☐ **nonexistent.**

balance sheet A financial statement that reports what an individual or a family owns and owes; also called a *net worth statement* or *statement of financial position.*

Personal Financial Statements

Every journey starts somewhere. You need to know where you are before you can go somewhere else. Personal financial statements tell you the starting point of your financial journey. Most financial documents come from financial institutions, businesses, or the government. However, two documents you create yourself are the personal balance sheet and the cash flow statement, also called *personal financial statements.*

These reports provide information about your current financial position and present a summary of your income and spending. The main purposes of personal financial statements are to (1) report your current financial position; (2) measure your progress toward financial goals; (3) maintain information about your financial activities; and (4) provide data for preparing tax forms or applying for credit.

Your Personal Balance Sheet: The Starting Point

The current financial position of an individual or family is a common starting point for financial planning. A **balance sheet,** also called a *net worth statement* or *statement of financial position,* reports what you own and what you owe. You prepare a personal balance sheet to determine your current financial position using the following process:

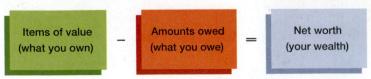

For example, if your possessions are worth $4,500 and you owe $800 to others, your net worth is $3,700. As shown in Exhibit 2–2, preparation of a balance sheet involves three main steps.

Exhibit 2–2 Creating a Personal Balance Sheet

Step 1

Prepare a total of all items of value (assets). Include amounts in bank accounts, investments, and the cost (or estimated current value) of your possessions.

Step 2

List and total the amounts owed to others (liabilities). This list will include current debts, charge account/credit card balances, and amounts due on loans and mortgages.

Step 3

Subtract total liabilities from total assets to determine net worth. This amount indicates the current financial position of an individual or a household.

Sandra and Mark Scott
Personal Balance Sheet as of October 31, 2016

Assets

Liquid Assets

Checking account balance (Chap. 4)	$ 1,450	
Savings/money market accounts (Chap. 4)	5,235	
Cash value of life insurance (Chap. 10)	3,685	
Total liquid assets		$ 10,370

Real Estate

Current market value of home (Chap. 7)		$ 189,900

Personal Possessions

Market value of automobile	8,000	
Furniture and appliances	5,900	
Home entertainment system	2,600	
Home computer	1,400	
Jewelry	2,200	
Total household assets		$ 20,100

Investment Assets (Chaps. 11–13)

Retirement accounts (Chap. 14)	26,780	
Mutual funds (Chap. 12)	11,890	
Total investment assets		38,670
Total assets		**$ 259,040**

Liabilities

Current Liabilities

Medical bills (Chap. 9)	$ 150	
Charge account and credit card balances (Chap. 5)	3,340	
Balance due on auto loan	1,750	
Total current liabilities		$ 5,240

Long-Term Liabilities

Mortgage (Chap. 7)	91,600	
Home improvement loan (Chap. 5)	1,760	
Student loan	1,200	
Total long-term liabilities		94,560
Total liabilities		**$ 99,800**

Net worth (assets minus liabilities)	**$ 159,240**

STEP 1: Listing Items of Value

Available cash and money in bank accounts combined with other items of value are the foundation of your current financial position. **Assets** are cash and other tangible property with a monetary value. The balance sheet for Sandra and Mark Scott lists their assets in four categories:

1. **Liquid assets** are cash and items of value that can easily be converted to cash. Money in checking and savings accounts is *liquid* and is available to the Scott family for current spending. The cash value of their life insurance may be borrowed if needed. While assets other than liquid assets can also be converted into cash, the process is not quite as easy.

assets Cash and other property with a monetary value.

liquid assets Cash and items of value that can easily be converted to cash.

2. *Real estate* includes a home, a condominium, vacation property, or other land that a person or family owns.

3. *Personal possessions* are a major portion of assets for most people. Included in this category are automobiles and other personal belongings. Although these items have value, they may be difficult to convert to cash. You may decide to list your possessions on the balance sheet at their original cost. However, these values probably need to be revised over time, since a five-year-old television set, for example, is worth less now than when it was new. Thus you may wish to list your possessions at their current value (also referred to as *market value*).

4. *Investment assets* are funds set aside for long-term financial needs. The Scott family will use their investments for such things as financing their children's education, purchasing a vacation home, and saving for retirement. Since investment assets usually fluctuate in value, the amounts listed should reflect their value at the time the balance sheet is prepared.

STEP 2: Determining Amounts Owed

liabilities Amounts owed to others.

current liabilities Debts that must be paid within a short time, usually less than a year.

long-term liabilities Debts that are not required to be paid in full until more than a year from now.

After looking at the total assets of the Scott family, you might conclude that they have a strong financial position. However, their debts must also be considered. **Liabilities** are amounts owed to others but do not include items not yet due, such as next month's rent. A liability is a debt you owe now, not something you may owe in the future. Liabilities fall into two categories:

1. **Current liabilities** are debts you must pay within a short time, usually less than a year. These liabilities include such things as medical bills, tax payments, insurance premiums, cash loans, and charge accounts.

2. **Long-term liabilities** are debts you do not have to pay in full until more than a year from now. Common long-term liabilities include auto loans, educational loans, and mortgages. A *mortgage* is an amount borrowed to buy a house or other real estate that will be repaid over a period of 15, 20, or 30 years.

STEP 3: Computing Net Worth

net worth The difference between total assets and total liabilities.

A person's **net worth** is the difference between total assets and total liabilities. This relationship can be stated as

$$\text{Assets} - \text{Liabilities} = \text{Net worth}$$

Net worth is the amount you would have left if all assets were sold for the listed values and all debts were paid in full. Also, total assets equal total liabilities plus net worth. The balance sheet of a business is commonly expressed as

$$\text{Assets} = \text{Liabilities} + \text{Net worth}$$

As Exhibit 2–2 shows, Sandra and Mark Scott have a net worth of $159,240. Since very few people, if any, liquidate all assets, the amount of net worth has a more practical purpose: It provides a measurement of your current financial position.

> **EXAMPLE: Net Worth**
>
> If a household has $193,000 of assets and liabilities of $88,000, the net worth would be $105,000 ($193,000 minus $88,000).

Figure It Out!

Ratios for Evaluating Financial Progress

Financial ratios provide guidelines for measuring the changes in your financial situation. These relationships can indicate progress toward an improved financial position.

Ratio	Calculation	Example	Interpretation
Debt ratio	Liabilities divided by net worth	$25,000/$50,000 = 0.5	Shows relationship between debt and net worth; a low debt ratio is best.
Current ratio	Liquid assets divided by current liabilities	$4,000/$2,000 = 2	Indicates $2 in liquid assets for every $1 of current liabilities; a high current ratio is desirable to have cash available to pay bills.
Liquidity ratio	Liquid assets divided by monthly expenses	$10,000/$4,000 = 2.5	Indicates the number of months in which living expenses can be paid if an emergency arises; a high liquidity ratio is desirable.
Debt-payments ratio	Monthly credit payments divided by take-home pay	$540/$3,600 = 0.15	Indicates how much of a person's earnings goes for debt payments (excluding a home mortgage); most financial advisors recommend a debt-payments ratio of less than 20 percent.
Savings ratio	Amount saved each month divided by gross income	$648/$5,400 = 0.12	Financial experts recommend monthly savings of 5–10 percent.

Based on the following information, calculate the ratios requested:

- Liabilities $12,000
- Liquid assets $2,200
- Monthly credit payments $150
- Monthly savings $130

- Net worth $36,000
- Current liabilities $550
- Take-home pay $900
- Gross income $1,500

(1) Debt ratio _____

(2) Debt-payments ratio _____

(3) Current ratio _____

(4) Savings ratio _____

ANSWERS: 1. $12,000/$36,000 = 0.33; **2.** $150/$900 = 0.166; **3.** $2,200/$550 = 4.0; **4.** $130/$1,500 = 0.086, 8.66 percent.

A person may have a high net worth but still have financial difficulties. Having many assets with low liquidity means not having the cash available to pay current expenses. **Insolvency** is the inability to pay debts when they are due; it occurs when a person's liabilities far exceed available assets.

Individuals and families can increase their net worth by (1) increasing their savings; (2) reducing spending; (3) increasing the value of investments and other possessions; and (4) reducing amounts owed. Remember, your net worth is *not* money available to use, but an indication of your financial position on a given date.

insolvency The inability to pay debts when they are due because liabilities far exceed the value of assets.

Your Cash Flow Statement: Inflows and Outflows

Each day, financial events can affect your net worth. When you receive a paycheck or pay living expenses, your total assets and liabilities change. **Cash flow** is the actual inflow and outflow of cash during a given time period. Income from employment will probably represent your most important *cash inflow;* however, other income, such as interest earned on a

cash flow The actual inflow and outflow of cash during a given time period.

cash flow statement A financial statement that summarizes cash receipts and payments for a given period; also called a *personal income and expenditure statement.*

savings account, should also be considered. In contrast, payments for items such as rent, food, and loans are *cash outflows.*

A **cash flow statement,** also called a *personal income and expenditure statement* (Exhibit 2–3), is a summary of cash receipts and payments for a given period, such as a month or a year. This report provides data on your income and spending patterns, which will be helpful when preparing a budget.

A checking account can provide information for your cash flow statement. Deposits to the account are your *inflows;* checks written, cash withdrawals, and debit card payments are your *outflows.* Of course, in using this system, when you do not deposit entire amounts received, you must also note the spending of these nondeposited amounts in your cash flow statement.

Exhibit 2–3   Creating a Cash Flow Statement

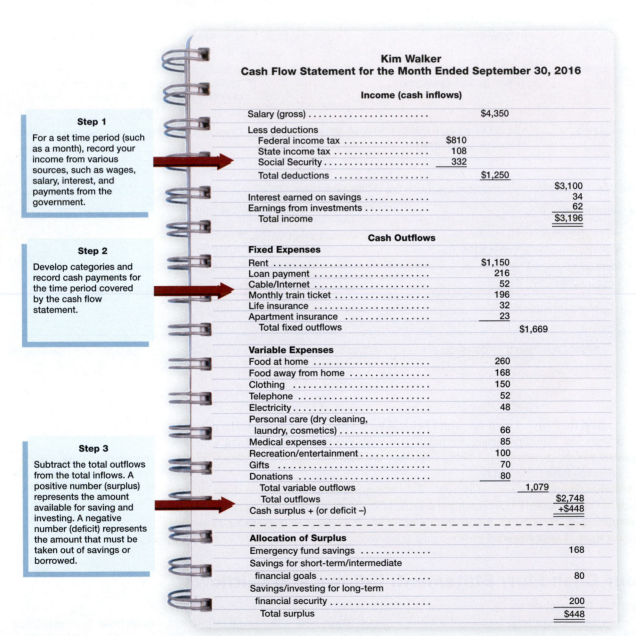

Step 1

For a set time period (such as a month), record your income from various sources, such as wages, salary, interest, and payments from the government.

Step 2

Develop categories and record cash payments for the time period covered by the cash flow statement.

Step 3

Subtract the total outflows from the total inflows. A positive number (surplus) represents the amount available for saving and investing. A negative number (deficit) represents the amount that must be taken out of savings or borrowed.

Kim Walker
Cash Flow Statement for the Month Ended September 30, 2016

Income (cash inflows)

Salary (gross)		$4,350
Less deductions		
Federal income tax	$810	
State income tax	108	
Social Security	332	
Total deductions	$1,250	
		$3,100
Interest earned on savings		34
Earnings from investments		62
Total income		$3,196

Cash Outflows

Fixed Expenses

Rent	$1,150	
Loan payment	216	
Cable/Internet	52	
Monthly train ticket	196	
Life insurance	32	
Apartment insurance	23	
Total fixed outflows		$1,669

Variable Expenses

Food at home	260	
Food away from home	168	
Clothing	150	
Telephone	52	
Electricity	48	
Personal care (dry cleaning, laundry, cosmetics)	66	
Medical expenses	85	
Recreation/entertainment	100	
Gifts	70	
Donations	80	
Total variable outflows		1,079
Total outflows		$2,748
Cash surplus + (or deficit −)		+$448

Allocation of Surplus

Emergency fund savings		168
Savings for short-term/intermediate financial goals		80
Savings/investing for long-term financial security		200
Total surplus		$448

The process for preparing a cash flow statement involves three steps:

Total cash received during the time period	−	Cash outflows during the time period	=	Cash surplus or deficit

STEP 1: Record Income

To create a cash flow statement, start by identifying the funds received. **Income** is the inflows of cash for an individual or a household. For most people, the main source of income is money received from a job. Other common income sources include commissions, self-employment income, interest, dividends, gifts, grants, scholarships, government payments, pensions, retirement income, alimony, and child support.

In Exhibit 2–3, notice that Kim Walker's monthly salary (or *gross income*) of $4,350 is her main source of income. However, she does not have use of the entire amount. **Take-home pay,** also called *net pay,* is a person's earnings after deductions for taxes and other items. Kim's deductions for federal, state, and Social Security taxes are $1,250. Her take-home pay is $3,100. This amount, plus earnings from savings and investments, is the income she has available for use during the current month.

Take-home pay is also called *disposable income,* the amount a person or household has available to spend. **Discretionary income** is money left over after paying for housing, food, and other necessities. Studies report that discretionary income ranges from less than 5 percent for people under age 25 to more than 40 percent for older people.

STEP 2: Record Cash Outflows

Cash payments for living expenses and other items make up the second component of a cash flow statement. Kim Walker divides her cash outflows into two major categories: fixed expenses and variable expenses. Every individual and household has different cash outflows, but these main categories, along with the subcategories Kim uses, can be adapted to most situations.

1. *Fixed expenses* are payments that do not vary from month to month. Rent or mortgage payments, installment loan payments, cable/Internet service, and a monthly train ticket for commuting to work are examples of constant or fixed cash outflows. For Kim, another type of fixed expense is the amount she sets aside each month for payments due once or twice a year. For example, Kim pays $384 every March for life insurance. Each month, she records a fixed outflow of $32 for deposit in a special savings account so that the money will be available when her insurance payment is due.
2. *Variable expenses* are flexible payments that change from month to month. Common examples of variable cash outflows are food, clothing, utilities (such as electricity and telephone), recreation, medical expenses, gifts, and donations. The use of a checkbook or some other recordkeeping system is necessary for an accurate total of cash outflows.

STEP 3: Determine Net Cash Flow

The difference between income and outflows can be either a positive (*surplus*) or a negative (*deficit*) cash flow. A deficit exists if more cash goes out than comes in during a given month. This amount must be made up by withdrawals from savings or by borrowing.

When you have a cash surplus, as Kim did (Exhibit 2–3), this amount is available for saving, investing, or paying off debts. Each month, Kim sets aside money for her *emergency fund* in a savings account that she would use for unexpected expenses or to pay living costs if she did not receive her salary. She deposits the rest of the surplus in savings and investment plans that have two purposes. The first is the achievement of short-term and

income Inflows of cash to an individual or a household.

take-home pay Earnings after deductions for taxes and other items; also called *disposable income.*

discretionary income Money left over after paying for housing, food, and other necessities.

intermediate financial goals, such as a new car, a vacation, or reenrollment in school; the second is long-term financial security—her retirement.

A cash flow statement provides the foundation for preparing and implementing a spending, saving, and investment plan. The cash flow statement reports the *actual* spending of a household. In contrast, a budget, which has a similar format, documents *projected* income and spending.

Sheet 6 Creating a Personal Balance Sheet
Sheet 7 Creating a Personal Cash Flow Statement

PRACTICE QUIZ 2-2

1. What are the main purposes of personal financial statements?

2. What does a personal balance sheet tell you about your financial situation?

3. For the following items, identify each as an asset (A), liability (L), cash inflow (CI), or cash outflow (CO):

_____ monthly rent   _____ automobile loan

_____ interest on savings account   _____ collection of rare coins

_____ retirement account   _____ mortgage amount

_____ electric bill   _____ market value of automobile

4. Jan Franks has liquid assets of $6,300 and monthly expenses of $2,100. Based on the liquidity ratio, she has _____ months in which living expenses could be paid if an emergency arises.

Apply Yourself!

Use online or library research to obtain information about the assets commonly held by households in the United States. How have the values of assets, liabilities, and net worth of U.S. consumers changed in recent years?

LO2.3

Develop and implement a personal budget.

ACTION ITEM

My budgeting attitude is:

☐ "I don't have enough money to have a budget."

☐ "I use an app to monitor spending."

☐ "My detailed plan helps me avoid money troubles."

budget A specific plan for spending income; also called a *spending plan*.

A Plan for Effective Budgeting

A **budget,** or *spending plan,* is necessary for successful financial planning. The common financial problems of overusing credit, lacking a regular savings program, and failing to ensure future financial security can be minimized through budgeting. The main purposes of a budget are to help you live within your income, spend your money wisely, reach your financial goals, prepare for financial emergencies, and develop wise financial management habits. With a budget, you will be in control of your life. Without a budget, others will be in control, such as those to whom you owe money. Use a budget to tell your money where to go, rather than having overspending and debt control your life. Budgeting may be viewed in seven main steps.

Step 1: Set Financial Goals

Your future plans are the foundation for a financial direction. Financial goals are plans for your spending, saving, and investing. As discussed in Chapter 1, financial goals should take a SMART approach with goals that are **S**pecific, **M**easurable, **A**ction-oriented, **R**ealistic, and **T**ime-based. Exhibit 2–4 gives examples of common financial goal topics based on life situation and time.

Step 2: Estimate Income

As Exhibit 2–5 shows, after setting goals, you need to estimate available money for a given time period. A common budgeting period is a month, since many payments, such as rent or mortgage, utilities, and credit cards, are due each month. In determining available income, include only money that you are sure you'll receive. Bonuses, gifts, or unexpected income should not be considered until the money is actually received.

Budgeting income may be difficult if your earnings vary by season or your income is irregular, as with sales commissions. In these situations, estimate your income on the low side to help avoid overspending and other financial difficulties.

did you know?

According to Lynnette Khalfani (themoneycoach.net), LIFE is the major budget buster:

L   is "Listed" expenses (housing, utilities, food, clothing) that are underestimated.

I   involves "Impulse buying," whether in stores or online.

F   are "Forgotten" bills, such as annual insurance payments.

E   are "Emergencies," such as unexpected auto or home repairs.

Step 3: Budget an Emergency Fund and Savings

To set aside money for unexpected expenses as well as future financial security, the Robinsons have budgeted several amounts for savings and investments (see Exhibit 2–5). Financial advisors suggest that an emergency fund representing three to six months of living expenses be established for use in periods of unexpected financial difficulty. This amount will vary based on a person's life situation and employment stability.

The Robinsons also set aside an amount each month for their automobile insurance payment, which is due every six months. Both this amount and the emergency fund are put into a savings account.

A frequent budgeting mistake is to save the amount you have left at the end of the month. When you do that, you often have *nothing* left for savings. Since saving is vital for long-term financial security, remember to always "pay yourself first."

Step 4: Budget Fixed Expenses

Definite obligations make up this portion of a budget. As Exhibit 2–5 shows, the Robinsons have fixed expenses for housing, taxes, and loan payments. They make a monthly payment of $29 for life insurance. The budgeted total for their fixed expenses is $806, or 28 percent of estimated available income.

You will notice that a budget has a similar format to the previously discussed cash flow statement. A budget, however, involves *projected* or planned income and expenses. The cash flow statement reports the *actual* income and expenses.

Assigning amounts to spending categories requires careful consideration. The amount you budget for various items will depend on your current needs and plans for the future.

Exhibit 2–4

Common Financial Goals

Personal Situation	Short-Term Goals (less than 2 years)	Intermediate Goals (2–5 years)	Long-Term Goals (over 5 years)
Single person	• Complete college • Pay off auto loan	• Take a vacation to Europe • Pay off education loan • Attend graduate school	• Buy a vacation home in the mountains • Provide for retirement income
Married couple (no children)	• Take an annual vacation • Buy a new car	• Remodel home • Build a stock portfolio	• Buy a retirement home • Provide for retirement income
Parent (young children)	• Increase life insurance • Increase savings	• Increase investments • Buy a new car	• Accumulate a college fund for children • Move to a larger home

Exhibit 2–5 Developing a Monthly Budget

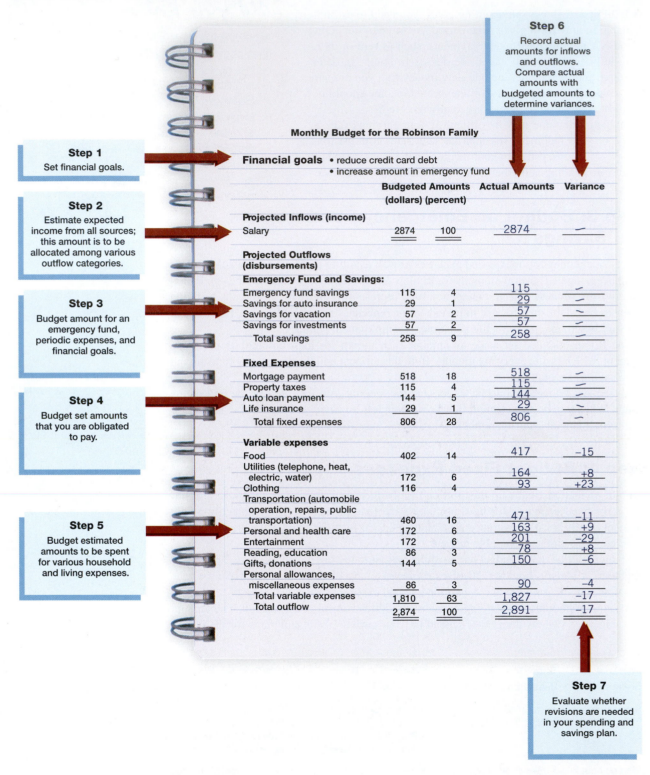

Step 1

Set financial goals.

Step 2

Estimate expected income from all sources; this amount is to be allocated among various outflow categories.

Step 3

Budget amount for an emergency fund, periodic expenses, and financial goals.

Step 4

Budget set amounts that you are obligated to pay.

Step 5

Budget estimated amounts to be spent for various household and living expenses.

Step 6

Record actual amounts for inflows and outflows. Compare actual amounts with budgeted amounts to determine variances.

Step 7

Evaluate whether revisions are needed in your spending and savings plan.

Monthly Budget for the Robinson Family

Financial goals • reduce credit card debt
• increase amount in emergency fund

	Budgeted Amounts (dollars)	(percent)	Actual Amounts	Variance
Projected Inflows (income)				
Salary	2874	100	2874	—
Projected Outflows (disbursements)				
Emergency Fund and Savings:				
Emergency fund savings	115	4	115	—
Savings for auto insurance	29	1	29	—
Savings for vacation	57	2	57	—
Savings for investments	57	2	57	—
Total savings	258	9	258	—
Fixed Expenses				
Mortgage payment	518	18	518	—
Property taxes	115	4	115	—
Auto loan payment	144	5	144	—
Life insurance	29	1	29	—
Total fixed expenses	806	28	806	—
Variable expenses				
Food	402	14	417	–15
Utilities (telephone, heat, electric, water)	172	6	164	+8
Clothing	116	4	93	+23
Transportation (automobile operation, repairs, public transportation)	460	16	471	–11
Personal and health care	172	6	163	+9
Entertainment	172	6	201	–29
Reading, education	86	3	78	+8
Gifts, donations	144	5	150	–6
Personal allowances, miscellaneous expenses	86	3	90	–4
Total variable expenses	1,810	63	1,827	–17
Total outflow	2,874	100	2,891	–17

Exhibit 2–6 suggests budget allocations for different life situations. Although this information can be of value when creating budget categories, maintaining a detailed record of your spending for several months is a better source for your personal situation. However, don't become discouraged. Use a simple system, such as a notebook or your checkbook. This "spending diary" will help you know where your money is going. (See Appendix D.)

Exhibit 2–6 Typical After-Tax Budget Allocations for Different Life Situations

Budget Category	Student	Working Single (no dependents)	Couple (children under 18)	Single Parent (young children)	Parents (children over 18 in college)	Couple (over 55, no dependent children)
Housing (rent or mortgage payment; utilities; furnishings and appliances)	0–25%	30–35%	25–35%	20–30%	25–30%	25–35%
Transportation	5–10	15–20	15–20	10–18	12–18	10–18
Food (at home and away from home)	15–20	15–25	15–25	13–20	15–20	18–25
Clothing	5–12	5–15	5–10	5–10	4–8	4–8
Personal and health care (including child care)	3–5	3–5	4–10	8–12	4–6	6–12
Entertainment and recreation	5–10	5–10	4–8	4–8	6–10	5–8
Reading and education	10–30	2–4	3–5	3–5	6–12	2–4
Personal insurance and pension payments	0–5	4–8	5–9	5–9	4–7	6–8
Gifts, donations, and contributions	4–6	5–8	3–5	3–5	4–8	3–5
Savings	0–10	4–15	5–10	5–8	2–4	3–5

SOURCES: Bureau of Labor Statistics (http://stats.bls.gov); *American Demographics; Money; The Wall Street Journal.*

Step 5: Budget Variable Expenses

Planning for variable expenses is not as easy as budgeting for savings or fixed expenses. Variable expenses will fluctuate by household situation, time of year, health, economic conditions, and a variety of other factors. A major portion of the Robinsons' planned spending—over 60 percent of their budgeted income—is for variable living costs. They base their estimates on past spending as well as expected changes in their cost of living.

Step 6: Record Spending Amounts

After having established a spending plan, you will need to keep track of your actual income and expenses. This process is similar to preparing a cash flow statement. In Exhibit 2–5, notice that the Robinsons estimated specific amounts for income and expenses. These are presented under "Budgeted Amounts." The family's actual spending was not always the same as planned. A **budget variance** is the difference between the amount budgeted and the actual amount received or spent. The total variance for the Robinsons was a $17 **deficit,** since their actual spending exceeded their planned spending by this amount. They would have had a **surplus** if their actual spending had been less than they had planned.

budget variance The difference between the amount budgeted and the actual amount received or spent.

deficit The amount by which actual spending exceeds planned spending.

surplus The amount by which actual spending is less than planned spending.

EXAMPLE: Budget Variance

If a family budgets $380 a month for food and spends $363, this would result in a $17 budget *surplus.* However, if the family spent $406 on food during the month, a $26 budget *deficit* would exist.

Personal Finance in Practice

A Money Management SWOT Analysis

SWOT (**s**trengths, **w**eaknesses, **o**pportunities, **t**hreats) is a planning tool used by companies and other organizations. This technique can also be used for your money management and budgeting activities. Listed below are examples of possible items for each SWOT category. Now, in the area provided, assess your strengths, weaknesses, opportunities, and threats related to budgeting and money management. Do online research and talk with others to get ideas for your personal SWOT items.

Internal (personal) Factors	External (economic, social) Influences
Strengths	**Opportunities**
• saving 5–10 percent of income • informed on personal finance topics • no credit card debt • flexible job skills *Your strengths:* _____ _____	• phone apps for monitoring finances • part-time work to supplement income • availability of no-fee bank account • low-interest-rate education loan *Potential opportunities:* _____ _____
Weaknesses	**Threats**
• high level of credit card debt • no emergency fund • automobile in need of repairs • low current cash inflow *Your weaknesses:* _____ _____	• lower market value of retirement fund • possible reduced hours at part-time job • reduced home market value • increased living costs (inflation) *Potential threats:* _____ _____

Creating a money management SWOT analysis is only a start. Next you need to select actions to build on your strengths, minimize your weaknesses, take advantage of opportunities, and avoid being a victim of threats. Through research and innovation, weaknesses and threats can become strengths and opportunities.

Variances for income should be viewed as the opposite of variances for expenses. Less income than expected would be a deficit, whereas more income than expected would be a surplus. Spending more than planned for an item may be justified by reducing spending for another item or putting less into savings. However, revising your budget and financial goals may be necessary.

Step 7: Review Spending and Saving Patterns

Like most decision-making activities, budgeting is a circular, ongoing process. You will need to review and perhaps revise your spending plan on a regular basis.

REVIEW YOUR FINANCIAL PROGRESS The results of your budget may be obvious: having extra cash in checking or falling behind in your bill payments. However, such obvious results may not always be present. Occasionally, you will have to review areas where spending has been more or less than expected. You can prepare an annual summary to compare actual spending with budgeted amounts for each month. A spreadsheet program can be useful for this purpose. This summary will help you see areas where changes in your budget may be necessary. This review process is vital to both successful short-term money management and long-term financial security.

REVISE YOUR GOALS AND BUDGET ALLOCATIONS What should you cut first when a budget shortage occurs? This question doesn't have easy answers, and answers will vary for different households. The most common overspending areas are entertainment and food, especially away-from-home meals. Purchasing less expensive brand items, buying quality used products, and avoiding credit card purchases are common budget adjustment techniques. When household budgets must be cut, spending is most frequently reduced for vacations, dining out, cleaning and lawn services, cable/Internet service, and charitable donations.

At this point in the budgeting process, you may also revise your financial goals. Are you making progress toward achieving your objectives? Have changes in personal or economic conditions affected the desirability of certain goals? Have new goals surfaced that should be given a higher priority? Addressing these issues while creating an effective saving method will help ensure accomplishment of your financial goals.

> *did you know?*
>
> Most households can have an additional $500 or more a month available by not receiving a tax refund, by cutting insurance costs, by wiser food shopping, by using less energy, by having a less expensive phone and cable plan, and by not being in debt.

SUCCESSFUL BUDGETING Having a spending plan will not eliminate financial worries. A budget will work only if you follow it. Changes in income, living expenses, and goals will require changes in your spending plan. Successful budgets are commonly viewed as being:

- *Well planned.* A good budget takes time and effort to prepare and should involve everyone affected by it.
- *Realistic.* If you have a moderate income, don't immediately expect to save enough money for an expensive car. A budget is designed not to prevent you from enjoying life but to help you achieve what you want most.
- *Flexible.* Unexpected expenses and life situation changes will require a budget that you can easily revise.
- *Clearly communicated.* Unless you and others involved are aware of the spending plan, it will not work. The budget should be written and available to all household members.

SELECTING A BUDGETING SYSTEM Although your bank statement will give you a fairly complete record of expenses, it does not serve the purpose of a spending plan. A budget requires that you outline how you will spend available income. Individuals and households commonly use these types of budgeting systems:

- A *mental budget* exists only in a person's mind. This simple system may be appropriate if you have limited resources and minimal financial responsibilities.
- A *physical budget* involves envelopes, folders, or containers to hold the money or slips of paper. Envelopes would contain the amount of cash or a note listing the amount to be used for "Food," "Rent," "Auto Payment," and other expenses.
- A *written budget* can be kept in a notebook or with multicolumn accounting paper.
- A *digital budget* may involve a spreadsheet program, specialized software such as Quicken, or an app.

The budgeting system you use will depend on your personal and financial situation. Most important is to select a system that best helps you achieve your financial goals.

Sheet 8 Developing a Personal Budget

PRACTICE QUIZ 2-3

1. What are the main purposes of a budget?

2. How does a person's life situation affect goal setting and amounts allocated for various budget categories?

3. For each of the following household expenses, indicate if the item is a FIXED or a VARIABLE expense.

_____ food away from home   _____ cable television

_____ rent   _____ electricity

_____ health insurance premium   _____ auto repairs

4. The Nollin family has budgeted expenses for a month of $4,560 and actual spending of $4,480. This would result in a budget SURPLUS or DEFICIT (circle one) of $_____.

Apply Yourself!

Conduct research to identify various budgeting and money management apps. Determine the features, ease of operation, and information provided by these apps. Which app would you consider using for your budgeting and money management activities?

LO2.4

Connect money management activities with saving for personal financial goals.

ACTION ITEM

My savings program is:

☐ **not started.**

☐ **a small amount.**

☐ **achieving a financial goal.**

Money Management and Achieving Financial Goals

Your personal financial statements and budget allow you to achieve your financial goals with

1. **Your balance sheet:** reporting your current financial position—where you are now.
2. **Your cash flow statement:** telling you what you received and spent over the past month.
3. **Your budget:** planning spending and saving to achieve financial goals.

Many people prepare a balance sheet on a periodic basis, such as every three or six months. Between those points in time, your budget and cash flow statement help you plan and measure spending and saving activities. For example, you might prepare balance sheets on January 1, June 30, and December 31. Your budget would serve to plan your spending and saving between these points in time, and your cash flow statement of income and outflows would document your actual spending and saving. This relationship may be illustrated in this way:

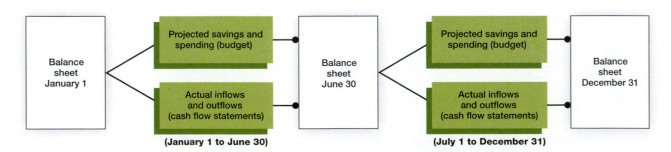

Changes in your net worth result from cash inflows and outflows. In periods when your outflows exceed your inflows, you must draw on savings or borrow (buy on credit). When

How to Stretch Your Money

You've launched your career, and the paychecks are rolling in. If this is the first time you've had to manage finances beyond your college meal plan, you may be surprised at how easily the money seems to evaporate. Even if you've been working a while, you may find that you're living paycheck to paycheck, without enough left over to meet your goals. That's why you need a strategy for how you'll spend and save it—in other words, a budget.

Yes, you need a budget. But look at it as an opportunity to set priorities.

Rather than view a budget as a straitjacket on your spending, think of it as a way to set priorities. "Is having HBO now more important than being able to retire with the standard of living you'd like?" asks Trent Porter, a certified financial planner and founder of Priority Financial Planning in Denver.

As a broad guideline. Alexa von Tobel, founder and CEO of money-management Web site LearnVest.com, suggests using the 50-20-30 rule. That means that up to 50% of your take-home pay goes toward essential spending: rent or mortgage payments, utility bills, groceries, and transportation to work. Designate at least 20% for savings (including for retirement, an emergency fund and other goals) plus paying off debt, such as student loans. Up to 30% is for lifestyle choices, such as a gym membership, your cell-phone plan, entertainment (including your cable bill), charitable giving, shopping and eating out.

Unless you work for yourself, your employer will make sure a portion of your pay finds its way to the IRS.

When money is tight, you're going to have to make some trade-offs. If rents are high where you are, you may have to live with a roommate or wait to get a car. If giving to charity or your church is crucial. cable may have to go. "It's not about deprivation," says von Tobel. "It's about spending thoughtfully."

Track your spending.

To meet your numbers, you'll have to keep track of what you spend. You may want to use a budgeting site, such as Mint.com or LearnVest.com. Their tools let you monitor your bank, retirement, credit card and investment accounts, automatically categorize your expenditures, and let you set target spending limits for various items, such as restaurants and shopping. They also help you organize your goals and monitor how much you're saving for them.

If a hard spending limit is more effective than just a warning at keeping you within your budget, nothing beats cash. Withdraw the equivalent of your budget over the course of the month in cash, divide the money into categories, and put money for each category into envelopes (the budget site Mvelopes.com lets you fund virtual envelopes and track the amount in them by linking

to your checking account and credit cards). Once you've spent all of the cash designated for eating out, for example, you're done with restaurants until next month.

> **GET THIS APP!**
> **MINT**
> **(Apple, Android, Windows) gives you a detailed snapshot of where your finances stand, including charts and graphs that show your spending and net income. Plus, it provides alerts when bills are due.**

As your circumstances change, your budget should be flexible enough to adjust. But that doesn't mean that you should upgrade to a flashier car or a downtown apartment as soon as you get a raise. Especially if your savings are missing the mark or you're paying off a lot of debt, ratchet up the amount you put toward those areas as your income reaches a more comfortable level.

Lisa Gerstner

SOURCE: Reprinted by permission from *Kiplinger's Personal Finance.* Copyright © 2014. The Kiplinger Washington Editors, Inc.

this happens, lower assets (savings) or higher liabilities (due to the use of credit) result in a lower net worth. When inflows exceed outflows, putting money into savings or paying off debts will result in a higher net worth.

Selecting a Saving Technique

Traditionally, the United States ranks low among industrial nations in savings rate. Low savings affect personal financial situations. Studies reveal that the majority of Americans do not set aside an adequate amount for emergencies.

Since most people find saving difficult, financial advisors suggest these methods to make it easier:

1. Write a check each payday to deposit in a separate savings account. Or use an automatic payment or a smartphone app to electronically transfer an amount to savings. This deposit can be a percentage of income, such as 5 or 10 percent, or a specific dollar amount.
2. *Payroll deduction* is available at many places of employment. Under a *direct deposit* system, an amount is automatically deducted from your salary and deposited in savings.
3. Saving coins or spending less on certain items can help you save. Each day, bring lunch instead of buying it, or avoid expensive coffee and snacks. Then, put the money saved in a container or use a phone app to transfer money to a savings or investment account.

How you save is far less important than making regular periodic savings deposits that will help you achieve financial goals. Small amounts of savings can grow faster than most people realize.

Calculating Savings Amounts

To achieve your financial objectives, you should convert your savings goals into specific amounts. Your use of a savings or investment plan is vital to the growth of your money. As Exhibit 2–7 shows, using the time value of money calculations introduced in Chapter 1 can help you calculate progress toward achieving your financial goals.

Exhibit 2–7

Using Savings to Achieve Financial Goals

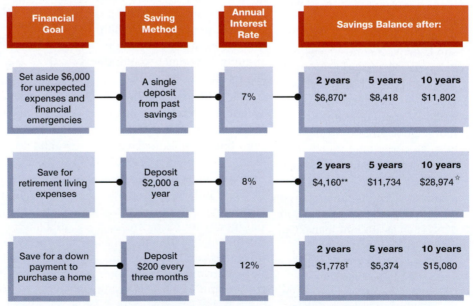

Financial Goal	Saving Method	Annual Interest Rate	Savings Balance after:		
			2 years	**5 years**	**10 years**
Set aside $6,000 for unexpected expenses and financial emergencies	A single deposit from past savings	7%	$6,870*	$8,418	$11,802
Save for retirement living expenses	Deposit $2,000 a year	8%	$4,160**	$11,734	$28,974 ☆
Save for a down payment to purchase a home	Deposit $200 every three months	12%	$1,778†	$5,374	$15,080

* Based on the future value of $1 tables in Chapter 1 and Chapter 1 Appendix.
** Based on the future value of a series of deposits tables in Chapter 1 and Chapter 1 Appendix.
☆ With annual $2,000 deposits, this same retirement account would grow to over $500,000 in 40 years.
† Based on quarterly compounding, explained in Chapter 4.

PRACTICE QUIZ 2-4

1. What relationship exists among personal financial statements, budgeting, and achieving financial goals?

2. What are some suggested methods to make saving easy?

3. If you wanted to obtain the following types of information, check the box for the document that you would find most useful.

Financial information needed	Balance sheet	Cash flow statement	Budget
Amounts owed for medical expenses			
Spending patterns for the past few months			
Planned spending patterns for the next month			
Current value of investment accounts			
Amounts to deposit in savings accounts			

Apply Yourself!

Talk to a young single person, a young couple, and a middle-aged person about their financial goals and saving habits. What actions do they take to determine and achieve various financial goals?

YOUR PERSONAL FINANCE DASHBOARD

MONTHLY BUDGET

CASH FLOW ANALYSIS

A personal finance dashboard with key performance indicators can help you monitor your financial situation and guide you toward financial independence. A monthly cash flow analysis will help you achieve various financial goals.

By comparing your cash inflows (income) and cash outflows (spending), you will determine if you have a *surplus* or *deficit*. A surplus allows you to save more or pay off debts. A deficit reduces your savings or increases the amount you owe.

YOUR SITUATION: Do you regularly maintain a record of cash inflows and outflows? Does your cash flow situation reflect a deficit with unnecessary spending? How can you reduce spending to improve your cash flow situation?

POSSIBLE ACTIONS TO TAKE ·····················

✓ *Reconsider your responses to the "Action Items" (in the text margin) for more effective money management and budgeting.*

✓ *Develop a recordkeeping system for your financial documents as shown in Exhibit 2–1.*

✓ *Prepare a balance sheet and a cash flow statement on a regular basis to monitor your financial situation and progress (see the "Personal Financial Statements" section).*

✓ *Consider using an online budgeting website or app for your money management activities. Use a web search to locate one that fits your needs.*

✓ *Develop a regular savings plan to set aside some amount each week. Start small . . . but save something. For savings ideas go to www.americasaves .org or www.choosetosave.org.*

Chapter Summary

LO2.1 Successful money management requires coordination of personal financial records, personal financial statements, and budgeting activities. An organized system of financial records and documents should provide ease of access as well as security for financial documents that may be impossible to replace.

LO2.2 A personal balance sheet, also known as a *net worth statement,* is prepared by listing all items of value (assets) and all amounts owed to others (liabilities). The difference between your total assets and your total liabilities is your net worth. A cash flow statement, also called a *personal income and expenditure statement,* is a summary of cash receipts and payments for a given period, such as a month or a year.

LO2.3 The budgeting process consists of seven steps: (1) set financial goals; (2) estimate income; (3) budget an emergency fund and savings; (4) budget fixed expenses; (5) budget variable expenses; (6) record spending amounts; and (7) review spending and saving patterns.

LO2.4 The relationship among the personal balance sheet, cash flow statement, and budget provides the basis for achieving long-term financial security. Future value and present value calculations may be used to compute the increased value of savings for achieving financial goals.

Key Terms

assets 49
balance sheet 48
budget 54
budget variance 57
cash flow 51
cash flow statement 52
current liabilities 50

deficit 57
discretionary income 53
income 53
insolvency 51
liabilities 50
liquid assets 49

long-term liabilities 50
money management 45
net worth 50
safe deposit box 46
surplus 57
take-home pay 53

Key Formulas

Page	Topic	Formula
50	Net worth	Net worth = Total assets − Total liabilities *Example:* = $125,000 − $53,000 = $72,000
51	Debt ratio	Debt ratio = Liabilities/Net worth *Example:* = $7,000/$21,000 = 0.33
51	Current ratio	Current ratio = Liquid assets/Current liabilities *Example:* = $8,500/$4,500 = 1.88
51	Liquidity ratio	Liquidity ratio = Liquid assets/Monthly expenses *Example:* = $8,500/$3,500 = 2.4
51	Debt-payments ratio	Debt-payments ratio = Monthly credit payments/Take-home pay *Example:* = $760/$3,800 = 0.20
51	Savings ratio	Savings ratio = Amount saved per month/Gross monthly income *Example:* = $460/$3,800 = 0.12
57	Cash surplus (or deficit)	Cash surplus (or deficit) = Total inflows − Total outflows *Example:* = $5,600 − $4,970 = $630 (surplus)

1. Describe some common money management mistakes that can cause long-term financial concerns.   (LO2.1)
2. What do you believe to be the major characteristics of an effective system to keep track of financial documents and records?   (LO2.1)
3. How might financial ratios be used when planning and implementing financial activities?   (LO2.2)
4. Discuss with several people how a budget might be changed if a household faced a decline in income. What spending areas might be reduced first?   (LO2.3)
5. What are long-term effects of low savings for both individuals and the economy of a country?   (LO2.4)

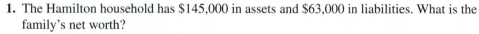

**Self-Test
Problems**

1. The Hamilton household has $145,000 in assets and $63,000 in liabilities. What is the family's net worth?
2. Harold Daley budgeted $210 for food for the month of July. He spent $227 on food during July. Does he have a budget surplus or deficit, and what amount?

Self-Test Solutions

1. Net worth is determined by assets ($145,000) minus liabilities ($63,000), resulting in a net worth of $82,000.
2. The budget *deficit* of $17 is calculated by subtracting the actual spending ($227) from the budgeted amount ($210).

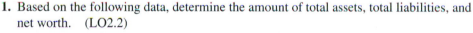

Problems

1. Based on the following data, determine the amount of total assets, total liabilities, and net worth.   (LO2.2)

Liquid assets, $3,870	Investment assets, $8,340
Current liabilities, $2,670	Household assets, $87,890
Long-term liabilities, $76,230	

   a. Total assets $ _____
   b. Total liabilities $ _____
   c. Net worth $ _____

2. Using the following balance sheet items and amounts, calculate the total liquid assets and total current liabilities.   (LO2.2)

Money market account, $2,600	Medical bills, $262
Mortgage, $158,000	Checking account, $780
Retirement account, $87,400	Credit card balance, $489

   a. Total liquid assets $ _____
   b. Total current liabilities $ _____

3. Use the following items to determine the total assets, total liabilities, net worth, total cash inflows, and total cash outflows.   (LO2.2)

Rent for the month, $650	Monthly take-home salary, $2,185
Spending for food, $345	Cash in checking account, $450
Savings account balance, $1,890	Balance of educational loan, $2,160
Current value of automobile, $8,800	Telephone bill paid for month, $65
Credit card balance, $235	Loan payment, $80
Auto insurance, $230	Household possessions, $3,400
Video equipment, $2,350	Payment for electricity, $90
Lunches/parking at work, $180	Donations, $160
Personal computer, $1,200	Value of stock investment, $860
Clothing purchase, $110	Restaurant spending, $130

a. Total assets $ _____
b. Total liabilities $ _____
c. Net worth $ _____
d. Total cash inflows $ _____
e. Total cash outflows $ _____

4. For each of the following situations, compute the missing amount.   (LO2.2)

   a. Assets $65,000; liabilities $18,000; net worth $ _____
   b. Assets $86,500; liabilities $ _____ ; net worth $18,700
   c. Assets $34,280; liabilities $12,965; net worth $ _____
   d. Assets $ _____ ; liabilities $38,345; net worth $52,654

5. Based on the following financial data, calculate the ratios requested.   (LO2.2)

Liabilities, $7,800	Net worth, $58,000
Liquid assets, $4,600	Current liabilities, $1,300
Monthly credit payments, $640	Take-home pay, $2,575
Monthly savings, $130	Gross income, $2,850

   a. Debt ratio _____
   b. Current ratio _____
   c. Debt-payments ratio _____
   d. Savings ratio _____

6. The Fram family has liabilities of $128,000 and a net worth of $340,000. What is their debt ratio? How would you assess this?   (LO2.2)

7. Carl Lester has liquid assets of $2,680 and current liabilities of $2,436. What is his current ratio? What comments do you have about this financial position?   (LO2.2)

8. For the following situations, calculate the cash surplus or deficit: (LO2.2)

Cash Inflows	Cash Outflows	Difference (surplus or deficit)
$3,460	$3,306	$_____ _____
4,693	4,803	$_____ _____
4,287	4,218	$_____ _____

9. The Brandon household has a monthly income of $5,630 on which to base their budget. They plan to save 10 percent and spend 32 percent on fixed expenses and 56 percent on variable expenses.   (LO2.3)

   a. What amount do they plan to set aside for each major budget section?
      Savings $ _____
      Fixed expenses $ _____
      Variable expenses $ _____
   b. After setting aside these amounts, what amount would remain for additional savings or for paying off debts?

10. Fran Powers created the following budget and reported the actual spending listed. Calculate the variance for each of these categories, and indicate whether it was a *deficit* or a *surplus*.   (LO2.3)

Item	Budgeted	Actual	Variance	Deficit/Surplus
Food	$360	$298	_____	_____
Transportation	320	334	_____	_____
Housing	950	982	_____	_____
Clothing	110	134	_____	_____
Personal	275	231	_____	_____

11. Ed Weston recently lost his job. Before unemployment occurred, the Weston household (Ed; wife, Alice; two children, ages 12 and 9) had a monthly take-home income of $3,165. Each month, the money went for the following items: $880 for rent, $180

for utilities, $560 for food, $480 for automobile expenses, $300 for clothing, $280 for insurance, $250 for savings, and $235 for personal and other items. After the loss of Ed's job, the household's monthly income is $1,550 from his wife's wages and his unemployment benefits. The Westons also have savings accounts, investments, and retirement funds of $28,000.   (LO2.3)

a. What budget items might the Westons consider reducing to cope with their financial difficulties?

b. How should the Westons use their savings and retirement funds during this financial crisis? What additional sources of funds might be available to them during this period of unemployment?

12. Use future value and present value calculations (see tables in the appendix for Chapter 1) to determine the following: (LO2.4)

a. The future value of a $600 savings deposit after eight years at an annual interest rate of 6 percent.

b. The future value of saving $1,800 a year for five years at an annual interest rate of 5 percent.

c. The present value of a $2,000 savings account that will earn 3 percent interest for four years.

13. Brenda plans to reduce her spending by $50 a month. What would be the future value of this reduced spending over the next 10 years? (Assume an annual deposit to her savings account, and an annual interest rate of 3 percent.)   (LO2.4)

14. Kara George received a $5,000 gift for graduation from her uncle. If she deposits this in an account paying 3 percent, what will be the value of this gift in 12 years?   (LO2.4)

 **To reinforce the content in this chapter, more problems are provided at connect.mheducation.com.**

ADJUSTING THE BUDGET

Case in Point

In a recent month, the Constantine family had a budget deficit, which is something they want to avoid so they do not have future financial difficulties. Jason and Karen Constantine and their children (ages 10 and 12) plan to discuss the situation after dinner this evening.

While at work, Jason was talking with his friend Ken Lopez. Ken had been a regular saver since he was very young, starting with a small savings account. Those funds were then invested in various stocks and mutual funds. While in college, Ken was able to pay for his education while continuing to save between $50 and $100 a month. He closely monitored his spending. Ken realized that the few dollars here and there for snacks and other minor purchases quickly add up.

Today, Ken works as a customer service manager for the online division of a retailing company. He lives with his wife and their two young children. The family's spending plan allows for all their needs and

also includes regularly saving and investing for the children's education and for retirement.

Jason asked Ken, "How come you never seem to have financial stress in your household?"

Ken replied, "Do you know where your money is going each month?"

"Not really," was Jason's response.

"You'd be surprised by how much is spent on little things you might do without," Ken responded.

"I guess so. I just don't want to have to go around with a notebook writing down every amount I spend," Jason said in a troubled voice.

"Well, you have to take some action if you want your financial situation to change," Ken countered.

That evening, the Constantine family met to discuss their budget situation:

Current Spending		Suggested Budget	
Rent	$950	Rent	$ ____
Electricity, water	120	Electricity, water	____
Telephone	55	Telephone	____
Cable, Internet	125	Cable, Internet	____
Food (at home)	385	Food (at home)	____
Food (away)	230	Food (away)	____
Auto payment	410	Auto payment	____
Gas, oil changes	140	Gas, oil changes	____
Insurance	125	Insurance	____
Clothing	200	Clothing	____
Personal, gifts	185	Personal, gifts	____
Donations	50	Donations	____
Savings	35	Savings	____
Total spending	$3,010	Total budgeted	$
Total monthly amount available...................................	$2,800	Total monthly amount available...................................	$2,800
Surplus (deficit)	($210)	Surplus (deficit)	$

Questions

1. What situations might have created the budget deficit for the Constantine family?

2. What amounts would you suggest for the various categories for the family budget?

3. Describe additional actions for the Constantine family related to their budget or other money management activities.

Continuing Case

MANAGING A BUDGET

Jamie Lee Jackson, age 24, now a busy full-time college student and part-time bakery clerk, has been trying to organize all of her priorities, including her budget. She has been wondering if she is allocating enough of her income toward savings, which includes accumulating enough money toward the $9,000 down payment she needs to open her dream cupcake café.

Jamie Lee has been making regular deposits to both her regular and her emergency savings accounts. She would really like to sit down and get a clearer picture of how much she is spending on various expenses, including rent, utilities, and entertainment, and how her debt compares to her savings and assets. She realizes that she must stay on track and keep a detailed budget if she is to realize her dream of being self-employed after college graduation.

Current Financial Situation

Assets:
Checking account: $1,250
Emergency fund savings account: $3,100
Car: $4,000

Liabilities:
Student loan: $5,400
Credit card balance: $400

Income:
Gross monthly salary: $2,125
Net monthly salary: $1,560

Monthly Expenses:
Rent obligation: $275
Utilities obligation: $125
Food: $120
Gas/Maintenance: $100
Credit card payment: $50

Savings:
Regular savings: $150
Emergency savings: $25

Entertainment:
Cake decorating class: $35
Movies with friends: $50

Questions

1. According to the text, a personal balance sheet is a statement of your net worth. It is an accounting of what you own as well as what you owe. Using the information provided, prepare a personal balance sheet for Jamie Lee.
2. Using the "Ratios for Evaluating Financial Progress" feature earlier in the chapter, what is Jamie Lee's debt ratio? When comparing Jamie Lee's liabilities and her net worth, is the relationship a favorable one?
3. Using the "Ratios for Evaluating Financial Progress" feature earlier in the chapter, what is Jamie Lee's savings ratio? Using the rule of thumb recommended by financial experts, is she saving enough?
4. Using Exhibit 2–6, Typical After-Tax Budget Allocations for Different Life Situations, calculate the budget allocations for Jamie Lee using her net monthly salary (or after-tax salary) amount. Is she within the recommended parameters for a student?

Spending Diary

"I AM AMAZED HOW LITTLE THINGS CAN ADD UP. . . . HOWEVER, SINCE KEEPING TRACK OF ALL MY SPENDING, I REALIZE THAT I NEED TO CUT DOWN ON SOME ITEMS SO I CAN PUT SOME MONEY AWAY INTO SAVINGS."

Directions Continue or start using the Daily Spending Diary sheets provided at the end of the book, or create your own format, to record *every cent* of your spending in the categories provided. This experience will help you better understand your spending patterns and help you plan for achieving financial goals. The Daily Spending Diary sheets are located in Appendix D at the end of the book and in Connect Finance.

Questions

1. What information from your daily spending diary might encourage you to reconsider various money management actions?
2. How can your daily spending diary assist you when planning and implementing a budget?

Name: _____ Date: _____

Financial Documents and Records

Purpose: To develop a system for maintaining and storing personal documents and records.

Financial Planning Activities: Indicate the location of the following records, and create files for the eight major categories of financial documents. This sheet is also available in an Excel spreadsheet format in Connect Finance.

Suggested Websites: money.cnn.com   www.kiplinger.com   www.usa.gov

Item	Home file	Safe deposit box	Other (specify location—computer file, online)
1. Money management records			
• budget, financial statements			
2. Personal/employment records			
• current résumé, Social Security card			
• educational transcripts			
• birth, marriage, divorce certificates			
• citizenship, military papers			
• adoption, custody papers			
3. Tax records			
4. Financial services/consumer credit records			
• unused or canceled checks			
• savings, passbook statements			
• credit card information, statements			
• credit contracts			
5. Consumer purchase, housing, and automobile records			
• warranties, receipts			
• owner's manuals			
• lease or mortgage papers, title deed, property tax info			
• automobile title			
• auto registration			
• auto service records			
6. Insurance records			
• insurance policies			
• home inventory			
• medical information (health history)			
7. Investment records			
• broker statements			
• dividend reports			
• stock/bond records			
• rare coins, stamps, and collectibles			
8. Estate planning and retirement			
• will			
• pension, Social Security info			

Suggested App:
• Manilla

What's Next for Your Personal Financial Plan?

• Plan a physical or online program for storing your financial documents and records.

• Decide if various documents may no longer be needed.

Name: _____   **Date:** _____

Creating a Personal Balance Sheet

Purpose: To determine your current financial position.

Financial Planning Activities: List current values of the assets; list amounts owed for liabilities; subtract total liabilities from total assets to determine net worth. This sheet is also available in an Excel spreadsheet format in Connect Finance.

Suggested Websites: www.kiplinger.com   money.cnn.com   www.lifeadvice.com

Balance sheet as of	_____	
Assets		
Liquid assets		
Checking account balance	_____	
Savings/money market accounts, funds	_____	
Cash value of life insurance	_____	
Other _____	_____	
Total liquid assets		_____
Household assets & possessions		
Current market value of home	_____	
Market value of automobiles	_____	
Furniture	_____	
Stereo, video, camera equipment	_____	
Jewelry	_____	
Other _____	_____	
Other _____	_____	
Total household assets		_____
Investment assets		
Savings certificates	_____	
Stocks and bonds	_____	
Individual retirement accounts	_____	
Mutual funds	_____	
Other _____	_____	
Total investment assets		_____
Total Assets	....	
Liabilities		
Current liabilities		
Charge account and credit card balances	_____	
Loan balances	_____	
Other _____	_____	
Other _____	_____	
Total current liabilities		_____
Long-term liabilities		
Mortgage	_____	
Other _____	_____	
Total long-term liabilities		_____
Total Liabilities	....	
Net Worth (assets minus liabilities)	....	

Suggested App:
• Balance

What's Next for Your Personal Financial Plan?

- Compare your net worth to previous balance sheets.
- Decide how often you will prepare a balance sheet.

Name: _____   Date: _____

Creating a Personal Cash Flow Statement

Purpose: To maintain a record of cash inflows and outflows for a month (or three months).

Financial Planning Activities: Record inflows and outflows of cash for a one- (or three-) month period. This sheet is also available in an Excel spreadsheet format in Connect Finance.

Suggested Websites: www.americasaves.org   money.cnn.com

For month ending	_____	
Cash Inflows		
Salary (take-home)	_____	
Other income	_____	
Other income	_____	
Total Income	....	_____
Cash Outflows		
Fixed expenses		
Mortgage or rent	_____	
Loan payments	_____	
Insurance	_____	
Other _____	_____	
Other _____	_____	
Total fixed outflows	....	_____
Variable expenses	_____	
Food	_____	
Clothing	_____	
Electricity	_____	
Telephone	_____	
Water	_____	
Transportation	_____	
Personal care	_____	
Medical expenses	_____	
Recreation/entertainment	_____	
Gifts	_____	
Donations	_____	
Other _____	_____	
Other _____	_____	
Total variable outflows	....	_____
Total Outflows	....	_____
Surplus/Deficit	....	_____
Allocation of surplus		
Emergency fund savings	_____	
Financial goal savings	_____	
Other savings _____	_____	

Suggested App:
- Expensify

What's Next for Your Personal Financial Plan?

- Decide which areas of spending need to be revised.
- Evaluate your spending patterns for preparation of a budget.

Name: _____ **Date:** _____

Developing a Personal Budget

Purpose: To compare projected and actual spending for a one- (or three-) month period.

Financial Planning Activities: Estimate projected spending based on your cash flow statement, and maintain records for actual spending for these same budget categories. This sheet is also available in an Excel spreadsheet format in Connect Finance.

Suggested Websites: www.betterbudgeting.com   www.asec.org   www.mymoney.gov

Income	Budgeted amounts		Actual amounts	Variance
	Dollar	Percent		
Salary				
Other _____				
Total income		100%		
Expenses				
Fixed expenses Mortgage or rent				
Property taxes				
Loan payments				
Insurance				
Other _____				
Total fixed expenses				
Emergency fund/savings Emergency fund				
Savings for _____				
Savings for _____				
Total savings				
Variable expenses Food				
Utilities				
Clothing				
Transportation costs				
Personal care				
Medical and health care				
Entertainment				
Education				
Gifts/donations				
Miscellaneous				
Other _____				
Other _____				
Total variable expenses				
Total expenses		100%		

Suggested App:
• Home Budget

What's Next for Your Personal Financial Plan?

• Evaluate the appropriateness of your budget for your current life situation.

• Assess whether your budgeting activities are helping you achieve your financial goals.

3

Taxes in Your Financial Plan

3 Steps to Financial Literacy . . .
Taxes in Your Financial Plan

1 Annually, estimate the proper tax withholding and other tax payments (as appropriate) based on current tax rates.
Website: www.irs.gov

2 Maintain complete and accurate tax records.
App: Expensify

3 Each year, review tax resources to ensure that you understand tax law changes for your financial situation.
Website: taxtopics.net

What's wrong with a large tax refund?
Each year, millions of American households receive federal tax refunds totaling over $225 billion, which represents several billion dollars in lost earnings from investing and saving. By not receiving a large tax refund, you can use the money during the year for saving or other financial needs. Monitoring your taxes throughout the year, rather than waiting until April 15, is a vital component of financial planning. At the end of the chapter, "Your Personal Finance Dashboard" will help you measure how well you have planned for your tax situation.

CHAPTER 3 LEARNING OBJECTIVES

In this chapter, you will learn to:

LO3.1 Identify the major tax types in our society.

LO3.2 Calculate taxable income and the amount owed for federal income tax.

LO3.3 Prepare a federal income tax return.

LO3.4 Select appropriate tax strategies for various life situations.

YOUR PERSONAL FINANCIAL PLAN SHEETS

9. Federal Income Tax Estimate
10. Tax Planning Activities

Taxes in Your Financial Plan

Taxes are an everyday financial fact of life. You pay taxes when you get a paycheck or make a purchase. However, most people concern themselves with taxes only immediately before April 15. Tax planning should be an ongoing process.

Planning Your Tax Strategy

Each year, the Tax Foundation determines how long the average person works to pay taxes. In recent years, "Tax Freedom Day" came in mid-April. This means that the time that elapsed from January 1 until mid-April represents the portion of the year people work to pay their taxes.

Tax planning starts with knowing current tax laws, next maintaining complete and appropriate tax records, then making purchase and investment decisions that can reduce your tax liability. Your primary goal should be to pay your fair share of taxes while taking advantage of appropriate tax benefits.

Types of Tax

Most people pay taxes in four major categories: taxes on purchases, taxes on property, taxes on wealth, and taxes on earnings.

TAXES ON PURCHASES You probably pay *sales tax* on many purchases. Many states exempt food and drugs from sales tax to reduce the financial burden on low-income households. In recent years, all but five states (Alaska, Delaware, Montana, New Hampshire, and Oregon) had a general sales tax. An **excise tax** is imposed by the federal and

LO3.1

Identify the major tax types in our society.

ACTION ITEM

I understand the various types of taxes I pay.

☐ **Yes** ☐ **No**

excise tax A tax imposed on specific goods and services, such as gasoline, cigarettes, alcoholic beverages, tires, and air travel.

state governments on specific goods and services, such as gasoline, cigarettes, alcoholic beverages, tires, air travel, hotels, and phone service.

TAXES ON PROPERTY *Real estate property tax* is a major source of revenue for local governments. This tax is based on the value of land and buildings. Many people have seen significant increases in property taxes in the last decade. Some areas impose a *personal property tax* on the value of automobiles, boats, furniture, and farm equipment.

estate tax A tax imposed on the value of a person's property at the time of death.

inheritance tax A tax levied on the value of property bequeathed by a deceased person.

TAXES ON WEALTH An **estate tax** is imposed on the value of a person's property at the time of death. This federal tax is based on the fair market value of the deceased person's investments, property, and bank accounts less allowable deductions and other taxes.

Money and property passed on to heirs may be subject to a state tax. An **inheritance tax** is levied on the value of property bequeathed by a deceased person. This tax is paid for the right to acquire the inherited property.

Individuals are allowed to give money or items valued at $14,000 or less in a year to a person without being subject to taxes. Gift amounts greater than $14,000 may have estate tax implications later. Amounts given for tuition payments or medical expenses are not subject to gift taxes.

digi – know?

The Tax Foundation (www.taxfoundation.org) posts an annual report of state tax changes.

TAXES ON EARNINGS The two main taxes on wages and salaries are Social Security and income taxes. The Federal Insurance Contributions Act (FICA) created the Social Security tax to fund the old-age, survivors, and disability insurance portion of the Social Security system and the hospital insurance portion (Medicare).

Income tax is a major financial planning factor for most people. Some workers are subject to federal, state, and local income taxes. Currently, only seven states do not have a state income tax. Additionally, two states, New Hampshire and Tennessee, tax only dividend and interest income.

Throughout the year, your employer will withhold income tax payments from your paycheck, or you may be required to make estimated tax payments if you own your own business. Both types of payments are only estimates; you may need to pay an additional amount, or you may get a tax refund. The following sections will assist you in preparing your federal income tax return and planning your future tax strategies.

PRACTICE QUIZ 3–1

1. What are the four major categories of taxes?

2. For each of the following financial planning situations, list the type of tax that is being described.

   a. A tax on the value of a person's house.
   b. The additional charge for gasoline and hotels.
   c. Payroll deductions for federal government retirement benefits.
   d. Amount owed on property received from a deceased person.
   e. Payroll deductions for a direct tax on earnings.

Apply Yourself!

Estimate the amount of all types of tax that you have paid in the last month.

Traveling? Better Budget for Taxes

You'll pay plenty for hotels, rental cars and restaurant meals.

For summer vacation, you've probably included the cost of a room in a hotel or resort, a rental car, some nice dinners, and a few souvenirs in the budget. But if you fail to include taxes, you could end up with a bad case of traveler's remorse.

This year, taxes on hotels, rental cars and restaurant meals are expected to cost travelers nearly $30 per day, on average, roughly the same as last year. But that's up from $29.17 in 2012 and about $28 in 2011, according to the Global Business Travel Association's annual survey of top U.S. destination cities. "For a family of four that might have budgeted $1,000 for their trip, they could end up $100 or $200 over budget," says Joseph Bates, vice-president of research for the GBTA.

The city with the highest total tax burden, which includes general sales taxes as well as travel-related taxes, is Chicago, where travelers pay an average of $41.04 in taxes per day. Second on the list is New York City, at $38.65 per day. Fort Lauderdale has the lowest tax burden, at $22.61 per day.

Travel-related tax increases enacted in 2013 include a 2% "transient occupancy tax" tacked on to existing tax rates for hotels in northern Virginia (which are popular with visitors to nearby Washington, D.C.) and an increase in Minnesota's rental-car tax from 6.2% to 9.2%.

Taxes on travel-related services have been on the rise since the 1990s, when protests against increases in property taxes led states, counties and other jurisdictions to search for alternative sources of revenue. Taxes on hotels, rental cars and restaurant meals were viewed as a way to raise money without increasing the tax burden on residents. But the GBTA argues that residents feel the pinch, too, because locals also eat in restaurants, stay in hotels for special occasions and rent cars when their own vehicles are in the shop.

Meeting planners increasingly factor in the cost of taxes when deciding where to hold conferences. "When you're talking about 1,000 people, those numbers add up," Bates says.

For leisure travelers, though, figuring out the amount of taxes in a specific destination can be difficult, says Carol Kokinis-Graves, senior state tax analyst for tax publisher CCH. State sales tax rates are readily available (see our "State by State Guide to Taxes," at kiplinger.com/links/taxmap), and most large cities provide information about taxes and fees on their Web sites. But many smaller cities and jurisdictions that impose their own taxes may not even have a Web presence, says Kokinis-Graves.

Still, you can avoid some sticker shock by planning ahead. Web sites such as Orbitz and Expedia don't include taxes and fees in their initial quotes for hotel rooms, but once you select a specific rate and provide the dates of your planned visit, you'll get the total cost. You don't need to provide your personal information or credit card number to get this figure. Web sites for some rental-car companies and travel discounters will give you the total rental cost upfront; with others, you must select the car you want to reserve to get that information.

Renting a car at an off-airport location could also save you the airport concession fee—typically 11% to 13% of your total rate. Just be sure to factor in the cost of cab fare. Some cities tax that, too.

Sandra Block

SOURCE: Reprinted by permission from *Kiplinger's Personal Finance.* Copyright 2014. The Kiplinger Washington Editors, Inc.

1. Why have taxes on travel-related services increased so dramatically?

2. What is a "transient occupancy tax"?

3. How can you determine the amount of taxes in advance?

Calculate taxable income and the amount owed for federal income tax.

ACTION ITEM

I understand how to calculate taxable income and federal tax owed.

☐ Yes   ☐ No

taxable income The net amount of income, after allowable deductions, on which income tax is computed.

earned income Money received for personal effort, such as wages, salary, commission, fees, tips, or bonuses.

investment income Money received in the form of dividends, interest, or rent from investments; also called *portfolio income.*

passive income Income resulting from business activities in which you do not actively participate.

exclusion An amount not included in gross income.

tax-exempt income Income that is not subject to tax.

tax-deferred income Income that will be taxed at a later date.

adjusted gross income (AGI) Gross income reduced by certain adjustments, such as contributions to an individual retirement account (IRA) and alimony payments.

tax shelter An investment that provides immediate tax benefits and a reasonable expectation of a future financial return.

tax deduction An amount subtracted from adjusted gross income to arrive at taxable income.

The Basics of Federal Income Tax

Each year, millions of Americans are required to pay their share of income taxes to the federal government. As shown in Exhibit 3–1, this process involves several steps.

Step 1: Determining Adjusted Gross Income

This process starts with steps to determine **taxable income,** which is the net amount of income, after allowable deductions, on which income tax is computed.

TYPES OF INCOME Most, but not all, income is subject to taxation. Your gross, or total, income can consist of three main components:

1. **Earned income** is usually in the form of wages, salary, commission, fees, tips, or bonuses.
2. **Investment income** (sometimes referred to as *portfolio income*) is money received in the form of dividends, interest, or rent from investments.
3. **Passive income** results from business activities in which you do not actively participate, such as a limited partnership.

Other types of income subject to federal income tax include alimony, awards, lottery winnings, credit card sign-up bonuses, and prizes. For example, cash and prizes won on television game shows are subject to both federal and state taxes.

Total income is also affected by exclusions. An **exclusion** is an amount not included in gross income. For example, the foreign income exclusion allows U.S. citizens working and living in another country to exclude a certain portion ($99,200 in 2014, adjusted each year for inflation) of their income from federal income taxes.

Exclusions may also be referred to as **tax-exempt income,** or income that is not subject to tax. For example, interest earned on most state and city bonds is exempt from federal income tax. **Tax-deferred income** is income that will be taxed at a later date.

ADJUSTMENTS TO INCOME **Adjusted gross income (AGI)** is gross income after certain reductions have been made. These reductions, called *adjustments to income,* include contributions to an IRA or a Keogh retirement plan, penalties for early withdrawal of savings, and alimony payments. Adjusted gross income is used as the basis for computing various income tax deductions, such as medical expenses.

Certain adjustments to income, such as tax-deferred retirement plans, are a type of tax shelter. **Tax shelters** are investments that provide immediate tax benefits and a reasonable expectation of a future financial return. In recent years, tax court rulings and changes in the tax code have disallowed various types of tax shelters that were considered excessive.

Step 2: Computing Taxable Income

DEDUCTIONS A **tax deduction** is an amount subtracted from adjusted gross income to arrive at taxable income. Every taxpayer receives at least the **standard deduction,** a set amount on which no taxes are paid. As of 2014, single people receive a standard deduction of $6,200 (married couples filing jointly receive $12,400). Blind people and individuals 65 and older receive higher standard deductions.

Many people qualify for more than the standard deduction. **Itemized deductions** are expenses a taxpayer is allowed to deduct from adjusted gross income. Common itemized deductions include:

- *Medical and dental expenses*—physician fees, prescription medications, hospital expenses, medical insurance premiums, hearing aids, eyeglasses, and medical travel that has not been reimbursed or paid by others. The amount of this deduction is the medical and dental expenses that exceed 10 percent (as of 2014)

Exhibit **3–1**   Computing Taxable Income and Your Tax Liability

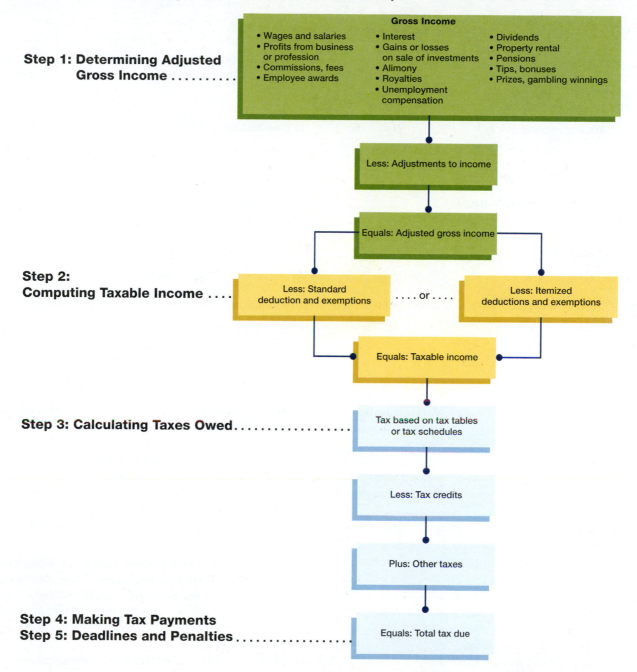

Step 1: Determining Adjusted
Gross Income . . . .

Gross Income

- Wages and salaries
- Profits from business or profession
- Commissions, fees
- Employee awards

- Interest
- Gains or losses on sale of investments
- Alimony
- Royalties
- Unemployment compensation

- Dividends
- Property rental
- Pensions
- Tips, bonuses
- Prizes, gambling winnings

Less: Adjustments to income

Equals: Adjusted gross income

Step 2:
Computing Taxable Income . . . .   Less: Standard deduction and exemptions   . . . . or . . . .   Less: Itemized deductions and exemptions

Equals: Taxable income

Step 3: Calculating Taxes Owed . . . .   Tax based on tax tables or tax schedules

Less: Tax credits

Plus: Other taxes

Step 4: Making Tax Payments
Step 5: Deadlines and Penalties . . . .   Equals: Total tax due

of adjusted gross income. For taxpayers over 65, it will remain at 7.5 percent of AGI through 2016.

- *Taxes*—state and local income tax, real estate property tax, and state or local personal property tax.
- *Interest*—mortgage interest, home equity loan interest, and investment interest expense up to an amount equal to investment income.
- *Contributions*—cash or property donated to qualified charitable organizations. Contribution totals greater than 20 percent of adjusted gross income are subject to limitations.
- *Casualty and theft losses*—financial losses resulting from natural disasters, accidents, or unlawful acts.

standard deduction A set amount on which no taxes are paid.

itemized deductions Expenses that can be deducted from adjusted gross income, such as medical expenses, real estate property taxes, home mortgage interest, charitable contributions, casualty losses, and certain work-related expenses.

Personal Finance in Practice

Is It Taxable Income? Is It Deductible?

Certain financial benefits individuals receive are not subject to federal income tax. Indicate whether each of the following items would or would not be included in taxable income when you compute your federal income tax.

Indicate whether each of the following items would or would not be deductible when you compute your federal income tax.

Is it taxable income . . . ?	Yes	No
1. Lottery winnings	___	___
2. Child support received	___	___
3. Worker's compensation benefits	___	___
4. Life insurance death benefits	___	___
5. Municipal bond interest earnings	___	___
6. Bartering income	___	___

Is it deductible . . . ?	Yes	No
7. Life insurance premiums	___	___
8. Gym membership	___	___
9. Fees for traffic violations	___	___
10. Mileage for driving to volunteer work	___	___
11. An attorney's fee for preparing a will	___	___
12. Income tax preparation fee	___	___

NOTE: These taxable income items and deductions are based on the 2014 tax year and may change due to changes in the tax code.

ANSWERS 1, 6, 10, 12—yes; 2, 3, 4, 5, 7, 8, 9, 11—no.

- *Moving expenses*—costs incurred for a change in residence associated with a new job that is at least 50 miles farther from your former home than your old main job location.
- *Job-related and other miscellaneous expenses*—unreimbursed job travel, union dues, required continuing education, work clothes or uniforms, investment expenses, tax preparation fees, safe deposit box rental (for storing investment documents), and so on. The amount of this deduction is the expenses that exceed 2 percent (as of 2014) of adjusted gross income.

The standard deduction *or* total itemized deductions, along with the value of your exemptions (see next section), are subtracted from adjusted gross income to obtain your taxable income. *Note:* For individual returns with incomes greater than $254,200 or joint returns greater than $305,000 in 2014, there are limitations to the amount of itemized deductions.

You are required to maintain records to document tax deductions, such as a home filing system (Exhibit 3–2). Canceled checks and receipts serve as proof of payment for deductions such as charitable contributions, medical expenses, and business-related expenses. Travel expenses can be documented in a daily log with records of mileage, tolls, parking fees, and away-from-home costs.

Generally, you should keep tax records for three years from the date you file your return. However, you may be held responsible for providing back documentation up to six years. Records such as past tax returns and housing documents should be kept indefinitely.

EXEMPTIONS An **exemption** is a deduction from adjusted gross income for yourself, your spouse, and qualified dependents. A dependent must not earn more than a set amount unless he or she is under age 19 or is a full-time student under age 24; you must provide

CAUTION!

Watch out for IRS agent impersonators. It has been reported that over 20,000 people have been contacted and lost over $1 million due to this scam. Most of these scams have occurred over the phone. The IRS will contact you by mail, not phone, regarding unpaid taxes. Information on these and other tax frauds is available at www.treasury.gov/tigta/.

exemption A deduction from adjusted gross income for yourself, your spouse, and qualified dependents.

Exhibit 3-2   A Tax Recordkeeping System

Tax Forms and Filing Information
• Current tax forms and instruction booklets and online resources
• Reference books on current tax laws and tax-saving techniques
• Social Security numbers of household members
• Copies of federal tax returns from previous years

Income Records
• W-2 forms reporting salary, wages, and taxes withheld
• W-2P forms reporting pension income
• 1099 forms reporting interest, dividends, and capital gains and losses from savings and investments
• 1099 forms for self-employment income, royalty income, and lump-sum payments from pension or retirement plans

Expense Records
• Receipts for medical, dependent care, charitable donations, and job-related expenses
• Mortgage interest (Form 1098) and other deductible interest
• Business, investment, and rental-property expense documents

more than half of the dependent's support; and the dependent must reside in your home or be a specified relative and must meet certain citizenship requirements. For 2014, taxable income was reduced by $3,950 for each exemption claimed. After deducting the amounts for exemptions, you obtain your taxable income, which is the amount used to determine taxes owed.

Step 3: Calculating Taxes Owed

Your taxable income is the basis for computing the amount of tax owed.

did you know?

The most frequently overlooked tax deductions are state sales taxes, reinvested dividends, out-of-pocket charitable contributions, student loan interest paid by parents, moving expenses to take a first job, military reservists' travel expenses, child care credit, estate tax on income in respect of a decedent, state tax you paid last spring, refinancing points, and jury pay paid to employer.

TAX RATES Use your taxable income in conjunction with the appropriate tax table or tax schedule. For 2014, the seven-rate system for federal income tax was as follows:

Rate on Taxable Income	Single Taxpayers	Married Taxpayers Filing Jointly	Heads of Household
10%	Up to $9,075	Up to $18,150	Up to $12,950
15	$9,076–$36,900	$18,151–$73,800	$12,951–$49,400
25	$36,901–$89,350	$73,801–$148,850	$49,401–$127,550
28	$89,351–$186,350	$148,851–$226,850	$127,551–$206,600
33	$186,351–$405,100	$226,851–$405,100	$206,601–$405,100
35	$405,101–$406,750	$405,101–$457,600	$405,101–$432,200
39.6	Over $406,751	Over $457,601	Over $432,201

A separate tax rate schedule also exists for married persons who file separate income tax returns.

The 10, 15, 25, 28, 33, 35 and 39.6 percent rates are referred to as **marginal tax rates.** These rates are used to calculate tax on the last (and next) dollar of taxable income. After deductions and exemptions, a person in the 35 percent tax bracket pays 35 cents in taxes for the next dollar of taxable income in that bracket.

In contrast, the **average tax rate** is based on the total tax due divided by taxable income. Except for taxpayers in the 10 percent bracket, this rate is less than a person's marginal tax rate. For example, a person with taxable income of $40,000 and a total tax bill of $4,200 would have an average tax rate of 10.5 percent ($4,200 ÷ $40,000).

marginal tax rate The rate used to calculate tax on the last (and next) dollar of taxable income.

average tax rate Total tax due divided by taxable income.

Tax Credits versus Tax Deductions

Many people confuse *tax credits* with *tax deductions.* Is one better than the other? A tax *credit,* such as eligible child care or dependent care expenses, results in a dollar-for-dollar reduction in the amount of taxes owed. A tax *deduction,* such as an itemized deduction in the form of medical expenses, mortgage interest, or charitable contributions, reduces the taxable income on which your taxes are based.

Here is how a $100 tax credit compares with a $100 tax deduction:

As you might expect, tax credits are less readily available than tax deductions. To qualify for a $100 child care tax credit, you may have to spend $500 in child care expenses. In some situations, spending on deductible items may be more beneficial than qualifying for a tax credit. A knowledge of tax law and careful financial planning will help you use both tax credits and tax deductions to maximum advantage.

TAX CREDIT	TAX DEDUCTION

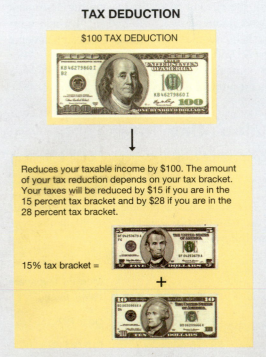

CALCULATIONS

1. If a person in a 28 percent tax bracket received a $1,000 tax *deduction,* how much would the person's taxes be reduced?

2. If a person in a 33 percent tax bracket received a $200 tax *credit,* how much would the person's taxes be reduced?

CALCULATING YOUR TAX Each of the tax rates represents a range of income levels. These are often referred to as "brackets." Thus, if you are married filing jointly and have a taxable income of $95,000, you and your spouse are in the 25 percent tax bracket. Although most computer programs will automatically calculate the tax owed, it is helpful to understand the process to calculate the tax due. (*Note:* For this example, we assume that you received no other income at different rates, such as capital gains.)

To calculate the tax on a specific amount of income, you must calculate the tax from each of the brackets as you progress up to your taxable income. (*Note:* This is the tax calculated prior to additional credits or other taxes, such as self-employment tax.)

Tax Due for Married Filing Jointly ($95,000 taxable income)

10% Bracket	• Range of income ($0–$18,150) • $18,150 x 10% = $1,815
15% Bracket	• Range of income ($18,150–$73,800) • $55,650 x 15% = $8,348
25% Bracket	• Range of income ($73,800–$95,000) • $21,200 x 25% = $5,300
Total Tax Due	• Total tax due (all brackets) • $1,815 + $8,348 + $5,300 = $15,463

ALTERNATIVE MINIMUM TAX Taxpayers with high amounts of certain deductions and various types of income may be subject to an additional tax. The *alternative minimum tax (AMT)* is designed to ensure that those who receive tax breaks also pay their fair share of taxes. The AMT was originally designed to prevent those with high incomes from using special tax breaks to pay little in taxes. However, in recent years, this tax is affecting increasing numbers of taxpayers. Some of the tax situations that can result in a person paying the AMT include high levels of deductions for state and local taxes, interest on second mortgages, medical expenses, and other deductions. Income items that can trigger the AMT are incentive stock options, long-term capital gains, and tax-exempt interest. Additional information about the AMT may be obtained at www.irs.gov.

TAX CREDITS The tax owed may be reduced by a **tax credit,** an amount subtracted directly from the amount of taxes owed. One example of a tax credit is the credit given for child care and dependent care expenses. Another tax credit for low-income workers is the *earned-income credit (EIC),* for working parents with taxable income under a certain amount. Families that do not earn enough to owe federal income taxes are also eligible for the EIC and receive a check for the amount of their credit. A *tax credit* differs from a deduction in that a tax credit has a full dollar effect in lowering taxes, whereas a *deduction* reduces the taxable income on which the tax liability is computed.

> **tax credit** An amount subtracted directly from the amount of taxes owed.

Recent tax credits also included:

- Foreign tax credit to avoid double taxation on income taxes paid to another country.
- Savers credit (formerly the retirement tax credit) to encourage investment contributions to individual and employer-sponsored retirement plans by low- and middle-income taxpayers.
- Adoption tax credit to cover expenses when adopting a child under age 18.
- Education credits to help offset college education expenses.

Step 4: Making Tax Payments

You pay federal income taxes through either payroll withholding or estimated tax payments.

WITHHOLDING The pay-as-you-go system requires an employer to deduct federal income tax from your pay. The withheld amount is based on the number of exemptions and the expected deductions claimed. For example, a married person with children would have less withheld than a single person with the same salary, since the married person will owe less tax.

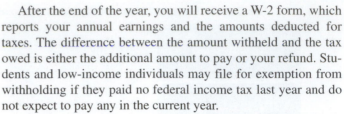
After the end of the year, you will receive a W-2 form, which reports your annual earnings and the amounts deducted for taxes. The difference between the amount withheld and the tax owed is either the additional amount to pay or your refund. Students and low-income individuals may file for exemption from withholding if they paid no federal income tax last year and do not expect to pay any in the current year.

Many taxpayers view an annual tax refund as a "windfall," extra money they count on each year. These taxpayers are forgetting the opportunity cost of withholding excessive amounts. Others view their extra tax withholding as "forced savings." This is giving the government a free loan. A payroll deduction plan for savings could serve the same purpose while also earning interest on your funds.

ESTIMATED PAYMENTS Income from savings, investments, independent contracting, royalties, and pension payments is reported on Form 1099. People who receive such income may be required to make tax payments during the year (April 15, June 15, September 15, and January 15 as the last payment for the previous tax year). These payments are based on an estimate of taxes due at year-end. Underpayment or failure to make estimated payments can result in penalties and daily interest charges.

Step 5: Deadlines and Penalties

Most people are required to file a federal income tax return by April 15. If you are not able to file on time, you can use Form 4868 to obtain an automatic six-month extension.

This extension is for the 1040 form and other documents, but it does not delay your payment liability. You must submit the estimated amount owed along with Form 4868 by April 15. Failure to file on time can result in a penalty for being just one day late. Underpayment of quarterly estimated taxes may require paying interest on the amount you should have paid. Underpayment due to negligence or fraud can result in penalties of 50 to 75 percent.

The good news is that if you claim a refund several months or years late, the IRS will pay you interest. However, refunds must be claimed within three years of filing the return or within two years of paying the tax.

Sheet 9 Federal Income Tax Estimate

PRACTICE QUIZ 3-2

1. How does tax-exempt income differ from tax-deferred income?

2. When would you use the standard deduction instead of itemized deductions?

3. What is the difference between your marginal tax rate and your average tax rate?

4. For each of the following, indicate if the item is a *tax deduction* or a *tax credit*.

   a. State personal income taxes paid
   b. Charitable donations
   c. Expenses for adopting a baby
   d. Moving expenses

Apply Yourself!

Using library resources or an online search, determine the amounts that are eligible for education credits for the current year.

Filing Your Federal Income Tax Return

As you prepare to do your taxes, you must first determine whether you are required to file a return. Next, you need to decide which tax form best serves you and if you are required to submit supplementary schedules or forms.

Who Must File?

Every citizen or resident of the United States and every U.S. citizen who is a resident of Puerto Rico is required to file a federal income tax return if his or her income is above a certain amount. The amount is based on the person's *filing status* and other factors such as age. For example, single persons under 65 had to file a return on April 15, 2014 (for tax year 2013) if their gross income exceeded $10,000. If your gross income is less than this amount but taxes were withheld, you should file a return to obtain your refund. Also, if you can be claimed as a dependent, the income limits are lower.

Your filing status is affected by marital status and dependents. The five filing status categories are:

- *Single*—never-married, divorced, or legally separated individuals with no dependents.
- *Married, filing joint return*—combines the spouses' incomes.
- *Married, filing separate returns*—each spouse is responsible for his or her own tax; under certain conditions, a married couple can benefit from this filing status.
- *Head of household*—an unmarried individual or a surviving spouse who maintains a household (paying for more than half of the costs) for a child or a dependent relative.
- *Qualifying widow or widower*—an individual whose spouse died within the past two years and who has a dependent; this status is limited to two years after the death of the spouse.

In some situations, you may have a choice of filing status. In such cases, compute your taxes under the alternatives to determine the most advantageous filing status.

LO3.3

Prepare a federal income tax return.

ACTION ITEM

I know the basics of preparing a federal income tax return.

☐ **Yes**   ☐ **No**

> **did you know?**
>
> *For determining your filing status:* If you get married on December 31, you are considered married for the entire year. The reverse is also true. If you get divorced by December 31, you are considered single for the entire year.

Which Tax Form Should You Use?

Although about 800 federal tax forms and schedules exist, you have a choice of three basic forms when filing your income tax (see "Personal Finance in Practice" following). Recently about 20 percent of taxpayers used Form 1040EZ or Form 1040A; about 60 percent used the regular Form 1040. Your decision in this matter will depend on your type of income, the amount of your income, the number of your deductions, and the complexity of your tax situation. Most tax preparation software programs will guide you in selecting the appropriate 1040 form.

Completing the Federal Income Tax Return

The major sections of Form 1040 (see Exhibit 3–3) correspond to tax topics discussed in the previous sections of this chapter:

1. *Filing status and exemptions.* Your tax rate is determined by your filing status and allowances for yourself, your spouse, and each person you claim as a dependent.
2. *Income.* Earnings from your employment (as reported by your W-2 form) and other income, such as savings and investment income, are reported in this section of Form 1040.

FORM 1040EZ

You may use Form 1040EZ if:

- You are single or married filing a joint return, under age 65, and claim no dependents.

- Your income consisted only of wages, salaries, and tips and not more than $1,500 of taxable interest.

- Your taxable income is less than $100,000.

- You do not itemize deductions or claim any adjustments to income or any tax credits.

FORM 1040A

This form would be used by people who have less than $100,000 in taxable income from wages, salaries, tips, unemployment compensation, interest, or dividends and use the standard deduction. With Form 1040A, you can also take deductions for individual retirement account (IRA) contributions and a tax credit for child care and dependent care expenses. If you qualify for either Form 1040EZ or Form 1040A, you may wish to use one of them to simplify filing your tax return. You may not want to use either the Form 1040EZ or Form 1040A if Form 1040 allows you to pay less tax.

FORM 1040

Form 1040 is an expanded version of Form 1040A that includes sections for all types of income. You are required to use this form if your income is over $100,000 or if you can be claimed as a dependent on your parents' return *and* you had interest or dividends over a set limit.

Form 1040 allows you to itemize your deductions. You can list various allowable expenses (medical costs, home mortgage interest, real estate property taxes) that will reduce taxable income and the amount you owe the government. You should learn about all the possible adjustments to income, deductions, and tax credits for which you may qualify.

FORM 1040X

This form is used to amend a previously filed tax return. If you discover income that was not reported, or if you find additional deductions, you should file Form 1040X to pay the additional tax or obtain a refund.

3. *Adjustments to income.* As discussed later in the chapter, if you qualify, you may deduct contributions (up to a certain amount) to an individual retirement account (IRA) or other qualified retirement program.

4. *Tax computation.* In this section, your adjusted gross income is reduced by your itemized deductions (see Exhibit 3–4) or by the standard deduction for your tax

situation. In addition, an amount is deducted for each exemption to arrive at your
taxable income. That income is the basis for determining the amount of your tax
(see Exhibit 3–5).

5. *Tax credits.* Any tax credits for which you qualify are subtracted at this point.

6. *Other taxes.* Any special taxes, such as self-employment tax, are included at this
point.

7. *Payments.* Your total withholding and other payments are indicated in this section.

8. *Refund or amount you owe.* If your payments exceed the amount of income tax
you owe, you are entitled to a refund. If the opposite is true, you must make an
additional payment. Taxpayers who want their refunds sent directly to a bank
can provide the necessary account information directly on Form 1040, 1040A, or
1040EZ.

Changing economic and political environments often result in new tax
regulations, some of which may be favorable for you while others are not. An
important element of tax planning is your refund. Each year, more than 90 million
American households receive an average tax refund of over $2,500 for a total of
over $225 billion. Invested at 5 percent for a year, these refunds represent about

Exhibit 3–3 Federal Income Tax Return—Form 1040

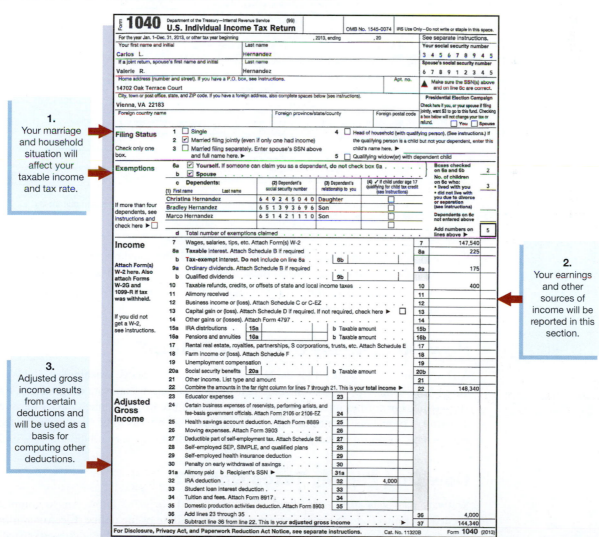

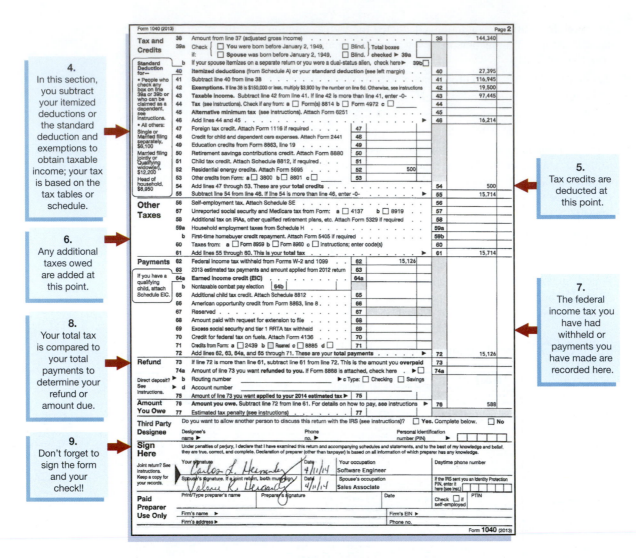

4.
In this section, you subtract your itemized deductions or the standard deduction and exemptions to obtain taxable income; your tax is based on the tax tables or schedule.

5.
Tax credits are deducted at this point.

6.
Any additional taxes owed are added at this point.

7.
The federal income tax you have had withheld or payments you have made are recorded here.

8.
Your total tax is compared to your total payments to determine your refund or amount due.

9.
Don't forget to sign the form and your check!!

NOTE: These forms were used in a recent year; the current forms may not be exactly the same. Obtain current income tax forms and current tax information from your local IRS office, select post offices and libraries, or at www.irs.gov.

$11.25 billion in lost earnings. By having less withheld and obtaining a smaller refund, you can save and invest these funds for your benefit during the year.

9. *Your signature.* Forgetting to sign a tax return is one of the most frequent filing errors.

How Do I File My State Tax Return?

All but seven states (Alaska, Florida, Nevada, South Dakota, Texas, Washington, and Wyoming) have some type of state income tax. In most states, the tax rate ranges from 1 to 10 percent. For further information about the income tax in your state, contact the state department of revenue. States usually require income tax returns to be filed when the federal income tax return is due. For planning your tax activities, see Exhibit 3–6.

How Do I File My Taxes Online?

Software packages such as *H&R Block At Home* and *TurboTax* allow you to complete needed tax forms and schedules and either print for mailing or file online. Electronic filing of federal taxes now exceeds 113 million returns annually. With e-file, taxpayers usually

Exhibit 3–4   Schedule A for Itemized Deductions—Form 1040

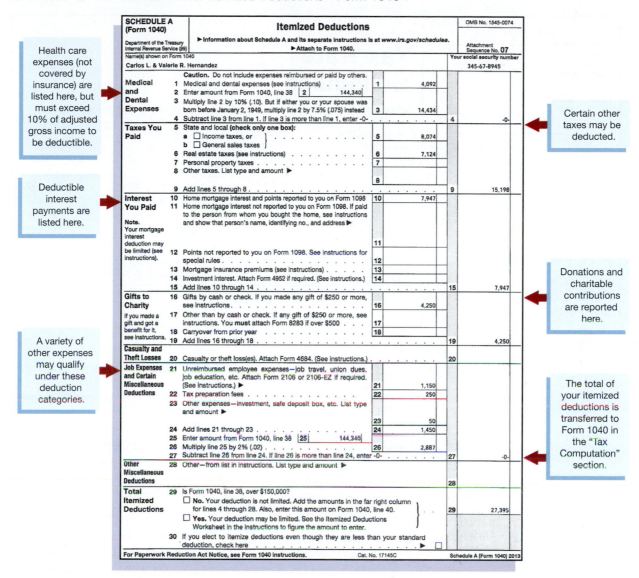

Health care expenses (not covered by insurance) are listed here, but must exceed 10% of adjusted gross income to be deductible.

Deductible interest payments are listed here.

A variety of other expenses may qualify under these deduction categories.

Certain other taxes may be deducted.

Donations and charitable contributions are reported here.

The total of your itemized deductions is transferred to Form 1040 in the "Tax Computation" section.

receive their refunds within three weeks. The cost for this service is usually between $15 and $40 and in some cases will be $0.

TAX PREPARATION SOFTWARE Today, most taxpayers use computers or online products for tax recordkeeping and tax form preparation. A spreadsheet program (or app) can be helpful in maintaining and updating income and expense data.

Using tax software can save you time when preparing your Form 1040 and accompanying schedules. When selecting tax software, consider the following factors:

1. Your personal situation—are you employed or do you operate your own business?
2. Special tax situations with regard to types of income, unusual deductions, and various tax credits.
3. Features in the software, such as "audit check," future tax planning, and filing your federal and state tax forms online.
4. Technical aspects, such as the hardware and operating system requirements, and online support that is provided.

Exhibit 3–5 Tax Tables and Tax Rate Schedules

Tax Table

If line 43 (taxable income) is—		And you are—			
At least	But less than	Single	Married filing jointly *	Married filing separately	Head of a house-hold
			Your tax is—		
97,000					
97,000	97,050	20,460	16,114	20,900	18,759
97,050	97,100	20,474	16,126	20,914	18,771
97,100	97,150	20,488	16,139	20,928	18,784
97,150	97,200	20,502	16,151	20,942	18,796
97,200	97,250	20,516	16,164	20,956	18,809
97,250	97,300	20,530	16,176	20,970	18,821
97,300	97,350	20,544	16,189	20,984	18,834
97,350	97,400	20,558	16,201	20,998	18,846
97,400	97,450	20,572	16,214	20,012	18,859
97,450	97,500	20,586	16,226	20,026	18,871
97,500	97,550	20,600	16,239	20,040	18,884
97,550	97,600	20,614	16,251	20,054	18,896
97,600	97,650	20,628	16,264	20,068	18,909
97,650	97,700	20,642	16,276	20,082	18,921
97,700	97,750	20,656	16,289	20,096	18,934
97,750	97,800	20,670	16,301	20,110	18,946
97,800	97,850	20,684	16,341	20,124	18,959
97,850	97,900	20,698	16,326	20,138	18,971
97,900	97,950	20,712	16,339	20,152	18,984
97,950	98,000	20,726	16,351	20,166	18,996

* This column must also be used by a qualifying widow(er).

Tax Rate Schedules

Schedule Y-1— If your filing status is **Married filing jointly** or **Qualifying widow(er)**

If your taxable income is:		The tax is:	of the amount over—
Over—	But not over—		
$0	$17,850	.... 10%	$0
17,850	72,500	$1,785.00 + 15%	17,850
72,500	146,400	9,982.50 + 25%	72,500
146,400	223,050	27,457.50 + 28%	146,400
223,050	398,350	49,919.50 + 33%	223,050
398,350	450,000	107,768.50 + 35%	398,350
450,000	....	125,856 + 39.6%	450,000

NOTE: These were the federal income tax rates for 2013 that are used for illustrative purposes for the tax return included in the chapter exhibits. Current rates may vary due to changes in the tax code and adjustments for inflation. Obtain current income tax booklets from www.irs.gov.

ELECTRONIC FILING In recent years, the IRS has made online filing easier and less expensive. Through the Free File Alliance, online tax preparation and e-filing are available free to millions of taxpayers. This partnership between the IRS and the tax software industry encourages more e-filing. The online filing process involves the following steps:

Step 1 Go to www.irs.gov and click "Free File" in the "Filing and Payment" section.

Step 2 The initial IRS webpage gives guidance regarding the process. Your eligibility for Free File is based on your income level. You can click on a Free File company to begin your tax return. You should determine your eligibility with a particular company. A brief description of the criteria for each is provided. A "How to use Free File" option is also available to help you understand the process.

Step 3 Next, connect to the chosen company's website to begin the preparation of your tax return.

Step 4 Finally, use the company's online software to prepare your return. Your federal tax return is then filed electronically and your tax data are stored at the vendor's site. Taxpayers who do not qualify for the Free File Alliance program may still be able to file online for a nominal fee or use fillable forms. You don't have to purchase the software; simply go to the software company's Internet site and pay a fee to use the tax program.

Taxpayers who use the Free File Alliance are cautioned to be careful consumers. A company may attempt to sell other financial products to inexperienced taxpayers, such as expensive refund anticipation loans. Also, taxpayers using the Free File service must be aware that their state tax return might not be included in the free program.

did you know?

Electronically filed federal income tax returns have an accuracy rate of 99 percent, compared to 81 percent for paper returns. Most electronic filing programs do your calculations and signal potential errors before you file.

Exhibit 3–6
Tax-Planner Calendar

January
- Establish a recordkeeping system for your tax information.
- If you expect a refund, file your tax return for the previous year.
- Make your final estimated quarterly payment for the previous year for income not covered by withholding.

February
- Check to make sure you received W-2 and 1099 forms from all organizations from which you had income during the previous year; these should have been received by January 31. If not, contact the organization.

March
- Organize your records and tax information in preparation for filing your tax return; if you expect a refund, file as soon as possible.

April
- April 15 is the deadline for filing your federal tax return; if it falls on a weekend, you have until the next business day (usually Monday).
- If necessary, file for an automatic extension for filing your tax forms.

May
- Review your tax return to determine whether any changes in withholding, exemptions, or marital status have not been reported to your employer.

June
- The second installment for estimated tax is due June 15 for income not covered by withholding.

July
- With the year half over, consider or implement plans for a personal retirement program such as an IRA or a Keogh plan.

August
- Tax returns are due August 15 for those who received the automatic four-month extension.
- Determine if you qualify for an IRA; if so, consider opening one.

September
- The third installment for estimated tax is due September 15 for income not covered by withholding.

October
- Determine the tax benefits of selling certain investments by year-end.
- Prepare a preliminary tax form to determine the most advantageous filing status.
- Tax returns are due October 15 for those who received the automatic six-month extension.

November
- Make any last-minute changes in withholding by your employer to avoid penalties for too little withholding.
- Determine if you qualify for an IRA; if so, consider opening one.
- If you haven't already, prepare a preliminary tax form to determine the most advantageous filing status.

December
- Determine if it would be to your advantage to make payments for next year before December 31 of the current year.
- Decide if you can defer income for the current year until the following year.

NOTE: Children born before the end of the year give you a full-year exemption, so plan accordingly!

What Tax Assistance Sources Are Available?

As with other aspects of personal financial planning, many tax resources are available to assist you.

IRS SERVICES If you prepare your own tax return or desire tax information, the IRS can assist in seven ways:

1. *Publications.* The IRS offers hundreds of free booklets and pamphlets that can be obtained at a local IRS office, by mail request, by telephone, or downloaded. Especially helpful is *Your Federal Income Tax* (IRS Publication 17). IRS publications and tax forms are available by phone at 1-800-TAX-FORM or online at www.irs.gov.

digi – know?

The irs.gov website ranks in the top 100 U.S. websites. In 2013, total visits were over 318 billion.

2. *Recorded messages.* The IRS Tele-Tax system gives you 24-hour access to about 150 recorded tax tips at 1-800-829-4477.

3. *Phone hotline.* Information about specific problems is available through an IRS-staffed phone line at 1-800-829-1040.

4. *Walk-in service.* You can visit a local IRS office (400 are available) to obtain tax assistance.

5. *Interactive tax assistant.* The IRS has developed a query-based interactive tool that allows taxpayers to get answers for basic and advanced questions.

6. *DVD.* The IRS also sells a DVD with over 2,000 tax forms, publications, and FAQs.

7. *IRS2Go App.* This tool provides options for checking your refund status, requesting tax records, locating free tax prep help, and other interactive tools.

TAX PUBLICATIONS   Each year, several tax guides are published and offered for sale. Publications such as *J.K. Lasser's Your Income Tax* and *The Ernst & Young Tax Guide* can be purchased online or at local stores. The IRS also offers Publication 17, *Your Federal Income Tax (for Individuals),* which is a free resource.

THE INTERNET   As with other personal finance topics, extensive information may be found on websites such as those mentioned earlier. Be sure to access reliable websites and print information for your records.

Tax Preparation Services

Over 40 million U.S. taxpayers pay someone to do their income taxes. The fee for this service can range from $40 at a tax preparation service for a simple return to more than $2,000 to a certified public accountant for a complicated return.

TYPES OF TAX SERVICES   Doing your own taxes may not be desirable, especially if you have sources of income other than salary. The sources available for professional tax assistance include the following:

- Tax services range from local, one-person operations to national firms with thousands of offices, such as H&R Block.
- Enrolled agents—government-approved tax experts—prepare returns and provide tax advice. You may contact the National Association of Enrolled Agents at 1-800-424-4339 for information about enrolled agents in your area.
- Many accountants offer tax assistance along with other business services. A certified public accountant (CPA) with special training in taxes can help with tax planning and the preparation of your annual tax return.
- Attorneys usually do not complete tax returns; however, you can use an attorney's services when you are involved in a tax-related transaction or when you have a difference of opinion with the IRS.

EVALUATING TAX SERVICES   When planning to use a tax preparation service, consider these factors:

- What training and experience does the tax professional possess?
- How will the fee be determined? (Avoid preparers who earn a percentage of your refund.)
- Does the preparer suggest you report various deductions that might be questioned?
- Will the preparer represent you if your return is audited?
- Is tax preparation the main business activity, or does it serve as a front for selling other financial products and services?

Additional information about tax preparers may be obtained at the websites for the National Association of Enrolled Agents (www.naea.org) and the National Association of Tax Professionals (www.natptax.com).

TAX SERVICE WARNINGS Even if you hire a professional tax preparer, you are responsible for supplying accurate and complete information. Hiring a tax preparer will not guarantee that you pay the *correct* amount. A study conducted by *Money* magazine of 41 tax preparers reported fees ranging from $375 to $3,600, with taxes due ranging from $31,846 to $74,450 for the same fictional family. If you owe more tax because your return contains errors or you have made entries that are not allowed, you are responsible for paying that additional tax, plus any interest and penalties.

Beware of tax preparers and other businesses that offer your refund in advance. These "refund anticipation loans" frequently charge very high interest rates for this type of consumer credit. Studies reveal interest rates sometimes exceeding 300 percent (on an annualized basis).

> **did you know?**
>
> Volunteer Income Tax Assistance (VITA) offers free tax help to low- and moderate-income taxpayers who cannot prepare their own tax returns. Certified volunteers provide this service at community centers, libraries, schools, shopping malls, and other locations. Most locations also offer free electronic filing. To locate the nearest VITA site, call 1-800-906-9887.

What If Your Return Is Audited?

The Internal Revenue Service reviews all returns for completeness and accuracy. If you make an error, your tax is automatically refigured and you receive either a bill or a refund. If you make an entry that is not allowed, you will be notified by mail. A **tax audit** is a detailed examination of your tax return by the IRS. In most audits, the IRS requests more information to support your tax return. Be sure to keep accurate records. Receipts, canceled checks, and other evidence can verify amounts that you claim. Avoiding common filing mistakes helps to minimize your chances of an audit (see Exhibit 3–7).

tax audit A detailed examination of your tax return by the Internal Revenue Service.

Exhibit 3–7   How to Avoid Common Filing Errors

- Organize all tax-related information for easy access.
- Follow instructions carefully. Many people deduct total medical and dental expenses rather than the amount of these expenses that exceeds 10 percent of adjusted gross income. The AGI threshold is 7.5 percent of your AGI if you or your spouse is age 65 or older. This will apply through December 31, 2016.
- Use the proper tax rate schedule or tax table column.
- Be sure to claim the correct number of exemptions and correct amounts of standard deductions.
- Consider the alternative minimum tax that may apply to your situation. Be sure to pay self-employment tax and tax on early IRA withdrawals.
- Check your math several times. Also check behind the tax software to ensure accuracy.
- Sign your return (both spouses must sign a joint return), or the IRS won't process it.
- Be sure to include the correct Social Security number(s) and to record amounts on the correct lines.
- Attach necessary documentation such as your W-2 forms and required supporting schedules.
- Make the check payable to "United States Treasury."
- Put your Social Security number, the tax year, and a daytime telephone number on your check—and be sure to sign the check!
- Keep a photocopy of your return.
- Put the proper postage on your mailing envelope.
- Finally, check everything again—and file on time!

WHO GETS AUDITED? About 1 percent of all tax filers—fewer than 1.5 million people—are audited each year. Although the IRS does not reveal its basis for auditing returns, several indicators are evident. People who claim large or unusual deductions increase their chances of an audit. Tax advisors suggest including a brief explanation or a copy of receipts for deductions that may be questioned.

TYPES OF AUDITS The simplest and most frequent type of audit is the *correspondence audit*. This mail inquiry requires you to clarify or document minor questions. The *office audit* requires you to visit an IRS office to clarify some aspect of your tax return.

The *field audit* is more complex. An IRS agent visits you at your home, your business, or the office of your accountant to have access to your records. A field audit may be done to verify whether an individual has a home office if this is claimed.

The IRS also conducts more detailed audits for about 50,000 taxpayers. These range from random requests to document various tax return items to line-by-line reviews by IRS employees.

YOUR AUDIT RIGHTS When you receive an audit notice, you have the right to request time to prepare. Also, you can ask the IRS for clarification of items being questioned. When audited, follow these suggestions:

- Decide whether you will bring your tax preparer, accountant, or lawyer.
- Be on time for your appointment; bring only relevant documents.
- Present tax evidence in a logical, calm, and confident manner; maintain a positive attitude.
- Make sure the information you present is consistent with the tax law.
- Keep your answers aimed at the auditor's questions. Answer questions clearly and completely. Be as brief as possible. The five best responses to questions during an audit are "Yes," "No," "I don't recall," "I'll have to check on that," and "What specific items do you want to see?"

If you disagree with the results of an audit, you may request a conference at the Regional Appeals Office. Although most differences of opinion are settled at this stage, some taxpayers take their cases further. A person may go to the U.S. tax court, the U.S. claims court, or the U.S. district court. Some tax disputes have gone to the U.S. Supreme Court.

PRACTICE QUIZ 3–3

1. In what ways does your filing status affect preparation of your federal income tax return?

2. What are the main sources available to help people prepare their taxes?

3. What actions can reduce the chances of an IRS audit?

4. Which 1040 form should each of the following individuals use? (Check one for each situation.)

Tax situation	1040EZ	1040A	1040
a. A high school student with an after-school job and interest earnings of $480 from savings accounts.			
b. A college student who, because of ownership of property, is able to itemize deductions rather than take the standard deduction.			
c. A young, entry-level worker with no dependents and income only from salary.			

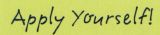

Compare tax services (and providers) in your area and online.

Tax Planning Strategies

LO3.4

Select appropriate tax strategies for various life situations.

For people to pay their fair share of taxes—no more, no less—they should practice **tax avoidance,** the use of legitimate methods to reduce one's taxes. In contrast, **tax evasion** is the use of illegal actions to reduce one's taxes. To minimize taxes owed, follow these guidelines:

- If you expect to have the *same* or a *lower* tax rate next year, *accelerate deductions* into the current year. Pay real estate property taxes or make charitable donations by December 31.
- If you expect to have a *lower* or the *same* tax rate next year, *delay the receipt of income* until next year so the funds will be taxed at a lower rate or at a later date.
- If you expect to have a *higher* tax rate next year, consider *delaying deductions,* since they will have a greater benefit. A $1,000 deduction at 25 percent lowers your taxes $250; at 28 percent, your taxes are lowered $280.
- If you expect to have a *higher* tax rate next year, *accelerate the receipt of income* to have it taxed at the current lower rate.

When considering financial decisions in relation to your taxes, remember that purchasing, investing, and retirement planning are the areas most heavily affected by tax laws.

ACTION ITEM

I understand tax strategies for now and in the future.

☐ **Yes**   ☐ **No**

tax avoidance The use of legitimate methods to reduce one's taxes.

tax evasion The use of illegal actions to reduce one's taxes.

Consumer Purchasing

The buying decisions most directly affected by taxes are the purchase of a residence, the use of credit, and job-related expenses.

PLACE OF RESIDENCE Owning a home is one of the best tax shelters. Both real estate property taxes and interest on the mortgage are deductible (as itemized deductions) and thus reduce your taxable income.

CONSUMER DEBT Current tax laws allow homeowners to borrow for consumer purchases. You can deduct interest on loans (of up to $100,000) secured by your primary or secondary home up to the actual dollar amount you have invested in it—the difference between the market value of the home and the amount you owe on it. These *home equity loans,* which are *second mortgages,* allow you to use that line of credit for various purchases. Some states place restrictions on home equity loans.

JOB-RELATED EXPENSES As previously mentioned, certain work expenses, such as union dues, some travel and education costs, business tools, and job search expenses (even if you were not successful), may be included as itemized deductions.

HEALTH CARE EXPENSES *Flexible spending accounts (FSAs),* also called *health savings accounts* and expense reimbursement accounts, allow you to reduce your taxable income when paying for medical expenses or child care costs. Workers are allowed to put pretax dollars into these employer-sponsored programs. These "deposits" result in a lower taxable income. Then, the funds in the FSA may be used to pay for various medical expenses and dependent care costs.

Investment Decisions

A major area of tax planning involves decisions related to investing.

TAX-EXEMPT INVESTMENTS Interest income from municipal bonds, which are issued by state and local governments, and other tax-exempt investments is not subject to federal income tax. Although municipal bonds have lower interest rates than other investments, the *tax-equivalent* income may be higher. For example, if you are in the

Figure It Out!

Short-Term and Long-Term Capital Gains

You will pay a lower tax rate on the profits from stocks and other investments if you hold the asset for more than 12 months. As of 2014, a taxpayer in the 28 percent tax bracket would pay $420 in taxes on a $1,500 short-term capital gain (assets held for less than a year). However, that same taxpayer would pay only $225 on the $1,500 (a 15 percent capital gains tax) if the investment were held for more than a year.

	Short-Term Capital Gain (assets held less than a year)	Long-Term Capital Gain (assets held a year or more)
Capital gain	$1,500	$1,500
Capital gains tax rate	28%	15%
Capital gains tax	$420	$225
Tax savings	$195 ($420 − $225)	

35 percent tax bracket, earning $100 of tax-exempt income would be worth more to you than earning $150 in taxable investment income. The $150 would have an after-tax value of $97.50—$150 less $52.50 (35 percent of $150) for taxes.

TAX-DEFERRED INVESTMENTS Although tax-deferred investments, with income taxed at a later date, are less beneficial than tax-exempt investments, they give you the advantage of paying taxes in the future rather than now. Examples of tax-deferred investments include:

- *Tax-deferred annuities,* usually issued by insurance companies. These investments are discussed in Chapter 10.
- *Section 529 savings plans* are state-run, tax-deferred plans to set aside money for a child's education. The 529 is a savings plan to help families set aside funds for future college costs. The 529 plans differ from state to state.
- *Retirement plans* such as IRA, Keogh, or 401(k) plans. The next section discusses the tax implications of these plans.

capital gains Profits from the sale of a capital asset such as stocks, bonds, or real estate.

Capital gains, profits from the sale of a capital asset such as stocks, bonds, or real estate, are also tax-deferred; you do not have to pay the tax on these profits until the asset is sold. In recent years, *long-term* capital gains (on investments held more than a year) have been taxed at a lower rate. See the nearby "Figure It Out!" box for an example.

The sale of an investment for less than its purchase price is, of course, a *capital loss.* Capital losses can be used to offset capital gains and up to $3,000 of ordinary income. Unused capital losses may be carried forward into future years to offset capital gains or ordinary income up to $3,000 per year.

SELF-EMPLOYMENT Owning your own business can have tax advantages. Self-employed persons may deduct expenses such as health and certain life insurance as business costs. However, business owners have to pay self-employment tax (Social Security) in addition to the regular tax rate.

CHILDREN'S INVESTMENTS A child under 18, or a full-time student under 24, with investment income of more than $2,000 is taxed at the parent's top rate. For investment income under $2,000, the child receives a deduction of $1,000 and the next $1,000 is taxed at his or her own rate, which is probably lower than the parent's rate.

Retirement and Education Plans

A major tax strategy of benefit to working people is the use of tax-deferred retirement plans such as individual retirement accounts (IRAs), Keogh plans, and 401(k) plans. Another tax strategy involves the use of education savings plans such as Coverdell Education Savings Accounts or 529 plans.

TRADITIONAL IRA The regular IRA deduction is available only to people who do not participate in employer-sponsored retirement plans or who have an adjusted gross income under a certain amount. As of 2014, the IRA contribution limit was $5,500. Older workers, age 50 and over, were allowed to contribute up to $6,500 as a "catch up" to make up for lost time saving for retirement.

In general, amounts withdrawn from deductible IRAs are included in gross income. An additional 10 percent penalty is usually imposed on withdrawals made before age 59½ unless the withdrawn funds are on account of death or disability, for medical expenses, or for qualified higher education expenses.

ROTH IRA The Roth IRA also allows a $5,500 (2014) annual contribution, which is not tax-deductible; however, the earnings on the account are tax-free after five years. The funds from the Roth IRA may be withdrawn before age 59½ if the account owner is disabled, or for the purchase of a first home ($10,000 maximum). Like the regular IRA, the Roth IRA is limited to people with an adjusted gross income under a certain amount.

Deductible IRAs provide tax relief up front as contributions reduce current taxes. However, taxes must be paid when the withdrawals are made from the deductible IRA. In contrast, the Roth IRA does not have immediate benefits, but the investment grows in value on a tax-free basis. Withdrawals from the Roth IRA are exempt from federal and state taxes.

KEOGH PLAN If you are self-employed and own your own business, you can establish a Keogh plan. This retirement plan, also called an HR10 plan, may combine a profit-sharing plan and a pension plan of other investments purchased by the employee. In general, with a Keogh people may contribute 25 percent of their annual income, up to a maximum of $52,000 (in 2014), to this tax-deferred retirement plan.

401(K) PLAN The part of the tax code called 401(k) authorizes a tax-deferred retirement plan sponsored by an employer. This plan allows you to contribute a greater tax-deferred amount ($17,500 in 2014) than you can contribute to an IRA. Older workers, age 50 and over, may be allowed to contribute an additional $5,500 if their employer allows. However, most companies set a limit on your contribution, such as 15 percent of your salary. Some employers provide a matching contribution in their 401(k) plans. For example, a company may contribute 50 cents for each $1 contributed by an employee. This results in an immediate 50 percent return on your investment.

Tax planners advise people to contribute as much as possible to a Keogh or 401(k) plan since (1) the increased value of the investment accumulates on a tax-free basis until the funds are withdrawn and (2) contributions reduce your adjusted gross income for computing your current tax liability.

COVERDELL EDUCATION SAVINGS ACCOUNT This account is designed to assist parents in saving for the education of their children. Withdrawals can be used for a variety of educational uses for kindergarten through college-age students. Once again, the annual contribution (limited to $2,000) is not tax-deductible and is limited to taxpayers with an adjusted gross income under a certain amount. However, as with the Roth IRA, the earnings accumulate tax-free.

529 PLAN   The 529 plan is an education savings plan that helps parents save for the college education of their children. Almost every state has a 529 plan available. There is no federal tax deduction, but the earnings grow tax-free and there are no taxes when the money is taken out of the account for qualified education expenses. Many states allow their residents to deduct contributions to their state plans up to a specified maximum.

Changing Tax Strategies

Each year, the tax code includes a myriad of changes. In the past few years, there have been debates over what types of tax reform would allow the U.S. economy to recover, how to avoid the "fiscal cliff," and how to stimulate economic growth. Congress frequently passes legislation that changes the tax code. These changes require that you regularly determine how to best take advantage of the tax laws for personal financial planning.

Recent tax changes have included the following:

- Advanced (premium) tax credit was initiated. This offers someone buying insurance through the health care exchanges an opportunity to reduce their premiums paid. If they do not get the full credit when they pay the premium, the difference will be available as a refundable tax credit at tax time.
- Penalties will be assessed for those who do not have health insurance. These penalties will be levied through a program with the IRS. Taxpayers will soon have to provide proof of health insurance with their tax return to avoid the penalty.
- Teachers will no longer be able to deduct up to $250 for unreimbursed educational expenses.
- Employers can now allow employees with health care flexible spending accounts to carry over up to $500 of unused funds.
- Streamlined options are available for the home office deduction for small businesses.

In addition to these and other recent tax changes, the IRS usually modifies the tax form and filing procedures yearly, so be sure to carefully consider changes in your personal situation and your income level. Well-informed taxpayers monitor their personal tax strategies to best serve daily living needs and to achieve long-term financial goals.

Flat or VAT Tax?

For many years, politicians have used tax reform as a platform to run for office. Some want to increase tax deductions to provide for certain segments, while others want to find ways to simplify the tax code. There is no denying that the tax code has become increasingly complex. The number of words in the tax code has reportedly grown from 1.4 million to more than 3.8 million in the last decade!

What are some options that are being proposed? First, a *flat tax* proposal has been around for many years. This would require that all taxpayers, regardless of income level and type, pay the same percentage. While seemingly relatively easy to implement, the reality is that this would be an increase in overall tax for quite a few people. The other alternative, a *value-added tax (VAT),* would add a tax to a product for each stage in the manufacturing process. It is believed that higher-income individuals would pay higher taxes since they are typically the larger consumers of goods. This has been implemented in other countries. That said, the administrative process can be a challenge for each of the companies involved in the process to remit the tax.

What do you think will happen to the tax code in 5 years? 10 years? 20 years?

Sheet 10 Tax Planning Activities

PRACTICE QUIZ 3-4

1. How does tax avoidance differ from tax evasion?

2. What common tax-saving methods are available to most individuals and households?

3. For the following tax situations, indicate if this item refers to tax-exempt income or tax-deferred income.

   a. Interest earned on municipal bonds
   b. Earnings on an individual retirement account
   c. Education IRA earnings used for college expenses
   d. Income of U.S. citizens working in another country

Apply Yourself!

Survey friends and relatives about their tax planning strategies. Do most people get a federal tax refund or owe taxes each year? Is their situation (refund or payment) planned?

YOUR PERSONAL FINANCE DASHBOARD

SMALL REFUND/SMALL AMOUNT OWED

LARGE REFUND

LARGE AMOUNT OWED

$500 $0 $500
$1000 $1000
$1500 $1500
$2000 $2000
$2500 $2500

TAX REFUND OR UNDERPAYMENT?

Another indicator of your financial health is your ability to organize and prepare key documents to maximize your tax situation. Whether you prepare your tax return or take it to someone to prepare, you need to have all of the key documents to pay your "fair share." You also need to monitor your tax situation throughout the year. This means understanding your tax situation and being aware of any changes.

YOUR SITUATION: Do you owe taxes each year? Do you receive an excessive tax refund?

Owing taxes each year could lead to underpayment penalties. Receiving a large tax refund could be hampering your savings ability. Paying your "fair share" in a timely manner is one of the foundations for progress toward financial independence.

POSSIBLE ACTIONS TO TAKE

 Reconsider your responses to the "Action Items" (in the text margin) to determine actions you might consider related to your tax planning activities.

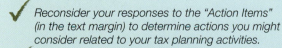 *Consider developing a system for organizing your tax records. See Exhibit 3–2 for an example.*

 Become aware of what is taxable income and what is deductible by using the "Personal Finance in Practice" box, "Is It Taxable Income?".

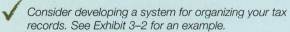 *Obtain the latest federal income tax forms and instructions, which are available at www.irs.gov. Information about state income taxes may be obtained at www.taxadmin.org.*

Continually update your knowledge of income tax changes to help you make better-informed financial decisions. Ask several people about the actions they take to stay informed and to reduce the amount paid in taxes.

Chapter Summary

LO3.1 Tax planning can influence spending, saving, borrowing, and investing decisions. An awareness of income taxes, sales taxes, excise taxes, property taxes, estate taxes, inheritance taxes, gift taxes, and Social Security taxes is vital for successful financial planning.

LO3.2 Taxable income is determined by subtracting adjustments to income, deductions, and allowances for exemptions from gross income. Your total tax liability is based on the published tax tables or tax schedules, less any tax credits.

LO3.3 The major sections of Form 1040 provide the basic framework for filing your federal income tax return. The main sources of tax assistance are IRS services and publications, other publications, the Internet, computer software, and professional tax preparers such as commercial tax services, enrolled agents, accountants, and attorneys.

LO3.4 You may reduce your tax burden through careful planning and making financial decisions related to consumer purchasing, and the use of debt, investments, and retirement planning.

Key Terms

adjusted gross income (AGI) 78
average tax rate 81
capital gains 96
earned income 78
estate tax 76
excise tax 75
exclusion 78

exemption 80
inheritance tax 76
investment income 78
itemized deductions 78
marginal tax rate 81
passive income 78
standard deduction 78
taxable income 78

tax audit 93
tax avoidance 95
tax credit 83
tax deduction 78
tax-deferred income 78
tax evasion 95
tax-exempt income 78
tax shelter 78

Discussion Questions

1. What factors might be considered when creating a tax that is considered fair by most people in a society? (LO3.1)
2. What are the ethical implications of not paying your fair share of taxes? (LO3.1)
3. How might tax-exempt income and tax credits be used by government to stimulate economic growth? (LO3.2)
4. What tax information sources would you be most likely to use? Why? (LO3.2)
5. Use IRS publications and other reference materials to answer a specific tax question. Contact an IRS office to obtain an answer for the same question. What differences, if any, exist between the information sources? (LO3.3)
6. What tax situation would cause a person who previously used Form 1040A to be required to file Form 1040? (LO3.3)
7. What are some advantages of electronic filing? (LO3.3)
8. What are some tax advantages and disadvantages of owning your own business? (LO3.4)

Self-Test Problems

1. A person had $3,102 withheld for federal income taxes and had a tax liability of $3,345. Would this be a refund or an additional amount due, and for what amount?
2. Based on the following information, what is the amount of taxable income?
   Gross salary, $46,900   Interest earnings, $65
   Dividend income, $160   One personal exemption, $3,950
   Itemized deductions, $6,150

Solutions

1. To determine the amount of refund or additional tax due, compare the amount of tax liability with the amount withheld. The $3,345 tax liability minus the $3,102 would result in an amount due of $243.
2. Taxable income is calculated by adding salary, income, and dividends, and then subtracting itemized deductions and exemptions:

$$\$46,900 + \$65 + \$160 - \$3,950 - \$6,150 = \$37,025$$

1. Daniel Simmons arrived at the following tax information:

Gross salary, $54,250	Interest earnings, $75
Dividend income, $140	One personal exemption, $3,950
Itemized deductions, $7,000	Adjustments to income, $850

   What amount would Daniel report as taxable income? (LO3.2)

2. If Samantha Jones had the following itemized deductions, should she use Schedule A or the standard deduction? The standard deduction for her tax situation is $6,200. (LO3.2)

   Donations to church and other charities, $3,050

   Medical and dental expenses exceeding 10 percent of adjusted gross income, $450

   State income tax, $920

   Job-related expenses exceeding 2 percent of adjusted gross income, $1,450

3. What would be the average tax rate for a person who paid taxes of $6,435 on taxable income of $40,780? (LO3.2)

4. Based on the following data, would Beth and Roger Simmons receive a refund or owe additional taxes? (LO3.2)

Adjusted gross income, $42,140	Itemized deductions, $12,240
Credit for child and dependent	Federal income tax withheld, $6,686
care expenses, $400	Tax rate on taxable income, 10 percent
Amount for personal exemptions,	
$11,850	

5. If $4,323 was withheld during the year and taxes owed were $4,122, would the person owe an additional amount or receive a refund? What is the amount? (LO3.2)

6. Noor Patel has had a busy year! She decided to take a cross-country adventure. Along the way, she won a new car on "The Price Is Right" (valued at $14,000) and won $500 on a scratch-off lottery ticket (the first time she ever played). She also signed up for a credit card to start the trip and was given a sign-up bonus of $100. How much will she have to include in her federal taxable income? (LO3.2)

7. Using the tax table on page 81, determine the amount of taxes for the following situations: (LO3.3)

   a. A head of household with taxable income of $55,000.

   b. A single person with taxable income of $35,000.

   c. Married taxpayers filing jointly with taxable income of $72,000.

8. If 300,000 people each receive an average refund of $2,500, based on an interest rate of 3 percent, what would be the lost annual income from savings on those refunds? (LO3.2)

9. Using the tax table in Exhibit 3–5, determine the amount of taxes for the following situations: (LO3.3)

   a. A head of household with taxable income of $97,525.

   b. A single person with taxable income of $97,001.

   c. A married person filing a separate return with taxable income of $97,365.

10. Wendy Brooks prepares her own income tax return each year. A tax preparer would charge her $75 for this service. Over a period of 10 years, how much does Wendy gain from preparing her own tax return? Assume she can earn 3 percent on her savings. (LO3.3)

11. Betty Sims has $30,000 of adjusted gross income and $5,000 of medical expenses. She will be itemizing her tax deductions this year. The most recent tax year has a medical expenses floor of 10 percent. How much of a tax deduction will Betty be able to take? (LO3.3)

12. Each year, the Internal Revenue Service adjusts the value of an exemption based on inflation (and rounds to the nearest $50). If the exemption in a recent year was worth $3,950 and inflation was 1.2 percent, what would be the amount of the exemption for the upcoming tax year? (LO3.3)

13. Would you prefer a fully taxable investment earning 10 percent or a tax-exempt investment earning 8.25 percent? Why? (Assume a 25 percent tax rate.) (LO3.4)

14. On December 30, you decide to make a $2,000 charitable donation.   (LO3.4)

   a. If you are in the 28 percent tax bracket, how much will you save in taxes for the current year?

   b. If you deposit that tax savings in a savings account for the next five years at 8 percent, what will be the future value of that account?

15. Reginald Sims deposits $2,500 each year in a tax-deferred retirement account. If he is in a 28 percent tax bracket, by what amount would his tax be reduced over a 20-year time period?   (LO3.4)

16. If a person in a 33 percent tax bracket makes a deposit of $5,000 to a tax-deferred retirement account, what amount would be saved on current taxes?   (LO3.4)

 **To reinforce the content in this chapter, more problems are provided at connect.mheducation.com.**

Case in Point

A SINGLE FATHER'S TAX SITUATION

Ever since his wife's death, Eric Stanford has faced difficult personal and financial circumstances. His job provides him with a fairly good income but keeps him away from his daughters, ages 8 and 10, nearly 20 days a month. This requires him to use in-home child care services that consume a major portion of his income. Since the Stanfords live in a small apartment, this arrangement has been very inconvenient.

Due to the costs of caring for his children, Eric has only a minimal amount withheld from his salary for federal income taxes. Thus more money is available during the year, but for the last few years he has had to make a payment in April—another financial burden.

Although Eric has created an investment fund for his daughters' college education and for his retirement, he has not sought investments that offer tax benefits. Overall, he needs to look at several aspects of his tax planning activities to find strategies that will best serve his current and future financial needs.

Eric has assembled the following information for the current tax year:

Earnings from wages, $71,604

Interest earned on savings, $50

IRA deduction, $3,000

Checking account interest, $45

Three exemptions at $3,950 each

Current standard deduction for filing status, $9,100

Amount withheld for federal income tax, $4,825

Tax credit for child care, $1,200

Child tax credit, $1,000

Filing status: head of household

Questions

1. What are Eric's major financial concerns in his current situation?

2. In what ways might Eric improve his tax planning efforts?

3. Calculate the following:

   a. What is Eric's taxable income? (Refer to Exhibit 3–1)

   b. What is his total tax liability? (Use tax rate table, page 81) What is his average tax rate?

   c. Based on his withholding, will Eric receive a refund or owe additional tax? What is the amount?

Continuing Case

FINANCIAL SERVICES: SAVINGS PLANS AND ACCOUNTS

Jamie Lee Jackson, age 26, is in her last semester of college and is waiting for a graduation day that is just around the corner! It is the time of year again when Jamie Lee must file her annual federal income taxes. Last year, she received an increase in salary from the bakery, which brought her gross monthly earnings to $2,550, and she also opened up an IRA, to which she contributed $300. Her savings accounts earn 2 percent interest per year, and she also received an unexpected $1,000 gift from her great aunt. Jamie was also lucky enough last year to win a raffle prize of $2,000, most of which was deposited into her regular savings account after paying off her credit card balance.

Current Financial Situation

Assets:

Checking account, $2,250

Savings account, $6,900 (interest earned last year: $125)

Emergency fund savings account, $3,900 (interest earned last year: $75)

IRA balance, $350 ($300 contribution made last year)

Car, $3,000

Liabilities:

Student loan, $10,800

Credit card balance, $0 (interest paid last year: $55)

Income:

Gross monthly salary, $2,550

Monthly Expenses:

Rent obligation, $275

Utilities obligation, $135

Food, $130

Gas/Maintenance, $110

Credit card payment, $0

Savings:

Regular savings monthly deposit, $175

Rainy day savings monthly deposit, $25

Entertainment:

Cake decorating class, $40

Movies with friends, $60

Questions

1. Jamie Lee is trying to decide between Form 1040EZ and Form 1040A to file her federal income tax return. Using the "Personal Finance in Practice" information found on page 86, choose the most appropriate federal tax filing form for Jamie to use and describe your reasoning for making this choice.

2. What impact on Jamie Lee's income would the gift of $1,000 from her great aunt have on her adjusted gross income? Would there be an impact on the adjusted gross income with her $2,000 raffle prize winnings? Explain your answer.

3. Using Exhibit 3–1 as a guide, calculate Jamie Lee's adjusted gross income amount by completing the table below:

Gross income	
(−) Adjustments to income	
= Adjusted gross income	

4. What would Jamie Lee's filing status be considered?

5. Jamie Lee has a marginal tax rate of 15% and an average tax rate of 11%. Explain why there is a difference between the two rates.

"SALES TAX ON VARIOUS PURCHASES CAN REALLY INCREASE THE AMOUNT OF MY TOTAL SPENDING."

Spending Diary

Directions Continue your Daily Spending Diary to record and monitor your spending in various categories. Your comments should reflect what you have learned about your spending patterns and help you consider possible changes you might want to make in your spending habits. The Daily Spending Diary sheets are located in Appendix D at the end of the book and in Connect Finance.

Questions

1. What taxes do you usually pay that are reflected (directly or indirectly) in your daily spending diary?

2. How might your spending habits be revised to better control or reduce the amount you pay in taxes?

Name: _____   Date: _____

Federal Income Tax Estimate

Purpose: To estimate your current federal income tax liability.

Financial Planning Activities: Based on last year's tax return, estimates for the current year, and current tax regulations and rates, estimate your current tax liability. This sheet is also available in an Excel spreadsheet format in Connect Finance.

Suggested Websites: www.irs.gov   www.taxlogic.com   www.walletpop.com/taxes

Gross income (wages, salary, investment income, and other ordinary income	$	
Less Adjustments to income (see current tax regulations)	−$	
Equals Adjusted gross income	=$	
Less Standard deduction **or**	Itemized deduction	
	Medical expenses (exceeding 10% of AGI, or 7.5% for those over 65), until 2016.	$
	State/local income, property taxes	$
	Mortgage, home equity loan, interest	$
	Charitable contributions	$
	Casualty and theft losses	$
	Moving expenses, job-related and miscellaneous expenses (exceeding 2% of AGI)	$
Amount −$	**Total**	−$
Less Personal exemptions	−$	
Equals Taxable income	=$	
Estimated tax (based on current tax tables or tax schedules)	$	
Less Tax credits	−$	
Plus Other taxes	+$	
Equals Total tax liability	=$	
Less Estimated withholding and payments	−$	
Equals Tax due (or refund)	=$	

Suggested App:
• TaxCaster
• TaxSlayer

What's Next for Your Personal Financial Plan?

• Develop a system for filing and storing various tax records related to income, deductible expenses, and current tax forms.

• Using the IRS and other websites, identify recent changes in tax laws that may affect your financial planning decisions.

Name: _____   Date: _____

Tax Planning Activities

Purpose: To consider actions that can prevent tax penalties and may result in tax savings.

Financial Planning Activities: Consider which of the following actions are appropriate to your tax situation. This sheet is also available in an Excel spreadsheet format in Connect Finance.

Suggested Websites: www.turbotax.com   taxes.about.com

	Action to be taken (if applicable)	Completed
Filing status/withholding		
• Change filing status or exemptions due to changes in life situation		
• Change amount of withholding due to changes in tax situation		
• Plan to make estimated tax payments (due the 15th of April, June, September, and January)		
Tax records/documents		
• Organize home files for ease of maintaining and retrieving data		
• Send current mailing address and correct Social Security number to IRS, place of employment, and other income sources		
Annual tax activities		
• Be certain all needed data and current tax forms are available well before deadline		
• Research tax code changes and uncertain tax areas		
Tax-savings actions		
• Consider tax-exempt and tax-deferred investments		
• If you expect to have the same or a lower tax rate next year, accelerate deductions into the current year		
• If you expect to have the same or a lower tax rate next year, delay the receipt of income until next year		
• If you expect to have a higher tax rate next year, delay deductions since they will have a greater benefit		
• If you expect to have a higher tax rate next year, accelerate the receipt of income to have it taxed at the current lower rate		
• Start or increase use of tax-deferred retirement plans		
• Other		

What's Next for Your Personal Financial Plan?

- Identify saving and investing decisions that would minimize future income taxes.
- Develop a plan for actions to take related to your current and future tax situation.

Suggested App:
- IRS2Go
- iDonatedIt

4

Financial Services: Savings Plans and Payment Accounts

3 Steps to Financial Literacy . . . an Increased Savings Rate

1 Identify areas in your budget that might be reduced or eliminated to save money.
App: MoneyBook

2 Determine the amount that you save each month from the reduced budget amounts.
Website: www.bankrate.com

3 Deposit your increased savings amount in an account in a bank or credit union.
Website: www.creditunion.coop

An increased rate of savings will reduce current financial difficulties and improve long-term financial security. Higher savings amounts will minimize your use of credit while also setting aside for future expensive purchases, vacations, and retirement. At the end of the chapter, "Your Personal Finance Dashboard" will provide additional information on increasing your savings rate.

CHAPTER 4 LEARNING OBJECTIVES

In this chapter, you will learn to:

LO4.1 Identify commonly used financial services.

LO4.2 Compare the types of financial institutions.

LO4.3 Assess various types of savings plans.

LO4.4 Evaluate different types of payment methods.

YOUR PERSONAL FINANCIAL PLAN SHEETS

11. Planning the Use of Financial Services
12. Comparing Savings Plans
13. Using Savings Plans to Achieve Financial Goals
14. Comparing Payment Methods; Bank Reconciliation

Planning Your Use of Financial Services

Lending practices, foreclosures, higher fees, and tougher account requirements have created a different environment for financial services. Today, you will find more emphasis on consolidation of accounts and online electronic banking while you encounter lower savings rates and higher loan rates.

More than 20,000 banks, savings and loan associations, credit unions, and other financial institutions provide payment, savings, and credit services. Today, "banking" may mean a credit union, an ATM, or a phone app to transfer funds. While some financial decisions relate directly to goals, your daily activities require other financial services. Exhibit 4–1 is an overview of financial services and institutions for managing cash flows and moving toward financial goals.

Managing Daily Money Needs

Buying groceries, paying the rent, and completing other routine spending activities require a *cash management plan*. Cash, check, credit card, debit card, and online/mobile transfer are the common payment choices. Mistakes made frequently when managing current cash needs include (1) overspending as a result of impulse buying and overusing credit; (2) having insufficient liquid assets to pay current bills; (3) using savings or borrowing to pay for current expenses; and (4) failing to put unneeded funds in an interest-earning savings account or investment plan.

LO4.1

Identify commonly used financial services.

ACTION ITEM

I am least informed about:

☐ **online banking.**

☐ **certificates of deposit.**

☐ **prepaid debit cards.**

Exhibit **4–1**

Financial Institutions and Banking Services

DEPOSIT INSTITUTIONS

- Commercial bank
- Credit union
- Savings and loan association
- Mutual savings bank

NON-DEPOSIT INSTITUTIONS

- Life insurance company
- Investment company
- Brokerage firm
- Credit card company
- Finance company
- Mortgage company

TYPES OF FINANCIAL SERVICES

Cash Availability	**Payment Services**
• Check cashing • ATM/ debit cards • Traveler's checks • Foreign currency exchange	• Checking account • Online payments • Cashier's checks • Money orders
Savings Services	**Credit Services**
• Regular savings account • Money market account • Certificates of deposit • U.S. savings bonds	• Credit cards, cash advances • Auto loans, education loans • Mortgages • Home equity loans
Investment Services	**Other Services**
• Individual retirement accounts (IRAs) • Brokerage service • Investment advice • Mutual funds	• Insurance; trust service • Tax preparation • Safe deposit boxes • Budget counseling • Estate planning

OTHER FINANCIAL SERVICE PROVIDERS

- Pawnshop
- Check-cashing outlet
- Payday loan company
- Rent-to-own center
- Car title loan company

NON-BANK FINANCIAL SERVICE PROVIDERS

- Retailer stores (prepaid debit cards, other services)
- Online banking service provider (E*Trade Bank)
- Online payment services (PayPal)
- P2P (peer-to-peer) lending intermediaries

Sources of Quick Cash

No matter how carefully you manage your money, at some time you will need more cash than you have available. To cope in that situation, you have two basic choices: liquidate savings or borrow. A savings account, certificate of deposit, mutual fund, or other investment may be accessed when you need funds. Or a credit card cash advance or a personal loan may be appropriate. Remember, however, that both using savings and increasing borrowing reduce your net worth and your potential to achieve long-term financial security.

Types of Financial Services

Banks and other financial institutions offer services to meet a variety of needs. These services may be viewed in these main categories:

1. *Savings* provides safe storage of funds for future use. Commonly referred to as *time deposits,* money in savings accounts and certificates of deposit are examples of savings plans.
2. *Payment services* offer an ability to transfer money to others for daily business activities. Checking accounts and other payment methods are generally called *demand deposits.*
3. *Borrowing* is used by most people at some time during their lives. Credit alternatives range from short-term accounts, such as credit cards and cash loans, to long-term borrowing, such as a home mortgage.

4. *Other financial services* include insurance, investments, tax assistance, and financial planning. A **trust** is a legal agreement that provides for the management and control of assets by one party for the benefit of another. This type of arrangement is usually created through a commercial bank or a lawyer. Parents who want to set aside certain funds for their children's education may use a trust.

To simplify financial services, many financial businesses offer consolidated accounts. An **asset management account,** also called a *cash management account,* provides a complete financial services program for a single fee. Investment companies and others offer this type of account, with checking, an ATM card, a credit card, online banking, and a line of credit as well as access for buying stocks, bonds, mutual funds, and other investments.

> **trust** A legal agreement that provides for the management and control of assets by one party for the benefit of another.
>
> **asset management account** An all-in-one account that includes savings, checking, borrowing, investing, and other financial services for a single fee; also called a *cash management account.*

Online and Mobile Banking

Banking online and through wireless mobile systems continues to expand (see Exhibit 4–2). While most traditional financial institutions offer online banking services, web-only banks have also become strong competitors. For example, E*Trade Bank operates online while also providing customers with access to ATMs. These "e-banks" and "e-branches" provide nearly every needed financial service.

Financial service activities through your smartphone or tablet have three access methods: (1) text banking, providing account information and conducting transactions through text messages; (2) mobile web banking with online access to the financial institution's website; and (3) banking apps to conduct transactions using the mobile application of a bank or credit union.

Mobile and online banking provide the benefits of convenience and saving time along with instant information access. However, concerns of privacy, security of data, ease of overspending, costly fees, and online scams must also be considered.

More traditional electronic banking can occur through an **automatic teller machine (ATM),** also called a *cash machine,* which can facilitate various types of transactions. To minimize ATM fees, compare several financial institutions. Use your own bank's ATM to avoid surcharges, and withdraw larger amounts to avoid fees on several small transactions.

> **automatic teller machine (ATM)** A computer terminal used to conduct banking transactions; also called a *cash machine.*

Exhibit **4–2** Mobile Banking Services

PAYMENTS/TRANSFERS
- **Access cash at ATM**
- **Balance inquiry**
- **Online payments**
- **Move funds among various accounts**
- **Person-to-person payments (transfer funds to another person's account)**
- **Instant payments for bills you forgot to pay**
- **Tap or wave your phone to make a purchase**
- **Access online images of canceled checks**

DEPOSITS
- **Direct deposit of paycheck and government payment**
- **Online transfer from other account**
- **Take photo of check to deposit (remote deposit)**

OTHER SERVICES
- **Direct deposit, transfers to savings accounts**
- **Text alerts for balances, payments, deposits**
- **Apply and receive approval for loans**
- **Compare current interest rates for loans**
- **Check rates, apply for insurance**
- **Buy, sell, monitor investments**
- **Locate ATM and bank branches using GPS**
- **Access or shoot photo of store, online coupons**

debit card A plastic access card used in computerized banking transactions; also called a *cash card.*

The **debit card,** or *cash card,* that activates ATM transactions is also used for purchases. A debit card is in contrast to a *credit card,* since you are spending your own funds rather than borrowing additional money. A lost or stolen debit card can be expensive. If you notify the financial institution within two days of the lost card, your liability for unauthorized use is $50. However, you can be liable for up to $500 of unauthorized use if you wait up to 60 days to notify your bank. After 60 days, your liability can be the total amount in your account, and even more if your card is linked to other bank accounts.

However, some card issuers use the same rules for lost or stolen debit cards as for credit cards: a $50 maximum. Of course, you are not liable for unauthorized use, such as a con artist using your account number to make a purchase. Remember to report the fraud within 60 days of receiving your statement to protect your right not to be charged for the transaction.

Prepaid Debit Cards

Prepaid debit cards have become the fastest-growing payment method. For many consumers, these cards are being used instead of traditional banking services. Prepaid debit cards are issued by many financial service providers including traditional financial institutions, retailers (such as Walmart), and non-bank companies specifically created to provide this financial service.

"Loading" (adding funds to) prepaid debit cards may occur by cash, check, direct deposit, online transfer, smartphone check photo, or credit card cash advance. Common uses include in-store and online purchases as well as person-to-person payments. A savings account feature may also be connected to the card.

A major concern with prepaid debit cards has been the extensive number of fees that a user can encounter due to few current regulations for these financial products. Beware of fees that may include an activation fee, a monthly fee, a transaction fee, a cash-withdrawal (ATM) fee, a balance-inquiry fee, a fee to add funds, a dormancy fee, and others.

However, the expanded use of prepaid cards has resulted in lower consumer debt since the debit card can help control spending and buying on credit. With credit cards you "pay later," with debit cards you "pay now," and with prepaid cards you "pay before."

Some prepaid cards have celebrity endorsements, which does not mean a better deal for consumers. Comparisons of features and fees for prepaid debit cards are available at www.nerdwallet.com/prepaid.

Debit and credit cards will likely give way to expanded wireless transactions, including cardless ATM access and in-store purchases. A smartphone, cash code, and PIN will be required. App customers may authorize cash to a phone contact. Recipients are sent a code to withdraw the approved amount. A credit card "lock and limit" app to control spending and block unauthorized transactions will also be available.

Financial Services and Economic Conditions

Changing interest rates, rising consumer prices, and other economic factors influence financial services. For successful financial planning, be aware of the current trends and future prospects for interest rates (see Exhibit 4–3). You can learn about these trends and prospects by reading *The Wall Street Journal* (www.wsj.com), *The Financial Times* (www.ft.com), the business section of daily newspapers, and business periodicals such as *Bloomberg Businessweek* (www.businessweek.com), *Forbes* (www.forbes.com), and *Fortune* (www.fortune.com).

When interest rates are rising...

- Use long-term loans to take advantage of current low rates.
- Select short-term savings instruments to take advantage of higher rates when they mature.

- Use short-term loans to take advantage of lower rates when you refinance the loans.
- Select long-term savings instruments to "lock in" earnings at current high rates.

When interest rates are falling...

Exhibit 4–3

Changing Interest Rates and Financial Service Decisions

Sheet 11 Planning the Use of Financial Services

PRACTICE QUIZ 4–1

1. What are the major categories of financial services?

2. What financial services are available through electronic banking systems?

3. How do changing economic conditions affect the use of financial services?

Apply Yourself!

Talk with others about their experiences with online and mobile banking. What apps have been beneficial? What concerns have been encountered?

Sources of Financial Services

Many types of businesses, including insurance companies, investment brokers, and credit card companies, offer financial services that were once exclusive to banks. Companies such as Ford, Walmart, and AT&T issue credit cards. Banks have also expanded their activities to provide investments, insurance, and real estate services.

Comparing Financial Institutions

The basic questions to ask when selecting a financial service provider are simple:

- Where can I get the best return on my savings?
- How can I minimize the cost of checking and payments services?
- Will I be able to borrow money if I need it?

As you use financial services, decide what you want from the organization that will serve your needs (see Exhibit 4–4). With the financial marketplace constantly changing, plan to continually consider various factors before selecting an organization.

The services offered will likely be a major factor. In addition, personal service may be important to you. Convenience may take the form of branch office and ATM locations as well as online services. Remember, convenience and service have a cost; compare fees and other charges at several financial institutions.

LO4.2

Compare the types of financial institutions.

ACTION ITEM

My primary financial service activities involve:

☐ **a bank or credit union.**

☐ **online payment or app.**

☐ **a prepaid debit card.**

Exhibit **4–4**

Selecting a Financial Institution

STEP 1. List your most important features for a financial institution related to:
- **Services:** checking, savings accounts; deposit insurance; loans; investments; mobile app
- **Costs, fees, earnings:** checking minimum balance, ATM fees; credit rates; savings rates
- **Convenience:** branch locations, hours; ATM locations; customer service; rewards program
- **Online, mobile banking:** ease of operation; services; privacy, security; other fees

STEP 2. Rank the top three or four specific features based on their importance to you.

STEP 3. Prepare a list of local, national, and online financial institutions (include the address, phone, and website).

STEP 4. Conduct three types of research: (1) talk with people who have used various financial institutions; (2) conduct online research on the services, policies, and fees; and (3) visit, as appropriate, the financial institution to observe the environment and to talk with staff members.

Additional research actions may include:
- Determining the minimum balance to avoid monthly service charges.
- Obtaining a fee disclosure statement, savings rate sheet, and sample loan application.
- Assessing whether the deposit insurance and online banking services meet your needs.

STEP 5. Balance your needs with the information collected, and select where you will do business. You may use more than one financial institution to take advantage of the best services offered by each. This action gives you flexibility to move your money if the fees at one place increase. Talk with a manager if you believe a fee was charged unfairly; the bank may reverse the charge to keep you as a customer. "Switch kits" are available to make changing banks easier. These forms and authorization letters facilitate a smooth transition of direct deposits and automatic payments from one financial institution to another.

NOTE: "Your Personal Financial Plan" sheets 11, 12, and 14 at the end of the chapter can be used for this process. Also, a fee disclosure form is available at www.pewtrusts.org/safechecking.

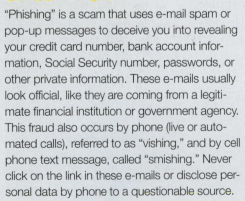

CAUTION!

"Phishing" is a scam that uses e-mail spam or pop-up messages to deceive you into revealing your credit card number, bank account information, Social Security number, passwords, or other private information. These e-mails usually look official, like they are coming from a legitimate financial institution or government agency. This fraud also occurs by phone (live or automated calls), referred to as "vishing," and by cell phone text message, called "smishing." Never click on the link in these e-mails or disclose personal data by phone to a questionable source.

commercial bank
A financial institution that offers a full range of financial services to individuals, businesses, and government agencies.

Finally, also consider safety and rates. Obtain information about earnings on savings and checking accounts and the rate you will pay for borrowed funds. Most financial institutions have deposit insurance to protect customers against losses; however, not all of them are insured by federal government programs.

Types of Financial Institutions

Despite changes in the banking environment, many familiar financial institutions still serve your needs. As previously shown in Exhibit 4–1, some organizations (such as banks and credit unions) offer a wide range of services, while others provide specialized assistance, such as home loans. Distinctions among the various types of financial institutions are disappearing. For example, today people can buy investments through their bank and credit union as well as from an investment company or brokerage firm.

Deposit institutions serve as intermediaries between suppliers (savers) and users (borrowers) of funds. The most common of these traditional organizations are:

- **Commercial banks,** which offer a full range of financial services, including checking, savings, lending, and most other services. Commercial banks, organized as corporations with investors (stockholders) contributing the needed capital to operate, have several types: national banks, regional banks, community banks, and online-only banks.

- **Savings and loan associations (S&Ls),** which traditionally specialized in savings accounts and mortgages. Today, many of these organizations have expanded to offer financial services comparable to those of a bank.
- **Mutual savings banks,** which are owned by depositors, also specialize in savings accounts and mortgages. Located mainly in the northeastern United States, the profits of a mutual savings bank go to the depositors through higher rates on savings.
- **Credit unions,** which are user-owned, nonprofit, cooperative organizations. Although members traditionally had a common bond such as work location, church, or community affiliation, credit union membership today is more flexible, with more than 80 million people belonging to one. Annual banking studies consistently report lower fees and lower loan rates with higher satisfaction levels for credit unions compared to other financial institutions.

Non-deposit institutions offer various financial services. These institutions include:

- Life insurance companies, which provide financial security for dependents with various life insurance policies, some containing savings and investment features. Expanded activities of life insurance companies include investment and retirement planning services.
- Investment companies, also called *mutual funds,* which offer a **money market fund**—a combination savings–investment plan. The company uses the money from many investors to purchase a variety of short-term financial instruments. However, unlike accounts at most deposit institutions, investment company accounts are not covered by federal deposit insurance.
- Brokerage firms, which employ investment advisors and financial planners, serve as an agent between the buyer and seller for stocks, bonds, and other investment securities. These companies obtain their earnings from commissions and fees. Expanded financial services are available from brokerage organizations, including checking accounts and online banking.
- Credit card companies, which specialize in funding short-term retail lending. However, these networks, including VISA, MasterCard, and Discover, have also expanded into various other banking and investing services.
- Finance companies, which provide loans to consumers and small businesses. These loans have short and intermediate terms with higher rates than most other lenders charge. Most finance companies also offer other financial planning services.
- Mortgage companies, which are organized primarily to provide loans for home purchases. The services of mortgage companies are presented in Chapter 7.

savings and loan association (S&L)
A financial institution that traditionally specialized in savings accounts and mortgage loans.

mutual savings bank
A financial institution that is owned by depositors and specializes in savings accounts and mortgage loans.

credit union A user-owned, nonprofit, cooperative financial institution that is organized for the benefit of its members.

money market fund A savings–investment plan offered by investment companies, with earnings based on investments in various short-term financial instruments.

did you know?

Bank customers may now access ATMs without a debit card. Using a smartphone, both a *cash code* and the PIN will be required for cash. App customers may authorize another person from phone contacts to obtain money. The recipient will be sent a cash code to allow withdrawal of an approved amount. Banks also offer a credit card "lock and limit" app to control security and spending. This feature is used to block overseas transactions where the card isn't present.

These and other types of financial institutions compete for your business. More and more of these companies are offering a combination of services (savings, checking, credit, insurance, investments) from one source. These one-stop financial service operations are sometimes referred to as *financial supermarkets.*

Problematic Financial Businesses

Would you pay $8 to cash a $100 check? Or pay $20 to borrow $100 for two weeks? Many people who do not have bank accounts (especially low-income consumers) make use of financial service companies that charge very high fees and excessive interest rates.

An estimated 17 million people in the United States are "unbanked," using a variety of "shadow" financial services rather than having a bank account. Another 20 percent of the population are "underbanked" and make use of many of these services in addition to having a bank account.

PAWNSHOPS Loans through pawnshops are based on the value of tangible possessions such as jewelry or other valuable items. Many low- and moderate-income families use these organizations to obtain cash loans quickly. Pawnshops charge higher fees than other financial institutions. Thousands of consumers are increasingly in need of small loans—usually $50 to $75, to be repaid in 30 to 45 days. Pawnshops have become the "neighborhood bankers" and the "local shopping malls," since they provide both lending and retail shopping services, selling items that owners do not redeem. While states regulate pawnshops, the interest rates charged can range from 3 percent a month to over 100 percent annually.

CHECK-CASHING OUTLETS Most financial institutions will not cash a check unless you have an account. The more than 6,000 check-cashing outlets (CCOs) charge anywhere from 1 to 20 percent of the face value of a check; the average cost is 2 to 3 percent. However, for a low-income family, that can be a significant portion of the total household budget. CCOs, sometimes called *currency exchanges,* also offer services, including electronic tax filing, money orders, private postal boxes, utility bill payment, and the sale of transit tokens. A person can usually obtain most of these services for less at other locations.

PAYDAY LOAN COMPANIES Many consumer organizations caution against using payday loans, also referred to as *cash advances, check advance loans, postdated check loans,* and *delayed deposit loans.* Desperate borrowers pay annual interest rates of as much as 780 percent and more to obtain needed cash from payday loan companies. The most frequent users of payday loans are workers who have become trapped by debts or poor financial decisions.

In a typical payday loan, a consumer writes a personal check for $115 to borrow $100 for 14 days. The payday lender agrees to hold the check until the next payday. This $15 finance charge for the 14 days translates into an annual percentage rate of 391 percent. Some consumers "roll over" their loans, paying another $15 for the $100 loan for the next 14 days. After a few rollovers, the finance charge can exceed the amount borrowed. To prevent this exploitation, some employers are offering pay advances through payroll provider services. The loans have rates in the 9 to 18 percent range.

RENT-TO-OWN CENTERS Rental businesses offer big-screen televisions, computers, seven-piece bedroom sets, and kitchen appliances. The rent-to-own (RTO) industry is defined as stores that lease products to consumers who can own the item if they complete a certain number of monthly or weekly payments. A $600 computer can result in $1,900 of payments. Many RTO purchases can result in annual interest rates of over 300 percent.

CAR TITLE LOAN COMPANIES When in need of money, people with poor credit ratings might obtain a cash advance using their automobile title as security for a high-interest loan. These loans, usually due in 30 days, typically have a cost similar to payday loans, often exceeding 200 percent. While the process is simple, the consequences can be devastating with the repossession of your car.

All of these expensive, high-risk financial service providers should be avoided. Instead, make an effort to properly manage your money and use the services of a reputable financial institution, such as a credit union.

PRACTICE QUIZ 4-2

1. What factors do consumers usually consider when selecting a financial institution to meet their saving and checking needs?

2. What are examples of deposit-type financial institutions?

3. Match the following descriptions with the appropriate financial institution:

   a. commercial bank   _____ Commonly used by people without a bank account.
   b. credit union   _____ Investment services accompany main business focus.
   c. life insurance company   _____ Traditionally provides widest range of financial services.
   d. check-cashing outlet   _____ Offers lower fees for members.

Apply Yourself!

Using the website for the Credit Union National Association (www.cuna.org) or other sources, obtain information about joining a credit union and the services offered by this type of financial institution.

Comparing Savings Plans

A savings plan is vital to attain financial goals. A range of savings alternatives exist (Exhibit 4–5). The many types of savings plans can be grouped into the following main categories.

Regular Savings Accounts

Regular savings accounts, previously called *passbook* or *statement accounts*, usually involve a low or no minimum balance and allow you to withdraw money as needed. Banks, savings and loan associations, and other financial institutions offer regular savings accounts. At a credit union, these savings plans are called *share accounts*.

Certificates of Deposit

Higher earnings are available to savers when they leave money on deposit for a set time period. A **certificate of deposit (CD)** is a savings plan requiring that a certain amount be left on deposit for a stated time period (ranging from 30 days to five or more years) to earn a specific rate of return.

These time deposits can be an attractive and safe savings alternative. However, most financial institutions impose a penalty for early withdrawal of CD funds. For CDs of one year or less, the penalty is usually three months of interest. CDs of more than a year will likely have a fine of six months' interest, while a five-year CD can result in a penalty as high as 20 to 25 percent of the total interest to maturity on the account.

TYPES OF CDS   While traditional certificates of deposit continue to be the most popular, financial institutions offer other types of CDs:

- *Rising-rate* or *bump-up CDs* may have higher rates at various intervals, such as every six months. However, beware of ads that highlight a higher rate in the future. This rate may be in effect only for the last few months of an 18- or 24-month CD.

LO4.3

Assess various types of savings plans.

ACTION ITEM

When selecting a savings plan, most important to me is:

☐ **bank location.**

☐ **federal deposit insurance.**

☐ **rate of return.**

certificate of deposit (CD) A savings plan requiring that a certain amount be left on deposit for a stated time period to earn a specified interest rate.

Start Saving Now

Get in the habit early, even if it's only a small amount with each paycheck.

I f you don't pay your rent or cell-phone bill, the consequences are immediate. If you fail to stash money in savings as soon as you start earning a paycheck, you probably won't notice the damage right away. But the long-term fallout can be devastating if it limits your choices—whether that's buying the house you want, sending your kids to a top college, or deciding when (or even if) you can retire.

Say you're 25 years old and you put $500 into a mutual fund that earns 8% a year, and you add $100 each month. You'll wind up with more than $335,000 by the time you're 65, excluding taxes. If you wait until you're 35, invest $2,500 and then add that $100 a month, all else being equal you'll have only about $167,000 by age 65.

Pay yourself first. If you skim savings off the top of each paycheck, the cash will disappear before you have a chance to miss it. With a 401(k) retirement plan at work, for example, your employer pulls the amount you designate from each paycheck. For other savings, you can schedule automatic transfers from your checking account. You may want to set up multiple savings accounts if that helps you track progress toward each goal more easily.

Saving for retirement is usually priority number one, but you should also create an emergency fund that holds enough cash to cover at least six months' worth of living expenses. Then, assuming you have a plan to pay off any debts, you can move on to saving for your other goals.

Choose a bank. Any savings that you may need to access in a pinch (and that includes your emergency fund) should reside in a bank, where your money is insured. Savings accounts and money market deposit accounts, which often pay more than regular savings accounts, are generally easy to access. At www.depositaccounts.com, look for accounts available in your area that pay top interest rates. Watch out for minimum-balance requirements and monthly maintenance or transfer charges.

You don't have to have a checking account and savings account in the same place. Banks are increasingly offering convenient features such as mobile check deposit, which allows you to submit a check by snapping a picture of it with your smart phone. Online banks, such as Ally Bank and Evantage Bank, let you perform many of the same transactions as a traditional bank.

Wherever you put your money, watch for fees. If you regularly get cash from other banks' ATMs, you could pay hundreds of dollars a year in extra charges.

Some banks will reimburse you for fees that other banks

GET THESE APPS!
SAVEDPLUS
(Android, Apple) automatically shifts money from your checking account into a savings account every time you make a purchase. You choose the percentage of the purchase amount.
MASTERCARD NEARBY
(Android, Apple, Windows) lets you search for nearby ATMs based on your current location, and it can filter for features such as 24-hour availability and fees.

charge you for using their ATMs; the State Farm Bank Free Checking Account, for one, will refund all ATM charges if you have direct deposit. Other institutions are members of large, surcharge-free ATM networks, such as the Allpoint network. Most banks waive monthly maintenance fees on checking accounts if you have a monthly direct deposit or maintain a minimum balance.

Lisa Gerstner

SOURCE: Reprinted by permission from *Kiplinger's Personal Finance.* Copyright © 2014. The Kiplinger Washington Editors, Inc.

1. What are current and long-term consequences of not saving?

2. Describe actions that you might consider to improve your savings attitude and habits.

3. Based on the information in this article, and your experiences, what suggestions would you offer for selecting a bank?

Exhibit **4–5** Savings Alternatives

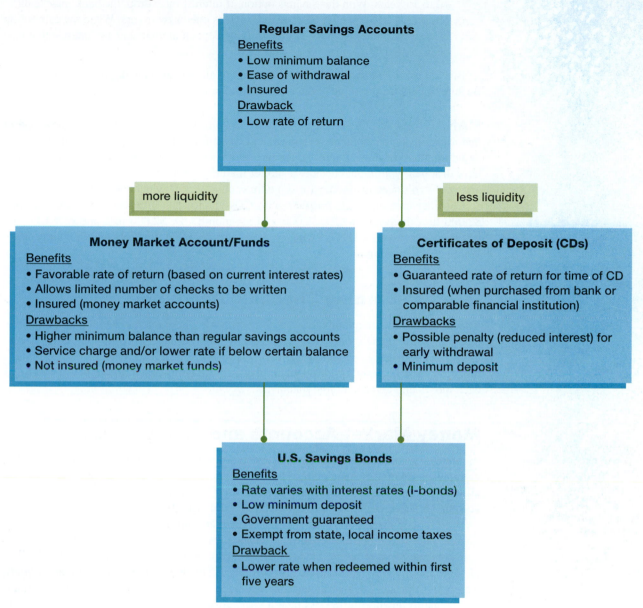

- *Liquid CDs* offer an opportunity to withdraw money without a penalty. However, you will likely be required to maintain a minimum balance in the account. This type of CD may have other restrictions such as a "waiting period" before any funds can be withdrawn or a limit on the number of withdrawals allowed.

- *A zero-coupon CD* is purchased at a deep discount (a small portion of the face value) with no interest payments. Your initial small deposit ($5,000, for example) grows to the maturity value of the CD ($10,000) in 10 years, which is approximately a 6 percent annual return.

- *Indexed CDs* have earnings based on the stock market. In times of strong stock performance, your earnings can be higher than those on other CDs. At other times, however, you may earn no interest and may even lose part of your savings. A CD based on the consumer price index can result in higher returns as inflation increases.

- *Callable CDs* start with higher rates and usually have long maturities, as high as 10 to 15 years. With this savings option, if interest rates drop, the bank may "call" (close) the account after a set period, such as one or two years. When the call option is exercised, the saver receives the original deposit amount and any interest that has been earned.

Beware of *promotional CDs,* which attempt to attract savers with gifts or special rates. Be sure to balance the value of the item against the lost interest.

MANAGING CDS When first buying or *rolling over* a CD (buying a new one at maturity), investigate potential earnings and costs. Do not allow your financial institution to automatically roll over your money into another CD for the same term. If interest rates have dropped, you might consider a shorter maturity. Or if you believe rates are at a peak and you won't need the money for some time, obtain a CD with a longer term.

Consider creating a CD *portfolio* with CDs maturing at different times, for example, $2,000 in a three-month CD, $2,000 in a six-month CD, $2,000 in a one-year CD, and $2,000 in a two-year CD. This will give you some degree of liquidity and flexibility when you reinvest your funds.

Interest-Earning Checking Accounts

Checking accounts frequently have a savings feature. These interest-earning accounts usually pay a low interest rate. However, recently, many financial institutions have offered high-rate checking accounts to customers who meet certain requirements. For example, a higher interest rate might be available if you use your debit card a certain number of times each month and agree to online statements.

Money Market Accounts and Funds

money market account
A savings account offered by banks, savings and loan associations, and credit unions that requires a minimum balance and has earnings based on market interest rates.

A **money market account** is a savings account that requires a minimum balance and has earnings based on the changing market level of interest rates. Money market accounts may allow a limited number of checks to be written and generally impose a fee when the account balance goes below the required minimum, usually $1,000.

Both money market accounts and money market funds offer earnings based on current interest rates, and both have minimum-balance restrictions and allow check writing. The major difference is in safety. Money market *accounts* at banks and savings and loan associations are covered by federal deposit insurance. This is not true of money market *funds,* which are a product of investment and insurance companies. Since money market funds invest mainly in short-term (less than a year) government and corporate securities, however, they are usually quite safe.

U.S. Savings Bonds

U.S. savings bonds are a low-risk savings program guaranteed by the federal government that have been used to achieve various financial goals. The Treasury Department offers several programs for buying savings bonds.

EE BONDS Series EE bonds may be purchased for any amount greater than $25. Electronic EE bonds are purchased online at face value; for example, you pay $50 for a $50 bond. These bonds may be obtained or purchased for any amount you desire, such as $143.58, giving savers more flexibility.

Paper savings bonds, while no longer issued at financial institutions, are still available through payroll savings plans or by using part or all of your federal tax refund. Paper EE bonds are sold at half the face value, and may be purchased for set values ranging from

$25 to $5,000, with maturity values of $50 to $10,000. Paper savings bonds continue to be redeemed at financial institutions. If a savings bond has been lost or stolen, it can be reissued in either a paper or an electronic format. To locate savings bonds issued since 1974, go to www.treasuryhunt.gov.

EE bonds increase in value as interest accrues monthly and compounds semiannually. If you redeem the bonds before five years, you forfeit the latest three months of interest; after five years, you are not penalized. A bond must be held for one year before it can be cashed. Series EE bonds continue to earn interest for 30 years. The main tax advantages of series EE bonds are (1) the interest earned is exempt from state and local taxes and (2) federal income tax on earnings is not due until the bonds are redeemed.

Redeemed series EE bonds may be exempt from federal income tax if the funds are used to pay tuition and fees at a college, university, or qualified technical school for yourself or a dependent. The bonds must be purchased by an individual who is at least 24 years old, and they must be issued in the names of one or both parents. This provision is designed to assist low- and middle-income households; people whose incomes exceed a certain amount do not qualify for this tax exemption.

did you know?

Most of the world's population lacks access to basic financial services. Many organizations serve these people with microloans, micro-savings accounts, and micro-insurance programs. The Grameen Bank (www.grameen-info.org) makes loans to the poorest of the poor in Bangladesh, without collateral. Opportunity International (www.opportunity.org) serves more than 2.5 million people in 20 countries with loans, savings, insurance, and business training. These efforts fight poverty and enhance community development.

HH BONDS Series HH bonds, which are no longer sold, were *current-income* bonds with interest deposited electronically to your bank account every six months. This interest was taxed as current income on a person's federal tax return, but it was exempt from state and local taxes.

I BONDS The I bond has an interest rate based on two components: (1) a fixed rate for the life of the bond and (2) an inflation rate that changes twice a year. Every six months a new, fixed base rate is set for new bonds. The additional interest payment is recalculated twice a year, based on the current annual inflation rate. I bonds are sold in any amount over $25 and are purchased at face value. As with EE bonds, the minimum holding period is one year. Interest earned on I bonds is added to the value of the bond and received when you redeem your bond. I bonds have the same tax and education benefits as EE bonds.

A person may purchase up to $10,000 worth of electronic savings bonds of each series (EE and I bonds) a year, for a total of $20,000. This amount applies to any person, so parents may buy an additional $25,000 in each child's name. Savings bonds are commonly registered one of three ways: (1) single owner, (2) two owners, either as co-owners or with one as primary owner, or (3) a beneficiary, who takes ownership of the bond when the original owner dies.

A TreasuryDirect account at www.treasurydirect.gov provides the benefits of:

- Twenty-four-hour access to buy, manage, and redeem series EE and I electronic savings bonds.
- Converting series EE and I paper savings bonds to electronic bonds through the SmartExchange feature.
- Purchasing electronic savings bonds as a gift.
- Enrolling in a payroll savings plan for purchasing electronic bonds.
- Investing in other Treasury securities such as bills, notes, bonds, and TIPS (Treasury Inflation-Protected Securities).
- Eliminating the risk that your savings bonds will be lost, stolen, or damaged.

Additional information and current value calculations may be obtained at www.savingsbonds.gov.

Evaluating Savings Plans

Selection of a savings plan is usually influenced by the rate of return, inflation, tax considerations, liquidity, safety, restrictions, and fees (see Exhibit 4–6).

rate of return The percentage of increase in the value of savings as a result of interest earned; also called *yield.*

RATE OF RETURN Earnings on savings can be measured by the **rate of return,** or *yield,* the percentage of increase in the value of your savings from earned interest. For example, a $100 savings account that earned $5 after a year would have a rate of return, or yield, of 5 percent. This rate of return was determined by dividing the interest earned ($5) by the amount in the savings account ($100). The yield on your savings usually will be greater than the stated interest rate.

compounding A process that calculates interest based on previously earned interest.

Compounding refers to interest that is earned on previously earned interest. Each time interest is added to your savings, the next interest amount is computed on the new balance in the account. The more frequent the compounding, the higher your rate of return will be. For example, $100 in a savings account that earns 6 percent compounded annually will increase $6 after a year. But the same $100 in a 6 percent account compounded daily will earn $6.19 for the year. Although this difference may seem slight, large amounts held in savings for long periods of time will result in far higher differences (see Exhibit 4–7).

The *Truth in Savings Act* requires financial institutions to disclose the following information on savings account plans: (1) fees on deposit accounts; (2) the interest rate; (3) the annual percentage yield (APY); and (4) other terms and conditions of the savings plan. Truth in Savings (TIS) defines **annual percentage yield (APY)** as the percentage rate expressing the total amount of interest that would be received on a $100 deposit based on the annual rate and frequency of compounding for a 365-day period. APY reflects the amount of interest a saver should expect to earn.

annual percentage yield (APY) The percentage rate expressing the total amount of interest that would be received on a $100 deposit based on the annual rate and frequency of compounding for a 365-day period.

INFLATION The rate of return you earn on your savings should be compared with the inflation rate. When inflation was over 10 percent, people with money in savings accounts earning 5 or 6 percent were experiencing a loss in the buying power of that money. In general, as the inflation rate increases, the interest rates offered to savers also increase.

Exhibit 4–6

Selecting a Savings Plan

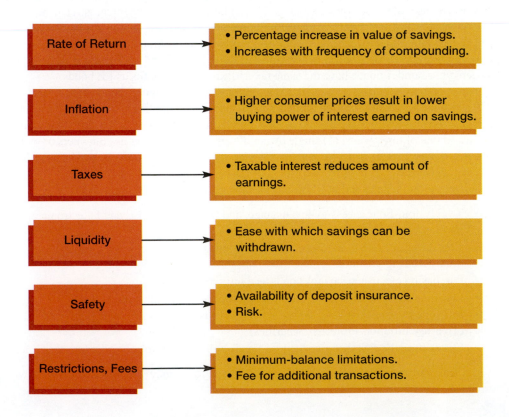

Rate of Return	• Percentage increase in value of savings. • Increases with frequency of compounding.
Inflation	• Higher consumer prices result in lower buying power of interest earned on savings.
Taxes	• Taxable interest reduces amount of earnings.
Liquidity	• Ease with which savings can be withdrawn.
Safety	• Availability of deposit insurance. • Risk.
Restrictions, Fees	• Minimum-balance limitations. • Fee for additional transactions.

EXAMPLE: Annual Percentage Yield

When the number of days in the term is 365 (that is, where the stated maturity is 365 days) or where the account does not have a stated maturity, the APY formula is simply

$$APY = 100 \left(\frac{Interest}{Principal} \right)$$

$$= 100 \left(\frac{66}{1,200} \right)$$

$$= 100 \ (0.055) = 5.5\%$$

TAXES Like inflation, taxes reduce interest earned on savings. For example, a 10 percent return for a saver in a 28 percent tax bracket means a real return of 7.2 percent (the "Figure It Out!" box shows how to compute the after-tax savings rate of return). As discussed in Chapter 3, several tax-exempt and tax-deferred savings plans and investments can increase your real rate of return.

LIQUIDITY *Liquidity* allows you to withdraw your money on short notice without a loss of value or fees. Some savings plans impose penalties for early withdrawal or have other restrictions. With certain types of savings certificates and accounts, early withdrawal may be penalized by a loss of interest or a lower earnings rate. Consider the degree of liquidity you desire in relation to your savings goals. To achieve long-term financial goals, many people trade off liquidity for a higher return.

SAFETY Most savings plans at banks, savings and loan associations, and credit unions are insured by agencies affiliated with the federal government. Federal Deposit Insurance Corporation (FDIC) coverage prevents a loss of money due to the failure of the insured

did you know?

To earn more interest on your savings: (1) compare local and online banks and credit unions; (2) combine several savings accounts into a larger amount that might quality for a higher rate; (3) search for special rates on checking accounts or specialty CDs. Helpful websites include bankrate.com, depositaccounts.com, and checkingfinder.com.

Exhibit 4–7

Compounding Frequency Affects the Savings Yield

Shorter compounding periods result in higher yields. This chart shows the growth of $10,000, earning a rate of 4 percent, but with different compounding methods.

End of year	COMPOUNDING METHOD			
	Daily	Monthly	Quarterly	Annually
1	$10,408	$10,407	$10,405	$10,400
2	10,832	10,831	10,827	10,816
3	11,275	11,272	11,267	11,249
4	11,735	11,731	11,724	11,699
5	12,214	12,208	12,198	12,165
10	14,918	14,904	14,883	14,800
15	18,221	18,196	18,160	18,004
20	22,254	22,215	22,154	21,902
Annual yield	4.08%	4.07%	4.05%	4.00%

Figure It Out!

After-Tax Savings Rate of Return

The taxability of interest on your savings reduces your real rate of return. In other words, you lose some portion of your interest to taxes. This calculation consists of the following steps:

1. Determine your top tax bracket for federal income taxes.

2. Subtract this rate, expressed as a decimal, from 1.0.

3. Multiply the result by the yield on your savings account.

4. This number, expressed as a percentage, is your after-tax rate of return.

For example,

1. You are in the 28 percent tax bracket.

2. $1.0 - 0.28 = 0.72$.

3. If the yield on your savings account is 6.25 percent, $0.0625 \times 0.72 = 0.045$.

4. Your after-tax rate of return is 4.5 percent.

You may use the same procedure to determine the *real rate of return* on your savings based on inflation. For example, if you are earning 6 percent on savings and inflation is 5 percent, your real rate of return (after inflation) is 5.7 percent: $0.06 \times (1 - 0.05) = 0.057$.

CALCULATION EXAMPLES:

1. What would be the after-tax return for a person who is receiving 4 percent on savings and is in a 15 percent tax bracket? _____ %

2. What would be the after-tax value of $100 earned in interest for a person who is in a 31 percent tax bracket? $ _____

institution. Credit unions may obtain deposit insurance through the National Credit Union Association (NCUA). Some state-chartered credit unions have opted for a private insurance program. While some financial institutions have failed in recent years, savers with deposits covered by federal insurance have not lost any money. Depositors have either been paid, or have had the accounts taken over by a financially stable institution.

The FDIC insures amounts of up to $250,000 per depositor per insured financial institution. Coverage amounts that exceed the limit are possible by using different ownership categories, such as individual, joint, and trust ownership accounts. For example, a joint account, held by two people, would be covered up to $500,000, with each account owner having $250,000 of coverage. Remember, however, that different branch offices count as the same institution, and mergers in the financial service industry may bring accounts from different banks together.

The FDIC and NCUA also provide deposit insurance for certain retirement accounts, up to $250,000, including traditional IRAs, Roth IRAs, Simplified Employee Pension (SEP) IRAs, and Savings Incentive Match Plans for Employees (SIMPLE) IRAs as well as self-directed Keogh accounts and various plans for state government employees. Of course, this coverage applies only to retirement accounts in financial institutions insured by the FDIC and NCUA. While some observers had expected the standard insurance amount to return to the previous level of $100,000 per depositor for all account categories except IRAs and other retirement accounts, Congressional action has kept the depositor coverage for every type of account at $250,000.

To determine if all of your deposits are insured, use the Electronic Deposit Insurance Estimator (EDIE) at www.fdic.gov/edie/index.html. This feature includes a step-by-step tutorial with depositor situations for different types of account and different ownership. Information about credit union deposit coverage is available at www.ncua.gov. Since not all financial institutions have federal deposit insurance, investigate this matter when you are selecting a savings plan. Additional information on the regulation and consumer protection aspects of financial institutions is included in Appendix C.

> ## EXAMPLE: Deposit Insurance
>
> If you have a $562,000 joint account with a relative in an FDIC-insured financial institution, $31,000 of your savings will not be covered by federal deposit insurance. One-half of the $562,000 exceeds the $250,000 limit by $31,000.

RESTRICTIONS AND FEES Other limitations can affect your choice of a savings program. For example, there may be a delay between the time interest is earned and the time it is added to your account. This means the interest will not be available for your immediate use. Also, some institutions charge a transaction fee for each deposit or withdrawal. In the past, financial institutions offered a "free gift" when a certain savings amount was deposited. To receive this gift, you had to leave your money on deposit for a certain time period, or you may have received less interest, since some of the earnings covered the cost of the "free" items.

Sheet 12 Comparing Savings Plans
Sheet 13 Using Savings Plans to Achieve Financial Goals

PRACTICE QUIZ 4–3

1. What are the main types of savings plans offered by financial institutions?

2. How does a money market *account* differ from a money market *fund*?

3. How do inflation and taxes affect earnings on savings?

4. In the following financial situations, check the box that is the major influence for the person when selecting a savings plan:

Financial planning situation	Rate of return	Inflation	Taxes	Liquidity	Safety
a. An older couple needs easy access to funds for living expenses.					
b. A person is concerned with loss of buying power of funds on deposit.					
c. A saver desires to maximize earnings from the savings plan.					
d. A middle-aged person wants assurance that the funds are safe.					

Apply Yourself!

Conduct online research to obtain past and current data on various interest rates (such as prime rate, T-bill rate, mortgage rate, corporate bond rate, and six-month CD rate). Information may be obtained at www.federalreserve.gov and other websites. How do these rates affect various personal financial decisions?

LO4.4

Evaluate different types of payment methods.

ACTION ITEM

My payment account balance is:

☐ **updated regularly.**

☐ **based on a rough estimate.**

☐ **only known by my financial institution.**

Comparing Payment Methods

Each year, paper checks account for a smaller and smaller portion of payments in our society. While check writing is being used less, checking accounts are still the common source for most debit card transactions and online payments. As shown in Exhibit 4–8, payment alternatives may be viewed in three main categories.

Electronic Payments

Transactions not involving cash, checks, or credit cards have expanded with technology, improved security, and increased consumer acceptance.

DEBIT CARD TRANSACTIONS   Nearly every store and online retailer processes debit card transactions, with the amount of the purchase deducted from your checking or other bank account. Most debit cards can be used two ways: (1) with your signature, like a credit card, and (2) with your personal identification number (PIN), like an ATM card. When the debit card is processed like a credit card, you have more security in case of a fraudulent transaction or a purchase dispute. But when using a debit card to check into a hotel, buy gas, or rent a car, a merchant may *freeze* an amount in your bank account above what you actually spend. This hold on your funds could result in an overdrawn account.

Use a credit card to . . .

. . . delay the payment for a purchase.

. . . build a credit history with wise buying.

. . . buy online or for major purchases.

. . . earn more generous rewards points for spending.

Use a debit card to . . .

. . . limit your spending to available money.

. . . avoid bills that will be paid in the future.

. . . avoid interest payment or an annual fee.

. . . obtain better protection if you process a transaction as a credit card.

CAUTION!

Banks and other financial institutions are increasing fees to cover lost revenue due to lower interest rates and bad loans. These charges include higher ATM fees, credit card annual fees and late payment fees, overdraft and stop-payment fees, charges for paper statements and to talk with a teller, and even a charge for closing your account within a certain time period. Compare charges before opening an account and consider changing financial institutions to get a better deal.

ONLINE PAYMENTS   Banks and online companies serve as third parties to facilitate online bill payments. These organizations include www.paypal.com, www.mycheckfree.com, www.paytrust.com, and Google Wallet (previously Google Checkout). Some online payment services give you a choice of using a credit card or a bank account, while others require one or the other. Linking a transaction to your checking account, rather than to a credit card, may not give you as much leverage when disputing a transaction.

People without a credit or debit card can use PayNearMe for online buying and other transactions. This service allows buyers to make a purchase and then pay cash at a local store. The consumer receives a receipt and the seller is notified of the payment. This cash transaction network may be used for online purchases, telephone orders, loan repayments, money transfers, and other transactions that might require a credit card. PayNearMe has partnerships with several major online and storefront retailers.

Exhibit 4–8

Payment Alternatives

Payments	Checking Accounts	Other Payment Methods
Debit (cash) and credit cards	Regular checking account	Certified check
Online, mobile payments	Activity checking account	Cashier's check
Stored-value (prepaid) cards	Interest-earning account	Money order
Smart cards ("digital wallet")		Traveler's checks
Peer-to-peer (P2P) payments		

Another payment alternative with no disclosure of credit card information is eBillme, which requires only an e-mail address to establish an account for making purchases. Then, you make your payment to eBillme through online banking or at a local walk-in site. When using these services, be sure to consider all fees, online security, and customer service availability.

MOBILE TRANSFERS Apps for mobile payment systems through smartphones, tablets, and other wireless devices are expanding. The *near-field communications* (NFC) technology stores credit card and bank account information. These wireless devices replace debit and credit cards for processing financial and purchasing transactions. A tap or wave of your phone at the point-of-sale terminal sensor completes the purchase. While these mobile transactions usually occur through a bank account, in the future these payments may bypass banks with charges directly on your phone bill.

Mobile banking is increasing the availability of "person-to-person" payments with the transfer of funds by e-mail or to a mobile phone number. The opportunity to send and receive money through links to bank accounts and cards may also occur with online payment services.

STORED-VALUE CARDS Prepaid cards for telephone service, transit fares, highway tolls, laundry service, and school lunches are common. While some of these stored-value cards are disposable, others can be reloaded with an additional amount. Also called *prepaid debit cards,* some stored-value cards may have activation charges, ATM fees, and other transaction costs. Recipients of government benefits may receive Social Security and other payments on a prepaid debit card, which is practical for people without a bank account.

SMART CARDS These "digital wallets" are similar to other ATM cards with an imbedded microchip. In addition to banking activities, the card may also store past purchases, insurance information, and your medical history. Recent developments in smart cards include an option that allows you to pay with reward points.

PEER-TO-PEER PAYMENTS Various services allow you to transfer money to another person. While most require registering debit card, credit card, or bank account information, some peer-to-peer (P2P) payments are conducted by e-mail and with a secured website. Fees for the P2P service can range from less than a dollar to a percentage of the amount transferred.

Checking Accounts

Even as electronic payments grow in popularity, a checking account is still necessary for most people. Checking accounts fall into three major categories: regular checking accounts, activity accounts, and interest-earning checking accounts.

REGULAR CHECKING ACCOUNTS *Regular checking accounts* usually have a monthly service charge that you may avoid by keeping a minimum balance in the account. Some financial institutions will waive the monthly fee if you keep a certain amount in savings. Avoiding the monthly service charge can be beneficial. For example, a monthly fee of $7.50 results in $90 a year. However, you lose interest on the minimum-balance amount in a non-interest-earning account.

ACTIVITY ACCOUNTS *Activity accounts* charge a fee for each check written and sometimes a fee for each deposit in addition to a monthly service charge. However, you do not have to maintain a minimum balance. An activity account is most appropriate for people who write only a few checks each month and are unable to maintain the required minimum balance.

INTEREST-EARNING CHECKING *Interest-earning checking accounts* usually require a minimum balance. If the account balance goes below this amount, you may not earn interest and will likely incur a service charge. These are called *share draft accounts* at credit unions.

Evaluating Checking and Payment Accounts

Would you rather have a checking account that pays interest and requires a $1,000 minimum balance or an account that doesn't pay interest and requires a $300 minimum balance? This decision requires evaluating factors such as restrictions, fees and charges, interest, and special services (see Exhibit 4–9).

RESTRICTIONS The most common limitation on a checking account is the required amount that must be kept on deposit to earn interest or avoid a service charge. In the past, financial institutions placed restrictions on the holding period for deposited checks. A waiting period was usually required before you could access the funds. The Check Clearing for the 21st Century Act (known as Check 21) shortens the processing time. This law establishes the *substitute check,* which is a digital reproduction of the original paper check, and is considered a legal equivalent of the original check.

FEES AND CHARGES Nearly all financial institutions require a minimum balance or impose service charges for checking accounts. When using an interest-bearing checking account, compare your earnings with any service charge or fee. Also, consider the cost of lost or reduced interest resulting from maintaining the minimum balance. Checking account fees have increased in recent years. Items such as check printing,

Exhibit 4–9

Checking Account
Selection Factors

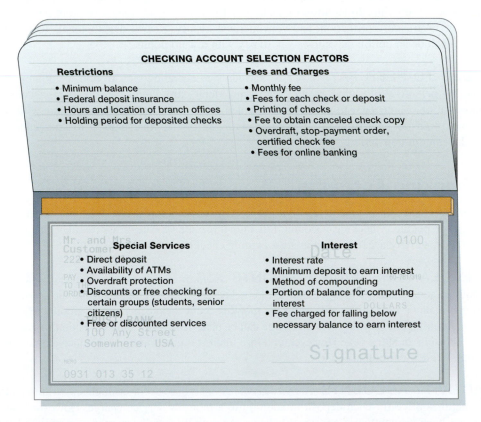

CHECKING ACCOUNT SELECTION FACTORS

Restrictions
- Minimum balance
- Federal deposit insurance
- Hours and location of branch offices
- Holding period for deposited checks

Fees and Charges
- Monthly fee
- Fees for each check or deposit
- Printing of checks
- Fee to obtain canceled check copy
- Overdraft, stop-payment order, certified check fee
- Fees for online banking

Special Services
- Direct deposit
- Availability of ATMs
- Overdraft protection
- Discounts or free checking for certain groups (students, senior citizens)
- Free or discounted services

Interest
- Interest rate
- Minimum deposit to earn interest
- Method of compounding
- Portion of balance for computing interest
- Fee charged for falling below necessary balance to earn interest

overdraft fees, and stop-payment orders have doubled or tripled in price at some financial institutions.

INTEREST The interest rate, the frequency of compounding, and the interest computation method will affect the earnings on your checking account.

SPECIAL SERVICES As financial institutions attempt to reduce paper and postage costs, canceled checks are no longer returned. Bank customers are provided with more detailed monthly statements and will likely have online access to view and print checks that have been paid.

Overdraft protection is an automatic loan made to checking account customers for checks written in excess of their balance. This service is convenient but costly. Most overdraft plans make loans based on $50 or $100 increments. An overdraft of just $1 might trigger a $50 loan and corresponding finance charges of perhaps 18 percent. But overdraft protection can be less costly than the fee charged for a check you write when you do not have enough money on deposit to cover it. That fee may be $30 or more. Many financial institutions will allow you to cover checking account overdrafts with an automatic transfer from a savings account for a nominal fee.

Beware of checking accounts packaged with several services (safe deposit box, traveler's checks, low-rate loans, and travel insurance) for a single monthly fee. This may sound like a good value; however, financial experts observe that only a small group of people make use of all services in the package.

overdraft protection An automatic loan made to checking account customers to cover the amount of checks written in excess of the available balance in the checking account.

Other Payment Methods

A *certified check* is a personal check with guaranteed payment. The amount of the check is deducted from your balance when the financial institution certifies the check. A *cashier's check* is a check issued by a financial institution. You may purchase one by paying the amount of the check plus a fee. You may purchase a *money order* in a similar manner from financial institutions, post offices, and stores. Certified checks, cashier's checks, and money orders allow you to make a payment that the recipient knows is valid.

Traveler's checks allow you to make payments when you are away from home. This payment form requires you to sign each check twice. First, you sign the traveler's checks when you purchase them. Then, to identify you as the authorized person, you sign them again as you cash them. Electronic traveler's checks, in the form of a prepaid travel card, are also available. The card allows travelers visiting other nations to get local currency from an ATM.

digi – know?

EMV credit and debit cards contain an integrated chip rather than a magnetic strip, to provide greater security and reduce fraud. This technology makes it very difficult to create counterfeit cards. The EMV name comes from Europay, MasterCard, and Visa, the companies involved in developing the chip-based payment cards that are commonly used in many countries around the world.

Managing Your Checking Account

Obtaining and using a checking account involve several activities.

OPENING A CHECKING ACCOUNT First, decide who the owner of the account is. Only one person is allowed to write checks on an *individual account*. A *joint account* has two or more owners. Both an individual account and a joint account require a signature card. This document is a record of the official signatures of the person or persons authorized to write checks on the account.

MAKING DEPOSITS A *deposit ticket* is used for adding funds to your checking account. On this document, you list the amounts of cash and checks being deposited. Each check you deposit requires an *endorsement*—your signature on the back of the check—to authorize the transfer of the funds into your account. The three common endorsement forms are:

- A *blank endorsement* is just your signature, which should be used only when you are actually depositing or cashing a check, since a check may be cashed by anyone once it has been signed.
- A *restrictive endorsement* consists of the words *for deposit only,* followed by your signature, which is especially useful when you are depositing checks.
- A *special endorsement* allows you to transfer a check to someone else with the words *pay to the order of* followed by the name of the other person and then your signature.

CAUTION!

Each year, consumers lose millions of dollars by accepting phony checks, money orders, and wire transfers for online transactions and other business activities. Information and videos on check scams may be obtained at www.fakechecks.org.

WRITING CHECKS Before writing a check, record the information in your check register and deduct the amount of the check from your balance. Many checking account customers use duplicate checks to maintain a record of their current balance.

The procedure for proper check writing has the following steps: (1) record the date; (2) write the name of the person or organization receiving the payment; (3) record the amount of the check in numerals; (4) write the amount of the check in words; checks for less than a dollar should be written as "only 79 cents," for example, and cross out the word *dollars* on the check; (5) sign the check; (6) note the reason for payment.

A *stop-payment order* may be necessary if a check is lost or stolen. Most banks do not honor checks with "stale" dates, usually six months old or older. The fee for a stop-payment commonly ranges from $20 to more than $30. If several checks are missing or you lose your checkbook, closing the account and opening a new one is likely to be less costly than paying several stop-payment fees.

RECONCILING YOUR CHECKING ACCOUNT Each month you will receive a *bank statement* summarizing deposits, checks paid, ATM withdrawals, interest earned, and fees such as service charges and printing of checks. The balance reported on the statement will usually differ from the balance in your checkbook. Reasons for a difference may include checks that have not yet cleared, deposits not received by the bank, and interest earned.

To determine the correct balance, prepare a *bank reconciliation,* to account for differences between the bank statement and your checkbook balance. This process involves the following steps:

1. Compare the checks written with those reported as paid on the statement. Use the canceled checks, or compare your check register with the check numbers reported on the bank statement. *Subtract* from the *bank statement balance* the total of the checks written but not yet cleared.
2. Determine whether any deposits made are not on the statement; *add* the amount of the outstanding deposits to the *bank statement balance.*
3. *Subtract* fees or charges on the bank statement and ATM withdrawals from your *checkbook balance.*
4. *Add* any interest earned to your *checkbook balance.*

At this point, the revised balances for both the checkbook and the bank statement should be the same. If the two do not match, check your math; make sure every check and deposit was recorded correctly.

Personal Finance in Practice

Are You Avoiding Identity Theft?

People who put their Social Security and driver's license numbers on their checks are making identity theft fairly easy. With one check, a con artist could know your Social Security, driver's license, and bank account numbers as well as your address, phone number, and perhaps even a sample of your signature.

An attorney had his wallet stolen. Within a week, the thieves ordered an expensive monthly cell phone package, applied for a Visa credit card, had a credit line approved to buy a Gateway computer, and received a PIN number from the Department of Motor Vehicles to change his driving record information online.

Identity fraud can range from passing bad checks and using stolen credit cards to theft of another person's total financial existence. The following quiz can help you avoid becoming one of the more than 1,000 people who each day have their identities stolen by con artists.

If you are a victim of identity theft, take the following actions:

- File a police report immediately in the area where the item was stolen. This proves you were diligent and is a first step toward an investigation (if there ever is one).

- Call the three national credit reporting organizations *immediately* to place a fraud alert on your name and Social Security number. The numbers are: Equifax, 1-800-525-6285; Experian (formerly TRW), 1-888-397-3742; and TransUnion, 1-800-680-7289.

- Contact the Social Security Administration fraud line at 1-800-269-0271.

Additional information on financial privacy and identity theft is available at www.identitytheft.org, www.idfraud.org, and www.privacyrights.org.

Which of the following actions have you taken to avoid identity theft?	Yes	No	Action needed
1. I have only my initials and last name on checks so others will not know how I sign my checks. I do not put the full account number on my checks when paying a bill, only the last four numbers.			
2. I have my work phone and a PO box (if applicable) on my checks instead of home information.			
3. I don't provide my Social Security number unless it is legally required.			
4. I have personal documents in a locked area and shred unneeded financial documents and CDs containing account or Social Security numbers. I clear the hard drives of old computers.			
5. I change passwords (letters, numbers, characters) and PINs often. I do not keep a list of these in my wallet, and I guard them when using them in a public place.			
6. I promptly collect my mail with account numbers and send bill payments from a post office or a public mailbox.			
7. I check my credit report regularly (all three major credit reporting agencies) to make sure it is correct. I have my name removed from mailing lists of credit agencies and companies offering credit promotions.			
8. I have a photocopy of the contents of my wallet (both sides of each item) as a record to cancel accounts if necessary.			
9. I am suspicious of companies and individuals who request verification of personal information.			
10. I use only secured, trusted websites when making purchases or when storing personal information online.			
11. I review my bank and credit card statements each month for questionable charges.			
12. I have a secured home wireless network with a password I created, a locked router, and encrypted information.			

EXAMPLE: Bank Reconciliation

To determine the true balance in your checking account:

Bank Statement		Your Checkbook	
Bank balance	$920	Checkbook balance	$1,041
Subtract: Outstanding checks	−187	Subtract: Fees, ATM withdrawals	−271
Add: Deposit in transit	+200	Add: Interest earned, direct deposits	+163
Adjusted bank statement balance	933	Adjusted checkbook balance	933

A failure to reconcile your bank account each month can result in **not** knowing:

• Your exact spending habits for wise money management.
• If the correct deposit amounts have been credited to your account.
• Any unauthorized ATM withdrawals.
• If your bank is overcharging you for fees.
• Errors that your bank may have made in your account.

 Sheet 14 Comparing Payment Methods; Bank Reconciliation

PRACTICE QUIZ 4–4

1. Are checking accounts that earn interest preferable to regular checking accounts? Why or why not?

2. What factors are commonly considered when selecting a checking account?

3. For the following situations, select and describe a payment method that would be appropriate for the needs of the person.

   a. A need to send funds for a purchase from an organization that requires guaranteed payment.
   b. Traveling to Asia, you desire to be able to access funds in the local currencies of various countries.
   c. A desire to pay bills using your home computer instead of writing checks.
   d. You write only a few checks a month and you want to minimize your costs.

4. Based on the following information, determine the true balance in your checking account.

Balance in your checkbook, $356	Balance on bank statement, $472
Service charge and other fees, $15	Interest earned on the account, $4
Total of outstanding checks, $187	Deposits in transit, $60

Apply Yourself!

Observe customers making payments in a retail store. How often are cash, checks, credit cards, debit cards, and other payment methods used?

YOUR PERSONAL FINANCE DASHBOARD

PERCENT SAVINGS RATE

A key indicator of your potential financial success is the percentage of income saved each month. Various financial institutions and savings instruments can be used to implement this element of your financial plan.

While most people in our society save nothing or very little, financial experts recommend a savings rate of between 5 and 10 percent. These funds might be used for emergencies, unexpected expenses, or short-term financial goals as well as long-term financial security.

YOUR SITUATION: Are you able to set aside an amount for savings each month? Are there expenses you can reduce, or sources of increased income that could add to the amount you save each month? An improving savings rate is the foundation for progress toward financial independence.

POSSIBLE ACTIONS TO TAKE

 Reconsider your responses to the "Action Items" (in the text margin) to determine actions you might take for improved actions for the wise use of financial services.

 Conduct a web search of online banks to obtain information on their services. Consider how changing interest rates might affect your decision to use various types of financial services.

 Consider various sources of financial services, such as credit unions, which often offer low-cost alternatives for financial services. For additional information about credit unions, go to www.cuna.org and www.creditunion.coop.

 Obtain current interest rates for CDs and other savings plans at www.bankrate.com. For the latest rates and information on U.S. savings bonds, go to www.savingsbonds.gov.

LO4.1 Financial products such as savings plans, checking accounts, loans, trust services, and electronic banking are used for managing daily financial activities.

LO4.2 Commercial banks, savings and loan associations, mutual savings banks, credit unions, life insurance companies, investment companies, finance companies, mortgage companies, pawnshops, and check-cashing outlets may be compared on the basis of services offered, rates and fees, safety, convenience, and special programs available to customers.

LO4.3 Commonly used savings plans include regular savings accounts, certificates of deposit, interest-earning checking accounts, money market accounts, money market funds, and U.S. savings bonds. Savings plans may be evaluated on the basis of rate of return, inflation, tax considerations, liquidity, safety, restrictions, and fees.

LO4.4 Debit cards, online payment systems, and stored-value cards are increasing in use for payment activities. Regular checking accounts, activity accounts, and interest-earning checking accounts can be compared with regard to restrictions (such as a minimum balance), fees and charges, interest, and special services.

Chapter Summary

Key Terms

annual percentage yield
(APY) 120

asset management
account 109

automatic teller machine
(ATM) 109

certificate of
deposit (CD) 115

commercial bank 112

compounding 120

credit union 113

debit card 110

money market
account 118

money market fund 113

mutual savings bank 113

overdraft protection 127

rate of return 120

savings and loan
association (S&L) 113

trust 109

Key Formulas

Page	Topic	Formula
121	Annual percentage yield (APY)	$APY = 100\left[\left(1 + \dfrac{\text{Interest}}{\text{Principal}}\right)^{365/\text{days in term}} - 1\right]$
		Principal = Amount of funds on deposit
		Interest = Total dollar amount earned on the principal
		Days in term = Actual number of days in the term of the account
122	When the number of days in the term is 365 or where the account does not have a stated maturity, the APY formula is simply	$APY = 100\left(\dfrac{\text{Interest}}{\text{Principal}}\right)$
		Example:
		$100\left[\left(1 + \dfrac{\$56.20}{\$1,000}\right)^{\frac{365}{365}} - 1\right] = 0.0562 = 5.62\%$
	After-tax rate of return	Interest rate $\times$ (1 − Tax rate)

Discussion Questions

1. How has online banking changed the way consumers select and use various financial services?   (LO4.1)
2. What relationship exists between changing interest rates and the rates of return for various savings accounts, money market accounts, and certificates of deposit of various lengths?   (LO4.1)
3. What actions would you recommend to someone who was considering using the services of a pawnshop, check-cashing outlet, or payday loan company?   (LO4.2)
4. What fees and deductions may be overlooked when balancing your checking account?   (LO4.4)
5. *a.* What are potential benefits of an overdraft protection service for your checking account?
   b. What costs should a person consider before deciding to use the overdraft protection service?   (LO4.4)

Self-Test Problems

1. What would be the annual percentage yield (APY) for a savings account that earned $174 on a balance of $3,250 over the past 365 days?
2. If you earned a 4.2 percent return on your savings, with a 15 percent tax rate, what is the after-tax rate of return?

Solutions

1. To calculate the APY when the number of days in the term is 365, use this formula:

$$APY = 100 \left(\frac{Interest}{Principal} \right)$$

$$= 100 \left(\frac{174}{3250} \right)$$

$$= 100 \, (0.0535) = 5.35\%$$

2. To calculate the after-tax rate of return use

Interest rate $\times$ (1 − Tax rate)

0.042 $\times$ (1 − 0.15) = 0.042 (0.85) = 0.0357 = 3.57%

Problems

1. An ATM with a service fee of $2 is used by a person 100 times in a year. What would be the future value in 10 years (use a 3 percent rate) of the annual amount paid in ATM fees?   (LO4.1)
2. If a person has ATM fees each month of $18 for six years, what would be the total cost of those banking fees?   (LO4.1)
3. A payday loan company charges 5 percent interest for a two-week period. What would be the annual interest rate from that company?   (LO4.2)
4. For each of these situations, determine the savings amount. Use the time value of money tables in Chapter 1 (Exhibit 1–3) or in the Chapter 1 appendix.   (LO4.3)

   a. What would be the value of a savings account started with $700, earning 4 percent (compounded annually) after 10 years?
   b. Brenda Young desires to have $15,000 eight years from now for her daughter's college fund. If she will earn 6 percent (compounded annually) on her money, what amount should she deposit now? Use the present value of a single amount calculation.
   c. What amount would you have if you deposited $1,800 a year for 30 years at 8 percent (compounded annually)?

5. What would be the annual percentage yield for a savings account that earned $56 in interest on $800 over the past 365 days?   (LO4.3)
6. With a 28 percent marginal tax rate, would a tax-free yield of 7 percent or a taxable yield of 9.5 percent give you a better return on your savings? Why?   (LO4.3)
7. Janie has a joint account with her mother with a balance of $562,000. Based on $250,000 of Federal Deposit Insurance Corporation coverage, what amount of Janie's savings would not be covered by deposit insurance?   (LO4.3)
8. A certificate of deposit often charges a penalty for withdrawing funds before the maturity date. If the penalty involves two months of interest, what would be the amount for early withdrawal on a $20,000, 5 percent CD?   (LO4.3)
9. What might be a savings goal for a person who buys a five-year CD paying 4.67 percent instead of an 18-month savings certificate paying 3.29 percent?   (LO4.4)
10. What is the annual *opportunity cost* of a checking account that requires a $300 minimum balance to avoid service charges? Assume an interest rate of 3 percent.   (LO4.4)
11. Compare the costs and benefits of these two checking accounts: (LO4.4)
    Account 1: A regular checking account with a monthly fee of $6 when the balance goes below $300.
    Account 2: An interest-earning checking account (paying 1.2 percent), with a monthly charge of $3 if the balance goes below $100.

12. A bank that provides overdraft protection charges 12 percent for each $100 (or portion of $100) borrowed when an overdraft occurs. (LO4.4)

   a. What amount of interest would the customer pay for a $188 overdraft? (Assume the interest is for the full amount borrowed for a whole year.)
   b. How much would be saved by using the overdraft protection loan if a customer has three overdraft charges of $30 each during the year?

13. What would be the net *annual* cost of the following checking accounts? (LO4.4)

   a. Monthly fee, $3.75; processing fee, 25 cents per check; checks written, an average of 14 a month.
   b. Interest earnings of 4 percent with a $500 minimum balance; average monthly balance, $600; monthly service charge of $15 for falling below the minimum balance, which occurs three times a year (no interest earned in these months).

14. Based on the following information, prepare a bank reconciliation to determine adjusted (corrected) balance: (LO4.4)

Bank balance, $680	Account fees, $12
Checkbook balance, $642	ATM withdrawals, $80
Outstanding checks, $112	Deposit in transit, $60
Direct deposits, $70	Interest earned, $8

 **To reinforce the content in this chapter, more problems are provided at connect.mheducation.com.**

Case in Point

EVALUATING BANKING SERVICES

"Wow! My account balance is a little lower than I expected," commented Melanie Harper as she reviewed her bank statement. "Wait a minute! There's nearly $20 in fees for ATM withdrawals and other service charges." "Oh no! I also went below the minimum balance required for my *free* checking account," Melanie groaned. "That cost me $7.50!"

Melanie is not alone in her frustration with fees paid for financial services. While careless money management caused many of these charges, others could have been reduced or eliminated by comparing costs at various financial institutions.

Melanie has decided to investigate various alternatives to her current banking services. Her preliminary research provided the following:

Mobile banking—allows faster access to account information, to quickly transfer funds, make payments and purchases. May include access to expanded financial services, such as low-cost, online investment trading and instant loan approval.

Prepaid debit card—would prevent overspending, staying within the budgeted amount loaded on the card. Cards are usually accepted in most retail locations and online. A variety of fees might be associated with the card.

Check-cashing outlet—would result in fees only when services are used, such as money orders, cashing a check, obtaining a prepaid cash card, or paying bills online.

Many people do not realize the amount they pay each month for various bank fees. Some basic research can result in saving several hundred dollars a year.

Questions

1. What benefits and drawbacks might Melanie encounter when using each of these financial services? Mobile banking . . . Prepaid debit card . . . Check-cashing outlet
2. What factors should Melanie consider when selecting among these various banking services?
3. What actions might you take to better understand the concerns associated with using various banking services?

FINANCIAL SERVICES: SAVINGS PLANS AND PAYMENT ACCOUNTS

Jamie Lee Jackson, age 26, is in her last semester of college and is anxiously waiting for a graduation day that is just around the corner! She still works part-time as a bakery clerk, has been sticking to her budget the past two years, and is on track to accumulate enough money for the $9,000 down payment she needs to open her cupcake café within the next two years.

Jamie Lee is still single, shares a small apartment with a friend, and continues to split all of the associated living expenses, such as rent and utilities. Unfortunately, she now has to seriously consider finding a place of her own.

One evening, after returning to the apartment after a long shift at the bakery, Jamie learned that her roommate had a couple of friends over earlier in the evening. As Jamie went to her room, she noticed that her top desk drawer had been left open and her debit/ATM card, as well as her checkbook and Social Security card, were missing. She immediately contacted the authorities, and the police instructed her to notify her financial institution immediately. But it was late Saturday night, and Jamie thought she had to now wait until Monday morning. Unfortunately, within no time, Jamie found that her checking account had been emptied!

Jamie Lee's luck worsened, as she had paid many of her monthly bills late last week. Her automobile insurance, two utility bills, and a layaway payment had all been paid for by check. Her bank almost immediately began sending overdraft alerts through her smartphone for the emptied checking account.

Current Financial Situation

Bank Accounts:

Checking account, $2,250 (before the theft)

Savings account, $6,900

Emergency fund savings account, $3,900

401(k) balance, $350

Questions

1. Jamie Lee is beside herself knowing that the thieves had unauthorized use of her debit/ATM card. What is Jamie's financial responsibility for the unauthorized use?
2. What would have been Jamie Lee's financial liability had she waited more than two days to report the debit/ATM card lost or stolen?
3. Using "Your Personal Financial Plan" sheet 11, what financial service would benefit Jamie Lee now, as she had legitimate checks written to cover her monthly bills that are now in excess of the available checking account balance due to the theft?

"MY CASH WITHDRAWALS HAVE RESULTED IN MANY ATM FEES THAT TAKE AWAY MONEY FROM OTHER BUDGET ITEMS."

Directions Start (or continue) your Daily Spending Diary or use your own format to record and monitor spending in various categories. Your comments should reflect what you have learned about your spending patterns and help you consider possible changes you might make. The Daily Spending Diary sheets are located in Appendix D at the end of the book and in Connect Finance.

Questions

1. Are there any banking fees that you encounter each month? What actions might be taken to reduce or eliminate these cash outflows?
2. What other areas of your daily spending might be reduced or revised?

Name: _____   **Date:** _____

Planning the Use of Financial Services

Purpose: To indicate currently used financial services and to determine services that may be needed in the future.

Financial Planning Activities: List (1) currently used services with financial institution information (name, address, phone); and (2) services that are likely to be needed in the future. This sheet is also available in an Excel spreadsheet format in Connect Finance.

Suggested Websites: www.bankrate.com   www.consumerfinance.gov   banking.about.com

Types of financial services	Current financial services used	Additional financial services needed
Payment services (checking, ATM, online bill payment, money orders)	Financial Institution	
Savings services (savings account, money market account, certificate of deposit, savings bonds)	Financial Institution	
Credit services (credit cards, personal loans, mortgage)	Financial Institution	
Other financial services (investments, trust account, tax planning)	Financial Institution	

What's Next for Your Personal Financial Plan?

- Assess whether the current types and sources of your financial services are appropriate.
- Determine additional financial services you may wish to make use of in the future.

Name: _____ **Date:** _____

Comparing Savings Plans

Purpose: To compare the costs and benefits associated with different savings plans.

Financial Planning Activities: Analyze advertisements and contact various financial institutions to obtain the information requested below. This sheet is also available in an Excel spreadsheet format in Connect Finance.

Suggested Websites: www.bankrate.com   www.nerdwallet.com   www.savingsaccounts.com

Type of savings plan (regular savings account, certificates of deposit, interest-earning checking accounts, money market accounts and funds, U.S. savings bonds)			
Financial institution			
Address/phone			
Website			
Annual interest rate			
Annual percentage yield (APY)			
Frequency of compounding			
Insured by FDIC, NCUA, other			
Maximum amount insured			
Minimum initial deposit			
Minimum time period savings that must be on deposit			
Penalties for early withdrawal			
Service charges/transaction fees, other costs, fees			
Additional services, other information			

Suggested
App:
• Savings Plan

What's Next for Your Personal Financial Plan?

• Based on this savings plan analysis, determine the best types for your current and future financial situation.
• When analyzing savings plans, what factors should you carefully investigate?

YOUR PERSONAL FINANCIAL PLAN

Name: _____   Date: _____

Using Savings Plans to Achieve Financial Goals

Purpose: Monitor savings to assist in reaching financial goals.

Financial Planning Activities: Record savings plan information along with the amount of your balance or income on a periodic basis. This sheet is also available in an Excel spreadsheet format in Connect Finance.

Suggested Websites: www.savingsbonds.gov   www.fdic.gov   www.banx.com

---

Regular savings account | **Savings goal/Amount needed/Date needed**

Acct. no. _____
Financial   Savings goal: Date _____ $ _____
institution _____   Balance: Date _____ $ _____
Address _____   Date _____ $ _____
         _____   Date _____ $ _____
Phone _____   Date _____ $ _____
Website _____

Certificate of deposit | **Savings goal/Amount needed/Date needed**

Acct. no. _____
Financial   Savings goal: Date _____ $ _____
institution _____   Balance: Date _____ $ _____
Address _____   Date _____ $ _____
         _____   Date _____ $ _____
Phone _____   Date _____ $ _____
Website _____

Money market fund/acct. | **Savings goal/Amount needed/Date needed**

Acct. no. _____
Financial   Savings goal: Date _____ $ _____
institution _____   Balance: Date _____ $ _____
Address _____   Date _____ $ _____
         _____   Date _____ $ _____
Phone _____   Date _____ $ _____
Website _____

U.S. savings bonds | **Savings goal/Amount needed/Date needed**

Purchase
location _____   Purchase date: _____ Maturity date: _____
         _____   Amount: _____
Address _____   Purchase date: _____ Maturity date: _____
         _____   Amount: _____
Phone _____
Website _____

Other savings | **Savings goal/Amount needed/Date needed**

Acct. no. _____
Financial   Initial deposit: Date _____ $ _____
institution _____   Balance: Date _____ $ _____
Address _____   Date _____ $ _____
         _____   Date _____ $ _____
Phone _____   Date _____ $ _____
Website _____

Suggested App:
• Save Genius

What's Next for Your Personal Financial Plan?

- Assess your current progress toward achieving various savings goals. Evaluate existing and new savings goals.
- Plan actions to expand the amount you are saving toward various savings goals.

Name: _____ Date: _____

Comparing Payment Methods; Bank Reconciliation

Purpose: To determine the adjusted cash balance for your checking account.

Financial Planning Activities: Compare checking accounts and payment services at various financial institutions (banks, savings and loan associations, credit unions, online banks). Enter data from your bank statement and checkbook for the amounts requested. This sheet is also available in an Excel spreadsheet format in Connect Finance.

Suggested Websites: www.bankrate.com   www.kiplinger.com   www.depositaccounts.com

Institution name			
Address			
Phone			
Website			
Type of account (regular checking, activity account, bill payment service)			
Minimum balance			
Monthly charge below balance			
"Free" checking for students?			
Online banking services, mobile app banking			
Branch/ATM locations			
Banking hours			
Other fees/costs			
Printing of checks			
Stop-payment order			
Overdrawn account			
Certified check			
ATM, other charges			
Other information			

Checking Account Reconciliation

Statement date:	**Statement Balance**		$_____
Step 1: Compare the checks written with those paid on statement. *Subtract* the total of the checks written but not cleared from the bank balance.	Check no.	Amount	−$_____
Step 2: Determine whether any deposits made are not on the statement; *add* the amount of the outstanding deposits to the *bank statement balance*.	Deposit date	Amount	+$_____
	Adjusted Balance		=$_____
	Checkbook Balance		
Step 3: *Subtract* fees or charges on the bank statement and ATM withdrawals from your *checkbook balance*.	Item	Amount	−$_____
Step 4: *Add* interest or direct deposits earned to your *checkbook balance*.			+$_____
Note: At this point, the two adjusted balances should be the same. If not, carefully check your math and make sure that deposits and checks recorded in your checkbook and on your statement are for the correct amounts.	**Adjusted Balance**		=$_____

Suggested App:
- MoneyPass (ATM locator)

5 Consumer Credit: Advantages, Disadvantages, Sources, and Costs

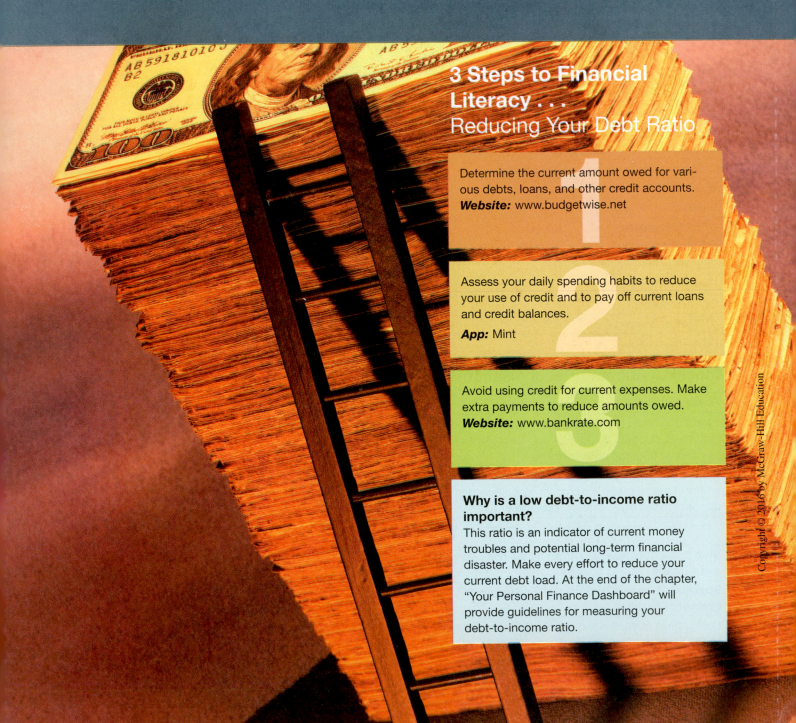

3 Steps to Financial Literacy . . .
Reducing Your Debt Ratio

Determine the current amount owed for various debts, loans, and other credit accounts. **Website:** www.budgetwise.net

Assess your daily spending habits to reduce your use of credit and to pay off current loans and credit balances. **App:** Mint

Avoid using credit for current expenses. Make extra payments to reduce amounts owed. **Website:** www.bankrate.com

Why is a low debt-to-income ratio important?
This ratio is an indicator of current money troubles and potential long-term financial disaster. Make every effort to reduce your current debt load. At the end of the chapter, "Your Personal Finance Dashboard" will provide guidelines for measuring your debt-to-income ratio.

CHAPTER 5 LEARNING OBJECTIVES

In this chapter, you will learn to:

LO5.1 Analyze advantages and disadvantages of using consumer credit.

LO5.2 Assess the types and sources of consumer credit.

LO5.3 Determine whether you can afford a loan and how to apply for credit.

LO5.4 Determine the cost of credit by calculating interest using various interest formulas.

LO5.5 Develop a plan to protect your credit and manage your debts.

YOUR PERSONAL FINANCIAL PLAN SHEETS

15. Consumer Credit Usage Patterns
16. Credit Card/Charge Account Comparison
17. Consumer Loan Comparison

What Is Consumer Credit?

Credit is an arrangement to receive cash, goods, or services now and pay for them in the future. **Consumer credit** refers to the use of credit for personal needs (except a home mortgage) by individuals and families, in contrast to credit used for business purposes. Many people use credit to live beyond their means, largely because of a change in perception about credit. Past generations viewed credit as a negative and used it very sparingly. Society today has popularized credit with phrases such as "Life takes Visa," "Priceless" campaigns, and even references to a "Plunk factor" when using a sought-after credit card. That said, when used appropriately, credit can be a very useful tool.

Consumer credit is based on trust in people's ability and willingness to pay bills when due. It works because people by and large are honest and responsible. But how does consumer credit affect our economy, and how is it affected by our economy?

The Importance of Consumer Credit in Our Economy

Consumer credit dates back to colonial times. Although credit was originally a privilege of the affluent, farmers came to use it extensively. No direct finance charges were imposed; instead, the cost of credit was added to the prices of goods. With the advent of the automobile in the early 1900s, installment credit, in which the debt is repaid in equal installments over a specified period of time, exploded on the American scene.

All economists now recognize consumer credit as a major force in the American economy. Any forecast or evaluation of the economy includes consumer spending trends and consumer credit as a sustaining force.

LO5.1

Analyze advantages and disadvantages of using consumer credit.

ACTION ITEM

I pay any bills I have when they are due.

☐ **Always**

☐ **Most of the time**

☐ **Sometimes**

credit An arrangement to receive cash, goods, or services now and pay for them in the future.

consumer credit The use of credit for personal needs (except a home mortgage).

Uses and Misuses of Credit

Using credit to purchase goods and services may allow consumers to be more efficient or more productive, or it may lead to more satisfying lives. Many valid reasons can be found for using credit. A medical emergency may leave a person strapped for funds. A homemaker returning to the workforce may need a car. An item may cost less money now than it will cost later. Borrowing for a college education may be another valid reason. But borrowing for everyday living expenses or financing a Corvette on credit when a Ford Focus is all your budget allows is probably not reasonable.

Using credit increases the amount of money a person can spend to purchase goods and services now. But the trade-off is that it decreases the amount of money that will be available to spend in the future. However, many people expect their incomes to increase and therefore expect to be able to make payments on past credit purchases and still make new purchases. This should be carefully considered.

Here are some questions you should consider before you decide how and when to make a major purchase, for example, a car:

- Do I have the cash I need for the down payment?
- Do I want to use my savings for this purchase?
- Does the purchase fit my budget?
- Could I use the credit I need for this purchase in some better way?
- Could I postpone the purchase?
- What are the opportunity costs of postponing the purchase (alternative transportation costs, a possible increase in the price of the car)?
- What are the dollar costs and the psychological costs of using credit (interest, other finance charges, being in debt and responsible for making a monthly payment)?

If you decide to use credit, make sure the benefits of purchasing now (increased efficiency or productivity, a more satisfying life, etc.) outweigh the costs (financial and psychological) of using credit. Thus, credit, when effectively used, can help you have more and enjoy more. When misused, credit can result in default, bankruptcy, and loss of creditworthiness.

Advantages of Credit

Consumer credit enables people to enjoy goods and services now—a car, a home, an education—or it can provide for emergencies, and it can pay for them all through payment plans based on future income.

Credit cards permit the purchase of goods even when funds are low. Customers with previously approved credit may receive other extras, such as advance notice of sales and the right to order by phone or to buy on approval. Many retailers will accept returned merchandise without a receipt because they can look up the purchase made by a credit card. Credit cards also provide shopping convenience and the efficiency of paying for several purchases with one monthly payment.

Credit is more than a substitute for cash. Many of the services it provides are taken for granted. Every time you turn on the water tap, click the light switch, or telephone a friend, you are using credit.

Using credit is safe, since charge accounts and credit cards let you shop and travel without carrying a large amount of cash. It offers convenience, since you need a credit card to make a hotel reservation, rent a car, and shop by phone or Internet. You may also use credit cards for identification when cashing checks, and the use of credit provides you with a record of expenses.

The use of credit cards can provide up to a 50-day "float," the time lag between when you make the purchase and when the lender deducts the balance from your checking account when payment is due. This float, offered by many credit card issuers, includes a grace period of 20 to 25 days. During the grace period, no finance charges are assessed on current purchases if the balance is paid in full each month within 25 days after billing.

In addition, many major credit cards provide the following benefits to their customers at no extra cost:

- Accidental death and dismemberment insurance when you travel on a common carrier (train, plane, bus, or ship), up to $250,000.
- Auto rental collision damage waiver (CDW) for damage due to collision or theft for $50,000 or more.
- Roadside dispatch referral service for emergency roadside assistance, such as towing, locksmith services, and more.
- Redemption of your points or miles for gift cards or cash, or to book travel—from airfare, hotels, and rental cars to vacation packages.
- No foreign transaction fees for some cards, such as CapitalOne.

Finally, credit indicates stability. The fact that lenders consider you a good risk usually means you are a responsible individual. However, if you do not repay your debts in a timely manner, you will find that credit has many disadvantages.

Disadvantages of Credit

Perhaps the greatest disadvantage of using credit is the temptation to overspend, especially during periods of inflation. Buying today and paying tomorrow, using cheaper dollars, seems ideal. But continual overspending can lead to serious trouble.

Whether or not credit involves *security* (or collateral)—something of value to back the loan—failure to repay a loan may result in loss of income, valuable property, and your good reputation. It can even lead to court action and bankruptcy. Misuse of credit can create serious long-term financial problems, cause damage to family relationships, and delay progress toward financial goals. Therefore, you should approach credit with caution and avoid using it more than your budget permits.

Although credit allows immediate satisfaction of needs and desires, it does not increase total purchasing power. Credit purchases must be paid out of future income; therefore, credit ties up the use of future income. Furthermore, if your income does not increase to cover rising costs, your ability to repay credit commitments will diminish. Before buying goods and services on credit, consider whether they will have lasting value, whether they will increase your personal satisfaction during present and future income periods, and whether your current income will continue or increase.

Finally, credit costs money. It is a service for which you must pay. Paying for purchases over a period of time is more costly than paying for them with cash. Purchasing with credit rather than cash involves one obvious trade-off: The items purchased may cost more due to monthly finance charges and the compounding effect of interest on interest.

Summary: Advantages and Disadvantages of Credit

The use of credit provides immediate access to goods and services, flexibility in money management, safety and convenience, a cushion in emergencies, a means of increasing resources, and a good credit rating if you pay back your debts in a timely manner. But remember, the use of credit is a two-sided coin. An intelligent decision as to its use demands careful evaluation of your current debt, your future income, the added cost, and the consequences of overspending.

PRACTICE QUIZ 5–1

1. What is consumer credit?

2. Why is consumer credit important to our economy?

3. List two good reasons to borrow and two unnecessary reasons to borrow.

Apply Yourself!

Using web research and discussion with family members and friends, prepare a list of advantages and disadvantages of using credit.

LO5.2

Assess the types and sources of consumer credit.

ACTION ITEM

If I need more money for my expenses, I borrow it.

☐ **Never**

☐ **Sometimes**

☐ **Often**

closed-end credit One-time loans that the borrower pays back in a specified period of time and in payments of equal amounts.

open-end credit A line of credit in which loans are made on a continuous basis and the borrower is billed periodically for at least partial payment.

Types of Credit

Two basic types of consumer credit exist: closed-end and open-end credit. With **closed-end credit,** you pay back one-time loans in a specified period of time and in payments of equal amounts. With **open-end credit,** loans are made on a continuous basis and you are billed periodically for at least partial payment. Exhibit 5–1 shows examples of closed-end and open-end credit.

Closed-End Credit

Closed-end credit is used for a specific purpose and involves a specified amount. Mortgage loans, automobile loans, and installment loans for purchasing furniture or appliances are examples of closed-end credit. Generally, the seller holds title to the merchandise until the payments have been completed and can take possession of the item if the bill is unpaid.

The three most common types of closed-end credit are installment sales credit, installment cash credit, and single lump-sum credit. *Installment sales credit* is a loan that allows you to receive merchandise, usually high-priced items such as large appliances or furniture. You make a down payment and usually sign a contract to repay the balance, plus interest and service charges, in equal installments over a specified period.

Installment cash credit is a direct loan of money for personal purposes, home improvements, or vacation expenses. You make no down payment and make payments in specified amounts over a set period.

Single lump-sum credit is a loan that must be repaid in total on a specified day, usually within 30 to 90 days. Lump-sum credit is generally, but not always, used to purchase a single item. As Exhibit 5–2 shows, consumer installment credit reached a peak of over $3 trillion in 2013. This number has declined slightly since then but still remains at a very high level.

Exhibit 5–1

Examples of Closed-End and Open-End Credit

Closed-End Credit	**Open-End Credit**
• Mortgage loans • Automobile loans • Installment loans (installment sales contract, installment cash credit, single lump-sum credit)	• Cards issued by department stores, bank cards (Visa, MasterCard) • Travel and entertainment (T&E) (American Express, Diners Club) • Overdraft protection

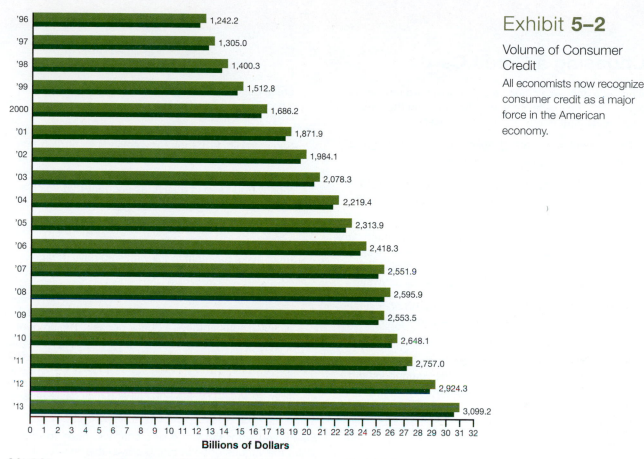

SOURCE: www.federalreserve.gov/RELEASES/g19/current, accessed April 22, 2014.

Exhibit 5–2

Volume of Consumer Credit

All economists now recognize consumer credit as a major force in the American economy.

Open-End Credit

Using a credit card issued by a department store, using a bank credit card (Visa, MasterCard) to make purchases at different stores, charging a meal at a restaurant, and using overdraft protection are examples of open-end credit. As you will soon see, you do not apply for open-end credit to make a single purchase, as you do with closed-end credit. Rather, you can use open-end credit to make any purchases you wish if you do not exceed your **line of credit,** the maximum dollar amount of credit the lender has made available to you. You may have to pay **interest,** a periodic charge for the use of credit, or other finance charges. Usually you have the option to pay the bill in full within 30 days without interest charges or to make set monthly installments based on the account balance plus interest. Some creditors allow you a grace period of 20 to 25 days to pay a bill in full before you incur any interest charges.

Many banks extend **revolving check credit.** Also called a *bank line of credit,* this is a prearranged loan for a specified amount that you can use by writing a special check. Repayment is made in installments over a set period. The finance charges are based on the amount of credit used during the month and on the outstanding balance.

Credit Cards

Credit cards are extremely popular. The average cardholder has more than nine credit cards, including bank, retail, and gasoline cards. Cardholders who pay off their balances in full each month are often known as *convenience* users. Cardholders who do not pay off their balances every month are known as *borrowers.*

Most credit card companies offer a grace period, a time period during which no finance charges will be added to your account. A **finance charge** is the total dollar amount you pay

line of credit The dollar amount, which may or may not be borrowed, that a lender makes available to a borrower.

interest A periodic charge for the use of credit.

revolving check credit A prearranged loan from a bank for a specified amount; also called a *bank line of credit.*

finance charge The total dollar amount paid to use credit.

Choosing a Credit Card

When you choose a credit card, shopping around can yield big returns. Follow these suggestions to find the card that best meets your needs and to use it wisely:

1. Department stores and gasoline companies are good places to obtain your first credit card.

2. Bank credit cards are offered through banks and savings and loan associations. Annual fees and finance charges vary widely, so shop around.

3. If you plan on paying off your balance every month, look for a card that has a grace period and carries no annual fee or a low annual fee. You might have a higher interest rate, but you plan to pay little or no interest anyway.

4. Watch out for creditors that offer low or no annual fees but instead charge a transaction fee every time you use the card.

5. If you plan to carry a balance, look for a card with a low monthly finance charge. Be sure that you understand how the finance charge is calculated.

6. To avoid delays that may result in finance charges, follow the card issuer's instructions as to where, how, and when to make bill payments.

7. Beware of offers of easy credit. No one can guarantee to get you credit.

8. If your card offers a grace period, take advantage of it by paying off your balance in full each month. With a grace period of 25 days, you actually get a free loan when you pay bills in full each month.

9. If you have a bad credit history and have trouble getting a credit card, look for a savings institution that will give you a secured credit card. With this type of card, your line of credit depends on how much money you keep in a savings account that you open at the same time.

10. Travel and entertainment cards often charge higher annual fees than most credit cards. Usually, you must make payment in full within 30 days of receiving your bill, or no further purchases will be approved on the account.

11. Be aware that debit cards are not credit cards but simply a substitute for a check or cash. The amount of the sale is subtracted from your checking account.

12. Think twice before you make a telephone call to a 900 number to request a credit card. You will pay from $2 to $50 for the 900 call and may never receive a credit card.

Before you enter the world of credit, you need to understand the various options that are available to you. Which of the preceding factors would be most important in your choice of a credit card?

SOURCES: American Institute of Certified Public Accountants, U.S. Office of Consumer Affairs, and Federal Trade Commission.

to use credit. Usually, if you pay your entire balance before the due date stated on your monthly bill, you will not have to pay a finance charge. Borrowers carry balances beyond the grace period and pay finance charges. Many credit cards offer "teaser rates." These introductory rates are good for a short period of time, typically 6 to 12 months. The rates may rise significantly after the introductory period. These should be carefully considered before transferring a balance or making significant purchases that you may not be able to repay during the introductory period.

Many credit card companies now offer reward programs that provide cash, rebates, or airline tickets. These types of cards usually have higher finance charges, and the value of the reward should be compared to the cost of the card if you do not intend to pay off the balance monthly.

The cost of a credit card depends on the type of credit card you have and the terms set forth by the lender. As a cardholder, you may have to pay interest or other finance charges. Some credit card companies charge cardholders an annual fee, usually about $40. However, many companies have eliminated annual fees in order to attract more customers. If you are looking for a credit card, be sure to shop around for one with no annual fee. The nearby "Personal Finance in Practice" box offers some other helpful hints for choosing a credit card.

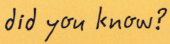

did you know?

An average household carries more than $7,000 in credit card debt.

DEBIT CARDS Don't confuse credit cards with debit cards. Although they may look alike, they're very different. A debit card electronically subtracts money from your savings or checking account to pay for goods and services. A credit card extends credit and delays your payment. Debit cards are most frequently used at automatic teller machines (ATMs). More and more, however, they are also used to purchase goods in stores and to make other types of payments.

Raquel Garcia is serious about avoiding debt. The 18-year-old customer representative for U-Haul recently canceled her credit card. Now she gets her entire paycheck deposited onto a prepaid debit card, which she uses for all her purchases. Since she can access only what's in the account, Garcia no longer worries about breaking her budget: "I'm spending just what I need."

did you know?

In 2013, an estimated 194 million debit card holders will use 580 million cards for 54 trillion transactions amounting to over $2 trillion.

SOURCE: *Statistical Abstract of the United States 2014*, Table 1211.

STORED VALUE (OR GIFT) CARDS Stored-value cards, gift cards, or pre-paid cards resemble a typical debit card, using magnetic stripe technology to store information and track funds. However, unlike traditional debit cards, stored value cards are prepaid, providing you with immediate money. Gift card sales have exploded over the last few years. The convenience factor for the gift giver is huge. It is estimated that sales of gift cards reached over $118 billion at the beginning of 2014. Substantial growth has also occurred in the area of digital gift cards. These cards are sent via e-mail to recipients, who will receive an access code to activate and use their e-cards online to make purchases.

Bankruptcy courts treat gift cards the same way they handle unsecured debt: If a retailer goes bankrupt, holders get pennies on the dollar at most—and in many cases nothing. One market research firm estimates that holders of gift cards recently lost more than $75 million when the number of retailer bankruptcies increased sharply.

SMART CARDS Some lenders are starting to offer a new kind of credit card called a smart card. A smart card is a plastic card equipped with a computer chip that can store 500 times as much data as a normal credit card. Smart cards can combine credit card balances, a driver's license, health care identification, medical history, and other information all in one place. A smart card, for example, can be used to buy an airline ticket, store it digitally, and track frequent flyer miles.

TRAVEL AND ENTERTAINMENT CARDS Travel and entertainment (T&E) cards are really not credit cards because the balance is due in full each month. However, most people think of T&E cards—such as Diners Club or American Express cards—as credit cards because they don't pay for goods or services when they purchase them.

SMARTPHONES Some phones are now equipped to make purchases. This concept, called **mobile commerce,** has seen a significant increase in interest from consumers, retailers, and finance companies. For example, some credit card companies, instead of providing a physical credit card, provide stickers that attach to a phone that will allow the customer to scan the code. In addition, retailers such as Starbucks have apps that are scannable barcodes to quickly pay using a mobile phone.

mobile commerce The ability to purchase using a mobile device.

Sources of Consumer Credit

Many sources of consumer credit are available, including commercial banks and credit unions. Exhibit 5–3 summarizes the major sources of consumer credit. Study and compare the differences to determine which source might best meet your needs and requirements.

Loans

Loans involve borrowing money with an agreement to repay it, as well as interest, within a certain amount of time. If you were considering taking out a loan, your immediate thought might be to go to your local bank. However, you might want to explore some other options first.

Exhibit 5–3 Sources of Consumer Credit

Credit Source	Type of Loan	Lending Policies
Commercial banks	Single-payment loan Personal installment loans Passbook loans Check-credit loans Credit card loans Primary mortgages Second mortgages	• Seek customers with established credit history • Often require collateral or security • Prefer to deal in large loans, such as vehicle, home improvement, and home modernization, with the exception of credit card and check-credit plans • Determine repayment schedules according to the purpose of the loan • Vary credit rates according to the type of credit, time period, customer's credit history, and the security offered • May require several days to process a new credit application
Consumer finance companies	Personal installment loans Primary mortgages Second mortgages	• Often lend to consumers without established credit history • Often make unsecured loans • Often vary rates according to the size of the loan balance • Offer a variety of repayment schedules • Make a higher percentage of small loans than other lenders • Maximum loan size limited by law • Process applications quickly, frequently on the same day the application is made
Credit unions	Personal installment loans Share draft-credit plans Credit card loans Primary mortgages Second mortgages	• Lend to members only • Make unsecured loans • May require collateral or cosigner for loans over a specified amount • May require payroll deductions to pay off loan • May submit large loan applications to a committee of members for approval • Offer a variety of repayment schedules
Life insurance companies	Single-payment or partial-payment loans	• Lend on cash value of life insurance policy • No date or penalty on repayment • Deduct amount owed from the value of policy benefit if death or other maturity occurs before repayment
Federal savings banks (savings and loan associations)	Personal installment loans (generally permitted by state-chartered savings associations) Home improvement loans Education loans Savings account loans Primary mortgages Second mortgages	• Will lend to all creditworthy individuals • Often require collateral • Loan rates vary depending on size of loan, length of payment, and security involved

Consumer credit is available from several types of sources. Which sources seem to offer the widest variety of loans?

INEXPENSIVE LOANS Parents or other family members are often the source of the least expensive loans—loans with low interest. They may charge only interest they would have earned on the money if they had deposited it in a savings account. They may even give you a loan without interest. Be aware, however, that loans can complicate family relationships. You can borrow (or invest) money with microlending organizations, such as kiva.org. Borrowers with good credit can borrow at interest rates lower than those charged by banks and credit unions.

MEDIUM-PRICED LOANS Often you can obtain medium-priced loans—loans with moderate interest—from commercial banks, savings and loan associations, and credit unions. Borrowing from credit unions has several advantages. They provide personalized service, and usually they're willing to be patient with borrowers who can provide good reasons for late or missed payments. However, you must be a member of a credit union in order to get a loan.

EXPENSIVE LOANS The easiest loans to obtain are also the most expensive. Finance companies and retail stores that lend to consumers will frequently charge high interest rates, ranging from 12 to 25 percent. Banks also lend money to their credit card holders through cash advances—loans that are billed to the customer's credit card account. Most cards charge higher interest for a cash advance and charge interest from the day the cash advance is made. As a result, taking out a cash advance is much more expensive than charging a purchase to a credit card. Read the nearby "Figure It Out!" box to learn why you should avoid such cash advances.

HOME EQUITY LOANS A home equity loan is a loan based on your home equity—the difference between the current market value of your home and the amount you still owe on the mortgage.

EXAMPLE: Home Equity Loans

Depending on your income and the equity in your home, you can apply for a line of credit for anywhere from $10,000 to $250,000 or more.

Some lenders let you borrow only up to 75 percent of the value of your home, less the amount of your first mortgage. At some banks you may qualify to borrow up to 85 percent! This higher lending limit may make the difference in your ability to get the money you need for home improvements, education, or other expenses.

Use the following chart to calculate your home loan value, which is the approximate amount of your home equity line of credit.

	Example	Your Home
Approximate market value of your home	$100,000	$ _____
Multiply by 0.75	× 0.75	× 0.75
Approximate loan value	75,000	_____
Subtract balance due on mortgage(s)	50,000	_____
Approximate credit limit available	$ 25,000	$ _____

Figure It Out!

Cash Advances

A cash advance is a loan billed to your credit card. You can obtain a cash advance with your credit card at a bank or an automated teller machine (ATM) or by using checks linked to your credit card account.

Most cards charge a special fee when a cash advance is taken out. The fee is based on a percentage of the amount borrowed, usually about 2 or 3 percent.

Some credit cards charge a minimum cash advance fee, as high as $5. You could get $20 in cash and be charged $5, a fee equal to 25 percent of the amount you borrowed.

Most cards do not have a grace period on cash advances. This means you pay interest every day until you repay the cash advance, even if you do not have an outstanding balance from the previous statement.

On some cards, the interest rate on cash advances is higher than the rate on purchases. Be sure you check the details on the contract sent to you by the card issuer.

Here is an example of charges that could be imposed for a $300 cash advance that you pay off when the bill arrives:

Cash advance fee = $6 (2% of $300)

Interest for one month = $5 (20% APR on $300)

Total cost for one month = $11($6 + $5)

In comparison, a $300 purchase on a card with a grace period could cost $0 if paid off promptly in full.

The bottom line: It is usually much more expensive to take out a cash advance than to charge a purchase to your credit card. Use cash advances only for real emergencies.

Unlike interest on most other types of credit, the interest you pay on a home equity loan is tax-deductible. You should use these loans only for major items such as education, home improvements, or medical bills, and you must use them with care. If you miss payments on a home equity loan, the lender can take your home.

PRACTICE QUIZ 5–2

1. What are two types of consumer credit?

2. Define the following key terms:

   a. Closed-end credit
   b. Open-end credit
   c. Line of credit
   d. Interest
   e. Finance charge

3. What are the major sources of:

   a. Inexpensive loans
   b. Medium-priced loans
   c. Expensive loans

4. What is the difference between a credit and a debit card?

Apply Yourself!

Research three credit cards. List their fees and any advantages they offer. Record your findings.

Visit www.creditcards.com and www.bankrate.com for more information.

Applying for Credit

Can You Afford a Loan?

The only way to determine how much credit you can assume is to first learn how to make an accurate and sensible personal or family budget (see Chapter 2).

Before you take out a loan, ask yourself whether you can meet all of your essential expenses and still afford the monthly loan payments. You can make this calculation in two ways. One is to add up all your basic monthly expenses and then subtract this total from your take-home pay. If the difference will not cover the monthly payment and still leave funds for other expenses, you cannot afford the loan.

A second and more reliable method is to ask yourself what you plan to give up to make the monthly loan payment. If you currently save a portion of your income that is greater than the monthly payment, you can use these savings to pay off the loan. But if you do not, you will have to forgo spending on entertainment, new appliances, or perhaps even necessities. Are you prepared to make this trade-off? Although precisely measuring your credit capacity is difficult, you can follow certain rules of thumb.

General Rules of Credit Capacity

DEBT PAYMENTS-TO-INCOME RATIO The debt payments-to-income ratio is calculated by dividing your monthly debt payments (not including house payment, which is a long-term liability) by your net monthly income. Experts suggest that you spend no more than 20 percent of your net (after-tax) income on consumer credit payments. Thus, as Exhibit 5–4 shows, a person making $1,250 per month after taxes should spend no more than $250 on credit payments per month.

The 20 percent is the maximum; however, 15 percent or less is much better. The 20 percent estimate is based on the average family, with average expenses; it does not take major emergencies into account. If you are just beginning to use credit, you should not consider yourself safe if you are spending 20 percent of your net income on credit payments.

DEBT-TO-EQUITY RATIO The debt-to-equity ratio is calculated by dividing your total liabilities by your net worth. In calculating this ratio, do not include the value of your home and the amount of its mortgage. If your debt-to-equity ratio is about 1—that is, if your consumer installment debt roughly equals your net worth (not including your home or the mortgage)—you have probably reached the upper limit of debt obligations.

None of the above methods is perfect for everyone; the limits given are only guidelines. Only you, based on the money you earn, your obligations, and your financial plans for the future, can determine the exact amount of credit you need and can afford. You must be your own credit manager.

The Five Cs of Credit

When you're ready to apply for a loan or a credit card, you should understand the factors that determine whether a lender will extend credit to you.

When a lender extends credit to consumers, it takes for granted that some people will be unable or unwilling to pay their debts. Therefore, lenders establish policies for determining

LO5.3

Determine whether you can afford a loan and how to apply for credit.

ACTION ITEM

If I want to see a copy of my credit report, I can contact:

☐ **a credit reporting agency.**

☐ **a bank.**

☐ **the dean of my college.**

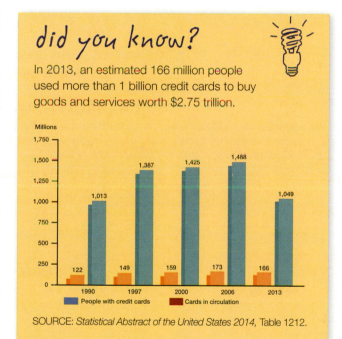

did you know?

In 2013, an estimated 166 million people used more than 1 billion credit cards to buy goods and services worth $2.75 trillion.

SOURCE: *Statistical Abstract of the United States 2014*, Table 1212.

Exhibit 5–4

How to Calculate Debt Payments-to-Income Ratio

Spend no more than 20 percent of your net (after-tax) income on credit payments

Monthly gross income	$1,682
Less:	
All taxes	270
Social Security	112
Monthly IRA contribution	50
Monthly net income	$1,250
Monthly installment credit payments:	
Visa	25
MasterCard	35
Discover card	15
Education loan	—
Personal bank loan	—
Auto loan	175
Total monthly payments	$ 250
Debt payments-to-income ratio ($250/$1,250)	20.00%

who will receive credit. Most lenders build such policies around the "five Cs of credit": character, capacity, capital, collateral, and conditions.

CHARACTER: WILL YOU REPAY THE LOAN? Creditors want to know your **character**—what kind of person they are lending money to. They want to know that you're trustworthy and stable. They may ask for personal or professional references, and they may check to see whether you have a history of trouble with the law. Some questions a lender might ask to determine your character are:

- Have you used credit before?
- How long have you lived at your present address?
- How long have you held your current job?

character The borrower's attitude toward his or her credit obligations.

CAPACITY: CAN YOU REPAY THE LOAN? Your income and the debts you already have will affect your **capacity**—your ability to pay additional debts. If you already have a large amount of debt in proportion to your income, lenders probably won't extend more credit to you. Some questions a creditor may ask about your income and expenses are:

- What is your job, and how much is your salary?
- Do you have other sources of income?
- What are your current debts?

capacity The borrower's financial ability to meet credit obligations.

CAPITAL: WHAT ARE YOUR ASSETS AND NET WORTH? Assets are any items of value that you own, including cash, property, personal possessions, and investments. Your **capital** is the amount of your assets that exceed your liabilities, or the debts you owe. Lenders want to be sure that you have enough capital to pay back a loan. That way, if you lost your source of income, you could repay your loan from your savings or by selling some of your assets. A lender might ask:

- What are your assets?
- What are your liabilities?

capital The borrower's assets or net worth.

COLLATERAL: WHAT IF YOU DON'T REPAY THE LOAN? Creditors look at what kinds of property or savings you already have, because these can be offered as **collateral** to secure the loan. If you fail to repay the loan, the creditor may take whatever you pledged as collateral. A creditor might ask:

- What assets do you have to secure the loan (such as a vehicle, your home, or furniture)?
- Do you have any other valuable assets (such as bonds or savings)?

collateral A valuable asset that is pledged to ensure loan payments.

CONDITIONS: WHAT IF YOUR JOB IS INSECURE? General economic **conditions,** such as unemployment and recession, can affect your ability to repay a loan. The basic question focuses on security—of both your job and the firm that employs you.

conditions The general economic conditions that can affect a borrower's ability to repay a loan.

The information gathered from your application and the credit bureau establishes your credit rating. A *credit rating* is a measure of a person's ability and willingness to make credit payments on time. The factors that determine a person's credit rating are income, current debt, information about character, and how debts have been repaid in the past. If you always make your payments on time, you will probably have an excellent credit rating. If not, your credit rating will be poor, and a lender probably won't extend credit to you. A good credit rating is a valuable asset that you should protect.

Creditors use different combinations of the five Cs to reach their decisions. Some creditors set unusually high standards, and others simply do not offer certain types of loans. Creditors also use various rating systems. Some rely strictly on their own instincts and experience. Others use a credit scoring or statistical system to predict whether an applicant is a good credit risk. When you apply for a loan, the lender is likely to evaluate your application by asking questions such as those included in the checklist in the nearby "Personal Finance in Practice" box.

Your Credit Report

When you apply for a loan, the lender will review your credit history very closely. The record of your complete credit history is called your *credit report,* or *credit file.* Your credit records are collected and maintained by credit bureaus. Most lenders rely heavily on credit reports when they consider loan applications. Exhibit 5–5 provides a checklist for building and protecting your credit history.

CREDIT BUREAUS A credit bureau is an agency that collects information on how promptly people and businesses pay their bills. The three major credit bureaus are Experian, TransUnion, and Equifax. Each of these bureaus maintains more than 200 million credit files on individuals, based on information they receive from lenders. Several thousand smaller credit bureaus also collect credit information about consumers. These firms make money by selling the information they collect to creditors who are considering loan applications.

Credit bureaus get their information from banks, finance companies, stores, credit card companies, and other lenders. These sources regularly transmit information about the types of credit they extend to customers, the amounts and terms of the loans, and the customers' payment habits. Credit bureaus also collect some information from other sources, such as court records.

WHAT'S IN YOUR CREDIT FILES? A typical credit bureau file contains your name, address, Social Security number, and birth date. It may also include the following information:

- Your employer, position, and income
- Your previous address

Exhibit 5–5

Checklist for Building and Protecting Your Credit History

It is simple and sensible to build and protect your own credit history. Here are some steps to get you started:

- Open a checking or savings account, or both.
- Apply for a local department store credit card.
- Take out a small loan from your bank. Make payments on time.

A Creditor Must . . .	Remember That a Creditor Cannot . . .
1. Evaluate all applicants on the same basis.	1. Refuse you individual credit in your own name if you are creditworthy.
2. Consider income from part-time employment.	2. Require your spouse to cosign a loan. Any creditworthy person can be your cosigner if one is required.
3. Consider the payment history of all joint accounts, if this accurately reflects your credit history.	3. Ask about your family plans or assume that your income will be interrupted to have children.
4. Disregard information on accounts if you can prove that it doesn't affect your ability or willingness to repay.	4. Consider whether you have a telephone listing in your name.

If you want a good credit rating, you must use credit wisely. Why is it a good idea to apply for a local department store credit card or a small loan from your bank?

SOURCE: Reprinted by permission of the Federal Reserve Bank of Minneapolis.

CAUTION!

Are you impatient? Researchers have discovered a link between credit scores and impatience. This can lead to more stress.

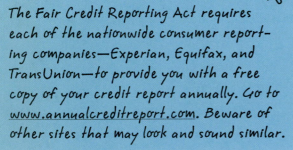

digi – know?

The Fair Credit Reporting Act requires each of the nationwide consumer reporting companies—Experian, Equifax, and TransUnion—to provide you with a free copy of your credit report annually. Go to www.annualcreditreport.com. Beware of other sites that may look and sound similar.

- Your previous employer
- Your spouse's name, Social Security number, employer, and income
- Whether you rent or own your home
- Checks returned for insufficient funds

In addition, your credit file contains detailed credit information. Each time you use credit to make a purchase or take out a loan of any kind, a credit bureau is informed of your account number and the date, amount, terms, and type of credit. Your file is updated regularly to show how many payments you've made, how many payments were late or missed, and how much you owe. Any lawsuits or judgments against you may appear as well. Federal law protects your rights if the information in your credit file is incorrect.

FAIR CREDIT REPORTING Fair and accurate credit reporting is vital to both creditors and consumers. In 1971 the U.S. Congress enacted the Fair Credit Reporting Act, which regulates the use of credit reports. This law requires the deletion of out-of-date information and gives consumers access to their files as well as the right to correct any misinformation that the files may include. The act also places limits on who can obtain your credit report.

WHO CAN OBTAIN A CREDIT REPORT? Your credit report may be issued only to properly identified persons for approved purposes. It may be supplied in response to a court order or by your own written request. A credit report may also be provided for use in connection with a credit transaction, underwriting of insurance, or some legitimate business need. Friends, neighbors, and other individuals cannot be given access to credit information about you. In fact, if they even request such information, they may be subject to a fine, imprisonment, or both.

TIME LIMITS ON UNFAVORABLE DATA Most of the information in your credit file may be reported for only seven years. However, if you've declared personal bankruptcy, that fact may be reported for 10 years. A credit reporting agency can't disclose information in your credit file that's more than 7 or 10 years old unless you're being reviewed for a credit application of $75,000 or more, or unless you apply to purchase life insurance of $150,000 or more.

INCORRECT INFORMATION IN YOUR CREDIT FILE Credit bureaus are required to follow reasonable procedures to ensure that the information in their files is correct. Mistakes can and do occur, however. If you think that a credit bureau may be reporting incorrect data from your file, contact the bureau to dispute the information. The credit bureau must check its records and change or remove the incorrect items. If you challenge the accuracy of an item on your credit report, the bureau must remove the item unless the lender can verify that the information is accurate.

If you are denied credit, insurance, employment, or rental housing based on the information in a credit report, you can get a free copy of your report. Remember to request it within 60 days of notification that your application has been denied.

WHAT ARE YOUR LEGAL RIGHTS? You have legal rights to sue a credit bureau or creditor that has caused you harm by not following the rules established by the Fair Credit Reporting Act.

Credit Scores

A credit score is a number that reflects the information in your credit report. The score summarizes your credit history and helps creditors predict how likely it is that you will repay a loan and make timely payments. Lenders use credit scores in deciding whether to grant you credit, what terms are offered, or the interest rate you will pay on a loan.

Information used to calculate your credit score usually includes the following:

- The number and type of account you have (credit cards, auto loans, mortgages, etc.);
- Whether you pay your bills on time;
- How much of your available credit you are currently using;
- Whether you have any collection actions against you;
- The amount of your outstanding debt; and
- The age of your accounts.

FICO AND VANTAGESCORE Typical questions in a credit application appear in Exhibit 5–6. The information in your credit report is used to calculate your FICO credit score—a number generally between 350 and 850 that rates how risky a borrower is. The higher the score, the less risk you pose to creditors. Your FICO score is available from www.myfico.com for a fee. Free credit reports do not provide your credit score.

According to Anthony Sprauve, senior consumer credit specialist at FICO, "The consequences of not maintaining a sound credit score can be very costly. A low score can bar you from getting a new loan, doom you to a higher interest rate and even cost you a new job or apartment." Exhibit 5–7 shows a numerical depiction of your creditworthiness and how you can improve your credit score.

did you know?

WHAT'S IN YOUR FICO® SCORE?
The data from your credit report is generally grouped into five categories. The percentages in the pie diagram reflect how important each of the categories is in determining your FICO® score.

Pie chart categories:
- 15% Length of credit history
- 35% Payment history
- 30% Amounts owed
- 10% Types of credit used
- 10% New credit

SOURCE: "How Your FICO Credit Score Is Calculated," FICO website at http://www.myfico.com/CreditEducation/. This information is provided by the Fair Isaac Corporation and is used with permission. Copyright © 2001–2013 Fair Isaac Corporation. All rights reserved. FICO is a trademark of Fair Isaac Corporation. Further use, reproduction, or distribution is governed by the FICO Copyright Usage Requirements, which can be found at www.fico.com

Exhibit 5–6

Sample Credit
Application Questions

- Amount of loan requested.
- Proposed use of the loan.
- Your name and birth date.
- Social Security and driver's license numbers.
- Present and previous street addresses.
- Present and previous employers and their addresses.
- Present salary.
- Number and ages of dependents.
- Other income and sources of other income.

- Have you ever received credit from us?
- If so, when and at which office?
- Checking account number, institution, and branch.
- Savings account number, institution, and branch.
- Name of nearest relative not living with you.
- Relative's address and telephone number.
- Your marital status.
- Information regarding joint applicant: same questions as above.

VantageScore is a new scoring technique, the first to be developed collaboratively by the three credit reporting companies. This model allows for a more predictive score for consumers, even for those with limited credit histories, reducing the need for creditors to manually review credit information. VantageScore features a common score range of 501–990 (higher scores represent lower likelihood of risk). A key benefit of VantageScore is that as long as the three major credit bureaus have the same information regarding your credit history, you will receive the same score from each of them. A different score alerts you that there are discrepancies in your report.

Some consumers have very little recorded credit. They may not have credit cards or car or home loans, but they have consistently paid their rent, phone, and utility bills. There is an alternative way to provide a consistent payment record. The Payment Reporting Builds Credit (PRBC) system will check on payment patterns and report to a creditor the history of payments that are typically not included on a traditional credit report.

Exhibit 5–7 TransUnion Personal Credit Score

The higher your FICO score, the less risk you pose to creditors.

You can purchase your credit score for $7.95 by calling 1-866-SCORE-TU or 1-866-726-7388.

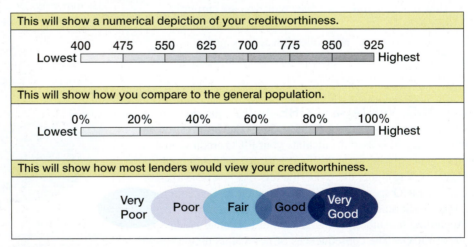

- **How can I improve my credit score?**
A credit score is a snapshot of the contents of your credit report at the time it is calculated. The first step in improving your score is to review your credit report to ensure it is accurate. Long-term, responsible credit behavior is the most effective way to improve future scores. Pay all bills, as well as parking, traffic, and even library fines, on time, lower balances, and use credit wisely to improve your score over time.

You should also know what factors a lender cannot consider, according to the law. The *Equal Credit Opportunity Act* (ECOA) gives all credit applicants the same basic rights. It states that race, nationality, age, sex, marital status, and certain other factors may not be used to discriminate against you in any part of a credit dealing.

Other Factors Considered in Determining Creditworthiness

AGE The Equal Credit Opportunity Act is very specific about how a person's age may be used as a factor in credit decisions. A creditor may request that you state your age on an application, but if you're old enough to sign a legal contract (usually 18–21 years old, depending on state law), a creditor may not turn you down or decrease your credit because of your age. Creditors may not close your credit account because you reach a certain age or retire.

PUBLIC ASSISTANCE You may not be denied credit because you receive Social Security or public assistance. However, certain information related to this source of income can be considered in determining your creditworthiness.

HOUSING LOANS The ECOA also covers applications for mortgages or home improvement loans. In particular, it bans discrimination against you based on the race or nationality of the people in the neighborhood where you live or want to buy your home, a practice called *redlining*.

WHAT IS THE BEST INTEREST RATE? Effective January 1, 2011, lenders that provide mortgages, credit cards, auto loans, and most other financial products must disclose important details to their customers if they utilize risk-based pricing. Risk-based pricing seeks to differentiate consumers based on their credit information and charge higher rates for more risky customers. Customers who do not receive the best possible (or preferred rate) must be informed of their current credit score or the fact that risk-based pricing was used and the fact that other customers received better rates. Customers may also be entitled to be told what the negative factors were as well as be provided with a scale of their ranking based upon credit score. This may allow customers an opportunity to review their credit report and ensure accuracy prior to paying an unnecessarily higher interest rate.

What If Your Application Is Denied?

If your credit application is denied, the ECOA gives you the right to know the reasons. If the denial is based on a credit report from the credit bureau, you're entitled to know the specific information in the report that led to the denial. After you receive this information, you can contact the credit bureau and ask for a copy of your credit report. The bureau cannot charge a fee for this service as long as you ask to see your files within 60 days of notification that your credit application has been denied. You're entitled to ask the bureau to investigate any inaccurate or incomplete information and correct its records (see Exhibit 5–8).

Personal Finance in Practice

The Five Cs of Credit

Here is what lenders look for in determining your credit-worthiness.

CREDIT HISTORY

1. Character: Will you repay the loan?   Yes   No

Do you have a good attitude toward
credit obligations?   _____   _____

Have you used credit before?   _____   _____

Do you pay your bills on time?   _____   _____

Have you ever filed for bankruptcy?   _____   _____

Do you live within your means?   _____   _____

STABILITY

How long have you lived at your
present address?   _____ yrs.

Do you own your home?   _____

How long have you been employed
by your present employer?   _____ yrs.

INCOME

2. Capacity: Can you repay the loan?

Your salary and occupation? $_____; _____

Place of occupation?   _____

How reliable is your
income?   Reliable _____;   Not reliable _____

Any other sources of income? $_____

EXPENSES
Number of dependents?   _____

Do you pay any alimony or
child support?   Yes _____; No _____

Current debts? $_____

NET WORTH

3. Capital: What are your assets and net worth?

What are your assets? $_____

What are your liabilities? $_____

What is your net worth? $_____

LOAN SECURITY

4. Collateral: What if you don't repay the loan?

What assets do you have to secure
the loan? (Car, home, furniture?)   _____

What sources do you have besides
income? (Savings, stocks, bonds,
insurance?)   _____

JOB SECURITY

**5. Conditions: What general economic conditions can
affect your repayment of the loan?**

How secure is
your job?   Secure _____; Not secure _____

How secure is the
firm you work for?   Secure _____; Not secure _____

SOURCE: Adapted from William M. Pride, Robert J. Hughes, and Jack R. Kapoor, *Business,* 11th ed., 2012 (Mason, OH: South-Western Cengage Learning, 2010), pages 555–557.

What Can You Do to Improve Your Credit Score?

A credit score is a snapshot of the contents of your credit report at the time it is calculated. The first step in improving your score is to review your credit report to ensure it is accurate. Long-term responsible credit behavior is the most effective way to improve future scores. Pay bills on time, lower balances, and use credit wisely to improve your score over time.

1. **Get copies of your credit report—then make sure information is correct.** Go to www.annualcreditreport.com. This is the only authorized online source for a free credit report. Under federal law, you can get a free report from each of the three national credit reporting companies every 12 months. You can also call 877-322-8228 or complete the *Annual Credit Report Request Form* and mail it to Annual Credit Report Request Service, P.O. Box 105281, Atlanta, GA 30348-5281.

Exhibit **5–8**   What If You Are Denied Credit?

Steps you can take if you are denied credit

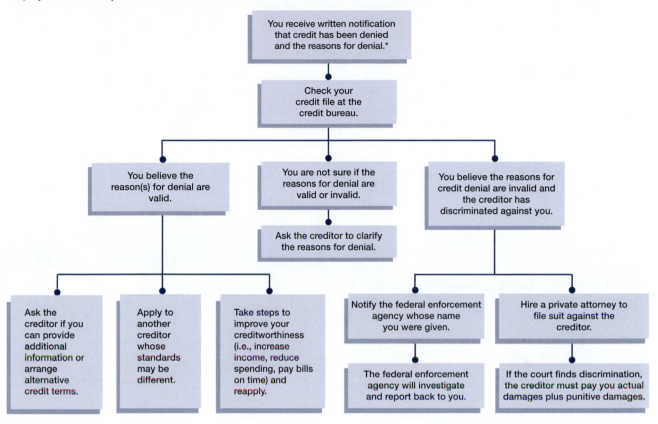

*If a creditor receives no more than 150 applications during a calendar year, the disclosures may be oral.

SOURCE: Reprinted courtesy of Office of Public Information, Federal Reserve Bank of Minneapolis, Minneapolis, MN 55480.

2. **Pay your bills on time.** One of the most important steps you can take to improve your credit score is to pay your bills by the due date. You can set up automatic payments from your bank account to help you pay on time, but be sure you have enough money in your account to avoid overdraft fees.

3. **Understand how your credit score is determined.** Your credit score is usually based on the answers to these questions.

   - **Do you pay your bills on time?** The answer to this question is very important. If you have paid bills late, had an account referred to a collection agency, or have ever declared bankruptcy, this history will show up in your credit report.
   - **What is your outstanding debt?** Many scoring models compare the amount of debt you have and your credit limits. If the amount you owe is close to your credit limit, it is likely to have a negative effect on your score.
   - **How long is your credit history?** A short credit history may have a negative effect on your score, but a short history can be offset by other factors, such as timely payments and low balances.
   - **Have you applied for new credit recently?** If you have applied for too many new accounts recently, that may negatively affect your score. However, if you request a copy of your own credit report, or if creditors are monitoring your account or looking at credit reports to make prescreened credit offers, these inquiries about your credit history are not counted as applications for credit.

- **How many and what types of credit accounts do you have?** Many credit-scoring models consider the number and type of credit accounts you have. A mix of installment loans and credit cards may improve your score. However, too many finance company accounts or credit cards might hurt your score. To learn more about credit scoring, see the Federal Trade Commission's website, *Facts for Consumers,* at www.ftc.gov.

4. **Learn the legal steps to take to improve your credit report.** The Federal Trade Commission's *Building a Better Credit Report* has information on correcting errors in your report, tips on dealing with debt and avoiding scams—and more.

5. **Beware of credit-repair scams.** Sometimes doing it yourself is the best way to repair your credit. The Federal Trade Commission's *Credit Repair: How to Help Yourself* explains how you can improve your creditworthiness and lists legitimate resources for low-cost or no-cost help.

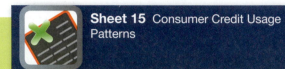

Sheet 15 Consumer Credit Usage Patterns

PRACTICE QUIZ 5-3

1. What are the two general rules of measuring credit capacity? How is it calculated?

2. Define the following key terms:

    a. character
    b. capacity
    c. capital
    d. collateral
    e. conditions

3. What are the factors a lender cannot consider according to the law when offering credit?

4. What is a credit bureau?

5. Write the steps you should take if you are denied credit.

Apply Yourself!

Talk to a person who has discovered an error on his or her credit report. What was their experience to get it corrected?

LO5.4

Determine the cost of credit by calculating interest using various interest formulas.

ACTION ITEM

If I know the finance charge and the annual percentage rate, I can compare credit prices.

☐ **Always**

☐ **Most of the time**

☐ **Sometimes**

The Cost of Credit

If you are thinking of borrowing money or opening a credit account, your first step should be to figure out how much it will cost you and whether you can afford it. Then you should shop for the best terms. Two key concepts that you should remember are the finance charge and the annual percentage rate.

Finance Charge and Annual Percentage Rate

Credit costs vary. If you know the finance charge and the annual percentage rate, you can compare credit prices from different sources. The *finance charge* is the total dollar amount you pay to use credit. It includes interest costs and sometimes other costs such as service charges, credit-related insurance premiums, or appraisal fees.

For example, borrowing $100 for a year might cost you $10 in interest. If there is also a service charge of $1, the finance charge will be $11. The **annual percentage rate (APR)** is the percentage cost (or relative cost) of credit on a yearly basis. The APR is your key to comparing costs, regardless of the amount of credit or how much time you have to repay it.

Suppose you borrow $100 for one year and pay a finance charge of $10. If you can keep the entire $100 for one year and then pay it all back at once, you are paying an APR of 10 percent.

annual percentage rate (APR) The percentage cost (or relative cost) of credit on a yearly basis. The APR yields a true rate of interest for comparisons with other sources of credit.

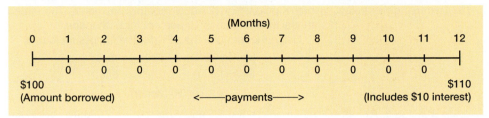

On average, you had full use of $100 throughout the year. To calculate the average use, add the loan balance during the first and last month, and then divide by 2:

$$\text{Average balance} = \frac{\$100 + \$100}{2} = \$100$$

But if you repay the $100 and the finance charge (a total of $110) in 12 equal monthly payments, you don't get use of $100 for the whole year. In fact, as shown next, you get use of increasingly less of that $100 each month. In this case, the $10 charge for credit amounts to an APR of 18.5 percent.

Amount Borrowed	Month Number	Payment Made	Loan Balance
$100	1	$ 0	$100.00
	2	8.33	91.67
	3	8.33	83.34
	4	8.33	75.01
	5	8.33	66.68
	6	8.33	58.35
	7	8.33	50.02
	8	8.33	41.69
	9	8.33	33.36
	10	8.33	25.03
	11	8.33	16.70
	12	8.33	8.37

Note that you are paying 10 percent interest even though you had use of only $91.67 during the second month, not $100. During the last month, you owed only $8.37 (and had use of $8.37), but the $10 interest is for the entire $100. As calculated in the previous example, the average use of the money during the year is $100 + $8.37 ÷ 2, or $54.18. The nearby "Figure It Out!" box shows how to calculate the APR.

Tackling the Trade-Offs

When you choose your financing, there are trade-offs between the features you prefer (term, size of payments, fixed or variable interest, or payment plan) and the cost of your loan. Here are some major trade-offs you should consider.

Figure It Out!

The Arithmetic of the Annual Percentage Rate (APR)

There are two ways to calculate the APR: using an APR formula and using the APR tables. The APR tables are more precise than the formula. The formula, given below, only approximates the APR:

$$r = \frac{2 \times n \times I}{P(N + 1)}$$

where

  r = Approximate APR

  n = Number of payment periods in one year (12, if payments are monthly; 52, if weekly)

  I = Total dollar cost of credit

  P = Principal, or net amount of loan

  N = Total number of payments scheduled to pay off the loan

Let us compare the APR when a $100 loan is paid off in one lump sum at the end of the year and when the same loan is paid off in 12 equal monthly payments. The stated annual interest rate is 10 percent for both loans.

Using the formula, the APR for the lump-sum loan is

$$r = \frac{2 \times 1 \times \$10}{\$100(1 + 1)} = \frac{\$20}{\$100(2)} = \frac{\$20}{\$200} = 0.10,$$

or 10 percent

Using the formula, the APR for the monthly payment loan is

$$r = \frac{2 \times 12 \times \$10}{\$100(12 + 1)} = \frac{\$240}{\$100(13)} = \frac{\$240}{\$1,300}$$

$$= 0.1846, \text{ or } 18.46 \text{ percent (rounded to } 18.5 \text{ percent)}$$

TERM VERSUS INTEREST COSTS Many people choose longer-term financing because they want smaller monthly payments, but the longer the term for a loan at a given interest rate, the greater the amount you must pay in interest charges. Consider the following analysis of the relationship between the term and interest costs.

Suppose you're buying a $10,000 used car. You put $2,000 down, and you need to borrow $8,000. Compare the following four credit arrangements:

	APR	Length of Loan	Monthly Payment	Total Finance Charge	Total Cost
Creditor A	5%	3 years	$240	$ 632	$8,632
Creditor B	5	4 years	184	843	8,843
Creditor C	6	4 years	188	1,018	9,018
Creditor D	6	5 years	155	1,280	9,280

How do these choices compare? The answer depends partly on what you need. The lowest-cost loan is available from creditor A. If you are looking for lower monthly payments, you could repay the loan over a longer period of time. However, you would have to pay more in total costs. A loan from creditor B—also at a 5 percent APR, but for four years—would add about $211 to your finance charge.

If that four-year loan were available only from creditor C, the APR of 6 percent would add another $175 to your finance charges. The lowest payment—but the most costly— would be the five-year loan. Other terms, such as the size of the down payment, will also make a difference. Be sure to look at all the terms before you make your choice.

LENDER RISK VERSUS INTEREST RATE You may prefer financing that requires low fixed payments with a large final payment or only a minimum of up-front cash. But both of these requirements can increase your cost of borrowing because they create more risk for your lender.

If you want to minimize your borrowing costs, you may need to accept conditions that reduce your lender's risk. Here are a few possibilities:

- *Variable interest rate.* A variable interest rate is based on fluctuating rates in the banking system, such as the prime rate. With this type of loan, you share the interest rate risks with the lender. Therefore, the lender may offer you a lower initial interest rate than it would with a fixed-rate loan.
- *A secured loan.* If you pledge property or other assets as collateral, you'll probably receive a lower interest rate on your loan.
- *Up-front cash.* Many lenders believe you have a higher stake in repaying a loan if you pay cash for a large portion of what you are financing. Doing so may give you a better chance of getting the other terms you want.
- *A shorter term.* As you have learned, the shorter the period of time for which you borrow, the smaller the chance that something will prevent you from repaying and the lower the risk to the lender. Therefore, you may be able to borrow at a lower interest rate if you accept a shorter-term loan, but your payments will be higher.

Calculating the Cost of Credit

The most common method of calculating interest is the simple interest formula. Other methods, such as simple interest on the declining balance and add-on interest, are variations of this formula.

SIMPLE INTEREST **Simple interest** is the interest computed on principal only and without compounding; it is the dollar cost of borrowing money. This cost is based on three elements: the amount borrowed, which is called the *principal;* the rate of interest; and the amount of time for which the principal is borrowed.

simple interest Interest computed on principal only and without compounding.

You can use the following formula to find simple interest:

$$\text{Interest} = \text{Principal} \times \text{Rate of interest} \times \text{Time}$$

or

$$I = P \times r \times T$$

EXAMPLE: Using the Simple Interest Formula

Suppose you have persuaded a relative to lend you $1,000 to purchase a laptop computer. Your relative agreed to charge only 5 percent interest, and you agreed to repay the loan at the end of one year. Using the simple interest formula, the interest will be 5 percent of $1,000 for one year, or $50, since you have the use of $1,000 for the entire year:

$$I = \$1,000 \times 0.05 \times 1$$
$$= \$50$$

Using the APR formula discussed earlier,

$$\text{APR} = \frac{2 \times n \times I}{P(N+1)} = \frac{2 \times 1 \times \$50}{\$1,000(1+1)} = \frac{\$100}{\$2,000} = 0.05, \text{ or 5 percent}$$

Note that the stated rate, 5 percent, is also the annual percentage rate.

SIMPLE INTEREST ON THE DECLINING BALANCE When simple interest is paid back in more than one payment, the method of computing interest is known as the declining balance method. You pay interest only on the amount of principal that you have not yet repaid. The more often you make payments, the lower the interest you'll pay. Most credit unions use this method.

EXAMPLE: Using the Simple Interest Formula on the Declining Balance

Using simple interest on the declining balance to compute interest charges, the interest on a 5 percent, $1,000 loan repaid in two payments, one at the end of the first half-year and another at the end of the second half-year, would be $37.50, as follows:
First payment:

$$I = P \times r \times T$$
$$= \$1,000 \times 0.05 \times 1/2$$
$$= \$25 \text{ interest plus } \$500, \text{ or } \$525$$

Second payment:

$$I = P \times r \times T$$
$$= \$500 \times 0.05 \times 1/2$$
$$= \$12.50 \text{ interest plus the remaining balance of } \$500, \text{ or } \$512.50$$

Total payment on the loan:

$$\$525 + \$512.50 = \$1,037.50$$

Using the APR formula,

$$\text{APR} = \frac{2 \times n \times I}{P(N + 1)} = \frac{2 \times 2 \times \$37.50}{\$1,000(2 + 1)} = \frac{\$150}{\$3,000} = 0.05, \text{ or 5 percent}$$

ADD-ON INTEREST With the add-on interest method, interest is calculated on the full amount of the original principal, no matter how frequently you make payments. When you pay off the loan with one payment, this method produces the same annual percentage rate (APR) as the simple interest method. However, if you pay in installments, your actual rate of interest will be higher than the stated rate. Interest payments on this type of loan do not decrease as the loan is repaid. The longer you take to repay the loan, the more interest you'll pay.

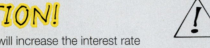

CAUTION!

Many banks will increase the interest rate because of one late payment. They'll also slap on a penalty fee, which can run as high as $50 a pop.

COST OF OPEN-END CREDIT The Truth in Lending Act requires that open-end creditors inform consumers as to how the finance charge and the APR will affect their costs. For example, they must explain how they calculate the finance charge. They must also inform you when finance charges on your credit account begin to accrue, so that you know how much time you have to pay your bills before a finance charge is added.

COST OF CREDIT AND EXPECTED INFLATION Inflation reduces the buying power of money. Each percentage point increase in inflation means a decrease of about 1 percent in the quantity of goods and services you can buy with the same amount of money. Because of this, lenders incorporate the expected rate of inflation when deciding how much interest to charge.

Remember the earlier example in which you borrowed $1,000 from your aunt at the bargain rate of 5 percent for one year? If the inflation rate was 4 percent that year, your aunt's actual rate of return on the loan would have been only 1 percent (5 percent stated interest minus 4 percent inflation rate). A professional lender who wanted to receive 5 percent interest on your loan might have charged you 9 percent interest (5 percent interest plus 4 percent anticipated inflation rate).

AVOID THE MINIMUM MONTHLY PAYMENT TRAP On credit card bills and with certain other forms of credit, the *minimum monthly payment* is the smallest amount you can pay and remain a borrower in good standing. Lenders often encourage you to make the minimum payment because it will then take you longer to pay off the loan. However, if you are paying only the minimum amount on your monthly statement, you need to plan your budget more carefully. The longer it takes for you to pay off a bill, the more interest you pay. The finance charges you pay on an item could end up being more than the item is worth.

Consider the following examples. In each example, the minimum payment is based on 1/36 of the outstanding balance or $20, whichever is greater.

Original Balance	Interest Rate	Years to Repay	Interest Paid	Total Interest Paid as Percentage of Original Balance
$500*	19.8%	2.5 years	$ 150	30%
$500*	12	2.5 years	78	16
$2,000**	19	22 years	4,800	240
$2,000***	19	7 years	1,120	56

*Minimum payment is 1/36 of the outstanding balance or $20, whichever is greater.
**2% minimum payment.
***4% minimum payment.

Sheet 16 Credit Card/Charge Account Comparison
Sheet 17 Consumer Loan Comparison

PRACTICE QUIZ 5-4

1. What are the two key concepts to remember when you borrow money?

2. What are the three major trade-offs you should consider as you take out a loan?

3. Using terms from the following list, complete the sentences below. Write the term you have chosen in the space provided.

   finance charge   minimum monthly payment

   annual percentage rate   add-on interest method

   simple interest

   a. The _____ is the cost of credit on a yearly basis expressed as a percentage.
   b. The total dollar amount paid to use credit is the _____.
   c. The smallest amount a borrower can pay on a credit card bill and remain a borrower in good standing is the _____.
   d. With the _____, interest is calculated on the full amount of the original principal, no matter how often you make payments.
   e. _____ is the interest computed only on the principal, the amount that you borrow.

Apply Yourself!

Use the Internet to obtain information about the costs of closed-end and open-end credit. Visit www.bankrate.com and www.lendingtree.com for more information.

LO5.5

Develop a plan to protect your credit and manage your debts.

ACTION ITEM

If I have serious credit problems, I should:

☐ **contact my creditors to explain the problems.**

☐ **contact only the most persistent creditors.**

☐ **not contact my creditors and hope they will forget about me.**

Fair Credit Billing Act (FCBA) Sets procedures for promptly correcting billing mistakes, refusing to make credit card payments on defective goods, and promptly crediting payments.

Protecting Your Credit

Have you ever received a bill for merchandise you never bought or that you returned to the store or never received? Have you ever made a payment that was not credited to your account or been charged twice for the same item? If so, you are not alone.

Billing Errors and Disputes

The **Fair Credit Billing Act (FCBA),** passed in 1975, sets procedures for promptly correcting billing mistakes, refusing to make credit card or revolving credit payments on defective goods, and promptly crediting your payments. This act is one of the main reasons why it is more advantageous to buy higher dollar value items with a credit card than a debit card. This act provides the consumer recourse against the retailer.

Follow these steps if you think that a bill is wrong or want more information about it. First notify your creditor in writing, and include any information that might support your case. (A telephone call is not sufficient and will not protect your rights.) Then pay the portion of the bill that is not in question.

Your creditor must acknowledge your letter within 30 days. Then, within two billing periods (but not longer than 90 days), the creditor must adjust your account or tell you why the bill is correct. If the creditor made a mistake, you don't have to pay any finance charges on the disputed amount. If no mistake is found, the creditor must promptly send you an explanation of the situation and a statement of what you owe, including any finance charges that may have accumulated and any minimum payments you missed while you were questioning the bill.

PROTECTING YOUR CREDIT RATING According to law, a creditor may not threaten your credit rating or do anything to damage your credit reputation while you're negotiating a billing dispute. In addition, the creditor may not take any action to collect the amount in question until your complaint has been answered.

DEFECTIVE GOODS AND SERVICES Theo used his credit card to buy a new mountain bike. When it arrived, he discovered that some of the gears didn't work properly. He tried to return it, but the store would not accept a return. He asked the store to repair or replace the bike—but still he had no luck. According to the Fair Credit Billing Act, he may tell his credit card company to stop payment for the bike because he has made a sincere attempt to resolve the problem with the store.

Identity Crisis: What to Do If Your Identity Is Stolen

"I don't remember charging those items. I've never been in that store." Maybe you never charged those goods and services, but someone else did—someone who used your name and personal information to commit fraud. When imposters use your personal information for their own purposes, they are committing a crime.

The biggest problem? You may not know that your identity has been stolen until you notice that something is wrong: You may get bills for a credit card account you never opened, or you may see charges to your account for things that you didn't purchase.

If you think that your identity has been stolen and that someone is using it to charge purchases or obtain credit in some other way, the Federal Trade Commission recommends that you take the following three actions immediately:

1. *Contact the credit bureaus.* Tell them to flag your file with a fraud alert, including a statement that creditors should call you for permission before they open any new accounts in your name.
2. *Contact the creditors.* Contact the creditors for any accounts that have been tampered with or opened fraudulently. Follow up in writing.

3. *File a police report.* Keep a copy of the police report in case your creditors need proof of the crime. If you're still having identity problems, stay alert to new instances of identity theft. You can also contact the Privacy Rights Clearinghouse. Call 1-619-298-3396.

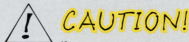

CAUTION!

If you see an error on your credit report, contact the three major credit bureaus immediately: Equifax (1-800-685-1111), Experian (1-888-397-3742), and TransUnion (1-800-916-8800).

Protecting Your Credit from Theft or Loss

Some thieves will pick through your trash in the hope of coming across your personal information. You can prevent this from happening by tearing or shredding any papers that contain personal information before you throw them out. Another tactic that an identity thief may use is *skimming.* Skimming involves the recording of the data on the magnetic strip of a credit or debit card. Thieves also target ATM machines by adding a device on the machine that will capture your PIN number. This allows them to make fake cards and have access to your account. The best way to avoid falling victim is to carefully look at the machine to see if there are extra wires, strings, or cords that should not be there. Notify the bank immediately if your card is not returned.

digi – know?

Opting out may also reduce identify theft. You can stop preapproved credit card offers by logging on to *www.optoutprescreen.com*.

According to a 2014 survey by American Consumer Credit Counseling, 64 percent of Americans do not trust retailers with their credit and debit card information. Due to recent data breaches at Target and Neiman Marcus, 42 percent of respondents are more likely to pay with cash or check.

If you believe that an identity thief has accessed your bank accounts, close the accounts immediately. If your checks have been stolen or misused, stop payment on them. If your debit card has been lost or stolen, cancel it and get another with a new personal identification number (PIN).

Lost credit cards are a key element in credit card fraud. To protect your card, you should take the following actions:

- Be sure that your card is returned to you after a purchase. Unreturned cards can find their way into the wrong hands.
- Keep a record of your credit card number. You should keep this record separate from your card.
- Notify the credit card company immediately if your card is lost or stolen. Under the Consumer Credit Protection Act, the maximum amount that you must pay if someone uses your card illegally is $50. However, if you manage to inform the company before the card is used illegally, you have no obligation to pay at all.

Read the accompanying "From the Pages of . . . Kiplinger's Personal Finance" feature on how to combat data theft.

Protecting Your Credit Information on the Internet

The Internet is becoming almost as important to daily life as the telephone and television. Increasing numbers of consumers use the Internet for financial activities, such as investing, banking, and shopping.

When you make purchases online, make sure that your transactions are secure, that your personal information is protected, and that your "fraud sensors" are sharpened. Although you can't control fraud or deception on the Internet, you can take steps to recognize it, avoid it, and report it. Here's how:

- Use a secure browser.
- Keep records of your online transactions.

How to Combat Data Theft

We tell you how you could be affected and give you the tools to protect your credit and financial information.

Highly publicized security breaches at retailers Target and Neiman Marcus have left consumers looking for guidance on how to guard their financial information. We have answers to your questions about what to do in the event of a data breach.

Should I request a new card? Asking your bank or credit card issuer to send you a new card with a new number is the best way to nip potential theft in the bud. And it's an especially good idea if you suspect that your debit card data has been stolen, given that a debit card provides direct access to your bank account—and that its legal protections are less robust than those of a credit card. Victims of credit card fraud are legally responsible for up to $50. With debit cards, your liability could be unlimited. As soon as you get your new card, notify any service—say, your electric utility or cable company—that charge automatic bill payments to the card so that you aren't hit with fees for missed payments. If you do incur any fees, explain the situation to the company and ask to have them waived.

What if I decide not to get a new card? Keep close tabs on your bank or credit card account. Log in daily for the first couple of months to check for suspicious activity, suggests

Beverly Harzog, a credit card expert and author of *Confessions of a Credit Junkie.* After that, try to check in about once a week. A weekly check-in is a good habit to maintain for all of your bank and credit accounts, regardless of whether you think they've been compromised.

Could I be scammed in other ways? If a data breach extends to customer names, phone numbers, and e-mail and mailing addresses, you could be vulnerable to phishing scams—fake messages designed to pry even more personal information from you. Fraudsters could also piece together, say, your credit card number, name and e-mail address to create a convincing e-mail that appears to be from your financial institution, says Jody Farmer, vice-president of strategic marketing at CreditCards.com. Scammers posing as representatives from a business or government agency may attempt to contact you. If you're not sure that a message is legitimate, don't click on any links that it contains or provide any personal information that it requests. Look up the institution's phone number and call to verify that it contacted you.

Should I worry about my identity being stolen? If a retailer offers free credit monitoring,

it wouldn't hurt to sign up. You can also check your credit reports from the three major bureaus—Equifax, Experian and TransUnion—free once a year at www.annualcreditreport.com.

I'm still nervous about ID theft. What else can I do? You could place a freeze on your credit reports as a preventive measure, says Adam Levin, chairman and co-founder of Identity Theft 911. Lenders won't be able to offer new credit in your name without your permission. You'll have to request the freeze separately with each of the three credit agencies. Keep in mind that a credit freeze could cause delays if you expect to shop for new credit. A less drastic action is to place a fraud alert on your reports, which requires lenders to take extra precautions to verify your identity before granting new credit. An initial fraud alert lasts 90 days, and you'll get a free copy of your credit report from each of the bureaus. If you set up an alert with one bureau, it will notify the other two.

Lisa Gerstner

SOURCE: Reprinted by permission from *Kiplinger's Personal Finance.* Copyright 2014. The Kiplinger Washington Editors, Inc.

1. In the event of a data breach, why is it wise to request a new card?

2. What precautions should you take if you decide not to get a new card?

3. What are the pros and cons of placing a freeze on your credit report as a preventive measure?

- Review your monthly bank and credit card statements.
- Read the privacy and security policies of websites you visit.
- Keep your personal information private.
- Never give your password to anyone online.
- Don't download files sent to you by strangers.

Cosigning a Loan

If a friend or relative ever asks you to cosign a loan, think twice. *Cosigning* a loan means that you agree to be responsible for loan payments if the other party fails to make them. When you cosign, you're taking a chance that a professional lender will not take. The lender would not require a cosigner if the borrower were considered a good risk.

If you cosign a loan and the borrower does not pay the debt, you may have to pay up to the full amount of the debt as well as any late fees or collection costs. The creditor can even collect the debt from you without first trying to collect from the borrower. The creditor can use the same collection methods against you that can be used against the borrower. If the debt is not repaid, that fact will appear on your credit record.

Most private student loans today have a cosigner, typically a parent or a grandparent. Your loan may contain provisions that allow the creditor to put you in default, even if you've been making your payments on time. In 2014, according to the Consumer Financial Protection Bureau, "We've received complaints that private lenders are placing borrowers into default and making balance due all at once when the cosigner dies or files for bankruptcy."

Complaining about Consumer Credit

If you believe that a lender is not following the consumer credit protection laws, first try to solve the problem directly with the lender. If that fails, use formal complaint procedures. This section describes how to file a complaint with the federal agencies that administer credit protection laws. Exhibit 5–9 provides contact information for the various federal agencies.

Consumer Credit Protection Laws

If you have a particular problem with a bank in connection with any of the consumer credit protection laws, you can get advice and help from the Federal Reserve System. You don't need to have an account at the bank to file a complaint. You may also take legal action against a creditor. If you decide to file a lawsuit, you should be aware of the various consumer credit protection laws described below.

TRUTH IN LENDING AND CONSUMER LEASING ACTS If a creditor fails to disclose information as required under the Truth in Lending Act or the Consumer Leasing Act, or gives inaccurate information, you can sue for any money loss you suffer. You can also sue a creditor that does not follow rules regarding credit cards. In addition, the Truth in Lending Act and the Consumer Leasing Act permit class action of all the people who have suffered the same injustice.

FAIR CREDIT AND CHARGE CARD DISCLOSURE ACT This act was initially written as an amendment to the Truth in Lending Act. This act requires that solicitations for credit cards in the mail, over the phone, in print, or online must provide the necessary terms of the account. This includes finance charges as well as cash advance or annual fees. This also includes any changes to the account.

Exhibit **5–9** Federal Government Agencies That Enforce the Consumer Credit Laws

If you think you've been discriminated against by:	You may file a complaint with the following agency:	
Consumer reporting agencies, creditors, and others not listed below	Federal Trade Commission: Consumer Response Center - FCRA Washington, DC 20580	1-877-382-4357
National banks, federal branches/agencies of foreign banks (word "National" or initials "N.A." appear in or after bank's name)	Office of the Comptroller of the Currency Compliance Management, Mail Stop 6-6 Washington, DC 20219	1-800-613-6743
Federal Reserve System member banks (except national banks and federal branches/agencies of foreign banks)	Federal Reserve Board Division of Consumer & Community Affairs Washington, DC 20551	1-202-452-3693
Federal credit unions (words "Federal Credit Union" appear in institution's name)	National Credit Union Administration 1775 Duke Street Alexandria, VA 22314	1-703-519-4600
State-chartered banks that are not members of the Federal Reserve System	Federal Deposit Insurance Corporation Consumer Response Center, 2345 Grand Avenue, Suite 100 Kansas City, MO 64108-2638	1-877-275-3342

The law gives you certain rights as a consumer of credit. What types of complaints about a creditor might you report to these government agencies?

EQUAL CREDIT OPPORTUNITY ACT (ECOA) If you think that you can prove that a creditor has discriminated against you for any reason prohibited by the ECOA, you may sue for actual damages plus punitive damages—a payment used to punish the creditor who has violated the law—up to $10,000.

FAIR CREDIT BILLING ACT A creditor that fails to follow the rules that apply to correcting any billing errors will automatically give up the amount owed on the item in question and any finance charges on it, up to a combined total of $50. This is true even if the bill was correct. You may also sue for actual damages plus twice the amount of any finance charges.

FAIR CREDIT REPORTING ACT You may sue any credit bureau or creditor that violates the rules regarding access to your credit records, or that fails to correct errors in your credit file. You're entitled to actual damages plus any punitive damages the court allows if the violation is proven to have been intentional.

CONSUMER CREDIT REPORTING REFORM ACT The Consumer Credit Reporting Reform Act of 1977 places the burden of proof for accurate credit information on the credit bureau rather than on you. Under this law, the creditor must prove that disputed information is accurate. If a creditor or the credit bureau verifies incorrect data, you can sue for damages.

ELECTRONIC FUND TRANSFER ACT If a financial institution does not follow the provisions of the Electronic Fund Transfer Act, you may sue for actual damages plus punitive damages of not less than $100 or more than $1,000. You are also entitled to court costs and attorney fees in a successful lawsuit. Class-action suits are also permitted.

CREDIT CARD ACCOUNTABILITY RESPONSIBILITY AND DISCLOSURE ACT OF 2009 (CARD ACT) This act became effective in February 2010. It changed many of the rules by which the credit card companies could provide credit and administer accounts. Credit card companies must now provide 45 days' notice of rate increases. Also, the time between receiving the statement and the payment due date has been extended to 21 days. Additionally, the credit card companies must apply payments first to the debts that carry the higher interest rates, such as cash advances. They must also provide a more detailed statement that includes the time and total interest amount to pay off the balance if only the minimum payment is made. The rules by which the credit card companies can extend credit to persons under the age of 21 have also changed. Young people must be able to show proof of income or have a signature by a person willing to accept responsibility for the account.

Consumer Financial Protection Bureau

If you are unable to find a resolution to a credit card situation, you may still have one more option. The Consumer Financial Protection Bureau (CFPB) has created a one-stop complaint website for credit card issues. You must visit the website, describe the circumstances of your complaint, and indicate any monies lost due to the issue. You can continue to check back on the website to monitor the progress of your complaint as the CFPB investigates. The website is https://help.consumerfinance.gov/app/ask_cc_complaint.

In 2014, the CFPB ordered Bank of America to pay $727 million to about 1.4 million consumers who were harmed by practices related to its credit card payment protection products, "Credit Protection Plus" and "Credit Protection Deluxe." According to the CFPB, Bank of America also illegally charged approximately 1.9 million consumers for credit monitoring and credit reporting services. In addition, Bank of America will pay a $20 million penalty to the CFPB.

Managing Your Debts

A sudden illness or the loss of your job may prevent you from paying your bills on time. If you find you cannot make your payments, contact your creditors at once and try to work out a modified payment plan with them.

Warning Signs of Debt Problems

Chris is in his late 20s. A college graduate, he has a steady job and earns an annual income of $40,000. With the latest model sports car parked in the driveway of his new home, it would appear that Chris has the ideal life.

However, Chris is deeply in debt. He is drowning in a sea of bills. Almost all his income is tied up in debt payments. The bank has already begun foreclosure proceedings on his home, and several stores have court orders to repossess practically all of his new furniture and electronic gadgets. His current car payment is overdue, and he is behind in payments on all his credit cards. If he doesn't come up with a plan of action, he'll lose everything.

Chris's situation is all too common. Some people who seem to be wealthy are just barely keeping their heads above water financially. Generally, the problem they share is financial immaturity. They lack self-discipline and don't control their impulses. They use poor judgment or fail to accept responsibility for managing their money.

Chris and others like him aren't necessarily bad people. They simply haven't thought about their long-term financial goals. Someday you could find yourself in a situation similar to Chris's. Here are some warning signs that you may be in financial trouble:

- You make only the minimum monthly payment on credit cards.
- You're having trouble making even the minimum monthly payment on your credit card bills.
- The total balance on your credit cards increases every month.
- You miss loan payments or often pay late.
- You use savings to pay for necessities such as food and utilities.
- You receive second and third payment due notices from creditors.

Personal Finance in Practice

New Credit Card Rules

The Federal Reserve has enacted new rules for credit card companies that mean new credit card protections for you. Here are some key changes in the rules for credit card companies as of February 22, 2010.

Your Credit Card Company Has to Tell You:

1. **When they plan to increase your rate or other fees.** Your credit card company must send you a notice 45 days before they can

   - increase your interest rate;
   - change certain fees (such as annual fees, cash advance fees, and late fees) that apply to your account; or
   - make other significant changes to the terms of your card.

   If your credit card company plans to make changes to the terms of your card, it must give you the option to cancel the card before certain fee increases take effect.

   For example, the credit card company can require you to pay off the balance in five years, or it can double the percentage of your balance used to calculate your minimum payment (which will result in faster repayment than under the terms of your account).

   The company does **not** have to send you a 45-day advance notice if

   - you have a variable interest rate tied to an index;
   - your introductory rate expires and reverts to the previously disclosed "go-to" rate; or
   - your rate increases because you haven't made your payments as agreed.

2. **How long it will take to pay off your balance.** Your monthly credit card bill will include information on how long it will take you to pay off your balance if you only make minimum payments. It will also tell you how much you would need to pay each month in order to pay off your balance in three years. For example, suppose you owe $3,000 and your interest rate is 14.4 percent—your bill might look like this:

New balance	$3,000.00
Minimum payment due	$ 90.00
Payment due date	4/20/15

Late Payment Warning: If we do not receive your minimum payment by the date listed above, you may have to pay a $35 late fee and your APRs may be increased up to the Penalty APR of 28.99%.

Minimum Payment Warning: If you make only the minimum payment each period, you will pay more interest and it will take you longer to pay off your balance. For example:

If you make no additional charges using this card and each month you pay . . .	You will pay off the balance shown on this statement in about . . .	And you will end up paying an estimated total of . . .
Only the minimum payment	11 years	$4,745
$103	3 years	$3,712
		(Savings = $1,033)

SOURCE: Board of Governors of the Federal Reserve System, http://www.federalreserve.gov/creditcard/flash/readingyourbill.pdf, accessed April 28, 2014.

- You borrow money to pay off old debts.
- You exceed the credit limits on your credit cards.
- You've been denied credit because of a bad credit bureau report.

If you are experiencing two or more of these warning signs, it's time for you to rethink your priorities before it's too late.

Debt Collection Practices

The Federal Trade Commission enforces the Fair Debt Collection Practices Act (FDCPA). This act prohibits certain practices by debt collectors—businesses that collect debts for creditors. The act does not erase the legitimate debts that consumers owe, but it does control the ways in which debt collection agencies may do business.

Financial Counseling Services

If you're having trouble paying your bills and need help, you have several options. You can contact your creditors and try to work out an adjusted repayment plan, or you can contact a nonprofit financial counseling program.

CONSUMER CREDIT COUNSELING SERVICES
The Consumer Credit Counseling Service (CCCS) is a nonprofit organization affiliated with the National Foundation for Consumer Credit (NFCC). Local branches of the CCCS provide debt counseling services for families and individuals with serious financial problems. The CCCS is not a charity, a lending institution, or a government agency. CCCS counseling is usually free. However, when the organization supervises a debt repayment plan, it sometimes charges a small fee to help pay administrative costs.

According to the NFCC, millions of consumers contact CCCS offices each year for help with their personal financial problems. To find an office near you, call 1-800-388-CCCS or go to www.nfcc.org. All information is kept confidential.

Credit counselors know that most individuals who are overwhelmed with debt are basically honest people who want to clear up their unmanageable *indebtedness,* the condition of being deeply in debt. Too often, such problems arise from a lack of planning or a miscalculation of earnings. The CCCS is concerned with preventing problems as much as it is with solving them. As a result, its activities are divided into two parts:

- Aiding families with serious debt problems by helping them to manage their money better and set up a realistic budget.
- Helping people prevent indebtedness by teaching them the importance of budget planning, educating them about the pitfalls of unwise credit buying, and encouraging credit institutions to withhold credit from people who cannot afford it.

See the nearby "Personal Finance in Practice" box for help in choosing a credit counselor.

OTHER COUNSELING SERVICES
In addition to the CCCS, universities, credit unions, military bases, and state and federal housing authorities sometimes provide nonprofit credit counseling services. These organizations usually charge little or nothing for their assistance. You can also check with your bank or local consumer protection office to see whether it has a listing of reputable financial counseling services, such as the Debt Counselors of America.

Declaring Personal Bankruptcy

What if a debtor suffers from an extreme case of financial woes? Can there be any relief? The answer is bankruptcy proceedings. *Bankruptcy* is a legal process in which some or all of the assets of a debtor are distributed among the creditors because the debtor is unable to pay his or her debts. Bankruptcy may also include a plan for the debtor to repay creditors on an installment basis. Declaring bankruptcy is a last resort because it severely damages your credit rating.

Anita Singh illustrates the face of bankruptcy. A 43-year-old freelance photographer from California, she was never in serious financial trouble until she began running up big medical costs. She reached for her credit cards to pay the bills. Because Anita didn't have health insurance, her debt quickly mounted and soon reached $17,000—too much to pay off with her $25,000-a-year income. Her solution was to declare personal bankruptcy to get relief from creditors' demands. Medical bills are the leading cause of bankruptcy.

Personal Finance in Practice

Choosing a Credit Counselor

Reputable credit counseling organizations employ counselors who are certified and trained in consumer credit, debt management, and budgeting. Here are a few important questions to ask when choosing a credit counselor:

1. **What services do you offer?** Look for an organization that offers a range of services, including budget counseling, savings and debt management classes, and trained certified counselors.

2. **Are you licensed to offer services in my state?** Many states require that credit counseling agencies register or obtain a license before offering their services.

3. **Do you offer free information?** Avoid organizations that charge for information about the nature of their services.

4. **Will I have a formal written agreement or contract with you?** Don't commit to participate in a debt management program over the telephone. Get all verbal promises in writing. Read all documents carefully before you sign them. If you are told you need to act immediately, consider finding another organization.

5. **What are the qualifications of your counselors?** Are they accredited or certified by an outside organization? Which one? If not, how are they trained? Try to use an organization whose counselors are trained by an outside organization that is not affiliated with creditors.

6. **Have other consumers been satisfied with the service they received?** Once you have identified credit counseling organizations that suit your needs, check them out with your state attorney general, local consumer protection agency, and Better Business Bureau.

7. **What are your fees? Are there setup and/or monthly fees?** Get a detailed quote in writing, and specifically ask whether all fees are covered in the quote. If an organization won't help you because you can't afford to pay, look elsewhere for help.

8. **How are your employees paid? Are the employees or the organization paid more if I sign up for certain services, pay a fee, or make a contribution to your organization?** Employees who are counseling you to purchase certain services may receive a commission if you choose to sign up for those services. Many credit counseling organizations receive additional compensation from creditors if you enroll in a debt management program.

9. **What do you do to keep personal information about your clients (for example, name, address, phone number, financial information) confidential and secure?** Credit counseling organizations handle your most sensitive financial information. The organization should have safeguards in place to protect the privacy of this information and prevent misuse.

THE U.S. BANKRUPTCY ACT OF 1978 Exhibit 5–10 illustrates the rate of personal bankruptcy in the United States. The vast majority of bankruptcies in the United States, like Anita Singh's, are filed under a part of U.S. bankruptcy code known as Chapter 7. You have two choices in declaring personal bankruptcy: Chapter 7 (a straight bankruptcy) and Chapter 13 (a wage earner plan bankruptcy). Both choices are undesirable, and neither should be considered an easy way to get out of debt.

Chapter 7 Bankruptcy In a Chapter 7 bankruptcy, an individual is required to draw up a petition listing his or her assets and liabilities. A person who files for relief under the bankruptcy code is called a *debtor*. The debtor submits the petition to a U.S. district court and pays a filing fee.

Chapter 7 is a straight bankruptcy in which many, but not all, debts are forgiven. Most of the debtor's assets are sold to pay off creditors. Certain assets, however, receive some protection. Among the assets usually protected are Social Security payments, unemployment compensation, and the net value of your home, vehicle, household goods and appliances, tools used in your work, and books.

The courts must charge a $306 case filing fee, a $46 miscellaneous administrative fee, and a $15 trustee fee. If the debtor is unable to pay the fees even in installments, the court may waive the fees.

Exhibit 5–10 U.S. Consumer Bankruptcy Filings, 1980–2013

Consumer bankruptcies have increased significantly over the past 30 years. Consumer bankruptcy filings rose from about 287,000 in 1980 to almost 2 million in 2005. Bankruptcies decreased after the Bankruptcy Abuse Prevention and Consumer Protection Act was passed. However, poor economic conditions have caused the numbers to increase yet again despite the legislation.

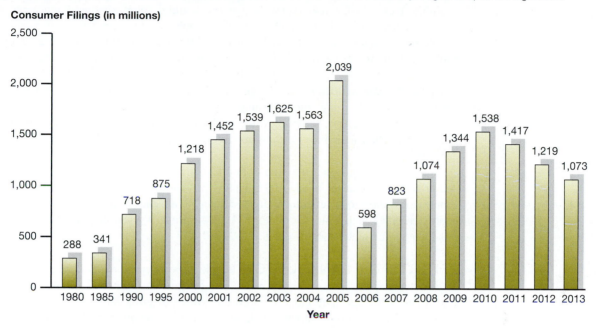

SOURCE: Administrative Office of the U.S. Courts, http://www.uscourts.gov/Statistics/JudicialBusiness/2013/us-bankruptcy-courts.aspx, accessed April 28, 2014.

In filing a petition, a debtor must provide the following information:

- A list of all creditors and the amount and nature of their claims.
- The source, amount, and frequency of the debtor's income.
- A list of all the debtor's property.
- A detailed list of the debtor's monthly expenses.

The release from debt does not affect alimony, child support, certain taxes, fines, certain debts arising from educational loans, or debts that you fail to disclose properly to the bankruptcy court. Furthermore, debts arising from fraud, driving while intoxicated, or certain other acts or crimes may also be excluded.

The Bankruptcy Abuse Prevention and Consumer Protection Act of 2005   On April 20, 2005, President George W. Bush signed the Bankruptcy Abuse Prevention and Consumer Protection Act, which is perhaps the largest overhaul of the Bankruptcy Code since it was enacted in 1978. Signing the bill, the president declared, "Bankruptcy should always be the last resort in our legal system. In recent years too many people have abused the bankruptcy laws. Under the new law, Americans who have the ability to pay will be required to pay back at least a portion of their debts. The law will help make credit more affordable, because when bankruptcy is less common, credit can be extended to more people at better rates. Debtors seeking to erase all debts will now have to wait eight years from their last bankruptcy before they can file again. The law will also allow us to clamp down on bankruptcy mills that make their money by advising abusers on how to game the system."

Among other provisions, the law requires that:

- The director of the Executive Office for U.S. Trustees develop a financial management training curriculum to educate individual debtors on how to better manage their finances, and test, evaluate, and report to Congress on the curriculum's effectiveness.

- Debtors complete an approved instructional course in personal financial management.
- The clerk of each bankruptcy district maintain a list of credit counseling agencies and instructional courses on personal financial management.

Furthermore, the law may require that states should develop personal finance curricula designed for use in elementary and secondary schools.

The bottom line: The new law made it more difficult for consumers to file a Chapter 7 bankruptcy and forces them into a Chapter 13 repayment plan.

Chapter 13 Bankruptcy   In Chapter 13 bankruptcy, a debtor with a regular income proposes a plan for using future earnings or assets to eliminate his or her debts over a period of time. In such a bankruptcy, the debtor normally keeps all or most of his or her property. A debtor must provide the same information that is required to file a Chapter 7 bankruptcy.

During the period when the plan is in effect, which can be as long as five years, the debtor makes regular payments to a Chapter 13 trustee, or representative, who then distributes the money to the creditors. Under certain circumstances, the bankruptcy court may approve a plan that permits the debtor to keep all property, even though he or she repays less than the full amount of the debts.

EFFECTS OF BANKRUPTCY People have varying experiences in obtaining credit after they file for bankruptcy. Some find the process more difficult, whereas others find it easier because they have removed the burden of prior debts or because creditors know that they cannot file another bankruptcy case for a certain period of time. Obtaining credit may be easier for people who file a Chapter 13 bankruptcy and repay some of their debts than for those who file a Chapter 7 bankruptcy and make no effort to repay any of their debts.

PRACTICE QUIZ 5-5

1. What steps might you take if there is a billing error in your monthly statement?

2. What steps would you take if someone stole your identity?

3. How might you protect your credit information on the Internet?

4. What are some warning signs of debt problems?

5. Distinguish between Chapter 7 and Chapter 13 bankruptcy.

Apply Yourself!

Search online to find branches of the Consumer Credit Counseling Service across the country. Choose one in your area and one in another part of the country. Visit the websites to find out who funds the offices.

YOUR PERSONAL FINANCE DASHBOARD

DEBT PAYMENTS-TO-INCOME RATIO

A key indicator of your creditworthiness is your capacity to handle a certain level of debt. Lenders will review your current debt payments-to-income ratio. Based upon this, they will determine how much credit they will extend and at what interest rate. Lenders will be more reluctant to lend to individuals who are near the top of the acceptable range of 20 percent.

YOUR SITUATION: Are you able to pay your credit cards off each month when the bill is due? If you carry a balance, is it steadily increasing? Are there debts that you can eliminate to reduce the amount of your overall debt payments?

An improving debt payments-to-income ratio is the foundation for progress toward financial independence.

POSSIBLE ACTIONS TO TAKE

✓ *Reconsider your responses to the "Action Items" (in the text margin) to determine actions you might consider related to the wise use of credit.*

✓ *Seek information from several sources when evaluating the sources of credit, including various websites and Exhibit 5–3.*

✓ *Determine how you intend to use your credit card before choosing one. Follow the suggestions to find the card that best meets your needs and use it wisely. See the "Personal Finance in Practice" box on page 146.*

✓ *Get copies of your credit report and make sure the information is correct. The only authorized online source for a free credit report is www.annualcredit-report.com, or call 877-322-8228.*

Chapter Summary

LO5.1 Consumer credit is the use of credit by individuals and families for personal needs. Among the advantages of using credit are the ability to purchase goods when needed and pay for them gradually, the ability to meet financial emergencies, convenience in shopping, and establishment of a credit rating. Disadvantages are that credit costs money, encourages overspending, and ties up future income.

LO5.2 Closed-end and open-end credit are two types of consumer credit. With closed-end credit, the borrower pays back a one-time loan in a stated period of time and with a specified number of payments. With open-end credit, the borrower is permitted to take loans on a continuous basis and is billed for partial payments periodically.

The major sources of consumer credit are commercial banks, savings and loan associations, credit unions, finance companies, life insurance companies, and family and friends. Each of these sources has unique advantages and disadvantages.

Parents or family members are often the source of the least expensive loans. They may charge you only the interest they would have earned had they not made the loan. Such loans, however, can complicate family relationships.

LO5.3 Two general rules for measuring credit capacity are the debt payments-to-income ratio and the debt-to-equity ratio. In reviewing your creditworthiness, a creditor seeks information from one of the three national credit bureaus or a regional credit bureau.

Creditors determine creditworthiness on the basis of the five Cs: character, capacity, capital, collateral, and conditions.

LO5.4 Compare the finance charge and the annual percentage rate (APR) as you shop for credit. Under the Truth in Lending Act, creditors are required to state the cost of borrowing so that you can compare credit costs and shop for credit.

LO5.5 If a billing error occurs on your account, notify the creditor in writing within 60 days. If the dispute is not settled in your favor, you can place your version of it in your credit file. You may also withhold payment on any defective goods or services you have purchased with a credit card as long as you have attempted to resolve the problem with the merchant.

If you have a complaint about credit, first try to deal directly with the creditor. If that fails, you can turn to the appropriate consumer credit law. These laws include the Truth in Lending Act, the Consumer Leasing Act, the Equal Credit Opportunity Act, the Fair Credit Billing Act, the Fair Credit Reporting Act, the Consumer Credit Reporting Reform Act, and the Electronic Fund Transfer Act.

If you cannot meet your obligations, contact your creditors immediately. Also, contact your local Consumer Credit Counseling Service or other debt counseling organizations.

A debtor's last resort is to declare bankruptcy, permitted by the U.S. Bankruptcy Act of 1978. Consider the financial and other costs of bankruptcy before taking this extreme step. A debtor can declare Chapter 7 (straight) bankruptcy or Chapter 13 (wage earner plan) bankruptcy.

Key Terms

annual percentage rate (APR) 161	conditions 153	line of credit 145
capacity 152	consumer credit 141	mobile commerce 147
capital 152	credit 141	open-end credit 144
character 152	Fair Credit Billing Act (FCBA) 166	revolving check credit 145
closed-end credit 144	finance charge 145	simple interest 163
collateral 153	interest 145	

Key Formulas

Page	Topic	Formula
162	Calculating annual percentage rate (APR)	$\text{APR} = \dfrac{2 \times \text{Number of payment periods in one year} \times \text{Dollar cost of credit}}{\text{Loan amount (Total number of payments to pay off the loan} + 1)}$ $= \dfrac{2 \times n \times I}{P(N + 1)}$
163	Calculating simple interest	Interest (in dollars) = Principal borrowed × Interest rate × Length of loan in years $I = P \times r \times T$

Discussion Questions

1. Vicky is trying to decide whether to finance her purchase of a used Mustang convertible. What questions should Vicky ask herself before making her decision? (LO5.1)
2. List advantages and disadvantages of using credit. (LO5.1)
3. To finance a sofa for his new apartment, Caleb signed a contract to pay for the sofa in six equal installments. What type of consumer credit is Caleb using? (LO5.2)
4. Alka plans to spend $5,000 on a plasma television and home theater system. She is willing to spend some of her $9,000 in savings. However, she wants to finance the rest and pay it off in small monthly installments out of the $400 a month she earns working

part-time. How might she obtain a low-interest loan and make low monthly payments? (LO5.2)

5. Samuel applied for a loan to purchase a new car. His application was denied. What should he do now? (LO5.3)

6. Diane wants to purchase a home in the next five years. She knows how important a good credit score is for getting a lower interest rate. What are some ways she can continue to improve her credit score over the next few years? (LO5.3)

7. Why is it important to avoid the minimum monthly payment trap? (LO5.4)

8. Grayson just received his credit card statement. He noticed a charge for $40 to a store he has never patronized. What steps should he take to handle this? (LO5.5)

9. What factors (including psychological) would you consider in assessing the choices in declaring personal bankruptcy? Why should personal bankruptcy be the choice of last resort? (LO5.5)

Self-Test Problems

1. Suppose that your monthly net income is $1,500. Your monthly debt payments include your student loan payment and a gas credit card, and they total $200. What is your debt payments-to-income ratio?

2. Suppose you borrow $1,000 at 6 percent and will repay it in one payment at the end of one year. Use the simple interest formula to determine the amount of interest you will pay.

Solutions

1. Use the debt payments-to-income ratio formula: Monthly debt payments/Monthly net income.

$$\text{Debt payments-to-income ratio} = \frac{\$200}{\$1,500} = 0.13, \text{ or } 13\%$$

2. Using the simple interest formula (Interest = Principal × Rate of interest × Time), the interest is $60, computed as follows:

$$\$60 = \$1,000 \times 0.06 \times 1 \text{ (year)}$$

Problems

1. A few years ago, Simon Powell purchased a home for $110,000. Today, the home is worth $150,000. His remaining mortgage balance is $50,000. Assuming that Simon can borrow up to 80 percent of the market value, what is the maximum amount he can borrow? (LO5.2)

2. Louise McIntyre's monthly gross income is $2,000. Her employer withholds $400 in federal, state, and local income taxes and $160 in Social Security taxes per month. Louise contributes $80 each month for her IRA. Her monthly credit payments for Visa and MasterCard are $35 and $30, respectively. Her monthly payment on an automobile loan is $285. What is Louise's debt payments-to-income ratio? Is Louise living within her means? (LO5.3)

3. Robert Sampson owns a $140,000 townhouse and still has an unpaid mortgage of $110,000. In addition to his mortgage, he has the following liabilities:

Visa	$565
MasterCard	480
Discover card	395
Education loan	920
Personal bank loan	800
Auto loan	4,250
Total	$7,410

Robert's net worth (not including his home) is about $21,000. This equity is in mutual funds, an automobile, a coin collection, furniture, and other personal property. What is Robert's debt-to-equity ratio? Has he reached the upper limit of debt obligations? Explain.   (LO5.3)

4. Madeline Rollins is trying to decide whether she can afford a loan she needs in order to go to chiropractic school. Right now Madeline is living at home and works in a shoe store, earning a gross income of $820 per month. Her employer deducts a total of $145 for taxes from her monthly pay. Madeline also pays $95 on several credit card debts each month. The loan she needs for chiropractic school will cost an additional $120 per month. Help Madeline make her decision by calculating her debt payments-to-income ratio with and without the college loan. (Remember the 20 percent rule.)   (LO5.3)

5. Joshua borrowed $500 for one year and paid $50 in interest. The bank charged him a $5 service charge. What is the finance charge on this loan?   (LO5.4)

6. In problem 5, Joshua borrowed $500 on January 1, 2014, and paid it all back at once on December 31, 2014. What was the APR?   (LO5.4)

7. If Joshua paid the $500 in 12 equal monthly payments, what is the APR?   (LO5.4)

8. Sidney took a $200 cash advance by using checks linked to her credit card account. The bank charges a 2 percent cash advance fee on the amount borrowed and offers no grace period on cash advances. Sidney paid the balance in full when the bill arrived. What was the cash advance fee? What was the interest for one month at an 18 percent APR? What was the total amount she paid? What if she had made the purchase with her credit card and paid off her bill in full promptly?   (LO5.4)

9. Brooke lacks cash to pay for a $600 washing machine. She could buy it from the store on credit by making 12 monthly payments of $52.74 each. The total cost would then be $632.88. Instead, Brooke decides to deposit $50 a month in the bank until she has saved enough money to pay cash for the washing machine. One year later, she has saved $642—$600 in deposits plus interest. When she goes back to the store, she finds that the washing machine now costs $660. Its price has gone up 10 percent—the current rate of inflation. Was postponing her purchase a good trade-off for Brooke?   (LO5.4)

10. What are the interest cost and the total amount due on a six-month loan of $1,500 at 13.2 percent simple annual interest?   (LO5.4)

11. After visiting several automobile dealerships, Richard selects the car he wants. He likes its $10,000 price, but financing through the dealer is no bargain. He has $2,000 cash for a down payment, so he needs an $8,000 loan. In shopping at several banks for an installment loan, he learns that interest on most automobile loans is quoted at add-on rates. That is, during the life of the loan, interest is paid on the full amount borrowed even though a portion of the principal has been paid back. Richard borrows $8,000 for a period of four years at an add-on interest rate of 11 percent.   (LO5.4)

    a. What is the total interest on Richard's loan?
    b. What is the total cost of the car?
    c. What is the monthly payment?
    d. What is the annual percentage rate (APR)?

 To reinforce the content in this chapter, more problems are provided at connect.mheducation.com.

Case in Point

FINANCING SUE'S HONDA ACCORD

After shopping around, Sue Wallace decided on the car of her choice, a used Honda Accord. The dealer quoted her a total price of $10,000. Sue decided to use $2,000 of her savings as a down payment and borrow $8,000. The salesperson wrote this information on a sales contract that Sue took with her when she set out to find financing.

When Sue applied for a loan, she discussed loan terms with the bank lending officer.

The officer told her that the bank's policy was to lend only 80 percent of the total price of a used car. Sue showed the officer her copy of the sales contract, indicating that she had agreed to make a $2,000, or 20 percent, down payment on the $10,000 car, so this requirement caused her no problem. Although the bank was willing to make 48-month loans at an annual percentage rate of 9 percent on used cars, Sue chose a 36-month repayment schedule. She believed she could afford the higher payments, and she knew she would not have to pay as much interest if she paid off the loan at a faster rate. The bank lending officer provided Sue with a copy of the Truth-in-Lending Disclosure Statement shown here.

TRUTH-IN-LENDING DISCLOSURE STATEMENT (LOANS)

Annual Percentage Rate	Finance Charge	Amount Financed	Total of Payments 36
The cost of your credit as a yearly rate.	The dollar amount the credit will cost you.	The amount of credit provided to you or on your behalf.	The amount you will have paid after you have made all payments as scheduled.
9%	$1,158.32	$8,000.00	$9,158.32

You have the right to receive at this time an itemization of the Amount Financed.

☐ I want an itemization.　　☐ I do not want an itemization.

Your payment schedule will be:

Number of Payments	Amount of Payments	When Payments Are Due
36	$254.40	1st of each month

Sue decided to compare the APR she had been offered with the APR offered by another bank, but the 11 percent APR of the second bank (bank B) was more expensive than the 9 percent APR of the first bank (bank A). Here is her comparison of the two loans:

	Bank A 9% APR	Bank B 11% APR
Amount financed	$8,000	$8,000
Finance charge	1,158.32	1,428.75
Total of payments	9,158.32	9,428.75
Monthly payments	254.40	261.91

The 2 percent difference in the APRs of the two banks meant Sue would have to pay $8 extra every month if she got her loan from the second bank. Of course, she got the loan from the first bank.

Questions

1. What is perhaps the most important item shown on the disclosure statement? Why?
2. What is included in the finance charge?
3. What amount will Sue receive from the bank?
4. Should Sue borrow from bank A or bank B? Why?

CONSUMER CREDIT: ADVANTAGES, DISADVANTAGES, SOURCE, AND COSTS

Continuing Case

Jamie Lee Jackson, age 27, full-time student and part-time bakery employee, has just moved into a bungalow-style, unfurnished home of her own. The house is only a one-bedroom, but the rent is manageable and it has plenty of room for Jamie Lee. She decided to give notice to her roommate that she would be leaving the apartment and the shared expenses after the incident with the stolen checkbook and credit cards a few weeks back. Jamie had to dip into her emergency savings account to help cover the deposit and moving expenses, because she had not planned to move out of the apartment and be on her own this soon.

Jamie is in need of a few appliances, as there is a small laundry room but no washer or dryer, nor is there a refrigerator in the kitchen. She will also need a living room set and a television, because Jamie only had a bedroom set to move in with. Jamie is so excited to finally have the say in how she will furnish the bungalow, and she began shopping for her home as soon as the lease was signed.

The home appliance store was the first stop, where Jamie chose a stacking washer and dryer set that would fit comfortably in the laundry space provided. A stainless steel refrigerator with a built-in television screen was her next choice, and the salesperson quickly began to write up the order. She informed Jamie that if she opened up a credit card through the appliance store, she would receive a discount of 10 percent off her total purchase. As she waited for her credit to be approved, she decided to continue shopping for her other needed items.

Living room furniture was next on the list. Jamie went to a local retailer who offered seemingly endless choices of complete sofa sets that included the coffee and end tables as well as matching lamps. Jamie chose a contemporary-style set and again was offered the tempting deal of opening a credit card through the store in exchange for a percentage off her purchase and free delivery.

Jamie's last stop was the local big box retailer, where she chose a 52" 1080p LED HDTV. For the third time, a percentage off her first purchase at the big box retailer was all that was needed to get Jamie to sign on the dotted line of the credit card application. She was daydreaming of how wonderful her new home would look when a call from the appliance store came through asking her to return to the store.

Jamie Lee received the unfortunate news that her credit application at the appliance store had been denied. She left the store only to be greeted at the next two stores where she had chosen the living room set and television with the same bad news—credit application denied! She was informed that her credit score was too low for approval. "How could this be?" Jamie wondered and immediately contacted the credit bureau for further explanation.

Current Financial Situation

Assets:

Checking account, $1,800

Savings account, $7,200

Emergency fund savings account, $2,700

IRA balance, $410

Car, $2,800

Liabilities:

Student loan balance, $10,800 (Jamie is still a full-time student, so no payments are required on the loan until after graduation)

Credit card balance, $4,250 (total of three store credit cards)

Income:

Gross monthly salary from the bakery, $2,750 (net income, $2,175)

Monthly Expenses:

Rent, $350

Utilities, $70

Food, $125

Gas/Maintenance, $130

Credit card payment, $0

Questions

1. What steps should Jamie Lee take to discover the reason for the denial of her credit applications?

2. Jamie discovers that she has become the victim of identity theft, as her credit report indicates that two credit cards have been opened in her name without her authorization! The police had already been notified the evening of the theft incident in the apartment, but what other measures should Jamie Lee take now that she has become aware of the identity theft?

3. Fortunately for Jamie, she was able to show proof of the theft to the credit bureau and her credit applications for her apartment furnishings were approved. The purchase total for the appliances, living room furniture, and television amounted to $4,250. The minimum payments among the three accounts total $325 a month. What is Jamie Lee's debt payments-to-income ratio?

4. Oh, no! The television was finally delivered today, but was left on the porch by the delivery company. When Jamie Lee was finally able to attach all the wires and cables according to the owner's manual, it played for half an hour and then shut off. Jamie Lee was unable to get the television to turn back on, although she read the trouble-shooting guide in the manual and contacted tech support from the manufacturer. Jamie Lee lugged the television back to the store, but they would not accept a return on electronics. What should Jamie Lee do now?

5. Jamie Lee now has to juggle the three monthly credit card bills for each of the retailers where she purchased her home furnishings. She is interested in getting one loan to consolidate the three store consumer credit cards so she may make a single payment on the goods per month. Using "Your Personal Financial Plan" sheet 17, compare the consumer loan options that Jamie Lee may consider. What are your recommendations for her to consolidate her monthly consumer charge bills?

Spending Diary

"I ADMIRE PEOPLE WHO ARE ABLE TO PAY OFF THEIR CREDIT CARDS EACH MONTH."

Directions Your ability to monitor spending and credit use is a fundamental skill for wise money management and long-term financial security. Use the Daily Spending Diary sheets provided at the end of the book to record all of your spending in the categories provided. Be sure to indicate the use of a credit card with (CR). The Daily Spending Diary sheets are available in Appendix D at the end of the book and in Connect Finance.

Questions

1. Describe any aspects of your spending habits that might indicate an overuse of credit.
2. How might your Daily Spending Diary provide information for wise credit use?

Name: _____ Date: _____

Consumer Credit Usage Patterns

Purpose: To create a record of current consumer debt balances.

Financial Planning Activities: Record account names, numbers, and payments for current consumer debts. This sheet is also available in an Excel spreadsheet format in Connect Finance.

Suggested Websites: www.ftc.gov   www.creditcards.com

Automobile, Education, Personal, and Installment Loans

Financial institution	Account number	Current balance	Monthly payment
_____	_____	_____	_____
_____	_____	_____	_____
_____	_____	_____	_____
_____	_____	_____	_____

Charge Accounts and Credit Cards

_____	_____	_____	_____
_____	_____	_____	_____
_____	_____	_____	_____
_____	_____	_____	_____
_____	_____	_____	_____

Other Loans (overdraft protection, home equity, life insurance loan)

_____	_____	_____	_____
_____	_____	_____	_____
_____	_____	_____	_____

Totals   _____   _____

Suggested App:
• Lemon Wallet

$$\text{Debt payments-to-income ratio} = \frac{\text{Total monthly payments}}{\text{Net (after-tax) income}}$$

What's Next for Your Personal Financial Plan?

• Survey three or four individuals to determine their uses of credit.
• Talk to several people to determine how they first established credit.

Name: _____   **Date:** _____

Credit Card/Charge Account Comparison

Purpose: To compare the benefits and costs associated with different credit cards and charge accounts.

Financial Planning Activities: Analyze ads and credit applications and contact various financial institutions to obtain the information requested below. This sheet is also available in an Excel spreadsheet format in Connect Finance.

Suggested Websites: www.bankrate.com   www.creditcards.com   www.consumerfinance.gov

Type of credit/charge account			
Name of company/account			
Address/phone			
Website			
Type of purchases that can be made			
Annual fee (if any)			
Annual percentage rate (APR) (interest calculation information)			
Credit limit for new customers			
Minimum monthly payment			
Other costs: • credit report • late fee • other _____			
Restrictions (age, minimum annual income)			
Other information for consumers to consider			
Frequent flyer or other bonus points			

What's Next for Your Personal Financial Plan?

• Make a list of the pros and cons of using credit or debit cards.

• Contact a local credit bureau to obtain information on the services provided and the fees charged.

Name: _____   Date: _____

Consumer Loan Comparison

Purpose: To compare the costs associated with different sources of loans.

Financial Planning Activities: Contact or visit a bank, credit union, and consumer finance company to obtain information on a loan for a specific purpose. This sheet is also available in an Excel spreadsheet format in Connect Finance.

Suggested Websites: www.eloan.com   www.wellsfargo.com   www.ftc.gov

Type of financial institution			
Name			
Address			
Phone			
Website			
What collateral is required?			
Amount of down payment			
Length of loan (months)			
Amount of monthly payment			
Total amount to be repaid (monthly amount × number of months + down payment)			
Total finance charge/ cost of credit			
Annual percentage rate (APR)			
Other costs • credit life insurance • credit report • other _____			
Is a cosigner required?			
Other information			

What's Next for Your Personal Financial Plan?

- Ask several individuals how they would compare loans at different financial institutions.
- Survey several friends and relatives to determine if they ever cosigned a loan. If yes, what were the consequences of cosigning?

6 Consumer Purchasing Strategies and Wise Buying of Motor Vehicles

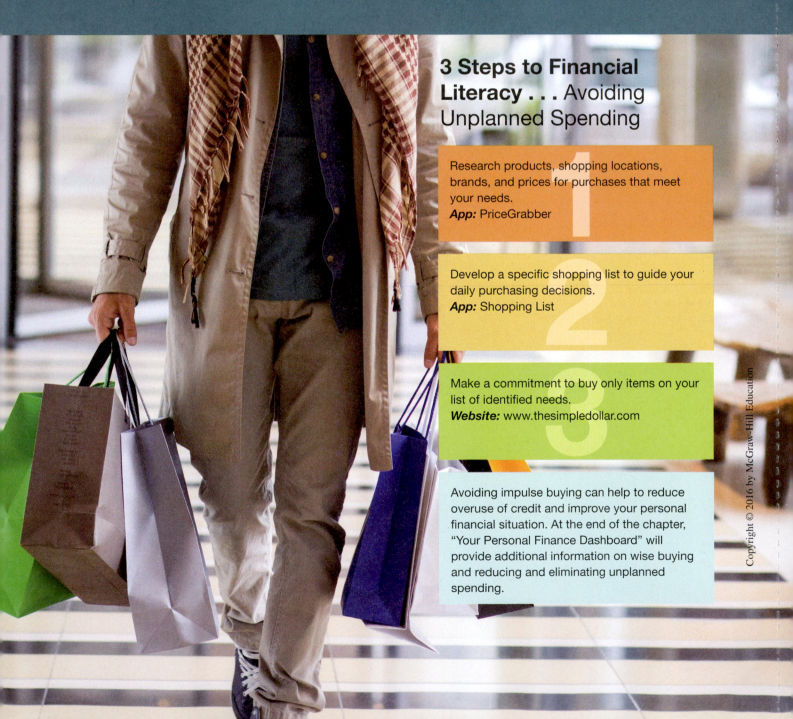

3 Steps to Financial Literacy . . . Avoiding Unplanned Spending

Research products, shopping locations, brands, and prices for purchases that meet your needs.
App: PriceGrabber

1

Develop a specific shopping list to guide your daily purchasing decisions.
App: Shopping List

2

Make a commitment to buy only items on your list of identified needs.
Website: www.thesimpledollar.com

3

Avoiding impulse buying can help to reduce overuse of credit and improve your personal financial situation. At the end of the chapter, "Your Personal Finance Dashboard" will provide additional information on wise buying and reducing and eliminating unplanned spending.

CHAPTER 6 LEARNING OBJECTIVES

In this chapter, you will learn to:

LO6.1 Identify strategies for effective consumer buying.

LO6.2 Implement a process for making consumer purchases.

LO6.3 Describe steps to take to resolve consumer problems.

LO6.4 Evaluate legal alternatives available to consumers.

YOUR PERSONAL FINANCIAL PLAN SHEETS

18. Consumer Purchase Comparison
19. Used-Car Purchase Comparison
20. Buying vs. Leasing a Vehicle
21. Legal Services Cost Comparison

Consumer Buying Activities

Daily buying decisions involve a trade-off between current spending and saving for the future. A wide variety of economic, social, and personal factors affect daily buying habits. These factors are the basis for spending, saving, investing, and achieving personal financial goals. In very simple terms, the only way you can have long-term financial security is to not spend all of your current income. In addition, overspending leads to misuse of credit and financial difficulties.

Practical Purchasing Strategies

Comparison shopping is the process of considering alternative stores, brands, and prices. In contrast, *impulse buying* involves unplanned purchasing, which can result in financial problems. Several buying techniques are commonly suggested for wise buying.

TIMING PURCHASES Certain items go on sale the same time each year. You can obtain bargains by buying winter clothing in mid- or late winter, or summer clothing in mid- or late summer. Many people save by buying holiday items and other products at reduced prices in late December and early January.

PURCHASE LOCATION Your decision to use a particular retailer is probably influenced by location, price, product selection, and services available. Competition and technology have changed retailing with superstores, specialty shops, and

LO6.1

Identify strategies for effective consumer buying.

ACTION ITEM

I stay informed on wise buying strategies.

☐ **Agree**

☐ **Disagree**

did you know?

To save money when shopping, (1) check your budget; (2) create a list, and don't stray from it; (3) avoid shopping as a social activity; (4) be careful not to let anxiety influence your purchases; and (5) remember that bargaining can result in the thrill of success for a deal on an item that you don't need.

online buying. This expanded shopping environment provides consumers with greater choice, potentially lower prices, and the need to carefully consider buying alternatives.

BRAND COMPARISON   Food and other products come in various brands. *National-brand* products are highly advertised items available in many stores. *Store-brand* and *private-label* products, sold by one chain of stores, are low-cost alternatives to famous-name products. Since store-brand products are frequently manufactured by the same companies that produce brand-name items, these lower-cost alternatives can result in extensive savings. The use of one or more of the many product comparison websites can assist you when comparing brands.

LABEL INFORMATION   Certain label information is helpful; however, other information is nothing more than advertising. Federal law requires that food labels contain certain information. Product labeling for appliances includes information about operating costs to assist you in selecting the most energy-efficient models. *Open dating* describes the freshness or shelf life of a perishable product. Phrases such as "Use before May 2016" or "Not to be sold after October 8" appear on most food products. However, these labels can be confusing. Most expiration dates relate to quality, not safety. Items used after the "sell by" date are likely to be safe for consumption. Canned and packaged food items, if not opened, will usually be safe beyond the expiration date.

PRICE COMPARISON   *Unit pricing* uses a standard unit of measurement to compare the prices of packages of different sizes. To calculate the unit price, divide the price of the item by the number of units of measurement, such as ounces, pounds, gallons, or number of sheets (for items such as paper towels and facial tissues). Then compare the unit prices for various sizes, brands, and stores.

EXAMPLE: Unit Pricing

To calculate the unit price of an item, divide the cost by the number of units. For example, a 64-ounce product costing $8.32 would be calculated in this manner:

Unit price = $8.32 ÷ 64
        = $0.13, or 13 cents an ounce

Coupons and rebates also provide better pricing for wise consumers. A family saving about $8 a week on their groceries by using coupons will save $416 over a year and $2,080 over five years (not counting interest). Coupons are available online through websites such as www.coolsavings.com and www.couponsurfer.com and through apps such as Coupon Cloud and Grocery Smarts. A *rebate* is a partial refund of the price of a product.

When comparing prices, remember that:

- More store convenience (location, hours, sales staff) usually means higher prices.
- Ready-to-use products have higher prices.
- Large packages are usually the best buy; however, compare using unit pricing.
- "Sale" may not always mean saving money.
- The use of online sources and shopping apps can save time.

Exhibit 6–1 summarizes techniques that can assist you in your online buying decisions.

CAUTION!

Buying fake and counterfeit products, online and elsewhere, may be cheap and easy, but also very dangerous. While buying a fake purse or watch may not cost much money, other products can cost lives. Counterfeit prescription medications are sold in many settings. A knock-off airbag used as a replacement part in a vehicle after an accident may not deploy properly.

Exhibit **6–1**   Wise Online Buying Activities

1. Conduct online research.
- Compare brands and features
- Use label and warranty information
- Use product testing reports to assess quality, safety, nutrition

2. Compare stores.
- Consider both stores and online
- Evaluate price, service, product quality, warranties, shipping cost and time, return policy
- Determine reputation, location

3. Make purchase.
- Use secure buying website
- Seek discounts, coupons
- Select payment method based on security, fees, other factors

4. Plan for future purchases.
- Keep receipts, other documents
- Know return, complaint process
- Watch e-mails for special offers
- Evaluate time, effort involved

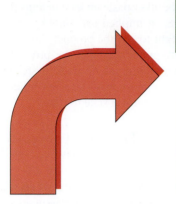
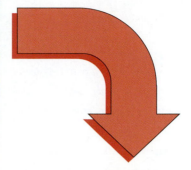

Warranties

Most products come with some guarantee of quality. A **warranty** is a written guarantee from the manufacturer or distributor that specifies the conditions under which the product can be returned, replaced, or repaired. An *express warranty,* usually in written form, is created by the seller or manufacturer and has two forms: the full warranty and the limited

warranty A written guarantee from the manufacturer or distributor of a product that specifies the conditions under which the product can be returned, replaced, or repaired.

warranty. A *full warranty* states that a defective product can be fixed or replaced during a reasonable amount of time.

A *limited warranty* covers only certain aspects of the product, such as parts, or requires the buyer to incur part of the costs for shipping or repairs. An *implied warranty* covers a product's intended use or other basic understandings that are not in writing. For example, an implied *warranty of title* indicates that the seller has the right to sell the product. An implied *warranty of merchantability* guarantees that the product is fit for the ordinary uses for which it is intended: A toaster must toast bread, and an MP3 player must play music or other recorded files. Implied warranties vary from state to state.

USED-CAR WARRANTIES The Federal Trade Commission (FTC) requires used cars to have a buyer's guide sticker telling whether the vehicle comes with a warranty and, if so, what protection the dealer will provide. If no warranty is offered, the car is sold "as is" and the dealer assumes no responsibility for any repairs, regardless of any oral claims. FTC used-car regulations do not apply to vehicles purchased from private owners.

While a used car may not have an express warranty, most states have implied warranties to protect used-car buyers. An implied warranty of merchantability means the product is guaranteed to do what it is supposed to do. The used car is guaranteed to run—at least for a while!

NEW-CAR WARRANTIES New-car warranties provide buyers with an assurance of quality. These warranties vary in the time, mileage, and parts they cover. The main conditions of a new-car warranty are (1) coverage of basic parts against defects; (2) power train coverage for the engine, transmission, and drive train; and (3) the corrosion warranty, which usually applies only to holes due to rust, not to surface rust. Other important conditions of a warranty are a statement regarding whether the warranty is transferable to other owners of the car and details about the charges, if any, that will be made for major repairs in the form of a *deductible*.

service contract An agreement between a business and a consumer to cover the repair costs of a product.

SERVICE CONTRACTS A **service contract** is an agreement between a business and a consumer to cover the repair costs of a product. Frequently called *extended warranties,* they are not warranties. For a fee, these agreements insure the buyer against losses due to the cost of certain repairs and losses. Beware of service contracts that offer coverage for three years but really only cover two since the item has a manufacturer's one-year warranty.

Automotive service contracts can cover repairs not included in the manufacturer's warranty. Service contracts range from $400 to more than $1,000; however, they do not always include everything you might expect. These contracts usually cover failure of the engine cooling system; however, some contracts exclude coverage of such failures if caused by overheating.

Because of costs and exclusions, service contracts may not be a wise financial decision. You can minimize your concern about expensive repairs by setting aside a fund of money to pay for them. Then, if you need repairs, the money to pay for them will be available.

Research-Based Buying

Major buying decisions should be based on a specific decision-making process, which may be viewed in four phases.

> ## did you know?
>
> When buying gifts or household items, you can make a difference in the life of an artisan in a developing country by making an online purchase from Ten Thousand Villages (www.tenthousandvillages.com). This organization works to help artisans earn a fair wage and to improve their quality of life by paying for food, education, health care, and housing. There are also more than 100 Ten Thousand Villages stores in the United States and Canada.

PHASE 1: PRESHOPPING ACTIVITIES

Start the buying process with actions that include:

- Problem identification to set a goal and focus your purchasing activities.
- Information gathering to benefit from the buying experiences of others.

PHASE 2: EVALUATING ALTERNATIVES

With every decision, consider various options:

- Attribute assessment with a comparison of product features.
- Price analysis including consideration of the costs at various buying locations.
- Comparison shopping activities to evaluate shopping locations.

PHASE 3: SELECTION AND PURCHASE

When making your final choice, actions may include:

- Negotiation activities to obtain lower price or added quality.
- Payment alternatives including use of cash and various credit plans.
- Assessment of acquisition and installation that might be encountered.

PHASE 4: POSTPURCHASE ACTIVITIES

After making a purchase, several actions are encouraged:

- Proper maintenance and operation.
- Identification and comparison of after-sale service alternatives.
- Resolution of any purchase concerns that may occur.

 Sheet 18 Consumer Purchase Comparison

PRACTICE QUIZ 6-1

1. What types of brands are commonly available to consumers?

2. In what situations can comparing prices help in purchasing decisions?

3. How does a service contract differ from a warranty?

4. Match the following descriptions with the warranties listed here. Write your answer in the space provided.

express warranty   limited warranty

full warranty   service contract

implied warranty

a. _____ Covers only aspects of the item purchased.
b. _____ Is commonly referred to as an extended warranty.
c. _____ Usually is in a written form.
d. _____ Covers a product's intended use; it may not be in writing.
e. _____ Covers fixing or replacement of a product for a set time period.

Apply Yourself!

Talk to people about their brand loyalty. For what products are people most brand loyal? What factors (price, location, information) may influence a person to change brands? Compare your findings to online research reports for brand loyalty.

Which Route Is Best for You?

	CPO	NON-CPO	PRIVATE PARTY
	Certified pre-owned vehicles are as close to a new-car-buying experience as you can get. You'll pay an extra $1,500 to $2,500 compared with non-CPO vehicles.	Dealers sell vehicles they acquire at auction or through trade-ins that aren't scooped up by the CPO programs. You'll likely pay at least 10% more to a dealer than to a private party.	The cheapest way to buy a used car. Private sellers can sell a used car for a higher price to you than they could to a dealer, but they can't inflate the price as much.
Condition	Excellent—models are five years old or newer with fewer than 60,000 miles. **Because many CPOs are off-lease, they have had only one owner.**	Mostly cosmetic reconditioning. **Don't expect repairs to be made.** Most dealers offer a vehicle history report from Auto-Check.com or Carfax .com.	It varies. **Ask for maintenance records** and get a vehicle history report on AutoCheck.com or Carfax.com.
Inspection	A 100- to 200-point inspection. Vehicles are repaired and reconditioned. **Worn parts are replaced, saving money on future maintenance.**	A dealer's service department inspects the car, but **get your own mechanic to go over the car** before you buy.	**You're on your own.** If the seller won't agree to let you take it to a mechanic, move on to the next prospect.
Warranty	Usually a year or two extension of new-car comprehensive and power-train warranty, **backed by the manufacturer, not the dealer.**	You get **what's left of the new-car warranty.** Resist the hard sell on an extended warranty. Some states have laws to protect used-car buyers.	As with a dealer sale, you get **what's left of the new-car warranty.** If you get stuck with a lemon, you have little or no recourse.
Financing	Carmakers' finance companies offer lower rates than you'd pay on non-CPO loans. **You may save hundreds of dollars in interest.**	The F&I department will arrange financing, **but dealers may get a commission.** Get prequalified at your bank or credit union and compare offers.	**You'll have to pay cash.** If you need a loan, consider drawing on a home-equity line, or get a used-car loan at a bank or credit union.

Jessica L. Anderson

1. From your perspective, what are the benefits and drawbacks of each of the three alternatives for buying a motor vehicle?

2. What factors should a person consider before buying an extended warranty?

3. What actions would you suggest when using any of the three alternatives presented in the article?

Major Consumer Purchases: Buying Motor Vehicles

LO6.2
Implement a process for making consumer purchases.

As shown in Exhibit 6–2, the steps for effective purchasing can be used for wise buying of motor vehicles.

Phase 1: Preshopping Activities

ACTION ITEM
I carefully plan major purchases with research and comparison shopping.

☐ **Agree**

☐ **Disagree**

First define your needs and obtain relevant product information. These activities are the foundation for buying decisions to help you achieve your goals.

PROBLEM IDENTIFICATION Effective decision making should start with an open mind. Some people always buy the same brand when another brand at a lower price would also serve their needs, or when another brand at the same price may provide better quality. A narrow view of the problem is a weakness in problem identification. You may think the problem is "I need to have a car" when the real problem is "I need transportation."

INFORMATION GATHERING Information is power. The better informed you are, the better buying decisions you will make. Some people spend very little time gathering and evaluating buying information. At the other extreme are people who spend much time obtaining consumer information. While information is necessary for wise purchasing, too much information can create confusion and frustration. The following information sources are frequently helpful:

1. *Personal contacts* allow you to learn about product performance, brand quality, and prices from others.
2. *Business organizations* offer advertising, product labels, and packaging that provide information about price, quality, and availability.
3. *Media information* (television, radio, newspapers, magazines, websites) can provide valuable information with purchasing advice.
4. *Independent testing organizations,* such as Consumers Union, provide information about the quality of products and services each month in *Consumer Reports.*

Exhibit **6–2** A Research-Based Approach for Purchasing a Motor Vehicle

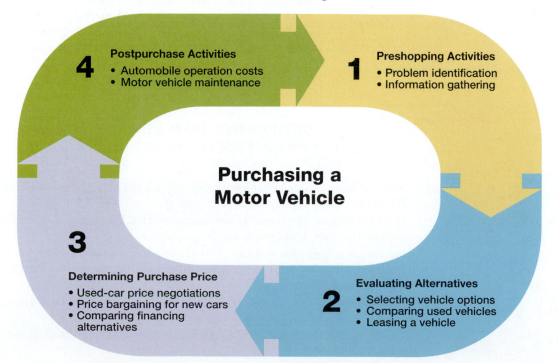

Purchasing a Motor Vehicle

4 Postpurchase Activities
• Automobile operation costs
• Motor vehicle maintenance

1 Preshopping Activities
• Problem identification
• Information gathering

3 Determining Purchase Price
• Used-car price negotiations
• Price bargaining for new cars
• Comparing financing alternatives

2 Evaluating Alternatives
• Selecting vehicle options
• Comparing used vehicles
• Leasing a vehicle

5. *Government agencies,* local, state, and federal, provide publications, toll-free telephone numbers, websites, and community programs.

6. *Online reviews* can provide buying guidance and shopping suggestions. However, be cautious since many are the result of fictitious online postings.

Basic information about car buying may be obtained at www.edmunds.com, www.caranddriver.com, www.autoweb.com, www.autotrader.com, and autos.msn.com. Consumers Union (www.consumerreports.org) offers a computerized car cost data service. Car-buying services, such as www.acscorp.com and www.autobytel.com, allow you to order your vehicle online.

digi – know?

Near-field communications (NFC) allow consumers to make purchases by waving their smartphones in front of a sensor when paying. Technology companies, financial service providers, and retailers are combining to become a part of this mobile-payments network. NFC also offers coupons and other deals that can result in people spending more than they might otherwise.

Phase 2: Evaluating Alternatives

Every purchasing situation usually has several acceptable alternatives. Ask yourself: Is it possible to delay the purchase or to do without the item? Should I pay for the item with cash or buy it on credit? Which brands should I consider? How do the price, quality, and service compare at different stores? Is it possible to rent the item instead of buying it? Considering such alternatives will result in more effective purchasing decisions.

Research shows that prices can vary for all types of products. For a camera, prices may range from under $100 to well over $500. The price of aspirin may range from less than $1 to over $3 for 100 five-grain tablets. While differences in quality and attributes may exist among the cameras, the aspirin tablets are equivalent in quantity and quality.

Many people view comparison shopping as a waste of time. Although this may be true in certain situations, comparison shopping can be beneficial when (1) buying expensive or complex items; (2) buying items that you purchase often; (3) comparison shopping can be done easily, such as with advertisements, catalogs, or online; (4) different sellers offer different prices and services; and (5) product quality or prices vary greatly.

CAUTION!

Every year, more than 450,000 people buy used vehicles with mileage gauges rolled back. According to the National Highway Traffic Safety Administration, consumers pay over $2,300 more than they should for vehicles with fraudulent mileage totals.

SELECTING VEHICLE OPTIONS Optional equipment for cars may be viewed in three categories: (1) mechanical devices to improve performance, such as power steering, power brakes, and cruise control; (2) convenience options, including power seats, air conditioning, audio systems, power locks, rear window defoggers, and tinted glass; and (3) aesthetic features that add to the vehicle's visual appeal, such as metallic paint, special trim, and upholstery.

COMPARING USED VEHICLES The average used car costs about $10,000 less than the average new car. Common sources of used cars include:

- New-car dealers, which offer late-model vehicles and may give you a warranty. Prices usually are higher than at other sources.
- Used-car dealers, which usually have older vehicles. Warranties, if offered, will be limited. However, lower prices may be available.
- Individuals selling their own cars. This can be a bargain if the vehicle was well maintained, but few consumer protection regulations apply to private-party sales. Caution is suggested.
- Auctions and dealers that sell automobiles previously owned by businesses, auto rental companies, and government agencies.
- Used-car superstores, such as CarMax, which offer a large inventory of previously owned vehicles.

Figure It Out!

Net Present Value of a Consumer Purchase: Is a Hybrid Car Worth the Cost?

The time value of money (explained in Chapter 1) may be used to evaluate the financial benefits of a consumer purchase. For example, when deciding to buy a hybrid car, the money saved on gas would be considered a cash *inflow* (since money not going out is like money coming in). The cost difference between a hybrid and a fuel-version vehicle would be the current cash *outflow*. If the car has an expected life of eight years, the *net present value* calculations might be as shown here:

Step 1: Estimate the annual savings on gas (for example, 2,000 miles at $4 a gallon), with a vehicle getting 50 miles per gallon rather than 25 miles per gallon.

Step 2: Calculate the present value (PV) of a series using either the time value of money tables (Chapter 1 Appendix) or a financial calculator. Assume a 2 percent interest rate, eight years.

Step 3: Subtract the difference in cost of hybrid car (compared with a gasoline-powered car).

Annual gas savings $2,400	→	PV of annual savings $7,032	−	Vehicle cost difference $6,000

The result: $1,032 is a positive (favorable) net present value of the savings from a hybrid car compared to a gasoline-powered car. A negative net present value would indicate that the financial aspects of the purchase are not desirable.

This analysis for buying a hybrid car can vary based on other factors, such as vehicle maintenance costs, miles driven per year, and gas prices. Hybrid car cost calculators are also available online. Remember that this decision will also be influenced by personal attitudes and social factors. This calculation format may be used to assess the financial benefits of other consumer purchases by comparing the present value of the cost savings over time with the price of the item.

Certified pre-owned (CPO) vehicles are nearly new cars that come with the original manufacturer's guarantee of quality. The rigorous inspection and repair process means a higher price than other used vehicles. CPO programs were originally created to generate demand for the many low-mileage vehicles returned at the end of a lease.

The appearance of a used car can be deceptive. A well-maintained engine may be inside a body with rust; a clean, shiny exterior may conceal major operational problems. Therefore, conduct a used-car inspection as outlined in Exhibit 6–3. Have a trained and trusted mechanic of *your* choice check the car to estimate the costs of potential repairs. This service will help you avoid surprises.

LEASING A MOTOR VEHICLE *Leasing* is a contractual agreement with monthly payments for the use of an automobile over a set time period, typically three, four, or five years. At the end of the lease term, the vehicle is usually returned to the leasing company.

Leasing offers several advantages: (1) Only a small cash outflow may be required for the security deposit, whereas buying can require a large down payment; (2) monthly lease payments are usually lower than monthly financing payments; (3) the lease agreement provides detailed records for business purposes; and (4) you are usually able to obtain a more expensive vehicle, more often.

Leasing also has major drawbacks: (1) You have no ownership interest in the vehicle; (2) you must meet requirements similar to qualifying for credit; and (3) additional costs may be incurred for extra mileage, certain repairs, turning the car in early, or even a move to another state.

Exhibit 6–3

Checking Out a
Used Car

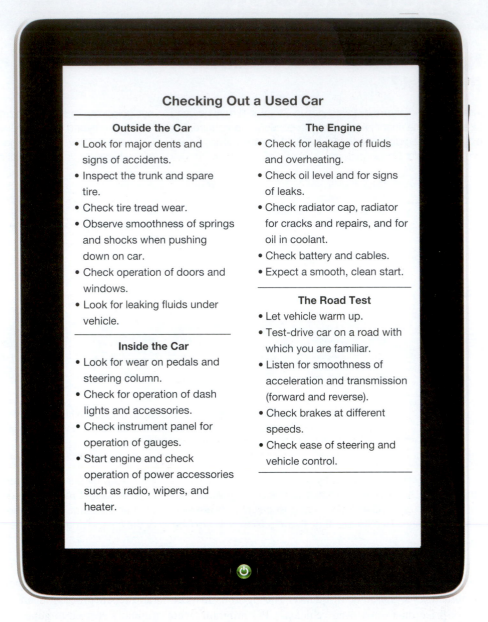

Checking Out a Used Car

Outside the Car
- Look for major dents and signs of accidents.
- Inspect the trunk and spare tire.
- Check tire tread wear.
- Observe smoothness of springs and shocks when pushing down on car.
- Check operation of doors and windows.
- Look for leaking fluids under vehicle.

Inside the Car
- Look for wear on pedals and steering column.
- Check for operation of dash lights and accessories.
- Check instrument panel for operation of gauges.
- Start engine and check operation of power accessories such as radio, wipers, and heater.

The Engine
- Check for leakage of fluids and overheating.
- Check oil level and for signs of leaks.
- Check radiator cap, radiator for cracks and repairs, and for oil in coolant.
- Check battery and cables.
- Expect a smooth, clean start.

The Road Test
- Let vehicle warm up.
- Test-drive car on a road with which you are familiar.
- Listen for smoothness of acceleration and transmission (forward and reverse).
- Check brakes at different speeds.
- Check ease of steering and vehicle control.

When leasing, you arrange for the dealer to sell the vehicle through a financing company. As a result, be sure you know the true cost, including

1. The *capitalized cost,* which is the price of the vehicle. The average car buyer pays about 92 percent of the list price for a vehicle; the average leasing arrangement has a capitalized cost of 96 percent of the list price.
2. The *money factor,* which is the interest rate being paid on the capitalized cost.
3. The *payment schedule,* which is the amount paid monthly and the number of payments.
4. The *residual value,* or the expected value of the vehicle at the end of the lease.

After the final payment, you may return, keep, or sell the vehicle. If the current market value is greater than the residual value, you may be able to sell it for a profit. However, if the residual value is more than the market value (which is the typical case), returning the vehicle to the leasing company is usually the best decision.

Phase 3: Determining Purchase Price

Once you've done your research and evaluations, other activities and decisions may be appropriate. Products such as real estate or automobiles may be purchased using price

Figure It Out!

Buying versus Leasing an Automobile

To compare the costs of purchasing and leasing a vehicle, use the following framework. This analysis involves two situations based on comparable payment amounts.

Purchase Costs	Example	Your Figures
Total vehicle cost, including sales tax ($20,000)		
Down payment (or full amount if paying cash)	$ 2,000	$_____
Monthly loan payment: $385 × 48-month length of financing (this item is zero if vehicle is not financed)	18,480	_____
Opportunity cost of down payment (or total cost of the vehicle if it is bought for cash): $2,000 × 4 years of financing/ownership × 3 percent	240	_____
Less: Estimated value of vehicle at end of loan term/ownership period	−6,000	_____
Total cost to buy	$14,720	_____

Leasing Costs	Example	Your Figures
Security deposit ($300)		
Monthly lease payments: $385 × 36-month length of lease	$13,860	$ _____
Opportunity cost of security deposit: $300 security deposit × 3 years × 3 percent	27	_____
End-of-lease charges* (if applicable)	800	_____
Total cost to lease	$14,687	_____

*Such as charges for extra mileage.

negotiation. Negotiation may also be used in other buying situations to obtain a lower price or additional features. Two vital factors in negotiation are (1) having all the necessary information about the product and buying situation and (2) dealing with a person who has the authority to give you a lower price or additional features, such as the owner or store manager.

USED-CAR PRICE NEGOTIATION Begin to determine a fair price by checking newspaper ads for the prices of comparable vehicles. Other sources of current used-car prices are *Edmund's Used Car Prices* and the *Kelley Blue Book.*

A number of factors influence the basic price of a used car. The number of miles the car has been driven, along with features and options, affect price. A low-mileage car will have a higher price than a comparable car with high mileage. The condition of the vehicle and the demand for the model also affect price.

PRICE BARGAINING FOR NEW CARS An important new-car price information source is the *sticker price* label, printed on the vehicle with the suggested retail price. This label presents the base price of the car with costs of added features. The dealer's cost, or *invoice price,* is an amount less than the sticker price. The difference between the sticker price and the dealer's cost is the range available for negotiation. This range is larger for full-size, luxury cars; subcompacts usually do not have a wide negotiation range. Information about dealer's cost is available from sources such as *Edmund's New Car Prices* and *Consumer Reports.*

Set-price dealers use no-haggling car selling with the prices presented to be accepted or rejected as stated. *Car-buying services* are businesses that help buyers obtain a specific new car at a reasonable price. Also referred to as an *auto broker,* these businesses offer desired models with options for prices ranging between $50 and $200 over the dealer's cost. First, the auto broker charges a small fee for price information on desired models. Then, if you decide to buy a car, the auto broker arranges the purchase with a dealer near your home.

To prevent confusion in determining the true price of the new car, do not mention a trade-in vehicle until the cost of the new car has been settled. Then ask how much the dealer is willing to pay for your old car. If the offer price is not acceptable, sell the old car on your own. A typical negotiating conversation might go like this:

Customer: "I'm willing to give you $15,600 for the car. That's my top offer."

Auto salesperson: "Let me check with my manager." After returning, "My manager says $16,200 is the best we can do."

Customer (who should be willing to walk out at this point): "I can go to $15,650."

Auto salesperson: "We have the car you want, ready to go. How about $15,700?"

If the customer agrees, the dealer receives $100 more than the customer's "top offer." Other sales techniques you should avoid include:

- *Lowballing,* when quoted a very low price that increases when add-on costs are included at the last moment.
- *Highballing,* when offered a very high amount for a trade-in vehicle, with the extra amount made up by increasing the new-car price.
- The question "How much can you afford per month?" Be sure to also ask how many months.
- The offer to hold the vehicle for a small deposit only. Never leave a deposit unless you are ready to buy a vehicle or are willing to lose that amount.
- Unrealistic statements, such as "Your price is only $100 above our cost." Usually, hidden costs have been added in to get the dealer's cost.
- Sales agreements with preprinted amounts. Cross out numbers you believe are not appropriate for your purchase.

COMPARING FINANCING ALTERNATIVES You may pay cash; however, most people buy cars on credit. Auto loans are available from banks, credit unions, consumer finance companies, and other financial institutions. Many lenders will *preapprove* you for a certain loan amount, which separates financing from negotiating the car price. Until the new-car price is set, you should not indicate that you intend to use the dealer's credit plan.

The lowest interest rate or the lowest payment does not necessarily mean the best credit plan. Also consider the loan length. Otherwise, after two or three years, the value of your car may be less than the amount you still owe; this situation is referred to as *upside-down* or *negative equity.* If you default on your loan or sell the car at this time, you will have to pay the difference.

---

did you know?

The *sharing economy* allows consumers to save money or earn income through car and bicycle rentals, home sharing, and shared nanny services. You may also borrow drills, saws, ladders, or lawn mowers with a community toolshed. About 5,000 sharing programs operate through websites and apps. To avoid dangers, use a sharing service that carefully screens participants.

EXAMPLE: Upside Down

A $26,000 vehicle is purchased with an initial loan of $18,000. After a period of time, the vehicle may only be worth $12,000 while you still owe $15,000. To avoid this situation, make a large down payment, have a short loan term (less than five years), and pay off the loan faster than the decline in value of the vehicle.

Automobile manufacturers frequently present opportunities for low-interest financing. They may offer rebates at the same time, giving buyers a choice between a rebate and a low-interest loan. Carefully compare low-interest financing and the rebate. Special rebates are sometimes offered to students, teachers, credit union members, real estate agents, and other groups.

Phase 4: Postpurchase Activities

Maintenance and ownership costs are associated with most major purchases. Correct use can result in improved performance and fewer repairs. When you need repairs not covered by a warranty, follow a pattern similar to that used when making the original purchase. Investigate, evaluate, and negotiate a variety of servicing options.

In the past, when major problems occurred with a new car and the warranty didn't solve the difficulty, many consumers lacked a course of action. As a result, all 50 states and the District of Columbia enacted *lemon laws* that require a refund for the vehicle after the owner has made repeated attempts to obtain servicing. These laws apply when four attempts are made to get the same problem corrected or when the vehicle has been out of service for more than 30 days within 12 months of purchase or the first 12,000 miles. The terms of the state laws vary.

AUTOMOBILE OPERATION COSTS Over your lifetime, you can expect to spend more than $200,000 on automobile-related expenses. Your driving costs will vary based on two main factors: the size of your automobile and the number of miles you drive. These costs involve two categories:

1. Fixed Ownership Costs	2. Variable Operating Costs
Depreciation	Gasoline and oil
Interest on auto loan	Tires
Insurance	Maintenance and repairs
License, registration, taxes, and fees	Parking and tolls

The largest fixed expense associated with a new automobile is *depreciation,* the loss in the vehicle's value due to time and use. Since money is not paid out for depreciation, many people do not consider it an expense. However, this decreased value is a cost that owners incur. Well-maintained vehicles and certain high-quality, expensive models, such as BMW and Lexus, depreciate at a slower rate.

Costs such as gasoline, oil, and tires increase with the number of miles driven. Planning expenses is easier if the number of miles you drive is fairly constant. Unexpected trips and vehicle age will increase such costs.

MOTOR VEHICLE MAINTENANCE People who sell, repair, or drive automobiles for a living stress the importance of regular care. While owner's manuals and articles suggest mileage or time intervals for certain servicing, more frequent oil changes or tune-ups can minimize major repairs and maximize vehicle life. Exhibit 6–4 suggests maintenance areas to consider.

AUTOMOBILE SERVICING SOURCES The following businesses offer automobile maintenance and repair service:

- Car dealers provide a service department with a wide range of car care services. Service charges at a car dealer may be higher than those of other repair businesses.
- Service stations can provide convenience and reasonable prices for routine maintenance and repairs. However, the number of full-service stations has declined in recent years.

Exhibit 6–4

Extending Vehicle Life with Proper Maintenance

- Get regular oil changes (every 3 months or 3,000 miles).
- Check fluids (brake, power steering, transmission).
- Inspect hoses and belts for wear.
- Get a tune-up (new spark plugs, fuel filter, air filter) every 12,000–15,000 miles.
- Check and clean battery cables and terminals.
- Check spark plug wires after 50,000 miles.
- Flush radiator and service transmission every 25,000 miles.
- Keep lights, turn signals, and horn in good working condition.
- Check muffler and exhaust pipes.
- Check tires for wear; rotate tires every 7,500 miles.
- Check condition of brakes.

Exhibit 6–5

Common Automobile Repair Frauds

The majority of automobile servicing sources are fair and honest. Sometimes, however, consumers waste dollars when they fall prey to the following unethical actions:

- When checking the oil, the attendant puts the dipstick only partway down and then shows you that you need oil.
- An attendant cuts a fan belt or punctures a hose. Watch carefully when someone checks under your hood.
- A garage employee puts some liquid on your battery and then tries to convince you that it is leaking and you need a new battery.
- Removing air from a tire instead of adding air to it can make an unwary driver open to buying a new tire or paying for an unneeded patch on a tire that is in perfect condition.
- The attendant puts grease near a shock absorber or on the ground and then tells you your present shocks are dangerous and you need new ones.
- You are charged for two gallons of antifreeze with a radiator flush when only one gallon was put in.

Dealing with reputable businesses and a basic knowledge of your automobile are the best methods of avoiding deceptive repair practices.

- Independent auto repair shops can service your vehicle at fairly competitive prices. Since the quality of these repair shops varies, talk with previous customers.
- Mass merchandise retailers, such as Sears and Walmart, may emphasize sale of tires and batteries as well as brakes, oil changes, and tune-ups.
- Specialty shops offer brakes, tires, automatic transmissions, and oil changes at a reasonable price with fast service.

To avoid unnecessary expenses, be aware of the common repair frauds presented in Exhibit 6–5. Remember to deal with reputable auto service businesses. Be sure to get a written, detailed estimate in advance as well as a detailed, paid receipt for the service completed. Studies of consumer problems consistently rank auto repairs as one of the top consumer ripoffs. Many people avoid problems and minimize costs by working on their own vehicles.

Sheet 19 Used-Car Purchase Comparison
Sheet 20 Buying vs. Leasing a Vehicle

PRACTICE QUIZ 6-2

1. What are the major sources of consumer information?

2. What actions are appropriate when buying a used car?

3. When might leasing a motor vehicle be appropriate?

4. What maintenance activities could increase the life of your vehicle?

5. The following abbreviations appeared in an ad for selling used cars. Interpret these abbreviations.

AC _____   Pwr Mrrs _____

ABS _____   P/S _____

Apply Yourself!

Using an online search, print ads, and store visits, compare the prices charged by different automotive service locations for a battery, tune-up, oil change, and tires.

Resolving Consumer Complaints

LO6.3

Describe steps to take to resolve consumer problems.

ACTION ITEM

I am well informed on how to take action for a consumer complaint.

☐ **Agree**

☐ **Disagree**

Most customer complaints result from defective products, low quality, short product lives, unexpected costs, deceptive pricing, and poor repairs. Federal consumer agencies estimate annual consumer losses from fraudulent business activities at $10 billion to $40 billion for telemarketing and mail order, $3 billion for credit card fraud and credit "repair" scams, and $10 billion for investment swindles.

People do not anticipate problems with purchases but should be prepared for them. To minimize consumer problems, before making a purchase (1) obtain recommendations from friends, family members, and online reviews; (2) verify company affiliations, certifications, and licenses; and (3) understand the sale terms, return policies, and warranty provisions. Most people do not anticipate or have problems with their purchases. However, since problems do arise, it's best to be prepared for them. The process for resolving differences between buyers and sellers includes the steps presented in Exhibit 6–6.

Before starting this process, know your rights and the laws that apply to your situation. Information on consumer rights is available online and through phone apps, such as the one that allows airline passengers to monitor the status of their flights. Information on delays, cancelations, and other situations can be submitted to keep airlines accountable.

To help ensure success when you make a complaint, keep a file of receipts, names of people you talked to, dates of attempted repairs, copies of letters you wrote, and costs incurred. Written documents can help to resolve a problem in your favor. An automobile owner kept detailed records and receipts for all gasoline purchases, oil changes, and repairs. When a warranty dispute occurred, the owner was able to prove proper maintenance and received a refund for the defective vehicle. Your perseverance is vital since companies might ignore your request or delay their response.

did you know?

The most common sources of consumer fraud involve (1) prizes, contests, and sweepstakes; (2) work at home, starting your own business, phony training courses, employment scams; (3) fraudulent diets and health claims, easy weight loss; (4) credit repair, debt collection, mortgage scams; (5) phony charities; (6) high-return investments and multilevel marketing; (7) foreign money offers, such as the Nigerian bank scam; (8) online purchases and auctions; (9) home and auto repairs; and (10) travel deals.

Step 1: Initial Communication

Most consumer complaints are resolved at the original sales location. As you talk with the salesperson, customer service person, or store manager, avoid yelling, threatening a lawsuit, or demanding unreasonable action. A calm, rational, yet persistent approach is recommended.

Key Website for Company Addresses

www.consumeraction.gov

Exhibit 6–6

Resolving Consumer
Complaints

STEP 1. Initial Communication
- Return to place of purchase or contact online retailer.
- Provide a detailed explanation and the action you desire.
- Be pleasant yet persistent in your efforts to obtain a resolution.

STEP 2. Communicate with the Company
- Send an e-mail with the details of the situation (Exhibit 6–7).
- Post your concerns on the company's online social media sites.
- Comment on a blog or a consumer review website.

STEP 3. Consumer Agency Assistance
- Seek guidance from a local, state, or federal consumer agency.
- Determine if any laws have been violated in the situation.
- Consider the use of mediation or arbitration.

STEP 4. Legal Action
- Consider bringing your case to small claims court.
- Determine if a class-action suit is appropriate.
- Seek assistance from a lawyer or legal aid organization.

Step 2: Communicate with the Company

Express your dissatisfaction to the corporate level if a problem is not resolved at the local store. Use a letter or e-mail such as the one in Exhibit 6–7. You can obtain companies' contact information at www.consumeraction.gov or with an online search. The websites of companies usually provide information for contacting the organization. You can obtain a company's consumer hotline number by calling 1-800-555-1212, the toll-free information number. Most companies print the toll-free hotline number and website information on product packages.

Exhibit 6–7   Sample Complaint E-mail

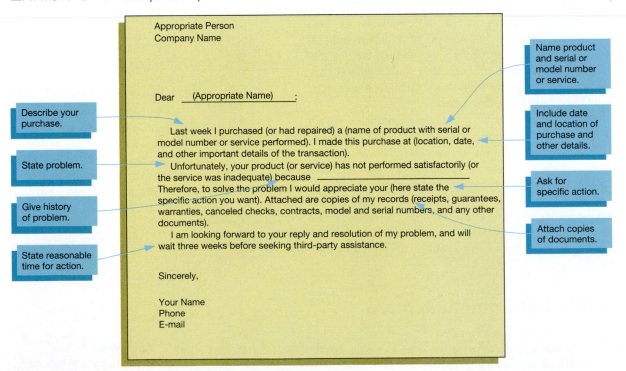

Appropriate Person
Company Name

Dear ___(Appropriate Name)___ :

Last week I purchased (or had repaired) a (name of product with serial or model number or service performed). I made this purchase at (location, date, and other important details of the transaction).
Unfortunately, your product (or service) has not performed satisfactorily (or the service was inadequate) because _____
Therefore, to solve the problem I would appreciate your (here state the specific action you want). Attached are copies of my records (receipts, guarantees, warranties, canceled checks, contracts, model and serial numbers, and any other documents).
I am looking forward to your reply and resolution of my problem, and will wait three weeks before seeking third-party assistance.

Sincerely,

Your Name
Phone
E-mail

Labels:
- Describe your purchase.
- State problem.
- Give history of problem.
- State reasonable time for action.
- Name product and serial or model number or service.
- Include date and location of purchase and other details.
- Ask for specific action.
- Attach copies of documents.

NOTE: Keep copies of your letter and all related documents and information.

SOURCE: *Consumer's Resource Handbook* (www.pueblo.gsa.gov).

Step 3: Consumer Agency Assistance

If you do not receive satisfaction from the company, organizations are available to assist with automobiles, appliances, health care, and other consumer concerns. **Mediation** involves the use of a third party to settle grievances. In mediation, an impartial person—the *mediator*—tries to resolve a conflict between a customer and a business through discussion and negotiation. Mediation is a nonbinding process. It can save time and money compared to other dispute settlement methods.

Arbitration is the settlement of a difference by a third party—the *arbitrator*—whose decision is legally binding. After both sides agree to arbitration, each side presents its case. Arbitrators are selected from volunteers trained for this purpose. Most major automobile manufacturers and many industry organizations have arbitration programs to resolve consumer complaints.

A vast network of government agencies is available. Problems with local restaurants or food stores may be handled by a city or county health department. Every state has agencies to handle problems involving deceptive advertising, fraudulent business practices, banking, insurance companies, and utility rates. Federal agencies are available to help with consumer concerns (see Appendix C).

mediation The attempt by an impartial third party to resolve a difference between two parties through discussion and negotiation.

 CAUTION!

Without realizing it, many consumers sign contracts with provisions that stipulate arbitration as the method to resolve disputes. As a result, consumers face various risks, including rules vastly different from a jury trial, higher costs for the arbitrator's time, and selection of an arbitrator by the defendant.

arbitration The settlement of a difference by a third party whose decision is legally binding.

Step 4: Legal Action

The next section considers various legal alternatives available to resolve consumer problems.

PRACTICE QUIZ 6–3

1. What are common causes of consumer problems and complaints?

2. How can most consumer complaints be resolved?

3. How does arbitration differ from mediation?

Apply Yourself!

Conduct online research to determine the most frequent sources of consumer complaints.

Legal Options for Consumers

If the previous actions fail to resolve your complaint, one of the following may be appropriate.

Small Claims Court

In **small claims court,** a person may file a claim involving amounts below a set dollar limit. The maximum varies from state to state, ranging from $500 to $10,000; most states have a limit of between $1,500 and $3,000. The process usually takes place without a lawyer, although in many states attorneys are allowed in small claims court. To effectively use small claims court, experts suggest that you:

• Become familiar with court procedures and filing fees (usually from $5 to $50).
• Observe other cases to learn about the process.

LO6.4

Evaluate legal alternatives available to consumers.

ACTION ITEM

I know the legal actions to take for consumer problems.

☐ **Agree**

☐ **Disagree**

small claims court A court that settles legal differences involving amounts below a set limit and employs a process in which the litigants usually do not use a lawyer.

class-action suit A legal action taken by a few individuals on behalf of all the people who have suffered the same alleged injustice.

- Present your case in a polite, calm, and concise manner.
- Submit evidence such as photographs, contracts, receipts, and other documents.
- Use witnesses who can testify on your behalf.

Class-Action Suits

Occasionally a number of people have the same complaint. A **class-action suit** is a legal action taken by a few individuals on behalf of all the people who have suffered the same alleged injustice. These people are represented by one or more lawyers. Once a situation qualifies as a class-action suit, all of the affected parties must be notified. A person may decide not to participate in the class-action suit and instead file an individual lawsuit. Recent class-action suits included auto owners who were sold unneeded replacement parts for their vehicles and a group of investors who sued a brokerage company for unauthorized buy-and-sell transactions that resulted in high commission charges.

did you know?

Websites such as LegalZoom, Nolo, and Rocket Lawyer are available to assist with basic legal documents, such as creating a will. Beyond this minimal document preparation, consumers are encouraged to consult a lawyer.

Using a Lawyer

In some situations, you may seek the services of an attorney. Common sources of lawyers are referrals from friends, advertisements, and the local division of the American Bar Association.

In general, straightforward legal situations such as appearing in small claims court, renting an apartment, or defending yourself on a minor traffic violation may not need legal counsel. More complicated matters such as writing a will, settling a real estate purchase, or suing for injury damages will likely require the services of an attorney.

When selecting a lawyer, consider several questions: Is the lawyer experienced in your type of case? Will you be charged on a flat fee basis, at an hourly rate, or on a contingency basis? Is there a fee for the initial consultation? How and when will you be required to make payment for services?

Other Legal Alternatives

legal aid society One of a network of publicly supported community law offices that provide legal assistance to consumers who cannot afford their own attorney.

Legal services can be expensive. A **legal aid society** is one of a network of publicly supported community law offices that provide legal assistance to people who cannot afford their own attorney. These community agencies provide this assistance at a minimal cost or without charge.

Prepaid legal services provide unlimited or reduced-fee legal assistance for a set fee. Some programs provide basic services, such as telephone consultation and preparation of a simple will, for an annual fee. Prepaid legal programs are designed to prevent minor troubles from becoming complicated legal problems.

Personal Consumer Protection

While many laws, agencies, legal tools, and online sources are available to protect your rights, none will be of value unless you use them. Consumer protection experts suggest that to prevent being taken by deceptive business practices, you should

1. Do business only with reputable companies with a record of satisfying customers.
2. Avoid signing contracts and other documents you do not understand.
3. Be cautious about offerings that seem too good to be true—they probably are!
4. Compare the cost of buying on credit with the cost of paying cash; also, compare the interest rates the seller offers with those offered by a bank or a credit union.
5. Avoid rushing to get a good deal; successful con artists depend on impulse buying.

How to File a Suit in Small Claims Court

In every state, small claims courts are available to handle legal disputes involving minor amounts. While specific procedures vary from state to state, these actions are usually involved:

Step 1. Notify the defendant to request a payment for damages with a deadline, such as within 30 days. Note in your letter that you will initiate legal action after that point in time.

Step 2. Determine the appropriate location for filing the case. Also, decide if your type of case is allowed in small claims court in your state, and if the amount is within the state limit. (Information on state limits is available at www.nolo.com/legal-encyclopedia/article-30031.html.)

Step 3. Obtain and complete the required filing documents. These forms can be obtained at the courthouse or may be available online. The petition will include the plaintiff's name (you), the defendant (person or organization being sued), the amount being requested, a detailed and clear description of the claim with dates of various actions, and copies of any pertinent documents (contracts, receipts).

Step 4. File the documents and pay the required fee. The petition will be served to the defendant notifying that person of the suit. After being served, the defendant is usually required to file a written response, denying or not contesting the claim. If the defendant does not respond, a default judgment will most likely be entered.

Step 5. Next, a hearing date will be set. Prepare evidence with a clear and concise presentation of (a) the details of what happened and when; (b) evidence, such as contracts, leases, receipts, canceled checks, credit card statements, or photographs; and (c) the testimony of people who witnessed aspects of the dispute or who are knowledgeable about the type of situation. If both parties decide to settle before the hearing, be sure that you receive payment before the case is dismissed.

Step 6. At the hearing, be as clear and concise as possible, and bring supporting documentation with you. A subpoena may be needed requiring witnesses whom you wish present at the hearing to appear in court.

Step 7. Once you receive a favorable judgment, you still have to collect the funds. While the court does not collect the money for you, the party may pay when the judgment is rendered. If not, a letter from you or an attorney may result in payment. Or more formal debt collection actions might be necessary.

Every state has different procedures and regulations related to small claims court. Conduct a web search to obtain information for your specific location. Careful and detailed preparation of your case is the key to a successful small claims court case.

Sheet 21 Legal Services Cost Comparison

PRACTICE QUIZ 6–4

1. In what types of situations would small claims court and class-action suits be helpful?

2. Describe situations in which you might use the services of a lawyer.

3. For the following situations, identify the legal action that would be most appropriate to take.

   a. A low-income person wants to obtain the services of a lawyer to file a product-liability suit.
   b. A person is attempting to obtain a $150 catering deposit that was never returned.
   c. A consumer wants to settle a dispute out of court with the use of a legally binding third party.
   d. A group of telephone customers were overcharged by $1.10 a month over the past 22 months.

Apply Yourself!

Interview someone who has had a consumer complaint. What was the basis of the complaint? What actions were taken? Was the complaint resolved in a satisfactory manner?

YOUR PERSONAL FINANCE DASHBOARD

UNPLANNED SPENDING PERCENT

Unplanned spending, often called *impulse buying,* is a common danger in preventing effective financial planning. While people may spend to feel good about themselves, that action often results in budget problems, higher debt levels, and greater financial stress.

Measuring the key performance indicator of unplanned spending as part of your personal finance dashboard can contribute to your financial progress. Careful spending will result in lower debt, increased savings, and achieving your financial goals.

YOUR SITUATION: Are you able to minimize the amount you spend on unplanned purchases? Are there areas of spending you might reduce? A low unplanned spending ratio can result in improved financial security.

POSSIBLE ACTIONS TO TAKE

 Reconsider your responses to the "Action Items" (in the text margin) to determine actions you might take to improve your daily spending habits.

 Talk with experienced shoppers, such as friends, relatives, and others, to learn more about their buying habits or tips that save time and money.

 Consult Appendix C for various sources of consumer information, government agencies, and organizations to assist you with buying decisions and to avoid potential consumer problems.

 Avoid becoming a victim of various consumer scams; these deceptions can be very creative. Conduct a web search to learn about small claims court procedures and other types of consumer legal actions available in your state.

Chapter Summary

LO6.1 Timing purchases, comparing stores and brands, using label information, computing unit prices, and evaluating warranties are common strategies for effective purchasing.

LO6.2 A research-based approach to consumer buying involves (1) preshopping activities, such as problem identification and information gathering; (2) evaluating alternatives; (3) determining the purchase price; and (4) postpurchase activities, such as proper operation and maintenance.

LO6.3 Most consumer problems can be resolved by following these steps: (1) Return to the place of purchase; (2) contact the company's main office; (3) obtain assistance from a consumer agency; and (4) take legal action.

LO6.4 Small claims court, class-action suits, the services of a lawyer, legal aid societies, and prepaid legal services are legal means for handling consumer problems that cannot be resolved through communication with the company involved or with help from a consumer protection agency.

Key Terms

arbitration 205

class-action suit 206

legal aid society 206

mediation 205

service contract 192

small claims court 205

warranty 191

1. Describe how advertisements, news articles, online sources, and personal observations might be used to make wiser buying decisions. (LO6.1)
2. When using the research-based approach for purchasing described in this chapter, which actions do you believe are overlooked by most shoppers? (LO6.2)
3. What are potential concerns associated with obtaining furniture, appliances, and other items from a rent-to-own business? (LO6.3)
4. What is a "certified pre-owned" vehicle? What are the benefits and drawbacks of this type of purchase? (LO6.2)
5. While fraud usually involves deceptions against consumers, what are some "frauds" that consumers commit against businesses? (LO6.3)

1. An item was bought on credit with a $60 down payment and monthly payments of $70 for 36 months. What was the total cost of the item?
2. A food package with 32 ounces costs $1.76. What is the unit cost of the package?

Solutions

1. 36 × $70 = $2,520 plus the $60 down payment for a total of $2,580.
2. $1.76 ÷ 32 = 5.5 cents an ounce.

1. An online buying club offers a membership for $300, for which you will receive a 10 percent discount on all brand-name items you purchase. How much would you have to buy to cover the cost of the membership? (LO6.1)
2. John Walters is comparing the cost of credit to the cash price of an item. If John makes an $80 down payment and pays $35 a month for 24 months, how much more will that amount be than the cash price of $685? (LO6.1)
3. Calculate the unit price of each of the following items: (LO6.1)

    a. Motor oil—2.5 quarts for $1.95 _____ *cents/quart*
    b. Cereal—15 ounces for $2.17 _____ *cents/ounce*
    c. Canned fruit—13 ounces for 89 cents _____ *cents/ounce*
    d. Facial tissue—300 tissues for $2.25 _____ *cents/100 tissues*

4. A service contract for a video projection system costs $70 a year. You expect to use the system for five years. Instead of buying the service contract, what would be the future value of these annual amounts after five years if you earn 3 percent on your savings? (LO6.1)
5. A work-at-home opportunity is available in which you will receive 3 percent of the sales for customers you refer to the company. The cost of your "franchise fee" is $600. How much would your customers have to buy to cover the cost of this fee? (LO6.1)
6. What would be the net present value of a microwave oven that costs $159 and will save you $68 a year in time and food away from home? Assume an average return on your savings of 4 percent for five years. (*Hint:* Calculate the present value of the annual savings, then subtract the cost of the microwave.) (LO6.1)
7. If a person saves $62 a month by using coupons and doing comparison shopping, (*a*) what is the amount for a year? (*b*) What would be the future value of this annual amount over 10 years, assuming an interest rate of 4 percent? (LO6.1)
8. Based on financial and opportunity costs, which of the following do you believe would be the wiser purchase? (LO6.2)

    Vehicle 1: A three-year-old car with 45,000 miles, costing $16,700 and requiring $1,385 of immediate repairs.

Vehicle 2: A five-year-old car with 62,000 miles, costing $14,500 and requiring $1,760 of immediate repairs.

9. Based on the following data, prepare a financial comparison of buying and leasing a motor vehicle with a $24,000 cash price:

Down payment (to finance vehicle), $4,000	Down payment for lease, $1,200
Monthly loan payment, $560	Monthly lease payment, $440
Length of loan, 48 months	Length of lease, 48 months
Value of vehicle at end of loan, $7,200	End-of-lease charges, $600

What other factors should a person consider when choosing between buying and leasing? (LO6.2)

10. Based on the data provided here, calculate the items requested: (LO6.2)

Annual depreciation, $2,500	Annual mileage, 13,200
Current year's loan interest, $650	Miles per gallon, 24
Insurance, $680	License and registration fees, $65
Average gasoline price, $3.50 per gallon	Oil changes/repairs, $370
Parking/tolls, $420	

a. The total annual operating cost of the motor vehicle.
b. The operating cost per mile.

11. Based on the following, calculate the costs of buying versus leasing a motor vehicle. (LO6.2)

Purchase Costs
Down payment, $1,500
Loan payment, $450 for 48 months
Estimated value at end of loan, $4,000
Opportunity cost interest rate, 4 percent

Leasing Costs
Security deposit, $500
Lease payment, $450 for 36 months
End-of-lease charges, $600

12. A class-action suit against a utility company resulted in a settlement of $1.4 million for 62,000 customers. If the legal fees, which must be paid from the settlement, are $300,000, what amount will each plaintiff receive? (LO6.4)

 **To reinforce the content in this chapter, more problems are provided at connect.mheducation.com.**

Case in Point

ONLINE CAR BUYING

With a click of the mouse, Mackenzie enters the auto "showroom." In the past few months she had realized that the repair costs for her 11-year-old car were accelerating. She thought it was time to start shopping for a new car online and decided to start her Internet search for a vehicle by looking at small and midsized SUVs.

Her friends suggested that Mackenzie research more than one type of vehicle. They reminded her that comparable models were available from various auto manufacturers.

In her online car-buying process, Mackenzie next did a price comparison. She obtained more than one price quote by using various online sources. She then prepared an overview of her online car-buying experiences.

Mackenzie's next step was to make her final decision. After selecting what she planned to buy, she finalized the purchase online and decided to take delivery at a local dealer.

In recent years, less than 5 percent of car buyers have actually purchased vehicles over the Internet. That number is increasing; however, car-buying experts strongly recommend that you make a personal examination of the vehicle before taking delivery.

Online Car-Buying Action	Online Activities	Websites Consulted
Information gathering	• Review available vehicle models and options. • Evaluate operating costs and safety features.	autos.msn.com www.consumerreports.org www.caranddriver.com www.motortrend.com
Comparing prices	• Identify specific make, model, and features desired. • Locate availability and specific price in your geographic area.	www.autobytel.com www.edmunds.com www.kbb.com www.nadaguides.com
Finalizing purchase	• Make payment or financing arrangements. • Conduct in-person inspection. • Arrange for delivery.	www.autobytel.com www.autonation.com www.autoweb.com www.carsdirect.com

Questions

1. Based on Mackenzie's experience, what benefits and drawbacks are associated with online car buying?

2. What additional actions might Mackenzie consider before buying a motor vehicle?

3. What do you consider to be the benefits and drawbacks of shopping online for motor vehicles and other items?

4. What actions might a car buyer take if a lemon is purchased?

Continuing Case

CONSUMER PURCHASING STRATEGIES AND WISE BUYING OF MOTOR VEHICLES

It sputtered and squeaked and, with a small hesitation followed by an exaggerated shudder, it was finally over. Ol' Reliable, the car Jamie Lee had driven since she first earned her driver's license at the age of 17, completed its last mile. Thirteen years and 140,000 miles later, it was time for a new vehicle.

After skimming the Sunday newspaper and browsing the online advertisements, Jamie Lee was ready to visit car dealers to see what vehicles would interest her. She was unsure if she would purchase a new car or used, and how she would pay for the car. "No money down and only $219 a month," Jamie Lee read, "with approved credit." It sounded like an offer she would be interested in. Jamie Lee knew she had a good credit rating, as she made sure she paid all of her bills on time each month and had kept a close eye on her credit score ever since she was the victim of identity theft several years ago. The more she thought about the brand-new car, the more excited she became. That new car fit her personality perfectly!

As Jamie Lee inquired about the advertised vehicle with the salesperson, her excitement quickly turned to dismay. The automobile advertised was available for $219 a month with no money down, based on approved credit, but Jamie Lee unexpectedly found that there were further qualifications in order to get the advertised price. The salesman explained that the information in the fine print of the newspaper advertisement stated that the price was based on all of the following criteria: being active in the military, a college graduate within the last three months, a current lessee of the automobile company, and having a top-tier credit score, which, he noted, was above 800. If Jamie Lee did not meet all of the qualifications, she would not receive the price advertised in the promotion. He could get her in that vehicle, but it would cost her an additional $110 per month. Jamie budgeted a maximum of $275 for her monthly car payment. She could not afford the vehicle.

Jamie Lee had to start over from scratch. She decided that she must fully research the vehicle purchase process before browsing at another dealership. She felt she was getting caught up in the moment and vowed to do her research before speaking with another salesperson.

Questions

1. Jamie Lee is considering a used vehicle, but cannot decide where to begin her search. Using "Your Personal Financial Plan" sheet 19, name the sources available to Jamie Lee for a used-car purchase. What are the advantages and disadvantages of each?

2. Jamie Lee is attracted to the low monthly payment advertised for a vehicle lease. She may well be able to afford a more expensive car than she originally thought. Jamie Lee really needs to think this through. What are the advantages and disadvantages to leasing a vehicle?

3. Jamie Lee sat down with a salesperson to discuss a new vehicle and its $24,000 purchase price. Jamie Lee has heard that "no one really pays the vehicle sticker price." What guidelines may be suggested for negotiating the purchase price of a vehicle?

4. Jamie Lee has decided to purchase a certified pre-owned vehicle. What might she expect as far as reliability and a warranty on the used car?

Spending Diary

"USING THE DAILY SPENDING DIARY HAS HELPED ME CONTROL IMPULSE BUYING. WHEN I HAVE TO WRITE DOWN EVERY AMOUNT, I'M MORE CAREFUL WITH MY SPENDING. I CAN NOW PUT MORE IN SAVINGS."

Directions Start (or continue) your Daily Spending Diary or use your own format to record and monitor spending in various categories. Most people who have participated in this activity have found it beneficial for monitoring and controlling their spending habits. The Daily Spending Diary sheets are located in Appendix D at the end of the book and in Connect Finance.

Questions

1. What daily spending items are amounts that might be reduced or eliminated to allow for higher savings amounts?

2. How might a Daily Spending Diary result in wiser consumer buying and more saving for the future?

Name: _____ Date: _____

Consumer Purchase Comparison

Purpose: To research and evaluate brands and store services for purchase of a major consumer item.

Financial Planning Activities: When considering the purchase of a major consumer item, use ads, catalogs, an Internet search, store visits, and other sources to obtain the information below. This sheet is also available in an Excel spreadsheet format in Connect Finance.

Suggested Websites: www.consumerreports.org   www.consumerworld.org
www.clarkhoward.com

Product

Exact description (size, model, features, etc.)

Research the item in consumer periodicals and online for information regarding your product

article/periodical _____   **website** _____

date/pages _____   **date** _____

What buying suggestions are presented in the articles?

Which brands are recommended in these articles? Why?

Contact or visit two or three stores that sell the product to obtain the following information:

	Store 1	Store 2	Store 3
Company			
Address			
Phone/website			
Brand name/cost			
Product difference from item above			
Warranty (describe)			
Which brand and at which store would you buy this product? Why?			

What's Next for Your Personal Financial Plan?

- Which consumer information sources are most valuable for your future buying decisions?
- List guidelines to use in the future when making major purchases.

Name: _____ Date: _____

Used-Car Purchase Comparison

Purpose: To research and evaluate different types and sources of used vehicles.

Financial Planning Activities: When considering a used-car purchase, use advertisements, online sources, and visits to new- and used-car dealers to obtain the information below. This sheet is also available in an Excel spreadsheet format in Connect Finance.

Suggested Websites: www.carbuyingtips.com   www.kbb.com   www.safercar.gov

Automobile (year, make, model)			
Name			
Address			
Phone			
Website (if applicable)			
Cost			
Mileage			
Condition of auto			
Condition of tires			
Radio			
Air conditioning			
Other options			
Warranty (describe)			
Items in need of repair			
Inspection items: • Rust, major dents?			
• Oil or fluid leaks?			
• Condition of brakes?			
• Proper operation of heater, wipers, other accessories?			
Other information			

Suggested App:
• KBB

What's Next for Your Personal Financial Plan?

• Maintain a record of automobile operating costs.
• Prepare a plan for regular maintenance of your vehicle.

Buying vs. Leasing a Vehicle

Purpose: To compare costs of buying or leasing an automobile or other vehicle. This analysis should compare two situations with comparable payment amounts, even though the length of the agreements may differ.

Financial Planning Activities: Obtain costs related to leasing and buying a vehicle. This sheet is also available in an Excel spreadsheet format in Connect Finance.

Suggested Websites: www.leasesource.com   www.kiplinger.com/tools

Purchase Costs

Total vehicle cost, including sales tax ($ _____)

Down payment (or full amount if paying cash) $ _____

Monthly loan payment: $ _____ times _____ month loan $ _____
(this item is zero if vehicle is not financed)

Opportunity cost of down payment (or total cost of the vehicle if bought for cash):

$ _____ times number of years of financing/ownership times _____
percent (interest rate which funds could earn) $ _____

Less: estimated value of vehicle at end of loan term/ownership $ _____

Total cost to buy . . . . $ _____

Leasing Costs

Security deposit $ _____

Monthly lease payments: $ _____ times _____ months $ _____

Opportunity cost of security deposit: $ _____ times years
times _____ percent $ _____

End-of-lease charges (if applicable)* $ _____

Total cost to lease . . . . $ _____

*With a closed-end lease, charges for extra mileage or excessive wear and tear; with an open-end lease, end-of-lease payment if appraised value is less than estimated ending value.

What's Next for Your Personal Financial Plan?

- Prepare a list of future actions to use when buying, financing, and leasing a car.
- Maintain a record of operating costs and maintenance actions for your vehicle.

Suggested
App:
• iLeaseMyCar

21

Name: _____   **Date:** _____

Legal Services Cost Comparison

Purpose: To compare cost of services from various sources of legal assistance.

Financial Planning Activities: Contact various sources of legal services (lawyer, prepaid legal service, legal aid society) to compare costs and available services. This sheet is also available in an Excel spreadsheet format in Connect Finance.

Suggested Websites: www.nolo.com   www.abanet.org

Type of legal service			
Organization name			
Address			
Phone			
Website			
Contact person			
Recommended by			
Areas of specialization			
Maximum initial deposit			
Cost of initial consultation			
Cost of simple will			
Cost of real estate closing			
Cost method for other services—flat fee, hourly rate, or contingency basis			
Other information			

Suggested App:
• Ask a Lawyer

What's Next for Your Personal Financial Plan?

• Determine the best alternative for your future legal needs.

• Maintain a file of legal documents and other financial records.

7

Selecting and Financing Housing

3 Steps to Financial Literacy . . . Building Home Equity

1 Save for a large down payment by reducing unnecessary spending for various monthly budget items.
Website: www.americasaves.org

2 Make monthly payments on time to avoid late penalties and to maintain your credit rating.
App: BillMinder

3 Pay an additional principal amount each month, which will also result in saving thousands of dollars on interest.
Website: www.bankrate.com

What are the financial benefits of increased home equity?
You will have the financial security of less debt and will be able to borrow against the equity if needed. At the end of the chapter, "Your Personal Finance Dashboard" will provide guidelines for measuring the progress of your home equity amount along with suggested actions for wise housing decisions.

CHAPTER 7 LEARNING OBJECTIVES

In this chapter, you will learn to:

LO7.1 Assess costs and benefits of renting.

LO7.2 Implement the home-buying process.

LO7.3 Determine costs associated with purchasing a home.

LO7.4 Develop a strategy for selling a home.

YOUR PERSONAL FINANCIAL PLAN SHEETS

22. Renting vs. Buying Housing
23. Apartment Rental Comparison
24. Housing Affordability and Mortgage Qualification
25. Mortgage Company Comparison

Evaluating Renting and Buying Alternatives

As you walk around various neighborhoods, you are likely to see a variety of housing types. When assessing housing alternatives, start by identifying factors that will influence your choice.

Your Lifestyle and Your Choice of Housing

Although the concept of *lifestyle*—how you spend your time and money—may seem intangible, it materializes in consumer purchases. Every buying decision is a statement about your lifestyle. Personal preferences are the foundation of a housing decision, but financial factors may modify the final choice.

Traditional financial guidelines suggest that "you should spend no more than 25 or 30 percent of your take-home pay on housing" or "your home should cost about 2½ times your annual income." Changes in various economic and social conditions have resulted in revised guidelines. Your budgeting activities and other financial records will provide information to determine an appropriate amount for your housing expenses.

Renting versus Buying Housing

The choice between renting and buying your residence should be analyzed based on lifestyle and financial factors. Mobility is a primary motivator of renters, whereas buyers usually want permanence (see Exhibit 7–1). As you can see in the "Figure It Out!" box, the choice between renting and buying may not be clear-cut. In general, renting is less costly in the short run, but home ownership usually has long-term financial advantages.

LO7.1

Assess costs and benefits of renting.

ACTION ITEM

Most important about a place to live is:

☐ **proximity to work or school.**

☐ **cost.**

☐ **flexibility for future moves.**

Exhibit 7–1

Comparing Renting and Buying Housing

Advantages	Disadvantages
RENTING	
• Easy to move	• No tax benefits
• Fewer responsibilities for maintenance	• Limitations regarding remodeling
• Minimal financial commitment	• Restrictions regarding pets, other activities
BUYING	
• Pride of ownership	• Financial commitment
• Financial benefits	• Higher living expenses than renting
• Lifestyle flexibility	• Limited mobility

Rental Activities

Are you interested in a "2-bd.garden apt, a/c, crptg, mod bath, lndry, sec $850"? Not sure? Translated, this means a two-bedroom garden apartment (at or below ground level) with air conditioning, carpeting, a modern bath, and laundry facilities. An $850 security deposit is required.

At some point in your life, you are likely to rent. As a tenant, you pay for the right to live in a residence owned by someone else. Exhibit 7–2 presents the activities involved in finding and living in a rental unit.

Exhibit 7–2   Housing Rental Activities

At the End of the Lease

4
• Clean the apartment; leave it in the same condition as when you moved in.
• Tell landlord where to send your security deposit.
• Require that any deductions from your security deposit be documented.

The Search

1
• Select an area and rental amount.
• Compare costs and facilities of comparable units.
• Talk to current and past residents.

Living in Rental Property

3
• Keep all facilities in good condition.
• Contact the owners regarding needed repairs.
• Respect the rights of others regarding noise.
• Obtain renter's insurance for personal belongings and liability situations (see Chapter 8).

Before Signing a Lease

2
• Verify lease starting date, costs, and facilities.
• Talk to a lawyer about unclear aspects of the lease.
• Note in writing, signed by the owner, the condition of the rental unit.
• Remember, if two names are on the lease, one person can be held responsible for the full rent.

Housing Rental Activities

Figure It Out!

Renting versus Buying Your Place of Residence

Comparing the costs of renting and buying involves consideration of a variety of factors. The following framework and example provide a basis for assessing these two housing alternatives. The apartment in the example has a monthly rent of $1,250, and the home costs $200,000. A 28 percent tax rate is assumed.

Although the numbers in this example favor buying, remember that in any financial decision, calculations provide only part of the answer. You should also consider your needs and values and assess the opportunity costs associated with renting and buying.

	Example	Your Figures
Rental Costs		
Annual rent payments	$ 15,000	$ _____
Renter's insurance	210	_____
Interest lost on security deposit (amount of security deposit times after-tax savings account interest rate)	36	_____
Total annual cost of renting	$ 15,246	_____
Buying Costs		
Annual mortgage payments	$ 15,168	_____
Property taxes (annual costs)	4,800	_____
Homeowner's insurance (annual premium)	600	_____
Estimated maintenance and repairs (1%)	2,000	_____
After-tax interest lost on down payment and closing costs	750	_____
Less (financial benefits of home ownership):		
Growth in equity	−1,120	− _____
Tax savings for mortgage interest (annual mortgage interest times tax rate)	−3,048	− _____
Tax savings for property taxes (annual property taxes times tax rate)	−1,344	− _____
Estimated annual appreciation (1.5%)*	−3,000	− _____
Total annual cost of buying	$ 14,806	_____

*This is a nationwide average; actual appreciation of property will vary by geographic area and economic conditions.

SELECTING A RENTAL UNIT An apartment is the most common type of rental housing. Apartments range from modern, luxury units with extensive recreational facilities to simple one- and two-bedroom units in quiet neighborhoods. If you need more room, consider renting a house. If less space is needed, rent a room in a private house. The main information sources for rental units are newspaper ads, real estate and rental offices, and people you know. When comparing rental units, consider the factors in Exhibit 7–3.

ADVANTAGES OF RENTING Renting offers mobility when a location change is necessary or desirable. Renters have

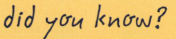

Lease-to-purchase and *rent-with-option* allow renters to become homeowners; however, problems can occur. Beware of offers that may seem beneficial but can turn into financial disasters. For example, an up-front deposit and other purchase funds could be lost if a late rent payment is made.

Exhibit **7–3**

Selecting an Apartment

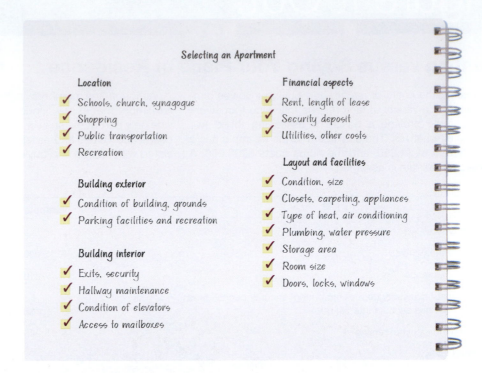

Selecting an Apartment

Location
- ✔ Schools, church, synagogue
- ✔ Shopping
- ✔ Public transportation
- ✔ Recreation

Building exterior
- ✔ Condition of building, grounds
- ✔ Parking facilities and recreation

Building interior
- ✔ Exits, security
- ✔ Hallway maintenance
- ✔ Condition of elevators
- ✔ Access to mailboxes

Financial aspects
- ✔ Rent, length of lease
- ✔ Security deposit
- ✔ Utilities, other costs

Layout and facilities
- ✔ Condition, size
- ✔ Closets, carpeting, appliances
- ✔ Type of heat, air conditioning
- ✔ Plumbing, water pressure
- ✔ Storage area
- ✔ Room size
- ✔ Doors, locks, windows

fewer responsibilities than homeowners since they usually do not have to be concerned with maintenance and repairs. Taking possession of a rental unit is less expensive than buying a home.

DISADVANTAGES OF RENTING Renters do not enjoy the financial advantages of homeowners. Tenants cannot take tax deductions for mortgage interest and property taxes or benefit from the increased real estate value. Renters are generally limited in the types of activities they can pursue in their place of residence. Noise from a stereo system or parties may be monitored closely. Tenants are often subject to restrictions regarding pets and decorating.

lease A legal document that defines the conditions of a rental agreement.

LEGAL DETAILS Most tenants sign a **lease,** a legal document that defines the conditions of a rental agreement. This document presents:

- A description of the property, including the address.
- The name and address of the owner/landlord (the *lessor*).
- The name of the tenant (the *lessee*).
- The effective date of the lease, and the length of the lease.
- The amount of the security deposit, and amount and due date of the monthly rent.
- The date and amount due of charges for late rent payments.
- A list of the utilities, appliances, furniture, or other facilities that are included in the rental amount.
- Restrictions regarding certain activities (pets, remodeling); tenant's right to sublet.
- Charges for damages or for moving out of the rental unit later (or earlier) than the lease expiration date.
- The conditions under which the landlord may enter the apartment.

Standard lease forms include conditions you may not want to accept. The fact that a lease is printed does not mean you must accept it as is. If you have a high credit score, you may be able to negotiate a lower rent or a reduced security deposit. Also, discuss with the landlord any lease terms you consider unacceptable.

Some leases give you the right to *sublet* the rental unit. Subletting may be necessary if you must vacate the premises before the lease expires. Subletting allows you to have another person take over rent payments and live in the rental unit.

While most leases are written, oral leases are also valid. In those situations, one party must give a 30-day written notice to the other party before terminating the lease or imposing a rent increase. A lease provides protection to both landlord and tenant. The tenant is protected from rent increases unless the lease contains a provision allowing an increase. The lease gives the landlord the right to take legal action against a tenant for nonpayment of rent or destruction of property.

COSTS OF RENTING A *security deposit,* frequently required when you sign a lease, is usually one month's rent. This money is held by the landlord to cover the cost of any damages. Some state and local laws may require that landlords pay interest on a security deposit if they own buildings with a certain number of rental units. After you vacate the rental unit, your security deposit should be refunded within a reasonable time. If money is deducted, you have the right to an itemized list of repair costs.

As a renter, you will incur other expenses. For many apartments, water is covered by the rent; however, other utilities may not be included. If you rent a house, you will probably pay for heat, electricity, water, telephone, and cable television. When you rent, be sure to obtain insurance coverage on your personal property.

did you know?

Millions of people in the United States and around the world lack adequate housing. Habitat for Humanity (www.habitat.org) has built more than 300,000 houses, providing shelter to over 1.5 million people. The efforts of Habitat continue through local and global volunteering as well as donations of money and building supplies.

⚠ CAUTION!

Renter's insurance is one of the most overlooked expenses of apartment dwellers. Damage or theft of personal property (clothing, furniture, stereo equipment, jewelry) is usually not covered by the landlord's insurance policy.

Sheet 22 Renting vs. Buying Housing
Sheet 23 Apartment Rental Comparison

PRACTICE QUIZ 7–1

1. What are the main benefits and drawbacks of renting a place of residence?

2. Which components of a lease are likely to be most negotiable?

3. For the following situations, would you recommend that the person rent or buy housing? (Circle your answer.)

    a. A person who desires to reduce income taxes paid.   rent   buy

    b. A person who expects to be transferred for work soon.   rent   buy

    c. A person with few assets for housing expenses.   rent   buy

Apply Yourself!

Interview a tenant and a landlord to obtain their views about potential problems associated with renting. How do their views on tenant–landlord relations differ?

Buy or Rent?

It's a good time to buy, but renting is better if you're not ready to stay put at least five years.

If you're uncertain where life might take you next—for a job, a relationship or just a change of scenery—renting beats buying. It costs a lot less in terms of time, effort and money to break a lease than to sell or rent out a home that you own. Plus, the landlord is responsible for maintenance and repairs.

Buying can be a great investment—or a lousy one, depending on the market where you live when you buy and when you sell. If you buy and home values go down, you may have to wait to sell to get back the money you invested in a down payment and mortgage closing costs.

It usually makes sense to buy only if you plan to stay in your home for five to seven years. That's generally long enough to recoup the upfront cost to get a mortgage and the back-end costs to sell and pay an agent's commission. If you fit that profile, now is a good time to buy; most cities in the U.S. have recovered from the housing market bust that began in mid 2006, and mortgage rates are still superlow. Once you become a homeowner and prices rise, you'll be rewarded with the power of leverage—you may put only 20% (or less) down, but you get 100% of the appreciation. Regardless of whether your home's value goes up, you'll benefit from the tax deductions for mortgage interest and property taxes if you itemize deductions on your federal tax return. And you will probably be able to keep up to $250,000 of profit tax-free when you sell ($500,000 if you're married and file your income taxes jointly).

If you're on the fence about buying or renting, take a look at the price-to-rent ratio where you live (the median sale price of a home divided by the average annual rent for a comparable one). In general, if the ratio is less than 15, the market rewards home buyers; if it's more than 20, it rewards renters. Right now, the ratio nationally is a balanced 14.8, according to Marcus & Millichap, a real estate research firm. Ratios between 15 and 20 can go either way, depending on factors such as taxes and the potential for appreciation. The ratios in such millennial meccas as New York City, San Francisco and Washington, D.C., typically favor renters, but a spike in rents and low mortgage rates is tipping the ratios in favor of buyers. (For a look at the largest 100 cities, see "Rent vs. Buy: Which is Cheaper for You?" at www.trulia.com/rent_vs_buy/ and use the calculator to assess your situation.)

INSURE YOUR STUFF

Just because you don't own a home doesn't mean you shouldn't insure the things you own. Buy renters insurance to reimburse you for the cost to replace your belongings (a replacement-cost policy) if they're stolen or destroyed, as well as provide liability coverage. The average cost of a policy is $16 a month, says the National Association of Insurance Commissioners. Compare policies at NetQuote.com or InsWeb.com. You'll usually get a discount if you buy coverage through the same company that insures your car.

Even with your down payment in hand, landing your dream home could be a challenge, especially in markets where the inventory of homes for sale is low (often the same markets where rents are inflated) and the best homes attract multiple bids. What you can do: Get preapproved for financing to make your bid more attractive. And ask the seller's agent if you can get the home inspected *before* you make an offer so you don't have to include it as a contingency in the contract.

Patricia Mertz Esswein

1. What risks are associated with buying a home?

2. How can the price-to-rent ratio be of value to you when deciding whether to rent or buy?

3. What factors are most likely to influence your decision regarding whether to rent or buy?

Home-Buying Activities

Many people dream of having a place of residence they can call their own. Home owner-ship is a common financial goal. Exhibit 7–4 presents the process for achieving this goal.

Step 1: Determine Home Ownership Needs

In the first phase of this process, consider the benefits and drawbacks of this major finan-cial commitment. Also, evaluate the types of housing units and determine the amount you can afford.

EVALUATE HOME OWNERSHIP Stability of residence and a personalized living location are important motives of many home buyers. One financial benefit is the deduct-ibility of mortgage interest and real estate tax payments, reducing federal income taxes.

A disadvantage of home ownership is financial uncertainty. Obtaining money for a down payment and securing mortgage financing may be problems. Changing property val-ues in an area can affect your financial investment. Home ownership does not provide ease of changing living location as does renting. If changes in your situation necessitate selling your home, doing so may be difficult.

Owning your place of residence can be expensive. The homeowner is responsible for maintenance and costs of repainting, repairs, and home improvements. Real estate taxes are a major expense of homeowners. Higher property values and increased tax rates mean higher real estate taxes.

TYPES OF HOUSING AVAILABLE Home buyers generally choose from the following options:

1. *Single-family dwellings* include previously owned houses, new houses, and custom-built houses.
2. *Multiunit dwellings* are dwellings with more than one living unit. A *duplex* is a building with separate homes. A *townhouse* may contain two, four, or six living units.

LO7.2

Implement the home-buying process.

ACTION ITEM

The best housing purchase for me would be:

☐ **a house.**

☐ **a condo or townhouse.**

☐ **a mobile home.**

Exhibit 7–4 The Home-Buying Process

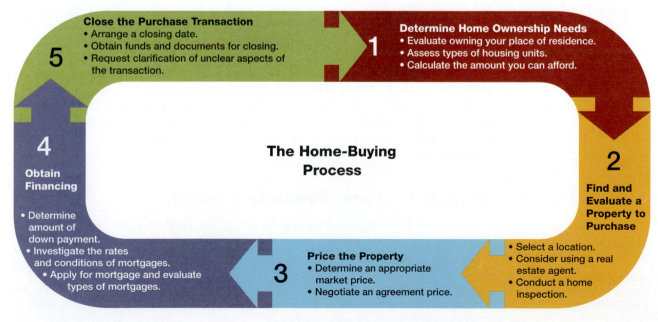

5 Close the Purchase Transaction
- Arrange a closing date.
- Obtain funds and documents for closing.
- Request clarification of unclear aspects of the transaction.

1 Determine Home Ownership Needs
- Evaluate owning your place of residence.
- Assess types of housing units.
- Calculate the amount you can afford.

The Home-Buying Process

4 Obtain Financing
- Determine amount of down payment.
- Investigate the rates and conditions of mortgages.
- Apply for mortgage and evaluate types of mortgages.

2 Find and Evaluate a Property to Purchase
- Select a location.
- Consider using a real estate agent.
- Conduct a home inspection.

3 Price the Property
- Determine an appropriate market price.
- Negotiate an agreement price.

condominium An individually owned housing unit in a building with several such units.

3. **Condominiums** are individually owned housing units in a building. Ownership does not include *common areas,* such as hallways, outside grounds, and recreational facilities. These areas are owned by the condominium association, which oversees the management and operation. Condominium owners pay a monthly fee for maintenance, repairs, improvements, and insurance of the building and common areas. A condominium is not the building structure; it is a legal form of home ownership.

cooperative housing A form of housing in which a building containing a number of housing units is owned by a nonprofit organization whose members rent the units.

4. **Cooperative housing** is a form of housing in which the units in a building are owned by a nonprofit organization. The shareholders purchase stock to obtain the right to live in a unit in the building. While the residents do not own the units, they have the legal right to occupy a unit for as long as they own stock in the cooperative association. The title for the property belongs to the co-op. This ownership arrangement is different from condominiums, in which residents own the individual living unit.

5. *Manufactured homes* are assembled in a factory and then moved to the living site. *Prefabricated homes* have components built in a factory and then assembled at the housing site. *Mobile home* is not a completely accurate term since very few are moved from their original sites. Although typically smaller than 1,000 square feet, they can offer features such as a fully equipped kitchen, fireplace, cathedral ceiling, and whirlpool bath. The site for a mobile home may be either purchased or leased.

6. *Building a home* is for people who want certain specifications. Before starting such a project, be sure you possess the necessary knowledge, money, and perseverance. When choosing a contractor to coordinate the project, consider (*a*) the contractor's experience and reputation; (*b*) the contractor's relationship with the architect, materials suppliers, electricians, plumbers, carpenters, and other personnel; and (*c*) payment arrangements during construction. Your written contract should include a time schedule, cost estimates, a description of the work, and a payment schedule.

did you know?

The CLUE® (Comprehensive Loss Underwriting Exchange) report provides a five-year history of insurance losses at a property that a home buyer is considering for purchase. This disclosure report is an independent source of information. You can find further information at www.choicetrust.com.

DETERMINE WHAT YOU CAN AFFORD The amount you spend on housing is affected by funds available for a down payment, your income, and your current living expenses. Other factors you should consider are current mortgage rates, the potential future value of the property, and your ability to make monthly payments. To determine how much you can afford to spend on a home, have a loan officer at a mortgage company or other financial institution *prequalify* you. This service is provided without charge.

You may not get all the features you want in your first home, but financial advisors suggest getting into the housing market by purchasing what you can afford. As you move up in the housing market, your second or third home can include more of the features you want.

While the home you buy should be in good condition, you may wish to buy a *handyman's special*—a home that needs work and that you are able to get at a lower price. You will then need to put more money into the house for repairs and improvements or do some of the work yourself.

Step 2: Find and Evaluate a Home

Next, select a location, consider using the services of a real estate agent, and conduct a home inspection.

zoning laws Restrictions on how the property in an area can be used.

SELECT A LOCATION Location is considered the most important factor when buying a home. You may prefer an urban, a suburban, or a rural setting. Or perhaps you want to live in a small town or in a resort area. Be aware of **zoning laws,** restrictions on how the property in an area can be used. The location of businesses and future construction projects may influence your decision.

If you have a family, assess the school system. Educators recommend that schools be evaluated on program variety, achievement level of students, percentage of students who go on to college, dedication of faculty members, facilities, school funding, and involvement of parents. Homeowners without children also benefit from strong schools, since the educational advantages of a community help maintain property values.

SERVICES OF REAL ESTATE AGENTS Real estate agents have information about housing in areas of interest to you. Their main services include (1) showing you homes to meet your needs; (2) presenting your offer to the seller based on a market analysis; (3) negotiating a settlement price; (4) assisting you in obtaining financing; and (5) representing you at the closing. A real estate agent may also recommend lawyers, insurance agents, home inspectors, and mortgage companies to serve your needs.

Since the home seller usually pays the commission, a buyer may not incur a direct cost. However, this expense is reflected in the price paid for the home. In some states, the agent could be working for the seller. In others, the agent may be working for the buyer, the seller, or as a *dual agent,* working for both the buyer and the seller. When dual agency exists, some states require that buyers sign a disclosure acknowledging that they are aware the agent is working for both buyer and seller. This agreement, however, can limit the information provided to each party. Many states have *buyer agents* who represent the buyer's interests and may be paid by either the seller or the buyer.

THE HOME INSPECTION An evaluation by a trained home inspector can minimize future problems. Being cautious will save you headaches and unplanned expenses. Exhibit 7–5 presents a detailed format for inspecting a home. Some states, cities, and lenders require inspection documents for pests, radon, or mold. The mortgage company will usually conduct an *appraisal,* which is not a home inspection but an assessment of the market value of the property.

Step 3: Price the Property

After selecting a home, determine an offer price and negotiate a final buying price.

DETERMINE THE HOME PRICE The amount you offer will be affected by recent selling prices in the area, current demand for housing, the time the home has been on the market, the owner's need to sell, financing options, and features and condition of the home. Each of these factors can affect your offer price. For example, you will have to offer a higher price in times of low interest rates and high demand for homes. On the other hand, a home that has been on the market for over a year could mean an opportunity to offer a lower price. Your offer will be in the form of a *purchase agreement,* or contract, which is your legal offer to purchase the home.

NEGOTIATE THE PURCHASE PRICE If your initial offer is accepted, you have a valid contract. If your offer is rejected, you have several options. A *counteroffer* from the owner indicates a willingness to negotiate a price. If the counteroffer is only slightly lower than the asking price, you are expected to move closer to that price with your next offer. If the counteroffer is quite a bit off the asking price, you are closer to arriving at the purchase price. If no counteroffer is forthcoming, you may wish to make another offer to see whether the seller is willing to do any negotiating. Negotiations may involve things other than price, such as closing date or inclusion of existing items, such as appliances.

> **did you know?**
>
> A two-story addition, a remodeled bathroom, an updated kitchen, addition of a deck, and a refinished basement are the upgrades most likely to add value to a home.

Exhibit **7–5** Conducting a Home Inspection

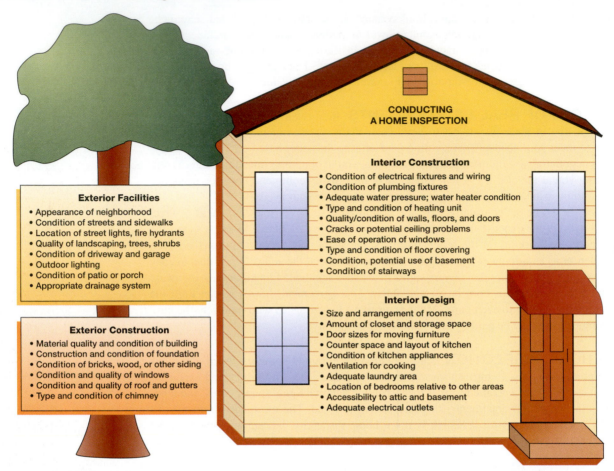

CONDUCTING A HOME INSPECTION

Exterior Facilities
- Appearance of neighborhood
- Condition of streets and sidewalks
- Location of street lights, fire hydrants
- Quality of landscaping, trees, shrubs
- Condition of driveway and garage
- Outdoor lighting
- Condition of patio or porch
- Appropriate drainage system

Exterior Construction
- Material quality and condition of building
- Construction and condition of foundation
- Condition of bricks, wood, or other siding
- Condition and quality of windows
- Condition and quality of roof and gutters
- Type and condition of chimney

Interior Construction
- Condition of electrical fixtures and wiring
- Condition of plumbing fixtures
- Adequate water pressure; water heater condition
- Type and condition of heating unit
- Quality/condition of walls, floors, and doors
- Cracks or potential ceiling problems
- Ease of operation of windows
- Type and condition of floor covering
- Condition, potential use of basement
- Condition of stairways

Interior Design
- Size and arrangement of rooms
- Amount of closet and storage space
- Door sizes for moving furniture
- Counter space and layout of kitchen
- Condition of kitchen appliances
- Ventilation for cooking
- Adequate laundry area
- Location of bedrooms relative to other areas
- Accessibility to attic and basement
- Adequate electrical outlets

earnest money A portion of the price of a home that the buyer deposits as evidence of good faith to indicate a serious purchase offer.

As part of the offer, the buyer must present **earnest money,** a portion of the purchase price deposited as evidence of good faith. At the closing of the home purchase, the earnest money is applied toward the down payment. This money is returned if the sale cannot be completed due to circumstances beyond the buyer's control.

Home purchase agreements may contain a *contingency clause,* stating the agreement is binding only if a certain event occurs. For example, the contract may be valid only if the buyer obtains financing for the home purchase within a certain time period, or it may make the purchase of a home contingent on the sale of the buyer's current home.

PRACTICE QUIZ 7–2

1. What are the advantages and disadvantages of owning a home?

2. What guidelines can be used to determine the amount to spend for a home purchase?

3. How can the quality of a school system benefit even homeowners in a community who do not have school-age children?

Apply Yourself!

Talk with a real estate agent about the process involved in selecting and buying a home. Ask about housing prices in your area and the services the agent provides.

The Finances of Home Buying

While looking for a place to buy, also consider your financing options. Most home buyers will meet with a banker or mortgage broker early in the process to determine the amount they can afford for their home. Financing a home purchase requires obtaining a mortgage, having an awareness of types of mortgages, and settling the real estate transaction.

LO7.3

Determine costs associated with purchasing a home.

ACTION ITEM

The type of mortgage I would likely use is:

☐ **fixed-rate mortgage.**

☐ **interest-only mortgage.**

☐ **FHA or VA mortgage.**

Step 4: Obtain Financing

THE DOWN PAYMENT The amount of cash available for a down payment affects the size of the mortgage required. If you can make a large down payment, such as 20 percent or more, you will likely obtain a mortgage relatively easily. Personal savings, sales of investments or other assets, and assistance from relatives are common down payment sources. Parents can help their children purchase a home by giving them a cash gift or a loan.

Private mortgage insurance (PMI) is usually required if the down payment is less than 20 percent. This protects the lender from financial loss due to default. After building up 20 percent equity in a home, a home buyer should contact the lender to cancel PMI. The Homeowners Protection Act requires that a PMI policy be terminated automatically when a homeowner's equity reaches 22 percent of the property value at the time the mortgage was executed. Homeowners can request termination earlier if they can provide proof that the equity in the home has grown to 22 percent of the current market value.

THE MORTGAGE A **mortgage** is a long-term loan on a specific piece of property such as a home or other real estate. Payments on a mortgage are usually made over 10, 15, 20, 25, or 30 years. Applying for a mortgage involves three main phases:

1. You complete the mortgage application and meet with the lender to present evidence of employment, income, ownership of assets, and amounts of existing debts.
2. The lender obtains a credit report and verifies your application and financial status.
3. The mortgage is either approved or denied, with the decision based on your financial history and an evaluation of the home you want to buy.

 CAUTION!

A real estate "short sale" occurs when the new selling price is less than the amount owed on the previous mortgage. This alternative to foreclosure can result in a "bargain" for a home buyer. However, beware that it may take a long time before the lender accepts the offer, if the offer is accepted at all. Also, the home is usually sold "as is," which means some items expected to be in the home may be missing or damaged. When doing a short sale, be sure to use a lawyer and a negotiator, and obtain a release from any deficiencies for previous loan amounts.

mortgage A long-term loan on a specific piece of property such as a home or other real estate.

Today, with a credit score of 620 a person can obtain home financing. The higher the credit score the lower the mortgage rate, given the same loan amount and down payment.

The recent "subprime" crisis, when many mortgages were issued to borrowers with poor credit histories, resulted in numerous loan defaults. As a result, lenders are facing new regulations. To assure your creditworthiness for a home loan, pay down your credit cards, make payments on time to existing loan accounts, and accumulate funds for a down payment. This process will indicate the maximum mortgage for which you qualify.

As shown in Exhibit 7–6, the major factors that affect the affordability of your mortgage are your income, other debts, the amount available for a down payment, the length of the loan, and current mortgage rates. The results of this calculation are (*a*) the monthly mortgage payment you can afford, (*b*) the mortgage amount you can afford, and (*c*) the home purchase price you can afford.

These sample calculations are typical of those most financial institutions use; the actual qualifications for a mortgage may vary by lender and by the type of mortgage. The loan commitment is the financial institution's decision to provide the funds needed to purchase a specific property. The approved mortgage application usually *locks in* an interest rate for 30 to 90 days.

Exhibit 7–6 Housing Affordability and Mortgage Qualification Amounts

	Example A	Example B
Step 1: Determine your monthly gross income (annual income divided by 12).	$48,000 ÷ 12	$48,000 ÷ 12
Step 2: With a down payment of at least 5 percent, lenders use 33 percent of monthly gross income as a guideline for PITI (principal, interest, taxes, and insurance) and 38 percent of monthly gross income as a guideline for PITI plus other debt payments.	$ 4,000 × 0.38 $ 1,520	$ 4,000 × 0.33 $ 1,320
Step 3: Subtract other debt payments (e.g., payments on an auto loan) and an estimate of the monthly costs of property taxes and homeowner's insurance.	−380 −300	— −300
(a) Affordable monthly mortgage payment	$ 840	$ 1,020
Step 4: Divide this amount by the monthly mortgage payment per $1,000 based on current mortgage rates—an 8 percent, 30-year loan, for example (see Exhibit 7–7)—and multiply by $1,000.	÷ $ 7.34 × $ 1,000	÷ $ 7.34 × $ 1,000
(b) Affordable mortgage amount	$114,441	$138,965
Step 5: Divide your affordable mortgage amount by 1 minus the fractional portion of your down payment (e.g., 1 − 0.1 with a 10 percent down payment).	÷ 0.9	÷ 0.9
(c) Affordable home purchase price	$127,157	$154,405

NOTE: The two ratios lending institutions use (step 2) and other loan requirements may vary based on a variety of factors, including the type of mortgage, the amount of the down payment, your income level, credit score, and current interest rates. For example, with a down payment of 10 percent or more and a credit score exceeding 720, the ratios might increase to 40/45 percent in this exhibit.

The mortgage loan for which you can qualify is larger when interest rates are low than when they are high. For example, a person who can afford a monthly mortgage payment of $700 will qualify for a 30-year loan of

$130,354 at 5 percent $95,368 at 8 percent

$116,667 at 6 percent $86,956 at 9 percent

$105,263 at 7 percent $79,726 at 10 percent

As interest rates rise, fewer people are able to afford the cost of an average-priced home.

EXAMPLE: Calculate Mortgage Payment

To determine the amount of your monthly mortgage payment, multiply the factor from Exhibit 7–7 by the number of thousands of the loan amount. For a 30-year, 7 percent, $223,000 mortgage:

Monthly payment amount = 223 × $6.65

= $1,482.95

In addition to using the mortgage payment factors from Exhibit 7–7, the monthly payment may be calculated using a formula, a financial calculator, Excel spreadsheet, website, or app.

Term Rate	30 Years	25 Years	20 Years	15 Years
3.0%	$4.22	$4.74	$5.55	$6.91
3.5	4.49	5.01	5.80	7.15
4.0	4.77	5.28	6.06	7.40
4.5	5.07	5.56	6.33	7.65
5.0	5.37	5.85	6.60	7.91
5.5	5.68	6.14	6.88	8.17
6.0	6.00	6.44	7.16	8.43
6.5	6.32	6.67	7.45	8.71
7.0	6.65	7.06	7.75	8.98
7.5	6.99	7.39	8.06	9.27
8.0	7.34	7.72	8.36	9.56

Exhibit 7-7

Mortgage Payment Factors (principal and interest factors per $1,000 of loan amount)

Loan payment amounts may also be determined using these methods:

Formula	Financial Calculator	Excel®
$M = P[i(1 + i)n]/[(1 + i)n - 1]$	(payments per year) 12 P/YR	=PMT (rate/12,30*12,loan amount)
M = mortgage payment (monthly)	(total loan payments) 360 N	= denotes a formula
P = principal of the loan (loan amount)	(interest rate) 6 I/YR	rate/12 provides monthly rate
i = interest rate divided by 12	(loan amount) 180000 PV	total number of payments, such as 12 per year for 30 years
n = number of months of the loan	(calculate monthly payment) PMT	loan amount − beginning mortgage balance

Various websites and apps are also available to determine monthly mortgage payments.

When comparing mortgage companies, remember that the interest rate you are quoted is not the only factor to consider. The required down payment and the points charged will affect the interest rate. **Points** are prepaid interest charged by the lender. Each *discount point* is equal to 1 percent of the loan amount and should be viewed as a premium you pay for obtaining a lower mortgage rate. In deciding whether to take a lower rate with more points or a higher rate with fewer points, consider the following guidelines:

points Prepaid interest charged by the lender.

- If you plan to live in your home a long time (over five years), the lower mortgage rate is probably the best action.
- If you plan to sell your home in the next few years, the higher mortgage rate with fewer discount points may be better.

Online research may be used to compare current mortgage rates, and you can apply for a mortgage online.

FIXED-RATE, FIXED-PAYMENT MORTGAGES
As Exhibit 7–8 shows, fixed-rate, fixed-payment mortgages are a major type of mortgage. The *conventional mortgage* usually has equal payments over 15, 20, or 30 years based on a fixed interest rate. Mortgage payments are set to allow **amortization** of the loan; that is, the balance owed is reduced with each payment. Since the amount borrowed is large, the payments made during the early years of the mortgage are applied mainly to interest, with only small reductions in the loan principal. As the amount owed declines, the monthly payments have

amortization The reduction of a loan balance through payments made over a period of time.

Exhibit 7–8

Types of Mortgages

Loan Type	Benefits	Drawbacks
1. Conventional 30-year mortgage	• Fixed monthly payments for 30 years provide certainty of principal and interest payments.	• Higher initial rates than adjustables.
2. Conventional 15- or 20-year mortgage	• Lower rate than 30-year fixed; faster equity buildup and quicker payoff of loan.	• Higher monthly payments.
3. FHA/VA fixed-rate mortgage (30-year and 15-year)	• Low down payment requirements and may be assumable with no prepayment penalties.	• May require additional processing time.
4. Adjustable-rate mortgage (ARM)—payment changes on 1-, 3-, 5-, 7-, or 10-year schedules	• Lower initial rates than fixed-rate loans, particularly on the 1-year adjustable. Offers possibility of future rate and payment decreases. Loans with rate "caps" may protect borrowers against increases in rates.	• Shifts far greater interest rate risk onto borrowers than fixed-rate loans. May push up monthly payments in future years.
5. Interest-only mortgage	• Lower payments; more easily affordable.	• No decrease in amount owed; no building equity unless home value increases; usually must convert to a higher fixed-rate mortgage after 10 years.

an increasing impact on the loan balance. Near the end of the mortgage term, almost all of each payment is applied to the balance.

For example, a $125,000, 30-year, 6 percent mortgage would have monthly payments of $749.44. The payments would be divided as follows:

	Interest		Principal	Remaining Balance	
For the first month	$625.00	($75,000 × 0.10 × 1/12)	$124.44	$124,875.56	($125,000 − $124.44)
For the second month	624.72	($74,966.82 × 0.10 × 1/12)	124.72	$124,750.84	($124,875.56 − $124.72)
For the 360th month	3.73		745.71	-0-	

In the past, many conventional mortgages were *assumable*. This feature allowed a home buyer to continue with the seller's original agreement. Assumable mortgages were especially attractive if the mortgage rate was lower than market interest rates at the time of the sale. Today, due to volatile interest rates, assumable mortgages are seldom offered.

GOVERNMENT-GUARANTEED FINANCING PROGRAMS These include loans insured by the Federal Housing Authority (FHA) and loans guaranteed by the Veterans Administration (VA). These government agencies do not provide the mortgage money; rather, they help home buyers obtain low-interest, low-down-payment loans.

To qualify for an FHA-insured loan, a person must meet certain conditions related to the down payment and fees. Most low- and middle-income people can qualify for the FHA loan program. The VA-guaranteed loan program assists eligible armed services veterans with home purchases. As with the FHA program, the funds for VA loans come from a financial institution or a mortgage company, with the risk reduced by government participation. A VA loan can be obtained without a down payment.

ADJUSTABLE-RATE, VARIABLE-PAYMENT MORTGAGES The **adjustable-rate mortgage (ARM),** also referred to as a *flexible-rate mortgage* or a *variable-rate mortgage,* has an

adjustable-rate mortgage (ARM) A home loan with an interest rate that can change during the mortgage term due to changes in market interest rates; also called a *flexible-rate mortgage* or a *variable-rate mortgage.*

interest rate that increases or decreases during the life of the loan. ARMs usually have a lower initial interest rate than fixed-rate mortgages; however, the borrower, not the lender, bears the risk of future interest rate increases.

A *rate cap* restricts the amount by which the interest rate can increase or decrease during the ARM term. This limit prevents the borrower from having to pay an interest rate significantly higher than the one in the original agreement. A *payment cap* keeps the payments on an adjustable-rate mortgage at a given level or limits the amount to which those payments can rise. When mortgage payments do not rise but interest rates do, the amount owed can increase in months in which the mortgage payment does not cover the interest owed. This increased loan balance, called *negative amortization,* means the amount of the home equity is decreasing instead of increasing.

Consider several factors when evaluating adjustable-rate mortgages: (1) Determine the frequency of and restrictions on allowed changes in interest rates; (2) consider the frequency of and restrictions on changes in the monthly payment; (3) investigate the possibility that the loan will be extended due to negative amortization, and find out if a limit exists on the amount of negative amortization; and (4) find out what index is used to set the mortgage interest rate.

INTEREST-ONLY MORTGAGE

An *interest-only mortgage* allows a home buyer to have lower payments for the first few years of the loan. During that time, none of the mortgage payment goes toward the loan amount. Once the initial period ends, the mortgage adjusts to be interest-only at the new payment rate. Or a borrower may obtain a different type of mortgage to start building equity.

Remember, with an interest-only mortgage, higher payments will occur later in the loan. These are based on the amount of the original loan since no principal has been paid. Interest-only mortgages can be especially dangerous if the value of the property declines.

OTHER FINANCING METHODS

A *buy-down* is an interest rate subsidy from a home builder, a real estate developer, or the borrower that reduces the mortgage payments during the first few years of the loan. This assistance is intended to stimulate sales among home buyers who cannot afford conventional financing. After the buy-down period, the mortgage payments increase to the level that would have existed without the financial assistance.

A *second mortgage,* more commonly called a *home equity loan,* allows a homeowner to borrow on the paid-up value of the property. Lending institutions offer a variety of home equity loans, including a line of credit program that allows the borrower to obtain additional funds. You need to be careful when using a home equity line of credit. This revolving credit plan can keep you continually in debt as you request new cash advances. A home equity loan allows you to deduct the interest on consumer purchases on your federal income tax return. However, it creates the risk of losing the home if required payments on both the first and second mortgages are not made.

Reverse mortgages (also called *home equity conversion mortgages*) provide homeowners who are 62 or older with tax-free income in the form of a loan that is paid back (with interest) when the home is sold or the homeowner dies.

did you know?

By taking out a 15-year instead of a 30-year mortgage, a home buyer borrowing $200,000 can save more than $150,000 in interest over the life of the loan. The faster equity growth and savings on interest with the shorter mortgage will also occur if a home buyer pays an additional amount toward principal each month.

⚠ CAUTION!

Mortgage fraud costs lenders more than $1 billion a year. These scams occur when people misrepresent their income or home value in an effort to obtain a loan. While banks and lenders are usually the victims, individual investors may also face losses. Communities are affected when the deception results in vacant buildings that are in disrepair. To avoid participating in mortgage fraud, be sure to verify that a mortgage company is properly licensed and report any incorrect information in the lending process.

did you know?

Obtaining funds for a home purchase from parents can increase the value of the home you can afford. With *shared-equity financing,* parents or other relatives who provide part of the down payment share in the appreciation of the property. A contract among the parties should detail (a) who makes the mortgage payments and gets the tax deduction, (b) how much each person will pay of the real estate taxes, and (c) how and when the equity will be shared.

During the term of your mortgage, you may want to *refinance* your home, that is, obtain a new mortgage on your current home at a lower interest rate. Before taking this action consider the refinancing costs in relation to the savings gained with a lower monthly payment.

Another financing decision involves making extra payments on your mortgage. Since this amount will be applied to the loan principal, you will save interest and pay off the mortgage in a shorter time. Paying an additional $25 a month on a $75,000, 30-year, 10 percent mortgage will save you more than $34,000 in interest and enable you to pay off the loan in less than 25 years. Beware of organizations that promise to help you make additional payments on your mortgage. You can do this on your own, without the fee they are likely to charge you.

Step 5: Close the Purchase Transaction

closing costs Fees and charges paid when a real estate transaction is completed; also called *settlement costs.*

Before finalizing the transaction, a *walk-through* allows you to inspect the condition of the home. Use a camera or video recorder to collect evidence for any last-minute items you may need to negotiate.

The *closing* is a meeting of the buyer, seller, and lender of funds, or representatives of each party, to complete the transaction. Documents are signed, last-minute details are settled, and appropriate amounts are paid. A number of expenses are incurred at the closing. The **closing costs,** also referred to as *settlement costs,* are the fees and charges paid when a real estate transaction is completed; these commonly include the items listed in Exhibit 7–9.

title insurance Insurance that, during the mortgage term, protects the owner or the lender against financial loss resulting from future defects in the title and from other unforeseen property claims not excluded by the policy.

Title insurance has two phases. First, the title company defines the boundaries of the property being purchased and conducts a search to determine whether the property is free of claims such as unpaid real estate taxes. Second, during the mortgage term, the title company protects the owner and the lender against financial loss resulting from future defects in the title and from other unforeseen property claims not excluded by the policy.

deed A document that transfers ownership of property from one party to another.

Also due at closing time is the deed recording fee. The **deed** is the document that transfers ownership of property from one party to another. With a *warranty deed,* the seller

Exhibit 7–9

Common Closing Costs

At the transaction settlement of a real estate purchase and sale, the buyer and seller will encounter a variety of expenses that are commonly referred to as *closing costs.*

	COST RANGE ENCOUNTERED	
	By the Buyer	**By the Seller**
Title search fee	$150–$375	—
Title insurance (lender/owner policies)	$700–$1,500	$2,000+
Attorney's fee	$400–$700	$50–$700
Property survey	—	$100–$400
Appraisal fee (or nonrefundable application fee)	$400–$600	—
Recording fees; transfer taxes	$95–$130	$70–$100
Settlement fee	$750–$1,000	—
Termite inspection	$70–$150	—
Lender's origination fee	1–3% of loan amount	—
Reserves for home insurance and property taxes	Varies	—
Interest paid in advance (from the closing date to the end of the month) and "points"	Varies	—
Real estate broker's commission	—	4–7% of purchase price

NOTE: The amounts paid by the buyer are in addition to the down payment.

Personal Finance in Practice

What Additional Home-Buying Information Do You Need?

For each of the following main aspects of home buying, list questions, additional information, or actions you might need to take. Locate websites that provide information for these areas.

- **Location.** Consider the community and geographic region. A $250,000 home in one area may be an average-priced house, while in another part of the country it may be fairly expensive real estate. The demand for homes is largely affected by the economy and the availability of jobs.

_____

- **Down payment.** While making a large down payment reduces your mortgage payments, you will also need the funds for closing costs, moving expenses, repairs, or furniture.

_____

- **Mortgage application.** When applying for a home loan, you will usually be required to provide copies of paystubs, W-2, and recent tax returns, a residence and employment history, information about bank and investment accounts, a listing of debts, and evidence of auto and any real estate ownership.

_____

- **Points.** You may need to select between a higher rate with no discount points and a lower rate requiring points paid at closing. (Some states limit the amount of closing costs.)

_____

- **Closing costs.** Settlement costs can range from 2 to 6 percent of the loan amount; this amount is in addition to your down payment.

_____

- **PITI.** Your monthly payment for principal, interest, taxes, and insurance is an important budget item. Beware of buying "too much house" and not having enough for other living expenses.

_____

- **Maintenance costs.** As any homeowner will tell you, owning a home can be expensive. Set aside funds for repair and remodeling expenses.

_____

Websites to consult:

_____

_____

guarantees the title is good. This document certifies that the seller is the true owner of the property, there are no claims against the title, and the seller has the right to sell the property.

The Real Estate Settlement Procedures Act (RESPA) helps home buyers understand the closing process and closing costs. This legislation requires that loan applicants be given an estimate of the closing costs before the actual closing. Obtaining this information early allows a home buyer to plan for the closing costs.

escrow account Money, usually deposited with the lending financial institution, for the payment of property taxes and homeowner's insurance.

At the closing and when you make your monthly payments, you will probably deposit money to be used for home expenses. For example, the lender will require that you have property insurance. An **escrow account** is money, usually deposited with the lending institution, for the payment of property taxes and home insurance.

As a new home buyer, you might also consider purchasing an agreement that gives you protection against defects in the home. *Implied warranties* created by state laws may cover some problem areas; other repair costs can occur. Home builders and real estate sales companies offer warranties to buyers. Coverage offered usually provides protection against electrical, plumbing, heating, appliances, and other mechanical defects. Most home warranty programs have various limitations.

Home Buying: A Summary

For most people, buying a home is the most expensive decision they will undertake. As a reminder, the nearby "Personal Finance in Practice" box provides an overview of the major elements to consider when making this critical financial decision.

Sheet 24 Housing Affordability and Mortgage Qualification

Sheet 25 Mortgage Company Comparison

PRACTICE QUIZ 7-3

1. What are the main sources of money for a down payment?

2. What factors affect a person's ability to qualify for a mortgage?

3. How do changing interest rates affect the amount of mortgage a person can afford?

4. Under what conditions might an adjustable-rate mortgage be appropriate?

5. For the following situations, select the type of home financing action that would be most appropriate:

   a. A mortgage for a person who desires to finance a home purchase at current interest rates for the entire term of the loan. _____

   b. A home buyer who wants to reduce the amount of monthly payments since interest rates have declined over the past year. _____

   c. A homeowner who wants to access funds that could be used to remodel the home. _____

   d. A person who served in the military, who does not have money for a down payment. _____

   e. A retired person who wants to obtain income from the value of her home. _____

Apply Yourself!

Conduct online research on various types of mortgages and current rates. Prepare a summary of your findings along with recommended actions for selecting a mortgage.

LO7.4

Develop a strategy for selling a home.

A Home-Selling Strategy

Most people who buy a home will eventually be on the other side of a real estate transaction. Selling your home requires preparing it for selling, setting a price, and deciding whether to sell it yourself or use a real estate agent.

Preparing Your Home for Selling

The effective presentation of your home can result in a fast and financially favorable sale. Real estate salespeople recommend that you make needed repairs and paint worn exterior

Personal Finance in Practice

Lowering Your Property Taxes

Property taxes vary from area to area and usually range from 2 to 4 percent of the market value of the home. Taxes are based on the *assessed value*, the amount that your local government determines your property to be worth for tax purposes. Assessed values normally are lower than the market value, often about half. A home with a market value of $180,000 may be assessed at $90,000. If the tax rate is $60 per $1,000 of assessed value, this would result in annual taxes of $5,400 ($90,000 divided by $1,000 times $60). This rate is 6 percent of the assessed value but only 3 percent of the market value.

Although higher home values are desirable, this increase means higher property assessments. Quickly increasing property taxes are frustrating, but there are actions you can take:

Suggested Action	Your Action
Step 1: Know the appeal deadline. Call the local assessor's office. You will usually have between 14 and 90 days to initiate your appeal. Late requests are usually not accepted. Send your appeal by certified mail to have proof that you met the deadline; keep copies of all documents.	
Step 2: Check for mistakes. The assessment office may have incorrect information. Obvious mistakes may include incorrect square footage, or an assessment may report a home with four bedrooms when there are only three.	
Step 3: Determine the issues to emphasize. A property tax appeal can be based on a mistake in the assessment or a higher assessment than comparable homes. Note items that negatively affect the value of your home. For example, a bridge is no longer in operation near your home, making your house much less accessible—and less valuable. Or if a garage has been taken down to increase garden space, the home's value likely would be lower. Compare your assessment with homes of the same size, age, and general location. Obtain comparisons for 5 to 10 homes.	
Step 4: Prepare for the hearing. Gather your evidence and prepare an organized presentation. Use photos of comparable properties. A spreadsheet can make it easy for the hearing officials to view your evidence. Suggest a specific corrected assessment, and give your reasons. Observe the hearing of another person to become familiar with the process.	

Beware of companies that charge fees to dispute your property assessment. Be especially wary of letters that look like they come from government agencies, but are really from private companies. Avoid offers that require an up-front fee to challenge your assessment or that request a certified copy of your property deed.

and interior areas. Clear the garage and exterior areas, and keep the lawn cut and the leaves raked. Keep the kitchen and bathroom clean. Remove excess furniture and dispose of unneeded items to make the house, closets, and storage areas look larger. When showing your home, open drapes and turn on lights. Consider environmentally friendly features such as energy-saving light bulbs and water-saving faucets. This effort will give your property a positive image and make it attractive to potential buyers.

Determining the Selling Price

Putting a price on your home can be difficult. You risk not selling it immediately if the price is too high, and you may not get a fair amount if the price is too low. An **appraisal,** an estimate of the current value of the property, can provide a good indication of the price you should set.

An appraisal is likely to cost between $200 and $300. This expense can help people selling a home on their own to get a realistic view of the property's value. An asking price is influenced by recent selling prices of comparable homes in your area, demand in the housing market, and current mortgage rates.

ACTION ITEM

When selling a home, I would:

☐ **use a real estate agent.**

☐ **use an online service.**

☐ **sell by owner.**

appraisal An estimate of the current value of a property.

The home improvements you have made may or may not increase the selling price. A hot tub or an exercise room may have no value for potential buyers. Among the most desirable improvements are energy-efficient features, a remodeled kitchen, an additional or remodeled bathroom, added rooms and storage space, a converted basement, a fireplace, and an outdoor deck or patio. Daily maintenance, timely repairs, and home improvements will increase the future sales price.

Sale by Owner

Each year, about 10 percent of home sales are made by the home's owners. If you sell your home without using a real estate agent, advertise in local newspapers and create a detailed information sheet. Distribute the sheet at stores and in other public areas. When selling your home on your own, obtain information about the availability of financing and financing requirements. This will help potential buyers determine whether a sale is possible. Use the services of a lawyer or title company to assist you with the contract, the closing, and other legal matters.

Require potential buyers to provide names, addresses, telephone numbers, and background information. Show your home only by appointment and only when two or more adults are at home. Selling your own home can save several thousand dollars in commission, but an investment of your time and effort is required.

Listing with a Real Estate Agent

If you sell your home with the assistance of a real estate agent, consider the person's knowledge of the community and the agent's willingness to actively market your home. A real estate agent will provide you with various services, such as suggesting a selling price, making potential buyers and other agents aware of your home, providing advice on features to highlight, conducting showings of your home, and handling the financial aspects of the sale. Marketing efforts are likely to include presentation of your home on various websites.

A real estate agent can also help screen potential buyers to determine whether they will qualify for a mortgage. Discount real estate brokers are available to assist sellers who are willing to take on certain duties and want to reduce selling costs.

PRACTICE QUIZ 7-4

1. What actions are recommended when planning to sell your home?

2. What factors affect the selling price of a home?

3. What should you consider when deciding whether to sell your home on your own or use the services of a real estate agent?

Apply Yourself!

Visit a couple of homes for sale. What features do you believe would appeal to potential buyers? What efforts were made to attract potential buyers to the open houses?

YOUR PERSONAL FINANCE DASHBOARD

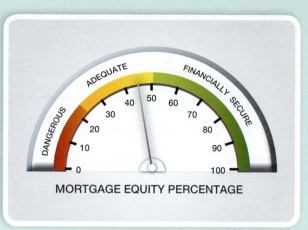

MORTGAGE EQUITY PERCENTAGE

DANGEROUS — ADEQUATE — FINANCIALLY SECURE

0 10 20 30 40 50 60 70 80 90 100

For home buyers, *home equity,* the amount of your ownership in the property, can be an indicator of financial progress. Equity is calculated by subtracting the mortgage amount owed from the current market value of the home. For example, a home worth $200,000 with $80,000 still owed on the mortgage would have equity of $120,000, which is 60 percent of the home's value.

In recent years, as the market value of many homes declined, home equity also declined for many homeowners. Building equity through shorter mortgages and additional principal payments can be a key financial strategy.

YOUR SITUATION: Are you able to make additional mortgage payments toward the loan principal to build the equity in your home?

POSSIBLE ACTIONS TO TAKE

 Reconsider your responses to the "Action Items" (in the text margin) to determine actions you might take to make wiser housing decisions.

 Use various information sources when planning a housing decision, including discussions with people you know and these helpful websites: homebuying.about.com, realestate.msn.com, www.hud.gov/buying, and www.homefair.com.

 Before signing a lease, be sure you understand the elements of this legal document. For additional information on leases, go to apartments.about.com or search online for lease information.

 Consider what size mortgage you can afford when starting the home-buying process at www.mortgage101.com or www.erate.com. Current mortgage rate information is available at www.bankrate.com, www.hsh.com, and www.interest.com, as well as from local financial institutions.

 When planning to sell a home on your own, you can find assistance at www.owners.com. Also of value is talking with people who have sold their own homes.

LO7.1   Assess renting and buying alternatives in terms of their financial and opportunity costs. The main advantages of renting are mobility, fewer responsibilities, and lower initial costs. The main disadvantages of renting are few financial benefits, a restricted lifestyle, and legal concerns.

LO7.2   Home buying involves five major stages: (1) determining home ownership needs, (2) finding and evaluating a property to purchase, (3) pricing the property, (4) financing the purchase, and (5) closing the real estate transaction.

LO7.3   The costs associated with purchasing a home include the down payment; mortgage origination costs; closing costs such as a deed fee, prepaid interest, attorney's fees, payment for title insurance, and a property survey; and an escrow account for homeowner's insurance and property taxes.

LO7.4   When selling a home, you must decide whether to make certain repairs and improvements, determine a selling price, and choose between selling the home yourself and using the services of a real estate agent.

Chapter Summary

adjustable-rate mortgage (ARM) 232	condominium 226	lease 222
amortization 231	cooperative housing 226	mortgage 229
appraisal 237	deed 234	points 231
closing costs 234	earnest money 228	title insurance 234
	escrow account 236	zoning laws 226

Discussion Questions

1. What do you believe are the most important factors a person should consider when selecting housing?   (LO7.1)
2. What are some common mistakes a person might make when renting an apartment or other housing?   (LO7.1)
3. What actions would you recommend to a person who was considering buying a home that needed several improvements?   (LO7.2)
4. Describe how knowledge of current interest rates would help you better plan when obtaining a mortgage.   (LO7.3)
5. Prepare a list of actions to take when selling a home.   (LO7.4)

Self-Test Problems

1. What would be the monthly payment for a $180,000, 20-year mortgage at 6 percent?
2. What is the total amount of a 30-year mortgage with monthly payments of $850?

Solutions

1. Using Exhibit 7–7, multiply 180 times $7.16 to determine the monthly payment of $1,288.80
2. 360 payments (30 years × 12 months) are multiplied by $850 for a total of $306,000.

Problems

1. Based on the following data, would you recommend buying or renting?   (LO7.1)

Rental Costs	*Buying Costs*
Annual rent, $7,380	Annual mortgage payments, $9,800 ($9,575 is interest)
Insurance, $145	Property taxes, $1,780
Security deposit, $650	Down payment/closing costs, $4,500
	Growth in equity, $225
	Insurance/maintenance, $1,050
	Estimated annual appreciation, $1,700

Assume an after-tax savings interest rate of 6 percent and a tax rate of 28 percent.

2. When renting, various move-in costs will be encountered. Estimate the following amounts: (LO7.1)

First month's rent	$_____
Security deposit	$_____
Security deposit for utilities (if applicable)	$_____
Moving truck, other moving expenses	$_____
Household items (dishes, towels, bedding)	$_____
Furniture and appliances (as required)	$_____
Renter's insurance	$_____
Refreshments for friends who helped you move	$_____
Other items: _____	$_____

3. Many locations require that renters be paid interest on their security deposits. If you have a security deposit of $1,800, how much would you expect a year at 2 percent? (LO7.1)

4. Condominiums usually require a monthly fee for various services. At $235 a month, how much would a homeowner pay over a 10-year period for living in this housing facility? (LO7.2)

5. Ben and Carla Covington plan to buy a condominium. They will obtain a $220,000, 30-year mortgage at 5 percent. Their annual property taxes are expected to be $1,800. Property insurance is $480 a year, and the condo association fee is $220 a month. Based on these items, determine the total monthly housing payment for the Covingtons. (LO7.2)

6. Estimate the affordable monthly mortgage payment, the affordable mortgage amount, and the affordable home purchase price for the following situation (see Exhibit 7–6). (LO7.3)

Monthly gross income, $2,950

Other debt (monthly payment), $160

30-year loan at 6 percent

Down payment to be made—15 percent of purchase price

Monthly estimate for property taxes and insurance, $210

7. Based on Exhibit 7–7, what would be the monthly mortgage payments for each of the following situations? (LO7.3)

   a. A $160,000, 15-year loan at 6.5 percent.
   b. A $215,000, 30-year loan at 5 percent.
   c. A $190,000, 20-year loan at 6 percent.

8. Which mortgage would result in higher total payments? (LO7.3)

   Mortgage A: $985 a month for 30 years.
   Mortgage B: $780 a month for 5 years and $1,056 a month for 25 years.

9. If an adjustable-rate 30-year mortgage for $120,000 starts at 4.0 percent and increases to 5.5 percent, what is the amount of increase of the monthly payment? (Use Exhibit 7–7.) (LO7.3)

10. Kelly and Tim Jarowski plan to refinance their mortgage to obtain a lower interest rate. They will reduce their mortgage payments by $56 a month. Their closing costs for refinancing will be $1,670. How long will it take them to cover the cost of refinancing? (LO7.3)

11. In an attempt to have funds for a down payment in five years, James Dupont plans to save $3,800 a year for the next five years. With an interest rate of 4 percent, what amount will James have available for a down payment after the five years? (LO7.3)

12. Based on Exhibit 7–9, if you were buying a home, what would be the approximate total closing costs (excluding the down payment)? As an alternative, obtain actual figures for the closing items by contacting various real estate organizations or by doing online research. (LO7.3)

13. You estimate that you can save $3,450 by selling your home yourself rather than using a real estate agent. What would be the future value of that amount if invested for five years at 3 percent? (LO7.4)

 **connect** To reinforce the content in this chapter, more problems are provided at connect.mheducation.com.

|FINANCE

HOUSING DECISIONS

When Mark and Valerie Bowman first saw the house, they didn't like it. However, it was a dark, rainy day. They viewed the house more favorably on their second visit, which they had expected to be a waste of time. Despite cracked ceilings, the need for new paint, and a kitchen built in the 1980s, the Bowmans saw a potential to create a place they could call their own.

Case in Point

Beth Young purchased her condominium several years ago. She obtained a mortgage rate of 6.5 percent, a very good rate then. Recently, when interest rates dropped, Beth was considering refinancing her mortgage at a lower rate.

Matt and Peggy Zoran had been married for five years and were still living in an apartment. Several of their friends had purchased homes recently. However, Matt and Peggy were not sure they wanted to follow this example. Although they liked their friends' homes and had viewed online videos of homes on the market, they also liked the freedom from maintenance responsibility they enjoyed as renters.

Questions

1. How could the Bowmans benefit from buying a home that needed improvements?
2. How might Beth Young have found out when mortgage rates were at a level that would make refinancing her condominium more affordable?
3. Although the Zorans had good reasons for continuing to rent, what factors might make it desirable for an individual or a family to buy a home?
4. What actions might each of these home buyers take to use websites or apps to enhance their home-buying and financing activities? Based on a web search, what advice would you offer when using the online sources for various phases of the home-buying process?

Continuing Case

SELECTING AND FINANCING HOUSING

Five years have passed and Jamie Lee, 34, is considering taking the plunge: Not only is she engaged to be married, but she is also deciding on whether to purchase a new home.

Jamie Lee's cupcake café is a success! It has been open over a year now and has earned itself rave reviews in the local press and from its regular customers, who just cannot get enough of her delicious cupcakes. One such customer, who stopped by on a whim in the café's first week of business, is Ross. After a whirlwind courtship, Ross, a self-employed web page designer, proposed and Jamie Lee agreed to be his wife.

The bungalow that Jamie Lee has been renting for the past five years is too small for the soon-to-be newlyweds, so Jamie Lee and Ross are trying to decide if they should move to another rental or purchase a home of their own. They agreed to visit their local banker to get an idea of how much home they can afford with their combined incomes.

Current Financial Situation

Assets (Jamie Lee and Ross combined):
Checking account, $4,300
Savings account, $55,200
Emergency fund savings account, $19,100
IRA balance, $24,000
Cars, $12,000 (Jamie Lee) and $20,000 (Ross)

Liabilities (Jamie Lee and Ross combined):
Student loan balance, $0
Credit card balance, $0
Car loans, $8,000

Income:
Jamie Lee, $45,000 gross income ($31,500 net income after taxes)
Ross, $70,000 gross income ($59,000 net income after taxes)

Monthly Expenses (Jamie Lee and Ross combined):
Utilities, $160
Food, $325
Gas/Maintenance, $275
Credit card payment, $0
Car loan payment, $289
Entertainment, $300

Questions

1. Using "Your Personal Financial Plan" sheet 22, compare the advantages and the disadvantages of renting a home or apartment to those of purchasing a home.

2. Jamie Lee and Ross are estimating that they will be putting $40,000 from their savings account toward a down payment on their home purchase. Using the traditional financial guideline suggestion of "two and a half times your salary plus your down payment," calculate approximately how much Jamie Lee and Ross can spend on a house.

3. Using "Your Personal Financial Plan" sheet 24, calculate the affordable mortgage amount that would be suggested by a lending institution based on Jamie Lee and Ross's income. How does this amount compare with the traditional financial guideline found in Question 2?

   Use the following amounts for Jamie Lee and Ross's calculations:
   * 10 percent down payment
   * 28 percent for TIPI
   * $500.00 per month for estimated combined property taxes and insurance
   * 5 percent interest rate for 30 years (see Exhibit 7–7)

4. Jamie Lee and Ross found a brand-new three-bedroom, 2½-bath home for sale in a quiet neighborhood. The listing price is $275,000. They placed a bid of $260,000 on the home. The seller's counteroffer was $273,000. What should Jamie Lee and Ross do next to demonstrate to the owner that they are serious buyers?

5. Jamie Lee and Ross received a signed contract from the seller accepting their $273,000 offer! The seller also agreed to pay two points toward Jamie Lee and Ross's mortgage. Calculate the benefit of having points paid toward the mortgage if Jamie Lee and Ross are putting a $40,000 down payment on the home.

6. Calculate Jamie Lee and Ross's mortgage payment, using the 5 percent rate for 30 years on the mortgage balance of $233,000.

Spending Diary

"AFTER I PAY MY RENT, UTILITIES, AND RENTER'S INSURANCE, I HAVE VERY LITTLE FOR OTHER EXPENSES."

Directions Your Daily Spending Diary will help you manage your housing expenses to create a better overall spending plan. As you record daily spending, your comments should reflect what you have learned about your spending patterns and help you consider possible changes you might want to make. The Daily Spending Diary sheets are located in Appendix D at the end of the book and in Connect Finance.

Questions

1. What portion of your daily spending involves expenses associated with housing?
2. What types of housing expenses might be reduced with more careful spending habits?

22

Name: _____   **Date:** _____

Renting vs. Buying Housing

Purpose: To compare the cost of renting or buying your place of residence.

Financial Planning Activities: Obtain estimates for comparable housing units for the data requested below. This sheet is also available in an Excel spreadsheet format in Connect Finance.

Suggested Websites: www.homefair.com   www.newbuyer.com/homes   finance.move.com   www.dinkytown.net

Rental Costs

Annual rent payments (monthly rent $_____ × 12) $_____

Renter's insurance $_____

Interest lost on security deposit (deposit times after-tax savings account interest rate) $_____

Total annual cost of renting $

Buying Costs

Annual mortgage payments $_____

Property taxes (annual costs) $_____

Homeowner's insurance (annual premium) $_____

Estimated maintenance and repairs $_____

After-tax interest lost because of down payment/closing costs $_____

Less: financial benefits of home ownership

Growth in equity $ –_____

Tax savings for mortgage interest (annual mortgage interest times tax rate) $ –_____

Tax savings for property taxes (annual property taxes times tax rate) $ –_____

Estimated annual appreciation $ –_____

Total annual cost of buying $

Suggested App:
• Realtor

What's Next for Your Personal Financial Plan?

• Determine if renting or buying is most appropriate for you at the current time.
• List some circumstances or actions that might change your housing needs.

Apartment Rental Comparison

Purpose: To evaluate and compare rental housing alternatives.

Financial Planning Activities: Obtain the information requested below to compare costs and facilities of three apartments. This sheet is also available in an Excel spreadsheet format in Connect Finance.

Suggested Websites: www.apartments.com   www.apartmentguide.com   apartments.about.com

Name of renting person or apartment building			
Address			
Phone			
Monthly rent			
Amount of security deposit			
Length of lease			
Utilities included in rent			
Parking facilities			
Storage area in building			
Laundry facilities			
Distance to schools			
Distance to public transportation			
Distance to shopping			
Pool, recreation area, other facilities			
Estimated utility costs: • Electric • Cable/Internet • Gas • Water			
Other costs			
Other information			

Suggested
App:
• PadMapper

What's Next for Your Personal Financial Plan?

- Which of these rental units would best serve your current housing needs?
- What additional information should be considered when renting an apartment?

Name: _____   Date: _____

Housing Affordability and Mortgage Qualification

Purpose: To estimate the amount of affordable mortgage payment, mortgage amount, and home purchase price.

Financial Planning Activities: Enter the amounts requested to estimate the amount of affordable mortgage payment, mortgage amount, and home purchase price. This sheet is also available in an Excel spreadsheet format in Connect Finance.

Suggested Websites: www.realestate.com   homeloanlearningcenter.com   mtgprofessor.com

Step 1

Determine your monthly gross income (annual income divided by 12). $ _____

Step 2

With a down payment of at least 10 percent, lenders use 28 percent of monthly gross income as a guideline for TIPI (taxes, insurance, principal, and interest), 36 percent of monthly gross income as a guideline for TIPI plus other debt payments (enter 0.28 or 0.36).   × _____

Step 3

Subtract other debt payments (such as payments on an auto loan), if applicable.   − _____

Subtract estimated monthly costs of property taxes and homeowner's insurance.   − _____

Affordable monthly mortgage payment . . . . $ _____

Step 4

Divide this amount by the monthly mortgage payment per $1,000 based on current mortgage rates (see Exhibit 7–7). For example, for an 8 percent, 30-year loan, the number would be $7.34.   ÷ _____

Multiply by $1,000.   × _____ $1,000 _____

Affordable mortgage amount . . . . $ _____

Step 5

Divide your affordable mortgage amount by 1 minus the fractional portion of your down payment (for example, 0.9 for a 10 percent down payment).   ÷ _____

Affordable home purchase price . . . . $ _____

Note: The two ratios used by lending institutions (Step 2) and other loan requirements are likely to vary based on a variety of factors, including the type of mortgage, the amount of the down payment, your income level, credit score, and current interest rates. If you have other debts, lenders will calculate both ratios and then use the one that allows you greater flexibility in borrowing.

Suggested App:
• Mortgage Calculator

What's Next for Your Personal Financial Plan?

• Identify actions you might need to take to qualify for a mortgage.
• Discuss your mortgage qualifications with a mortgage broker or other lender.

Name: _____ **Date:** _____

Mortgage Company Comparison

Purpose: To compare the services and costs for different home mortgage alternatives.

Financial Planning Activities: Obtain the information requested below to compare the services and costs for different home mortgage sources. This sheet is also available in an Excel spreadsheet format in Connect Finance.

Suggested Websites: www.hsh.com   www.eloan.com   www.bankrate.com   mtgprofessor.com

Amount of mortgage: $_____	Down payment: $_____	Years: _____
Company		
Address		
Phone		
Website		
Contact person		
Application fee, credit report, property appraisal fees		
Loan origination fee		
Other fees, charges (commitment, title, tax transfer)		
Fixed-rate mortgage		
Monthly payment		
Discount points		
Adjustable-rate mortgage		
• Time until first rate charge		
• Frequency of rate charge		
Monthly payment		
Discount points		
Payment cap		
Interest rate cap		
Rate index used		
Commitment period		
Other information		

What's Next for Your Personal Financial Plan?

- What additional information should be considered when selecting a mortgage?
- Which of these mortgage companies would best serve your current and future needs?

Suggested App:
• Bankrate Mortgages

8

Home and Automobile Insurance

3 Steps to Financial Literacy . . . Percent of Personal Property Coverage

1 Prepare a household inventory with a description and the value of belongings, furniture, clothing, electronics, and other personal property. *App:* III Inventory

2 Compare various insurance companies and levels of coverage to obtain home or renter's insurance for your life situation. *Website:* www.insure.com

3 Determine if additional personal property coverage is needed based on the value of your household inventory. *Website:* www.insweb.com

Each year homeowners and renters in the United States lose billions of dollars from more than 3 million burglaries, 500,000 fires, and 200,000 cases of damage from other perils. A major portion of these claims is due to losses for personal property. At the end of the chapter, "Your Personal Finance Dashboard" will provide guidelines for measuring the level of your personal property coverage.

CHAPTER 8 LEARNING OBJECTIVES

In this chapter, you will learn to:

LO8.1 Identify types of risks and risk management methods and develop a risk management plan.

LO8.2 Assess the insurance coverage and policy types available to homeowners and renters.

LO8.3 Analyze the factors that influence the amount of coverage and cost of home insurance.

LO8.4 Identify the important types of automobile insurance coverage.

LO8.5 Evaluate factors that affect the cost of automobile insurance.

YOUR PERSONAL FINANCIAL PLAN SHEETS

26. Current Insurance Policies and Needs
27. Home Inventory
28. Determining Needed Property Insurance
29. Apartment/Home Insurance Comparison
30. Automobile Insurance Cost Comparison

Insurance and Risk Management

In today's world of the "strange but true," you can get insurance for just about anything. You might purchase a policy to protect yourself in the event that you're abducted by aliens. Some insurance companies will offer you protection if you think that you have a risk of turning into a werewolf. If you're a fast runner, you might be able to get a discount on a life insurance policy. Some people buy wedding disaster insurance just in case something goes wrong on the big day. You may never need these types of insurance, but you'll certainly need insurance on your home, your vehicle, and your personal property. The more you know about insurance, the better able you will be to make decisions about buying it.

What Is Insurance?

Insurance is protection against possible financial loss. You can't predict the future. However, insurance allows you to be prepared for the worst. It provides protection against many risks, such as unexpected property loss, illness, and injury. Many kinds of insurance exist, and they all share some common characteristics. They give you peace of mind, and they protect you from financial loss when trouble strikes.

An **insurance company,** or **insurer,** is a risk-sharing business that agrees to pay for losses that may happen to someone it insures. A person joins the risk-sharing group by purchasing a contract known as a **policy.** The purchaser of the policy is called a **policyholder.** Under the policy, the insurance company agrees to take on the risk. In return the policyholder pays the company a **premium,** or fee. The protection provided by the terms of an

Copyright © 2016 by McGraw-Hill Education

LO8.1

Identify types of risks and risk management methods and develop a risk management plan.

ACTION ITEM

Can you list several risk management methods?

☐ Yes ☐ No

insurance Protection against possible financial loss.

insurance company A risk-sharing firm that assumes financial responsibility for losses that may result from an insured risk.

insurer An insurance company.

policy A written contract for insurance.

policyholder A person who owns an insurance policy.

premium The amount of money a policyholder is charged for an insurance policy.

coverage The protection provided by the terms of an insurance policy.

insured A person covered by an insurance policy.

risk Chance or uncertainty of loss; also used to mean "the insured."

peril The cause of a possible loss.

hazard A factor that increases the likelihood of loss through some peril.

negligence Failure to take ordinary or reasonable care in a situation.

insurance policy is known as **coverage,** and the people protected by the policy are known as the **insured.**

Types of Risk

You face risks every day. You can't cross the street without some danger that a motor vehicle might hit you. You can't own property without running the risk that it will be lost, stolen, damaged, or destroyed.

"Risk," "peril," and "hazard" are important terms in insurance. In everyday use, these terms have almost the same meanings. In the insurance business, however, each has a distinct meaning.

Risk is the chance of loss or injury. In insurance it refers to the fact that no one can predict trouble. This means that an insurance company is taking a chance every time it issues a policy. Insurance companies frequently refer to the insured person or property as the risk.

Peril is anything that may possibly cause a loss. It's the reason someone takes out insurance. People buy policies for protection against a wide range of perils, including fire, windstorms, explosions, robbery, and accidents.

Hazard is anything that increases the likelihood of loss through some peril. For example, defective house wiring is a hazard that increases the chance that a fire will start.

The most common risks are personal risks, property risks, and liability risks. *Personal risks* involve loss of income or life due to illness, disability, old age, or unemployment. *Property risks* include losses to property caused by perils, such as fire or theft, and hazards. *Liability risks* involve losses caused by negligence that leads to injury or property damage. **Negligence** is the failure to take ordinary or reasonable care to prevent accidents from happening. If a homeowner doesn't clear the ice from the front steps of her house, for example, she creates a liability risk because visitors could fall on the ice.

Personal risks, property risks, and liability risks are types of *pure,* or *insurable, risk.* The insurance company will have to pay only if some event that the insurance covers actually happens. Pure risks are accidental and unintentional. Although no one can predict whether a pure risk will occur, it's possible to predict the costs that will accrue if one does.

A *speculative risk* is a risk that carries a chance of either loss or gain. Starting a small business that may or may not succeed is an example of speculative risk. Speculative risks are not insurable.

Risk Management Methods

Risk management is an organized plan for protecting yourself, your family, and your property. It helps reduce financial losses caused by destructive events. Risk management is a long-range planning process. Your risk management needs will change at various points in your life. If you understand how to manage risks, you can provide better protection for yourself and your family. Most people think of risk management as buying insurance. However, insurance is not the only way of dealing with risk. Four general risk management techniques are commonly used.

RISK AVOIDANCE You can avoid the risk of a traffic accident by not driving to work. A car manufacturer can avoid the risk of product failure by not introducing new cars. These are both examples of risk avoidance. They are ways to avoid risks, but they require serious trade-offs. You might have to give up your job if you can't get there. The car manufacturer might lose business to competitors who take the risk of producing exciting new cars.

did you know?

The poor of the world often lack the ability to protect their assets. However, in recent years, microinsurance has evolved to serve consumers and businesses not covered by traditional insurance programs. These low-premium, low-coverage policies provide low-income households protection from losses that would have a major impact on their financial situation.

In some cases, though, risk avoidance is practical. By taking precautions in high-crime areas, you might avoid the risk that you will be robbed.

RISK REDUCTION You can't avoid risks completely. However, you can decrease the likelihood that they will cause you harm. For example, you can reduce the risk of injury in an automobile accident by wearing a seat belt. You can reduce the risk of developing lung cancer by not smoking. By installing fire extinguishers in your home, you reduce the potential damage that could be caused by a fire. Your risk of illness might be lower if you eat properly and exercise regularly.

RISK ASSUMPTION Risk assumption means taking on responsibility for the negative results of a risk. It makes sense to assume a risk if you know that the possible loss will be small. It also makes sense when you've taken all the precautions you can to avoid or reduce the risk.

When insurance coverage for a particular item is expensive, that item may not be worth insuring. For instance, you might decide not to purchase collision insurance on an older car. If an accident happens, the car may be wrecked, but it wasn't worth much anyway. *Self-insurance* is setting up a special fund, perhaps from savings, to cover the cost of a loss. Self-insurance does not eliminate risks, but it does provide a way of covering losses as an alternative to an insurance policy. Some people self-insure because they can't obtain insurance from an insurance company.

RISK SHIFTING The most common method of dealing with risk is to shift it. That simply means to transfer it to an insurance company. In exchange for the fee you pay, the insurance company agrees to pay for your losses.

Most insurance policies include deductibles. Deductibles are a combination of risk assumption and risk shifting. A **deductible** is the set amount that the policyholder must pay per loss on an insurance policy. For example, if a falling tree damages your car, you may have to pay $200 toward the repairs. Your insurance company will pay the rest.

Exhibit 8–1 summarizes various risks and effective ways of managing them.

> **deductible** The set amount that the policyholder must pay per loss on an Insurance policy.

Planning an Insurance Program

Your personal insurance program should change along with your needs and goals. Dave and Ellen are a young couple. How will they plan their insurance program to meet their needs and goals?

Exhibit 8–2 outlines the steps in developing a personal insurance program.

STEP 1: SET INSURANCE GOALS Dave and Ellen's main goal should be to minimize personal, property, and liability risks. They also need to decide how they will cover costs resulting from a potential loss. Income, age, family size, lifestyle, experience, and responsibilities will be important factors in the goals they set. The insurance they buy must reflect those goals. Dave and Ellen should try to come up with a basic risk management plan that achieves the following:

- Reduces possible loss of income caused by premature death, illness, accident, or unemployment.
- Reduces possible loss of property caused by perils, such as fire or theft, or hazards.
- Reduces possible loss of income, savings, and property because of personal negligence.

STEP 2: DEVELOP A PLAN TO REACH YOUR GOALS Planning is a way of taking control of life instead of just letting life happen to you. Dave and Ellen need to determine

did you know?

Deductibles are a combination of risk assumption and risk shifting. The insured person assumes part of the risk, paying the first $100, $250, or $500 of a claim. The majority of the risk for a large claim is shifted to another party, the insurance company.

Exhibit 8–1 Examples of Risks and Risk Management Strategies

RISKS		STRATEGIES FOR REDUCING FINANCIAL IMPACT		
Personal Events	Financial Impact	Personal Resources	Private Sector	Public Sector
Disability	Loss of one income Loss of services Increased expenses	Savings, investments Family observing safety precautions	Disability insurance	Disability insurance

Illness	Loss of one income
	Catastrophic hospital
	  expenses
		Health-enhancing
		  behavior
			Health insurance
			Health maintenance
			  organizations
				Military health care
				Medicare, Medicaid

Death	Loss of one income
	Loss of services
	Final expenses
		Estate planning
		Risk reduction
			Life insurance	Veteran's life
				  insurance
				Social Security
				  survivor's benefits

Retirement	Decreased income
	Unplanned living
	  expenses
		Savings
		Investments
		Hobbies, skills
			Retirement and/or
			  pensions
				Social Security
				Pension plan for
				  government
				  employees

Property loss	Catastrophic storm
	  damage to
	  property
	Repair or
	  replacement cost
	  of theft
		Property repair and
		  upkeep
		Security plans
			Automobile
			  insurance
			Homeowner's
			  insurance
			Flood insurance (joint
			  program with
			  government)
				Flood insurance (joint
				  program with
				  business)

Liability	Claims and
	  settlement costs
	Lawsuits and legal
	  expenses
	Loss of personal
	  assets and income
		Observing safety
		  precautions
		Maintaining property
			Homeowner's
			  insurance
			Automobile
			  insurance
			Malpractice insurance	

what risks they face and what risks they can afford to take. They also have to determine what resources can help them reduce the damage that could be caused by serious risks.

Furthermore, they need to know what kind of insurance is available. The cost of different kinds of insurance and the way the costs vary among companies will be the key factors in their plan. Finally, this couple needs to research the reliability record of different insurance companies.

Exhibit 8–2

Creating a Personal Insurance Program

Personal Finance in Practice

How Can You Plan an Insurance Program?

Did you:	Yes	No
• Seek advice from a competent and reliable insurance advisor?	☐	☐
• Determine what insurance you need to provide your family with sufficient protection if you die?	☐	☐
• Consider what portion of the family protection is met by Social Security and by group insurance?	☐	☐
• Decide what other needs insurance must meet (funeral expenses, savings, retirement annuities, etc.)?	☐	☐
• Decide what types of insurance best meet your needs?	☐	☐
• Plan an insurance program and implement it except for periodic reviews of changing needs and changing conditions?	☐	☐
• Avoid buying more insurance than you need or can afford?	☐	☐
• Consider dropping one policy for another that provides the same coverage for less money?	☐	☐

NOTE: Yes answers reflect wise actions for insurance planning.

Dave and Ellen must ask four questions as they develop their risk management plan:

- What do they need to insure?
- How much should they insure it for?
- What kind of insurance should they buy?
- Whom should they buy insurance from?

STEP 3: PUT YOUR PLAN INTO ACTION Once they've developed their plan, Dave and Ellen need to follow through by putting it into action. During this process they might discover that they don't have enough insurance protection. If that's the case, they could purchase additional coverage or change the kind of coverage they have. Another alternative would be to adjust their budget to cover the cost of additional insurance. Finally, Dave and Ellen might expand their savings or investment programs and use those funds in the case of an emergency.

The best risk management plans will be flexible enough to allow Dave and Ellen to respond to changing life situations. Their goal should be to create an insurance program that can grow or shrink as their protection needs change.

STEP 4: CHECK YOUR RESULTS Dave and Ellen should take the time to review their plan every two or three years, or whenever their family circumstances change.

Until recently, Dave and Ellen were satisfied with the coverage provided by their insurance policies. However, when the couple bought a house six months ago, the time had come for them to review their insurance plan. With the new house the risks became much greater. After all, what would happen if a fire destroyed part of their home?

The needs of a couple renting an apartment differ from those of a couple who own a house. Both couples face similar risks, but their financial responsibility differs greatly. When you're developing or reviewing a risk management plan, ask yourself if you're providing the financial resources you'll need to protect yourself, your family, and your property. The nearby "Personal Finance in Practice" box suggests several guidelines to follow in planning your insurance programs.

Property and Liability Insurance in Your Financial Plan

Major natural disasters have caused catastrophic amounts of property loss in the United States and other parts of the world. According to the Insurance Information Institute, the first months of 2011 were violent in terms of catastrophes on a global scale. Mega catastrophes worldwide caused an estimated $350 billion in economic losses, shattering the previous record of $230 billion set in 2005. In 2005 Hurricanes Katrina, Rita, and Wilma caused $50 billion in damages. In 1992 Hurricane Andrew resulted in $22.3 billion worth of insurance **claims,** or requests for payment to cover financial losses. Superstorm Sandy, the deadliest and most destructive tropical cyclone of 2012, caused more than $18 billion in insured losses and became the third costliest hurricane in the history of the U.S. insurance industry.

claim A request for payment to cover financial losses.

Most people invest large amounts of money in their homes and motor vehicles. Therefore, protecting these items from loss is extremely important. Each year homeowners and renters in the United States lose billions of dollars from more than 3 million burglaries, 500,000 fires, and 200,000 cases of damage from other perils. The cost of injuries and property damage caused by vehicles is also enormous.

Think of the price you pay for home and motor vehicle insurance as an investment in protecting your most valuable possessions. The cost of such insurance may seem high. However, the financial losses from which it protects you are much higher.

Two main types of risk are related to your home and your car or other vehicle. One is the risk of damage to or loss of your property. The second type involves your responsibility for injuries to other people or damage to their property.

POTENTIAL PROPERTY LOSSES People spend a great deal of money on their houses, vehicles, furniture, clothing, and other personal property. Property owners face two basic types of risk. The first is physical damage caused by perils such as fire, wind, water, and smoke. These perils can damage or destroy property. For example, a windstorm might cause a large tree branch to smash the windshield of your car. You would have to find another way to get around while it was being repaired. The second type of risk is loss or damage caused by criminal behavior such as robbery, burglary, vandalism, and arson.

liability Legal responsibility for the financial cost of another person's losses or injuries.

LIABILITY PROTECTION You also need to protect yourself from liability. **Liability** is legal responsibility for the financial cost of another person's losses or injuries. You can be held legally responsible even if the injury or damage was not your fault. For example, suppose that Terry falls and gets hurt while playing in her friend Lisa's yard. Terry's family may be able to sue Lisa's parents even though Lisa's parents did nothing wrong. Similarly, suppose that Sanjay accidentally damages a valuable painting while helping Ed move some furniture. Ed may take legal action against Sanjay to pay the cost of the painting.

Usually, if you're found liable, or legally responsible in a situation, it's because negligence on your part caused the mishap. Examples of such negligence include letting young children swim in a pool without supervision or cluttering a staircase with things that could cause someone to slip and fall.

Sheet 26 Current Insurance Policies and Needs

PRACTICE QUIZ 8-1

1. What are the three types of risk? Give an example for each.

2. What are the four methods of managing risks? Give an example for each.

3. List the four steps in planning for your insurance program.

4. Give an example of each kind of risk—personal, property, and liability.

Home and Property Insurance

Your home and personal belongings are probably a major portion of your assets. Whether you rent your dwelling or own a home, property insurance is vital. **Homeowner's insurance** is coverage for your place of residence and its associated financial risks, such as damage to personal property and injuries to others (see Exhibit 8–3).

Homeowner's Insurance Coverages

A homeowner's insurance policy provides coverage for the following:

- The building in which you live and any other structures on the property.
- Additional living expenses.
- Personal property.
- Personal liability and related coverage.
- Specialized coverage.

BUILDING AND OTHER STRUCTURES The main purpose of homeowner's insurance is to protect you against financial loss in case your home is damaged or destroyed. Detached structures on your property, such as a garage or toolshed, are also covered. Homeowner's coverage even includes trees, shrubs, and plants.

ADDITIONAL LIVING EXPENSES If a fire or other event damages your home, additional living expense coverage pays for you to stay somewhere else. For example, you may need to stay in a motel or rent an apartment while your home is being repaired. These extra living expenses will be paid by your insurance. Some policies limit additional living expense coverage to 10 to 20 percent of the home's coverage amount. They may also limit payments to a maximum of six to nine months. Other policies may pay additional living expenses for up to a year.

PERSONAL PROPERTY Homeowner's insurance covers your household belongings, such as furniture, appliances, and clothing, up to a portion of the insured value of the home. That portion is usually 55, 70, or 75 percent. For example, a home insured for $160,000 might have $112,000 (70 percent) worth of coverage for household belongings.

Personal property coverage typically limits the payout for the theft of certain items, such as $5,000 for jewelry. It provides protection against the loss or damage of articles that you take with you when you are away from home. For example, items you take on vacation

LO8.2

Assess the insurance coverage and policy types available to homeowners and renters.

ACTION ITEM

Do you have enough home and property insurance?

☐ Yes ☐ No

homeowner's insurance Coverage for a place of residence and its associated financial risks.

Exhibit **8–3** Home Insurance Coverage

| Building and other structures | Personal property | Loss of use/additional living expenses while home is uninhabitable | Personal liability and related coverages |

or use at college are usually covered up to the policy limit. Personal property coverage even extends to property that you rent, such as a rug cleaner, while it's in your possession.

Most homeowner's policies include optional coverage for personal computers, including stored data, up to a certain limit. Your insurance agent can determine whether the equipment is covered against data loss and damage from spilled drinks or power surges.

If something does happen to your personal property, you must prove how much it was worth and that it belonged to you. To make the process easier, you can create a household inventory. A **household inventory** is a list or other documentation of personal belongings, with purchase dates and cost information. You can get a form for such an inventory from an insurance agent. Exhibit 8–4 provides a list of items you might include if you decide to compile your own inventory. For items of special value, you should have receipts, serial numbers, brand names, and proof of value.

household inventory A list or other documentation of personal belongings, with purchase dates and cost information.

Exhibit 8–4   Household Inventory Contents

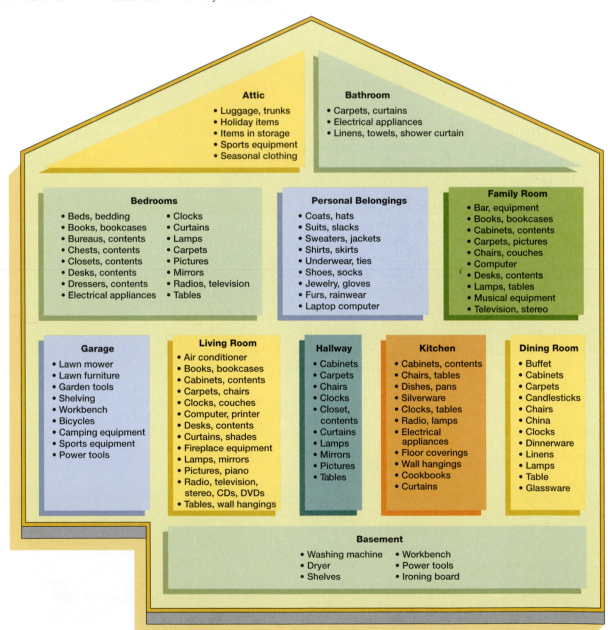

Your household inventory can include a video recording or photographs of your home and its contents. Make sure that the closet and storage area doors are photographed open. On the back of the photographs, indicate the date and the value of the objects. Update your inventory, photos, and related documents on a regular basis. Keep a copy of each document in a secure location, such as a safe deposit box.

If you own valuable items, such as expensive musical instruments, or need added protection for computers and related equipment, you can purchase a personal property floater. A **personal property floater** is additional property insurance that covers the damage or loss of a specific item of high value. The insurance company will require a detailed description of the item and its worth. You'll also need to have the item appraised, or evaluated by an expert, from time to time to make sure that its value hasn't changed.

PERSONAL LIABILITY AND RELATED COVERAGE Every day people face the risk of financial loss due to injuries to other people or their property. The following are examples of this risk:

- A guest falls on a patch of ice on the steps to your home and breaks his arm.
- A spark from the barbecue in your backyard starts a fire that damages a neighbor's roof.
- Your son or daughter accidentally breaks an antique lamp while playing at a neighbor's house.

In each of these situations, you could be held responsible for paying for the damage. The personal liability portion of a homeowner's policy protects you and members of your family if others sue you for injuries they suffer or damage to their property. This coverage includes the cost of legal defense.

Not all individuals who come to your property are covered by your liability insurance. Friends, guests, and babysitters are probably covered. However, if you have regular employees, such as a housekeeper, a cook, or a gardener, you may need to obtain worker's compensation coverage for them.

Most homeowner's policies provide basic personal liability coverage of $100,000, but often that's not enough. An **umbrella policy,** also called a *personal catastrophe policy,* supplements your basic personal liability coverage. This added protection covers you for all kinds of personal injury claims. For instance, an umbrella policy will cover you if someone sues you for saying or writing something negative or untrue or for damaging his or her reputation. Extended liability policies are sold in amounts of $1 million or more and are useful for wealthy people. If you are a business owner, you may need other types of liability coverage as well.

Medical payments coverage pays the cost of minor accidental injuries to visitors on your property. It also covers minor injuries caused by you, members of your family, or even your pets, away from home. Settlements under medical payments coverage are made without determining who was at fault. This makes it fast and easy for the insurance company to process small claims, generally up to $5,000. If the injury is more serious, the personal liability portion of the homeowner's policy covers it. Medical payments coverage does not cover injury to you or the other people who live in your home.

If you or a family member should accidentally damage another person's property, the supplementary coverage of homeowner's insurance will pay for it. This protection is usually limited to $500 or $1,000. Again, payments are made regardless of fault. If the damage is more expensive, however, it's handled under the personal liability coverage.

SPECIALIZED COVERAGE FOR PSYCHOLOGICAL AND FINANCIAL WELL-BEING Homeowner's insurance usually doesn't cover losses from floods and earthquakes. If you live in an area that has frequent floods or earthquakes, you need to purchase special coverage. In some places the National Flood Insurance Program makes flood insurance available. This

personal property floater Additional property insurance to cover the damage or loss of a specific item of high value.

umbrella policy Supplementary personal liability coverage; also called a *personal catastrophe policy.*

medical payments coverage Home insurance that pays the cost of minor accidental injuries on one's property.

did you know?

For $50 to $80 a year, homeowners can obtain $10,000 for sewage and drain backup damage. Heavy rains that clog a sewer line can cause damage to furniture and other items in a finished basement.

Personal Finance in Practice

Flood Facts

- Floods and flash floods happen in all 50 states.
- Everyone lives in a flood zone.
- Most homeowner's insurance does not cover flood damage.
- If you live in a Special Flood Hazard Area (SFHA) or high-risk area and have a federally backed mortgage, your mortgage lender requires you to have flood insurance.
- Just an inch of water can cause costly damage to your property.
- Flash floods often bring walls of water 10 to 20 feet high.
- A car can easily be carried away by just two feet of floodwater.
- Hurricanes, winter storms, and snowmelt are common (but often overlooked) causes of flooding.
- New land development can increase flood risk, especially if the construction changes natural runoff paths.
- Federal disaster assistance is usually a loan that must be paid back with interest. For a $50,000 loan at 4 percent interest, your monthly payment would be about $240 a month ($2,880 a year) for 30 years. Compare that to a $100,000 flood insurance premium, which is about $400 a year ($33 a month).
- If you live in a moderate-to-low risk area and are eligible for the Preferred Risk Policy, your flood insurance premium may be as low as $129 a year, including coverage for your property's contents.

- You are eligible to purchase flood insurance as long as your community participates in the National Flood Insurance Program.
- It takes 30 days after purchase for a policy to take effect, so it's important to buy insurance before the floodwaters start to rise.
- In a high-risk area, your home is more than twice as likely to be damaged by flood than by fire.
- Anyone can be financially vulnerable to floods. People outside of high-risk areas file over 20 percent of NFIP claims and receive one-third of disaster assistance for flooding.
- The average annual U.S. flood losses in the past 10 years (2003–2012) were nearly $4 billion.
- When your community participates in the Community Rating System (CRS), you can qualify for an insurance premium discount of up to 45 percent.
- Since 1978, the NFIP has paid over $48.1 billion for flood insurance claims and related costs (as of July 8, 2013).
- Over 5.5 million people currently hold flood insurance policies in more than 21,000 communities across the United States.

For more policy and claim statistics, visit the National Flood Insurance Program.

SOURCE: www.floodsmart.gov/floodsmart/pages/flood_facts.jsp, accessed May 23, 2014.

---

protection is separate from a homeowner's policy. An insurance agent or the Federal Emergency Management Agency (FEMA) of the Federal Insurance Administration can give you additional information about this coverage. Read the nearby "Personal Finance in Practice" box to learn more about flood insurance.

endorsement An addition of coverage to a standard insurance policy.

You may be able to get earthquake insurance as an **endorsement**—addition of coverage—to a homeowner's policy or through a state-run insurance program. The most serious earthquakes occur in the Pacific Coast region. However, earthquakes can happen in other regions, too. If you plan to buy a home in an area that has a high risk of floods or earthquakes, you may have to buy the necessary insurance in order to be approved for a mortgage loan.

Renter's Insurance

For people who rent, home insurance coverage includes personal property protection, additional living expenses coverage, and personal liability and related coverage. Renter's insurance does not provide coverage on the building or other structures.

There are two standard renter's insurance policies. The *broad form* covers your personal property against perils specified in the policy, such as fires and thefts, and the *comprehensive form* protects your personal property against all perils not specifically excluded in the policy. When shopping for renter's insurance, be aware that these policies:

- Normally pay only the actual cash value of your losses. Replacement cost coverage is available for an extra premium.
- Fully cover your personal property only at home. When traveling, your luggage and other personal items are protected up to a certain percentage of the policy's total amount of coverage.
- Automatically provide liability coverage if someone is injured on your premises.
- May duplicate other coverage. For instance, if you are still a dependent, your personal property may be covered by your parents' homeowner's policy. This coverage is limited, however, to an amount equal to a certain percentage of the total personal property coverage provided by the policy.

The most important part of renter's insurance is the protection it provides for your personal property. Many renters believe that they are covered under the landlord's insurance. In fact, that's the case only when the landlord is proved liable for some damage. For example, if bad wiring causes a fire and damages a tenant's property, the tenant may be able to collect money from the landlord. Renter's insurance is relatively inexpensive and provides many of the same kinds of protection as a homeowner's policy.

Home Insurance Policy Forms

Home insurance policies are available in several forms. The forms provide different combinations of coverage. Some forms are not available in all areas.

The basic form (HO-1) protects against perils such as fire, lightning, windstorms, hail, volcanic eruptions, explosions, smoke, theft, vandalism, glass breakage, and riots.

The broad form (HO-2) covers an even wider range of perils, including falling objects and damage from ice, snow, or sleet.

The special form (HO-3) covers all basic- and broad-form risks, plus any other risks except those specifically excluded from the policy. Common exclusions are flood, earthquake, war, and nuclear accidents. Personal property is covered for the risks listed in the policy.

The tenant's form (HO-4) protects the personal property of renters against the risks listed in the policy. It does not include coverage on the building or other structures.

The comprehensive form (HO-5) expands the coverage of the HO-3. The HO-5 includes endorsements for items such as replacement cost coverage on contents and guaranteed replacement cost coverage on buildings.

Condominium owner's insurance (HO-6) protects personal property and any additions or improvements made to the living unit. These might include bookshelves, electrical fixtures, wallpaper, or carpeting. The condominium association purchases insurance on the building and other structures.

CAUTION!

Computers and other equipment used in a home-based business are not usually covered by a home insurance policy. Contact your insurance agent to obtain needed coverage.

Manufactured housing units and mobile homes usually qualify for insurance coverage with conventional policies. However, some mobile homes may need special policies with higher rates because the way they are built increases their risk of fire and wind damage. The cost of mobile home insurance coverage depends on the home's location and the way it's attached to the ground. Mobile home insurance is quite expensive: A $40,000 mobile home can cost as much to insure as a $120,000 house.

In addition to the risks previously discussed, home insurance policies include coverage for:

- Credit card fraud, check forgery, and counterfeit money.
- The cost of removing damaged property.

Exhibit 8–5 Not Everything Is Covered

CERTAIN PERSONAL PROPERTY IS NOT COVERED BY HOMEOWNER'S INSURANCE:

- Items insured separately, such as jewelry, furs, boats, or expensive electronic equipment
- Animals, birds, or fish
- Motorized vehicles not licensed for road use, except those used for home maintenance
- Sound devices used in motor vehicles, such as radios and CD players

- Aircraft and parts
- Property belonging to tenants
- Property contained in a rental apartment
- Property rented by the homeowner to other people
- Business property

- Emergency removal of property to protect it from damage.
- Temporary repairs after a loss to prevent further damage.
- Fire department charges in areas with such fees.

Not everything is covered by home insurance (see Exhibit 8–5). Read the nearby "Kiplinger's Personal Finance" box for more information.

Separate coverage may be available for personal property that is not covered by a homeowner's insurance policy.

 Sheet 27 Home Inventory

PRACTICE QUIZ 8-2

1. Define the following terms:

   a. Homeowner's insurance
   b. Household inventory
   c. Personal property floater
   d. Renter's insurance

2. Identify the choice that best completes the statement or answers the question:

   a. The personal liability portion of a homeowner's insurance policy protects the insured against financial loss when his or her (i) house floods, (ii) jewelry is stolen, (iii) guests injure themselves, (iv) reputation is damaged.
   b. Renter's insurance includes coverage for all of the following *except* (i) the building, (ii) personal property, (iii) additional living expenses, (iv) personal liability.
   c. The basic home insurance policy form protects against several perils, including (i) sleet, (ii) lightning, (iii) flood, (iv) earthquake.

3. Define the following terms:

   a. Umbrella policy
   b. Medical payments coverage
   c. Endorsement

4. List at least four personal property items that are not covered by a homeowner's insurance policy.

Apply Yourself!

You are about to rent your first apartment. You have approximately $10,000 worth of personal belongings. Contact an insurance agent to find out the cost of renter's insurance.

Game Plan

"If my home is damaged by a summer storm, will my insurance cover repairs?"

Where water-related damage is concerned, the answer depends on whether the water came from above or below. In general, if the damage was caused by wind-driven rain that came in through your roof, windows or doors, your insurance will cover the cost of repairs.

But if the damage is caused by flooding, a far more common problem during storm season, your homeowners insurance will not cover it. The only way to protect yourself from flood-related damage is to buy flood insurance from the federal National Flood Insurance Program. Premiums range from about $200 a year to more than $2,000, depending on your area's risk of flooding.

Never assume you don't need flood insurance just because you don't live in a coastal area. In 2011, torrential rainfall from Hurricane Irene caused widespread flooding throughout the Northeast. Vermont was hard hit, and many of the victims didn't have flood insurance. "A lot of Vermont residents never thought they'd be involved in major flooding," says Richard McGrath, chief executive of McGrath Insurance Group, in Sturbridge, Mass.

You can purchase federal flood insurance through a local insurance agent. Don't wait until storm clouds gather to buy a policy; typically, there's a 30-day waiting period before premiums take effect. For price quotes, go to FloodSmart.gov.

Sewage backup. If heavy rains overwhelm your storm-water system, sewage could back up into your house—an expensive and smelly mess. Most standard homeowners policies don't include sewage-backup coverage, but you can purchase a rider that will pay for $10,000 to $20,000 of damages for about $50 to $75 a year, McGrath says.

Damage from trees. Old-growth trees lose their charm in a hurry when lightning, wind or heavy rain knocks them down. If the tree hits your house, garage or other insured structure, the damage is usually covered by your homeowners insurance, says Jeanne Salvatore, spokeswoman for the Insurance Information Institute.

Damage from a neighbor's tree—or even from one a block away that was uprooted in a windstorm—is also covered. If your insurer believes your neighbor contributed to the problem by failing to take care of the tree, it may try to collect against your neighbor's policy, Salvatore says. In that case, you could get a break on all or part of your deductible. But it works both ways: If your tree damages your neighbor's property, you could be held responsible. Your insurer could refuse to cover damage to your property if it believes you were negligent.

Most policies won't pay to remove a tree that falls in your yard but doesn't hit anything—although you may be eligible for some coverage if the fallen tree blocks your driveway or prevents you from getting into your house.

Get a tax break? You may be able to recover some of the costs your insurance doesn't reimburse when you file your taxes.

Losses from hurricanes, floods and other disasters that aren't covered by your policy are deductible, as long as you itemize. You won't be able to deduct the entire amount of your losses, however. First, you'll have to reduce the amount of your loss by $100. Then, you can deduct only the amount that exceeds 10% of your adjusted gross income. For example, if you suffered $20,000 in unreimbursed losses and your AGI is $100,000, you would subtract $100, then subtract $10,000 (10% of your AGI) from the $19,900 balance, bringing your deduction to $9,900.

Sandra Block

1. How can you protect yourself from flood-related damage to your home?

2. Should you consider purchasing flood-related insurance if you don't live in a coastal area?

3. Can you be held responsible if your tree damages your neighbor's property?

LO8.3

Analyze the factors that
influence the amount of
coverage and cost of home
insurance.

ACTION ITEM

Do you have enough
insurance coverage for your
home?

☐ **Yes** ☐ **No**

actual cash value (ACV)
A claim settlement method
in which the insured receives
payment based on the
current replacement cost of
a damaged or lost item, less
depreciation.

replacement value A
claim settlement method in
which the insured receives
the full cost of repairing or
replacing a damaged or lost
item.

Home Insurance Cost Factors

How Much Coverage Do You Need?

You can get the best insurance value by choosing the right coverage amount and knowing the factors that affect insurance costs (see Exhibit 8–6). Your insurance should be based on the amount of money you would need to rebuild or repair your house, not the amount you paid for it. As construction costs rise, you should increase the amount of coverage. In fact, today most insurance policies automatically increase coverage as construction costs rise.

In the past, many homeowner's policies insured the building for only 80 percent of the replacement value. If the building were destroyed, the homeowner would have to pay for part of the cost of replacing it, which could be expensive. Today most companies recommend full coverage.

If you are borrowing money to buy a home, the lender will require that you have property insurance. Remember, too, that the amount of insurance on your home determines the coverage on your personal belongings. Coverage for personal belongings is usually from 55 to 75 percent of the insurance amount on your home.

Insurance companies base claim settlements on one of two methods. Under the **actual cash value (ACV)** method, the payment you receive is based on the replacement cost of an item minus depreciation. Depreciation is the loss of value of an item as it gets older. This means you would receive less for a five-year-old bicycle than you originally paid for it.

Under the **replacement value** method for settling claims, you receive the full cost of repairing or replacing an item. Depreciation is not considered. Many companies limit the replacement cost to 400 percent of the item's actual cash value. Replacement value coverage is more expensive than actual cash value coverage.

EXAMPLE: Replacement Cost and Time Value of Money

To save on future home insurance costs, you need a new roof and a burglar alarm system that will cost $10,000 five years from now. You can earn 3 percent on your savings. How much should you deposit now to obtain $10,000 five years from today?

PV = $10,000 × 0.863 = $8,630   (from Exhibit 1–C)

Exhibit 8–6

Determining the Amount
of Home Insurance You
Need

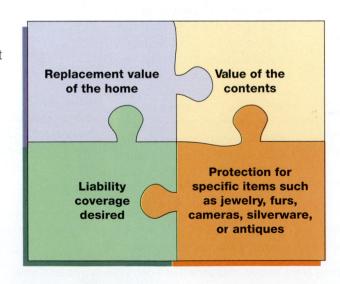

Factors That Affect Home Insurance Costs

The cost of your home insurance will depend on several factors, such as the location of the building and the type of building and construction materials. The amount of coverage and type of policy you choose will also affect the cost of home insurance. Furthermore, different insurance companies offer different rates.

LOCATION OF HOME The location of your home affects your insurance rates. Insurance companies offer lower rates to people whose homes are close to a water supply or fire hydrant or located in an area that has a good fire department. On the other hand, rates are higher in areas where crime is common. People living in regions that experience severe weather, such as tornadoes and hurricanes, may also pay more for insurance.

TYPE OF STRUCTURE The type of home and its construction influence the price of insurance coverage. A brick house, for example, will usually cost less to insure than a similar structure made of wood. However, earthquake coverage is more expensive for a brick house than for a wood dwelling because a wooden house is more likely to survive an earthquake. Also, an older house may be more difficult to restore to its original condition. That means that it will cost more to insure.

COVERAGE AMOUNT AND POLICY TYPE The policy and the amount of coverage you select affect the premium you pay. Obviously, insuring a $300,000 home costs more than insuring a $100,000 home.

The deductible amount in your policy also affects the cost of your insurance. If you increase the amount of your deductible, your premium will be lower because the company will pay out less in claims. The most common deductible amount is $250. Raising the deductible from $250 to $500 or $1,000 can reduce the premium you pay by 15 percent or more.

> **EXAMPLE: Increase a Deductible to Reduce the Premium**
>
> Suppose your home insurance policy premium is $800 with a $250 deductible. If you increase the amount of your deductible to $500, you reduce the premium by 10 percent, or $80.

HOME INSURANCE DISCOUNTS Most companies offer discounts if you take action to reduce risks to your home. Your premium may be lower if you have smoke detectors or a fire extinguisher. If your home has dead-bolt locks and alarm systems, which make a break-in harder for thieves, insurance costs may be lower. Some companies offer discounts to people who don't file any claims for a certain number of years.

COMPANY DIFFERENCES You can save more than 30 percent on homeowner's insurance by comparing rates from several companies. Some insurance agents work for only one company. Others are independent agents who represent several different companies. Talk to both types of agent. You'll get the information you need to compare rates.

Don't select a company on the basis of price alone; also consider service and coverage. Not all companies settle claims in the same way. Suppose that all homes on Evergreen Terrace are dented on one side by large hail. They all have the same kind of siding. Unfortunately, the homeowners discover that this

did you know?

In some areas, a home can be automatically rejected for insurance coverage if it has had two or three claims of any sort in the past three years. Homes that have had water damage, storm damage, and burglaries are most vulnerable to rejection.

type of siding is no longer available so all the siding on all of the houses will need to be replaced. Some insurance companies will pay to replace all the siding. Others will pay only to replace the damaged parts.

State insurance commissions and consumer organizations can give you information about different insurance companies. *Consumer Reports* rates insurance companies on a regular basis.

Read the nearby "Personal Finance in Practice" box to learn how you can lower the cost of homeowner's and renter's insurance.

Sheet 28 Determining Needed Property Insurance

Sheet 29 Apartment/Home Insurance Comparison

PRACTICE QUIZ 8-3

1. In the space provided, write "T" if you believe the statement is true, "F" if the statement is false.

   a. Today most insurance policies automatically increase coverage as construction costs rise. _____
   b. In the past, many homeowner's policies insured the building for only 50 percent of the replacement value. _____
   c. Most mortgage lenders do not require that you buy home insurance. _____
   d. Coverage for personal belongings is usually from 55 to 75 percent of the insurance amount on your home. _____

2. What are the two methods insurance companies use in settling claims?

3. List the five factors that affect home insurance costs.

Apply Yourself!

Research the web to learn about the natural disasters that occur most frequently in your part of the country. How would you protect your home from such natural disasters?

LO8.4

Identify the important types of automobile insurance coverage.

ACTION ITEM

Do you have an adequate amount of automobile insurance?

☐ Yes ☐ No

financial responsibility law State legislation that requires drivers to prove their ability to cover the cost of damage or injury caused by an automobile accident.

Automobile Insurance Coverages

Motor vehicle crashes cost over $150 billion in lost wages and medical bills every year. Traffic accidents can destroy people's lives physically, financially, and emotionally. Buying insurance can't eliminate the pain and suffering that vehicle accidents cause. It can, however, reduce the financial impact.

Every state in the United States has a **financial responsibility law,** a law that requires drivers to prove that they can pay for damage or injury caused by an automobile accident. All states have laws requiring people to carry motor vehicle insurance. These laws impose heavy fines, suspension of a driver's license, community service, and even imprisonment if you don't carry car insurance. Indeed, opportunity costs of driving without insurance can be very high. Very few people have the money they would need to meet financial responsibility requirements on their own.

The coverage provided by motor vehicle insurance falls into two categories. One is protection for bodily injury. The other is protection for property damage (see Exhibit 8–7).

Motor Vehicle Bodily Injury Coverages

Most of the money that motor vehicle insurance companies pay out in claims goes for legal expenses, medical expenses, and other costs that arise when someone is injured. The main types of bodily injury coverage are bodily injury liability, medical payments, and uninsured motorist protection.

Personal Finance in Practice

How to Lower the Cost of Insurance

How can you lower your cost of homeowner's and renter's insurance? Shop around and compare the cost. Here are a few tips that can save you hundreds of dollars annually.

1. **Consider a higher deductible.** Increasing your deductible by just a few hundred dollars can make a big difference in your premium.

2. **Ask your insurance agent about discounts.** You may be able to secure a lower premium if your home has safety features such as dead-bolt locks, smoke detectors, an alarm system, storm shutters, or fire retardant roofing material. Persons over 55 years of age or long-term customers may also be offered discounts.

3. **Insure your house, NOT the land under it.** After a disaster, the land is still there. If you don't subtract the value of the land when deciding how much homeowner's insurance to buy, you will pay more than you should.

4. **Make certain you purchase enough coverage to replace what is insured.** "Replacement" coverage

gives you the money to rebuild your home and replace its contents. An actual cash value policy is cheaper but pays only what your property is worth at the time of the loss—your cost minus depreciation.

5. **Ask about special coverage you might need.** You may have to pay extra for computers, cameras, jewelry, art, antiques, musical instruments, stamp collections, and other items.

6. **Remember that flood and earthquake damage are not covered by a standard homeowner's policy.** The cost of a separate earthquake policy will depend on the likelihood of earthquakes in your area. Homeowners who live in areas prone to flooding should take advantage of the National Flood Insurance Program. Call 1-888-CALLFLOOD or visit www.fema.gov/national-flood-insurance-program.

7. **If you are a renter do NOT assume your landlord carries insurance on your personal belongings.** Purchase a special policy for renters.

BODILY INJURY LIABILITY **Bodily injury liability** is insurance that covers physical injuries caused by a vehicle accident for which you were responsible. If pedestrians, people in other vehicles, or passengers in your vehicle are injured or killed, bodily injury liability coverage pays for expenses related to the crash.

Liability coverage is usually expressed by three numbers, such as 100/300/50. These amounts represent thousands of dollars of coverage. The first two numbers refer to bodily injury coverage. In this example, $100,000 is the maximum amount that the insurance company will pay for the injuries of any one person in any one accident. The second number, $300,000, is the maximum amount the company will pay all injured parties (two or more) in any one accident. The third number, $50,000, indicates the limit for payment for damage to the property of others (see Exhibit 8–8).

bodily injury liability Coverage for the risk of financial loss due to legal expenses, medical costs, lost wages, and other expenses associated with injuries caused by an automobile accident for which the insured was responsible.

MEDICAL PAYMENTS COVERAGE **Medical payments coverage** is insurance that applies to the medical expenses of anyone who is injured in your vehicle, including you. This type of coverage also provides additional medical benefits for you and members

medical payments coverage Automobile insurance that covers medical expenses for people injured in one's car.

Exhibit 8–7 Two Major Categories of Automobile Insurance

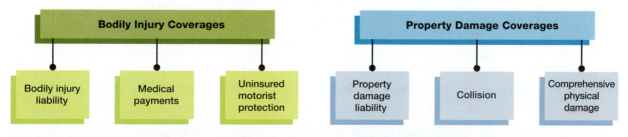

Buying bodily injury and property damage coverage can reduce the financial impact of an accident. *What type of expenses would be paid for by bodily injury liability coverage?*

Exhibit 8–8

Automobile Liability
Insurance Coverage

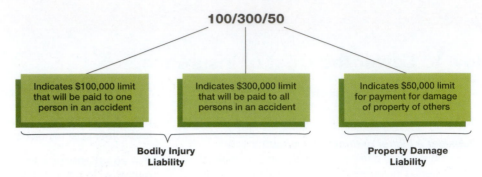

100/300/50

Indicates $100,000 limit that will be paid to one person in an accident

Indicates $300,000 limit that will be paid to all persons in an accident

Indicates $50,000 limit for payment for damage of property of others

Bodily Injury Liability

Property Damage Liability

The three numbers used to describe liability coverage refer to the limits on different types of payments. *Why do you think the middle number is the highest?*

of your family; it pays medical expenses if you or your family members are injured while riding in another person's vehicle or if any of you are hit by a vehicle.

UNINSURED MOTORIST PROTECTION Unfortunately, you cannot assume that everyone who is behind the wheel is carrying insurance. How can you guard yourself and your passengers against the risk of getting into an accident with someone who has no insurance? The answer is uninsured motorist protection.

uninsured motorist protection Automobile insurance coverage for the cost of injuries to a person and members of his or her family caused by a driver with inadequate insurance or by a hit-and-run driver.

   Uninsured motorist protection is insurance that covers you and your family members if you are involved in an accident with an uninsured or hit-and-run driver. In most states it does not cover damage to the vehicle itself. Penalties for driving uninsured vary by state, but they generally include stiff fines and suspension of driving privileges.

   Underinsured motorist coverage protects you when another driver has some insurance, but not enough to pay for the injuries he or she has caused.

Motor Vehicle Property Damage Coverage

One afternoon, during a summer storm, Carrie was driving home from her job as a hostess at a pancake house. The rain was coming down in buckets, and she couldn't see very well. As a result, she didn't realize that the car in front of her had stopped to make a left turn, and she hit the car. The crash totaled Carrie's new car. Fortunately, she had purchased property damage coverage. Property damage coverage protects you from financial loss if you damage someone else's property or if your vehicle is damaged. It includes property damage liability, collision, and comprehensive physical damage. (See the nearby "Personal Finance in Practice: Are You Covered?" feature.)

property damage liability Automobile insurance coverage that protects a person against financial loss when that person damages the property of others.

PROPERTY DAMAGE LIABILITY **Property damage liability** is motor vehicle insurance that applies when you damage the property of others. In addition, it protects you when you're driving another person's vehicle with the owner's permission. Although the damaged property is usually another car, the coverage also extends to buildings and to equipment such as street signs and telephone poles.

collision Automobile insurance that pays for damage to the insured's car when it is involved in an accident.

COLLISION **Collision** insurance covers damage to your vehicle when it is involved in an accident. It allows you to collect money no matter who was at fault. However, the amount you can collect is limited to the actual cash value of your vehicle at the time of the accident. If your vehicle has many extra features, make sure that you have a record of its condition and value.

COMPREHENSIVE PHYSICAL DAMAGE Comprehensive physical damage coverage protects you if your vehicle is damaged in a nonaccident situation. It covers your

Personal Finance in Practice

ARE YOU COVERED?

Often people believe their insurance will cover various financial losses. For each of the following situations, name the type of home or automobile insurance that would protect you.

1. While you are on vacation, clothing and other personal belongings are stolen._____

2. Your home is damaged by fire, and you have to live in a hotel for several weeks._____

3. You and members of your family suffer injuries in an automobile accident caused by a hit-and-run driver.
_____

4. A delivery person is injured on your property and takes legal action against you._____

5. Your automobile is accidentally damaged by some people playing baseball._____

6. A person takes legal action against you for injuries you caused in an automobile accident.
_____

7. Water from a local lake rises and damages your furniture and carpeting._____

8. Your automobile needs repairs because you hit a tree.
_____

9. You damaged a valuable tree when your automobile hit it, and you want to pay for the damage._____

10. While riding with you in your automobile, your nephew is injured in an accident and incurs various medical expenses._____

ANSWERS (1) Personal property coverage of home insurance; (2) additional living expenses of home insurance; (3) uninsured motorist protection; (4) personal liability coverage of home insurance; (5) comprehensive physical damage; (6) bodily injury liability; (7) flood insurance—requires coverage separate from home insurance; (8) collision; (9) property damage liability of automobile insurance; (10) medical payments.

---

vehicle against risks such as fire, theft, falling objects, vandalism, hail, floods, tornadoes, earthquakes, and avalanches.

No-Fault Insurance

To reduce the time and cost of settling vehicle injury cases, various states are trying a number of alternatives. Under the **no-fault system,** drivers who are involved in accidents collect money from their own insurance companies. It doesn't matter who caused the accident. Each company pays the insured up to the limits of his or her coverage. Because no-fault systems vary by state, you should investigate the coverage of no-fault insurance in your state.

no-fault system An automobile insurance program in which drivers involved in accidents collect medical expenses, lost wages, and related injury costs from their own insurance companies.

Other Automobile Insurance Coverages

Several other kinds of motor vehicle insurance are available to you. *Wage loss insurance* pays for any salary or income you might have lost because of being injured in a vehicle accident. Wage loss insurance is usually required in states with a no-fault insurance system. In other states it's available by choice.

Towing and emergency road service coverage pays for mechanical assistance in the event that your vehicle breaks down. This can be helpful on long trips or during bad weather. If necessary, you can get your vehicle towed to a service station. However, once your vehicle arrives at the repair shop, you are responsible for paying the bill. If you belong to an automobile club, your membership may include towing coverage. If that's the case, paying for emergency road service coverage could be a waste of money. *Rental reimbursement coverage* pays for a rental car if your vehicle is stolen or being repaired.

PRACTICE QUIZ 8–4

1. List the three main types of bodily injury coverage.

2. In the space provided, write "T" if the statement is true, "F" if it is false.

   a. Financial responsibility law requires drivers to prove that they can pay for damage or injury caused by an automobile accident. _____

   b. Insurance that covers physical injuries caused by a vehicle accident for which you were responsible is called uninsured motorist protection. _____

   c. Automobile liability coverage is usually expressed by three numbers, 100/300/50. _____

   d. The first two numbers in 100/300/50 refer to the limit for payment for damage to the property of others. _____

   e. Uninsured motorist protection is insurance that covers you and your family members if you are involved in an accident with an uninsured motorist or hit-and-run driver. _____

   f. Collision insurance covers damage to your vehicle when it is involved in an accident. _____

3. What is no-fault insurance? What is its purpose?

4. List at least three other kinds of automobile insurance that are available to you.

Apply Yourself!

Research the make and model of vehicles that are most frequently stolen, consequently resulting in higher insurance rates.

LO8.5

Evaluate factors that affect the cost of automobile insurance.

ACTION ITEM

Do you know what factors determine your motor vehicle insurance premium?

☐ Yes   ☐ No

did you know?

Foods and drinks that were reported as the most common distractions in auto accidents: coffee, hot soup, tacos, chili-covered foods, hamburgers, chicken, jelly- or cream-filled doughnuts, and soft drinks.

Automobile Insurance Costs

Motor vehicle insurance is not cheap. The average household spends more than $1,200 for motor vehicle insurance yearly. The premiums are related to the amount of claims insurance companies pay out each year. Your automobile insurance cost is directly related to coverage amounts and factors such as the vehicle, your place of residence, and your driving record.

Amount of Coverage

The amount you will pay for insurance depends on the amount of coverage you require. You need enough coverage to protect yourself legally and financially.

LEGAL CONCERNS As discussed earlier, most people who are involved in motor vehicle accidents cannot afford to pay an expensive court settlement with their own money. For this reason, most drivers buy liability insurance.

In the past, bodily injury liability coverage of 10/20 was usually enough. However, some people have been awarded millions of dollars in recent cases, so coverage of 100/300 is usually recommended.

PROPERTY VALUES Just as medical expenses and legal settlements have increased, so has the cost of vehicles. Therefore, you should consider a policy with a limit of $50,000 or even $100,000 for property damage liability.

Motor Vehicle Insurance Premium Factors

Vehicle type, rating territory, and driver classification are three other factors that influence insurance costs.

VEHICLE TYPE   The year, make, and model of a vehicle will affect insurance costs. Vehicles that have expensive replacement parts and complicated repairs will cost more to insure. Also, premiums will probably be higher for vehicle makes and models that are frequently stolen.

RATING TERRITORY   In most states your rating territory is the place of residence used to determine your vehicle insurance premium. Different locations have different costs. For example, rural areas usually have fewer accidents and less frequent occurrences of theft. Your insurance would probably cost less there than if you lived in a large city.

DRIVER CLASSIFICATION   Driver classification is based on age, sex, marital status, driving record, and driving habits. In general, young drivers (under 25) and elderly drivers (over 70) have more frequent and more serious accidents. As a result these groups pay higher premiums. Your driving record will also influence your insurance premiums. If you have accidents or receive tickets for traffic violations, your rates will increase.

The cost and number of claims that you file with your insurance company will also affect your premium. If you file expensive claims, your rates will increase. If you have too many claims, your insurance company may cancel your policy. You will then have more difficulty getting coverage from another company. To deal with this problem, every state has an assigned risk pool. An **assigned risk pool** includes all the people who can't get motor vehicle insurance. Some of these people are assigned to each insurance company operating in the state. These policyholders pay several times the normal rates, but they do get coverage. Once they establish a good driving record, they can reapply for insurance at regular rates.

Insurance companies may also consider your credit score when deciding whether to sell, renew, or cancel a policy and what premium to charge. However, an insurer cannot refuse to issue you a home or auto insurance policy solely based on your credit report. Read the nearby "Personal Finance in Practice" box to understand how insurance companies use credit information.

Reducing Vehicle Insurance Premiums

Two ways in which you can reduce your vehicle insurance costs are by comparing companies and taking advantage of discounts.

COMPARING COMPANIES   Rates and services vary among motor vehicle insurance companies. Even among companies in the same area, premiums can vary by as much as 100 percent. You should compare the service and rates of local insurance agents. Most states publish this type of information.

> ### digi – know?
>
> Global positioning systems (GPS) and other technology are being used to encourage safer driving and reduce auto insurance costs. In Britain, one insurance company adjusts premiums each month based on a driver's braking and acceleration habits. The Car Chip (www.carchipconnect.com) allows parents to monitor the speed and braking actions of young drivers.

assigned risk pool
Consists of people who are unable to obtain automobile insurance due to poor driving or accident records and must obtain coverage at high rates through a state program that requires insurance companies to accept some of them.

> ### did you know?
>
> An automobile insurance company once paid $3,600 for damages to a car in an accident caused by a mouse. The critter apparently got into the car while it was parked and then crawled up the driver's pant leg while the car was on an interstate highway. The driver lost control of the vehicle and crashed into a roadside barrier. Another claim resulted when a barbecued steak fell off a 17th-floor balcony and dented a car.

Is It Ethical for Insurance Companies to Use Credit Information?

The Fair Credit Reporting Act (FCRA, discussed in Chapter 5) allows insurance companies to examine your credit report without your permission. These companies believe that consumers who are financially responsible have fewer and less costly losses and therefore should pay less for their insurance. Insurance companies use credit scores in two ways:

- *Underwriting*—deciding whether to issue you a new policy or to renew your existing policy. Some state laws prohibit insurance companies from refusing to issue you a new policy or from renewing your existing policy based solely on information obtained from your credit report. In addition, some state laws prohibit insurance companies from using your credit information as the sole factor in accepting you and placing you into a specific company within their group of companies.

- *Rating*—deciding what price to charge you for your insurance, either by placing you into a specific

rating tier, or level, or by placing you into a specific company within their group of companies. Some insurance companies use credit information along with other more traditional rating factors such as motor vehicle records and claims history. Where permitted by state law, some insurance companies may use credit reports only to determine your rate.

The FCRA requires an insurance company to tell you if it has taken "adverse action" against you because of your credit report information. If the company tells you that you have been adversely affected, it must also tell you the name of the national credit bureau that supplied the information so you can get a free copy of your credit report. The best way to know for sure if your credit score is affecting your acceptance with an insurer for the best policy at the best rate is to ask.

CAUTION!

Your insurance company may charge an extra fee if you are involved in an accident or cited for a serious traffic violation. Worse, the insurer may not renew your insurance policy.

Furthermore, you can check a company's reputation with sources such as *Consumer Reports* or your state insurance department.

PREMIUM DISCOUNTS The penalties of poor driving behavior can be severe. For example, car insurance premiums increased 18 percent if you had only one moving violation in 2010; for two moving violations the average premium increased 34 percent compared to drivers with no violations. Annual premiums jumped to 53 percent higher if you had three violations.

The best way for you to keep your rates down is to maintain a good driving record by avoiding accidents and traffic tickets. In addition, most insurance companies offer various discounts. If you are under 25, you can qualify for reduced rates by taking a driver training program or maintaining good grades in college.

Furthermore, installing security devices will decrease the chance of theft and lower your insurance costs. Being a nonsmoker can qualify you for lower motor vehicle insurance premiums as well. Discounts are also offered for insuring two or more vehicles with the same company.

Increasing the amounts of deductibles will also lead to a lower premium. If you have an old car that's not worth much, you may decide not to pay for collision and comprehensive coverage. However, before you make this move, you should compare the value of your car for getting to college or work with the cost of these coverages.

Choose your car carefully. Some makes and models are more costly to insure than others. Contact your insurance agent before purchasing your car. And finally, maintain a good credit history. Many insurers are now examining your credit reports.

The nearby "Figure It Out!" box presents motor vehicle insurance cost comparison.

Figure It Out!

Motor Vehicle Insurance—How Much Will It Cost?

Before Mario bought the car he wanted, he needed to be sure he could afford the insurance for it. In this example he chose low liability, uninsured motorist coverage, and high deductibles to keep his insurance payments as low as possible. Clearly insurer B offered a lower price for the same coverage.

Investigating Insurance Companies		
	Insurer A	**Insurer B**
Bodily Injury Coverage:		
• Bodily injury liability $50,000 each person; $100,000 each accident	$472	$358
• Uninsured motorist protection	208	84
• Medical payments coverage $2,000 each person	48	46
Property Damage Coverage:		
• Property damage liability $50,000 each accident	182	178
• Collision with $500 deductible	562	372
• Comprehensive physical damage with $500 deductible	263	202
Car rental	40	32
Discounts: good driver, air bags, garage parking	(165)	
Annual total	$1,610	$1,272

RESEARCH

Identify a make, model, and year of a vehicle you might like to own. Research two insurance companies and get prices using this example. You can get their rates by telephone. Many also have websites. Using your workbook or on a separate sheet of paper, record your findings. How do they compare? Which company would you choose and why?

EXAMPLE: Time Value of Money—Insuring Two Vehicles with the Same Insurer

Suppose you insure your cars with two separate companies, paying $600 and $800 a year. If you insure both cars with the same company, you may save 10 percent on the annual premiums, or $140 a year. What is the future value of the annual savings over 10 years based on an annual interest rate of 3 percent?

The total premium $600 plus $800 = $1,400

Ten percent of 1,400 = $1,400 × 0.10 = $140

Future value of $140 over 10 years at 3 percent:

$140 × 11.464 = $1,604.96 (from Exhibit 1-B)

Sheet 30 Automobile Insurance Cost Comparison

PRACTICE QUIZ 8–5

1. In the space provided, write "A" if you agree with the statement, "D" if you disagree.

   a. Motor vehicle insurance is not cheap. _____
   b. The average household spends less than $500 for motor vehicle insurance yearly. _____

Copyright © 2016 by McGraw-Hill Education

c. Most people who are involved in an automobile accident can afford to pay an expensive court settlement with their own money. _____

d. Liability coverage of 100/300 is usually recommended. _____

e. You should consider a policy with a limit of $50,000 or even $100,000 for property damage liability. _____

f. The year, make, and model of a vehicle do not affect insurance costs. _____

g. Your automobile insurance would probably cost more in rural areas than if you lived in a large city. _____

2. List the five factors that determine driver classification.

3. What are the two ways by which you can reduce your vehicle insurance costs?

Apply Yourself!

Using web research, find the laws in your state regarding uninsured motorist protection.

YOUR PERSONAL FINANCE DASHBOARD

PERCENT OF PERSONAL PROPERTY COVERAGE

A personal finance dashboard can help you determine if you have proper coverage for household belongings. Homeowner's insurance protects you against financial loss in case your home is damaged or destroyed.

Your household belongings, such as furniture, appliances, and clothing, are covered by the personal property portion of a homeowner's insurance policy up to a portion of the insured value of the home. That portion may range from 55 to 75 percent.

YOUR SITUATION: Have you established a specific and measurable portion of coverage for your household belongings? Do you have adequate additional living expense coverage if a fire or other event damages your home? Some policies limit additional living expense coverage to 10 to 20 percent of a home's total coverage amount. Have you considered a personal property floater for additional property insurance that covers the damage or loss of a specific item of high value?

POSSIBLE ACTIONS TO TAKE

 Reconsider your responses to the "Action Items" (in the text margin) to determine actions you might take to improve your home and automobile insurance coverages.

 Seek advice from a competent and reliable insurance advisor. Then decide what types of insurance best meet your needs.

 Determine how you can lower the cost of homeowner's and renter's insurance. See the "Personal Finance in Practice" box on the topic in this chapter.

 If you live in a flood-prone area, visit the Federal Emergency Management Agency's (FEMA) website at www.FloodSmart.gov. For more information about federal flood insurance, contact the National Flood Insurance Program at 1-800-638-6620.

LO8.1 The main types of risk are personal risk, property risk, and liability risk. Risk management methods include avoidance, reduction, assumption, and shifting.

Planning an insurance program is a way to manage risks.

Property and liability insurance protect your homes and motor vehicles against financial loss.

LO8.2 A homeowner's policy provides coverage for buildings and other structures, additional living expenses, personal property, personal liability and related coverages, and specialized coverages.

Renter's insurance provides many of the same kinds of protection as homeowner's policies.

LO8.3 The factors that affect home insurance coverage and costs include the location, the type of structure, the coverage amount and policy type, discounts, and the choice of insurance company.

LO8.4 Motor vehicle bodily injury coverages include bodily injury liability, medical payments coverage, and uninsured motorist protection.

Motor vehicle property damage coverages include property damage liability, collision, and comprehensive physical damage.

LO8.5 Motor vehicle insurance costs depend on the amount of coverage you need as well as vehicle type, rating territory, and driver classification.

actual cash value (ACV) 262

assigned risk pool 269

bodily injury liability 265

claim 254

collision 266

coverage 250

deductible 251

endorsement 258

financial responsibility law 264

hazard 250

homeowner's insurance 255

household inventory 256

insurance 249

insurance company 249

insured 250

insurer 249

liability 254

medical payments coverage 257, 265

negligence 250

no-fault system 267

peril 250

personal property floater 257

policy 249

policyholder 249

premium 249

property damage liability 266

replacement value 262

risk 250

umbrella policy 257

uninsured motorist protection 266

1. Survey friends and relatives to determine the types of insurance coverages they have. Also, obtain information about the process used to select these coverages. (LO8.1)
2. Outline a personal insurance plan with the following phases: *(a)* Identify personal, financial, and property risks; *(b)* set goals you might achieve when obtaining needed insurance coverages; and *(c)* describe actions you might take to achieve these insurance goals. (LO8.1)
3. Talk to a financial planner or an insurance agent about the financial difficulties faced by people who lack adequate home and auto insurance. What common coverages do many people overlook? (LO8.2)
4. Contact two or three insurance agents to obtain information about home or renter's insurance. Use "Your Personal Financial Plan" sheet 29 to compare the coverages and costs. (LO8.2)
5. Examine a homeowner's or renter's insurance policy. What coverages does the policy include? Does the policy contain unclear conditions or wording? (LO8.3)
6. Contact two or three insurance agents to obtain information about automobile insurance. Use "Your Personal Financial Plan" sheet 30 to compare costs and coverages for various insurance companies. (LO8.5)

1. Eric Fowler and his wife Susan just purchased their first home, which cost $130,000. They purchased a homeowner's policy to insure the home for $120,000 and personal property for $75,000. They declined any coverage for additional living expenses. The deductible for the policy is $500.

   Soon after Eric and Susan moved into their new home, a strong windstorm caused damage to their roof. They reported the roof damage to be $17,000. While the roof was under repair, the couple had to live in a nearby hotel for three days. The hotel bill amounted to $320. Assuming the insurance company settles claims using the replacement value method, what amount will the insurance company pay for the damages to the roof?

2. Eric's Ford Mustang and Susan's Toyota Prius are insured with the same insurance agent. They have 50/100/15 vehicle insurance coverage. The very week of the windstorm, Susan had an accident. She lost control of her car, hit a parked car, and damaged a storefront. The damage to the parked car was $4,300 and the damage to the store was $15,400. What amount will the insurance company pay for Susan's car accident?

Solutions

1. Home damages:

   Home value: $130,000
   Insured amount: $120,000
   Damage amount reported: $17,000
   Additional living expenses incurred: $320
   Total expenses incurred from windstorm: $17,320
   Deductible on the policy: $500
   Insurance company covered amount ($17,000 − $500 deductible): $16,500
   Eric and Susan's costs ($500 + $320 hotel bill): $820

2. Car accident:

   Store damage amount: $15,400
   Parked car damage amount: $4,300
   Total damages: $19,700
   Insurance company covered amount (50/100/15): $15,000
   Eric and Susan's costs ($19,700 − $15,000): $4,700

1. Most home insurance policies cover jewelry for $1,000 and silverware for $2,500 unless items are covered with additional insurance. If $4,500 worth of jewelry and $6,000 worth of silverware were stolen from a family, what amount of the claim would not be covered by insurance? (LO8.2)

2. What amount would a person with actual cash value (ACV) coverage receive for two-year-old furniture destroyed by a fire? The furniture would cost $2,000 to replace today and had an estimated life of five years. (LO8.2)

3. What would it cost an insurance company to replace a family's personal property that originally cost $25,000? The replacement costs for the items have increased 15 percent. (LO8.2)

4. If Carissa Dalton has a $130,000 home insured for $100,000, based on the 80 percent coinsurance provision, how much would the insurance company pay on a $5,000 claim? (LO8.2)

5. For each of the following situations, what amount would the insurance company pay? (LO8.2)

   a. Wind damage of $835; the insured has a $500 deductible.
   b. Theft of a stereo system worth $1,150; the insured has a $250 deductible.
   c. Vandalism that does $425 of damage to a home; the insured has a $500 deductible.

6. Becky Fenton has 25/50/10 automobile insurance coverage. If two other people are awarded $35,000 each for injuries in an auto accident in which Becky was judged at fault, how much of this judgment would the insurance cover? (LO8.4)

7. Kurt Simmons has 50/100/15 auto insurance coverage. One evening he lost control of his vehicle, hitting a parked car and damaging a storefront along the street. Damage to the parked car was $5,400, and damage to the store was $12,650. What amount will the insurance company pay for the damages? What amount will Kurt have to pay? (LO8.4)

8. Karen and Mike currently insure their cars with separate companies, paying $700 and $900 a year. If they insured both cars with the same company, they would save 10 percent on the annual premiums. What would be the future value of the annual savings over 10 years based on an annual interest rate of 4 percent? (LO8.4)

9. When Carolina's house burned down, she lost household items worth a total of $50,000. Her house was insured for $160,000 and her homeowner's policy provided coverage for personal belongings up to 55 percent of the insured value of the house. Calculate how much insurance coverage Carolina's policy provides for her personal possessions and whether she will receive payment for all of the items destroyed in the fire. (LO8.2)

10. Dave and Ellen are newly married and living in their first house. The yearly premium on their homeowner's insurance policy is $450 for the coverage they need. Their insurance company offers a 5 percent discount if they install dead-bolt locks on all exterior doors. The couple can also receive a 2 percent discount if they install smoke detectors on each floor. They have contacted a locksmith, who will provide and install dead-bolt locks on the two exterior doors for $60 each. At the local hardware store, smoke detectors cost $8 each, and the new house has two floors. Dave and Ellen can install them themselves. What discount will Dave and Ellen receive if they install the dead-bolt locks? If they install smoke detectors? (LO8.2)

11. In the preceding example, assuming their insurance rates remain the same, how many years will it take Dave and Ellen to earn back in discounts the cost of the dead-bolts? The cost of the smoke detectors? Would you recommend Dave and Ellen invest in the safety items? Why or why not? (LO8.2)

12. Shaan and Anita currently insure their cars with separate companies, paying $650 and $575 a year. If they insure both cars with the same company, they will save 10 percent on their annual premiums. What would be the future value of the annual savings over 10 years based on an annual interest rate of 6 percent? (LO8.5)

 **To reinforce** the content in this chapter, more problems are provided at connect.mheducation.com.

WE RENT, SO WHY DO WE NEED INSURANCE?

"Have you been down in the basement?" Nathan asked his wife Erin as he entered their apartment.

"No, what's up?" responded Erin.

"It's flooded because of all that rain we got last weekend!" he exclaimed.

"Oh no! We have the extra furniture my mom gave us stored down there. Is everything ruined?" Erin asked.

"The couch and coffee table are in a foot of water; the love seat was the only thing that looked OK. Boy, I didn't realize the basement of this building wasn't waterproof. I'm going to call our landlady to complain."

As Erin thought about the situation, she remembered that when they moved in last fall, Kathy, their landlady, had informed them that her insurance policy covered the building but not the property belonging to each tenant. Because of this, they had purchased renter's insurance. "Nathan, I think our renter's insurance will cover the damage. Let me give our agent a call."

When Erin and Nathan purchased their insurance, they had to decide whether they wanted to be insured for cash value or for replacement costs. Replacement was more expensive, but it meant they would collect enough to go out and buy new household items at today's prices. If they had opted for cash value, the couch for which Erin's mother had paid $1,000 five years ago would be worth less than $500 today.

Erin made the call and found out their insurance did cover the furniture in the basement, and at replacement value after they paid the deductible. The $300 they had invested in renter's insurance last year was well worth it!

Not every renter has as much foresight as Erin and Nathan. Fewer than 4 in 10 renters have renter's insurance. Some aren't even aware they need it. They may assume they are covered by the landlord's insurance, but they aren't. This mistake can be costly.

Think about how much you have invested in your possessions and how much it would cost to replace them. Start with your stereo equipment or the flat screen television and DVD player that you bought last year. Experts suggest that people who rent start thinking about these things as soon as they move into their first apartment. Your policy should cover your personal belongings and provide funds for living expenses if you are dispossessed by a fire or other disaster.

Questions

1. Why is it important for people who rent to have insurance?
2. Does the building owner's property insurance ever cover the tenant's personal property?
3. What is the difference between cash value and replacement value?
4. When shopping for renter's insurance, what coverage features should you look for?

Continuing Case

HOME AND AUTOMOBILE INSURANCE

Jamie Lee and Ross have had several milestones in the past year. They are newlyweds, recently purchased their first home, and now have twins on the way!

Jamie Lee and Ross have to seriously consider their insurance needs. Since they have family, a home, and, now, babies on the way, they need to develop a risk management plan to help them should an unexpected event arise.

Current Financial Situation

Assets *(Jamie Lee and Ross combined):*
Checking account, $4,300
Savings account, $22,200
Emergency fund savings account, $20,500
IRA balance, $26,000
Cars, $10,000 (Jamie Lee) and $18,000 (Ross)

Liabilities *(Jamie Lee and Ross combined):*
Student loan balance, $0
Credit card balance, $2,000
Car loans, $6,000

Income:
Jamie Lee, $50,000 gross income ($37,500 net income after taxes)
Ross, $75,000 gross income ($64,000 net income after taxes)

Monthly Expenses *(Jamie Lee and Ross combined):*
Mortgage, $1,252
Property taxes and insurance, $500
Utilities, $195
Food, $400
Gas/Maintenance, $275
Credit card payment, $250
Car loan payment, $289
Entertainment, $300

Questions

1. Based on their current life status, what are some of the goals Jamie Lee and Ross should set to achieve when developing their insurance plan?

2. What four questions should Jamie Lee and Ross ask themselves as they develop the risk management plan?

3. Once Jamie Lee and Ross put their insurance plan into action, what should they do to maintain their plan?

4. Jamie and Ross decided to conduct a checkup on their homeowner's insurance policy. They noticed that they had omitted covering Jamie Lee's diamond wedding band set from their policy. What if it got lost or stolen? It was a major purchase and, besides the emotional value, the cost to replace the diamond jewelry would be very high. What type of policy should Jamie Lee and Ross consider to cover the diamond wedding rings?

5. Mr. Ferrell, Jamie Lee and Ross's insurance agent, suggested a flood insurance policy in addition to their regular homeowner's policy. Jamie Lee and Ross looked quizzically at the agent, as they do not live within two miles of a body of water. What is the basis for Mr. Ferrell's claim for the necessity of the flood policy?

6. Using "Your Personal Financial Plan" sheet 27, create a home inventory for Jamie Lee and Ross. Consider items of value that may be located in each of the rooms of the house and determine a dollar amount for each item. What is the total cost of the items?

7. Considering the value of Jamie Lee and Ross's automobiles, what type of automobile insurance coverage would you suggest for them?

8. What financial strategy would you suggest to Jamie Lee and Ross to enable them to save money on their insurance premiums?

Spending Diary

"MY SPENDING TAKES MOST OF MY MONEY. SO AFTER PAYING FOR CAR INSURANCE, MY BUDGET IS REALLY TIGHT."

Directions As you continue (or start) using your Daily Spending Diary sheets, you should be able to make better choices for your spending priorities. The financial data you develop will help you better understand your spending patterns and help you plan for achieving financial goals. The Daily Spending Diary sheets are located in Appendix D at the end of the book and in Connect Finance.

Questions

1. What information from your Daily Spending Diary might encourage you to use your money differently?

2. How can your spending habits be altered to ensure that you will be able to afford appropriate home and auto insurance coverage?

Name: _____   Date: _____

Current Insurance Policies and Needs

Purpose: To establish a record of current and needed insurance coverage.

Financial Planning Activities: List current insurance policies and areas where new or additional coverage is needed. This sheet is also available in an Excel spreadsheet format in Connect Finance.

Suggested Websites: www.insure.com   www.insweb.com   www.accuquote.com

Current Coverage	Needed Coverage
Property	
Company _____	
Policy no. _____	
Coverage amounts _____	
Deductible _____	
Annual premium _____	
Agent _____	
Address _____	
Phone _____	
Website _____	
Automobile Insurance	
Company _____	
Policy no. _____	
Coverage amounts _____	
Deductible _____	
Annual premium _____	
Agent _____	
Address _____	
Phone _____	
Website _____	
Disability Income Insurance	
Company _____	
Policy no. _____	
Coverage _____	
Contact _____	
Phone _____	
Website _____	
Health Insurance	
Company _____	
Policy no. _____	
Policy provisions _____	
Contact _____	
Phone _____	
Website _____	
Life Insurance	
Company _____	
Policy no. _____	
Type of policy _____	
Amount of coverage _____	
Cash value _____	
Agent _____	
Phone _____	
Website _____	

What's Next for Your Personal Financial Plan?

- Talk with friends and relatives to determine the types of insurance coverage they have.
- Conduct a web search for various types of insurance on which you need additional information.

Name: _____ Date: _____

Home Inventory

Purpose: To create a record of personal belongings for use when settling home insurance claims.

Financial Planning Activities: For each area of the home, list your possessions including a description (model, serial number), cost, and date of acquisition. Also consider photographs and videos of your possessions. This sheet is also available in an Excel spreadsheet format in Connect Finance.

Suggested Websites: www.insweb.com   www.money.com   www.ambest.com

Item, Description	Cost	Date Acquired
Attic		
Bathroom		
Bedrooms		
Family room		
Living room		
Hallways		
Kitchen		
Dining room		
Basement		
Garage		
Other items		

Suggested App:
• III Inventory

What's Next for Your Personal Financial Plan?

• Determine common items that may be overlooked when preparing a home inventory.
• Talk to a local insurance agent to point out the areas of protection that many people tend to overlook.

Name: _____   Date: _____

Determining Needed Property Insurance

Purpose: To determine property insurance needed for a home or apartment.

Financial Planning Activities: Estimate the value and your needs for the categories below. This sheet is also available in an Excel spreadsheet format in Connect Finance.

Suggested Websites: www.iii.org   www.quicken.com   www.naic.org

Real Property (this section not applicable to renters)

Current replacement value of home $ _____

Personal Property

Estimated value of appliances, furniture, clothing, and other household $ _____
items (conduct an inventory)

Type of coverage for personal property (check one)

    Actual cash value   [   ]

    Replacement value   [   ]

Additional coverage for items with limits on standard personal property coverage such as jewelry; firearms; silverware; and photographic, electronic, and computer equipment

Item	Amount
_____	_____
_____	_____
_____	_____

Personal Liability

Amount of additional personal liability coverage desired for possible personal $ _____
injury claims

Specialized Coverages

If appropriate, investigate flood or earthquake coverage excluded from $ _____
home insurance policies

Note: Use sheet 29 to compare companies, coverages, and costs for apartment or home insurance.

What's Next for Your Personal Financial Plan?

- Outline the steps involved in planning an insurance program.
- Outline special types of property and liability insurance such as personal computer insurance, trip cancellation insurance, and liability insurance.

Apartment/Home Insurance Comparison

Purpose: To research and compare companies, coverages, and costs for apartment or home insurance.

Financial Planning Activities: Contact three insurance agents to obtain the information requested below. This sheet is also available in an Excel spreadsheet format in Connect Finance.

Suggested Websites: www.freeinsurancequotes.com   www.insure.com   www.insureuonline.org

YOUR PERSONAL FINANCIAL PLAN

Type of building   ☐ apartment   ☐ home   ☐ condominium

Location _____

Type of construction _____ Age of building _____

Company name			
Agent's name, address, and phone			
Coverage: Dwelling $ Other structure $ (does not apply to apartment/condo coverage)	**Premium**	**Premium**	**Premium**
Personal property $			
Additional living expenses $			
Personal liability Bodily injury $ Property damage $			
Medical payments Per person $ Per accident $			
Deductible amount			
Other coverage $			
Service charges or fees			
Total Premium			

What's Next for Your Personal Financial Plan?

- List the reasons most commonly given by renters for not having renter's insurance.
- Determine cost differences for home insurance among various local agents and online providers.

30

YOUR PERSONAL FINANCIAL PLAN

Name: _____ Date: _____

Automobile Insurance Cost Comparison

Purpose: To research and compare companies, coverages, and costs for auto insurance.

Financial Planning Activities: Contact three insurance agents to obtain the information requested below. This sheet is also available in an Excel spreadsheet format in Connect Finance.

Suggested Websites: www.autoinsuranceindepth.com   www.progressive.com   www.standardandpoors.com

Automobile (year, make, model, engine size) _____

Driver's age _____ Sex _____   Total miles driven in a year _____

Full- or part-time driver? _____

Driver's education completed? _____

Accidents or violations within the past three years? _____

Company name			
Agent's name, address, and phone			
E-mail, website			
Policy length (6 months, 1 year)			
Coverage: Bodily injury liability Per person $ Per accident $	**Premium**	**Premium**	**Premium**
Property damage liability per accident $			
Collision deductible $			
Comprehensive deductible $			
Medical payments per person $			
Uninsured motorist liability Per person $ Per accident $			
Other coverage			
Service charges			
Total Premium			

Suggested App:
• iCompare Car Insurance

What's Next for Your Personal Financial Plan?

• Research actions that you might take to reduce automobile insurance costs.

• Talk to friends, relatives, and insurance agents to determine methods of reducing the cost of auto insurance.

9 Health and Disability Income Insurance

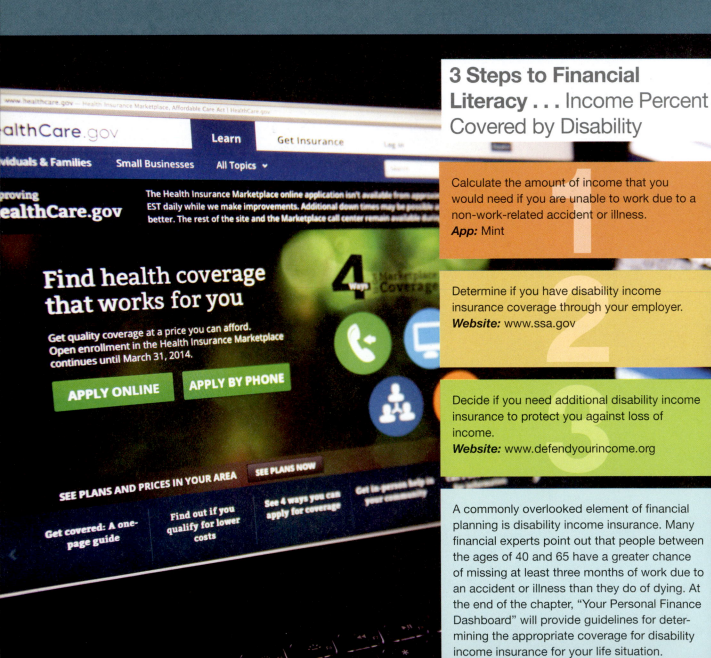

3 Steps to Financial Literacy . . . Income Percent Covered by Disability

1 Calculate the amount of income that you would need if you are unable to work due to a non-work-related accident or illness.
App: Mint

2 Determine if you have disability income insurance coverage through your employer.
Website: www.ssa.gov

3 Decide if you need additional disability income insurance to protect you against loss of income.
Website: www.defendyourincome.org

A commonly overlooked element of financial planning is disability income insurance. Many financial experts point out that people between the ages of 40 and 65 have a greater chance of missing at least three months of work due to an accident or illness than they do of dying. At the end of the chapter, "Your Personal Finance Dashboard" will provide guidelines for determining the appropriate coverage for disability income insurance for your life situation.

Graw-Hill Educa

CHAPTER 9 LEARNING OBJECTIVES

In this chapter, you will learn to:

LO9.1 Recognize the importance of health insurance in financial planning.

LO9.2 Analyze the costs and benefits of various types of health insurance coverage as well as major provisions in health insurance policies.

LO9.3 Assess the trade-offs of different health insurance plans.

LO9.4 Evaluate the differences among health care plans offered by private companies and by the government.

LO9.5 Explain the importance of disability income insurance in financial planning and identify its sources.

LO9.6 Explain why the costs of health insurance and health care have been increasing.

YOUR PERSONAL FINANCIAL PLAN SHEETS

31. Assessing Current and Needed Health Care Insurance
32. Disability Income Insurance Needs

Health Insurance and Financial Planning

What Is Health Insurance?

Health insurance is a form of protection that eases the financial burden people may experience as a result of illness or injury. You pay a *premium,* or fee, to the insurer. In return the company pays most of your medical costs. Although plans vary in what they cover, they may reimburse you for hospital stays, doctors' visits, medications, and sometimes vision and dental care.

Health insurance includes both medical expense insurance, as discussed above, and disability income insurance. *Medical expense insurance* typically pays only the actual medical costs. *Disability income insurance* provides payments to make up for some of the income of a person who cannot work as a result of injury or illness. In this chapter the term "health insurance" refers to medical expense insurance.

Health insurance plans can be purchased in several different ways: group health insurance, individual health insurance, and COBRA.

GROUP HEALTH INSURANCE Most people who have health insurance are covered under group plans. Typically, these plans are employer sponsored. This means that the employer offers the plans and usually pays some or all of the premiums. However, not all employers provide health insurance to their employees. The Affordable Care Act of 2010 requires large employers to provide health insurance coverage for all employees. Other organizations, such as labor unions and professional associations, also offer group plans. Group insurance plans cover you and your immediate family. The Health Insurance Portability and Accountability Act of 1996 (HIPAA) set new federal standards to ensure that workers would not lose their health insurance if they changed jobs. As a result, a parent with a sick child, for example, can move from one group health plan to another without a

LO9.1

Recognize the importance of health insurance in financial planning.

ACTION ITEM

I am aware of several different ways of purchasing health insurance.

☐ **Yes** ☐ **No**

Starting a New Job? Make Your Health Benefits Work for You

The Department of Labor's Employee Benefits Security Administration (EBSA) administers several important health benefit laws covering employer-based health plans. These laws govern your basic rights to information about how your health plan works, how to qualify for benefits, and how to make claims for benefits. In addition, there are specific laws protecting your right to health benefits when you lose coverage or change jobs.

- **Realize that your options are important.** There are many different types of health benefit plans. Find out which one your employer offers, and then check out the plan, or plans, offered. Your employer's human resource office, the health plan administrator, or your union can provide information to help you match your needs and preferences with the available plans. If your employer offers a high-deductible health plan, look into setting up a Health Savings Account to save money for future medical expenses on a tax-free basis. The more information you have, the better your health care decisions will be.

- **Review the benefits available.** Do the plans cover preventive care, well-baby care, vision or dental care? Are there deductibles? Answers to these questions can help determine the out-of-pocket expenses you may face. Matching your needs and those of your family members will result in the best possible benefits. Cheapest may not always be best. Your goal is high-quality health benefits.

- **Read your plan's Summary Plan Description (SPD).** Provided by your health plan administrator, the SPD outlines your benefits and your legal rights under the Employee Retirement Income Security Act (ERISA), the federal law that protects your health benefits. It should contain information about the coverage of dependents, what services will require a copay, and the circumstances under which your employer can change or terminate a health benefits plan. Save the SPD and all other health plan brochures and documents, along with memos or correspondence from your employer relating to health benefits.

- **Assess your benefit coverage as your family status changes.** Marriage, divorce, childbirth or adoption, or the death of a spouse are life events that may require changes in your health benefits. You, your spouse, and dependent children may be eligible for a special enrollment period under provisions of the Health Insurance Portability and Accountability Act (HIPAA). Even without life-changing events, the information provided by your employer should tell you how you can change benefits or switch plans, if more than one plan is offered.

- **Know that changing jobs and other life events can affect your health benefits.** Under COBRA, you, your covered spouse, and your dependent children may be eligible to purchase extended health coverage under your employer's plan if you lose your job, change employers, get divorced, or upon occurrence of certain other events.

- **Look for wellness programs.** More and more employers are establishing wellness programs that encourage employees to work out, stop smoking, and generally adopt healthier lifestyles.

- **Plan for retirement.** Before you retire, find out what health benefits, if any, extend to you and your spouse during your retirement years. Consult with your employer's human resources office, your union, and the plan administrator, and check your SPD.

- **Know how to file an appeal if your health benefits claim is denied.** Understand how your plan handles grievances and where to make appeals of the plan's decisions. Keep records and copies of correspondence. Check your health benefits package and your SPD to determine who is responsible for handling problems with benefit claims.

SOURCE: U.S. Department of Labor (www.dol.gov/ebsa/publications), accessed May 28, 2014.

lapse in coverage. Moreover, the parent will not have to pay more for coverage than other employees do.

Are you starting a new job? Read the nearby "Personal Finance in Practice" box to make your group health benefits work for you.

The cost of group insurance is relatively low because many people are insured under the same *policy*—a contract with a risk-sharing group, or insurance company. However, group insurance plans vary in the amount of protection that they provide. For example, some plans limit the amount that they will pay for hospital stays and surgical procedures. If your plan does not cover all of your health insurance needs, you have several choices.

If you are married, you may be able to take advantage of a coordination of benefits (COB) provision, which is included in most group insurance plans. This provision allows you to combine the benefits from more than one insurance plan. The benefits received from all the plans are limited to 100 percent of all allowable medical expenses. For example, a couple could use benefits from one spouse's group plan and from the other spouse's plan up to 100 percent.

If this type of provision is not available to you, or if you are single, you can buy individual health insurance for added protection.

INDIVIDUAL HEALTH INSURANCE Some people do not have access to an employer-sponsored group insurance plan because they are self-employed. Others are simply dissatisfied with the coverage that their group plan provides. In these cases individual health insurance may be the answer. You can buy individual health insurance directly from the company of your choice. Plans usually cover you as an individual or cover you and your family. Individual plans can be adapted to meet your own needs. You should comparison shop, however, because rates vary.

THE CONSOLIDATED OMNIBUS BUDGET RECONCILIATION ACT OF 1986 (COBRA). If you are covered under your employer's health plan and you lose your job, have your hours reduced, or get laid off, and your employer's health plan continues to exist, you and your dependents may qualify to purchase temporary extended health coverage under COBRA at group rates under the employer's plan. Divorce, legal separation, loss of dependent child status, the covered employee's death, or entitlement to Medicare may also give your covered spouse and dependent children the right to elect continued coverage under COBRA. Your plan must be notified of these events. Generally, COBRA covers group health plans maintained by employers with 20 or more employees. The group health plan is required to provide you with a written notice indicating your eligibility for COBRA coverage. If you are eligible, you will have 60 days from the date the notice is sent or from the date your coverage ends—whichever is later—to elect COBRA. If the employer is too small to be subject to COBRA, state law may require the plan's insurer to provide some continuation coverage. Caution: Not everyone qualifies for COBRA. You have to work for a private company or state or local government to benefit.

PRACTICE QUIZ 9-1

1. What is health insurance?

2. What are the three ways of purchasing health insurance?

3. For the following statements, circle "T" for true or "F" for false.

   a. Health insurance is available only as a benefit from an employer.   T   F
   b. You can continue your health insurance even if you leave a job.   T   F

Apply Yourself!

Ask someone in a human resources office of an organization to obtain information on the health insurance provided as an employee benefit.

ACTION ITEM

I am aware of several types of health insurance coverage available to me.

☐ Yes ☐ No

basic health insurance coverage Hospital expense insurance, surgical expense insurance, and physician expense insurance.

hospital expense insurance Pays part or all of hospital bills for room, board, and other charges.

deductible An amount the insured must pay before benefits become payable by the insurance company.

surgical expense insurance Pays part or all of the surgeon's fees for an operation.

physician expense insurance Provides benefits for doctors' fees for nonsurgical care, X-rays, and lab tests.

coinsurance A provision under which both the insured and the insurer share the covered losses.

Health Insurance Coverage

Several types of health insurance coverage are available, either through a group plan or through individual purchase. Some benefits are included in nearly every health insurance plan; other benefits are seldom offered.

Types of Health Insurance Coverage

BASIC HEALTH INSURANCE COVERAGE **Basic health insurance coverage** includes hospital expense coverage, surgical expense coverage, and physician expense coverage.

Hospital Expense **Hospital expense coverage** pays for some or all of the daily costs of room and board during a hospital stay. Routine nursing care, minor medical supplies, and the use of other hospital facilities are covered as well. For example, covered expenses would include anesthesia, laboratory fees, dressings, X-rays, local ambulance service, and the use of an operating room.

Be aware, though, that most policies set a maximum amount they will pay for each day you are in the hospital. They may also limit the number of days they will cover. Recall from Chapter 8 that many policies require a deductible. A **deductible** is a set amount that the policyholder must pay toward medical expenses before the insurance company pays benefits.

Surgical Expense **Surgical expense insurance** pays all or part of the surgeon's fees for an operation, whether it is done in a hospital or in the doctor's office. Policies often have a list of the services that they cover, which specifies the maximum payment for each type of operation. For example, a policy might allow $500 for an appendectomy. If the entire surgeon's bill is not covered, the policyholder has to pay the difference. People often buy surgical expense coverage in combination with hospital expense coverage.

Physician Expense **Physician expense insurance** meets some or all the costs of physician care that do not involve surgery. This form of health insurance covers treatment in a hospital, a doctor's office, or even a patient's home. Plans may cover routine doctor visits, X-rays, and lab tests. Like surgical expense, physician expense specifies maximum benefits for each service. Physician expense coverage is usually combined with surgical and hospital coverage in a package called basic health insurance.

Major Medical Expense Insurance Coverage Most people find that basic health insurance meets their usual needs. The cost of a serious illness or accident, however, can quickly go beyond the amounts that basic health insurance will pay. Chen had emergency surgery, which meant an operation, a two-week hospital stay, a number of lab tests, and several follow-up visits. He was shocked to discover that his basic health insurance paid less than half of the total bill, leaving him with debts of more than $10,000.

Chen would have been better protected if he had had major medical expense insurance. This coverage pays the large costs involved in long hospital stays and multiple surgeries. In other words, it takes up where basic health insurance coverage leaves off. Almost every type of care and treatment prescribed by a physician, in and out of a hospital, is covered. Maximum benefits can range from $5,000 to more than $1 million per illness per year.

Of course, this type of coverage isn't cheap. To control premiums, most major medical plans require a deductible. Some plans also include a coinsurance provision. **Coinsurance** is the percentage of the medical expenses the policyholder must pay in addition to the deductible amount. Many policies require policyholders to pay 20 or 25 percent of expenses after they have paid the deductible.

[
EXAMPLE: Deductibles and Coinsurance

Ariana's policy includes an $800 deductible and a coinsurance provision requiring her to pay 20 percent of all bills. If her bill total is $3,800, for instance, the company will first exclude $800 from coverage, which is Ariana's deductible. It will then pay 80 percent of the remaining $3,000, or $2,400. Therefore, Ariana's total costs are $1,400 ($800 for the deductible and $600 for the coinsurance).
]

Some major medical policies contain a stop-loss provision. **Stop-loss** is a provision that requires the policyholder to pay all costs up to a certain amount, after which the insurance company pays 100 percent of the remaining expenses, as long as they are covered in the policy. Typically, the policyholder will pay between $3,000 and $5,000 in out-of-pocket expenses before the coverage begins.

Major medical expense insurance may be offered as a single policy with basic health insurance coverage, or it can be bought separately. Comprehensive major medical insurance is a type of complete insurance that helps pay hospital, surgical, medical, and other bills. It has a low deductible, usually $500 to $1,000. Many major medical policies set limits on the benefits they will pay for certain expenses, such as surgery and hospital room and board.

stop-loss A provision under which an insured pays a certain amount, after which the insurance company pays 100 percent of the remaining covered expenses.

HOSPITAL INDEMNITY POLICIES A hospital indemnity policy pays benefits when you're hospitalized. Unlike most of the other plans mentioned, however, these policies don't directly cover medical costs. Instead you are paid in cash, which you can spend on medical or nonmedical expenses as you choose. Hospital indemnity policies are used as a supplement to—and not a replacement for—basic health or major medical policies. The average person who buys such a policy, however, usually pays much more in premiums than he or she receives in payments.

did you know?

The Coalition Against Insurance Fraud provides "scam alerts" on phony health coverage, including a list of 10 warning signs. Visit www.insurancefraud.org.

DENTAL EXPENSE INSURANCE Dental expense insurance provides reimbursement for the expenses of dental services and supplies. It encourages preventive dental care. The coverage normally provides for oral examinations (including X-rays and cleanings), fillings, extractions, oral surgery, dentures, and braces. As with other insurance plans, dental insurance may have a deductible and a coinsurance provision, stating that the policyholder pays from 20 to 50 percent after the deductible.

VISION CARE INSURANCE An increasing number of insurance companies are including vision care insurance as part of group plans. Vision care insurance may cover eye examinations, glasses, contact lenses, eye surgery, and the treatment of eye diseases.

PSYCHOLOGY OF DREAD DISEASE POLICIES Dread disease, trip accident, death insurance, and cancer policies are usually sold through the mail, in newspapers and magazines, or by door-to-door salespeople. These kinds of policies play upon unrealistic fears, and they are illegal in many states. They cover only specific conditions, which are already fully covered if you are insured under a major medical plan.

LONG-TERM CARE INSURANCE **Long-term care insurance (LTC)** provides coverage for the expense of daily help that you may need if you become seriously ill or disabled and are unable to care for yourself. It is useful whether you require a lengthy stay in a nursing home or just need help at home with daily activities such as dressing, bathing,

long-term care insurance (LTC) Provides day-in, day-out care for long-term illness or disability.

Get a Long-Term-Care Insurer to Pay Up

A long-term-care insurance policy can help cover the costs of care in a nursing home, an assisted-living facility or at home. Follow these steps, and you're more likely to get through the claims process smoothly.

1. Find out what triggers benefits. Most policies pay only if the patient needs help with at least two out of six activities of daily living (such as bathing or dressing) or there is evidence of cognitive impairment. But the requirements for making a claim vary. Work with your parent's doctor to provide the information the insurer needs.

2. Find out about home-care requirements. If you plan to provide care at home for your parent, call the insurer to find out about requirements for payouts—especially before you hire a caregiver to come into the home. Some insurers require home caregivers to be licensed or from an agency, for example. A few pay benefits even to relatives who provide care. Many insurers have care coordinators who can help you search for caregivers or facilities.

3. Understand the waiting period. Most policies have waiting periods of at least 60 days. However, some companies have a zero-day waiting period for home care but a longer waiting period for assisted living or nursing homes. Others count every calendar day from the time your parent met the requirement for needing help with activities of daily living or the cognitive-impairment requirement, even if he or she didn't receive care every day. Still others count only the days on which your parent received care—which can extend the waiting period. To speed things up, you may want to have a caregiver come in for a shorter period for more days rather than a longer period for fewer days.

4. Keep track of the paperwork. That includes forms you submit and communications with the facility and the

long-term-care insurer. Sometimes payouts are delayed because of paperwork issues. Keep records of all phone calls and dates that you or the doctor or the facility sent information, and follow up to make sure the paperwork has been received. Also ask your insurer or agent if there is anything you can do to streamline the paperwork; some insurers will arrange direct billing between the nursing home and insurer.

5. Appeal a denied claim. If you have a dispute, work through the insurer's appeals process, and contact your state insurance department for help (see www.naic.org for links).

Kimberly Lankford

1. Why is it important to work with your parent's doctor to provide the information the insurer needs for long-term-care benefits?

2. Why might you want to have a caregiver come in for a shorter period for more days rather than a longer period for fewer days?

3. Why is it important to keep track of the paperwork submitted to an insurance company?

4. What steps can you take if your claim is denied?

and household chores. Annual premiums range from less than $1,000 to over $16,000, depending on your age and extent of the coverage. The older you are when you enroll, the higher your annual premium. Typically, individual insurance plans are sold to the 50- to 80-year age group, pay benefits for a maximum of two to six years, and carry a dollar limit on the total benefits they will pay.

According to experts, long-term care protection makes sense for people with a net worth of $100,000 to $2 million. If your net worth is less than $100,000, you will exhaust your assets and qualify for Medicaid; if your assets are more than $2 million, you can fund your own long-term care. If you purchase a policy, consider at least a three-year term with a daily benefit that would cover the nursing-facility cost in your area. Recently, the national daily average of a nursing facility was $229 per day, or more than $83,585 per year. The nearby "Personal Finance in Practice" box can help you compare the features of long-term care policies.

Explore services available in your community to help meet long-term care needs. Care given by family members can be supplemented by visiting nurses, home health aides, friendly visitor programs, home-delivered meals, chore services, adult day care centers, and respite services for caregivers who need a break from daily responsibilities.

These services are becoming more widely available. Some or all of them may be found in your community. Your local area Agency on Aging or Office on Aging can help you locate the services you need. Call the Eldercare Locator at 1-800-677-1116 to locate your local office.

Major Provisions in a Health Insurance Policy

All health insurance policies have certain provisions in common. You have to be sure that you understand what your policy covers. What are the benefits? What are the limits? The following are details of provisions that are usually found in health insurance policies:

- *Eligibility:* The people covered by the policy must meet specified eligibility requirements, such as family relationship and, for children, a certain age.
- *Assigned benefits:* You are reimbursed for payments when you turn in your bills and claim forms. When you assign benefits, you let your insurer make direct payments to your doctor or hospital.
- *Internal limits:* A policy with internal limits sets specific levels of repayment for certain services. Even if your hospital room costs $600 a day, you won't be able to get more than $250 if an internal limit specifies that maximum.
- *Copayment:* A **copayment** is a flat fee that you pay every time you receive a covered service. The fee is usually between $20 and $30, and the insurer pays the balance of the cost of the service. This is different from coinsurance, which is the percentage of your medical costs for which you are responsible after paying your deductible.
- *Service benefits:* Policies with this provision list coverage in terms of services, not dollar amounts: You're entitled to X-rays, for instance, not $40 worth of X-rays per visit. Service benefits provisions are always preferable to dollar amount coverage because the insurer will pay all the costs.
- *Benefit limits:* This provision defines a maximum benefit, either in terms of a dollar amount or in terms of number of days spent in the hospital.
- *Exclusions and limitations:* This provision specifies services that the policy does not cover. It may include preexisting conditions (a condition you were diagnosed with before your insurance plan took effect), cosmetic surgery, or more.
- *Guaranteed renewable:* This provision means that the insurer can't cancel the policy unless you fail to pay the premiums. It also forbids insurers to raise premiums unless they raise all premiums for all members of your group.
- *Cancellation and termination:* This provision explains the circumstances under which the insurer can cancel your coverage. It also explains how you can convert your group contract into an individual contract.

copayment A provision under which the insured pays a flat dollar amount each time a covered medical service is received after the deductible has been met.

Shopping for a Long-Term Care Policy

What do you need to know when you are comparing LTC policies? You should consider asking the following questions:

	Policy 1	Policy 2		Policy 1	Policy 2
1. Are these services covered?			**7.** What is the waiting period before benefits begin for:		
Skilled Nursing Care	_____	_____	Home Health Care?	_____	_____
Home Health Care	_____	_____	Assisted Living Facility Care?	_____	_____
Custodial/Personal Care	_____	_____	Nursing Home Care?	_____	_____
Homemaker Services	_____	_____	Is the waiting period calendar days, or covered service days?	_____	_____
2. What is the daily allowance for these services?			**8.** How long will it be before pre-existing conditions are covered?	_____	_____
Skilled Nursing Care	_____	_____	**9.** What does the policy use to decide if you're eligible for benefits?		
Home Health Care	_____	_____	Inability to complete activities of daily living (ADLs)	_____	_____
Custodial/Personal Care	_____	_____	Doctor certification of medical necessity	_____	_____
Homemaker Services	_____	_____	Prior hospital stay	_____	_____
3. Does this policy pay for care in any licensed facility?	_____	_____	Cognitive impairment	_____	_____
If not, what won't it pay for?	_____	_____	Other	_____	_____
4. Does the policy pay for care received in:			**10.** Is the policy renewable?	_____	_____
Adult day care centers?	_____	_____	**11.** Does the policy offer inflation protection?	_____	_____
Assisted living facilities?	_____	_____	**12.** Are benefits adjusted for inflation?	_____	_____
One's home?	_____	_____	**13.** Are you allowed to buy more coverage?	_____	_____
5. How long will the policy pay benefits for:			**14.** Is there a waiver-of-premium provision? If so:		
Home Health Care?	_____	_____	How long must you be in a nursing home before it begins?	_____	_____
Skilled Nursing Care?	_____	_____	Does the waiver apply to home care?	_____	_____
Custodial/Personal Care?	_____	_____	**15.** What is the annual cost of the policy?	_____	_____
Homemaker Services?	_____	_____	With inflation adjustment	_____	_____
Adult Day Care Centers?	_____	_____	Without inflation adjustment	_____	_____
Assisted Living Facilities?	_____	_____	**16.** Is there a free trial period?	_____	_____
6. What is the policy's maximum lifetime benefit?					
For Home Care	_____	_____			
For Assisted Living Facility Care	_____	_____			
For Nursing Home Care	_____	_____			

SOURCE: Adapted from the National Association of Insurance Commissioners publication "A Shopper's Guide to Long-Term Care Insurance."

PRACTICE QUIZ 9-2

1. What three types of coverage are included in the basic health insurance?

2. What benefits are provided by:

   a. Hospital expense coverage?
   b. Surgical expense coverage?
   c. Physician expense coverage?

3. Match the following terms with an appropriate statement.

   coinsurance   a. Requires the policyholder to pay all costs up to a certain amount. _____

   stop-loss   b. The percentage of the medical expenses you must pay. _____

   hospital indemnity policy   c. A policy used as a supplement to basic health or major medical policies. _____

   exclusions and limitations   d. Defines who is covered by the policy. _____

   copayment   e. Specifies services that the policy does not cover. _____

   eligibility   f. A flat fee that you pay every time you receive a covered service. _____

Apply Yourself!

Raj is thinking about buying major medical insurance to supplement his basic health insurance from work. Describe a situation in which Raj would need major medical.

Health Insurance Trade-Offs

LO9.3

Assess the trade-offs of different health insurance plans.

Different health insurance policies may offer very different benefits. As you decide which insurance plan to buy, consider the following trade-offs.

Coverage Trade-Offs

REIMBURSEMENT VERSUS INDEMNITY A reimbursement policy pays you back for actual expenses. An indemnity policy provides you with specific amounts, regardless of how much the actual expenses may be.

ACTION ITEM

In choosing health insurance coverage, I should get a basic plan and a major medical supplement policy.

☐ Yes ☐ No

EXAMPLE: Reimbursement versus Indemnity

Katie and Seth are both charged $200 for an office visit to the same specialist. Katie's reimbursement policy has a deductible of $300. Once she has met the deductible, the policy will cover the full cost of such a visit. Seth's indemnity policy will pay him $125, which is what his plan provides for a visit to any specialist.

INTERNAL LIMITS VERSUS AGGREGATE LIMITS A policy with internal limits will cover only a fixed amount for an expense, such as the daily cost of room and board during a hospital stay. A policy with aggregate limits will limit only the total amount

Copyright © 2016 by McGraw-Hill Education

did you know?

International health care insurance provides health coverage no matter where you are in the world. The policy term is flexible so you can purchase only for the time you will be out of the country. Check online or contact your current health care provider for coverage information.

of coverage (the maximum dollar amount paid for all benefits in a year), such as $1 million in major expense benefits, or it may have no limits.

DEDUCTIBLES AND COINSURANCE The cost of a health insurance policy can be greatly affected by the size of the deductible (the set amount that the policyholder must pay toward medical expenses before the insurance company pays benefits). It can also be affected by the terms of the *coinsurance provision* (which states what percentage of the medical expenses the policyholder must pay in addition to the deductible amount).

OUT-OF-POCKET LIMITS Some policies limit the amount of money you must pay for the deductible and coinsurance. After you have reached that limit, the insurance company covers 100 percent of any additional costs. Out-of-pocket limits help you lower your financial risk, but they also increase your premiums.

BENEFITS BASED ON REASONABLE AND CUSTOMARY CHARGES Some policies consider the average fee for a service in a particular geographical area. They then use the amount to set a limit on payments to policyholders. If the standard cost of a certain procedure is $1,500 in your part of the country, then your policy won't pay more than that amount.

Which Coverage Should You Choose?

Now that you are familiar with the available types of health insurance and some of their major provisions, how do you choose one? The type of coverage you choose will be affected by the amount you can afford to spend on the premiums and the level of benefits that you feel you want and need. It may also be affected by the kind of coverage your employer offers, if you are covered through your employer.

You can buy basic health coverage, major medical coverage, or both basic and major medical coverage. Any of these three choices will take care of at least some of your medical expenses. Ideally, you should get a basic plan and a major medical supplement. Another option is to purchase a comprehensive major medical policy that combines the value of both plans in a single policy. Exhibit 9–1 describes the most basic features you should look for.

Exhibit 9–1

Health Insurance Must-Haves

A health insurance plan should:

- Offer basic coverage for hospital and doctor bills.

- Provide at least 120 days' hospital room and board in full.

- Provide at least a $1 million lifetime maximum for each family member.

- Pay at least 80 percent for out-of-hospital expenses after a yearly deductible of $500 per person or $1,000 per family.

- Impose no unreasonable exclusions.

- Limit your out-of-pocket expenses to no more than $3,000 to $5,000 a year, excluding dental, vision care, and prescription costs.

Although health insurance plans vary greatly, all plans should have the same basic features. Would you add anything to this list of must-haves?

PRACTICE QUIZ 9-3

1. As you decide which health insurance plan to buy, what trade-offs would you consider?

2. Match the following terms with an appropriate statement.

reimbursement	*a.* A policy that will cover only a fixed amount of an expense. _____
indemnity	*b.* A policy that pays you back for actual expenses. _____
internal limits	*c.* A policy that provides you with specific amounts, regardless of how much the actual expenses may be. _____
deductible	*d.* After you have reached a certain limit, the insurance company covers 100 percent of any additional cost. _____
out-of-pocket limit	*e.* The set amount that you must pay toward medical expenses before the insurance company pays benefits. _____

3. What basic features should be included in your health insurance plan?

Apply Yourself!

Prepare a list of trade-offs that are important to you in a health insurance policy.

Private Health Care Plans and Government Health Care Programs

Private Health Care Plans

Most health insurance in the United States is provided by private organizations rather than by the government. Private health care plans may be offered by a number of sources: private insurance companies; hospital and medical service plans; health maintenance organizations; preferred provider organizations; home health care agencies; and employer self-funded health plans.

PRIVATE INSURANCE COMPANIES Several hundred private insurance companies are in the health insurance business. They provide mostly group health plans to employers, which in turn offer them to their employees as a benefit. Premiums may be fully or partially paid by the employer, with the employee paying any remainder. These policies typically pay you for medical costs you incur, or they send the payment directly to the doctor, hospital, or lab that provides the services.

HOSPITAL AND MEDICAL SERVICE PLANS Blue Cross and Blue Shield are statewide organizations similar to private health insurance companies. Each state has its own Blue Cross and Blue Shield. The "Blues" provide health insurance to millions of Americans. **Blue Cross** provides hospital care benefits. **Blue Shield** provides benefits for surgical and medical services performed by physicians.

LO9.4

Evaluate the differences among health care plans offered by private companies and by the government.

ACTION ITEM

I am aware of health care plans offered by private companies and by the government.

☐ **Yes** ☐ **No**

Blue Cross An independent membership corporation that provides protection against the cost of hospital care.

Blue Shield An independent membership corporation that provides protection against the cost of surgical and medical care.

managed care Prepaid health plans that provide comprehensive health care to members.

health maintenance organization (HMO) A health insurance plan that provides a wide range of health care services for a fixed, prepaid monthly premium.

preferred provider organization (PPO) A group of doctors and hospitals that agree to provide health care at rates approved by the insurer.

point-of-service (POS) plan A network of selected contracted, participating providers; also called an *HMO-PPO hybrid* or *open-ended HMO.*

HEALTH MAINTENANCE ORGANIZATIONS

Rising health care costs have led to an increase in managed care plans. According to a recent industry survey, 23 percent of employed Americans are enrolled in some form of managed care. **Managed care** refers to prepaid health plans that provide comprehensive health care to their members. Managed care is designed to control the cost of health care services by controlling how they are used. Managed care is offered by health maintenance organizations (HMOs), preferred provider organizations (PPOs), and point-of-service plans (POSs).

Health maintenance organizations are an alternative to basic health insurance and major medical expense insurance. A **health maintenance organization (HMO)** is a health insurance plan that directly employs or contracts with selected physicians and other medical professionals to provide health care services in exchange for a fixed, prepaid monthly premium.

HMOs are based on the idea that preventive services will minimize future medical problems. Therefore, these plans typically cover routine immunizations and checkups, screening programs, and diagnostic tests. They also provide customers with coverage for surgery, hospitalization, and emergency care. If you have an HMO, you will usually pay a small copayment for each covered service. Supplemental services may include vision care and prescription services, which are typically available for an additional fee.

When you first enroll in an HMO, you must choose a plan physician from a list of doctors provided by the HMO. The physician provides or arranges for all of your health care services. You must receive care through your plan physician; if you don't, you are responsible for the cost of the service. The only exception to this rule is in the case of a medical emergency. If you experience a sudden illness or injury that would threaten your life or health if not treated immediately, you may go to the emergency room of the nearest hospital. All other care must be provided by hospitals and doctors under contract with the HMO.

HMOs are not for everyone. Many HMO customers complain that their HMO denies them necessary care. Others feel restricted by the limited choice of doctors.

Exhibit 9–2 provides some tips on using and choosing an HMO: Because HMOs require you to use only certain doctors, you should make sure that these doctors are near your home or office. You should also be able to change doctors easily if you don't like your first choice. Similarly, second opinions should always be available at the HMO's expense, and you should be able to appeal any case in which the HMO denies care. Finally, look at the costs and benefits: Will you incur out-of-pocket expenses or copayments? What services will the plan provide?

PREFERRED PROVIDER ORGANIZATIONS

A variation on the HMO is a **preferred provider organization (PPO),** a group of doctors and hospitals that agree to provide specified medical services to members at prearranged fees. PPOs offer these discounted services to employers either directly or indirectly through an insurance company. The premiums for PPOs are slightly higher than the premiums for HMOs.

PPO plan members often pay no deductibles and may make minimal copayments. Whereas HMOs require members to receive care from HMO providers only, PPOs allow members greater flexibility. Members can either visit a preferred provider (a physician whom you select from a list, as in an HMO) or go to their own physicians. Patients who decide to use their own doctors do not lose coverage as they would with an HMO. Instead they must pay deductibles and larger copayments.

Increasingly, the difference between PPOs and HMOs is becoming less clear. A **point-of-service (POS) plan** combines features of both HMOs and PPOs. POSs use a network of participating physicians and medical professionals who have contracted to provide services for certain fees. As with your HMO, you choose a plan physician who manages your

Exhibit 9–2 Tips on Using and Choosing an HMO

How to Use an HMO

When you first enroll in an HMO, you must choose a plan physician (family practitioner, internist, pediatrician, or obstetrician-gynecologist) who provides or arranges for all of your health care services. It is extremely important that you receive your care through the plan physician. If you don't, you are responsible for the cost of the service rendered.

The only exceptions to the requirement that care be received through the plan physician are medical emergencies. A medical emergency is a sudden onset of illness or a sudden injury that would jeopardize your life or health if not treated immediately. In such instances, you may use the facilities of the nearest hospital emergency room. All other care must be provided by hospitals and doctors under contract with the HMO.

How to Choose an HMO

If you decide to enroll in an HMO, you should consider these additional factors:

1. *Accessibility.* Since you must use plan providers, it is extremely important that they be easily accessible from your home or office.

2. *Convenient office hours.* Your plan physician should have convenient office hours.

3. *Alternative physicians.* Should you become dissatisfied with your first choice of a physician, the HMO should allow you the option to change physicians.

4. *Second opinions.* You should be able to obtain second opinions.

5. *Type of coverage.* You should compare the health care services offered by various HMOs, paying particular attention to whether you will incur out-of-pocket expenses or copayments.

6. *Appeal procedures.* The HMO should have a convenient and prompt system for resolving problems and disputes.

7. *Price.* You should compare the prices various HMOs charge to ensure that you are getting the most services for your health care dollar.

What to Do When an HMO Denies Treatment or Coverage

- *Get it in writing.* To better defend your case, ask for a letter detailing the clinical reasons your claim was denied and the name and medical expertise of the HMO staff member responsible.

- *Know your rights.* The plan document or your HMO's member services department will tell you how experimental treatments are defined and covered and how the appeals process works.

- *Keep records.* Make copies of any correspondence, including payments and any reimbursements. Also, keep a written log of all conversations relevant to your claim.

- *Find advocates.* Enlist the help of your doctor, employer, and state insurance department to lobby your case before the HMO.

SOURCE: Reprinted from the May 18, 1997, issue of *BusinessWeek* by special permission © 1999 McGraw-Hill Companies, Inc.

care and controls referrals to specialists. As long as you receive care from a plan provider, you pay little or nothing, just as you would with an HMO. However, you're allowed to seek care outside the network at a higher charge, as with a PPO.

HOME HEALTH CARE AGENCIES Rising hospital costs, new medical technology, and the increasing number of elderly people have helped make home care one of the fastest-growing areas of the health care industry. Home health care consists of home health agencies; home care aide organizations; and hospices, facilities that care for the terminally ill. These providers offer medical care in a home setting in agreement with a medical order, often at a fraction of the cost hospitals would charge for a similar service.

EMPLOYER SELF-FUNDED HEALTH PLANS Some companies choose to self-insure. The company runs its own insurance plan, collecting premiums from employees and paying medical benefits as needed. However, these companies must cover any costs that exceed the income from premiums. Unfortunately, not all corporations have the financial assets necessary to cover these situations, which can mean a financial disaster for the company and its employees.

NEW HEALTH CARE ACCOUNTS Health savings accounts (HSAs), which Congress authorized in 2003, are the newest addition to the alphabet soup of health insurance available to American workers. Now you and your employer must sort through HSAs,

Personal Finance in Practice

HSAs: How They Work in 2014

1. Your company offers a health insurance policy with an annual deductible of at least $1,250.

2. You can put pretax dollars into an HSA each year, up to the amount of the deductible—but no more than $6,550 for family coverage or $3,300 for individual coverage, plus a $1,000 catch-up contribution for those who are over 55.

3. You withdraw the money from your HSA tax-free, but it can be used only for your family's medical expenses. After the deductible and copays are met, insurance still typically covers 80 percent of health costs.

4. HSA plans are required to have maximum out-of-pocket spending limits, $6,350 for individuals, $12,700 for families. That's when your company's insurance kicks in again at 100 percent coverage.

5. Your company can match part or all of your HSA contributions if it wishes, just as it does with 401(k)s.

6. You can invest your HSA in stocks, bonds, or mutual funds. Unused money remains in your account at the end of the year and grows tax-free.

7. You can also take your HSA with you if you change jobs or retire.

8. To help you shop for health care now that you're spending your own money, employers say they will give you detailed information about prices and quality of doctors and hospitals in your area.

SOURCE: U.S. Department of the Treasury (www.irs.gov/pub/irs-drop/rp-13-25.pdf), accessed May 24, 2014.

health reimbursement accounts (HRAs), and flexible spending accounts (FSAs). Each has its own rules about how money is spent, how it can be spent, and how it is taxed.

How do FSAs, HRAs, and HSAs differ? FSAs allow you to contribute pretax dollars to an account managed by your employer. You use the money for health care spending but forfeit anything left over at the end of the year.

HRAs are tied to high-deductible policies. They are funded *solely* by your employer and give you a pot of money to spend on health care. You can carry over unspent money from year to year, but you lose the balance if you switch jobs. Premiums tend to be lower than for traditional insurance but higher than for HSAs. You can invest the funds in stocks, bonds, and mutual funds. The money grows tax-free but can be spent only on health care.

HSAs allow you to contribute money to a tax-free account that can be used for out-of-pocket health care expenses if you buy high-deductible health insurance policies to cover catastrophic expenses. Exhibit 9–3 summarizes the important features of HSAs, FSAs, and HRAs. Also, read the "Personal Finance in Practice" box to learn how HSAs work in 2014.

In addition to the private sources of health insurance and health care discussed in this section, government health care programs cover over 50 million people. The next section discusses these programs.

Government Health Care Programs

The health insurance coverage discussed thus far is normally purchased through private companies. Some consumers, however, are eligible for health insurance coverage under programs offered by federal and state governments.

MEDICARE Perhaps the best-known government health program is Medicare. *Medicare* is a federally funded health insurance program available mainly to people over 65 and to people with disabilities. Medicare has four parts: hospital insurance (Part A), medical insurance (Part B), Medicare Advantage Plan (Part C), and Prescription Drug Coverage (Part D). Medicare hospital insurance is funded by part of the Social Security payroll tax. Part A helps pay for inpatient hospital care, inpatient care in a skilled nursing facility, home health care, and hospice care. Program participants pay a single annual deductible.

Health Savings Accounts (HSAs)	Flexible-Spending Accounts (Arrangements) (FSAs)	Health Reimbursement Accounts (HRAs)
• Employer sponsored • Set aside tax-free dollars you can use to pay for medical expenses that are not covered by insurance • Tied to a high-deductible policy • Unspent money can be carried over and accumulate year to year • Can invest the funds in stocks, bonds, and mutual funds • The money grows tax-free but can be spent only on health care • You own the funds; you take any unspent funds with you if you leave the employer	• Employer sponsored • Set aside tax-free dollars you can use to pay for medical expenses that are not covered by insurance • Not tied to a high-deductible policy • Money left over can't be carried over; if you don't use it, you lose it to your employer	• Employer sponsored • Funded solely by your employer to spend on your health care • Reimbursement of claims is tax-deductible for employers • Tied to high-deductible policies • The maximum annual contribution is determined by your employer's plan document • Can carry over unspent money from year to year, but you lose the balance if you change jobs • Premiums tend to be lower than for traditional insurance but higher than for HSAs

Exhibit 9–3

Comparison of HSAs, FSAs, and HRAs

Part B helps pay for doctors' services and a variety of other medical services and supplies not covered or not fully covered by Part A. Part B has a deductible and a 20 percent coinsurance provision. Medicare medical insurance is a supplemental program paid for by individuals who feel that they need it. A regular monthly premium is charged. The federal government matches this amount. For a brief summary of Medicare Parts A, B, C, and D, see the nearby "Personal Finance in Practice" box.

Medicare is constantly in financial trouble. Health care costs continue to grow, and the proportion of senior citizens in society is rising. This situation puts Medicare in danger of running out of funds. According to recent projections, the program will be bankrupt by the year 2035 if no changes are made.

The Balanced Budget Act of 1997 created the new Medicare Choice program. This program allows many Medicare members to choose a managed care plan in addition to their Medicare coverage. For some additional costs, members can receive greater benefits. Exhibit 9–4 compares features of different Medicare options.

What Is Not Covered by Medicare?   Although Medicare is very helpful for meeting medical costs, it does not cover everything. In addition to the deductibles and coinsurance payments, Medicare will not cover some medical expenses at all. These are certain types of skilled or long-term nursing care, out-of-hospital prescription drugs, routine checkups, dental care, and most immunizations. Medicare also severely limits the types of services it will cover and the amount it will pay for those services. If your doctor does not accept Medicare's approved amount as payment in full, you're responsible for the difference.

Medigap   Those eligible for Medicare who would like more coverage may buy **Medigap (MedSup) insurance.** Medigap insurance supplements Medicare by filling the gap between Medicare payments and medical costs not covered by Medicare. It is offered by private companies. For more information about Medicare supplement insurance, visit www.medicare .gov/publications, or call 1-800-Medicare and request the booklet "Choosing a Medigap Policy: A Guide to Health Insurance for People with Medicare." You may also visit http://www.medicare.gov/supplement-other-insurance/medigap/whats-medigap.html or call your state insurance department.

Medigap (MedSup) insurance Supplements Medicare by filling the gap between Medicare payments and medical costs not covered by Medicare.

A Brief Look at Medicare

Medicare is health insurance for people age 65 or older, under age 65 with certain disabilities, and any age with end-stage renal disease (permanent kidney failure requiring dialysis or a kidney transplant).

Most people get their Medicare health care coverage in one of two ways. Your costs vary depending on your plan, coverage, and the services you use.

ORIGINAL MEDICARE PLAN	
Part A (Hospital)	Part B (Medical)
Medicare provides this coverage. Part B is optional. You have your choice of doctors. Your costs may be higher than in Medicare Advantage Plans.	

+

Part D (Prescription Drug Coverage)
You can choose this coverage. Private companies approved by Medicare run these plans. Plans cover different drugs. Medically necessary drugs must be covered.

+

Medigap (Medicare Supplement Insurance) Policy
You can choose to buy this private coverage (or an employer or union may offer similar coverage) to fill in gaps in Part A and Part B coverage. Costs vary by policy and company.

or

MEDICARE ADVANTAGE PLANS LIKE HMOS AND PPOS
Called "Part C," this option combines your Part A (Hospital) and Part B (Medical)
Private insurance companies approved by Medicare provide this coverage. Generally, you must see doctors in the plan. Your costs may be lower than in the Original Medicare Plan, and you may get extra benefits.

+

Part D (Prescription Drug Coverage)
Most Part C plans cover prescription drugs. If they don't, you may be able to choose this coverage. Plans cover different drugs. Medically necessary drugs must be covered.

For information about Medicare, visit www.medicare.gov or call 1-800-MEDICARE (1-800-633-4227).

SOURCE: *Medicare & You* (Washington, DC: The Centers for Medicare and Medicaid Services, 2014).

MEDICAID The other well-known government health program is *Medicaid,* a medical assistance program offered to certain low-income individuals and families. Medicaid is administered by states, but it is financed by a combination of state and federal funds. Unlike Medicare, Medicaid coverage is so comprehensive that people with Medicaid do not need supplemental insurance. Typical Medicaid benefits include physicians' services, inpatient and outpatient hospital services, lab services, skilled nursing and home health services, prescription drugs, eyeglasses, and preventive care for people under the age of 21.

Health Insurance and the Patient Protection and Affordable Care Act of 2010

Americans had been debating for years that the nation needs health care reform to ensure that we get high-quality, affordable health care. The Patient Protection and Affordable Care Act of 2010 sets aside $635 billion over the next 10 years to help finance this reform. Here are the key provisions of the act that will take effect now and in the years to come. The act:

- Offers tax credits for small businesses to make employee coverage more affordable.
- Prohibits denying coverage to children with preexisting medical conditions.
- Provides access to affordable insurance for those who are uninsured because of a preexisting condition through a temporary subsidized high-risk pool.

Exhibit **9–4**　A Comparison of Various Medicare Plans

	Current Options	New Options (Medicare and Choice)	Plan Description
Original Medicare	✔	✔	• You choose your health care providers.
			• Medicare pays your providers for covered services.
			• Most beneficiaries choose Medicare supplemental insurance to cover deductible and copayments.
Medicare health maintenance organization (HMO)	✔	✔	• You must live in the plan's service area.
			• You agree to use the plan network of doctors, hospitals, and other health providers, except in an emergency.
			• Medicare pays the HMO to provide all medical services.
Preferred provider organization (PPO)		✔	• Works like an HMO, except you have the choice to see a health provider out of the network.
			• If you do see an out-of-network provider, you will pay a higher cost.
Provider-sponsored organization (PSO)		✔	• Works like a Medicare HMO, except the networks are managed by health care providers (doctors and hospitals) rather than an insurance company.
Private fee for service		✔	• Medicare pays a lump sum to a private insurance health plan.
			• Providers can bill more than what the plan pays; you are responsible for paying the balance.
			• The plan may offer more benefits than Original Medicare.
Medical savings account (MSA)		✔	• Medicare MSAs are a special type of savings account that can be used to pay medical bills.
			• Centers for Medicare and Medicaid Services (CMS) will make an annual lump-sum deposit into enrollee's account (only Medicare can deposit funds into this account).
			• MSAs work with a special private insurance company and carry a very high deductible.
			• Funds withdrawn for nonmedical purposes are taxable and subject to a penalty.

SOURCE: *Medicare & You* (Washington, DC: The Centers for Medicare and Medicaid Services, 2014).

- Bans insurance companies from dropping people from coverage when they get sick.
- Eliminates copayments for preventive services and exempts preventive services from deductibles under the Medicare program.
- Requires new health plans to allow young people up to their 26th birthday to remain on their parents' insurance policy.
- Prohibits health insurance companies from placing lifetime caps on coverage.
- Restricts the use of annual limits to ensure access to needed care in all plans.
- Requires new private plans to cover preventive services with no copayment and with preventive services being exempt from deductibles.
- Ensures that consumers in new plans have access to an effective internal and external appeals process to appeal decisions by their health insurance plans.

The Affordable Care Act: Checklist for You and Your Family

Whether you are uninsured or just want to explore new options, the Health Insurance Marketplace will give you and your family more choice and selection in health plans.

SEVEN STEPS YOU CAN TAKE TO GET READY NOW

1. **Learn about different types of health insurance.** Through the marketplace , you'll be able to choose a health plan that gives you the right balance of costs and coverage.

2. **Make a list of questions before it's time to choose your health plan.** For example, "Can I stay with my current doctor?" or "Will this plan cover my health costs when I'm traveling?"

3. **Make sure you understand how insurance works, including deductibles, out-of-pocket maximums, copayments, etc.** Consider these details while you're shopping around. Visit the HealthCare.gov website to learn more about how insurance works.

4. **Start gathering basic information about your household income.** Most people will qualify to get a break on costs, and you'll need income information to find out how much.

5. **Set your budget.** There will be different types of health plans to meet a variety of needs and budgets, and breaking them down by cost can help narrow your choices.

6. **Ask your employers whether they plan to offer health insurance, especially if you work for a small business.**

7. **Explore current options.** You will be able to get help with insurance now, through existing programs or changes that are in effect already from the new health care law. Use HealthCare.gov resources to get information about health insurance for adults up to age 26, children in families with limited incomes, and Medicare for people who are over 65 or are disabled.

SOURCE: HealthCare.gov website at http://www.healthcare.gov/marketplace/get-ready/consumer-checklist/index.html, accessed May 28, 2014.

- Provides aid to states in establishing offices of health insurance consumer assistance to help individuals with the filing of complaints and appeals.
- Increases funds for community health centers to allow for nearly a doubling of the number of patients seen by the centers over the next five years.
- Provides new investments to increase the number of primary care practitioners, including doctors, nurses, nurse practitioners, and physician assistants.
- Requires health insurance companies to submit justification for all requested premium increases.
- Requires that most Americans purchase health insurance by 2014.
- Creates state-based health insurance marketplaces (also called *insurance exchanges*) through which individuals can purchase coverage, with subsidies available to lower-income individuals.
- Expands the Medicaid program for the nation's poorest individuals.
- Requires employers with more than 20 employees to provide health insurance to their employees or pay penalties.[1]

The law is expansive and will be implemented over several years, but all major provisions took effect in January 2014. On June 28, 2012, the Supreme Court, in a 5 to 4 vote, upheld the majority of the landmark Affordable Care Act. Under the law, if you don't have health insurance, you will have to pay 1 percent of your income to the IRS starting in 2014. However, there are some exceptions for religious beliefs and financial hardship.

According to the Health and Human Services secretary,

Three years ago, the Affordable Care Act ushered in a new day for health care. Since then, more than 6.3 million seniors and people with disabilities with Medicare have saved more

[1]HealthCare.gov website at www.healthcare.gov, accessed March 20, 2013.

than $6.1 billion on prescription drugs. Nearly 71 million Americans got expanded access to preventive services at no charge through their private insurance plans, and 47 million women now have guaranteed access to additional preventive services without cost sharing. More than 3.1 million young adults who were uninsured were able to gain coverage by being able to stay on their parents' insurance policies until they turned 26. And parents no longer have to worry about insurers denying coverage to their children because of a pre-existing condition.

Americans are getting more value for their health care dollars due to the health care law. Affordable Care Act initiatives are promoting coordinated care; paying for quality, not quantity; and dramatically reducing fraud and waste, contributing to the slowest growth in national health spending in 50 years.[2]

The act's opponents, however, claim that

Three years later, the act has failed to live up to its name, leaving a trail of broken promises in its wake. Instead of lowering costs as promised and making the system simpler for patients, the law has added a litany of new rules, regulations and fines. The pledge that 'If you like your current health care plan, you'll be able to keep it' is already broken. In fact, the Congressional Budget Office estimated that 7 million people will lose their coverage, no matter how much they like it. Even though the law promised that families could save $2,500 in health care premiums, the average family premium has, in fact, increased by more than $3,000 since 2008. Moreover, the House Ways and Means Committee reported that the law includes about $1.1 trillion in new taxes that will hit Americans at all income levels. And a recent Government Accountability Office report shows that the law will add $6.2 trillion to the primary deficit. Nothing is free; it's being paid with higher taxes and insurance premiums.[3]

An ethical dilemma: Is a government-run health care system that provides universal health care to all the most ethical? The current health care issues and the health care reform will have long-term effects on federal and state governments, insurance companies, health care providers, pharmaceutical companies, and, most important, patients. Most Americans believe that an ethical health care system should provide high, if not the highest, quality of health care and freedom of choice; and it must be affordable and available to all citizens. Will "Obamacare" have long-term positive or negative effects on the general population? Only time will tell!

The Affordable Care Act is intended to make our health insurance system work better for families. It also contains some of the strongest anti–health care fraud provisions in American history.

The Affordable Care Act and the Individual Shared Responsibility Provision

Under the Affordable Care Act, the federal government, state governments, insurers, employers, and individuals share the responsibility for health insurance coverage beginning in 2014. Many people already have qualifying health insurance coverage (called minimum essential coverage) and do not need to do anything more than maintain that coverage.

The individual shared responsibility provision requires you and each member of your family to

- Have minimum essential coverage, or
- Have an exemption from the responsibility to have minimum essential coverage, or
- Make a shared responsibility payment when you file your 2014 federal income tax return in 2015.

[2]Kathleen Sebelius, "Affordable Care Act at 3: Looking Forward and Expanding Access," Health Care Blog, HealthCare.gov, accessed March 22, 2013.

[3]Rob Engstrom, "Three Years Ago Today," U.S. Chamber of Commerce (Washington, DC), http://www.uschamber.com/healthcare, accessed March 23, 2013.

MINIMUM ESSENTIAL COVERAGE If you and your family need to acquire minimum essential coverage, you may have several of the following options:

- Health insurance coverage provided by your employer.
- Health insurance purchased through the Health Insurance Marketplace in the area where you live, where you may qualify for financial assistance.
- Coverage provided under a government-sponsored program for which you are eligible (including Medicare, Medicaid, and health care programs for veterans).
- Health insurance purchased directly from an insurance company.
- Other health insurance coverage that is recognized by the Department of Health and Human Services as minimum essential coverage.

You can learn more at HealthCare.gov about which health insurance options are available to you, how to purchase health insurance coverage, and how to get financial assistance with the cost of insurance. If you purchase health insurance through the marketplace and you meet certain requirements, you may be eligible for a premium tax credit to help pay your premiums.

EXEMPTIONS You may be exempt from the requirement to maintain minimum essential coverage and thus will not have to make a shared responsibility payment when you file your 2014 federal income tax return in 2015, if you meet certain criteria. You may be exempt if you

- Have no affordable coverage options because the minimum amount you must pay for the annual premiums is more than 8 percent of your household income, or
- Have a gap in coverage for less than three consecutive months, or
- Qualify for an exemption for one of several other reasons, including having a hardship that prevents you from obtaining coverage, or belonging to a group explicitly exempt from the requirement.

MAKING A PAYMENT If you or any of your dependents don't have minimum essential coverage and you don't have an exemption, you will need to make an individual shared responsibility payment on your tax return. Remember, choosing to make the individual shared responsibility payment instead of purchasing minimum essential coverage means you will also have to pay the entire cost of all your medical care.

For 2014, the annual payment amount was

- The greater of 1 percent of your household income that is above the tax return filing threshold for your filing status, or
- Your family's flat dollar amount, which is $95 per adult and $47.50 per child, limited to a family maximum of $285.

For more information about the individual shared responsibility provision and detailed examples of the payment calculation, visit irs.gov.

GOVERNMENT CONSUMER HEALTH INFORMATION WEBSITES

The Department of Health and Human Services operates more than 60 websites with a wealth of reliable information related to health and medicine. For example:

- *Healthfinder:* Healthfinder includes links to more than 1,000 websites operated by government and nonprofit organizations. It lists topics according to subject (www.hhs.gov).
- *MedlinePlus:* MedlinePlus is the world's largest collection of published medical information. It was originally designed for health professionals and researchers, but it's also valuable for students and others who are interested in health care and medical issues (www.nlm.nih.gov/medlineplus).
- *NIH Health Information Page:* The National Institutes of Health (NIH) operates a website called the NIH Health Information Page, which can direct you to

the consumer health information in NIH publications and on the Internet (www.nih.gov).

- *FDA:* The Food and Drug Administration (FDA) also runs a website. This consumer protection agency's site provides information about the safety of various foods, drugs, cosmetics, and medical devices (www.fda.gov).

PRACTICE QUIZ 9-4

1. What are the six sources of private health plans?

2. Match the following terms with the appropriate statement.

Blue Cross

a. A medical assistance program offered to certain low-income individuals and families. _____

Blue Shield

b. A health insurance plan that combines features of both HMOs and PPOs. _____

HMOs

c. A statewide organization that provides hospital care benefits. _____

PPOs

d. A federally funded health insurance program available mainly to people over 65 and to people with disabilities. _____

point-of-service (POS)

e. Health insurance plans that directly employ or contract with selected physicians to provide health services in exchange for a fixed, prepaid monthly premium. _____

Medicare

f. A statewide organization that provides benefits for surgical and medical services performed by physicians. _____

Medicaid

g. Groups of doctors and hospitals that agree to provide specified medical services to members at prearranged fees. _____

3. What health care services are not covered by Medicare?

Apply Yourself!

Talk to several people covered by Medicare and Medicaid to obtain information on the coverage provided and the difficulties sometimes faced.

Disability Income Insurance

The Need for Disability Income

Before disability insurance existed, people who were ill lost more money from missed paychecks than from medical bills. Disability income insurance was set up to protect against such loss of income. This kind of coverage is very common today, and several hundred insurance companies offer it.

Disability income insurance provides regular cash income when you're unable to work because of a pregnancy, a non-work-related accident, or an illness. It protects your earning power, your most valuable resource.

The exact definition of a disability varies from insurer to insurer. Some insurers will pay you when you are unable to work at your regular job. Others will pay only if you are so ill or badly hurt that you can't work at any job. A violinist with a hand injury, for instance, might have trouble doing his or her regular work but might be able to perform a range of other jobs. A good disability income insurance plan pays you if you can't

LO9.5

Explain the importance of disability income insurance in financial planning and identify its sources.

ACTION ITEM

Since I am a healthy adult, I don't need to worry about disability income insurance.

☐ **Yes**   ☐ **No**

disability income insurance Provides payments to replace income when an insured person is unable to work.

work at your regular job. A good plan will also pay partial benefits if you are able to work only part-time.

Many people make the mistake of ignoring disability insurance, not realizing that it's very important insurance to have. Disability can cause even greater financial problems than death. Disabled persons lose their earning power but still have to meet their living expenses. In addition, they often face huge costs for their medical treatment and special care that their disabilities require.

Sources of Disability Income

Before you buy disability income insurance from a private insurance company, remember that you may already have some form of insurance of this kind. This coverage may be available through worker's compensation if you're injured on the job. Disability benefits may also be available through your employer or through Social Security in case of a long-term disability.

WORKER'S COMPENSATION If your disability is a result of an accident or illness that occurred on the job, you may be eligible to receive worker's compensation benefits in your state. Benefits will depend on your salary and your work history.

EMPLOYER PLANS Many employers provide disability income insurance through group insurance plans. In most cases your employer will pay part or all of the cost of such insurance. Some policies may provide continued wages for several months only, whereas others will give you long-term protection.

did you know?

Nearly one in five Americans will become disabled for one year or more before the age of 65, according to the Life Foundation, a nonprofit organization dedicated to helping consumers make smart financial decisions. The number of workers who become disabled has risen by 35 percent since 2000, according to the Social Security Administration.

SOCIAL SECURITY Social Security may be best known as a source of retirement income, but it also provides disability benefits. If you're a worker who pays into the Social Security system, you're eligible for Social Security funds if you become disabled. How much you get depends on your salary and the number of years you've been paying into Social Security. Your dependents also qualify for certain benefits. However, Social Security has very strict rules. Workers are considered disabled if they have a physical or mental condition that prevents them from working and that is expected to last for at least 12 months or to result in death. Benefits start at the sixth full month the person is disabled. They stay in effect as long as the disability lasts.

PRIVATE INCOME INSURANCE PROGRAMS Privately owned insurance companies offer many policies to protect people from loss of income resulting from illness or disability. Disability income insurance gives weekly or monthly cash payments to people who cannot work because of illness or accident. The amount paid is usually 40 to 60 percent of a person's normal income. Some plans, however, pay as much as 75 percent.

Disability Income Insurance Trade-Offs

As with the purchase of health insurance, you must make certain trade-offs when you decide among different private disability insurance policies. Keep the following in mind as you look for a plan that is right for you.

WAITING OR ELIMINATION PERIOD Benefits won't begin the day you become disabled. You'll have to wait anywhere between one and six months before you can begin collecting. The span of time is called an elimination period. Usually a policy with a longer elimination period charges lower premiums.

DURATION OF BENEFITS Every policy names a specified period during which benefits will be paid. Some policies are valid for only a few years. Others are automatically canceled when you turn 65. Still others continue to make payments for life. You should look for a policy that pays benefits for life. If your policy stops payments when you turn 65, then permanent disability could be a major financial as well as physical loss.

AMOUNT OF BENEFITS You should aim for a benefit amount that, when added to other sources of income, will equal 70 to 80 percent of your take-home pay. Of course, the greater the benefit, the greater the cost, or premium.

ACCIDENT AND SICKNESS COVERAGE Some disability policies pay only for accidents. Coverage for sickness is important, though. Accidents are not the only cause of disability.

GUARANTEED RENEWABILITY If your health becomes poor, your disability insurer may try to cancel your coverage. Look for a plan that guarantees coverage as long as you continue to pay your premiums. The cost may be higher, but it's worth the extra security and peace of mind. You may even be able to find a plan that will stop charging the premiums if you become disabled, which is an added benefit.

Your Disability Income Needs

Once you have found out what your benefits from the numerous public and private sources would be, you should determine whether those benefits would meet your disability income needs. Ideally, you'll want to replace all the income you otherwise would have earned. This should enable you to pay your day-to-day expenses while you're recovering. You won't have work-related expenses and your taxes will be lower during the time you are disabled. In some cases you may not have to pay certain taxes at all. Use Exhibit 9–5 to determine how much income you will have available if you become disabled.

	Monthly Amount	After Waiting:	For a Period of:
Sick leave or short-term disability	_____	_____	_____
Group long-term disability	_____	_____	_____
Social Security	_____	_____	_____
Other government programs	_____	_____	_____
Individual disability insurance	_____	_____	_____
Credit disability insurance	_____	_____	_____
Other income:	_____	_____	_____
Savings	_____	_____	_____
Spouse's income	_____	_____	_____
Total monthly income while disabled:	$_____		

Exhibit 9–5

Calculating Disability Income

How much income will you have available if you become disabled?

Sheet 32 Disability Income Insurance Needs

PRACTICE QUIZ 9-5

1. What is the purpose of disability income insurance?

2. What are the four sources of disability income?

3. Match the following terms with an appropriate statement.

waiting or elimination period	*a.* A specified period during which benefits are paid. _____
duration of benefits	*b.* A plan that guarantees coverage as long as you continue to pay your premiums. _____
guaranteed renewability	*c.* A period of one to six months that must elapse before benefits can be collected. _____

Apply Yourself!

Contact an insurance agent to obtain cost information for an individual disability income insurance policy.

LO9.6

Explain why the costs of health insurance and health care have been increasing.

ACTION ITEM

To avoid high medical costs, I eat a balanced diet and keep my weight under control.

☐ **Yes**   ☐ **No**

High Medical Costs

Affordable health care has become one of the most important social issues of our time. News broadcasts abound with special reports on "America's health care crisis" or politicians demanding "universal health insurance."

What do an aging and overweight population, the cost of prescription drugs, the growing number of uninsured, and advancements in medical technology have in common? These and other factors all add up to rising health costs. The United States has the highest per capita medical expenditures of any country in the world. We spend twice as much on health care as the average for the 24 industrialized countries in Europe and North America.

Health care costs were estimated at $3.09 trillion in 2014 (see Exhibit 9–6). Since 1993, health care spending as a percentage of gross domestic product (GDP) has remained relatively constant at 13.6 percent, except in 1997, when it fell to 13.4 percent, and in 2011, when it increased to 17.7 percent. The latest projections from the Centers for Medicare and Medicaid Services show that improving economic conditions, the provisions of the Affordable Care Act, and the aging population will continue to increase health care spending in 2015 and beyond. Over the 2012–2022 period, national health spending is projected to grow at an average annual rate of 5.8 percent. By 2022, health spending financed by federal, state, and local governments is projected to account for 49 percent of national health spending and to reach a total of $2.4 trillion.

RAPID INCREASE IN MEDICAL EXPENDITURES Since federally sponsored health care began in 1965, U.S. health care expenditures rose from $41.6 billion, or about 6 percent of GDP, to $3.09 trillion in 2014, about 18 percent of GDP.

HIGH ADMINISTRATIVE COSTS In the United States, administrative costs consume nearly 26 percent of health care dollars, compared to 1 percent under Canada's socialized system. These costs include activities such as enrolling beneficiaries in a health plan, paying health insurance premiums, checking eligibility, obtaining authorizations

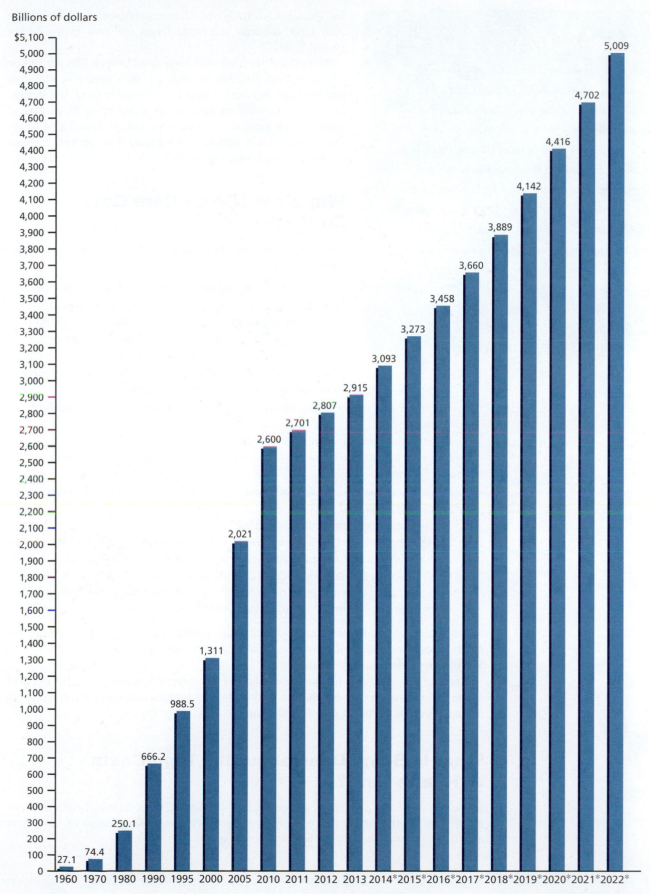

Exhibit 9–6 U.S. National Health Expenditures, 1960–2022

Billions of dollars

Year	Value
1960	27.1
1970	74.4
1980	250.1
1990	666.2
1995	988.5
2000	1,311
2005	2,021
2010	2,600
2011	2,701
2012	2,807
2013	2,915
2014*	3,093
2015*	3,273
2016*	3,458
2017*	3,660
2018*	3,889
2019*	4,142
2020*	4,416
2021*	4,702
2022*	5,009

* Projected.

SOURCES: U.S. Department of Health and Human Services. The Centers for Medicare and Medicaid Services. www.cms.gov, accessed May 24, 2014.

for specialist referrals, and filing reimbursement claims. More than 1,100 different insurance forms are now in use in the United States.

Is it ethical for insurance companies to spend 26 percent on administrative costs? No, according to the Centers for Medicare and Medicaid Services. Under the Affordable Care Act, starting in 2011, companies are required to spend 80 to 85 percent of premiums on medical care and improving the quality of health care. If they don't, insurance companies must provide a rebate to their customers starting in 2012.

Why Does Health Care Cost So Much?

The high and rising costs of health care are attributable to many factors, including:

- The use of sophisticated, expensive technologies.
- Duplication of tests and sometimes duplication of technologies that yield similar results.
- Increases in the variety and frequency of treatments, including allegedly unnecessary tests.
- The increasing number and longevity of elderly people.
- Regulations that result in cost shifting rather than cost reduction.
- The increasing number of accidents and crimes that require emergency medical services.
- Limited competition and restrictive work rules in the health care delivery system.
- Labor intensiveness and rapid average earnings growth for health care professionals and executives.
- Using more expensive medical care than necessary, such as going to an emergency room with a bad cold.
- Built-in inflation in the health care delivery system.
- Aging baby boomers' use of more health care services, whether they're going to the doctor more often or snapping up pricier drugs, from Celebrex to Viagra.
- Other major factors that cost billions of dollars each year, including fraud, administrative waste, malpractice insurance, excessive surgical procedures, a wide range of prices for similar services, and double health coverage.

According to the Government Accountability Office, fraud and abuse account for nearly 10 percent of all dollars spent on health care. In 2010, that was a loss of more than $97 billion to Medicare and Medicaid.

Because third parties—private health insurers and government—pay such a large part of the nation's health care bill, hospitals, doctors, and patients often lack the incentive to make the most economical use of health care services.

What Is Being Done about the High Costs of Health Care?

In the private sector, concerned groups such as employers, labor unions, health insurers, health care professionals, and consumers have undertaken a wide range of innovative activities to contain the costs of health care. These activities include:

- Programs to carefully review health care fees and charges and the use of health care services.
- The establishment of incentives to encourage preventive care and provide more services out of hospitals, where this is medically acceptable.
- Involvement in community health planning to help achieve a better balance between health needs and health care resources.
- The encouragement of prepaid group practices and other alternatives to fee-for-service arrangements.
- Community health education programs that motivate people to take better care of themselves.
- Physicians encouraging patients to pay cash for routine medical care and lab tests.

President Obama maintains that improving health information technology could lower costs; setting up electronic medical records would be a smart investment and could reduce medical errors. According to Karen Davis, president of Commonwealth Fund, a health policy research organization, "Improvements in health information technology could save $88 billion over 10 years, though no gains will be realized in the first few years."

What Can You Do to Reduce Personal Health Care Costs?

The best way to avoid the high cost of illness is to stay well. The prescription is the same as it has always been:

1. Eat a balanced diet and keep your weight under control.
2. Avoid smoking and don't drink to excess.
3. Get sufficient rest, relaxation, and exercise.
4. Drive carefully and watch out for accident and fire hazards in the home.
5. Protect yourself from medical ID theft.

did you know?

According to the Medical Identity Fraud Alliance, an estimated 1.85 million people in the United States were victims of medical identity theft in 2012.

Sheet 32 Disability Income Insurance Needs

PRACTICE QUIZ 9-6

1. What are the reasons for rising health care expenditures?
2. What are various groups doing to curb the high costs of health care?
3. What can individuals do to reduce health care costs?

Apply Yourself!

Create a list of personal actions that you can take to reduce the costs of health care.

YOUR PERSONAL FINANCE DASHBOARD

INCOME PERCENT COVERED BY DISABILITY

A personal finance dashboard with key performance indicators can help you monitor your financial situation and guide you toward financial independence. Disability can be more disastrous financially than death. If you are disabled, you lose your earning power, but you still have living expenses and often huge expenses for medical care.

YOUR SITUATION: Do you know how disability is defined? When do your benefits begin? How long do your benefits last? What is the amount of your benefits? Can benefits be reduced by Social Security disability and worker's compensation payments? Are the benefits adjusted for inflation? You should aim for benefit amounts that, when added to your other income, equal 70 or 80 percent of your gross pay.

POSSIBLE ACTIONS TO TAKE

 Reconsider your responses to the "Action Items" (in the text margin) to determine actions you might take to improve your health and disability income insurance requirements.

 Review your disability income policy and explanation of benefits.

 Check if your employer provides disability income insurance through group insurance plans. In most cases, your employer will pay part or all of the cost of such insurance.

 Contact the Social Security Administration. If you pay into the Social Security system, you are eligible for Social Security funds if you become disabled.

 After you find out what your benefits would be from numerous public and private sources, you should determine whether those benefits would meet your disability income needs.

 For more information on disability income insurance, visit www.iii.org and www.ahip.org.

Chapter Summary

LO9.1   Health insurance is protection that provides payments of benefits for a covered sickness or injury. Health insurance should be a part of your overall insurance program to safeguard your family's economic security. Health insurance plans can be purchased through group health insurance, individual health insurance, and COBRA.

LO9.2   Four basic types of health insurance are available under group and individual policies: hospital expense insurance, surgical expense insurance, physician expense insurance, and major medical expense insurance.

Major provisions of a health insurance policy include eligibility requirements, assigned benefits, internal limits, copayment, service benefits, benefit limits, exclusions and limitations, guaranteed renewability, and cancellation and termination.

LO9.3   Health insurance policy trade-offs include reimbursement versus indemnity, internal limits versus aggregate limits, deductibles and coinsurance, out-of-pocket limits, and benefits based on reasonable and customary charges.

LO9.4   Health insurance and health care are available from private insurance companies, hospital and medical service plans such as Blue Cross/Blue Shield, health maintenance organizations (HMOs), preferred provider organizations (PPOs), point-of-service plans (POSs), home health care agencies, and employer self-funded health plans.

The federal and state governments offer health coverage in accordance with laws that define the premiums and benefits. Two well-known government health programs are Medicare and Medicaid.

LO9.5 Disability income insurance provides regular cash income lost by employees as the result of an accident, illness, or pregnancy. Sources of disability income insurance include the employer, Social Security, worker's compensation, and private insurance companies.

LO9.6 Health care costs, except during 1994–1996, have gone up faster than the rate of inflation. Among the reasons for high and rising health care costs are the use of expensive technologies, duplication of tests and sometimes technologies, increases in the variety and frequency of treatments, unnecessary tests, the increasing number and longevity of elderly people, regulations that shift rather than reduce costs, the increasing number of accidents and crimes requiring emergency services, limited competition and restrictive work rules in the health care delivery system, rapid earnings growth among health care professionals, and built-in inflation in the health care delivery system.

Key Terms

basic health insurance coverage 288

Blue Cross 295

Blue Shield 295

coinsurance 288

copayment 291

deductible 288

disability income insurance 305

health maintenance organization (HMO) 296

hospital expense insurance 288

long-term care insurance (LTC) 289

managed care 296

Medigap (MedSup) insurance 299

physician expense insurance 288

point-of-service (POS) plan 296

preferred provider organization (PPO) 296

stop-loss 289

surgical expense insurance 288

Discussion Questions

1. What is the relationship between health insurance coverage and other aspects of financial planning? (LO 9.1)
2. Should employers be required to provide employees some type of health insurance coverage, even if it is a group plan, with each employee paying his or her full premium? (LO 9.1)
3. Larry and Liz are a young couple both working full-time and earning about $70,000 a year. They recently purchased a house and took out a large mortgage. Since both of them work, they own two cars and are still making payments on them. Liz has major medical health insurance through her employer, but Larry's coverage is inadequate. They have no children, but they hope to start a family in about three years. Liz's employer provides disability income insurance, but Larry's employer does not. Analyze the need for health and disability insurance for Liz and Larry. (LO9.2)
4. Pam is 31 and recently divorced, with children ages 3 and 6. She earns $40,000 a year as a secretary. Her employer provides her with basic health insurance coverage. She receives child support from the children's father, but he misses payments often and is always behind in payments. Her ex-husband, however, is responsible for the children's medical bills. Analyze the need for health and disability insurance for Pam. (LO9.2)
5. List the benefits included in your employee benefit package, such as health insurance, disability income insurance, and life insurance. Discuss the importance of such a benefit package to the consumer. (LO9.3)
6. Obtain sample health insurance policies from insurance agents or brokers, and analyze the policies for definitions, coverage, exclusions, limitations on coverage, and amounts of coverage. In what ways are the policies similar? In what ways do they differ? (LO9.3)

 is at Key Terms.

 is at Discussion Questions.

7. What do you consider to be an "ethical" health care system? Explain your answer. (LO9.4)
8. Visit the Social Security Administration's web page to determine your approximate monthly Social Security disability benefits should you become disabled in the current year. Or call your Social Security office to request the latest edition of *Social Security: Understanding the Benefits*. (LO9.5)

Self-Test Problems

1. The MacDonald family of five has health insurance coverage that pays 75 percent of out-of-hospital expenses after a $600 deductible per person. Mrs. MacDonald incurred doctor and prescription medication expenses of $1,380. What amount would the insurance company pay?

2. Under Rose's PPO, emergency room care at a network hospital is 80 percent covered after the member has met a $300 annual deductible. Assume that Rose went to a hospital within her PPO network and that she had not met her annual deductible yet. Her total emergency room bill was $850. What amount did Rose have to pay? What amount did the PPO cover?

3. Gene, an assembly line worker at an automobile manufacturing plant, has take-home pay of $900 a week. He is injured in an accident that kept him off work for 18 weeks. His disability insurance coverage replaces 65 percent of his earnings after a six-week waiting period. What amount would he receive in disability benefits?

Solutions

1. Total expenses = $ 1,380
   Deductible = $-\ 600$
   $ 780

   Insurance company will pay 75 percent of $780 or $780 × 0.75 = $585.

2. Total bill = $ 850
   Deductible = $-\ 300$
   $ 550

   Rose pays $550 × 0.20 = $110 + $300 = $410.

   PPO covers $440 ($850 − $410).

3. Insurance will replace 65 percent of $900, or $900 × 0.65 = $585 per week. Insurance will pay for 18 minus 6 weeks, or 12 weeks, or $585 × 12 = $7,020.

Problems

1. The Tucker family has health insurance coverage that pays 80 percent of out-of-hospital expenses after a $500 deductible per person. If one family member has doctor and prescription medication expenses of $1,100, what amount would the insurance company pay? (LO9.2)

2. A health insurance policy pays 65 percent of physical therapy costs after a $200 deductible. In contrast, an HMO charges $15 per visit for physical therapy. How much would a person save with the HMO if he or she had 10 physical therapy sessions costing $50 each? (LO9.2)

3. Becky's comprehensive major medical health insurance plan at work has a deductible of $750. The policy pays 85 percent of any amount above the deductible. While on a hiking trip, Becky contracted a rare bacterial disease. Her medical costs for treatment, including medicines, tests, and a six-day hospital stay, totaled $8,893. A friend told her that she would have paid less if she had a policy with a stop-loss feature that capped her out-of-pocket expenses at $3,000. Was her friend correct? Show your computations. Then determine which policy would have cost Becky less and by how much. (LO9.2)

4. Georgia, a widow, has take-home pay of $600 a week. Her disability insurance coverage replaces 70 percent of her earnings after a four-week waiting period. What amount would she receive in disability benefits if an illness kept Georgia from work for 16 weeks? (LO9.5)

5. Stephanie was injured in a car accident and was rushed to the emergency room. She received stitches for a facial wound and treatment for a broken finger. Under Stephanie's PPO plan, emergency room care at a network hospital is 80 percent covered after the member has met a $300 annual deductible. Assume that Stephanie went to a hospital within her PPO network. Her total emergency room bill was $850. What amount did Stephanie have to pay? What amount did the PPO cover? (LO9.2)

Questions 6, 7, and 8 are based on the following scenario:

Ronald Roth started his new job as controller with Aerosystems today. Carole, the employee benefits clerk, gave Ronald a packet that contains information on the company's health insurance options. Aerosystems offers its employees the choice between a private insurance company plan (Blue Cross/Blue Shield), an HMO, and a PPO. Ronald needs to review the packet and make a decision on which health care program fits his needs. The following is an overview of that information.

a. Blue Cross/Blue Shield plan: The monthly premium cost to Ronald will be $42.32. For all doctor office visits, prescriptions, and major medical charges, Ronald will be responsible for 20 percent and the insurance company will cover 80 percent of covered charges. The annual deductible is $500.

b. The HMO is provided to employees free of charge. The copayment for doctors' office visits and major medical charges is $10. Prescription copayments are $5. The HMO pays 100 percent after Ronald's copayment. No annual deductible.

c. The POS requires that the employee pay $24.44 per month to supplement the cost of the program with the company's payment. If Ron uses health care providers within the plan, he pays the copayments as described above for the HMO. He can also choose to use a health care provider out of the network and pay 20 percent of all charges after he pays a $500 deductible. The POS will pay for 80 percent of those covered visits. No annual deductible.

Ronald decided to review his medical bills from the previous year to see what costs he had incurred and to help him evaluate his choices. He visited his general physician four times during the year at a cost of $125 for each visit. He also spent $65 and $89 on prescriptions during the year. Using these costs as an example, what would Ron pay for each of the plans described above? (For the purposes of the POS computation, assume that Ron visited a physician outside of the network plan. Assume he had his prescriptions filled at a network-approved pharmacy.)

6. What annual medical costs will Ronald pay using the sample medical expenses provided if he enrolls in the Blue Cross/Blue Shield plan? (LO9.2)

7. What total costs will Ronald pay if he enrolls in the HMO plan? (LO9.2)

8. If Ronald selects the POS plan, what will his annual medical costs be? (LO9.2)

9. In 2005, Joelle spent $5,000 on her health care. If this amount increased by 6 percent per year, what would be the amount Joelle spent in 2015 for the same health care? (*Hint:* Use the time value of money table in Chapter 1 Appendix, Exhibit 1–A.) (LO9.6)

10. As of 2012, per capita spending on health care in the United States was about $9,000. If this amount increased by 7 percent a year, what would be the amount of per capita spending for health care in 8 years? (*Hint:* Use the time value of money table in Chapter 1 Appendix, Exhibit 1–A.) (LO9.6)

 To reinforce the content in this chapter, more problems are provided at connect.mheducation.com.

BUYING ADEQUATE HEALTH INSURANCE COVERAGE

Kathy Jones was a junior at Glenbard High School. She had two younger brothers. Her father, the assistant manager of a local supermarket, had take-home pay of $3,000 a month. He had a group health insurance policy and a $30,000 life insurance policy. He said that he could not afford to buy additional insurance. All of his monthly salary was used to meet current expenses, including car and house payments, food, clothing, transportation, children's allowances, recreation and entertainment, and vacation trips.

One evening, Kathy was talking with her father about insurance, which she was studying in an economics course. She asked what kind of insurance program her father had for their family. The question started Mr. Jones thinking about how well he was planning for his wife and children. Since the family had always been in good health, Mr. Jones felt that additional health and life insurance was not essential. Maybe after he received a raise in his salary and after his daughter was out of high school, he could afford to buy more insurance.

Questions

1. Do you think Kathy's father was planning wisely for the welfare of his family? Can you suggest ways in which this family could have cut monthly expenses and thus set aside some money for more insurance?

2. Although Mr. Jones's salary was not big enough to buy insurance for all possible risks, what protection do you think he should have had at this time?

3. Suppose Mr. Jones had been seriously injured and unable to work for at least one year. What would his family have done? How might this situation have affected his children?

Continuing Case

HEALTH AND DISABILITY INCOME INSURANCE

Jamie Lee and Ross, happy newlyweds with a new home and twins on the way, are anxiously awaiting their new bundles of joy. Ross was understandably nervous as he wondered if everything would go smoothly with Jamie's pregnancy. Fortunately, they coordinated benefits from the medical insurance group plan offered by Ross's employment at the graphics agency and Jamie Lee's own plan, although Ross's plan would be their primary. His employer offers a health care savings plan, but Ross had not previously realized the benefit of participating.

Jamie Lee has had maternity care that she has been comfortable with so far, but Ross needed to review their health insurance policies with the potential of extensive medical expenses just on the horizon. He wondered if his salary would be enough to pay for the expenses that were not covered for out-of-network doctors.

Current Medical Insurance Plan Provisions

Jamie Lee and Ross have a PPO, or *preferred provider organization,* plan.

In-Network Medical Care:
Jamie Lee and Ross currently have a $15 copayment on regular preventive care doctor visits and a $30 copayment on specialists that are preferred providers or participating members from the PPO plan's list.

Out-of-Network Medical Care:
Jamie Lee and Ross have the choice of seeking medical care from the professional of their choice outside the PPO member list, but will incur a deductible of $500 per person/$1,000 per family, per year.

After the deductible is met, there is a coinsurance of 80 percent/20 percent. The insurance company will cover 80 percent of the allowable medical fees and the policyholders will be responsible for the other 20 percent of the allowable medical fees.

Medical fees that are not allowed under the medical plan provisions would be 100 percent of the policyholders' responsibility.

Out-of-Pocket Limits:
Their health insurance plan provides an out-of-pocket limit of $7,500 per year.

Questions

1. Using the information on the ACA and health planning from the "Personal Finance in Practice" box in this chapter, what are some of the strategies that Ross can use to better prepare financially for the arrival of the twins?
2. How could Jamie Lee and Ross prepare for the birth of the twins with their existing PPO plan?
3. Jamie Lee and Ross learned that the hospital that they plan to use for the delivery is not a participating hospital. What will their financial responsibility be for the nonparticipating hospital expenses?
4. The doctor's office has estimated the hospital expense for Jamie Lee and the babies' delivery, without complications, to be approximately $18,000. Based on their health insurance policy, how much would Jamie Lee and Ross owe for this out-of-network hospital stay?
5. Surprise! The babies arrived five weeks early and Jamie Lee and Ross are the proud parents of *triplets:* two boys and a girl! Since they were preterm, they will need to spend a few extra days in the hospital for observation. How will Ross and Jamie Lee make provisions for adding the babies to their health insurance policy now that they have arrived?

Spending Diary

"SOME OF MY EATING HABITS NOT ONLY WASTE MONEY BUT ARE ALSO NOT BEST FOR MY HEALTH."

Directions Continue your Daily Spending Diary to record and monitor spending in various categories. Your comments should reflect what you have learned about your spending patterns and help you consider possible changes you might want to make in your spending habits. The Daily Spending Diary sheets are located in Appendix D at the end of the book and in Connect Finance.

Questions

1. What spending actions might directly or indirectly affect your health and physical well-being?
2. What amounts (if any) are currently required from your spending for the cost of health and disability insurance?

Name: _____   Date: _____

Assessing Current and Needed Health Care Insurance

Purpose: To assess current and needed medical and health care insurance

Financial Planning Activities: Assess current and needed medical and health care insurance. Investigate your existing medical and health insurance, and determine the need for additional coverages. This sheet is also available in an Excel spreadsheet format in Connect Finance.

Suggested Websites: www.insure.com   www.lifehappens.org   www.insurekidsnow.gov

---

Insurance company _____

Address _____

Type of coverage   ☐ individual health policy   ☐ group health policy
                   ☐ HMO   ☐ PPO   ☐ other

Premium amount (monthly/quarterly/semiannually/annually) _____

Main coverages _____

Amount of coverage for _____

• Hospital costs _____

• Surgery costs _____

• Physicians' fees _____

• Lab tests _____

• Outpatient expenses _____

• Maternity _____

• Major medical _____

Other items covered/amounts _____

Policy restrictions (deductible, coinsurance, maximum limits) _____

Items not covered by this insurance _____

Of items not covered, would supplemental coverage be appropriate for your personal situation? _____

What actions related to your current (or proposed additional) coverage are necessary? _____

What's Next for Your Personal Financial Plan?

• Talk to others about the impact of their health insurance on other financial decisions.

• Contact an insurance agent to obtain cost information for an individual health insurance plan.

Suggested App:
• Healthcare Bluebook

Disability Income Insurance Needs

Purpose: To determine financial needs and insurance coverage related to employment disability situations.

Financial Planning Activities: Use the categories below to determine your potential income needs and disability insurance coverage. This sheet is also available in an Excel spreadsheet format in Connect Finance.

Suggested Websites: www.ssa.gov   www.insweb.com   www.dol.gov

Monthly Expenses

	Current	When Disabled
Mortgage (or rent)	$ _____	$ _____
Utilities	$ _____	$ _____
Food	$ _____	$ _____
Clothing	$ _____	$ _____
Insurance payments	$ _____	$ _____
Debt payments	$ _____	$ _____
Auto/transportation	$ _____	$ _____
Medical/dental care	$ _____	$ _____
Education	$ _____	$ _____
Personal allowances	$ _____	$ _____
Recreation/entertainment	$ _____	$ _____
Contributions, donations	$ _____	$ _____
Total monthly expenses	$ _____	
Total monthly expenses when disabled		$ _____

Substitute Income   Monthly Benefit*

Group disability insurance	$ _____
Social Security	$ _____
State disability insurance	$ _____
Worker's compensation	$ _____
Credit disability insurance (in some auto loan or home mortgages)	$ _____
Other income (investments, etc.)	$ _____
Total projected income when disabled	$ _____

If projected income when disabled is less than expenses, additional disability income insurance should be considered.

*Most disability insurance programs have a waiting period before benefits start, and they may have a limit as to how long benefits are received.

What's Next for Your Personal Financial Plan?

- Survey several people to determine if they have disability insurance.
- Talk to an insurance agent to compare the costs of disability income insurance available from several insurance companies.

Suggested App:
- myCigna

10 Financial Planning with Life Insurance

3 Steps to Financial Literacy . . . Determining Your Life Insurance Coverage

Calculate the current and future financial needs of your dependents and household members.
App: Insurance Needs Calculator

1

Determine the amount of life insurance based on the financial needs from Step 1.
Website: www.bankrate.com

2

Compare types of life insurance policies and costs among various companies and sources of life insurance.
App: Life Insurance Quotes

3

Why is life insurance important?
Providing for the financial needs of family members and other dependents is the primary purpose of life insurance. At the end of the chapter, "Your Personal Finance Dashboard" will provide additional information on planning for an appropriate amount of life insurance.

CHAPTER 10 LEARNING OBJECTIVES

In this chapter, you will learn to:

LO10.1 Define life insurance and determine your life insurance needs.

LO10.2 Distinguish between the types of life insurance companies and analyze various life insurance policies these companies issue.

LO10.3 Select important provisions in life insurance contracts and create a plan to buy life insurance.

LO10.4 Recognize how annuities provide financial security.

YOUR PERSONAL FINANCIAL PLAN SHEETS

33. Determining Life Insurance Needs
34. Life Insurance Policy Comparison

What Is Life Insurance?

Even though putting a price on your life is impossible, you probably own some life insurance—through a group plan where you work, as a veteran, or through a policy you bought. Life insurance is one of the most important and expensive purchases you may ever make; therefore, it is important that you budget for this need. Deciding whether you need it and choosing the right policy from dozens of options take time, research, and careful thought. This chapter will help you make decisions about life insurance. It describes what life insurance is and how it works, the major types of life insurance coverage, and how you can use life insurance to protect your family.

When you buy life insurance, you're making a contract with the company issuing the policy. You agree to pay a certain amount of money—the premium—periodically. In return the company agrees to pay a death benefit, or a stated sum of money upon your death, to your beneficiary. A **beneficiary** is a person named to receive the benefits from an insurance policy.

The Purpose of Life Insurance

Most people buy life insurance to protect the people who depend on them from financial losses caused by their death. Those people could include a spouse, children, an aging parent, or a business partner or corporation. Life insurance benefits may be used to:

- Pay off a home mortgage or other debts at the time of death.
- Provide lump-sum payments through an endowment for children when they reach a specified age.
- Provide an education or income for children.
- Make charitable donations after death.
- Provide a retirement income.
- Accumulate savings.

LO10.1

Define life insurance and determine your life insurance needs.

ACTION ITEM

I need life insurance because someone depends on me for financial support.

☐ Yes   ☐ No

beneficiary A person designated to receive something, such as life insurance proceeds, from the insured.

• Establish a regular income for survivors.
• Set up an estate plan.
• Pay estate and gift taxes.

The Principle and Psychology of Life Insurance

No one can say with any certainty how long a particular person will live. Still, insurance companies are able to make some educated guesses. Over the years they've compiled tables that show about how long people live. Using these tables, the company will make a rough guess about a person's life span and charge him or her accordingly. The sooner a person is likely to die, the higher the premiums he or she will pay.

How Long Will You Live?

If history is a guide, you'll live longer than your ancestors did. In 1900 an American male could be expected to live 46.3 years. By 2014, in contrast, life expectancy had risen to 76.1 years for men and 80.9 for women. Exhibit 10–1 shows about how many years a person can be expected to live today. For instance, a 30-year-old woman can be expected to live another 51.9 years. That doesn't mean that she has a high probability of dying at age 81.9. This just means that 51.9 is the average number of additional years a 30-year-old woman may expect to live.

Do You Need Life Insurance?

Before you buy life insurance, you'll have to decide whether you need it at all. Generally, if your death would cause financial hardship for somebody, then life insurance is a wise purchase. Households with children usually have the greatest need for life insurance. Single people who live alone or with their parents, however, usually have little or no need for life insurance unless they have a great deal of debt or want to provide for their parents, a friend, relative, or charity.

Exhibit 10–1   Life Expectancy Tables, All Races, 2009

This table helps insurance companies determine insurance premiums. Use the table to find the average number of additional years a 20-year-old male and female are expected to live.

EXPECTATION OF LIFE IN YEARS			EXPECTATION OF LIFE IN YEARS		
Age	Male	Female	Age	Male	Female
0	76.0	80.9	50	29.4	33.1
1	75.5	80.4	55	25.3	28.7
5	71.6	76.4	60	21.3	24.4
10	66.6	71.5	65	17.6	20.3
15	61.7	66.5	70	14.2	16.5
20	56.9	61.6	75	11.0	12.9
25	52.2	58.8	80	8.2	9.7
30	47.6	51.9	85	5.9	7.0
35	42.9	47.1	90	4.1	4.9
40	38.3	42.3	95	2.9	3.4
45	33.7	37.7	100	2.1	2.4

SOURCE: CDC/NCHS, National Vital Statistics Report, Volume 62, Number 7, United States Life Tables, 2009, January 6, 2014, p. 3, accessed at www.cdc.gov/nchs/fastats/life-expectancy.htm, accessed October 16, 2014.

Estimating Your Life Insurance Requirements

In estimating your life insurance requirements, consider the insurance coverage that your employer offers you as a fringe benefit. Many employers provide employees with life insurance coverage equal to their yearly salary. For example, if you earn $55,000 per year, you may receive $55,000 of insurance coverage. Some employers offer insurance of two or more times the salary with increased contributions from employees. The premiums are usually lower than premiums for individual life insurance policies, and you don't have to pass a physical exam.

There are four general methods for determining the amount of insurance you may need: the easy method, the DINK method, the "nonworking" spouse method, and the "family need" method.

THE EASY METHOD Simple as this method is, it is remarkably useful. It is based on the insurance agent's rule of thumb that a "typical family" will need approximately 70 percent of your salary for seven years before they adjust to the financial consequences of your death. In other words, for a simple estimate of your life insurance needs, just multiply your current gross income by 7 (7 years) and 0.70 (70 percent).

EXAMPLE: The Easy Method

$40,000 current income × 7 = $280,000 × 0.70 = $196,000

Example from Your Life

$ _____ current income × 7 = $ _____ × 0.70 = $ _____

This method assumes your family is "typical." You may need more insurance if you have four or more children, if you have above-average family debt, if any member of your family suffers from poor health, or if your spouse has poor employment potential. On the other hand, you may need less insurance if your family is smaller.

THE DINK (DUAL INCOME, NO KIDS) METHOD If you have no dependents and your spouse earns as much or more than you do, you have very simple insurance needs. Basically, all you need to do is ensure that your spouse will not be unduly burdened by debts should you die. Here is an example of the DINK method:

EXAMPLE: The DINK Method

	Example	Your Figures
Funeral expenses	$ 5,000	$_____
One-half of mortgage	60,000	_____
One-half of auto loan	7,000	_____
One-half of credit card balance	1,500	_____
One-half of personal debt	1,500	_____
Other debts	1,000	_____
Total insurance needs	$76,000	$_____

Figure It Out!

A Worksheet to Calculate Your Life Insurance Needs

1. Five times your personal yearly income _____ (1)
2. Total approximate expenses above and beyond your daily living costs for you and your dependents (e.g., tuition, care for a disabled child or parent) amount to _____ (2)
3. Your emergency fund (3 to 6 months of living expenses) amounts to _____ (3)
4. Estimated amount for your funeral expenses (U.S. average is $5,000 to $10,000) + _____ (4)
5. Total estimate of your family's financial needs (add lines 1 through 4) = _____ (5)
6. Your total liquid assets (e.g., savings accounts, CDs, money market funds, existing life insurance both individual and group, pension plan death benefits, and Social Security benefits) − _____ (6)
7. Subtract line 6 from line 5 and enter the difference here = _____ (7)

The net result (line 7) is an estimate of the shortfall your family would face upon your death. Remember, these are just rules of thumb. For a complete analysis of your needs, consult a professional.

SOURCES: *About Life Insurance*, Metropolitan Life Insurance Company, February 1997, p. 3; *The TIAA Guide to Life Insurance Planning for People in Education* (New York: Teachers Insurance and Annuity Association, January 1997), p. 3.

This method assumes your spouse will continue to work after your death. If your spouse suffers poor health or is employed in an occupation with an uncertain future, you should consider adding an insurance cushion to see him or her through hard times.

THE "NONWORKING" SPOUSE METHOD Insurance experts have estimated that extra costs of up to $10,000 a year may be required to replace the services of a homemaker in a family with small children. These extra costs may include the cost of a housekeeper, child care, more meals out, additional carfare, laundry services, and so on. They do not include the lost potential earnings of the surviving spouse, who often must take time away from the job to care for the family.

To estimate how much life insurance a homemaker should carry, simply multiply the number of years before the youngest child reaches age 18 by $10,000:

EXAMPLE: The "Nonworking" Spouse Method

Youngest child's age = 8 years

10 years × $10,000 = $100,000

Example from Your Life

_____ years × $10,000 = $ _____

If there are teenage children, the $10,000 figure can be reduced. If there are more than two children under age 13, or if anyone in the family suffers poor health or has special needs, the $10,000 figure should be adjusted upward.

THE "FAMILY NEED" METHOD The first three methods assume you and your family are "typical" and ignore important factors such as Social Security and your liquid assets. The nearby "Figure It Out!" box provides a detailed worksheet for making a thorough estimate of your life insurance needs.

Although this method is quite thorough, if you believe it does not address all of your special needs, you should obtain further advice from an insurance expert or a financial planner.

As you determine your life insurance needs, don't forget to consider the life insurance you may already have. You may have ample coverage through your employer and through any mortgage and credit life insurance you purchased.

Before you consider types of life insurance policies, you must decide what you want your life insurance to do for you and your dependents. First, how much money do you want to leave to your dependents should you die today? Will you require more or less insurance protection to meet their needs as time goes on? Second, when would you like to be able to retire? What amount of income do you believe you and your spouse would need then? Third, how much will you be able to pay for your insurance program? Are the demands on your family budget for other living expenses likely to be greater or lower as time goes on?

When you have considered these questions and developed some approximate answers, you are ready to select the types and amounts of life insurance policies that will help you accomplish your objectives.

Sheet 33 Determining Life Insurance Needs

PRACTICE QUIZ 10-1

1. What is life insurance? What is its purpose?

2. For each of the following statements, indicate your response by writing "T" or "F."

   a. Life insurance is one of the least important and least expensive purchases. _____
   b. A beneficiary is a person named to receive the benefits from an insurance policy. _____
   c. Life insurance benefits may be used to pay off a home mortgage or other debts at the time of death. _____
   d. The sooner a person is likely to die, the higher the premiums he or she will pay. _____
   e. All people need to purchase a life insurance policy. _____

3. What are the four methods of determining life insurance needs?

Apply Yourself!

Interview relatives and friends to determine why they purchased life insurance. Summarize your findings.

Types of Life Insurance Companies and Policies

Types of Life Insurance Companies

You can purchase the new or extra life insurance you need from two types of life insurance companies: stock life insurance companies, owned by shareholders, and mutual life insurance companies, owned by policyholders. Of the 868 life insurance companies in the United States, about 75 percent are stock companies, and about 25 percent are mutual.

Stock companies generally sell **nonparticipating** (or *nonpar*) **policies,** while mutual companies specialize in the sale of **participating** (or *par*) **policies.** A participating policy has a somewhat higher premium than a nonparticipating policy, but a part of the premium is refunded to the policyholder annually. This refund is called the *policy dividend.* In 2012, mutual companies had $5.1 trillion of life insurance in force and stock life insurers had $13.7 trillion.

LO10.2

Distinguish between the types of life insurance companies and analyze various life insurance policies these companies issue.

ACTION ITEM

I am aware of different types of life insurance companies and policies they offer.

☐ **Yes**   ☐ **No**

nonparticipating policy
Life insurance that does not provide policy dividends; also called a *nonpar policy*.

participating policy Life insurance that provides policy dividends; also called a *par policy*.

A long debate about whether stock companies or mutual companies offer less expensive life insurance has been inconclusive. You should check with both stock and mutual companies to determine which type offers the best policy for your particular needs at the lowest price.

If you wish to pay exactly the same premium each year, you should choose a nonparticipating policy with its guaranteed premiums. However, you may prefer life insurance whose annual price reflects the company's experience with its investments, the health of its policyholders, and its general operating costs, that is, a participating policy.

Nevertheless, as with other forms of insurance, price should not be your only consideration in choosing a life insurance policy. You should consider the financial stability of and service provided by the insurance company.

did you know?

Seventy-five million—or two out of three—American families depend on life insurers' products for protection, long-term savings, and a guarantee of lifetime income during retirement.

Types of Life Insurance Policies

Both mutual insurance companies and stock insurance companies sell two basic types of life insurance: temporary and permanent insurance. Temporary insurance can be term, renewable term, convertible term, or decreasing term insurance. Permanent insurance is known by different names, including whole life, straight life, ordinary life, and cash-value life insurance. As you will learn in the next section, permanent insurance can be limited payment, variable, adjustable, or universal life insurance. Other types of insurance policies—group life and credit life insurance—are generally temporary forms of insurance. Exhibit 10–2 lists major types and subtypes of life insurance.

term insurance Life insurance protection for a specified period of time; sometimes called *temporary life insurance*.

TERM LIFE INSURANCE **Term insurance,** sometimes called *temporary life insurance,* provides protection against loss of life for only a specified term, or period of time. A term insurance policy pays a benefit only if you die during the period it covers, which may be 1, 5, 10, or 20 years, or up to age 70. If you stop paying the premiums, your coverage stops. Term insurance is often the best value for customers. You need insurance coverage most while you are raising children. As your children become independent and your assets increase, you can reduce your coverage. Of the new individual life policies purchased in 2012, 36 percent (or 3.6 million) were term insurance policies. Term insurance comes in many different forms. Here are some examples.

Renewable Term   The coverage of term insurance ends at the conclusion of the term, but you can continue it for another term—five years, for example—if you have a renewable option. However, the premium will increase because you will be older. It also usually has an age limit; you cannot renew after you reach a certain age.

Multiyear Level Term   The most popular, a multiyear level term, or *straight term*, policy guarantees that you will pay the same premium for the duration of your policy.

Exhibit 10–2

Major Types and Subtypes of Life Insurance

Term (temporary)	Whole, Straight, or Ordinary Life	Other Types
• Renewable term	• Limited payment	• Group life
• Multiyear level term	• Variable life	• Credit life
• Convertible term	• Adjustable life	• Endowment life
• Decreasing term	• Universal life	
• Return of premium		

Conversion Term   This type of policy allows you to change from term to permanent coverage. This will have a higher premium.

Decreasing Term   Term insurance is also available in a form that pays less to the beneficiary as time passes. The insurance period you select might depend on your age or on how long you decide that the coverage will be needed. For example, if you have a mortgage on a house, you might buy a 25-year decreasing term policy as a way to make sure that the debt could be paid if you died. The coverage would decrease as the balance on the loan decreased.

Return-of-Premium Term   Recently, insurance companies began to sell return-of-premium term life policies. These policies return all the premiums if you survive to the end of the policy term. Premiums are higher than the regular term policy but you do get all your money back.

WHOLE LIFE INSURANCE   The other major type of life insurance is known as whole life insurance (also called a *straight life policy*, a *cash-value policy*, or an *ordinary life policy*). **Whole life insurance** is a permanent policy for which you pay a specified premium each year for the rest of your life. In return the insurance company pays your beneficiary a stated sum when you die. The amount of your premium depends mostly on the age at which you purchase the insurance.

Whole life insurance may also serve as an investment. Part of each premium you pay is set aside in a savings account. When and if you cancel the policy, you are entitled to the accumulated savings, which is known as the **cash value.** Whole life policies are popular because they provide both a death benefit and a savings component. You can borrow from your cash value if necessary, although you must pay interest on the loan. Cash-value policies may make sense for people who intend to keep the policies for the long term or for people who want a more structured way to save. However, the Consumer Federation of America Insurance Group suggests that you explore other savings and investment strategies before investing your money in a permanent policy.

Remember, the primary purpose of buying life insurance is not for investment; it is to protect loved ones who depend on you for financial support upon your death. Furthermore, buying life insurance later in life can be expensive and you may not qualify because of poor health or chronic diseases.

The premium of a term insurance policy will increase each time you renew your insurance. In contrast, whole life policies have a higher annual premium at first, but the rate remains the same for the rest of your life. Several types of whole life policies have been developed to meet the needs of different customers. These include the limited payment policy, the variable life policy, the adjustable life policy, and universal life insurance.

Limited Payment Policy   Limited payment policies charge premiums for only a certain length of time, usually 20 or 30 years or until the insured reaches a certain age. At the end of this time, the policy is "paid up," and the policyholder remains insured for life. When the policyholder dies, the beneficiary receives the full death benefit. The annual premiums are higher for limited payment policies because the premiums have to be paid within a shorter period of time.

Variable Life Policy   With a variable life policy, your premium payments are fixed. As with a cash-value policy, part of your premium is placed in a separate account; this money is invested in a stock, bond, or money market fund. The death benefit is guaranteed, but the cash value of the benefit can vary considerably according to the ups and downs of the stock market. Your death benefit can also increase, depending on the earnings of that separate fund.

whole life insurance An insurance plan in which the policyholder pays a specified premium each year for as long as he or she lives; also called a *straight life policy*, a *cash-value life policy*, or an *ordinary life policy.*

cash value The amount received after giving up a life insurance policy.

> **did you know?**
>
> One hundred and forty-six million individual life insurance policies were in force at the beginning of 2013. Of the new individual policies issued in 2012, 64 percent were whole life policies.

Adjustable Life Policy   An adjustable life policy allows you to change your coverage as your needs change. For example, if you want to increase or decrease your death benefit, you can change either the premium payments or the period of coverage.

universal life insurance
A whole life policy that combines term insurance and investment elements.

Universal Life   **Universal life insurance** is essentially a term policy with a cash value. Part of your premium goes into an investment account that grows and earns interest. You are able to borrow or withdraw your cash value. Unlike a traditional whole life policy, a universal life policy allows you to change your premium without changing your coverage. Exhibit 10–3 compares the important features of term life, whole life, and universal life insurance.

OTHER TYPES OF LIFE INSURANCE POLICIES   Other types of life insurance policies include group life insurance, credit life insurance, and endowment life insurance.

Group Life Insurance   Group life insurance is basically a variation of term insurance. It covers a large number of people under a single policy. The people included in the group do not need medical examinations to get the coverage. Group insurance is usually offered through employers, who pay part or all of the costs for their employees, or through professional organizations, which allow members to sign up for the coverage. Group plans are easy to enroll in, but they can be much more expensive than similar term policies. In 2012, group insurance represented 39 percent of all life insurance policies in force and provided $8 trillion of protection.

Exhibit 10–3   Comparing the Major Types of Life Insurance

	Term Life	Whole Life	Universal Life
Premium	Lower initially, increasing with each renewal.	Higher initially than term; normally doesn't increase.	Flexible premiums.
Protects for	A specified period.	Entire life if you keep the policy.	A flexible time period.
Policy benefits	Death benefits only.	Death benefits and eventually a cash and loan value.	Flexible death benefits and eventually a cash and loan value.
Advantages	Low outlay. Initially, you can purchase a larger amount of coverage for a lower premium.	Helps you with financial discipline. Generally fixed premium amount. Cash value accumulation. You can take loan against policy.	More flexibility. Takes advantages of current interest rates. Offers the possibility of improved mortality rates (increased life expectancy because of advancements in medicine, which may lower policy costs).
Disadvantages	Premium increases with age. No cash value.	Costly if you surrender early. Usually no cash value for at least three to five years. May not meet short-term needs.	Same as whole life. Greater risks due to program flexibility. Low interest rates can affect cash value and premiums.
Options	May be renewable or convertible to a whole life policy.	May pay dividends. May provide a reduced paid-up policy. Partial cash surrenders permitted.	May pay dividends. Minimum death benefit. Partial cash surrenders permitted.

Credit Life Insurance   Credit life insurance is used to pay off certain debts, such as auto loans or mortgages, in the event that you die before they are paid in full. These types of policies are not the best buy for the protection that they offer. Decreasing term insurance is a better option.

Endowment Life Insurance   Endowment is life insurance that provides coverage for a specific period of time and pays an agreed-upon sum of money to the policyholder if he or she is still living at the end of the endowment period. If the policyholder dies before that time, the beneficiary receives the money.

PRACTICE QUIZ 10-2

1. What are the two types of life insurance companies?

2. For each of the following statements, indicate your response by writing "T" or "F."

    a. Stock life insurance companies generally sell participating (or par) policies. _____
    b. Mutual life insurance companies specialize in the sale of nonparticipating (nonpar) policies. _____
    c. If you wish to pay exactly the same premium each year, you should choose a nonpar policy. _____
    d. Permanent insurance is known as whole life, straight life, ordinary life, and cash-value life insurance. _____
    e. Term life insurance is the most expensive type of policy. _____

3. What are the five forms of term insurance?

4. What are the four forms of whole life insurance?

5. Define the following types of life insurance policies:

    a. Group life insurance.
    b. Credit life insurance.
    c. Endowment life insurance.

Apply Yourself!

Choose one stock and one mutual life insurance company. Obtain and compare premiums for $50,000 term, whole life, and universal life insurance.

Selecting Provisions and Buying Life Insurance

Key Provisions in a Life Insurance Policy

Study the provisions in your policy carefully. The following are some of the most common features.

NAMING YOUR BENEFICIARY   You decide who receives the benefits of your life insurance policy: your spouse, your child, or your business partner, for example. You can also name contingent beneficiaries, those who will receive the money if your primary beneficiary dies before or at the same time as you do. Update your list of beneficiaries as your needs change.

INCONTESTABILITY CLAUSE   The incontestability clause says that the insurer can't cancel the policy if it's been in force for a specified period, usually two years. After

LO10.3

Select important provisions in life insurance contracts and create a plan to buy life insurance.

ACTION ITEM

I have started budgeting for my life insurance premiums while I am still young and healthy.

☐ **Yes**   ☐ **No**

that time the policy is considered valid during the lifetime of the insured. This is true even if the policy was gained through fraud. The incontestability clause protects the beneficiaries from financial loss in the event that the insurance company refuses to meet the terms of the policy.

THE GRACE PERIOD When you buy a life insurance policy, the insurance company agrees to pay a certain sum of money under specified circumstances and you agree to pay a certain premium regularly. The *grace period* allows 28 to 31 days to elapse, during which time you may pay the premium without penalty. After that time, the policy lapses if you have not paid the premium.

POLICY REINSTATEMENT A lapsed policy can be put back in force, or reinstated, if it has not been turned in for cash. To reinstate the policy, you must again qualify as an acceptable risk, and you must pay overdue premiums with interest. There is a time limit on reinstatement, usually one or two years.

NONFORFEITURE CLAUSE One important feature of the whole life policy is the **nonforfeiture clause.** This provision prevents the forfeiture of accrued benefits if you choose to drop the policy. For example, if you decide not to continue paying premiums, you can exercise specified options with your cash value.

> **nonforfeiture clause** A provision that allows the insured not to forfeit all accrued benefits.

MISSTATEMENT OF AGE PROVISION The misstatement of age provision says that if the company finds out that your age was incorrectly stated, it will pay the benefits your premiums would have bought if your age had been correctly stated. The provision sets forth a simple procedure to resolve what could otherwise be a complicated legal matter.

POLICY LOAN PROVISION A loan from the insurance company is available on a whole life policy after the policy has been in force for one, two, or three years, as stated in the policy. This feature, known as the *policy loan provision,* permits you to borrow any amount up to the cash value of the policy. However, a policy loan reduces the death benefit by the amount of the loan plus interest if the loan is not repaid.

SUICIDE CLAUSE In the first two years of coverage, beneficiaries of someone who dies by suicide receive only the amount of the premiums paid. After two years beneficiaries receive the full value of death benefits.

RIDERS TO LIFE INSURANCE POLICIES An insurance company can change the conditions of a policy by adding a rider to it. A **rider** is a document attached to a policy that changes its terms by adding or excluding specified conditions or altering its benefits.

> **rider** A document attached to a policy that modifies its coverage.

Waiver of Premium Disability Benefit One common rider is a waiver of premium disability benefit. This clause allows you to stop paying premiums if you're totally and permanently disabled before you reach a certain age, usually 60. The company continues to pay the premiums at its own expense.

Accidental Death Benefit Another common rider to life insurance is an accidental death benefit, sometimes called **double indemnity.** Double indemnity pays twice the value of the policy if you are killed in an accident. Again, the accident must occur before a certain age, generally 60 to 65. Experts counsel against adding this rider to your coverage. The benefit is very expensive, and your chances of dying in an accident are slim.

> **double indemnity** A benefit under which the company pays twice the face value of the policy if the insured's death results from an accident.

Guaranteed Insurability Option   A third important rider is known as a guaranteed insurability option. This rider allows you to buy a specified additional amount of life insurance at certain intervals without undergoing medical exams. This is a good option for people who anticipate needing more life insurance in the future.

Cost-of-Living Protection   This special rider is designed to help prevent inflation from eroding the purchasing power of the protection your policy provides. A *loss, reduction,* or *erosion of purchasing power* refers to the impact inflation has on a fixed amount of money. As inflation increases the cost of goods and services, that fixed amount will not buy as much in the future as it does today. Exhibit 10–4 shows the effects of inflation on a $100,000 life insurance policy. However, your insurance needs are likely to be smaller in later years.

Accelerated Benefits   *Accelerated benefits,* also known as *living benefits,* are life insurance policy proceeds paid to the policyholder who is terminally ill before he or she dies. The benefits may be provided for directly in the policies, but more often they are added by riders or attachments to new or existing policies. A representative list of insurers that offer accelerated benefits is available from the National Insurance Consumer Helpline (NICH) at 1-800-942-4242. Although more than 150 companies offer some form of accelerated benefits, not all plans are approved in all states. NICH cannot tell you whether a particular plan is approved in any given state. For more information, check with your insurance agent or your state department of insurance.

Second-to-Die Option   A *second-to-die life insurance policy,* also called *survivorship life,* insures two lives, usually husband and wife. The death benefit is paid when the second spouse dies. Usually a second-to-die policy is intended to pay estate taxes when both spouses die. However, some attorneys claim that with the right legal advice, you can minimize or avoid estate taxes completely.

Now that you know the various types of life insurance policies and the major provisions of and riders to such policies, you are ready to make your buying decisions.

 CAUTION!

Each rating agency uses its own criteria to determine financial ratings. Even though all use an "A," "B," or "C" grading system, what is "A" for one might be "AA+" or "Aa1" for another.

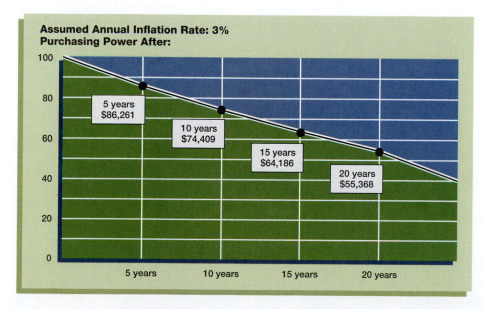

Exhibit 10–4

Effects of Inflation on a $100,000 Life Insurance Policy

SOURCE: *The TIAA Guide to Life Insurance Planning for People in Education* (New York: Teachers Insurance and Annuity Association, January 1997), p. 8.

Buying Life Insurance

You should consider a number of factors before buying life insurance. As discussed earlier in this chapter, these factors include your present and future sources of income, other savings and income protection, group life insurance, group annuities (or other pension benefits), Social Security, and, of course, the financial strength of the company.

FROM WHOM TO BUY?   Look for insurance coverage from financially strong companies with professionally qualified representatives. It is not unusual for a relationship with an insurance company to extend over a period of 20, 30, or even 50 years. For that reason alone you should choose carefully when deciding on an insurance company or an insurance agent. Fortunately, you have a choice of sources.

Sources   Protection is available from a wide range of private and public sources, including insurance companies and their representatives; private groups such as employers, labor unions, and professional or fraternal organizations; government programs such as Medicare and Social Security; and financial institutions and manufacturers offering credit insurance.

Rating Insurance Companies   Some of the strongest, most reputable insurance companies in the nation provide excellent insurance coverage at reasonable costs. In fact, the financial strength of an insurance company may be a major factor in holding down premium costs for consumers.

Locate an insurance company by checking the reputations of local agencies. Ask members of your family, friends, or colleagues about the insurers they prefer. Exhibit 10–5 describes the rating systems used by A. M. Best and the other big four rating agencies.

Choosing Your Insurance Agent   An insurance agent handles the technical side of insurance. However, that's only the beginning. The really important part of the agent's job is to apply his or her knowledge of insurance to help you select the proper kind of protection within your financial boundaries.

Is it ethical for an attorney who is also a licensed insurance agent to sell life insurance to clients? Yes, according to experts, if terms are fair and reasonable to you and you consent in writing to the terms of the transactions and to the conflict of interest.

Choosing a good agent is among the most important steps in building your insurance program. How do you find an agent? One of the best ways to begin is by asking your parents, friends, neighbors, and others for their recommendations. The "Personal Finance in Practice" box offers guidelines for choosing an insurance agent.

COMPARING POLICY COSTS   Each life insurance company designs the policies it sells to make them attractive and useful to many policyholders. One policy may have features another policy doesn't; one company may be more selective than another company; one company may get a better return on its investments than another company. These and other factors affect the prices of life insurance policies.

In brief, five factors affect the price a company charges for a life insurance policy: the company's cost of doing business, the return on its investments, the mortality rate it expects among its policyholders, the features the policy contains, and competition among companies with comparable policies.

Personal Finance in Practice

Checklist for Choosing an Insurance Agent

	Yes	No
1. Is your agent available when needed? Clients sometimes have problems that need immediate answers.	☐	☐
2. Does your agent advise you to have a financial plan? Each part of the plan should be necessary to your overall financial protection.	☐	☐
3. Does your agent pressure you? You should be free to make your own decisions about insurance coverage.	☐	☐
4. Does your agent keep up with changes in the insurance field? Agents often attend special classes or study on their own so that they can serve their clients better.	☐	☐
5. Is your agent happy to answer questions? Does he or she want you to know exactly what you are paying for an insurance policy?	☐	☐

Exhibit 10–5

Rating Systems of Major Rating Agencies
You Should Deal with Companies Rated Superior or Excellent

	A. M. Best	Standard & Poor's, Duff & Phelps	Moody's	Weiss Research
Superior	A++	AAA	Aaa	A+
	A+			
Excellent	A	AA+	Aa1	A
	A−	AA	Aa2	A−
		AA−	Aa3	B+
Good	B++	A+	A1	B
	B+	A	A2	B−
		A−	A3	C+
Adequate	B	BBB+	Baa1	C
	B−	BBB	Baa2	C−
		BBB−	Baa3	D+
Below average	C++	BB+	Ba1	D
	C+	BB	Ba2	D−
		BB−	Ba3	E+
Weak	C	B+	B1	E
	C−	B	B2	E−
	D	B−	B3	
Nonviable	E	CCC	Caa	F
	F	CC	Ca	
		C, D	C	

Personal Finance in Practice

Ten Golden Rules of Buying Life Insurance

Remember that your need for life insurance coverage will change over time. Your income may go up or down, or your family size might change. Therefore, it is wise to review your coverage periodically to ensure that it keeps up with your changing needs.

Follow these rules when buying life insurance	Done
1. Understand and know what your life insurance needs are before you make any purchase, and make sure the company you choose can meet those needs.	☐
2. Buy your life insurance from a company that is licensed in your state.	☐
3. Select an agent who is competent, knowledgeable, and trustworthy.	☐
4. Shop around and compare costs.	☐
5. Buy only the amount of life insurance you need and can afford.	☐
6. Ask about lower premium rates for nonsmokers.	☐
7. Read your policy and make sure you understand it.	☐
8. Inform your beneficiaries about the kinds and amount of life insurance you own.	☐
9. Keep your policy in a safe place at home, and keep your insurance company's name and your policy number in a safe deposit box.	☐
10. Check your coverage periodically, or whenever your situation changes, to ensure that it meets your current needs.	☐

SOURCE: American Council of Life Insurance, 1001 Pennsylvania Avenue NW, Washington, DC 20004-2599.

---

interest-adjusted index A method of evaluating the cost of life insurance by taking into account the time value of money.

Consider the time value of money in comparing policy costs. Ask your agent to give you interest-adjusted indexes. An **interest-adjusted index** is a method of evaluating the cost of life insurance by taking into account the time value of money. Highly complex mathematical calculations and formulas combine premium payments, dividends, cash-value buildup, and present value analysis into an index number that makes possible a fairly accurate cost comparison among insurance companies. The lower the index number, the lower the cost of the policy. The nearby "Figure It Out!" box shows how to use an interest-adjusted index to compare the costs of insurance.

OBTAINING AND EXAMINING A POLICY A life insurance policy is issued after you submit an application for insurance and the insurance company accepts the application. The company determines your insurability by means of the information in your application, the results of a medical examination, and the inspection report. When you receive a life insurance policy, read every word of the contract and, if necessary, ask your agent for a point-by-point explanation of the language. Many insurance companies have rewritten their contracts to make them more understandable. These are legal documents, and you should be familiar with what they promise, even though they use technical terms.

After you buy new life insurance, you have a 10-day "free-look" period during which you can change your mind. If you do so, the company will return your premium without penalty.

CHOOSING SETTLEMENT OPTIONS Selecting the appropriate settlement option is an important part of designing a life insurance program. The most common

Figure It Out!

Determining the Cost of Insurance: The Time Value of Money

In determining the cost of insurance, don't overlook the time value of money. You must include as part of that cost the interest (opportunity cost) you would earn on money if you did not use it to pay insurance premiums. For many years, insurers did not assign a time value to money in making their sales presentations. Only recently has the insurance industry widely adopted interest-adjusted cost estimates.

If you fail to consider the time value of money, you may get the false impression that the insurance company is giving you something for nothing. Here is an example. Suppose you are 35 and have a $10,000 face amount, 20-year, limited-payment, participating policy. Your annual premium is $210, or $4,200 over the 20-year period. Your dividends over the 20-year payment period total $1,700, so your total net premium is $2,500 ($4,200 − $1,700). Yet the cash value of your policy at the end of 20 years is $4,600. If you disregard the interest your premiums could otherwise have earned, you might get the impression that the insurance company is giving you $2,100 more than you paid ($4,600 − $2,500). But if you consider the time value of money (or its opportunity cost), the insurance company is

not giving you $2,100. What if you had invested the annual premiums in a conservative stock mutual fund? At an 8 percent annual yield, your account would have accumulated to $9,610 in 20 years. (See Exhibit 1–B.) Therefore, instead of having received $2,100 from the insurance company, you have paid the company $5,010 for 20 years of insurance protection:

Premiums you paid over 20 years	$4,200	
Time value of money	5,410	($9,610 − $4,200)
Total cost	9,610	
Cash value	4,600	
Net cost of insurance	5,010	($9,610 − $4,600)

Be sure to request interest-adjusted indexes from your agent; if he or she doesn't give them to you, look for another agent. As you have seen in the example, you can compare the costs among insurance companies by combining premium payments, dividends, cash-value buildup, and present value analysis into an index number.

---

settlement options are lump-sum payment, limited installment payment, life income option, and proceeds left with the company.

Lump-Sum Payment The insurance company pays the face amount of the policy in one installment to the beneficiary or to the estate of the insured. This form of settlement is the most widely used option.

Limited Installment Payment This option provides for payment of the life insurance proceeds in equal periodic installments for a specified number of years after your death.

Life Income Option Under the life income option, payments are made to the beneficiary for as long as she or he lives. The amount of each payment is based primarily on the sex and attained age of the beneficiary at the time of the insured's death.

Proceeds Left with the Company The life insurance proceeds are left with the insurance company at a specified rate of interest. The company acts as trustee and pays the interest to the beneficiary. The guaranteed minimum interest rate paid on the proceeds varies among companies.

SWITCHING POLICIES Think twice if your agent suggests that you replace the whole life or universal life insurance you already own. Before you give up this protection, make sure you are still insurable (check medical and any other qualification requirements). Ask your agent or company for an opinion about the new proposal to get both sides of the argument. The nearby "Personal Finance in Practice" box presents 10 important guidelines for purchasing life insurance.

 CAUTION!
Never buy coverage you don't understand. It is the agent's responsibility to explain your coverage in terms you can understand.

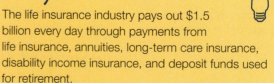 *did you know?*
The life insurance industry pays out $1.5 billion every day through payments from life insurance, annuities, long-term care insurance, disability income insurance, and deposit funds used for retirement.

Sheet 34 Life Insurance Policy Comparison

PRACTICE QUIZ 10-3

1. What are the key provisions in a life insurance policy?

2. What is a rider?

3. What are the various riders in a life insurance policy?

4. What factors do you consider in choosing an insurance agent?

5. What are the four most common settlement options?

6. Match the following terms with the appropriate definition:

endowment	a. A person named to receive the benefits from an insurance policy. _____
beneficiary	b. Provides coverage for a specific period of time and pays an agreed-upon sum of money to the policyholder if he or she is still living at the end of the period. _____
whole life insurance	c. A permanent policy for which the policyholder pays a specified premium for the rest of his or her life. _____
double indemnity	d. A rider to a life insurance policy that pays twice the value of the policy if the policyholder is killed in an accident. _____

Apply Yourself!

Examine your life insurance policies and the policies of other members of your family. Note the contractual provisions of each policy. What does the company promise to do in return for premiums?

LO10.4

Recognize how annuities provide financial security.

ACTION ITEM

An annuity protects me against the risk of outliving my assets.

☐ Yes ☐ No

annuity A contract that provides a regular income for as long as the person lives.

Financial Planning with Annuities

As you have seen so far, life insurance provides a set sum of money at your death. However, if you want to enjoy benefits while you are still alive, you might consider annuities. An annuity protects you against the risk of outliving your assets.

An **annuity** is a financial contract written by an insurance company that provides you with regular income. Generally, you receive the income monthly, often with payments arranged to continue for as long as you live. Annuities may be fixed, providing a specific income for life, or variable, with payouts above a guaranteed minimum level dependent on investment return. The payments may begin at once (*immediate annuity*) or at some future date (*deferred annuity*).

IMMEDIATE ANNUITIES People approaching retirement age can purchase immediate annuities. These annuities provide income payments at once. They are usually purchased with a lump-sum payment. When you are 65, you may no longer need all of your life insurance coverage—especially if you have grown children. You may decide to convert the cash value of your insurance policy into a lump-sum payment for an immediate annuity.

DEFERRED ANNUITIES With deferred annuities, income payments start at some future date. Meanwhile, interest accumulates on the money you deposit. Younger people often buy such annuities to save money toward retirement. A deferred annuity purchased with a lump-sum payment is known as a *single-premium deferred annuity*. A premium is the payment you make. These annuities are popular because of the greater potential for tax-free growth. If you are buying a deferred annuity on an installment basis, you may want one that allows flexible premiums, or payments. That means that your contributions can vary from year to year.

As with the life insurance principle, discussed earlier, the predictable mortality experience of a large group of individuals is fundamental to the annuity principle. By determining the average number of years a large number of persons in a given age group will live, the insurance company can calculate the annual amounts to pay to each person in the group over his or her entire life.

Because the annual payouts per premium amount are determined by average mortality experience, annuity contracts are more attractive for people whose present health, living habits, and family mortality experience suggest that they are likely to live longer than average. As a general rule, annuities are not advisable for people in poor health, although exceptions to this rule exist.

INDEX ANNUITIES A type of fixed annuity, an index annuity, has earnings that accumulate at a rate based on a formula linked to one or more equity-based indexes, such as the S&P 500. Index annuities may offer death benefit protection.

Why Buy Annuities?

A primary reason for buying an annuity is to give you retirement income for the rest of your life. You should fully fund your IRAs, Keoghs, and 401(k)s before considering annuities. We discuss retirement income in Chapter 14.

Although people have been buying annuities for many years, the appeal of variable annuities increased during the mid-1990s due to a rising stock market. A *fixed annuity* states that the annuitant (the person who is to receive the annuity) will receive a fixed amount of income over a certain period or for life. With a *variable annuity,* the monthly payments vary because they are based on the income received from stocks or other investments.

CAUTION!

An annuity is a long-term financial contract. You should enter into an annuity arrangement only after a thorough review of your personal finances and retirement goals.

Today, variable annuities are part of the retirement and investment plans of many Americans. Before buying any variable annuity, however, request a prospectus from the insurance company or from your insurance agent and read it carefully. The prospectus contains important information about the annuity contract, including fees and charges, investment options, death benefits, and annuity payout options. Compare the benefits and costs of the annuity to other variable annuities and to other types of investments, such as mutual funds, discussed in Chapter 13.

Some of the growth in the use of annuities can be attributed to the passage of the Employee Retirement Income Security Act (ERISA) of 1974. Annuities are often purchased for individual retirement accounts (IRAs), which ERISA made possible. They may also be used in Keogh-type plans for self-employed people. As you will see in Chapter 14, contributions to both IRA and Keogh plans are tax-deductible up to specified limits.

Costs of Annuities

You will pay several charges when you purchase a variable annuity. Be sure you understand all the costs before you invest. These costs will reduce the value of your account and the return on your investment. The most common costs are:

- *Surrender charges.* The insurance company will assess a "surrender" charge if you withdraw money within a certain period, usually within 6 to 8 years. Generally, the surrender charge declines gradually over a period of 7 to 10 years.

EXAMPLE: Surrender Charge

You purchase a variable annuity contract with a $10,000 purchase payment. The contract has a schedule of surrender charges, beginning with a 7 percent charge in the first year, and declining by 1 percent each year. In addition, you are allowed to withdraw 10 percent of your contract value each year free of surrender charges. In the first year, you decide to withdraw $5,000, or one-half of your contract value of $10,000 (assuming that your contract value has not increased or decreased because of investment performance). In this case, you could withdraw $1,000 (10 percent of contract value) free of surrender charges, but you would pay a surrender charge of 7 percent, or $280, on the other $4,000 withdrawn.

- *Mortality and expense risk charge.* This charge is equal to a certain percentage of your account value, usually 1.25 percent per year. The charge compensates the insurance company for insurance risks it assumes under the annuity contract. Profit from the mortality and expense risk charge is sometimes used to pay the insurer's costs of selling the variable annuity, such as a commission paid to your financial professional for selling the variable annuity to you.

EXAMPLE: Mortality and Expense Risk Charge

Your variable annuity has a mortality and expense risk charge at an annual rate of 1.25 percent of account value. Your average account value during the year is $20,000, so you will pay $250 in mortality and expense risk charges that year.

- *Administrative fees.* Your insurance company may deduct fees to cover recordkeeping and other administrative expenses. The fee may be charged as a flat account maintenance fee (perhaps $25 or $30 per year) or as a percentage of your account value (usually 0.15 percent per year).

EXAMPLE: Administrative Fees

Your variable annuity charges administrative fees at an annual rate of 0.15 percent of account value. Your average account value during the year is $50,000. You will pay $75 in administrative fees.

- *Fund expenses.* You will also indirectly pay the fees and expenses imposed by the mutual funds that are the underlying investment options for your variable annuity.

Read the "Kiplinger's Personal Finance" box to learn more about the costs and benefits of variable annuities.

Tax Considerations

When you buy an annuity, the interest on the principal, as well as the interest compounded on that interest, builds up free of current income tax. The Tax Reform Act of 1986 preserves

A Tolerable Annuity

I never thought that I would write a positive article about a variable annuity. As an investment advisor, I get sales pitches almost daily touting the huge commissions I could make by *selling* variable annuities. The trouble is, what's potentially a good deal for me is usually a lousy deal for my clients, who could be stuck paying annual fees of 3% or more.

But Vanguard is now offering a guaranteed-income provision for its variable annuity, and that is causing me to reconsider. For a total annual cost of 1.45% to 1.55%—about half the industry average—you get a balanced portfolio of stocks and bonds. Plus, you get a guarantee that you'll receive a fixed sum annually—no matter how much the markets may decline.

How it works. A variable annuity is a hybrid: part investment, part insurance. Say you invest $100,000 in the Vanguard variable annuity. If you're between 59½ and 64 years old, you can withdraw 4.5%, or $4,500, in the first year (4%, or $4,000, for a couple). If you're older, your initial withdrawal percentage is slightly higher.

Assume that the stock and bond markets rally and that your account grows 10%, to $110,000, the next year. Instead of withdrawing $4,500, you can withdraw $4,950 from your account in the second year—a 10% increase. Now assume that the markets fall the following year, and your account shrinks from $110,000 to $90,000. Thanks to the income guarantee, you will still receive $4,950 that year. In other words, your minimum annual withdrawal benefit can never shrink below its previous high-water mark.

Investment accounts are valued once a year for the purpose of computing your high-water mark. The value of your account rises and falls with the markets but also declines with your annual withdrawals.

The Vanguard variable annuity has three investment options. The best, in my view, is an actively managed balanced fund that is virtually identical to Vanguard Wellington (symbol VWELX), which keeps 60% to 70% in stocks and the remainder in bonds. Or you can choose an option that invests 60% in Vanguard stock index funds and 40% in the firm's bond index funds, or a more conservative plan that keeps 40% in stock index funds and 60% in bond index funds. The Wellington option costs 0.60% annually; the others cost 0.50% a year.

Unlike many variable annuities, the terms of Vanguard's annuity are flexible. Say your investment account grows over the next decade and you decide that you don't need the guaranteed-withdrawal benefit. You can ask Vanguard to remove the benefit. You'll still have a variable annuity, but your annual expenses will drop by 0.95 percentage point. Why not hold on to the guarantee? Because, over

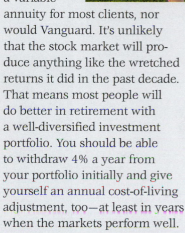

time, the additional charges of nearly 1% a year will be a significant drain on your returns.

I wouldn't recommend a variable annuity for most clients, nor would Vanguard. It's unlikely that the stock market will produce anything like the wretched returns it did in the past decade. That means most people will do better in retirement with a well-diversified investment portfolio. You should be able to withdraw 4% a year from your portfolio initially and give yourself an annual cost-of-living adjustment, too—at least in years when the markets perform well.

Is the Vanguard annuity right for you? If stocks make you nervous, check out Vanguard's low-cost variable annuity with a guaranteed payout. And it might be a good alternative if you have a higher-cost annuity you'd like to swap for a lower-cost one. To compare Vanguard's variable-annuity prices against others, try the free calculator at https://personal.vanguard.com/us/whatweoffer/annuities/costcalculator.

Bottom line: If you need guaranteed income and you are risk-averse, it's nice to know you can finally buy a product that meets your needs and doesn't charge an arm and a leg.

Steve Goldberg

SOURCE: Reprinted by permission from *Kiplinger's Personal Finance.* Copyright © 2012. The Kiplinger Washington Editors, Inc.

1. Why was the author of "A Tolerable Annuity" reluctant to write a positive article about a variable annuity?

2. What led the author to reconsider his opinion about variable annuities?

3. How does the Vanguard variable annuity differ from other variable annuities?

4. Does the author recommend a variable annuity for most clients? Explain your answer.

the tax advantage of annuities (and insurance) but curtails deductions for IRAs. With an annuity, there is no maximum annual contribution. Also, if you die during the accumulation period, your beneficiary is guaranteed no less than the amount invested.

Exhibit 10–6 shows the difference between an investment in an annuity and an investment in a certificate of deposit (CD). Remember, federal income tax on an annuity is deferred, whereas the tax on interest earned on a CD must be paid currently.

As with any other financial product, the advantages of annuities are tempered by drawbacks. In the case of variable annuities, these drawbacks include reduced flexibility and fees that lower investment return.

Exhibit 10–6

Tax-Deferred Fixed Annuity versus Taxable CD (a 30-year projection of performance; single deposit of $30,000)

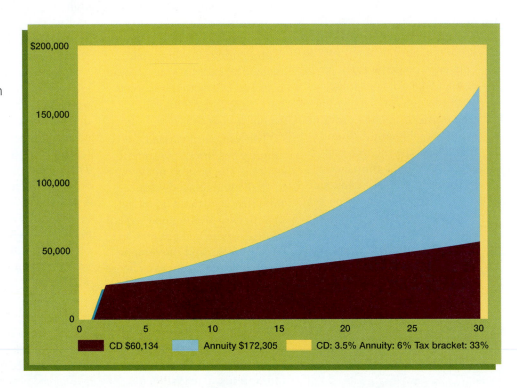

CD $60,134   Annuity $172,305   CD: 3.5% Annuity: 6% Tax bracket: 33%

PRACTICE QUIZ 10-4

1. What is an annuity?

2. What is the difference between an immediate and a deferred annuity?

3. As a general rule, are annuities advisable for people in poor health? Why or why not?

4. What are fixed and variable annuities?

Apply Yourself!

Interview friends, relatives, and others who have bought annuities. Which type of annuity did they purchase, and why?

YOUR PERSONAL FINANCE DASHBOARD

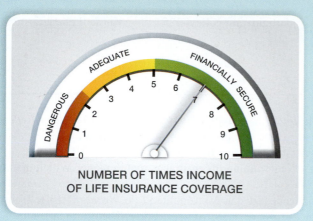

NUMBER OF TIMES INCOME
OF LIFE INSURANCE COVERAGE

A personal finance dashboard with key performance indicators can help you monitor your financial situation and guide you toward financial independence. Your need for life insurance will change with changes in your life. For example, if you are single or live with your parents, you may not need life insurance, unless you have a debt or want to provide for your parents, a friend, a relative, or charity. However, as children are born, your need for life insurance will increase. As children grow older and leave the nest, you will probably need less insurance.

YOUR SITUATION: Do you know if you need life insurance? Have you taken time to consider why you need life insurance and to find a sales agent who is knowledgeable and trustworthy? Have you evaluated the advantages and disadvantages of term life, whole life, and other life insurance options available to you?

POSSIBLE ACTIONS TO TAKE

✔ *Reconsider your responses to the "Action Items" (in the text margin) in the chapter to determine actions you might take to improve your life insurance requirements.*

✔ *Check if your employer provides life insurance through group insurance plans. In most cases, your employer will pay part or all of the cost of such insurance.*

✔ *Choose a reputable life insurance company; then obtain and compare premiums for $100,000 term, whole life, and universal life insurance.*

✔ *Examine your life insurance policy and note its contractual provisions. What does the company promise to do in return for premiums?*

✔ *For more information on life insurance, visit www.accuquote.com, www.acli.com, www.iii.org, www.InsureUonline.org, and www.insure.com.*

LO10.1 Life insurance protects the people who depend on you from financial losses caused by your death. You can use the easy method, the DINK method, the "nonworking" spouse method, or the "family need" method to determine your life insurance needs.

LO10.2 Two types of insurance companies—stock and mutual—sell nonparticipating and participating policies. Both sell two basic types of insurance: term life and whole life. Many variations and combinations of these types are available.

LO10.3 Most life insurance policies have standard features. An insurance company can change the conditions of a policy by adding a rider to it.

Before buying life insurance, consider all your present and future sources of income; then compare the costs and choose appropriate settlement options.

LO10.4 An annuity pays while you live, whereas life insurance pays when you die. With a fixed annuity, you receive a fixed amount of income over a certain period or for life. With a variable annuity, the monthly payments vary because they are based on the income received from stocks or other investments.

Chapter Summary

annuity 336

beneficiary 321

cash value 327

double indemnity 330

interest-adjusted index 334

nonforfeiture clause 330

nonparticipating
policy 325

participating policy 325

rider 330

term insurance 326

universal life
insurance 328

whole life insurance 327

Discussion Questions

1. Choose a current issue of *Money, Kiplinger's Personal Finance, Consumer Reports,* or *Worth* and summarize an article that provides information on human life expectancy and how life insurance may provide financial security.   (LO10.1)
2. Analyze the four methods of determining life insurance requirements. Which method is best, and why? (LO10.1)
3. Visit a few websites of companies such as Metropolitan Life, New York Life, Transamerica Life, Lincoln Benefit Life, or others of your choice. Then summarize the various types of insurance coverage available from these companies.   (LO10.2)
4. Contact your state insurance department to get information about whether your state requires interest-adjusted cost disclosure. Summarize your findings.   (LO10.3)
5. Review the settlement options on your family's life insurance policies, and discuss with your family which option would be the best choice for them at this time.   (LO10.3)
6. Is it legal or ethical for an insurance agent to suggest a variable life insurance policy to an 80-year-old man? Explain your answer.   (LO10.4)

Self-Test Problems

1. Suppose that yours is a typical family. Your annual income is $60,000. Use the easy method to determine your need for life insurance.
2. Using the "nonworking" spouse method, what should be the life insurance needs for a family whose youngest child is two years old?
3. Suppose your annual premium for a $20,000, twenty-year limited-payment policy is $420 over the twenty-year period. The cash value of your policy at the end of 20 years is $9,200. Assume that you could have invested the annual premium in a mutual fund yielding 7 percent annually. What is the net cost of your insurance for the 20-year period?

Solutions

1.

Current gross income	=	$60,000
Multiply gross income by 7 years	=	$420,000
Take 70 percent of $420,000	=	$420,000 × 0.70
Approximate insurance needed	=	$294,000

2.

Youngest child's age	=	2 years
16 years before the child is 18 years old		
Insurance needed 16 × $10,000	=	$160,000

3.

Premiums paid over 20 years	=	$420 × 20 = $8,400
Time value of 20-year annual payments of $420 at 7 percent yield.		
(See Exhibit 1–B; use a factor of 40.995)	=	40.995 × $420 = $17,218
Cash value	=	$9,200
Net cost of insurance	=	$17,218 − 9,200 = $8,018

342

1. You are the wage earner in a "typical family," with $40,000 gross annual income. Use the easy method to determine how much insurance you should carry.   (LO10.1)

2. You and your spouse are in good health and have reasonably secure careers. Each of you makes about $40,000 annually. You own a home with an $80,000 mortgage, and you owe $15,000 on car loans, $5,000 in personal debts, and $4,000 on credit card loans. You have no other debts. You have no plans to increase the size of your family in the near future. Estimate your total insurance needs using the DINK method.   (LO10.1)

3. Shaan and Anita are married and have two children, ages 4 and 7. Anita is a "non-working" spouse who devotes all of her time to household activities. Estimate how much life insurance Shaan and Anita should carry.   (LO10.1)

4. Obtain premium rates for $50,000 whole life, universal life, and term life policies from local insurance agents. Compare the costs and provisions of these policies.   (LO10.2)

5. Use the "Figure It Out!" worksheet in this chapter to calculate your own life insurance needs.   (LO10.1)

6. Use Exhibit 10–1 to find the average number of additional years a 25-year-old male and female are expected to live, based on the statistics gathered by the U.S. government as of 2009.   (LO10.1)

7. Mark and Parveen are the parents of three young children. Mark is a store manager in a local supermarket. His gross salary is $75,000 per year. Parveen is a full-time stay-at-home mom. Use the easy method to estimate the family's life insurance needs.   (LO10.1)

8. You are a dual-income, no-kids family. You and your spouse have the following debts (total): mortgage, $200,000; auto loan, $10,000; credit card balance, $4,000; other debts, $10,000. Further, you estimate that your funeral will cost $8,000. Your spouse expects to continue to work after your death. Using the DINK method, what should be your need for life insurance?   (LO10.1)

9. Using the "nonworking" spouse method, what should be the life insurance needs for a family whose youngest child is 10 years old?   (LO10.1)

10. Using the "nonworking" spouse method, what should be the life insurance needs for a family whose youngest child is five years old?   (LO10.1)

11. Your variable annuity charges administrative fees at an annual rate of 0.15 percent of account value. Your average account value during the year is $200,000. What is the administrative fee for the year?   (LO10.4)

12. Sophia purchased a variable annuity contract with $25,000 purchase payment. Surrender charges begin with 7 percent in the first year and decline by 1 percent each year. In addition, Sophia can withdraw 10 percent of her contract value each year without paying surrender charges. In the first year, Sophia needed to withdraw $6,000. Assume that the contract value had not increased or decreased because of investment performance. What was the surrender charge Sophia had to pay?   (LO10.4)

13. Shelly's variable annuity has a mortality and expense risk charge at an annual rate of 1.25 percent of account value. Her account value during the year is $50,000. What was Shelly's mortality and expense risk charge for the year?   (LO10.4)

connect |FINANCE To reinforce the content in this chapter, more problems are provided at connect.mheducation.com.

LIFE INSURANCE FOR THE YOUNG MARRIED

Jeff and Ann are both 28 years old. They have been married for three years, and they have a son who is almost two. They expect their second child in a few months.

Jeff is a teller in a local bank. He has just received a $30-a-week raise. His income is $480 a week, which, after taxes, leaves him with $1,648 a month. His company provides $20,000 of life insurance, a medical/hospital/surgical plan, and a major medical plan. All of these group plans protect him as long as he stays with the bank.

When Jeff received his raise, he decided that part of it should be used to add to his family's protection. Jeff and Ann talked to their insurance agent, who reviewed the insurance Jeff obtained through his job. Under Social Security, they also had some basic protection against the loss of Jeff's income if he became totally disabled or if he died before the children were 18.

But most of this protection was only basic, a kind of floor for Jeff and Ann to build on. For example, monthly Social Security payments to Ann would be approximately $1,250 if Jeff died leaving two children under age 18. Yet the family's total expenses would soon be higher after the birth of the second baby. Although the family's expenses would be lowered if Jeff died, they would be at least $250 a month more than Social Security would provide.

Questions

1. What type of policy would you suggest for Jeff and Ann? Why?
2. In your opinion do Jeff and Ann need additional insurance? Why or why not?

Continuing Case

FINANCIAL PLANNING WITH LIFE INSURANCE

Surprise! Jamie Lee and Ross were stunned to find that their family of two has grown to a family of five. They were expecting twins until they found out the day they were born that they were actually the parents of triplets!

Ross immediately had worries of being able to provide for the growing family: diapers, formula, college expenses times three. What if something happened to him or Jamie Lee? How would the surviving parent be able to provide for such a large family?

Current Financial Situation

Assets *(Jamie Lee and Ross combined):*
Checking account, $2,500
Savings account, $16,000
Emergency fund savings account, $19,100
IRA balance, $25,000
Cars, $11,500 (Jamie Lee) and $19,000 (Ross)

Liabilities *(Jamie Lee and Ross combined):*
Student loan balance, $0
Credit card balance, $3,500
Car loans, $7,000

Income:
Jamie Lee, $45,000 gross income ($31,500 net income after taxes)
Ross, $73,000 gross income ($60,800 net income after taxes)

Monthly Expenses
Mortgage, $1,225
Property taxes, $400
Homeowner's insurance, $200
Utilities, $160
Food, $500
Gas/Maintenance, $275
Credit card payment, $275
Car loan payment, $289
Entertainment, $125

Questions

1. Within days of the triplets' arrival, Jamie Lee and Ross began researching and comparing various agencies for the purchase of a life insurance policy. What characteristics should Ross look for when choosing a life insurance agency? What sources could he reference for help when choosing a life insurance agency?
2. Jamie Lee and Ross need to ensure that the surviving spouse and the children will not have financial hardship in the event of a loss. Using the easy method and considering Ross's salary in the calculation, how much life insurance will they need?

3. With so many policy variations to choose from, Ross and Jamie Lee are unsure which company is offering the most competitive rates. How will they be able to compare the rates between the various companies?

4. Jamie Lee and Ross have a limited budget for the life insurance necessity now that they have the additional present-day expenses of the triplets to consider. What type of life insurance would you recommend for the family at this life stage, and what are its associated advantages and disadvantages?

Spending Diary

"I'M NOT SURE SPENDING FOR LIFE INSURANCE IS NECESSARY FOR MY LIFE SITUATION."

Directions As you continue to record and monitor spending in various categories, be sure to consider how various decisions will affect your long-term financial security. Various comments you record might remind you to consider possible changes you might want to make in your spending habits. The Daily Spending Diary sheets are located in Appendix D at the end of the book and in Connect Finance.

Questions

1. Are there any spending amounts or items that you might consider reducing or eliminating?

2. What actions might you consider now or in the future regarding spending on life insurance?

Name: _____ **Date:** _____

Determining Life Insurance Needs

Purpose: To estimate life insurance coverage needed to cover expected expenses and future family living costs.

Financial Planning Activities: Estimate the amounts for the categories listed below. This sheet is also available in an Excel spreadsheet format in Connect Finance.

Suggested Websites: www.insure.com   www.kiplinger.com/tools/

Household expenses to be covered

Final expenses (funeral, estate taxes, etc.)	1 $ _____
Payment of consumer debt amounts	2 $ _____
Emergency fund	3 $ _____
College fund	4 $ _____

Expected living expenses:

Average living expense	$ _____
Spouse's income after taxes	$ − _____
Annual Social Security benefits	$ − _____
Net annual living expenses	$ _____
Years until spouse is 90	$ _____
Investment rate factor (see below)	$ _____

Total living expenses	5 $ _____
Total monetary needs (1 + 2 + 3 + 4 + 5)	$ _____
Less: Total current investments	$ _____
Life insurance needs	$ _____

Investment rate factors

Years until spouse is 90	25	30	35	40	45	50	55	60
Conservative investment	20	22	25	27	30	31	33	35
Aggressive investment	16	17	19	20	21	21	22	23

Note: Use "Your Personal Financial Plan" sheet 34 to compare life insurance policies.

What's Next for Your Personal Financial Plan?

- Survey several people to determine their reasons for buying life insurance.
- Talk to an insurance agent to compare the rates charged by different companies and for different age categories.

Name: _____ **Date:** _____

Life Insurance Policy Comparison

Purpose: To research and compare companies, coverages, and costs for different insurance policies.

Financial Planning Activities: Analyze ads and contact life insurance agents to obtain the information requested below. This sheet is also available in an Excel spreadsheet format in Connect Finance.

Suggested Websites: www.insure.com   www.accuquote.com

Age:

Company			
Agent's name, address, and phone			
Type of insurance (term, straight/whole, limited payment, endowment, universal)			
Type of policy (individual, group)			
Amount of coverage			
Frequency of payment (monthly, quarterly, semiannually, annually)			
Premium amount			
Other costs: • Service charges • Physical exam			
Rate of return (annual percentage increase in cash value; not applicable for term policies)			
Benefits of insurance as stated in ad or by agent			
Potential problems or disadvantages of this coverage			

Suggested App:
• LIFE Foundation

What's Next for Your Personal Financial Plan?

- Talk to a life insurance agent to obtain information on the methods he or she suggests for determining the amount of life insurance a person should have.
- Research the differences in premium costs between a mutual and a stock company.

11 Investing Basics and Evaluating Bonds

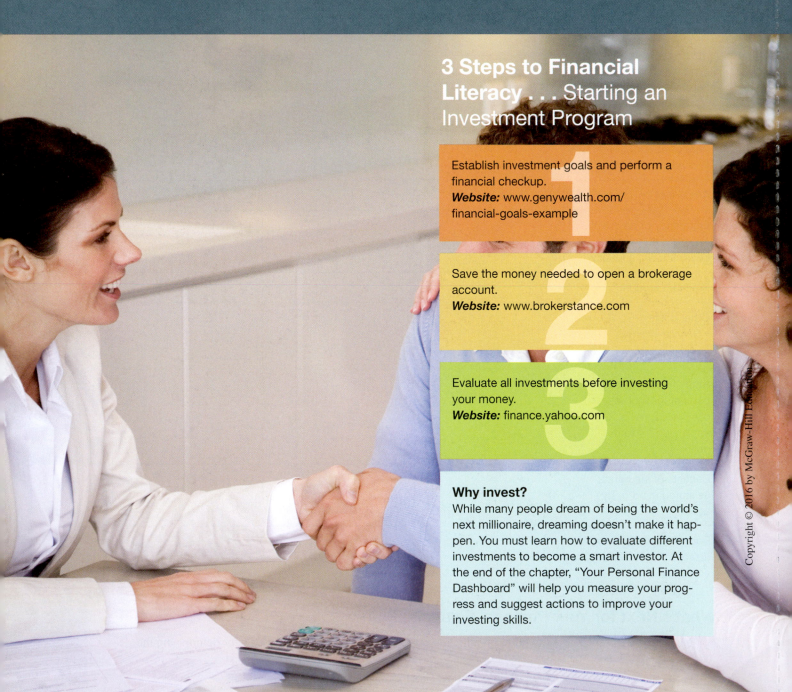

3 Steps to Financial Literacy . . . Starting an Investment Program

1 Establish investment goals and perform a financial checkup.
Website: www.genywealth.com/financial-goals-example

2 Save the money needed to open a brokerage account.
Website: www.brokerstance.com

3 Evaluate all investments before investing your money.
Website: finance.yahoo.com

Why invest?

While many people dream of being the world's next millionaire, dreaming doesn't make it happen. You must learn how to evaluate different investments to become a smart investor. At the end of the chapter, "Your Personal Finance Dashboard" will help you measure your progress and suggest actions to improve your investing skills.

CHAPTER 11 LEARNING OBJECTIVES

In this chapter, you will learn to:

LO11.1 Explain why you should establish an investment program.

LO11.2 Describe how safety, risk, income, growth, and liquidity affect your investment program.

LO11.3 Identify the factors that can reduce investment risk.

LO11.4 Understand why investors purchase government bonds.

LO11.5 Recognize why investors purchase corporate bonds.

LO11.6 Evaluate bonds when making an investment.

YOUR PERSONAL FINANCIAL PLAN SHEETS

35. Establishing Investment Goals
36. Assessing Risk for Investments
37. Evaluating Corporate Bonds

Preparing for an Investment Program

Many people ask the question: Why begin an investment program now? This chapter will help you understand the importance of beginning an investment program as soon as you can because the sooner you start an investment program, the more time your investments have to work for you.

Like other decisions, the decision to start an investment plan is one you must make for yourself. In fact, the *specific* goals you want to accomplish must be the driving force behind your investment plan.

Establishing Investment Goals

Some financial planners suggest that investment goals be stated in terms of money: By December 31, 2022, I will have total assets of $120,000. Other financial planners believe investors are more motivated to work toward goals that are stated in terms of the particular things they desire: By January 1, 2024, I will have accumulated enough money to purchase a second home in the mountains. Regardless of how they are stated, investment goals must be specific and measurable. The following questions will help you establish valid investment goals:

1. How much money do you need to satisfy your investment goals?
2. How much risk are you willing to assume in an investment program?
3. What possible economic or personal conditions could alter your investment goals?
4. Considering your economic circumstances and how long your investments can work for you, are your investment goals reasonable?
5. Are you willing to make the sacrifices necessary to ensure that you meet your investment goals?

LO11.1

Explain why you should establish an investment program.

ACTION ITEM

My investment goals are written down.

☐ **Yes**   ☐ **No**

Your investment goals are always oriented toward the future. For example, you may establish a short-term goal of accumulating $3,000 in a savings account over the next 12 months. You may then use the $3,000 to purchase stocks or mutual funds to help you obtain your intermediate or long-term investment goals.

Performing a Financial Checkup

In this section, we examine several factors you should consider before making your first investment.

ETHICAL CONCERNS: PAYING YOUR BILLS ON TIME
While there are many reasons why people can't pay their bills on time, the problem often starts with people wanting more than they can afford. From both a legal *and* ethical standpoint, you have an obligation to pay for credit purchases. Moreover, business firms that extend credit expect you will pay for a product or service purchased when you use credit.

If you don't pay for products or services purchased on credit, there are serious repercussions. For example:

- Merchandise can be repossessed.
- A business can sue to recover the cost of the product or service.
- Your credit score can be lowered to reflect late or missed payments.
- The cost of additional credit, if available, may be higher because of lower credit scores or late or missed payments.

Some consumers believe the only way out of their financial problems is to declare personal bankruptcy, but think about the long-term consequences. First, filing bankruptcy is not cheap and most lawyers expect to be paid (usually in cash) before they file the necessary legal documents and represent you in court. Second, remember that bankruptcy will affect your ability to obtain future credit for a home, automobile, or other consumer purchases.

WORK TO BALANCE YOUR BUDGET
Many individuals regularly spend more than they make. They purchase items on credit and then must make monthly installment payments and pay finance charges ranging between 12 and 18 percent or higher. With this situation, investing in certificates of deposit, bonds, stocks, mutual funds, or other investments that might earn 1 to 10 percent makes no sense until credit card and installment purchases, along with the accompanying finance charges, are reduced or eliminated. A good rule of thumb is to limit consumer credit payments to 20 percent of your net (after-tax) income. Eventually, the amount of cash remaining after the bills are paid will increase and can be used to start a savings program or finance investments. For help balancing your budget, visit one of the following websites: Quicken at www.quicken.com; MoneyStrands at www.money.strands.com; or Mint at www.mint.com.

MANAGE YOUR CREDIT CARD DEBT
While all cardholders have reasons for using their credit cards, it is *very* easy to get in trouble by using your credit cards. Watch for the following five warning signs:

1. Experts suggest that you pay your credit card balance in full each month. One of the first warning signs is the inability to pay your entire balance each month.
2. Don't use your credit cards to pay for many small purchases during the month. Often this leads to a "real surprise" when you open your credit card statement and realize how much you spent during the month.
3. Don't use the cash advance provision that accompanies most credit cards. The reason is simple: The annual percentage rate is usually higher for cash advances.

Why Frugality Is Liberating

It lets you focus on what you really want.

*C*lare K. Levison is a CPA and author of "Frugal Isn't Cheap." She is a financial-literacy spokeswoman for the American Institute of Certified Public Accountants. Here are excerpts from Kiplinger's recent interview with Levison:

Isn't *frugality* a synonym for deprivation?

Some financial gurus make frugality all about abstinence, but I think it's about being smart—prioritizing and taking responsibility for your choices. It's not so much "I won't" or "I can't," but "I'd rather." Ask yourself: What is most important to me? Where will I put my discretionary dollars? What will I truly enjoy? What will enhance my life? The goal—to quote my book's subhead—is to "Spend less, save more, and live better."

I encourage people to find one thing each day that they can do to save money. Get out of the habit of spending when you're bored. Stay out of the malls, discount stores and online shopping sites. Call up a friend and have a chat, take your dog for a walk, go to the library to see what new books are available. Take care of the stuff you already have. Clean out your bedroom closet. It doesn't sound like fun, but no one who does any of those things says, "Gosh, I wish I hadn't done that."

Should I cut up my plastic?

No. We're moving away from a cash-based society. Online banking and other tools make it easy to check your accounts so that you're aware of what you're spending. You probably check Facebook and text messages every day. Just add this to your list. When you reach your spending limit, stop!

What do you think of tactics such as extreme couponing?

It's a version of hoarding, and it doesn't provide as good a return as it should. You spend all your time clipping coupons, and you accumulate 500 jars of mayo that you can't consume in a reasonable time. "But it's free!" you say. No matter. If you don't need it, it's no bargain. And you clutter up your life.

How can I save more?

Put your saving on autopilot. Have as much as 20% of your paycheck direct-deposited to savings. Save 80% of any raises or bonuses. And make it *exciting*. Saving is liberating, because you're not beholden to a bank, credit card company or your parents. You'll have money when you need it, which equates to independence and freedom—and *that's* exciting. Think of fun things that motivate you. Saving for retirement may sound difficult and boring, but how about saving for a condo on the beach when you're *x* years old?

Pat Mertz Esswein

1. In today's world where consumers are bombarded with advertisements to buy "everything," what specific steps can you take to spend less, save more, and live better?

2. What are the advantages of having part of your paycheck automatically deposited in a savings or investment account?

3. Why is it important to be motivated to save and invest for specific things that you want either now or in the future?

4. Think about the number of cards you really need. Most experts recommend that an individual have one or two cards and use those cards for emergencies.

5. Get help if you think you are in trouble. You may want to review the discussion on organizations that help people manage their finances presented in Chapter 5.

emergency fund An amount of money you can obtain quickly in case of immediate need.

START AN EMERGENCY FUND An **emergency fund** is an amount of money you can obtain quickly in case of immediate need. This money should be deposited in a savings account or in a money market mutual fund that provides immediate access to cash if needed.

Most financial planners agree that an amount equal to at least three months' living expenses is reasonable.

EXAMPLE: Calculating an Amount for Emergencies

If your monthly expenses total $1,800, you should save at least $5,400 before you can begin investing.

$$\text{Minimum emergency fund} = \text{Monthly expenses} \times 3 \text{ months}$$
$$= \$1,800 \times 3 \text{ months}$$
$$= \$5,400$$

Example from Your Life

$ _____ × 3 months = $ _____
  monthly expenses

HAVE ACCESS TO OTHER SOURCES OF CASH FOR EMERGENCY NEEDS

line of credit A short-term loan that is approved before the money is actually needed.

To meet unexpected emergencies, you may also want to establish a line of credit at a commercial bank, savings and loan association, or credit union. A **line of credit** is a short-term loan that is approved before you actually need the money.

The cash advance provision offered by major credit card companies can also be used in an emergency. However, both lines of credit and credit cards have a ceiling, or maximum dollar amount, that limits the amount of available credit. If you have already exhausted both of these sources of credit on everyday expenses, they will not be available in an emergency.

Getting the Money Needed to Start an Investment Program

How badly do you want to achieve your investment goals? Are you willing to sacrifice some purchases to provide financing for your investments? The answers to both questions are extremely important. Take Rita Johnson, a 32-year-old nurse in a large St. Louis hospital. As part of a divorce settlement in 2007, she received a cash payment of almost $55,000. At first, she was tempted to spend this money on a new BMW and new furniture. But after some careful planning, she decided to save $25,000 in a certificate of deposit and invest the remainder in a conservative mutual fund. On May 31, 2014, these investments were valued at $79,000.

What is important to you? What do you value? Each of these questions affects your investment goals. At one extreme are people who save or invest as much of each paycheck as they can. At

Suggestion	Comments
1. Pay yourself first.	Many financial experts recommend that you (1) pay your monthly bills, (2) save or invest a reasonable amount of money, and (3) use the money left over for personal expenses and entertainment.
2. Take advantage of employer-sponsored retirement programs.	Some employers will match part or all of the contributions you make to a company-sponsored retirement program.
3. Participate in an elective savings program.	You can elect to have money withheld from your paycheck each payday and automatically deposited in a savings or investment account.
4. Make a special savings effort one or two months each year.	By cutting back to the basics, you can obtain money for investment purposes.
5. Take advantage of gifts, inheritances, and windfalls.	Use money from unexpected sources to fund an investment program.

Exhibit **11–1**

Five Suggestions to Help You Accumulate the Money Needed to Fund Your Investments

the other extreme are people who spend everything they earn and run out of money before their next paycheck. Most people find either extreme unacceptable and take a more middle-of-the-road approach. These people often spend money on the items that make their lives more enjoyable and still save enough to fund an investment program. Suggestions to help you obtain the money you need to fund an investment program are listed in Exhibit 11–1.

For many people, the easiest way to begin an investment program is to participate in an employer-sponsored retirement account—often referred to as a 401(k) or a 403(b) account. Many employers will match part or all of your contributions to retirement accounts. For example, an employer may contribute $0.50 for every $1.00 the employee contributes up to a certain percentage of their annual salary. More information on different types of retirement accounts is provided in Chapter 14.

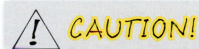

CAUTION!

Today, many employers are reducing or eliminating matching provisions in their employee retirement plans.

How the Time Value of Money Affects Your Investments

Many people never start an investment program because they have only small sums of money. But even small sums grow over a long period of time. Mary and Peter Miller, for example, began their investment program by investing $1,000 *each year* when they were in their 20s. Now 20 years later, their investment portfolio is worth over $40,000. How did they do it? They took advantage of the time value of money. Simply put: If you save money over a long period of time, make quality investments, and let the time value of money work, you can achieve the same type of result. The information in the nearby "Figure It Out!" box illustrates this important personal finance concept. For instance, assume you invest $2,500 each year for 30 years. Also, assume that the investment earns 6 percent each year. To determine how much your investment is worth at the end of 30 years, use the table in the "Figure It Out!" box and follow these steps:

1. Locate the table factor for 6 percent and 30 years.
2. The table factor is 79.058.
3. Multiply the $2,500 yearly investment by the 79.058 table factor.

$$\$2,500 \times 79.058 = \$197,645 \text{ total dollar return}$$

Figure It Out!

Using the Time Value of Money to Calculate Investment Returns

$2,000 invested each year at 4 percent for 40 years equals $190,052.

$2,000 invested each year at 11 percent for 40 years equals $1,163,660.

QUESTION

How do you calculate these amounts?

ANSWER: The calculations were based on the time value of money concept discussed in Chapter 1. The fact is that this type of calculation is so important to your investment program that it makes sense to review the concept. While you can calculate the answers by using a formula, many people find that it is easier to use a table factor from a future value table like the one illustrated below. To work the first problem, follow these steps:

1. Locate the table factor for 4 percent and 40 years.

2. The table factor is 95.026.

3. Multiply the $2,000 yearly deposit by the 95.026 table factor.

$$\$2,000 \times 95.026 = \$190,052$$

NOW IT'S YOUR TURN.

Using the table below, calculate the future value of a $1,500 annual investment that earns 7 percent a year for 25 years.

FUTURE VALUE (COMPOUNDED SUM) OF $1 PAID IN AT THE END OF EACH PERIOD OF A GIVEN NUMBER OF TIME PERIODS (AN ANNUITY)											
Period	**1%**	**2%**	**3%**	**4%**	**5%**	**6%**	**7%**	**8%**	**9%**	**10%**	**11%**
1	1.000	1.000	1.000	1.000	1.000	1.000	1.000	1.000	1.000	1.000	1.000
5	5.101	5.204	5.309	5.416	5.526	5.637	5.751	5.867	5.985	6.105	6.228
10	10.462	10.950	11.464	12.006	12.578	13.181	13.816	14.487	15.193	15.937	16.722
15	16.097	17.293	18.599	20.024	21.579	23.276	25.129	27.152	29.361	31.772	34.405
20	22.019	24.297	26.870	29.778	33.066	36.786	40.995	45.762	51.160	57.275	64.203
25	28.243	32.030	36.459	41.646	47.727	54.865	63.249	73.106	84.701	98.347	114.410
30	34.785	40.588	47.575	56.085	66.439	79.058	94.461	113.280	136.310	164.490	199.020
40	48.886	60.402	75.401	(95.026)	120.800	154.760	199.640	259.060	337.890	442.590	581.830

Tryout problem answer: $94,873.50

In this example, your investments total $75,000 ($2,500 × 30 years = $75,000). To determine your investment earnings during the 30-year period, subtract the total of all investments from the total dollar return at the end of 30 years ($197,645 − $75,000 = $122,645).

In this example, notice that the value of your investments increases each year because of two factors. First, it is assumed you will invest another $2,500 each year. Second, all investment earnings are allowed to accumulate and are added to your yearly deposits.

Also, notice that if investments earn a higher rate of return each year, *total* dollar returns increase dramatically. For example, a $2,000 annual investment that earns 11 percent a year is worth $1,163,660 at the end of 40 years, compared to $190,052 for a $2,000 investment that earns 4 percent each year for the same 40-year period. The rate of return and the length of time your money is invested *do* make a difference. The search for higher returns is one reason many investors choose stocks, mutual funds, and other investments that offer higher potential returns compared to certificates of deposit or government or corporate bonds.

 Sheet 35 Establishing Investment Goals

PRACTICE QUIZ 11–1

1. What factors should you consider when performing a financial checkup?

2. How can you obtain the money needed to begin investing?

3. In your own words, describe the time value of money concept and how it could affect your investment program.

Apply Yourself!

Visit the Mint website (www.mint.com) and describe the services available to individuals who need help managing their finances.

Factors Affecting the Choice of Investments

Although each investor may have specific, individual goals for investing, all investors must consider a number of factors before choosing an investment alternative.

Safety and Risk

The safety and risk factors are two sides of the same coin. *Safety* in an investment means minimal risk or loss. On the other hand, *risk* in an investment means a measure of uncertainty about the outcome. Investments range from very safe to very risky. At one end of the investment spectrum are very safe investments. Investments in this category include government bonds, savings accounts, certificates of deposit, and certain corporate bonds, stocks, and mutual funds. Real estate may also be a very safe investment. Investors pick investments that have less risk because they know there is very little chance that investments of this kind will become worthless.

At the other end of the investment spectrum are speculative investments. A **speculative investment** is a high-risk investment made in the hope of earning a relatively large profit in a short time. Such investments offer the possibility of a larger dollar return, but if they are unsuccessful, you may lose most or all of your initial investment. Speculative stocks, certain bonds, some mutual funds, some real estate, commodities, options, precious metals, precious stones, and collectibles are risk-oriented investments.

From an investor's standpoint, one basic rule sums up the relationship between the factors of safety and risk: *The potential return on any investment should be directly related to*

LO11.2

Describe how safety, risk, income, growth, and liquidity affect your investment program.

ACTION ITEM

I understand how the factors of safety and risk affect an investment decision.

☐ **Yes** ☐ **No**

speculative investment
A high-risk investment made in the hope of earning a relatively large profit in a short time.

the risk the investor assumes. The fact is there is some risk associated with all investments. In fact, you may experience two types of risks with many investments.

- First, investors often choose some investments because they provide a predictable source of income. For example, you may choose to purchase a stock because a corporation pays dividends. If the corporation experiences financial difficulties, it may reduce or omit dividend payments to stockholders. In other words, there is a risk that you will not receive income payments. With the exception of savings accounts and certificates of deposit, income payments are not guaranteed with most investments.
- A second type of risk associated with many investments is that an investment will decrease in value. For example, the value of Apple stock decreased approximately 10 percent in January 2014 when executives suggested that sales and profit growth may slow in the future.[1]

Exhibit 11–2 lists a number of factors related to safety and risk that can affect an investor's choice of investments.

Often beginning investors are afraid of the risk associated with many investments. But remember that without the risk, obtaining the larger returns that really make an investment program grow is impossible. To help you determine how much risk you are willing to assume, take the test for risk tolerance presented in Exhibit 11–3.

Components of the Risk Factor

When choosing an investment, you must carefully evaluate changes in the risk factor. In fact, the overall risk factor can be broken down into four components.

INFLATION RISK As defined in Chapter 1, inflation is a rise in the general level of prices. During periods of high inflation, there is a risk that the financial return on an investment will not keep pace with the inflation rate. To see how inflation reduces your buying power, let's assume you have deposited $10,000 in a certificate of deposit at 1 percent interest. At the end of one year, your money will have earned $100 in interest ($10,000 × 1% = $100). Assuming an inflation rate of 3 percent, it will cost you an additional $300 ($10,000 × 3% = $300), or a total of $10,300, to purchase the same amount of goods you could have purchased for $10,000 a year earlier. Thus, even though you earned $100, you lost $200 in purchasing power. And after paying taxes on the $100 interest, your loss of purchasing power is even greater.

INTEREST RATE RISK The interest rate risk associated with preferred stocks or government or corporate bonds is the result of changes in the interest rates in the economy. The value of these investments decreases when overall interest rates increase. In contrast,

Exhibit 11–2

Factors That Can Affect Your Tolerance for Risk and Your Investment Choices

Investments with Less Risk	Investments with Higher Risks
People with no financial training or investment background	Investors with financial training and investment background
Older investors	Younger investors
Lower-income investors	Higher-income investors
Families with children	Single individuals or married couples with no children
Employees worried about job loss	Employees with secure employment positions

[1]The Yahoo Finance website (http://finance.yahoo.com), accessed March 18, 2014.

Exhibit 11–3 A Quick Test to Measure Investment Risk

Read the statements below and choose the answer that most closely matches how you feel about investing.

	1–Not At All Like Me				5-Not Quite Sure			10–Fits Me Perfectly		
I would prefer to invest in the stock market than in more conservative investments like savings accounts, certificates of deposit, or bonds.	1	2	3	4	5	6	7	8	9	10
I like a lot of risk in my investments because I'm more likely to make money that way.	1	2	3	4	5	6	7	8	9	10
I look for short-term investments that I can buy and sell within a year.	1	2	3	4	5	6	7	8	9	10
Instead of a buy-and-hold strategy, I prefer to use the speculative techniques of buying stock on margin and selling short.	1	2	3	4	5	6	7	8	9	10
Sometimes, I use the money in my investment account for immediate cash needs or buy something I really want.	1	2	3	4	5	6	7	8	9	10

WHAT TYPE OF INVESTOR ARE YOU?
Total up your score from above, and write your score here: _____. Based on your score, what type of investor are you?

High-Risk Investor (38 to 50 points): You could be described as a speculative, aggressive investor. You enjoy the pursuit of high returns, and you realize that there will be ups and downs as you chase larger profits.

Moderate-Risk Investor (24 to 37 points): You are neither particularly conservative nor aggressive in your investment choices. You try to balance your desire to maximize your returns with your long-term desire for a comfortable and stable financial future and planning for retirement.

Low-Risk Investor (5 to 23 points): You could be described as a conservative investor. You aren't going to take risks to chase high returns, but you aren't going to suffer big losses either.

SOURCE: Adapted from the quiz "Determine your risk profile" on the Wells Fargo website (www.wellsfargo.com).

the value of these same investments increases when overall interest rates decrease. Assume you purchase a Microsoft corporate bond that pays 4.2 percent interest and hold it for three years before deciding to sell your bond. The value of your bond will decrease if interest rates for comparable bonds increase during the three-year period. On the other hand, the value of your Microsoft bond will increase if interest rates for comparable bonds decrease during the three-year period.

BUSINESS FAILURE RISK The risk of business failure is associated with investments in stock and corporate bonds or mutual funds that invest in stocks or bonds. With each of these investments, you face the possibility that bad management, unsuccessful products, competition, or a host of other factors will cause the business to be less profitable than originally anticipated or experience a loss. The business may even fail and be forced to file for bankruptcy, in which case your investment may become totally worthless.

MARKET RISK Economic growth is not as systematic and predictable as most investors might believe. Generally, a period of rapid expansion is followed by a period of recession. For instance, the business cycle—the recurring time period between economic expansion and recession—has lasted a little less than six years since World War II.[2]

The prices of stocks, bonds, mutual funds, and other investments may also fluctuate because of the behavior of investors in the marketplace and may have nothing to do with

[2]The Investopedia website (www.investopedia.com), accessed March 17, 2014.

the fundamental changes in the financial health of the corporations that issue these investments. Such fluctuations may be caused by political or social conditions. The price of petroleum stocks, for instance, may increase or decrease as a result of political activity in the Middle East.

Investment Income

Investors sometimes purchase certain investments because they want a predictable source of income. The most conservative investments—passbook savings accounts, certificates of deposit, and securities issued by the United States government—are also the most predictable sources of income. With these investments, you know exactly how much income will be paid on a specific date.

If investment income is a primary objective, you can also choose municipal bonds, corporate bonds, preferred stocks, utility stocks, or selected common stock issues. Other investments that may provide income potential are mutual funds and real estate rental property.

Investment Growth

To investors, *growth* means their investments will increase in value. Often the greatest opportunity for growth is an investment in common stock. Companies with earnings potential, sales revenues that are increasing, and managers who can solve the problems associated with rapid expansion are often considered to be growth companies. These same companies generally pay little or no dividends.

The money the companies keep can provide at least part of the financing they need for future growth and expansion and control the cost of borrowing money. As a result, they grow at an even faster pace. Growth financed by profits reinvested in the company normally increases the dollar value of a share of stock for the investor.

Other investments that may offer growth potential include mutual funds and real estate. For example, many mutual funds are referred to as growth funds or aggressive growth funds because of the growth potential of the individual securities included in the fund.

Investment Liquidity

liquidity The ability to buy or sell an investment quickly without substantially affecting the investment's value.

Liquidity is the ability to buy or sell an investment quickly without substantially affecting the investment's value. Investments range from near-cash investments to frozen investments from which it is virtually impossible to get your money. Interest-bearing checking and savings accounts are very liquid because they can be quickly converted to cash. Certificates of deposit impose penalties for withdrawing money before the maturity date. With other investments, you may be able to sell quickly, but market conditions, economic conditions, or many other factors may prevent you from regaining the amount you originally invested.

Sheet 36 Assessing Risk for Investments

PRACTICE QUIZ 11-2

1. Why are safety and risk two sides of the same coin?

2. In your own words, describe each of the four components of the risk factor.

3. How do income, growth, and liquidity affect the choice of an investment?

Factors That Reduce Investment Risk

Consider the following: Since 1926—almost 90 years—stocks have returned an average of almost 10 percent a year. During the same period, U.S. government securities earned just over 5 percent.[3] These facts suggest that everyone should invest in stocks because they offer the largest returns. In reality, stocks may have a place in your investment portfolio, but establishing an investment program is more than just picking a bunch of stocks or mutual funds that invest in stocks. Before making the decision to purchase stocks, consider the factors of portfolio management and asset allocation.

Asset Allocation and Diversification

Earlier in this chapter, we examined how safety, risk, income, growth, and liquidity affect your investment choices. Now let's compare the factors that affect the choice of investments with some typical investment alternatives. Exhibit 11–4 ranks each alternative in terms of safety, risk, income, growth, and liquidity. More detailed information on each investment alternative is provided later in this chapter and in Chapters 12 and 13.

ASSET ALLOCATION Asset allocation is the process of spreading your assets among several different types of investments to lessen risk. The term *asset allocation* is a fancy way of saying you need to diversify and avoid the pitfall of putting all your eggs in one basket. Asset allocation is often expressed in percentages. For example, what percentage of my assets do I want to put in stocks and mutual funds? What percentage do I want to put in bonds or certificates of deposit? The diversification provided by investing in *different* investments provides a measure of safety and reduces risk, because a loss in one type of investment is usually offset by gains from other types of investments. Typical investments include:

- Stocks issued by large corporations (large cap).
- Stocks issued by medium-size corporations (midcap).
- Stocks issued by small, rapidly growing companies (small cap).
- Foreign stocks.
- Bonds.
- Cash.

LO11.3

Identify the factors that can reduce investment risk.

ACTION ITEM

I use asset allocation to minimize risk when investing.

☐ Agree   ☐ Disagree

asset allocation The process of spreading your assets among several different types of investments to lessen risk.

---

[3]"Money 101 Lesson 4: Basics of Investing," *CNN/Money* (http://money.cnn.com/magazines/moneymag/money101/lesson4/index.htm), accessed March 19, 2014.

Exhibit **11–4**

Factors Used to Evaluate Traditional Investment Alternatives

Type of Investment	FACTORS TO BE EVALUATED				
	Safety	Risk	Income	Growth	Liquidity
Corporate stock	Average	Average	Average	High	Average
Corporate bonds	Average	Average	High	Low	Average
Government bonds	High	Low	Low	Low	High
Mutual funds	Average	Average	Average	Average	Average
Real estate	Average	Average	Average	Average	Low

Note: Mutual funds can also be included as an investment, but the typical mutual fund will invest in the securities just listed or a combination of these securities.

The percentage of your investments that should be invested in each asset class is determined by:

- Your age;
- Your investment objectives;
- How much you can save and invest each year;
- The dollar value of your current investments;
- The economic outlook for the economy; and
- Other factors.

Today, many personal finance websites provide asset allocation calculators to help you determine the right types of investments for your investment program. For example, the asset allocation calculator provided by Bankrate considers your age, tolerance for risk, how much you can save or invest each year, and some of the other factors mentioned above to determine the appropriate types of investments for your situation. To use this Bankrate calculator, go to www.bankrate.com and enter "asset allocation calculator" in the search window. Then supply the information required to build a customized investment program. You can also find other asset allocation calculators by using a search engine like Google or Yahoo!

To help you decide how much risk is appropriate for your investment program, many financial planners suggest that you think of your investment program as a pyramid consisting of four levels ranging from low risk to high risk, as illustrated in Exhibit 11–5. Regardless of which type of investment you choose for your investment program and the percentage you invest in each type, it may be necessary to adjust your asset allocation from time to time. Often, the main reasons for making changes are the amount of time that your investments have to work for you and your age.

THE TIME FACTOR The amount of time that your investments have to work for you is another important factor when managing your investment portfolio. Recall the investment returns presented earlier in this section. Since 1926, stocks have returned an average of almost 10 percent a year and returned more than other investment alternatives. And yet, during the same period, there were years when stocks decreased in value.[4] The point is that if you invested at the wrong time and then couldn't wait for the investment to recover, you lost money.

The amount of time you have before you need your investment money is crucial. If you can leave your long-term investments alone and let them work for 5 to 10 years or more, then you can invest in stocks and mutual funds. On the other hand, if you need your

[4]"Money 101 Lesson 4: Basics of Investing," *CNN/Money* (http://money.cnn.com/magazines/moneymag/money101/lesson4/index.htm), accessed March 19, 2014.

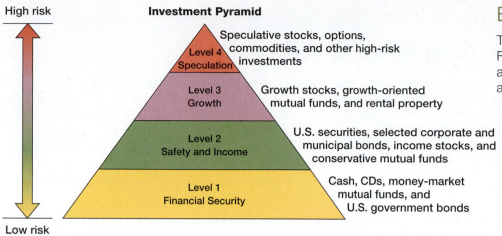

High risk

Investment Pyramid

**Level 4
Speculation** — Speculative stocks, options, commodities, and other high-risk investments

**Level 3
Growth** — Growth stocks, growth-oriented mutual funds, and rental property

**Level 2
Safety and Income** — U.S. securities, selected corporate and municipal bonds, income stocks, and conservative mutual funds

**Level 1
Financial Security** — Cash, CDs, money-market mutual funds, and U.S. government bonds

Low risk

Exhibit 11–5

Typical Investments for Financial Security, Safety and Income, Growth, and Speculation

investment money in two years or less, you should probably invest in short-term government bonds, highly rated corporate bonds, or certificates of deposit. By taking a more conservative approach for short-term investments, you reduce the possibility of having to sell your investments at a loss because of depressed market value or a staggering economy.

YOUR AGE A final factor to consider when choosing an investment is your age. Younger investors tend to invest a large percentage of their nest egg in growth-oriented investments. If their investments take a nosedive, they have time to recover. On the other hand, older investors tend to be more conservative and invest in government bonds, high-quality corporate bonds, and very safe corporate stocks or mutual funds. As a result, a smaller percentage of their nest egg is placed in growth-oriented investments.

Financial experts like Suze Orman, author of *The Road to Wealth,* suggest that you subtract your age from 110, and the difference is the percentage of your assets that should be invested in growth investments. For example, if you are 30 years old, subtract 30 from 110, which gives you 80. Therefore, 80 percent of your assets should be invested in growth-oriented investments while the remaining 20 percent should be kept in safer, conservative investments.[5]

Your Role in the Investment Process

Successful investors continually evaluate their investments. They never sit back and let their investments manage themselves. Some factors to consider when choosing different investments are described next.

EVALUATE POTENTIAL INVESTMENTS Let's assume you have $25,000 to invest. Also assume your investment will earn a 10 percent return the first year. At the end of one year, you will have earned $2,500 and your investment will be worth $27,500. Not a bad return on your original investment! Now ask yourself: How long would it take to earn $2,500 if I had to work for this amount of money at a job? For some people, it might take a month; for others, it might take longer. The point is that if you want this type of return, you should be willing to work for it, but the work takes a different form than a job. When choosing an investment, the work you invest is the time needed to research different investments so that you can make an informed decision. More information on evaluating different investment alternatives is presented at the end of this chapter and in Chapter 12 (stocks) and Chapter 13 (mutual funds).

[5]Suze Orman, *The Road to Wealth* (New York: Riverbend Books, 2001), p. 371.

Personal Finance in Practice

Psychology 101: Conquering the Fear of Investing

Just the thought of losing hard-earned cash on a "bad" investment often keeps would-be investors from making that first investment. Still, if you want to become financially secure and enjoy the peace of mind that establishing a well-planned investment program can provide, you must overcome the fear of investing. According to the experts, the five steps below can reduce fear and at the same time help you become a "smart" investor.

Take This Step	Why This Step Is Important
1. Don't start investing before you create an emergency fund.	By creating an emergency fund, you reduce the possibility of having to sell your investments at a loss because of depressed market value.
2. Do your homework before investing any money.	Learn to be a good investor. Begin by looking at investment websites like Yahoo! Finance (http://finance.yahoo.com) and the Motley Fool (www.fool.com).
3. Begin investing with small amounts of money.	Begin by investing small amounts of money that you can afford to lose. Once successful, you can add to existing investments or purchase additional investments.
4. After the purchase, monitor the value of all investments.	Monitor the value of your investments to determine if you should hold, sell, or increase your stake in a specific investment.
5. Continue to learn about investing.	Once you begin investing, it is important to continue to learn. Begin by determining the type of investments that interest you. Then develop a plan to organize information about specific investment alternatives.

MONITOR THE VALUE OF YOUR INVESTMENTS AND YOUR FINANCIAL HEALTH Monitoring the value of your investments will help if you have a personal financial crisis or the nation experiences an economic crisis. With either type of crisis, often many people are caught off guard and must scramble to find the money to pay their monthly bills. In some cases, individuals are forced to sell some or all of their investments at depressed prices just to buy food for the family and pay for everyday necessities.

To survive a crisis, many experts recommend that you take action to make sure your financial affairs are in order. Here are six steps you can take:

1. *Establish a larger than usual emergency fund.* Under normal circumstances, an emergency fund of three months' living expenses is considered adequate, but you may want to increase your fund in anticipation of a crisis.
2. *Know what you owe.* Make a list of all your debts and the amount of the required monthly payments; then identify the debts that *must* be paid. Typically these include the mortgage or rent, medicine, utilities, food, and transportation costs.
3. *Reduce spending.* Cut back to the basics and reduce the amount of money spent on entertainment, dining at restaurants, and vacations. The money saved from reduced spending can be used to increase your emergency fund or pay for everyday necessities.
4. *Notify credit card companies and lenders if you are unable to make payments.* Although not all lenders are willing to help, many will work with you and lower your interest rate, reduce your monthly payment, or extend the time for repayment.
5. *Monitor the value of your investment and retirement accounts.* Tracking the value of your stock, mutual fund, and retirement accounts, for example, will help you decide which investments to sell if you need cash for emergencies.

6. *Consider converting investments to cash to preserve value.* According to personal finance experts, most investors accumulate more money when they use a buy-and-hold approach over a long period of time. Still, there may be times when you could sell some of your investments and use the cash for emergencies or to weather an economic crisis.

Above all, don't panic. While financial problems are stressful, staying calm and considering all the options may help reduce the stress.

If you choose to invest in stocks, bonds, mutual funds, commodities, or options, you can determine the value of your holdings by looking at the price quotations reported on the Internet and in newspapers. Your real estate holdings may be compared with similar properties currently for sale in the surrounding area. Finally, you can determine the value of your precious metals, gemstones, and collectibles by checking with reputable dealers and investment firms. To monitor the value of their investments, many investors use a simple chart. To construct a chart, place the original purchase price of your investment in the middle on the side of the chart. Then use price increments of a logical amount to show increases and decreases in dollar value. Place individual dates along the bottom of the chart. For stocks, bonds, mutual funds, and similar investments, you may want to graph every two weeks and chart current values on, say, a Friday. For longer-term investments like real estate, you can chart current values every six months. Computer software or investment portfolio management tools are available on many investment websites to help you track the value of your investments. *A word of caution:* If an investment is beginning to have a large increase or decrease in value, you may want to check dollar values more frequently—in some cases, daily.

> **did you know?**
>
> If you really want to be socially responsible, then prove it by choosing green investments. To begin,
> - Learn what socially responsible investing is.
> - Research socially responsible companies and mutual funds.
> - Pick your investments and then monitor both their financial performance and their social responsibility record.
>
> For more information, visit the US SIF (The Forum for Sustainable and Responsible Investment) website at www.ussif.org.

KEEP ACCURATE RECORDS   Accurate recordkeeping can help you spot opportunities to maximize profits or reduce dollar losses when you sell your investments. Accurate recordkeeping can also help you decide whether you want to invest additional funds in a particular investment. At the very least, you should keep purchase records for each of your investments that include the actual dollar cost of the investment, plus any commissions or fees you paid. It is also useful to keep a list of the sources of information (Internet addresses, business periodicals, research publications, etc.), along with copies of the material you used to evaluate each investment. Then, when it is time to reevaluate an existing investment, you will know where to begin your search for current information. Finally, accurate recordkeeping is also necessary for tax purposes.

OTHER FACTORS THAT IMPROVE INVESTMENT DECISIONS   To achieve their financial goals, many people seek professional help. In many cases, they turn to stockbrokers, lawyers, accountants, bankers, or insurance agents. However, these professionals are specialists in one specific field and may not be qualified to provide the type of advice required to develop a thorough financial plan. Another source of investment help is a financial planner who has had training in securities, insurance, taxes, real estate, and estate planning.

Whether you are making your own decisions or have professional help, you must consider the tax consequences of selling your investments. Taxes were covered in Chapter 3, and it is not our intention to cover them again. And yet, you are responsible for determining how taxes affect your investment decisions. To find more information about how investments are taxed, visit the Internal Revenue Service website at www.irs.gov.

PRACTICE QUIZ 11-3

1. Assume you must choose an investment that will help you obtain your investment goals. Rank the following investments from 1 (low) to 5 (high) and then justify your choice for your investment portfolio. (See Exhibit 11–4 and Exhibit 11–5 for help evaluating each investment.)

Investment	Rank (1 = low; 5 = high)	Justification
Corporate stocks		
Corporate bonds		
Government bonds		
Mutual funds		
Real estate		

2. Why should investors be concerned with asset allocation and the time their investments have to work for them?

3. Why should you monitor the value of your investments?

Apply Yourself!

Use the Suze Orman method to determine the percentage of your investments that should be invested in growth investments.

LO11.4

Understand why investors purchase government bonds.

ACTION ITEM

I know why some people choose to invest in government or corporate bonds.

☐ Agree   ☐ Disagree

Conservative Investment Options: Government Bonds

Provide feedback on the following statements to see if government or corporate bond investments may be right for you:

Statement	Yes	No
1. Stocks seem to be overpriced and will probably go down in the next 12 to 24 months.	____	____
2. I need to convert my investments to cash in a short period of time.	____	____
3. I'm afraid I will lose the money invested in speculative investments.	____	____

If you answered yes to any of these questions, you may want to consider the more conservative investments described in this section and the next section.

The Psychology of Investing in Bonds

Bonds are a conservative investment option that may offer more income or growth potential than savings accounts or certificates of deposit. They are also a safer investment when compared to stocks, mutual funds, or other investments. Bonds are often considered a "safe harbor" in troubled economic times. For example, many stock and mutual fund investors lost money during the period from 2008 to 2011 because of the nation's economic crisis.

As an alternative to leaving your money in stocks and mutual funds, assuming that you thought the financial markets were headed for a period of decline, you could have moved money into government or corporate bonds. That's exactly what Joe Goode did before the 2008 economic crisis. Although his friends thought he was crazy for taking such a conservative approach, he actually avoided a downturn in the stock market. Now many of his friends wish they had made the same decision. According to Joe, he earned interest on his government and corporate bonds while preserving his investment funds for a return to the stock market when the economy began to improve.

Investors also purchase bonds as a way to use asset allocation to diversify their investment portfolio. If diversification is your goal, you may also purchase bond funds. Bond funds are an indirect way of owning bonds issued by the U.S. Treasury; state and local governments; and corporations. Many financial experts recommend bond funds for small investors because they offer diversification *and* professional management. The advantages and disadvantages of bond funds are discussed in more detail in Chapter 13—Investing in Mutual Funds.

Government Bonds and Debt Securities

The U.S. government and state and local governments issue bonds to obtain financing. A **government bond** is a written pledge of a government or a municipality to repay a specified sum of money, along with interest. In this section, we discuss bonds issued by each level of government and look at why investors purchase these bonds.

government bond
The written pledge of a government or a municipality to repay a specified sum of money, along with interest.

U.S. TREASURY BILLS, NOTES, AND BONDS

Traditionally, investors chose U.S. government securities because they were backed by the full faith and credit of the U.S. government and carried a decreased risk of default. Today, as a result of concerns about the national debt and downgrades or threats of downgrades by U.S. rating agencies, many investors are beginning to worry about what were once considered risk-free investments. Even with these concerns, investors from around the world still regard U.S. government securities as a very conservative and safe investment.

In this section, we discuss four principal types of securities issued by the U.S. Treasury: Treasury bills, Treasury notes, Treasury bonds, and Treasury Inflation-Protected Securities (TIPS). These securities can be purchased through Treasury Direct at www.treasurydirect.gov. Treasury Direct conducts auctions to sell Treasury securities, and buyers interested in purchasing these securities at such auctions may bid competitively or noncompetitively. If they bid competitively, they must specify the rate or interest yield they are willing to accept. If they bid noncompetitively, they are willing to accept the interest rate determined at auction. Treasury securities may also be purchased through banks or brokers, which charge a commission. For each type of U.S. government security, the minimum purchase is $100 with additional increments of $100 above the minimum.

U.S. government securities can be held until maturity or sold or redeemed before maturity. Interest paid on U.S. government securities (and growth in principal for TIPS) is taxable for federal income tax purposes but is exempt from state and local taxation. More information about U.S. government securities is provided in Exhibit 11–6.

municipal bond A debt security issued by a state or local government.

STATE AND LOCAL GOVERNMENT SECURITIES

A **municipal bond** is a debt security issued by a state or local government. Such securities are used to finance the ongoing activities of state and local governments and major projects such as airports, schools, toll roads, and toll bridges. They may be purchased directly from the government entity that issued them or through account executives.

digi – know?

Just about everything you want to know about U.S. Treasury bills, notes, bonds, and Treasury Inflation-Protected Securities can be found at Treasury Direct.

• In addition to the basics, you can access research information, financial calculators, and other tools to fine-tune your investment program.

• Take a look at www.treasurydirect.gov.

Exhibit **11–6**

Information about
Treasury Bills, Treasury
Notes, Treasury Bonds,
and Treasury Inflation-
Protected Securities
(TIPS)

Type of Security	Maturity	Interest	Notes
Treasury bills (T-bills)	4, 13, 26, or 52 weeks	Discounted securities because the actual purchase price is less than the maturity value.	At maturity, the government repays the face value of T-bills. The difference between the purchase price and the face value is interest.
Treasury notes	2, 3, 5, 7, and 10 years	Interest is paid every six months until maturity.	Interest rate is slightly higher than T-bills because of the longer maturity.
Treasury bonds	30 years	Interest is paid every six months until maturity.	Interest rate is slightly higher than T-bills and T-notes because of the longer maturity.
Treasury Inflation-Protected Securities (TIPS)	5, 10, or 30 years At maturity, you are paid the adjusted principal or original principal, whichever is greater.	Interest is paid every six months until maturity at a fixed rate applied to the adjusted principal.	The principal of TIPS securities increases with inflation and decreases with deflation.

general obligation bond
A bond backed by the full
faith, credit, and unlimited
taxing power of the
government that issued it.

revenue bond A bond that
is repaid from the income
generated by the project it is
designed to finance.

State and local securities are classified as either general obligation bonds or revenue bonds. A **general obligation bond** is backed by the full faith, credit, and unlimited taxing power of the government that issued it. A **revenue bond** is repaid from the income generated by the project it is designed to finance. Although both general obligation and revenue bonds are relatively safe, defaults have occurred in recent years.

If the risk of default worries you, you can purchase insured municipal bonds. A number of states offer to guarantee payments on selected securities, and there are private insurers. Even if a municipal bond issue is insured, however, financial experts worry about the insurer's ability to pay off in the event of default on a large bond issue. Most advise investors to determine the underlying quality of a bond whether or not it is insured.

One of the most important features of municipal bonds is that the interest on them may be exempt from federal taxes. Whether or not the interest on municipal bonds is tax exempt often depends on how the funds obtained from their sale are used. *You are responsible, as an investor, to determine whether or not interest on municipal bonds is taxable.* Municipal bonds exempt from federal taxation are generally exempt from state and local taxes only in the state where they are issued. Although the *interest* on municipal bonds may be exempt from taxation, a *capital gain* that results when you sell a municipal bond before maturity *and* at a profit may be taxable just like capital gains on other investments sold at a profit.

Because of their tax-exempt status, the interest rates on municipal bonds are lower than those on taxable bonds. By using the following formula, you can calculate the *taxable equivalent yield* for a municipal security:

$$\text{Taxable equivalent yield} = \frac{\text{Tax-exempt yield}}{1.0 - \text{Your tax rate}}$$

EXAMPLE: Determining Taxable Equivalent Yield

The taxable equivalent yield on a 5 percent, tax-exempt municipal bond for a person in the 28 percent tax bracket is 6.94 percent, as follows:

$$\text{Taxable equivalent yield} = \frac{0.05}{1.0 - 0.28}$$
$$= 0.0694, \text{ or } 6.94 \text{ percent}$$

Once you have calculated the taxable equivalent yield, you can compare the return on tax-exempt securities with the return on taxable investments.

PRACTICE QUIZ 11–4

1. What is the difference between a Treasury bill, a Treasury note, a Treasury bond, and TIPS?

2. Explain the difference between a general obligation bond and a revenue bond.

3. What are the risks involved when investing in state and local securities?

Apply Yourself!

Using the formula presented in this section, calculate the taxable equivalent yields for the following tax-exempt bonds.

Tax-Exempt Yield	Equivalent Yield for a Taxpayer in the 25% Tax Bracket	Equivalent Yield for a Taxpayer in the 28% Tax Bracket	Equivalent Yield for a Taxpayer in the 33% Tax Bracket
3%			
4%			
5.5%			

Conservative Investment Options: Corporate Bonds

A **corporate bond** is a corporation's written pledge to repay a specified amount of money with interest. The **face value** is the dollar amount the bondholder will receive at the bond's maturity. The usual face value of a corporate bond is $1,000. Between the time of purchase and the maturity date, the corporation pays interest to the bondholder.

The **maturity date** of a corporate bond is the date on which the corporation is to repay the borrowed money. Maturity dates for bonds generally range from 1 to 30 years after the date of issue.

The actual legal conditions for a corporate bond are described in a bond indenture. A **bond indenture** is a legal document that details all of the conditions relating to a bond issue. Since corporate bond indentures are very difficult for the average person to read and understand, a corporation issuing bonds appoints a trustee. The **trustee** is a financially independent firm that acts as the bondholders' representative. Usually the trustee is a commercial bank or some other financial institution. If the corporation fails to live up to all the provisions in the indenture agreement, the trustee may bring legal action to protect the bondholders' interests.

Why Corporations Sell Corporate Bonds

Bonds can be used to finance a corporation's ongoing business activities or when it is difficult to sell stock. The sale of bonds can also improve a corporation's financial leverage—the use of borrowed funds to increase the corporation's return on investment. Finally, the

LO11.5

Recognize why investors purchase corporate bonds.

ACTION ITEM

I appreciate the advantages of investing in corporate bonds.

☐ **Agree**   ☐ **Disagree**

corporate bond A corporation's written pledge to repay a specified amount of money with interest.

face value The dollar amount the bondholder will receive at the bond's maturity.

maturity date For a corporate bond, the date on which the corporation is to repay the borrowed money.

bond indenture A legal document that details all of the conditions relating to a bond issue.

trustee A financially independent firm that acts as the bondholders' representative.

debenture A bond that is backed only by the reputation of the issuing corporation.

mortgage bond A corporate bond secured by various assets of the issuing firm.

convertible bond A bond that can be exchanged, at the owner's option, for a specified number of shares of the corporation's common stock.

high-yield bond A corporate bond that pays higher interest but also has a higher risk of default.

interest paid to bond owners is a tax-deductible expense and thus can be used to reduce the taxes the corporation must pay to the federal and state governments.

Corporate bonds are a form of *debt financing*. Bond owners must be repaid at a future date, and interest payments on bonds are required. In the event of bankruptcy, bondholders have a claim to the assets of the corporation prior to that of stockholders.

TYPES OF BONDS Most corporate bonds are debentures. A **debenture** is a bond that is backed only by the reputation of the issuing corporation. If the corporation fails to make either interest payments or repayment at maturity, debenture bondholders become general creditors, much like the firm's suppliers.

To make a bond issue more appealing to conservative investors, a corporation may issue a mortgage bond. A **mortgage bond** (sometimes referred to as a *secured bond*) is a corporate bond secured by various assets of the issuing firm. Because of this added security, interest rates on mortgage bonds are usually lower than interest rates on unsecured debentures.

A special type of bond a corporation may issue is a convertible bond. A **convertible bond** can be exchanged, at the owner's option, for a specified number of shares of the corporation's common stock. This conversion feature allows investors to enjoy the lower risk of a corporate bond but also take advantage of the speculative nature of common stock. For example, assume you purchase a $1,000 convertible bond that is issued by Wesco—a leading wholesaler and distributor of electrical products. Each bond can be converted to 34.6433 shares of the company's common stock. This means you could convert the bond to common stock whenever the price of the company's common stock is $28.87 ($1,000 ÷ 34.6433 = $28.87) or higher. Generally, the interest rate on a convertible bond is 1 to 2 percent lower than that on traditional bonds because of the conversion factor.

Investors in search of higher interest can purchase a high-yield bond. A **high-yield bond** is a corporate bond that pays higher interest but also has a higher risk of default. Before investing in high-yield bonds, keep in mind these investments are often referred to as "junk bonds" in the financial world. High-yield (junk) bonds are sold by companies with a poor earnings history, companies with a questionable credit record, and newer companies with the unproven ability to increase sales and earn profits. They are also frequently used in connection with leveraged buyouts—a situation where investors acquire a company and sell high-yield bonds to pay for the company. So why do investors purchase high-yield bonds? The answer is simple: Corporations issuing high-yield bonds must offer investors interest rates that are three to four percentage ponts higher than safer bond issues. *Caution:* You should not invest in high-yield bonds unless you fully understand all of the risks associated with this type of investment.

call feature A feature that allows the corporation to call in, or buy, outstanding bonds from current bondholders before the maturity date.

sinking fund A fund to which annual or semiannual deposits are made for the purpose of redeeming a bond issue.

serial bonds Bonds of a single issue that mature on different dates.

PROVISIONS FOR REPAYMENT Today most corporate bonds are callable. A **call feature** allows the corporation to call in, or buy, outstanding bonds from current bondholders before the maturity date. In most cases, corporations issuing callable bonds agree not to call them for the first 5 to 10 years after the bonds have been issued. The money needed to call a bond may come from the firm's profits, the sale of additional stock, or the sale of a new bond issue that has a lower interest rate.

A corporation may use one of two methods to ensure that it has sufficient funds available to redeem a bond issue at maturity. First, the corporation may establish a sinking fund. A **sinking fund** is a fund to which annual or semiannual deposits are made for the purpose of redeeming a bond issue. To repay a $275 million bond issue, Union Pacific Corporation agreed to make annual sinking fund payments in order to retire 95 percent of the bonds in the issue prior to the bond maturity date.

Second, a corporation may issue serial bonds. **Serial bonds** are bonds of a single issue that mature on different dates. For example, Seaside Productions used a 20-year, $100 million bond issue to finance its expansion. None of the bonds mature during the first 10 years. Thereafter, 10 percent of the bonds mature each year until all the bonds are retired at the end of the 20-year period.

Detailed information about provisions for repayment, along with other vital information (including maturity date, interest rate, bond rating, call provisions, trustee, and details about security), is available from Moody's Investors Service, Standard & Poor's Corporation, Fitch Ratings Service, and Mergent, Inc.

Why Investors Purchase Corporate Bonds

Basically, investors purchase corporate bonds for three reasons: (1) interest income, (2) possible increase in value, and (3) repayment at maturity.

INTEREST INCOME Bondholders normally receive interest payments every six months until the bond's maturity. The formula to calculate the amount of interest is face value times the interest rate, as illustrated below.

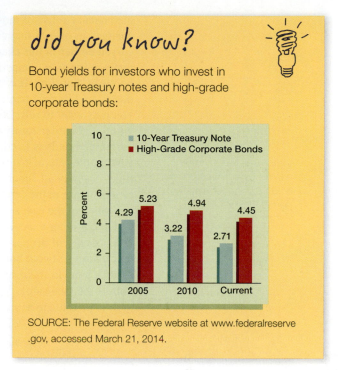

did you know?

Bond yields for investors who invest in 10-year Treasury notes and high-grade corporate bonds:

SOURCE: The Federal Reserve website at www.federalreserve .gov, accessed March 21, 2014.

EXAMPLE: Interest Calculation (IBM)

Assume you purchase a $1,000 bond issued by IBM that pays 4 percent interest each year. Using the following formula, you can calculate the annual interest amount.

Amount of annual interest = Face value × Interest rate

= $1,000 × 4 percent

= $1,000 × 0.04

= $40

Note: Yearly interest of $40 will be paid in two installments of $20 at the end of each six-month period.

The method used to pay bondholders their interest depends on whether they own registered bonds or registered coupon bonds. A **registered bond** is registered in the owner's name by the issuing company. Most registered bonds are now tracked electronically, using computers to record the owners' information. Interest checks for registered bonds are mailed directly to the bondholder of record. A variation of a registered bond is the registered coupon bond. A **registered coupon bond** is registered for principal only, not for interest. While only the registered owner can collect the principal at maturity, interest payments can be paid to anyone who presents one of the detachable coupons to the issuing corporation or the paying agent.

registered bond A bond that is registered in the owner's name by the issuing company.

registered coupon bond A bond that is registered for principal only, not for interest.

DOLLAR APPRECIATION OF BOND VALUE Most beginning investors think that a $1,000 bond is always worth $1,000. In reality, the price of a corporate bond may fluctuate until the maturity date. Changes in overall interest rates in the economy are the primary cause of most bond price fluctuations. Changing bond prices that result from changes in overall interest rates in the economy are an example of interest rate risk, discussed earlier in this chapter. When IBM issued the bond mentioned earlier, the 4 percent interest rate was competitive with the interest rates offered by other corporations issuing bonds at that time. If overall interest rates fall, the price of your IBM bond will increase due to its higher 4 percent interest rate. Because your IBM bond has increased in value, you may want to sell your bond at the current higher price. Or, if you prefer, you can hold your bond until maturity and receive the bond's face value. *Note:* While the interest rate for corporate bonds is fixed, the price and the yield for your IBM bond are not. In this case, **yield** is the rate of return earned by an investor who holds a bond for a stated period of time—usually a 12-month period. Changes in the yield for a bond are caused by an increase *or* a decrease in the current price of a bond. The actual steps required to calculate yield are described in the next section.

> **yield** The rate of return earned by an investor who holds a bond for a stated period of time.

On the other hand, if overall interest rates for comparable bonds rise, the price of your IBM bond will decrease due to its fixed 4 percent stated interest rate. Keep in mind, you can always sell your bond, but if the price has decreased below the price you paid, you will incur a loss. In this situation, many investors choose to hold the bond until maturity and collect the face value.

It is possible to approximate a bond's current market value using the following formula:

$$\text{Approximate market value} = \frac{\text{Dollar amount of annual interest}}{\text{Comparable interest rate}}$$

EXAMPLE: Calculating Approximate Market Value

Assume you purchase an IBM bond that pays 4 percent or annual interest of $40 and has a face value of $1,000. Also assume new corporate bond issues of comparable quality are currently paying 5 percent. The approximate market value is $800, as follows:

$$\text{Approximate market value} = \frac{\text{Dollar amount of annual interest}}{\text{Comparable interest rate}} = \frac{\$40}{5\%}$$

$$= \$800$$

The price of a bond may also be affected by the financial condition of the company or government unit issuing the bond, the factors of supply and demand, an upturn or downturn in the economy, and the proximity of the bond's maturity date.

BOND REPAYMENT AT MATURITY Corporate bonds are repaid at maturity. After you purchase a bond, you have two options: You may keep the bond until maturity and then redeem it, or you may sell the bond to another investor. In either case, the value of your bond is closely tied to the corporation's ability to repay its bond indebtedness. For example, the value of bonds issued by J.C. Penney dropped in value when the retailer's sales revenue dropped, the corporation experienced large dollar losses, and investors feared the company would be forced to file for bankruptcy protection.

A Typical Bond Transaction

Most bonds are sold through full-service brokerage firms, discount brokerage firms, or the Internet. If you use a full-service brokerage firm, your account executive should provide both information and advice about bond investments. As with other investments, the chief advantage of using a discount brokerage firm or trading online is lower commissions, but you must do your own research.

Generally, if you purchase a $1,000 corporate bond through an account executive or brokerage firm, you should expect to pay a minimum commission of between $5 and $25. If you purchase more bonds, the commission usually drops to $1 to $10 per bond. You should also expect to pay commissions when you sell bonds.

PRACTICE QUIZ 11-5

1. Calculate the annual interest and the semiannual interest payment for corporate bond issues with a face value of $1,000.

Annual Interest Rate	Annual Interest	Semiannual Interest Payment
6%		
6.5%		
7%		

2. In your own words, describe why corporations issue corporate bonds.

3. List the three reasons investors purchase corporate bonds.

Apply Yourself!

Historically, the dollar return for bonds is less than the return for stocks. Still, investors often choose corporate and government bonds for their investment portfolio. In the chart below, describe the advantages and disadvantages of bond investments.

Type of Bond	Advantages	Disadvantages
Corporate		
Government		

The Decision to Buy or Sell Bonds

One basic principle we have stressed throughout this chapter is the need to evaluate any potential investment. As you will see in this section, a number of sources of information can be used to evaluate bond investments.

The Internet

By accessing a corporation's web page and locating the topics "financial information," "annual report," or "investor relations," you can find many of the answers to the questions asked in "Your Personal Financial Plan" sheet 37, Evaluating Corporate Bonds.

When investing in bonds, you can use the Internet in three other ways. First, you can obtain price information on specific bond issues to track your investments. Second, you can trade bonds online and pay lower commissions than you would pay a full-service or discount brokerage firm. Third, you can get research about a corporation and its bond issues (including recommendations to buy or sell) by accessing specific bond websites.

LO11.6

Evaluate bonds when making an investment.

ACTION ITEM

I know how to evaluate bond investments.

☐ **Yes** ☐ **No**

The following are popular websites for corporate and government bond investors: www .bondsonline.com, www.fmsbonds.com, www.treasurydirect.gov, www.emuni.com, and bonds.yahoo.com. *Be warned:* Bond websites are not as numerous as websites that provide information on stocks, mutual funds, or other investment alternatives. And many of the better bond websites charge a fee for their research and recommendations.

You may want to visit the Moody's website (www.moodys.com), the Standard & Poor's website (www.standardandpoors.com), Fitch Ratings (www.fitchratings.com), and Mergent, Inc. (www.mergent.com) to obtain detailed information about both corporate and government bonds.

Financial Coverage for Bond Transactions

In bond quotations, prices are given as a percentage of the face value, which is usually $1,000. Thus, to find the actual current price for a bond, you must multiply the face value ($1,000) by the bond quotation.

EXAMPLE: Determining Bond Prices

To calculate the current price for a bond, you multiply the bond price quotation by the face value—usually $1,000. If the bond price quotation is 84, the current price is $840, as shown below.

Current price = Bond price quotation × Face value

$$= 84\% \times \$1,000$$
$$= 0.84 \times \$1,000$$
$$= \$840$$

While some information about bonds may be available in *The Wall Street Journal* or larger metropolitan newspapers, today most bond investors use the Internet to obtain detailed information on bond issues. Detailed information obtained from the Yahoo! Finance website (bonds.yahoo.com) for a $1,000 AT&T corporate bond, which pays 6.40 percent interest and matures in 2038, is provided in Exhibit 11–7.

Bond Ratings

To determine the quality and risk associated with bond issues, investors rely on the bond ratings provided by Moody's Investors Service, Inc., Standard & Poor's Corporation, Fitch Ratings, and Mergent. All four companies rank thousands of corporate and municipal bonds.

As Exhibit 11–8 illustrates, bond ratings range from AAA (the highest) to D (the lowest) for Standard & Poor's and Aaa (the highest) to C (the lowest) for Moody's. Fitch ratings and the ratings provided by Mergent are similar to the bond ratings provided by Standard & Poor's and Moody's. For both Moody's and Standard & Poor's, the first four individual categories represent investment-grade securities. Investment-grade securities are suitable for conservative investors who want a safe investment that provides a predictable source of income. Bonds in the next two individual categories are considered speculative in nature. Finally, the C and D categories are used to rank bonds where there are poor prospects of repayment or even continued payment of interest. Bonds in these categories may be in default.

Generally, the ratings for U.S. government securities issued by the Treasury Department and state and local government securities are similar to those of corporate bonds.

AT&T INC.	
Overview	
1. Price:	117.70
2. Coupon (%):	6.400
3. Maturity Date:	15-May-2038
4. Yield to Maturity (%):	5.114
5. Current Yield (%):	5.437
6. Fitch Ratings:	A
7. Coupon Payment Frequency:	Semi-Annual
8. First Coupon Date:	15-Nov-2008
9. Type:	Corporate
10. Callable:	No

1. Price quoted as a percentage of the face value: $1,000 × 117.70% = $1177.00

2. Coupon (%) is the rate of interest: 6.400 percent

3. Maturity Date is the date when bondholders will receive repayment of the face value: May 15, 2038

4. Yield to Maturity (%) takes into account the relationship among a bond's maturity value, the time to maturity, the current price, and the amount of interest: 5.114 percent

5. Current Yield (%) is determined by dividing the dollar amount of annual interest by the current price of the bond: $64 ÷ $1,177 = 5.437 percent

6. Fitch Ratings is issued by Fitch Bond Ratings and is used to assess the risk associated with this bond: A

7. Coupon Payment Frequency tells bondholders how often they will receive interest payments: Semi-Annual

8. First Coupon Date: November 15, 2008

9. Type: Corporate

10. Callable tells the bondholder if the bond is callable or not: No

SOURCE: Yahoo! Finance bond website (bonds.yahoo.com), accessed March 22, 2014.

Exhibit **11–7**

Bond Information Available by Accessing the Yahoo! Bond Website

Bond Yield Calculations

The **current yield** is determined by dividing the annual interest amount by the bond's current price. The following formula may help you complete this calculation:

$$\text{Current yield} = \frac{\text{Annual interest amount}}{\text{Current price}}$$

current yield Determined by dividing the yearly dollar amount of interest by the bond's current price.

EXAMPLE: Calculating Current Yield

Assume you own a D.R. Horton corporate bond that pays 6.5 percent interest on an annual basis. This means that each year you will receive $65 ($1,000 × 6.5% = $65). Also assume the current price of the D.R. Horton bond is $1,060. Because the current price is more than the bond's face value, the current yield decreases to 6.13 percent, as follows:

$$\text{Current yield} = \frac{\$65}{\$1,060}$$
$$= 0.0613, \text{ or } 6.13 \text{ percent}$$

Exhibit 11–8 Description of Bond Ratings Provided by Moody's Investors Service and Standard & Poor's Corporation

Quality	Moody's	Standard & Poor's	Description
High-grade	Aaa	AAA	Bonds that are judged to be of the best quality.
	Aa	AA	Bonds that are judged to be of high quality by all standards. Together with the first group, they comprise what are generally known as *high-grade* bonds.
Medium-grade	A	A	Bonds that possess many favorable investment attributes and are to be considered upper-medium-grade obligations.
	Baa	BBB	Bonds that are considered medium-grade obligations; i.e., they may possess certain speculative risks.
Speculative	Ba	BB	Bonds that are judged to have more speculative elements than higher-rated bond issues; their future may be determined by economic or adverse business conditions.
	B	B	Bonds that generally lack characteristics of the desirable investment and are subject to high risk of nonpayment of interest and principal.
Poor prospects or Default	Caa	CCC	Bonds that are of poor standing and very high risk.
	Ca		Bonds that represent obligations that are highly speculative and are likely in, or very near, default.
	C		Bonds that are in default with little prospect for recovery of principal and interest.
		CC	Bonds that are very close to default and Standard & Poor's expects default to be a virtual certainty.
		C	Standard & Poor's rating given to bonds that are highly vulnerable to nonpayment and have lower prospects of eventual recovery of principal or interest.
		D	Bond issues in default.

SOURCE: "Long-Term Corporate Obligation Ratings," Moody's website (www.moodys.com), accessed March 24, 2014, and Standard & Poor's Corporation, Global Credit Portal website (www.globalcreditportal.com), accessed March 24, 2014.

Whereas the interest rate for corporate bonds is fixed, the current yield is not. The reason for changes in the current yield is simple: During the time you own a bond, the price of a bond may go up or down. In the previous example, the current price of the D.R. Horton bond (that has a stated interest rate of 6.5 percent) was more than the bond's face value. As a result, the current yield decreased to 6.13 percent. Keep in mind that a bond's price can also decrease below its face value. When this happens, the current yield will increase and be higher than the stated interest rate.

This calculation allows you to compare the yield on a bond investment with the yields of other investment alternatives, which include savings accounts, certificates of deposit, common stock, preferred stock, and mutual funds. Naturally, the higher the current yield, the better! A current yield of 7 percent is better than a current yield of 6.13 percent.

Other Sources of Information

Investors can use two additional sources of information to evaluate potential bond investments. First, business and personal finance magazines can provide information about the economy and interest rates and investment information about a corporation or government entity that issues bonds.

Second, a number of federal agencies provide information that may be useful to bond investors in either printed form or on the Internet. Reports and research published by the Federal Reserve System, the U.S. Treasury, the Bureau of Economic Analysis, and the

Department of Commerce may be used to assess the nation's economy. You can also obtain information that corporations have reported to the Securities and Exchange Commission by accessing the SEC website at www.sec.gov. Finally, state and local governments will provide information about specific municipal bond issues.

 Sheet 37 Evaluating Corporate Bonds

PRACTICE QUIZ 11-6

1. What type of information about bonds is available on the Internet?

2. Calculate the current price for the following bonds:

Face Value	Bond Quotation	Current Price
$1,000	103	
$1,000	77.5	

3. Explain what the following bond ratings mean for investors:

   a. Aaa
   b. BBB
   c. CC

Apply Yourself!

Visit one of the bond websites listed in this section and describe how this type of information could help you evaluate a bond investment.

YOUR PERSONAL FINANCE DASHBOARD

MY FINANCIAL CHECKUP IS COMPLETE AND I'M READY TO INVEST

BEGINNING AN INVESTMENT PROGRAM

Once you have established your investment goals and completed your financial checkup, it's time to start investing—assuming you have enough money to finance your investments. Unfortunately, the money doesn't automatically appear.

YOUR SITUATION: Have you established specific and measurable investment goals? Have you performed a financial checkup to see if you are ready to begin investing? Do you have any money to invest? All three questions are important and should be answered before you begin to invest.

POSSIBLE ACTIONS TO TAKE

✓ Reconsider the three steps to start an investment program at the beginning of the chapter to determine actions you might take to improve your personal financial activities.

✓ Reevaluate your financial goals to make sure they reflect what is important to you.

✓ Establish an emergency fund that can be used to meet unexpected emergencies.

✓ Use the suggestions in Exhibit 11–1 to obtain the money needed to fund your investment program.

LO11.1 In addition to developing investment goals, you must make sure your personal financial affairs are in order. The next step is the accumulation of an emergency fund equal to at least three months' living expenses. Then, it's time to save the money needed to establish an investment program. The time value of money concept can help you achieve your goals—especially if you start sooner rather than later.

LO11.2 All investors must consider the factors of safety, risk, income, growth, and liquidity. Especially important is the relationship between safety and risk. Basically, this relationship can be summarized as follows: The potential return for any investment should be directly related to the risk the investor assumes. In addition to safety and risk, investors choose investments that provide income, growth, or liquidity.

LO11.3 Asset allocation is the process of spreading your assets among several different types of investments to lessen risk. In addition to asset allocation, the amount of time before you need your money is a critical component in the type of investments you choose. Finally, your age is a factor that influences investment choices. You can also improve your investment returns by evaluating all potential investments, monitoring the value of your investments, developing a plan if you experience an economic crisis, and keeping accurate and current records. Professional help and your tax situation may also affect your investment decisions.

LO11.4 Generally, U.S. government securities—Treasury bills, notes, bonds, and Treasury Inflation-Protected Securities—are chosen because most investors consider them to be a safe harbor in troubled economic times. Municipal bonds are also conservative investments and may provide tax-exempt income.

LO11.5 Bonds are issued by corporations to raise capital. Investors purchase corporate bonds for three reasons: (1) interest income, (2) possible increase in value, and (3) repayment at maturity. The method used to pay bondholders interest depends on whether they own registered bonds or registered coupon bonds. Most corporate bonds are bought and sold through full-service brokerage firms, discount brokerage firms, or the Internet. Investors pay commissions when bonds are bought and sold.

LO11.6 Today it is possible to obtain information and trade bonds online via the Internet. To determine the quality of a bond issue, most investors study the ratings provided by Standard & Poor's, Moody's, Mergent, Inc., and Fitch Ratings. Investors can also calculate a current yield to evaluate a decision to buy or sell bond issues. Finally, business magazines and government sources can be used to evaluate both government and corporate bonds and the economy.

Key Terms

asset allocation 359
bond indenture 367
call feature 368
convertible bond 368
corporate bond 367
current yield 373
debenture 368
emergency fund 352
face value 367

general obligation
  bond 366
government bond 365
high-yield bond 368
line of credit 352
liquidity 358
maturity date 367
mortgage bond 368
municipal bond 365

registered bond 369
registered coupon
  bond 369
revenue bond 366
serial bonds 368
sinking fund 368
speculative
  investment 355
trustee 367
yield 370

Page	Topic	Formula
352	Emergency fund	Minimum emergency fund = Monthly expenses $\times$ 3 months
366	Taxable equivalent yield	Taxable equivalent yield = $\dfrac{\text{Tax-exempt yield}}{1.0 - \text{Your tax rate}}$
369	Interest calculation for a bond	Amount of annual interest = Face value $\times$ Interest rate
370	Approximate market value	Approximate market value = $\dfrac{\text{Dollar amount of annual interest}}{\text{Comparable interest rate}}$
372	Current price for a bond	Current price = Bond price quotation $\times$ Face value
373	Current yield for a bond	Current yield = $\dfrac{\text{Annual interest amount}}{\text{Current price}}$

1. After performing a financial checkup, you realize that you have too much credit card debt. What steps can you take to reduce the amount of money you owe on your credit cards?   (LO11.1)
2. Is it ethical to spend more than you earn month after month? What repercussions could you encounter if you overspend on a regular basis?   (LO11.1)
3. Explain the following statement: The potential return on any investment should be directly related to the risk the investor assumes.   (LO11.2)
4. Assume you are 30 years old, single, and are just beginning to invest. How can you balance safety, risk, and growth when choosing investments? Which component do you consider to be the most important?   (LO11.2)
5. How does your age affect the type of investments you choose to obtain your financial goals?   (LO11.3)
6. Assume that you are choosing an investment for your retired parents. Would you choose a bond issued by the federal government, a state or local government, or a corporation? Justify your answer.   (LO11.4)
7. In what circumstances would a $1,000 corporate bond be worth more than $1,000? In what circumstances would the corporate bond be worth less than $1,000?   (LO11.5)
8. You are considering two different corporate bonds. One is rated AAA by Standard & Poor's and pays 4.5 percent annual interest. The other bond is rated B by Standard & Poor's and pays 6.2 percent annual interest. What do these ratings mean? Which bond would you choose and why?   (LO11.6)

1. For Ned Masterson, the last few years have been a financial nightmare. It all started when he lost his job. Because he had no income, he began using his credit cards to obtain the cash needed to pay everyday living expenses. Finally, after an exhaustive job search, he has a new job that pays $42,000 a year. While his take-home pay is $2,450 a month, he must now establish an emergency fund, pay off his $6,200 credit card debt, and start saving the money needed to begin an investment program.
   a. If monthly expenses are $1,750, how much money should Ned save for an emergency fund?
   b. Ned has decided that he will save $2,000 a year for the next five years in order to establish a long-term investment program. If his savings and investments earn 4 percent each year, how much money will he have at the end of five years? (Use the table in this chapter's "Figure It Out!" box to answer this question.)
2. Betty Forrester is 55 years old, wants to diversify her investment portfolio, and must decide if she should invest in tax-free municipal bonds or corporate bonds. The

tax-free bonds are highly rated and pay 4.25 percent. The corporate bonds are more speculative and pay 6.1 percent.

    a. If Betty is in the 33 percent tax bracket, what is the taxable equivalent yield for the municipal bond?

    b. If you were Betty, would you choose the municipal bonds or corporate bonds? Justify your answer.

3. Mary Glover purchased ten $1,000 corporate bonds issued by Avon Products. The annual interest rate for the bonds is 6.5 percent.

    a. What is the annual interest amount for each Avon Products bond?

    b. If the bonds have a current bond price quotation of 112, what is the current price of the bond?

    c. Given the above information, what is the current yield for an Avon Products bond?

Solutions

1. *a.* The minimum emergency fund is $5,250.

$$\text{Minimum emergency fund} = \text{Monthly expenses} \times 3 \text{ months}$$
$$= \$1,750 \times 3$$
$$= \$5,250$$

    b. Based on the information in the table in the "Figure It Out!" box, Ned will have invested $10,000 at the end of five years. If his savings and investments earn 4 percent, he will have $10,832 at the end of five years that can be used to fund additional investments. To solve this problem, you must use the table factor for 5 years and 4 percent, which is 5.416, and then multiply $2,000 × 5.416 = $10,832.

2. *a.* The taxable equivalent yield for the municipal bond is

$$\text{Taxable equivalent yield} = \frac{\text{Tax-exempt yield}}{1.0 - \text{Your tax rate}}$$
$$= \frac{0.0425}{1.0 - 0.33}$$
$$= 0.063, \text{ or } 6.3 \text{ percent}$$

    b. The taxable equivalent yield for the municipal bonds is 6.3 percent; the yield for the corporate bonds is 6.1 percent. Also, it should be noted that the corporate bonds are "speculative" and the interest income on the corporate bonds is taxable. In this case, Betty should choose the tax-free municipal bonds because the yield is higher and they are more conservative.

3. *a.* The annual interest for each bond is $65.

$$\text{Amount of annual interest} = \text{Face value} \times \text{Interest rate}$$
$$= \$1,000 \times 0.065$$
$$= \$65$$

    b. The current price is $1,120.

$$\text{Current price} = \text{Bond price quotation} \times \text{Face value}$$
$$= 112\% \times \$1,000$$
$$= 1.12 \times \$1,000$$
$$= \$1,120$$

    c. The current yield is

$$\text{Current yield} = \frac{\text{Annual interest amount}}{\text{Current price}}$$
$$= \frac{\$65}{\$1,120}$$
$$= 0.058 = 5.8 \text{ percent}$$

1. Jane and Bill Collins have total take-home pay of $4,500 a month. Their monthly expenses total $3,400. Calculate the minimum amount this couple needs to establish an emergency fund.   (LO11.1)

2. Use the information in the "Figure It Out!" box earlier in the chapter to complete the following table.   (LO11.1)

Annual Deposit	Rate of Return	Number of Years	Investment Value at the End of Time Period	Total Amount of Investment	Total Amount of Earnings
$2,000	2%	10			
$2,000	8%	10			
$2,000	4%	30			
$2,000	11%	30			

3. Assume you are 45 years old, want to retire in 20 years, and currently have an investment portfolio valued at $240,000 invested in technology stocks. After talking with a financial advisor, you feel you have "too many eggs in one basket," and need to diversify your investments. Based on this information, use the asset allocation method described in this chapter and the table below to diversify your investment portfolio. Then in a short paragraph explain why you chose these investments. (LO11.3)

Investment Alternative	Percentage You Would Like in This Category
Stocks issued by large corporations (large cap)	
Stocks issued by medium-sized corporations (midcap)	
Stocks issued by small, rapidly growing companies (small cap)	
Foreign stocks	
Bonds	
Cash	
Other investments (specify type)	
	100%

4. Based on the following information, construct a graph that illustrates price movement for a Washington Utilities bond fund.   (LO11.3)

January	$16.50	July	$14.00
February	$15.50	August	$13.10
March	$17.20	September	$15.20
April	$18.90	October	$16.70
May	$19.80	November	$18.40
June	$16.50	December	$19.80

5. Assume you are in the 28 percent tax bracket and purchase a 3.50 percent municipal bond. Use the formula presented in this chapter to calculate the taxable equivalent yield for this investment.   (LO11.4)

6. Assume you are in the 35 percent tax bracket and purchase a 3.75 percent municipal bond. Use the formula presented in this chapter to calculate the taxable equivalent yield for this investment.   (LO11.4)

7. Assume that three years ago you purchased a corporate bond that pays 5.8 percent. The purchase price was $1,000. What is the annual dollar amount of interest that you receive from your bond investment?   (LO11.5)

8. Twelve months ago, you purchased 10-year Treasury notes with a face value of $1,000. The interest rate is 2.90 percent. What is the dollar amount of interest you will receive each year?   (LO11.5)

9. Assume that you purchased a $1,000 convertible corporate bond. Also assume the bond can be converted to 38.4615 shares of the firm's stock. What is the dollar value that the stock must reach before investors would consider converting to common stock?   (LO11.5)

10. Five years ago, you purchased a $1,000 corporate bond issued by General Electric. The interest rate for the bond was 4 percent. Today comparable bonds are paying 5 percent.   (LO11.5)

    a. What is the approximate dollar price for which you could sell your General Electric bond?

    b. In your own words, describe why your bond decreased in value.

11. In 1994, you purchased a $1,000 corporate bond issued by Boeing. At the time, the interest rate for the bond was 6 percent. Today, comparable bonds are paying 4.30 percent.   (LO11.5)

    a. What is the approximate dollar price for which you could sell your Boeing bond?

    b. In your own words, describe why your bond increased in value.

12. Determine the current yield on a corporate bond investment that has a face value of $1,000, pays 4.60 percent, and has a current price of $950.   (LO11.6)

13. Choose a corporate bond that you would consider purchasing. Then, using information obtained on the Internet or in the library, answer the questions in "Your Personal Financial Plan" sheet 37. Based on your research, would you still purchase this bond?   (LO11.6)

 **To reinforce the content in this chapter, more problems are provided at connect.mheducation.com.**

Case in Point

A LESSON FROM THE PAST

Back in 2002, Mary Goldberg, a 34-year-old widow, got a telephone call from a Wall Street account executive who said that one of his other clients had given him her name. Then he told her his brokerage firm was selling a new corporate bond issue in New World Explorations, a company heavily engaged in oil exploration in the western United States. The bonds in this issue paid investors 11.2 percent a year. He then said that the minimum investment was $10,000 and that if she wanted to take advantage of this "once in a lifetime" opportunity, she had to move fast. To Mary, it was an opportunity that was too good to pass up, and she bit hook, line, and sinker. She sent the executive a check—and never heard from him again. A few days later (and after her check was paid by her bank), she went to the library to research her bond investment. Unfortunately, she found there was no such company as New World Explorations, and she had lost $10,000. Right then and there, she vowed she would never invest in bonds again. From now on, she would put her money in the bank, where it was guaranteed.

Over the years, she continued to save and deposit money in the bank and accumulated more than $32,000. Things seemed to be pretty much on track until one of her certificates of deposit (CD) matured. When she went to renew the CD, the bank officer told her interest rates had fallen and current CD interest rates ranged between 0.50 and 1.5 percent.

Faced with the prospects of lower interest rates, Mary decided to shop around for higher rates. She called several local banks and got pretty much the same answer. Then a friend suggested that she talk to Peter Manning, an account executive for Fidelity Investments. Manning told her there were conservative bonds that offered higher returns. But he warned her that these investments were *not* guaranteed. If she wanted higher returns, she would have to take some risks.

While Mary wanted higher returns, she also remembered how she had lost $10,000. When she told Peter Manning about her bond investment in the fictitious New World Explorations, he pointed out that she had made some pretty serious mistakes. For starters, she bought the bonds over the phone from someone she didn't know, and she bought them without doing any research. He assured her that the bonds he would recommend would be issued by real companies, and she would be able to find information on each of his recommendations at the library or on the Internet. For starters, he suggested the following two investments:

1. America West Airlines corporate bonds that pay 8.057 percent annual interest and mature on July 2, 2020. This bond has a current price of $1,160 and is rated BBB.

2. Berkshire Hathaway corporate bonds that pay 3.40 percent annual interest and mature on January 31, 2022. This bond has a current price of $1,030 and is rated AA.

Questions

1. According to Mary Goldberg, the chance to invest in New World Explorations was "too good to pass up," and she lost $10,000. Why do you think so many people are taken in by get-rich-quick schemes?

2. Using the information obtained in the library or on the Internet, answer the following questions about Peter Manning's investment suggestions.

   a. What does the rating for the America West Airlines bond mean?
   b. What is the current yield for an America West Airlines bond?
   c. What does the rating for the Berkshire Hathaway bond mean?
   d. What is the current yield for a Berkshire Hathaway bond?

3. Based on your research, which investment would you recommend to Mary Goldberg? Why?

Continuing Case

INVESTING BASICS AND EVALUATING BONDS

The triplets are now three-and-a-half years old and Jamie Lee and Ross, both 38, are finally beginning to settle down into a regular routine. The first three years were a blur of diapers, feedings, baths, mounds of laundry, and crying babies!

Jamie Lee and Ross finally went out to a welcome dinner out on the town. Ross's parents were watching the triplets. They were having a conversation about their future and the future of the kids. They figured college expenses will be $100,000, and their eventual retirement was a major worry for both of them. They have dreamed of owning a beach house when they retire. That could be another $350,000, 30 years from now. They wondered how could they possibly afford all of this.

They agreed that it was time to talk to an investment counselor, but they wanted to organize all of their financial information and discuss their family's financial goals before setting up the appointment.

Current Financial Situation

Assets (Jamie Lee and Ross combined):
Checking account, $4,500
Savings account, $20,000
Emergency fund savings account, $21,000
IRA balance, $32,000
Cars, $8,500 (Jamie Lee) and $14,000 (Ross)

Liabilities (Jamie Lee and Ross combined):
Student loan balance, $0
Credit card balance, $4,000
Car loans, $2,000

Income:
Jamie Lee, $45,000 gross income ($31,500 net income after taxes)

Ross, $80,000 gross income ($64,500 net income after taxes)

Monthly Expenses:
Mortgage, $1,225
Property taxes, $400
Homeowner's insurance, $200
IRA contribution, $300
Utilities, $250
Food, $600
Baby essentials (diapers, clothing, toys, etc.), $200
Gas/Maintenance, $275
Credit card payment, $400
Car loan payment, $289
Entertainment, $125

Questions

1. Describe the stage in the adult life cycle (Exhibit 1–1) that Jamie Lee and Ross are experiencing right now. What are some of the financial activities that they should be participating in at this stage?
2. After reviewing Jamie Lee and Ross's current financial situation, suggest specific and measurable short-term and long-term financial goals that can be implemented at this stage.
3. Using the investment goal guidelines, assess the validity of Jamie Lee and Ross's short- and long-term financial goals and objectives:

Financial Question	Short-Term Goals	Long-Term Goals
1. How much money do they need to satisfy their investment goals?		
2. How much risk are they willing to assume in an investment program?		
3. What possible economic or personal conditions could alter their investment goals?		
4. Considering their economic conditions, are their investment goals reasonable?		
5. Are they willing to make the sacrifices necessary to ensure that they meet their investment goals?		

4. Using the formula for allocating investments and the risk involved, assess how much of Jamie Lee and Ross's assets should be allocated in higher-risk growth investments? How should the remaining investments be distributed and what is the associated risk?
5. Jamie Lee and Ross need to evaluate their emergency fund of $21,000. Will their present emergency fund be sufficient to cover them should one of them lose their job?
6. Jamie Lee and Ross agree that by accomplishing their short-term goals, they can budget $5,000 a year toward their long-term investment goals. They are estimating that with the allocations recommended by their financial advisor, they will see an average return of 7 percent on their investments. The triplets will begin college in 15 years and will need $100,000 for tuition.

   Using the time value of money calculations found in the "Figure It Out!" information box found in this chapter, decide if Jamie Lee and Ross will be on track to reach their long-term financial goals of having enough money from their investments to pay the triplets' tuition.

Spending Diary

"WHILE I HAVE A FAIRLY LARGE AMOUNT IN A SAVINGS ACCOUNT, I SHOULD THINK ABOUT INVESTING SOME OF THIS MONEY IN OTHER WAYS."

Directions The use of your Daily Spending Diary can provide an important foundation for monitoring and controlling spending. This will allow the possibility of wiser use of your money now and in the future. The Daily Spending Diary sheets are located in Appendix D at the end of the book and in Connect Finance.

Questions

1. Explain how the use of a Daily Spending Diary could result in starting an investment program.
2. Based on your Daily Spending Diary, describe actions that you might take to identify and achieve various financial and investment goals.

Establishing Investment Goals

Purpose: To determine specific goals for an investment program.

Financial Planning Activities: Based on short- and long-term objectives for your investment efforts, enter the items requested below. This sheet is also available in an Excel spreadsheet format in Connect Finance.

Suggested Websites: www.fool.com   money.cnn.com

Description of investment goal	Dollar amount	Date needed	Possible investments to achieve this goal	Level of risk (high, medium, low)

Suggested App:
• The Motley Fool

What's Next for Your Personal Financial Plan?

• Use the suggestions listed in this chapter to perform a financial checkup.
• Discuss the importance of investment goals and financial planning with other household members.

YOUR PERSONAL FINANCIAL PLAN

YOUR PERSONAL FINANCIAL PLAN

Name: _____ Date: _____

Assessing Risk for Investments

Purpose: To assess the risk of various investments in relation to your personal risk tolerance and financial goals.

Financial Planning Activities: List various investments you are considering based on the type and level of risk associated with each. This sheet is also available in an Excel spreadsheet format in Connect Finance.

Suggested Websites: www.marketwatch.com   www.fool.com

Type of investment	Loss of market value (market risk)	Type of Risk		
		Inflation risk	Interest rate risk	Liquidity risk
High risk				
Moderate risk				
Low risk				

What's Next for Your Personal Financial Plan?

- Identify current economic trends that might increase or decrease the risk associated with your choice of investments.
- Based on the risk associated with the investments you chose, which investment would you choose to attain your investment goals?

Name: _____ Date: _____

Evaluating Corporate Bonds

Purpose: To determine if a specific corporate bond can help you attain your financial goals.

Financial Planning Activities: No checklist can serve as a foolproof guide for choosing a corporate bond. However, the following questions will help you evaluate a potential bond investment. This sheet is also available in an Excel spreadsheet format in Connect Finance.

Suggested Websites: bonds.yahoo.com www.bondsonline.com

Category 1: Information about the Corporation

1. What is the corporation's name, website address, and phone number? _____
_____

2. What type of products or services does this firm provide? _____
_____

3. Briefly describe the prospects for this company. (Include significant factors like product development, plans for expansion, plans for mergers, etc.)
_____
_____
_____

Category 2: Bond Basics

4. What type of bond is this? _____

5. What is the face value for this bond? _____

6. What is the interest rate for this bond? _____

7. What is the dollar amount of annual interest for this bond? _____

8. When are interest payments made to bondholders?
_____

9. Is the corporation currently paying interest as scheduled? ☐ Yes ☐ No

10. What is the maturity date for this bond? _____

11. What is Moody's rating for this bond? _____

12. What is Standard & Poor's rating for this bond?
_____

13. What do these ratings mean? _____
_____
_____

14. What was the original issue date? _____
_____

15. Who is the trustee for this bond issue? _____
_____

16. Is the bond callable? If so, when? _____
_____

17. Is the bond secured with collateral? If so, what?
☐ Yes ☐ No
_____

Category 3: Financial Performance

18. What are the firm's earnings per share for the last year? _____

19. Have the firm's earnings increased over the past five years? _____

20. What are the firm's projected earnings for the next year? _____

21. Do the analysts indicate that this is a good time to invest in this company? Why or why not?
_____
_____

22. Briefly describe any other information that you obtained from Moody's, Standard & Poor's, or other sources of information.
_____
_____

A Word of Caution

The above checklist is not a cure-all, but it does provide some very sound questions that you should answer before making a decision to invest in bonds. If you need other information, *you* are responsible for obtaining it and for determining how it affects your potential investment.

What's Next for Your Personal Financial Plan?

- Talk with various people who have invested in government, municipal, or corporate bonds.
- Discuss with other household members why bonds might be a logical choice for your investment program.

Suggested App:
- Yahoo! Finance

12 Investing in Stocks

3 Steps to Financial Literacy . . . Begin Investing in Stocks

Save the money needed to purchase your first stock.
Website: www.daveramsey.com/article/the-secret-to-saving-money

1

Evaluate different stocks that match your personal investment goals.
Website: money.cnn.com

2

Research the services and fees offered by different brokerage firms.
Website: www.brokerstance.com

3

Often people don't invest in stocks because it seems too complicated. In reality, it may be easier than you think. By following the three steps above, you can begin purchasing stock. As an incentive, keep in mind that since 1926—a period of over 90 years—stocks have returned an average annual return of almost 10 percent. Because stocks offer higher annual returns, many financial experts recommend stock investments for investors who are establishing a long-term investment program.

CHAPTER 12 LEARNING OBJECTIVES

In this chapter, you will learn to:

LO12.1 Identify the most important features of common and preferred stock.

LO12.2 Explain how you can evaluate stock investments.

LO12.3 Analyze the numerical measures that cause a stock to increase or decrease in value.

LO12.4 Describe how stocks are bought and sold.

LO12.5 Explain the trading techniques used by long-term investors and short-term speculators.

YOUR PERSONAL FINANCIAL PLAN SHEETS

38. Evaluating Corporate Stocks
39. Investment Broker Comparison

Common and Preferred Stock

LO12.1

Identify the most important features of common and preferred stock.

Why invest in stocks? To answer this question, consider the returns provided by stocks over a long period of time. Since 1926, the average annual return for stocks is almost 10 percent as measured by the Standard & Poor's 500 stock index—a bench mark of stock market performance often reported on financial news programs. In fact, stock returns were substantially higher than the returns provided by more conservative investments.[1] Simply put, investors who want larger returns choose stocks. Certainly, there have been periods when stocks declined in value. For proof, just ask any stock investor what happened to the value of his or her stock investments during the recent economic crisis. Still, the key to success with any investment program often is allowing your investments to work for you over a long period of time. A long-term investment program allows you to ride through the rough times and enjoy the good times. However, before you decide to invest your money, you should realize the importance of evaluating a potential stock investment.

ACTION ITEM

I understand the three ways investors can profit from stock investments.

☐ **Yes** ☐ **No**

Many investors face two concerns when they begin an investment program. First, they don't know where to get the information they need to evaluate potential investments. In reality, more information is available than most investors can read. Yet, as crazy as it sounds, some investors invest in stocks without doing any research at all. As we begin this chapter, you should know that *there is no substitute for researching a potential stock investment.*

Second, beginning investors sometimes worry that they won't know what the information means when they do find it. Yet common sense goes a long way when evaluating potential investments. For example, consider the following questions:

1. Is an increase in sales revenues a healthy sign for a corporation? (*Answer: yes*)
2. Should a firm's profits increase or decrease over time? (*Answer: increase*)

[1]"Money 101 Lesson 4: Basics of Investing," *CNN/Money* (http://money.cnn.com/magazines/moneymag/money101/lesson4/index.htm), accessed April 20, 2014.

Although the answers to these two questions are obvious, you will find more detailed answers to these and other questions in this chapter. In fact, that's what this chapter is all about. We want you to learn how to evaluate a stock and to make money from your investment decisions.

Why Corporations Issue Common Stock

common stock The most basic form of corporate ownership.

Common stock is the most basic form of ownership for a corporation. Corporations issue common stock to finance their business start-up costs and help pay for expansion and their ongoing business activities. Corporate managers prefer selling common stock as a method of financing for several reasons.

A FORM OF EQUITY *Important point:* Stock is equity financing. **Equity financing** is money received from the sale of shares of ownership in a business. One reason corporations prefer selling stock is because the money obtained from equity financing doesn't have to be repaid and the company doesn't have to buy back shares from the stockholders. On the other hand, a stockholder who buys common stock may sell his or her stock to another individual.

equity financing Money received from the owners or from the sale of shares of ownership in a business.

DIVIDENDS NOT MANDATORY *Important point:* Dividends are paid out of profits, and dividend payments must be approved by the corporation's board of directors. A **dividend** is a distribution of money, stock, or other property that a corporation pays to stockholders. Dividend policies vary among corporations, but most firms distribute between 30 and 70 percent of their earnings to stockholders. However, some corporations follow a policy of smaller or no dividend distributions to stockholders. In general, these are rapidly growing firms, like Amazon (online sales) or Google (online websites) or Facebook (social networking), that retain a large share of their earnings for research and development, expansion, or major projects. On the other hand, utility companies, such as Duke Energy, and other financially secure enterprises may distribute 70 to 90 percent of their earnings. Always remember that if a corporation has had a bad year, dividend payments may be reduced or omitted.

dividend A distribution of money, stock, or other property that a corporation pays to stockholders.

VOTING RIGHTS AND CONTROL OF THE COMPANY In return for the financing provided by selling common stock, management must make concessions to stockholders that may restrict corporate policies. For example, corporations are required by law to have an annual meeting at which stockholders have a right to vote, usually casting one vote per share of stock. Stockholders may vote in person or by proxy. A **proxy** is a legal form that lists the issues to be decided at a stockholders' meeting and requests that stockholders transfer their voting rights to some individual or individuals. The common stockholders elect the board of directors and must approve major changes in corporate policies.

proxy A legal form that lists the issues to be decided at a stockholders' meeting and requests that stockholders transfer their voting rights to some individual or individuals.

Why Investors Purchase Common Stock

Let's begin with two basic assumptions. First, no one invests in stocks in order to lose money. Second, every investor wants to earn a better-than-average return on stock investments. For more information about why people invest in stocks, read the next section.

THE PSYCHOLOGY OF STOCK INVESTING Why do people invest in stocks? Good question! The simple answer is that investors want the larger returns that stocks offer, even though they are aware of the potential for losses. Remember the statistics that were presented at the beginning of this chapter. Historically, long-term stock investors experience an average annual return of almost 10 percent. The bottom line: When compared to current interest rates for savings accounts, certificates of deposit, and bonds, stock investments offer a greater potential for larger returns.

From a psychological standpoint, many investors have trouble making the decision to buy or sell a stock. The following suggestions can be used to reduce anxiety when you make stock investment decisions.

- *Evaluate each investment.* Too often, investors purchase or sell a stock without doing their homework. A much better approach is to become an expert and learn all that you can about the company (and its stock).
- *Analyze the firm's finances.* Look at the company's financial information, which is available in the firm's annual report or on many investment websites. Examine trends for sales, profits, dividends, and other important financial data. More specific information on how to evaluate a firm's finances is provided later in this chapter.
- *Track the firm's product line.* If the firm's products become obsolete and the company fails to introduce state-of-the art new products, its sales—and, ultimately, profits—may take a nosedive.
- *Monitor economic developments.* An economic recovery or an economic recession may cause the value of a stock investment to increase or decrease. Also, watch the unemployment rate, inflation rate, interest rates, productivity rates, and similar economic indicators.
- *Be patient.* The secret of success for making money with stocks is often time. If you choose quality stocks based on quality research, and in some cases wait, eventually your stock investments will provide average or even above-average returns. And remember: There are no guarantees when investing in stocks. Larger returns are always accompanied by increased risk when investing in stocks.

How do you make money by buying common stock? Basically, there are three ways: income from dividends, dollar appreciation of stock value, and the *possibility* of increased value from stock splits.

INCOME FROM DIVIDENDS While the corporation's board members are under no legal obligation to pay dividends, most board members like to keep stockholders happy (and prosperous). Therefore, board members usually declare dividends if the corporation's profits are sufficient for them to do so. Since dividends are a distribution of profits, investors must be concerned about future profits.

Dividends for common stock may take the form of cash, additional stock, or company products. However, the last type of dividend is extremely unusual. If the board of directors declares a cash dividend, each common stockholder receives an equal amount per share. Although dividend policies vary, most corporations pay dividends on a quarterly basis.

Notice in Exhibit 12–1 that Microsoft declared a quarterly dividend of $0.28 per share to stockholders who owned the stock on the record date of May 15, 2014. The **record date**

record date The date on which a stockholder must be registered on the corporation's books in order to receive dividend payments.

Exhibit **12–1**

Dividend Information

Information about corporate dividends is available by using the Internet to access a corporation's website or other investment sites. The numbers above each of the columns correspond to the numbered entries in the list of explanations that appear at the bottom of the exhibit.

1 Company	2 Amount of Dividend	3 Record Date	4 Payable Date
Microsoft	$0.28	May 15, 2014	June 12, 2014

1. The name of the company paying the dividend is Microsoft.
2. The dollar amount of the quarterly dividend is $0.28.
3. The record date is Thursday, May 15, 2014. Stockholders must be registered on the corporate books by the record date in order to receive this quarterly dividend payment. The stock begins selling "ex-dividend" Tuesday, May 13, 2014—two business days before the record date.
4. The dividend will be paid on June 12, 2014, to stockholders who own the stock on the record date (May 15, 2014).

SOURCE: The Microsoft Corporation website at www.microsoft.com, accessed April 21, 2014.

is the date on which a stockholder must be registered on the corporation's books in order to receive dividend payments. When a stock is traded around the record date, the company must determine whether the buyer or the seller is entitled to the dividend. To solve this problem, this rule is followed: *Dividends remain with the stock until two business days before the record date.* On the second day before the record date, the stock begins selling *ex-dividend.* Investors who purchase an ex-dividend stock are not entitled to receive dividends for that quarter, and the dividend is paid to the previous owner of the stock.

For example, Microsoft declared a quarterly dividend of $0.28 per share to stockholders who owned its stock on Thursday, May 15, 2014. The stock went ex-dividend on Tuesday, May 13, 2014, *two business days* before the May 15 date. A stockholder who purchased the stock on Tuesday, May 13, or after was not entitled to this quarterly dividend payment. The actual dividend payment was paid on June 12, 2014, to stockholders who owned the stock on the record date. Investors are generally very conscious of the date on which a stock goes ex-dividend, and the dollar value of the stock may go down by the value of the dividend.

DOLLAR APPRECIATION OF STOCK VALUE The price for a share of stock is determined by how much a buyer is willing to pay for the stock. The price changes when information about the firm or its future prospects is released to the general public. For example, information about future sales revenues or expected earnings can increase or decrease the price for the firm's stock. In most cases, you purchase stock and then hold on to that stock for a period of time. If the price of the stock increases, you must decide whether to sell the stock at the higher price or continue to hold it. If you decide to sell the stock, the dollar amount of difference between the purchase price and the selling price represents your profit.

Let's assume that on January 15, 2011, you purchased 100 shares of Johnson & Johnson stock at a cost of $65 a share. Your cost for the stock was $6,500 plus $25 in commission charges, for a total investment of $6,525. (*Note:* Commissions, a topic covered later in this chapter, are charged when you purchase stock *and* when you sell stock.) Let's also assume you held your 100 shares until January 15, 2014 and then sold them for $95 a share. During the three-year period you owned Johnson & Johnson shares, the company paid dividends totaling $7.24 per share. Exhibit 12–2 shows your return on the investment. In this case, you made money because of dividend payments and through an increase in stock value from $65 to $95 per share. As Exhibit 12–2 shows, your total return is $3,674. Of course, if the stock's value should decrease, or if the firm's board of directors reduces or votes to omit dividends, your return may be less than the original investment.

POSSIBILITY OF INCREASED VALUE FROM STOCK SPLITS Investors can also increase potential profits through a stock split. A **stock split** is a procedure in which the shares of stock owned by existing stockholders are divided into a larger number of shares. In 2014, for example, the board of directors of Under Armour, the company that develops, manufactures, and markets athletic clothing, approved a 2-for-1 stock split. After the stock split, a stockholder who had previously owned 100 shares now owned 200 shares. The most common stock splits are 2-for-1 or 3-for-1.

Why do corporations split their stock? In many cases, a firm's management has a theoretical ideal price range for the firm's stock. If the market value of the stock rises above the ideal range, a stock split brings the market value back in line. In the case of Under

CAUTION!

One of the most common Internet stock frauds is called "Pump and Dump." Here's how it works: Glowing information about a company appears on a company's website, in newsletters, or in chat rooms or blogs. Based on this information, uninformed investors purchase the "hot" stock, creating high demand and pumping up the price. When the stock price peaks, the fraudsters behind the scheme dump their shares and the stock price falls.

To avoid this scam, the Securities and Exchange Commission advises investors to check any information that seems too good to be true and to use multiple information sources to research any stock before investing.

SOURCE: "Pump&Dump.con," The Securities and Exchange Commission (www.sec.gov), accessed April 23, 2014.

stock split A procedure in which the shares of stock owned by existing stockholders are divided into a larger number of shares.

Exhibit **12–2**

Sample Stock Transaction
for Johnson & Johnson

Assumptions			
100 shares of common stock purchased January 15, 2011, sold January 15, 2014; dividends of $7.24 per share for the investment period.			

Costs When Purchased		Return When Sold	
100 shares @ $65 =	$6,500	100 shares @ $95 =	$9,500
Plus commission	+25	Minus commission	− 25
Total investment	$6,525	Total return	$9,475

Transaction Summary	
Total return	$ 9,475
Minus total investment	−6,525
Profit from stock sale	$ 2,950
Plus dividends	+724
Total return for the transaction	$ 3,674

Armour, the 2-for-1 stock split reduced the market value to one-half of the stock's value on the day prior to the split. The lower market value for each share of stock was the result of dividing the dollar value of the company by a larger number of shares of common stock. Also, a decision to split a company's stock and the resulting lower market value make the stock more attractive to the investing public. This attraction is based on the belief that most corporations split their stock only when their financial future is improving and on the upswing.

Be warned: There are no guarantees that a stock's market value will go up after a split. This is important to understand, because investors often think that a stock split leads to immediate profits. Nothing could be further from the truth. Here's why: The total market capitalization—the value of the company's stock multiplied by the number of shares outstanding—does not change because a corporation splits its stock. A company that has a market capitalization of $100 million before a 2-for-1 stock split is still worth $100 million after the split. Simply put, there is twice as much stock, but each share is worth half of its previous value before the stock split occurred. If a stock's value does increase after a stock split, it increases because of the firm's financial performance after the split and not just because there are more shares of stock.

Preferred Stock

In addition to or instead of purchasing common stock, you may purchase preferred stock. **Preferred stock** is a type of stock that gives the owner the advantage of receiving cash dividends before common stockholders are paid any dividends. This is the most important priority an investor in preferred stock enjoys. Unlike the amount of the dividend on common stock, the dollar amount of the dividend on preferred stock is known before the stock is purchased.

Preferred stocks are often referred to as "middle" investments because they represent an investment midway between common stock and corporate bonds. When compared to corporate bonds, the yield on preferred stocks is often higher than the yield on bonds. And yet, because it is a type of equity financing, preferred stock is less secure than bonds (debt) issued by the same company. When compared to common stocks, preferred stocks are safer

preferred stock A type of stock that gives the owner the advantage of receiving cash dividends before common stockholders are paid any dividends.

investments that offer more secure dividends. They are often purchased by individuals who need a predictable source of income greater than that offered by common stock investments. For all other investors, preferred stocks lack the growth potential that common stocks offer and the safety of many corporate bond issues.

When compared to corporations selling common stock, preferred stock is issued less often by only a few corporations. Keep in mind that dividends on preferred stock, as on common stock, may be omitted by action of the board of directors. While preferred stock does not represent a legal debt that must be repaid, if the firm is dissolved or declares bankruptcy, preferred stockholders do have first claim to the corporation's assets after creditors (including bondholders).

PRACTICE QUIZ 12–1

1. Why do corporations sell stock? Why do investors purchase stock?

2. Why do corporations split their stock? Is a stock split good or bad for investors?

3. From an investor's viewpoint, what is the difference between common stock and preferred stock?

Apply Yourself!

Talk with different people and ask them if they include common or preferred stocks in their investment program. Also, ask them if they feel stocks could help you achieve your investment goals.

LO12.2

Explain how you can evaluate stock investments.

ACTION ITEM

I know how to evaluate a stock issue.

☐ Yes   ☐ No

Evaluating a Stock Issue

Many people purchase investments without doing *any* research. They wouldn't buy a car without a test drive or purchase a home without comparing different houses, but for some unknown reason they invest without doing their homework. The truth is that there is no substitute for a few hours of detective work when choosing an investment. In reality, it is important to evaluate not only the corporation that issues the individual stock you are interested in purchasing, but also the industry in which the corporation operates. For example, when the automobile industry encountered problems during the economic crisis, most companies within this industry found that increasing sales and profits was difficult if not impossible. Also, keep in mind that the nation's and even the world's economy—the big picture—may impact the way a corporation operates and cause a corporate stock to increase or decrease in value.

A wealth of information is available to stock investors, and a logical place to start the evaluation process for stock is with the classification of different types of stock investments described in Exhibit 12–3. Once you have identified a type of stock that may help you obtain your investment goals, you may want to use the Internet to evaluate a potential investment.

The Internet

In this section, we examine some websites that are logical starting points when evaluating a stock investment, but there are many more than those described. Let's begin with information about the corporation that is available on the Internet.

Type of Stock	Characteristics of This Type of Investment
Blue chip	A stock, issued by large, stable corporations with a history of paying dividends, that generally attracts conservative investors.
Cyclical	A stock that follows the business cycle of advances and declines in the economy.
Defensive	A stock that remains stable during declines in the economy.
Growth	A stock issued by a corporation that has the potential of earning profits above the average profits of all firms in the economy.
Income	An investment that pays higher-than-average dividends.
Large cap	A stock issued by a corporation that has a large amount of capitalization in excess of $10 billion.
Micro cap	A stock issued by a company that has a capitalization of between $50 million and $300 million or less.
Midcap	A stock issued by a corporation that has a capitalization of between $2 billion and $10 billion.
Penny	A stock that typically sells for less than $5 per share (or in some cases, less than $1 per share) and has a small amount of capitalization.
Small cap	A stock issued by a company that has a capitalization of between $300 million and $2 billion.

Exhibit 12–3

Classification of Stock Investments

When evaluating a stock investment, investors often classify stocks into these ten categories.

Today most corporations have a website, and the information these sites provide is especially useful. First, it is easily accessible. All you have to do is type in the corporation's URL address or use a search engine to locate the corporation's home page. Second, the information on the website may be more up to date and thorough than printed material obtained from the corporation or outside sources. Once at the corporation's home page, look for a link to "investor relations" or "financial information." Just by clicking on a button, you can access information on the firm's earnings and other financial factors that could affect the value of the company's stock.

You can also use websites like Google, Yahoo!, and other search engines to obtain information about stock investments. Take a look at Exhibit 12–4, which illustrates a portion of the summary page taken from Yahoo! Finance for Facebook, the world's largest social networking site. In addition to the current price, the Yahoo! Finance website provides even more specific information about a particular company like Facebook. By clicking on the buttons under the headings for the quotes, charts, news and info, company, analyst coverage, ownership, and financials that are part of the screen for each corporation, you can obtain even more information. How about picking a company like The Gap (symbol GPS) or Coca-Cola (symbol KO) and going exploring on the Internet? To begin, enter the web address for Yahoo! Finance (finance.yahoo.com). Then enter the symbol for one of the

did you know?

Saving the Planet One Investment at a Time!

Experts predict that the next "great" investments will be companies that produce alternative fuels, fuel cells, hybrid vehicles, and organic foods. To obtain information about investing in the companies that are developing environmentally friendly products and services, go to

www.sustainablebusiness.com
www.greenchipstocks.com
www.ecobusinesslinks.com

Exhibit **12–4**   A Portion of the Opening Page from the Yahoo! Finance Website for Facebook

Facebook, Inc. (FB) - NasdaqGS   Follow

62.22   **0.81(1.29%)**   10:14AM EDT - Nasdaq Real Time Price

Get the big picture on all your investments.

Sync your Yahoo portfolio now

Prev Close:	63.03	Day's Range:	61.96 - 63.46	
Open:	63.43	52wk Range:	22.67 - 72.59	
Bid:	62.40 x 500	Volume:	18,001,703	
Ask:	62.41 x 5400	Avg Vol (3m):	68,056,300	
1y Target Est:	74.61	Market Cap:	158.64B	
Beta:	1.772	P/E (ttm):	101.83	
Next Earnings Date:	23-Apr-14	EPS (ttm):	0.61	
		Div & Yield:	N/A (N/A)	

Facebook, Inc.
■ FB   Apr 23, 10:15am EDT

1d 5d 1m 3m 6m 1y 2y
customize chart

Quotes delayed, except where indicated otherwise. Currency in USD.

above corporations in the Quote Lookup box and click the Go tab. You'll be surprised at the amount of information you can obtain with a click of your mouse.

You can also use professional advisory services like Standard & Poor's Financial Services (www.netadvantage.standardandpoors.com), Mergent Online (www.mergentonline .com), and Value Line (www.valueline.com). While some of the information provided by these services is free, there is a charge for the more detailed online information you may need to evaluate a stock investment. For more information about professional advisory services and the type of information they provide, read the next section.

In addition to Internet search engines and professional advisory services, you can access personal finance websites like *CNN Money* (money.cnn.com) and *Kiplinger's Personal Finance* (www.kiplinger.com). Both websites provide a wealth of information for the stock investor. While there are many websites that can help you learn more about investing in stocks, the following three deserve special mention: The Street (www.thestreet .com), MarketWatch (www.marketwatch.com), and MSN Money (money.msn.com).

Stock Advisory Services

In addition to the Internet, sources of information you can use to evaluate potential stock investments are the printed materials provided by stock advisory services. The information ranges from simple alphabetical listings to detailed financial reports.

Value Line, Standard & Poor's reports, and Mergent are three widely used advisory services that provide detailed research for stock investors. Here we will examine a detailed report for Disney, one of the world's leading entertainment companies, that is published in *The Value Line Investment Survey* (see Exhibit 12–5).

While there is a lot of information about Disney in Exhibit 12–5, it helps to break down the entire Value Line report into different sections. For example:

- Overall ratings for timeliness, safety, and technical, along with price information and projections for the price of a share of stock, are included at the top of the report.
- Detailed information about revenues per share, earnings per share, dividends, book value, total revenues, net profit, capital structure, and other important financial information is included in the middle and along the left side of the report.
- Information about the type of business and prospects for the future is provided toward the bottom and in the right-hand corner.

Exhibit 12–5   Value Line Report for Walt Disney Corporation

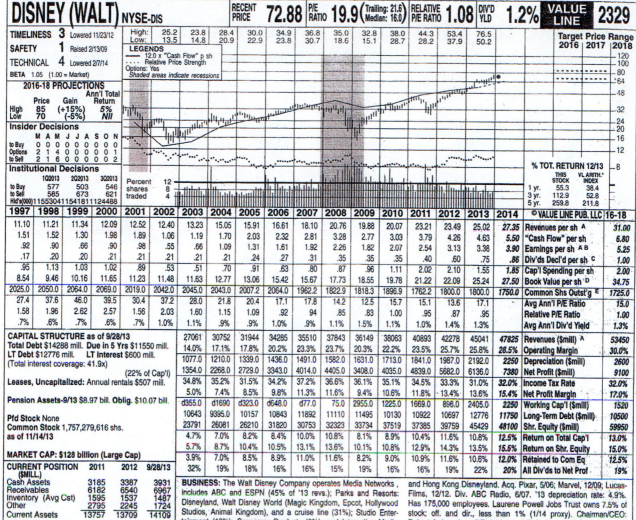

DISNEY (WALT) NYSE-DIS

| RECENT PRICE | 72.88 | P/E RATIO | 19.9 | (Trailing: 21.6) (Median: 16.0) | RELATIVE P/E RATIO | 1.08 | DIV'D YLD | 1.2% | VALUE LINE | 2329 |

TIMELINESS	3	Lowered 11/23/12
SAFETY	1	Raised 2/13/09
TECHNICAL	4	Lowered 2/7/14
BETA 1.05 (1.00 = Market)		

High/Low range (per year): High: 25.2 23.8 28.4 30.0 34.9 36.8 35.0 32.8 38.0 44.3 53.4 76.5 ; Low: 13.5 14.8 20.9 22.9 23.8 30.7 18.6 15.1 28.7 28.2 37.9 50.2

Target Price Range 2016 2017 2018

LEGENDS: — 12.0 x "Cash Flow" p sh · · · Relative Price Strength Options: Yes Shaded areas indicate recessions

2016-18 PROJECTIONS

	Price	Gain	Ann'l Total Return
High	85	(+15%)	5%
Low	70	(-5%)	Nil

Insider Decisions

	M	A	M	J	J	A	S	O	N
to Buy	0	0	0	0	0	0	0	0	0
Options	2	1	4	0	0	0	0	0	1
to Sell	2	1	6	0	0	0	0	0	2

Institutional Decisions

	1Q2013	2Q2013	3Q2013
to Buy	577	503	546
to Sell	585	673	621
Hld's(000)	1155304	1154181	1124486

Percent shares traded: 12 / 8 / 4

% TOT. RETURN 12/13

	THIS STOCK	VL ARITH.* INDEX
1 yr.	55.3	38.4
3 yr.	112.9	52.8
5 yr.	259.8	211.8

	1997	1998	1999	2000	2001	2002	2003	2004	2005	2006	2007	2008	2009	2010	2011	2012	2013	2014	© VALUE LINE PUB. LLC 16-18
Revenues per sh A	11.10	11.21	11.34	12.09	12.52	12.40	13.23	15.05	15.91	16.61	18.10	20.76	19.88	20.07	23.21	23.49	25.02	27.35	31.00
"Cash Flow" per sh	1.51	1.52	1.30	1.98	1.89	1.06	1.19	1.70	2.03	2.32	2.81	3.28	2.77	3.03	3.79	4.26	4.63	5.50	6.80
Earnings per sh A B	.92	.90	.66	.90	.98	.55	.66	1.09	1.31	1.61	1.92	2.26	1.82	2.07	2.54	3.13	3.38	3.90	5.25
Div'ds Decl'd per sh C	.17	.20	.20	.21	.21	.21	.21	.21	.24	.27	.31	.35	.35	.35	.40	.60	.75	.86	1.00
Cap'l Spending per sh	.95	1.13	1.03	1.02	.89	.53	.51	.70	.91	.63	.80	.87	.96	1.11	2.02	2.10	1.55	1.85	2.00
Book Value per sh D	8.54	9.46	10.16	11.65	11.23	11.48	11.63	12.77	13.06	15.42	15.67	17.73	18.55	19.78	21.22	22.09	25.24	27.50	34.75
Common Shs Outst'g E	2025.0	2050.0	2064.0	2069.0	2019.0	2042.0	2045.0	2043.0	2007.2	2064.0	1962.2	1822.9	1818.3	1896.9	1762.2	1800.0	1800.0	1750.0	1725.0
Avg Ann'l P/E Ratio	27.4	37.6	46.0	39.5	30.4	37.2	28.0	21.8	20.4	17.1	17.8	14.2	12.5	15.7	15.1	13.6	17.1		15.0
Relative P/E Ratio	1.58	1.96	2.62	2.57	1.56	2.03	1.60	1.15	1.09	.92	.94	.85	.83	1.00	.95	.87	.95		1.00
Avg Ann'l Div'd Yield	.7%	.6%	.7%	.6%	.7%	1.0%	1.1%	.9%	.9%	1.0%	.9%	1.1%	1.5%	1.1%	1.0%	1.4%	1.3%		1.3%
Revenues ($mill) A							27061	30752	31944	34285	35510	37843	36149	38063	40893	42278	45041	47825	53450
Operating Margin							14.0%	17.1%	17.8%	20.2%	23.3%	23.7%	20.3%	22.2%	23.5%	25.7%	25.8%	28.5%	30.0%
Depreciation ($mill)							1077.0	1210.0	1339.0	1436.0	1491.0	1582.0	1631.0	1713.0	1841.0	1987.0	2192.0	2250	2600
Net Profit ($mill)							1354.0	2268.0	2729.0	3343.0	4014.0	4405.0	3408.0	4035.0	4839.0	5682.0	6136.0	7380	9100
Income Tax Rate							34.8%	35.2%	31.5%	34.2%	37.2%	36.6%	36.1%	35.1%	34.5%	33.3%	31.0%	32.0%	32.0%
Net Profit Margin							5.0%	7.4%	8.5%	9.8%	11.3%	11.6%	9.4%	11.6%	11.8%	13.4%	13.6%	15.4%	17.0%
Working Cap'l ($mill)							d355.0	d1690	d323.0	d648.0	d77.0	75.0	2955.0	1225.0	1669.0	896.0	2405.0	2250	1520
Long-Term Debt ($mill)							10643	9395.0	10157	10843	11892	11110	11495	10130	10922	10697	12776	11750	10500
Shr. Equity ($mill)							23791	26081	26210	31820	30753	32323	33734	37519	37385	39759	45429	48100	59950
Return on Total Cap'l							4.7%	7.0%	8.2%	8.4%	10.0%	10.8%	8.1%	8.9%	10.4%	11.6%	10.8%	12.5%	13.0%
Return on Shr. Equity							5.7%	8.7%	10.4%	10.5%	13.1%	13.6%	10.1%	10.8%	12.9%	14.3%	13.5%	15.5%	15.0%
Retained to Com Eq							3.9%	7.0%	8.5%	8.9%	11.0%	11.6%	8.2%	9.0%	10.9%	11.6%	10.6%	12.0%	12.5%
All Div'ds to Net Prof							32%	19%	18%	16%	16%	16%	19%	16%	16%	19%	22%	20%	19%

CAPITAL STRUCTURE as of 9/28/13

Total Debt $14288 mill. Due in 5 Yrs $11550 mill.
LT Debt $12776 mill. LT Interest $600 mill.
(Total interest coverage: 41.9x)
(22% of Cap'l)

Leases, Uncapitalized: Annual rentals $507 mill.

Pension Assets-9/13 $8.97 bill. Oblig. $10.07 bill.

Pfd Stock None

Common Stock 1,757,279,616 shs.
as of 11/14/13

MARKET CAP: $128 billion (Large Cap)

CURRENT POSITION ($MILL.)

	2011	2012	9/28/13
Cash Assets	3185	3387	3931
Receivables	6182	6540	6967
Inventory (Avg Cst)	1595	1537	1487
Other	2795	2245	1724
Current Assets	13757	13709	14109
Accts Payable	6362	6393	6803
Debt Due	3055	3614	1512
Other	2671	2806	3389
Current Liab.	12088	12813	11704

ANNUAL RATES

of change (per sh)	Past 10 Yrs.	Past 5 Yrs.	Est'd '11-'13 to '16-'18
Revenues	6.5%	5.5%	5.5%
"Cash Flow"	12.0%	8.5%	10.0%
Earnings	15.0%	9.5%	11.5%
Dividends	11.0%	13.5%	11.5%
Book Value	7.0%	7.0%	8.5%

QUARTERLY REVENUES ($ mill.) A

Fiscal Year Ends	Dec.Per	Mar.Per	Jun.Per	Sep.Per	Full Fiscal Year
2010	9739	8580	10002	9742	38063
2011	10716	9077	10675	10425	40893
2012	10779	9629	11088	10782	42278
2013	11341	10554	11578	11568	45041
2014	11750	11625	12350	12100	47825

EARNINGS PER SHARE A B

Fiscal Year Ends	Dec.Per	Mar.Per	Jun.Per	Sep.Per	Full Fiscal Year
2010	.47	.48	.67	.44	2.07
2011	.68	.49	.78	.59	2.54
2012	.80	.63	1.01	.69	3.13
2013	.77	.83	1.01	.77	3.38
2014	.85	.90	1.15	1.00	3.90

QUARTERLY DIVIDENDS PAID C

Calendar	Mar.Per	Jun.Per	Sep.Per	Dec.Per	Full Year
2010	.35	--	--	--	.35
2011	.40	--	--	--	.40
2012	.60	--	--	.75	1.35
2013	--	--	--	--	
2014	.86				

BUSINESS

The Walt Disney Company operates Media Networks, includes ABC and ESPN (45% of '13 revs.); Parks and Resorts: Disneyland, Walt Disney World (Magic Kingdom, Epcot, Hollywood Studios, Animal Kingdom), and a cruise line (31%); Studio Entertainment (13%); Consumer Products (8%); and Interactive Media (3%). Earns Tokyo Disneyland royalties. Manages Disneyland Paris and Hong Kong Disneyland. Acq. Pixar, 5/06; Marvel, 12/09; Lucas-Films, 12/12. Div. ABC Radio, 6/07. '13 depreciation rate: 4.9%. Has 175,000 employees. Laurene Powell Jobs Trust owns 7.5% of stock; off. and dir., less than 1% (1/14 proxy). Chairman/CEO: Robert A. Iger. Inc.: DE. Address: 500 S. Buena Vista St., Burbank, CA 91521-7320. Tel.: 818-560-1000. Internet: www.disney.com.

The Walt Disney Co. is in good shape for the near term. The media conglomerate closed fiscal 2013 (ended September 28th) on a good note. Disney reported gains at all but its Studio Entertainment unit last year. Plus, its smallest business category, Interactive, posted the largest year-over-year increase. Looking ahead, we imagine the Parks & Resorts and Media Networks segments will continue to pave the way in the coming months. (Fiscal first-quarter results are scheduled to be released after we went to press with this report.) In all, we look for share net to climb another 15% this year, on a 5%-10% top-line advance.

The company is better positioning itself for the long haul. Management will probably work to lower operating costs, thus helping bolster margins and profits. Moreover, we think Disney will accelerate investments in technological enhancements (across its business lines) and brand-building efforts to help capture additional market share. And, in all likelihood, it will further strengthen its distribution channels and digital platforms to keep pace with industry peers and broaden its reach.

Disney is putting its cash to good use. Over the past couple of years, Disney invested heavily in the Parks & Resorts segment. But it is liable to scale back spending there now that much of that unit's expansion plans have taken place, such as the nearly complete construction of Disney Shanghai. Also, thanks to the benefits Disney is reaping from the Marvel and Lucas-Films acquisitions, it may eye other accretive additions. What's more, the company is increasing its stock-buyback program, and plans to earmark between $6 billion and $8 billion in fiscal 2014 (up from last year's $1 billion authorization). In addition, Disney's board raised its annual payout 15%, to $0.86 a share.

These shares appear to be fairly valued at this juncture. Much of the good news we anticipate over the 2016-2018 pull is already baked into the recent price. Nevertheless, this Dow-30 component has some conservative luster; the company earns perfect marks for Financial Strength (A++) and for Price Growth Persistence (100).

Orly Seidman   February 7, 2014

(A) Fiscal year ends Saturday closest to Sept. 30th. Fiscal 2009 contained 53 weeks. (B) Dil. egs. Excl. nonrec. gains/(losses): '97, 4¢; '98, 1¢; '99, (4¢); '02, (1¢); '02, 8¢; '03, (4¢); '04, 4¢; '05, (9¢); '06, 3¢; '07, 32¢; '08, 2¢; '09, 6¢; '10, (4¢); '11, (2¢). Excl. disc. ops.: '07, 1¢. Excl. loss from interest in Disney Internet Group: '00, 35¢. Next egs. report due early May. (C) Div'ds hist. paid in mid-Jan. Two div'ds paid in calendar 2012. (D) Incl. intang., at 9/28/13: $34.7 bill., $19.28/sh. (E) In millions.

Company's Financial Strength	A++
Stock's Price Stability	80
Price Growth Persistence	100
Earnings Predictability	90

Make the Most of an Annual Report

You don't have to be Warren Buffett to know what makes a company tick.

Way back when, if you owned stock in a company, you'd often find a glossy annual report in your mailbox. Nowadays, all you may receive is a letter telling you where to download the report on the company's Web site. And truth be told, annual reports are being supplanted by the Form 10-K, the annual filing required by the Securities and Exchange Commission. Don't be put off by the form's intimidating appearance. We've highlighted some key sections—and what to focus on in each.

Business. The first part of the 10-K provides a thorough look at what the firm does or makes, its divisions, and where in the world its products are made and sold. It also gives info on key customers and competitors, and where the company stands in its industry. You may even learn an interesting fact or two—for example, that there really were a Mr. Procter and a Mr. Gamble, and that they founded P&G in 1837.

Risk factors. Listed in order of importance, these are the factors that may adversely affect the company's business. Much of this section, found just after the "Business" description, may elicit a big *duh*, such as P&G's disclosure

that "our businesses face cost fluctuations and pressures that could affect our business results." But read carefully and you may ferret out less-obvious risks, such as a disproportionate share of sales coming from a single product or customer.

Management's discussion and analysis. In Part II of the 10-K, the company reports and analyzes its performance over the past year compared with the previous year's results.

Income statement. This is a basic report of sales, expenses and profits. Ideally, you want to see a trend of rising sales and earnings. A 10-K typically shows three years of results, as well as a five-year summary in the section called "Selected Financial Data." Focus on the trend in net earnings rather than earnings per share, in part because share buy-backs, which cut the number of outstanding shares, can skew earnings per share and thus camouflage a drop in overall profits.

Balance sheet. This is a snapshot of the company's assets (such as cash and inventory) and its liabilities (such as outstanding debt). Zero in on how much long-term debt the firm carries and whether retained profits, the earnings a company reinvests in its business, have grown in each

of the past three years. Great companies have little or no long-term debt on their balance sheets—or they generate enough profit annually to pay off that debt within three to five years.

Notes to financial statements. To some people, the 10-K notes matter as much as the statements. That's because Note 1 describes the accounting methods used to prepare the financial statements. If a company has made a change to its methodology from the previous year, that renders a comparison of the current year's financial statements with the previous year's useless.

Auditor's report. Look for this key sentence: "In our opinion, the financial statements present fairly. . . the financial position of the company." That means the company has honestly described its finances over the past year to the best knowledge of the accounting firm that is auditing the 10-K.

Nellie S. Huang

SOURCE: Reprinted by permission from *Kiplinger's Personal Finance.* Copyright © 2014. The Kiplinger Washington Editors, Inc.

1. In this article, the type of information contained in a firm's income statement and balance sheet—both statements contained in an annual report or a Securities and Exchange Commission 10-K report—is described. How can this information help you pick a stock that will help you attain your financial goals?

2. Often, financial experts suggest that investors should pay more attention to the notes that accompany a firm's financial statements because "that's where they bury the bodies." What type of information is contained in the notes and why is it important?

While other stock advisory services provide basically the same types of information as that in Exhibit 12–5, it is the investor's job to interpret such information and decide whether the company's stock is a good investment.

Newspaper Coverage and Corporate News

Although some newspapers have eliminated or reduced the amount of financial coverage, *The Wall Street Journal* and most metropolitan newspapers still contain some information about stocks. Although not all newspapers print exactly the same information, they usually provide the basic information. Stocks are listed alphabetically, so your first task is to move down the table to find the stock you're interested in. Then, to read the stock quotation, you simply read across the table. Typical information provided by newspapers includes the name of the company, stock symbol, and price information.

The federal government requires corporations selling new issues of securities to disclose in a prospectus information about corporate earnings, assets and liabilities, products or services, and the qualifications of top management. In addition to a prospectus, all publicly owned corporations may send their stockholders an annual report that contains detailed financial data. An electronic version of a corporation's annual report is available on a corporation's Internet website. You can also obtain a print version of an annual report from the corporation. For most corporations, all it takes is a call to a toll-free phone number, a written request to the corporation's headquarters, or a visit to a corporation's website.

In addition to corporate publications, you can access the Securities and Exchange Commission website (www.sec.gov) to obtain financial and other important information that a corporation has supplied to the federal government.

Finally, many periodicals, including *Bloomberg Businessweek, Fortune, Forbes, Money, Kiplinger's Personal Finance,* and similar publications, contain information about stock investing.

PRACTICE QUIZ 12–2

1. Describe how each of the following sources of investment information could help you evaluate a stock investment.

Source of Information	Type of Information	How Could This Help
The Internet		
Stock advisory services		
A newspaper		
Government publications		
Business periodicals		

2. What is the difference between a prospectus and an annual report?

3. Using Exhibit 12–5, pick three financial measures and describe how they could help you evaluate a corporate stock.

Apply Yourself!

Go to the library or get on the Internet and use Standard & Poor's, Value Line, or Mergent to research a stock that you think would help you attain your investment goals.

ACTION ITEM

I understand how financial calculations can help me pick a stock that will be profitable.

☐ **Agree** ☐ **Disagree**

Numerical Measures That Influence Investment Decisions

How do you determine whether the time is right to buy or sell a particular stock? Good question! Unfortunately, there is no simple answer. In addition to the material in the previous section, "Evaluating a Stock Issue," many investors rely on numerical measures to decide when to buy or sell a stock. We begin this section by examining the relationship between a stock's price and a corporation's earnings.

Why Corporate Earnings Are Important

Many financial experts believe that a corporation's ability or inability to generate earnings in the future may be one of the most significant factors that account for an increase or decrease in the value of a stock. Simply put, higher earnings generally equate to higher stock prices. Unfortunately, the reverse is also true. If a corporation's earnings decline, generally the stock's price will also decline. Corporate earnings are reported in the firm's annual report. You can also obtain information about a corporation's current earnings by using a professional advisory service or accessing the Yahoo! Finance website or one of the other websites described in the last section.

EARNINGS PER SHARE Many investors calculate earnings per share to evaluate the financial health of a corporation. **Earnings per share** are a corporation's earnings divided by the number of outstanding shares of a firm's common stock. See the "Earnings per Share" example box to see how this works.

Most stockholders consider the amount of earnings per share important because it is a measure of the company's profitability. No meaningful average for this measure exists, mainly because the number of shares of a firm's stock is subject to change via stock splits and stock dividends. *As a general rule, however, an increase in earnings per share is a healthy sign for any corporation and its stockholders.*

PRICE-EARNINGS RATIO Another calculation, the price-earnings ratio, can be used to evaluate a potential stock investment.

did you know?

The Dow Jones Industrial Average measures 30 different stocks that are considered leaders in the economy. (Closing values as of end of December for 2008, 2010, 2012, and April 15, 2014.)

2008	$8,776
2010	$11,578
2012	$13,104
2014 (April 15)	$16,253

SOURCE: The MarketWatch website at www.marketwatch.com, accessed April 23, 2014.

earnings per share
A corporation's earnings divided by the number of outstanding shares of a firm's common stock.

EXAMPLE: Earnings per Share

Assume General Mills's 2013 earnings were $1,855 million. Also assume that General Mills—the company known for producing consumer food products—has 666 million shares of common stock. Earnings per share are $2.79 as illustrated below.

$$\text{Earnings per share} = \frac{\text{Earnings}}{\text{Number of shares outstanding}}$$

$$= \frac{\$1,855 \text{ million}}{666 \text{ million}} = \$2.79$$

The **price-earnings (PE) ratio** is the price of a share of stock divided by the corporation's earnings per share of stock.

price-earnings (PE) ratio The price of a share of stock divided by the corporation's earnings per share of stock.

EXAMPLE: Price-Earnings (PE) Ratio

Consumer packaged goods manufacturer Procter & Gamble Corporation's common stock is selling for $82 a share. Also assume Procter & Gamble's earnings per share are $3.72. The corporation's price-earnings ratio is 22, as illustrated below.

$$\text{Price-earnings (PE) ratio} = \frac{\text{Price per share}}{\text{Earnings per share}}$$

$$= \frac{\$82}{\$3.72} = 22$$

The price-earnings ratio is a key factor that serious investors use to evaluate stock investments. Generally, a price-earnings ratio gives investors an idea of how much they are paying for a company's earning power. The higher the price-earnings ratio, the more investors are paying for earnings. For example, an investor might say that Procter & Gamble is selling for 22 times its current earnings. A high price-earnings ratio (over 20) often indicates investor optimism because of the expectation of higher earnings in the future. Always remember the relationship between earnings and stock value. If future earnings do increase, the stock usually becomes more valuable in the future. On the other hand, a low price-earnings ratio (under 20) indicates that investors have lower earnings expectations. If future earnings decrease or don't maintain the same level of growth, the stock will become less valuable in the future.

Like earnings per share, a corporation's PE ratio is often reported on investment websites. When researching a stock, comparing the PE ratios of one company to other companies in the same industry, to the market in general, or against the company's own historical PE ratios is usually helpful. Keep in mind that the PE ratio calculation is just another piece of the puzzle when researching a stock for investment purposes.

PROJECTED EARNINGS Both earnings per share and the price-earnings ratio are based on historical numbers. In other words, this is what the company has done in the past. With this fact in mind, many investors will also look at earnings estimates for a corporation. The MSN Money website or similar financial websites provide earnings estimates for major corporations. At the time of publication, for example, MSN Money provided the following earnings estimates for Starbucks, the company that provides rich-brewed coffee, espresso beverages, and complementary food products.[2]

Starbucks	This Year	Next Year
Yearly earnings estimates	$2.66 per share	$3.17 per share

From an investor's standpoint, a projected increase in earnings from $2.66 per share to $3.17 per share is a good sign. In the case of Starbucks, these estimates were determined by surveying different analysts who track Starbucks. By using the same projected earnings amount, it is possible to calculate a projected price-earnings ratio or a projected price per share of stock. Of course, you should remember that these are estimates and are not "etched in stone." Changes that affect the economy, industry, or company's sales and profit amounts could cause analysts to revise the above estimates.

[2]*MSN Money* (money.msn.com), accessed April 24, 2014.

Figure It Out!

Calculations Can Improve Investment Decisions!

Numbers, numbers, numbers! The truth is that if you are going to be a good investor, you must learn the numbers game. As mentioned in the text, many calculations can help you gauge the value of a potential stock investment. These same calculations can help you decide if the time is right to sell a stock investment.

Now it's your turn. Use the formulas in this section and the following financial information for Bozo Oil Company to

calculate the earnings per share, price-earnings (PE) ratio, and dividend yield:

After-tax income	$6,250,000
Dividend amount	$0.60
Price per share	$30
Number of shares outstanding	5,000,000

Dividend Yield and Total Return

dividend yield The annual dividend amount divided by the stock's current price per share.

One of the calculations investors use most frequently to monitor the value of their investments is the dividend yield. The **dividend yield** is the annual dividend amount divided by the stock's current price per share.

> ### EXAMPLE: Dividend Yield
>
> Assume you own common stock issued by Wal-Mart Stores Inc., the world's largest retailer. A share of stock pays an annual dividend of $1.92 and is currently selling for $78 a share. The current dividend yield is 2.5 percent, as illustrated below.
>
> $$\text{Dividend yield} = \frac{\text{Annual dividend amount}}{\text{Current price per share}}$$
>
> $$= \frac{\$1.92}{\$78} = 0.025 = 2.5 \text{ percent}$$

An increase in dividend yield is a healthy sign for any stock investment. A dividend yield of 2.5 percent is better than a 2 percent dividend yield.

total return A calculation that includes the yearly dividend amount as well as any increase or decrease in the original purchase price of the investment.

Although the dividend yield calculation is useful, you should also consider whether the stock's price per share is increasing or decreasing in dollar value. **Total return** is a calculation that includes not only the yearly dividend amount but also any increase or decrease in the original purchase price of the investment. While this concept may be used for any investment, let's illustrate it by using the assumptions for GameStop—the video game and electronics retailer.

> ### EXAMPLE: Total Return
>
> Assume you own 100 shares of GameStop stock that you purchased for $33 a share and hold your stock for one year before deciding to sell it at the current market price of $40 a share. During this one-year period, GameStop paid dividends totaling $1.32 per share. Your total return is $832, as illustrated below.
>
> $$\text{Total return} = \text{Dividends} + \text{Capital gain}$$
>
> $$= \$132 + \$700 = \$832$$

The dividend of $132 results from the payment of dividends for one year ($1.32 per-share dividend × 100 shares). The capital gain of $700 results from the increase in the stock price from $33 a share to $40 a share ($7 per-share increase × 100 shares = $700). (Of course, commissions to buy and sell your stock, a topic covered in the next section, would reduce your total return.)

Other Factors That Influence the Price of a Stock

The **beta** is a measure reported in many financial publications that compares the volatility associated with a specific stock issue with the volatility of the Standard & Poor's 500 stock index. The beta for the S&P is 1.0. The majority of stocks have betas between 0.5 and 2.0. Generally, conservative stocks have low betas while more speculative stocks have betas greater than one.

beta A measure reported in many financial publications that compares the volatility associated with a specific stock issue with the volatility of the Standard & Poor's 500 stock index.

EXAMPLE: Beta Calculation for Google

Assume that the overall stock market increases by 10 percent and that Google stock has a beta of 1.20. Based on the calculation below, Google is 20 percent more volatile than the stock market and will increase 12 percent when the market increases 10 percent.

Volatility for a stock = Increase in overall market × Beta for a specific stock

$$= 10 \text{ percent} \times 1.20$$

$$= 12 \text{ percent}$$

Because individual stocks generally move in the same direction as the stock market, most betas are positive, but it is possible for a stock to have a negative beta. A negative beta occurs when a corporation's stock moves in the opposite direction compared to the stock market as a whole.

Although little correlation may exist between the price of a stock and its book value, book value is widely reported in financial publications. Therefore, it deserves mention. The **book value** for a share of stock is determined by deducting all liabilities from the corporation's assets and dividing the remainder by the number of outstanding shares of common stock. For Southwest Airlines—a major passenger airline in the United States—book value is $10.48, as illustrated below.

book value Determined by deducting all liabilities from the corporation's assets and dividing the remainder by the number of outstanding shares of common stock.

EXAMPLE: Book Value

Assume Southwest Airlines has assets of $19,345 million and liabilities of $12,009 million. The company has also issued 700 million shares of stock.

$$\text{Book value} = \frac{\text{Assets} - \text{Liabilities}}{\text{Number of shares outstanding}}$$

$$= \frac{\$19,345 \text{ million} - \$12,009 \text{ million}}{700 \text{ million}} = \$10.48 \text{ per share}$$

Some investors believe they have found a bargain when a stock's share price is about the same as or lower than its book value. *Be warned:* Book value calculations may be misleading, because the dollar amount of assets used in the above formula may be understated or overstated on the firm's financial statements. From a practical standpoint, most financial experts suggest that book value is just another piece of the puzzle and you must consider other factors along with book value when evaluating a possible stock investment.

With regard to stock prices, two other factors should be mentioned. First, predicting the future value for a share of stock is a practical example of the time value of money concepts presented in Chapter 1. The price that a successful investor is willing to pay for a share of stock is determined by

- The amount of dividends you expect to receive in the future, or
- A potential increase in the price for a share of stock, and/or
- A combination of future dividends and a potential increase in the price of the stock.

stock market bubble
A situation in which stocks are trading at prices above their actual worth.

Second, always remember that the price for a share of stock is determined by what another investor is willing to pay for it. While most successful investors use investment research and financial calculations to choose stock investments, there are times when investors may pay a high, inflated price for a share of stock. For example, the term **stock market bubble** is used to describe a situation when stocks are trading at prices above their actual worth. Often the high stock prices are driven by investor optimism and irrational expectations. Unfortunately, stock market bubbles may burst because of an economic slowdown, high unemployment rates, higher interest rates, and other factors that affect the economy. The bubble for a specific stock can also burst when a company lowers estimates for future earnings, a company reduces or omits dividend payments to stockholders, or stockholders begin to sell the stock for any other reason.

 Sheet 38 Evaluating Corporate Stocks

PRACTICE QUIZ 12-3

1. Explain the relationship between corporate earnings and a stock's market value.

2. Write the formula for the following stock calculations, and then describe how this formula could help you make a decision to buy or sell a stock.

Calculation	What Is the Formula?	Why Is This Calculation Useful?
Earnings per share		
Price-earnings (PE) ratio		
Dividend yield		
Total return		
Beta		
Book value		

Apply Yourself!

Use an Internet website to locate the current price for a share of stock and earnings per share for Microsoft (symbol MSFT), 3M Company (symbol MMM), and Colgate-Palmolive (symbol CL).

Buying and Selling Stocks

To purchase common or preferred stock, you generally have to work through a brokerage firm. In turn, your brokerage firm must buy the stock in either the primary or secondary market. In the **primary market,** you purchase financial securities, via an investment bank or other representative, from the issuer of those securities. An **investment bank** is a financial firm that assists corporations in raising funds, usually by helping to sell new security issues.

New security issues sold through an investment bank can be issued by corporations that have sold stocks and bonds before and need to sell new issues to raise additional financing. New securities can also be initial public offerings. An **initial public offering (IPO)** occurs when a corporation sells stock to the general public for the first time. In May 2014, Papa Murphy's—the U.S. company famous for high-quality "Take 'N' Bake" pizza—used an IPO to sell 5.8 million shares and raised approximately $70 million.[3] The money from the IPO can be used for expansion or any other activity to create a larger and more successful company.

Be warned: The promise of quick profits often lures investors to purchase IPOs. An IPO is generally classified as a high-risk investment—one made in the hope of earning a relatively large profit in a short time. Depending on the corporation selling the new security, IPOs are usually too speculative for most people.

Once stocks are sold in the primary market, they can be sold time and again in the secondary market. The **secondary market** is a market for existing financial securities that are currently traded among investors. The fact that stocks can be sold in the secondary market improves the liquidity of stock investments because the money you pay for stock goes to the seller of the stock.

Secondary Markets for Stocks

When you purchase stock in the secondary market, the transaction is completed on a securities exchange or through the over-the-counter market.

SECURITIES EXCHANGES   A **securities exchange** is a marketplace where member brokers who represent investors meet to buy and sell securities. Generally, the securities issued by nationwide corporations are traded at the New York Stock Exchange or regional exchanges in the United States. There are also foreign securities exchanges—in Tokyo, London, or Paris, for example.

The New York Stock Exchange (NYSE), now owned by the Intercontinental Exchange Group, is one of the largest securities exchanges in the world. Most of the NYSE members represent brokerage firms that charge commissions on security trades made by their representatives for their customers. Other members are called *specialists* or *specialist firms.* A **specialist** buys *or* sells a particular stock in an effort to maintain a fair and orderly market.

Before a corporation's stock is approved for listing on the NYSE, the corporation must meet specific listing requirements. The various regional exchanges also have listing requirements, but typically these are less stringent than the NYSE requirements. The stock of corporations that cannot meet the NYSE requirements, find it too expensive to be listed on the NYSE, or choose not to be listed on the NYSE is often traded on one of the regional exchanges, or through the over-the-counter market.

THE OVER-THE-COUNTER MARKET   Not all securities are traded on organized exchanges. Stocks issued by several thousand companies are traded in the over-the-counter market. The **over-the-counter (OTC) market** is a network of dealers who buy and

---

LO12.4
Describe how stocks are bought and sold.

ACTION ITEM

I know how to buy and sell stocks.

☐ **Yes**   ☐ **No**

primary market A market in which an investor purchases financial securities, via an investment bank or other representative, from the issuer of those securities.

investment bank A financial firm that assists corporations in raising funds, usually by helping to sell new security issues.

initial public offering (IPO) Occurs when a corporation sells stock to the general public for the first time.

secondary market A market for existing financial securities that are currently traded among investors.

securities exchange A marketplace where member brokers who represent investors meet to buy and sell securities.

specialist Buys or sells a particular stock in an effort to maintain an orderly market.

over-the-counter (OTC) market A network of dealers who buy and sell the stocks of corporations that are not listed on a securities exchange.

---

[3]The IPOScoop website (www.iposcoop.com), accessed April 25, 2014.

Nasdaq An electronic marketplace for stocks issued by approximately 3,300 different companies.

sell the stocks of corporations that are not listed on a securities exchange. Today these stocks are not really traded over the counter. The term was coined more than 100 years ago when securities were sold "over the counter" in stores and banks.

Most over-the-counter securities are traded through Nasdaq (pronounced "nazzdack"). **Nasdaq** is an electronic marketplace for stocks issued by approximately 3,300 different companies.[4] In addition to providing price information, this computerized system allows investors to buy and sell shares of companies traded on Nasdaq. When you want to buy or sell shares of a company that trades on Nasdaq—say, Microsoft—your account executive sends your order into the Nasdaq computer system, where it shows up on the screen with all the other orders from people who want to buy or sell Microsoft. Then a Nasdaq dealer (sometimes referred to as a *market maker*) sitting at a computer terminal matches buy and sell orders for Microsoft. Once a match is found, your order is completed. They may also complete buy or sell orders from their own inventory of shares that they maintain to meet the demands of investors.

Brokerage Firms and Account Executives

account executive A licensed individual who works for a brokerage firm and buys or sells securities for clients; also called a *stockbroker.*

An **account executive,** or *stockbroker,* is a licensed individual who works for a brokerage firm and buys or sells investments for his or her clients. Before choosing an account executive, you should have already determined your financial objectives. Then you must be careful to communicate those objectives to the account executive so that he or she can do a better job of advising you. To help avoid a situation in which your account executive's recommendations are automatically implemented, you should be *actively* involved in the decisions related to your investment program and you should never allow your account executive to use his or her discretion without your approval. Watch your account for signs of churning. **Churning** is excessive buying and selling of securities to generate commissions. Finally, keep in mind that account executives generally are not liable for client losses that result from their recommendations. In fact, most brokerage firms require clients to sign a statement in which they promise to submit any complaints to an arbitration board. This arbitration clause generally prevents a client from suing an account executive or a brokerage firm.

churning Excessive buying and selling of securities to generate commissions.

Should You Use a Full-Service, Discount, or Online Brokerage Firm?

Today a healthy competition exists between full-service, discount, and online brokerage firms. While the most obvious difference between full-service, discount, and online firms is the amount of the commissions they charge when you buy or sell stock and other securities, there are at least three other factors to consider. First, consider how much research information is available. All three types of brokerage firms offer excellent research materials, but you may have to pay for research information and access to professional advisory reports if you choose a discount or online brokerage firm.

Second, consider how much help you need when making an investment decision. Many full-service brokerage firms argue that you need a professional to help you make important investment decisions. On the other side, many discount and online brokerage firms argue that you alone are responsible for making your investment decisions. They are quick to point out that the most successful investors are the ones involved in their investment programs.

[4]The Nasdaq website (www.nasdaq.com), accessed April 25, 2014.

And they argue that they have both personnel and materials dedicated to helping you learn how to become a better investor. Although there are many exceptions, the information below may help you decide whether to use a full-service, discount, or online brokerage firm.

• Full-service	Beginning investors with little or no experience.
	Individuals who are uncomfortable making investment decisions.
	Individuals who are uncomfortable trading stocks online.
• Discount	People who understand the "how to" of researching stocks and prefer to make their own decisions.
	Individuals who are uncomfortable trading stocks online.
• Online	People who understand the "how to" of researching stocks and prefer to make their own decisions.
	Individuals who are comfortable trading stocks online.

Finally, consider how easy it is to buy and sell stock and other securities when using a full-service, discount, or online brokerage firm. Questions to ask include:

1. Can I buy or sell stocks using the Internet or over the phone?
2. What is the typical commission for a stock transaction?
3. Do you have a toll-free telephone number for customer use?
4. Is there a charge for statements, research reports, and other financial reports?
5. Are there any fees in addition to the commissions I pay when I buy or sell stocks?

Computerized Transactions

Many people still prefer to use telephone orders to buy and sell stocks, but a growing number are using computers to complete security transactions. To meet this need, online, discount, and most full-service brokerage firms allow investors to trade online.

As a rule of thumb, the more active the investor is, the more sense it makes to use computers to trade online. Other reasons that justify using a computer include the size of your investment portfolio and the ability to manage your investments closely.

While buying and selling stock online can make the investment process easier and faster, you should realize that *you* are still responsible for analyzing the information and making the final decision to buy or sell a security. In fact, many investors still prefer to have an account executive help make important financial decisions. Finally, some investors are reluctant to trade online because they are afraid they will make mistakes or the computer will garble their accounts.

Sample Stock Transactions

Once you have decided on a particular stock transaction, it is time to execute an order to buy or sell. Let's begin by examining three types of orders used to trade stocks.

CAUTION!

To find out if other investors have lodged complaints about an account executive or a brokerage firm go to the Securities and Exchange Commission website at www.sec.gov.

did you know?

When you purchase stock, you have three choices when it comes to holding your securities until they are sold.

- **Physical Certificate**—The security is registered in your name on the corporate books and you receive an actual stock certificate.

- **Street Name Registration**—The security is registered in the name of the brokerage firm on the corporate books and the brokerage firm holds the security for you.

- **Direct Registration**—The security is registered in your name on the corporate books, and either the company or its transfer agent holds the security for you.

For more information about each type of stock registration, go to www.sec.gov.

SOURCE: The Securities and Exchange website at www.sec.gov, accessed April 22, 2014.

market order A request to buy or sell a stock at the current market price.

limit order A request to buy or sell a stock at a specified price.

stop-loss order An order to sell a particular stock at the next available opportunity after its market price reaches a specified amount.

A **market order** is a request to buy or sell a stock at the current market price. Payment for stocks is generally required within three business days after the transaction. Today it is common practice for investors to leave stock certificates with a brokerage firm. Because the stock certificates are in the broker's care, transfers when the stock is sold are much easier. The phrase "left in the street name" is used to describe investor-owned securities held by a brokerage firm. Investors can also use two other types of stock registration—see the nearby "Did You Know?" feature about stock registration.

A **limit order** is a request to buy or sell a stock at a specified price. When you purchase stock, a limit order ensures that you will buy at the best possible price but not above a specified dollar amount. When you sell stock, a limit order ensures that you will sell at the best possible price, but not below a specified dollar amount. For example, if you place a limit order to buy eBay stock for $50 a share, the stock will not be purchased until the price drops to $50 a share or lower. Likewise, if your limit order is to sell eBay for $50 a share, the stock will not be sold until the price rises to $50 a share or higher. *Be warned:* Limit orders are executed if and when the specified price or better is reached and *all* other previously received orders have been fulfilled.

Many stockholders are certain they want to sell their stock if it reaches a specified price. A limit order does not guarantee this will be done. With a limit order, as mentioned above, orders by other investors may be placed ahead of your order. If you want to guarantee that your order will be executed, you place a special type of limit order known as a stop-loss order. A **stop-loss order** is an order to sell a particular stock at the next available opportunity after its market price reaches a specified amount. This type of order is used to protect an investor against a sharp drop in price and thus stop the dollar loss on a stock investment. For example, assume you purchased General Motors stock at $40 a share. Two weeks after you made that investment, General Motors reports lower-than-expected sales revenues and profits and is facing multiple product liability lawsuits because of faulty ignition switches. Fearing that the market value of your stock will decrease, you enter a stop-loss order to sell your General Motors stock at $30. This means that if the price of the stock decreases to $30 or lower, the account executive will sell it. While a stop-loss order does not guarantee that your stock will be sold at the price you specified, it does guarantee that it will be sold at the next available opportunity. Both limit and stop-loss orders may be good for one day, one week, one month, or good until canceled (GTC).

Before you begin investing your "real" money, you may want to practice. Today, numerous investment websites provide simulations that allow you to practice stock investing for free. To find a stock investment simulation, use an Internet search engine like Google or Yahoo! Enter the term "stock practice" or "virtual stock game," select a site, follow the rules, and use the practice to fine-tune your investment skills.

Commission Charges

Most brokerage firms have a minimum commission ranging from $5 to $25 for buying and selling stock. Additional commission charges are based on the number of shares and the value of stock bought and sold. *Note:* Some brokerage firms offer free trades, but strings are attached. For example, free trades may be an introductory offer, good for a limited time, or you may have to maintain a large balance in your investment account.

Exhibit 12–6 shows the minimum amount to open an account and typical commissions charged by discount and online brokerage firms. Generally, full-service and discount brokerage firms charge higher commissions than those charged by online brokerage firms. As a rule of thumb, full-service brokers may charge approximately 1 percent of the transaction amount. In return for charging higher commissions, full-service brokers usually spend more time with each client, help make investment decisions, and provide free research information.

Exhibit 12–6 Typical Commission Charges for Stock Transactions

Brokerage Firm	Minimum to Open an Account	Internet Trades	Broker-Assisted Trades
E*Trade	$500	$9.99	$54.99
Charles Schwab	$1,000	$8.95	$33.95
Fidelity	$0	$7.95	$32.95
Scottrade	$500	$7.00	$27.00
TD Ameritrade	$0	$9.99	$44.99

 Sheet 39 Investment Broker Comparison

PRACTICE QUIZ 12-4

1. What is the difference between the primary market and the secondary market? What is an initial public offering (IPO)?

2. Assume you want to purchase stock. Would you use a full-service broker or a discount broker? Would you ever trade stocks online?

3. Explain the important characteristics of each of the following types of stock transaction orders:

   a. Market order.
   b. Limit order.
   c. Stop-loss order.

Apply Yourself!

Prepare a list of at least five questions that could help you interview a prospective account executive.

Long-Term and Short-Term Investment Strategies

Once you purchase stock, the investment may be classified as either long term or short term. Generally, individuals who hold an investment for a year or longer are referred to as *investors*. Individuals who routinely buy and then sell stocks within a short period of time are called *speculators* or *traders*.

Long-Term Techniques

In this section, we discuss the long-term techniques of buy and hold, dollar cost averaging, direct investment programs, and dividend reinvestment programs.

BUY-AND-HOLD TECHNIQUE Many long-term investors purchase stock and hold on to it for a number of years. When they do this, their investment can increase in value in three ways. First, they are entitled to dividends if the board of directors approves dividend payments to stockholders. Second, the price of the stock may go up, or appreciate in value. To see how an investor using the buy-and-hold technique can earn profits from dividends and an increase in stock value, review the Johnson & Johnson investment illustrated in Exhibit 12–2. Third, the stock may be split. Although there are no guarantees, stock splits may increase the future value of a stock investment over a long period of time.

LO12.5

Explain the trading techniques used by long-term investors and short-term speculators.

ACTION ITEM

I know the difference between long-term and short-term investment techniques.
☐ **Agree** ☐ **Disagree**

dollar cost averaging A long-term technique used by investors who purchase an equal dollar amount of the same stock at equal intervals.

direct investment plan A plan that allows stockholders to purchase stock directly from a corporation without having to use an account executive or a brokerage firm.

dividend reinvestment plan A plan that allows current stockholders the option to reinvest or use their cash dividends to purchase stock of the corporation.

DOLLAR COST AVERAGING **Dollar cost averaging** is a long-term technique used by investors who purchase an equal dollar amount of the same stock at equal intervals. Assume you invest $2,000 in Johnson & Johnson's common stock each year for a period of seven years. The results of your investment program are illustrated in Exhibit 12–7. Notice that when the price of the stock decreased in 2009, you purchased more shares. And when the price of the stock increased in 2014, you purchased fewer shares. The average cost for a share of stock, determined by dividing the total investment ($14,000) by the total number of shares, is $66.51 ($14,000 ÷ 210.5 = $66.51). Other applications of dollar cost averaging occur when employees purchase shares of their company's stock through a payroll deduction plan or as part of an employer-sponsored retirement plan over an extended period of time.

The two goals of dollar cost averaging are to minimize the average cost per share and to avoid the common pitfall of buying high and selling low. In the situation shown in Exhibit 12–7, you would lose money only if you sold your stock at less than the average cost of $66.51. Thus, with dollar cost averaging, you can make money if the stock is sold at a price higher than the average cost for a share of stock.

DIRECT INVESTMENT AND DIVIDEND REINVESTMENT PLANS
Today a large number of corporations offer direct investment plans. A **direct investment plan** allows you to purchase stock directly from a corporation without having to use an account executive or a brokerage firm. Similarly, a **dividend reinvestment plan** (often called a DRIP) allows you the option to reinvest your cash dividends to purchase stock of the corporation. For stockholders, the chief advantage of both types of plans is that these plans enable them to purchase stock without paying a commission charge to a brokerage firm. (*Note:* A few companies may charge a small fee for direct and dividend reinvestment plans, but the fee is less than the commissions most brokerage firms charge.) The fees,

Exhibit 12–7 Dollar Cost Averaging for Johnson & Johnson

Year	Investment	Stock Price	Shares Purchased
2008	$ 2,000	$58	34.5
2009	2,000	50	40.0
2010	2,000	63	31.7
2011	2,000	65	30.8
2012	2,000	70	28.6
2013	2,000	84	23.8
2014	2,000	95	21.1
Total	$14,000		210.5

Average cost = Total investment ÷ Total shares

= $14,000 ÷ 210.5

= $66.51

Personal Finance in Practice

How Do I Pick a Winning Stock?

Good question! Now for some answers. Stock investors who are willing to do their homework can make sense out of all the information and numbers that are available. Below are some suggestions for pulling it all together.

1. **Learn why the information and numbers are important.** There are many sources—this chapter, self-help investing books, and Internet sites—that will help you learn the "how to" of researching a stock investment.

2. **Develop a plan or system to help organize the data.** With so much information available, you need to organize the information so that it makes sense. One suggestion is to use "Your Personal Financial Plan" sheet 38 (Evaluating Corporate Stock) located at the end of this chapter as a starting point. You can customize this sheet by adding or deleting questions that help you

establish a database of information for each potential stock investment.

3. **Use software and financial calculators to fine-tune your investment selections.** Many investment websites have both software and financial calculators that will help you evaluate a corporate stock. For example, a financial calculator that provides detailed information is MSN Money's Stock Screener (money .msn.com).

A final word of caution! Making informed investment decisions takes hard work and time. While each of the above suggestions will help you accumulate the information you need to make a more informed decision, a better approach is to use all three suggestions and any other available information to get a more complete picture of a corporation and the investment potential for its stock.

---

minimum investment amounts, rules, and features for both direct investment and dividend reinvestment vary from one corporation to the next. Also, with the direct investment and dividend reinvestment plans, you can take advantage of dollar cost averaging, discussed in the previous section. For corporations, the chief advantage of both types of plans is that they provide an additional source of capital. As an added bonus, they are providing a service to their stockholders. For more information about direct investment plans and dividend reinvestment plans, go to www.directinvesting.com or www.dripinvesting.org.

Short-Term Techniques

Investors sometimes use more speculative, short-term techniques. In this section, we discuss buying stock on margin, selling short, and trading in options. *Be warned:* The methods presented in this section are risky; do not use them unless you fully understand the underlying risks. Also, you should not use them until you have experienced success using the more traditional long-term techniques described above.

BUYING STOCK ON MARGIN When buying stock on **margin,** you borrow part of the money needed to buy a particular stock. The margin requirement is set by the Federal Reserve Board and is subject to periodic change. The current margin requirement is 50 percent. This requirement means you may borrow up to half of the total stock purchase price. Although margin is regulated by the Federal Reserve, specific requirements and the interest charged on the loans used to fund margin transactions may vary among brokerage firms. Usually the brokerage firm either lends the money or arranges the loan with another financial institution.

Investors buy on margin because the financial leverage created by borrowing money can increase the return on an investment. Because they can buy up to twice as much stock by buying on margin, they can earn larger returns. Suppose you expect the market price of a share of ExxonMobil to *increase* in the next three to four months. Let's say you have enough money to purchase 100 shares of the stock. However, if you buy on margin, you can purchase an additional 100 shares for a total of 200 shares.

margin A speculative technique whereby an investor borrows part of the money needed to buy a particular stock.

EXAMPLE: Margin Transaction

If the price of ExxonMobil's stock increases by $7 a share, your profit will be:

Without margin: $ 700 = $7 increase per share × 100 shares

With margin: $1,400 = $7 increase per share × 200 shares

In the preceding example, buying more shares on margin enables you to earn double the profit (less the interest you pay on the borrowed money and customary commission charges).

Keep in mind that the stock in a margin transaction serves as collateral for the loan. If the value of a margined stock decreases to approximately 65 percent of the original price, you will receive a *margin call* from the brokerage firm. After the margin call, you must pledge additional cash or securities to serve as collateral for the loan. If you don't have acceptable collateral or cash, the margined stock is sold and the proceeds are used to repay the loan. The exact price at which the brokerage firm issues the margin call is determined by the amount of money you borrowed when you purchased the stock. Generally, the more money you borrow, the sooner you will receive a margin call if the value of the margined stock drops.

In addition to facing the possibility of larger dollar losses because you own more shares, you must pay interest on the money borrowed to purchase stock on margin. Most brokerage firms charge 1 to 3 percent above the prime rate. Normally, economists define the prime rate as the interest rate that the best business customers must pay. Interest charges can absorb the potential profits if the value of margined stock does not increase rapidly enough and the margined stocks must be held for long periods of time.

SELLING SHORT Your ability to make money by buying and selling securities is related to how well you can predict whether a certain stock's price will increase or decrease. Normally, you buy stocks and assume they will increase in value, a procedure referred to as *buying long.* But not all stocks increase in value. In fact, the value of a stock may decrease for many reasons, including lower sales, lower profits, reduced dividends, product failures, increased competition, product liability lawsuits, and labor strikes. In addition, the health of a nation's economy can make a difference.

selling short Selling stock that has been borrowed from a brokerage firm and must be replaced at a later date.

When stock prices are declining, you may use a procedure called *selling short* to make money. **Selling short** is selling stock that has been borrowed from a brokerage firm and must be replaced at a later date. When you sell short, you sell today, knowing you must buy or *cover* your short transaction at a later date. To make money in a short transaction, you must take these steps:

1. Arrange to *borrow a stock certificate* for a specific number of shares of a particular stock from a brokerage firm.
2. *Sell the borrowed stock,* assuming it will drop in value in a reasonably short period of time.
3. *Buy the stock at a lower price* than the price it sold for in step 2.
4. Use the stock purchased in step 3 to *replace the stock borrowed from the brokerage firm* in step 1.

When selling short, your profit is the difference between the amount received when the stock is sold in step 2 and the amount paid for the stock in step 3. For example, assume that you think General Motors stock is overvalued at $40 a share. You also believe the stock will *decrease* in value over the next four to six months because of lower sales revenues and profits and a large number of product liability lawsuits. You call your broker and arrange to borrow 100 shares of General Motors stock (step 1). The broker then sells your borrowed stock for you at the current market price of $40 a share (step 2). Also assume that four months later General Motors stock drops to $32 a share. You instruct your broker to purchase 100 shares of General Motors stock at the current lower price (step 3). The newly purchased stock is given to the brokerage firm to repay the borrowed stock (step 4).

EXAMPLE: Selling Short

Your profit from the General Motors short transaction was $800 because the price declined from $40 to $32.

$4,000 Selling price   = $40 price per share × 100 shares (step 2)

− $3,200 Purchase price = $32 price per share × 100 shares (step 3)

$ 800 Profit from selling short

There is usually no special or extra brokerage charge for selling short, since the brokerage firm receives its regular commission when the stock is bought and sold. Before selling short, consider two factors. First, since the stock you borrow from your broker is actually owned by another investor, you must pay any dividends the stock earns before you replace the stock. After all, you borrowed the stock and then sold the borrowed stock. Eventually, dividends can absorb the profits from your short transaction if the price of the stock does not *decrease* rapidly enough. Second, to make money selling short, you must be correct in predicting that a stock will *decrease* in value. If the value of the stock increases, you lose.

TRADING IN OPTIONS An **option** gives you the right—but not the obligation—to buy or sell a stock at a predetermined price during a specified period of time. If you think the market price of a stock will increase during a short period of time, you may decide to purchase a call option. A *call option* is sold by a stockholder and gives the purchaser the right to *buy* 100 shares of a stock at a guaranteed price before a specified expiration date. With a call option, the purchaser is betting that the price of the stock will increase in value before the expiration date. If the stock's price does increase, the purchaser will be able to purchase the stock for the lower price guaranteed by the call option and then sell it for a profit.

It is also possible to purchase a put option. A *put option* is the right to sell 100 shares of a stock at a guaranteed price before a specified expiration date. With a put option, the purchaser is betting that the price of the stock will decrease in value before the expiration date. If the stock's price does decrease, the purchaser will be able to purchase stock at the lower price and then sell the stock for a higher price that is guaranteed by the put option. If these price movements do not occur before the expiration date, you lose the money you paid for your call or put option.

Because of the increased risk involved in option trading, a more detailed discussion of how you profit or lose money with options is beyond the scope of this book. *Be warned:* Amateurs and beginning investors should stay away from options unless they fully understand all of the risks involved. For the rookie, the lure of large profits over a short period of time may be tempting, but the risks are real.

option The right to buy or sell a stock at a predetermined price during a specified period of time.

PRACTICE QUIZ 12-5

1. In your own words, describe the difference between an investor and a speculator.

2. Describe each of the following investment techniques:

   a. Buy and hold.
   b. Dollar cost averaging.
   c. Direct investment.
   d. Dividend reinvestment.
   e. Margin.
   f. Selling short.
   g. Options.

Apply Yourself!

In a short paragraph, describe why you would use a long-term technique or a short-term technique to achieve your investment goals.

YOUR PERSONAL FINANCE DASHBOARD

HAVE YOU SAVED ENOUGH MONEY TO OPEN A BROKERAGE ACCOUNT AND PURCHASE YOUR FIRST STOCK?

Beginning investors are often reluctant to begin investing because of three factors. First, they don't have the money to establish an investment program. Second, they don't know how to research different investment alternatives. Third, they must use the services of a brokerage firm in order to buy or sell stock.

YOUR SITUATION: Have you saved enough money to open a brokerage account? Depending on the brokerage firm, you will typically need between $500 and $1,000 to open an account. Next, you should research any potential investment. Finally, you should open an account with a brokerage firm. The material in this chapter along with information available on Internet websites and material in the library will help.

POSSIBLE ACTIONS TO TAKE

 Reconsider the three steps required to begin investing in stocks that were described at the beginning of the chapter.

 Review the five suggestions to help you accumulate the money needed to fund your investment program—see Exhibit 11–1 for a refresher.

 Review the material on "Evaluating a Stock Issue" and "Numerical Measures That Influence Investment Decisions" in this chapter.

 Use the information in this chapter and Internet research to choose a brokerage firm. Then open an account so you can begin buying and selling stocks that can help you achieve your financial goals.

LO12.1 Corporations sell stock (a form of equity) to finance their business start-up costs and help pay for their ongoing business activities. In return for providing the money needed to finance the corporation, stockholders have the right to elect the board of directors. They must also approve major changes to corporate policies.

People invest in stock because they want the larger returns that stocks offer. Possible reasons for stock investments include dividend income, appreciation of value, and the *possibility* of gain through stock splits. In addition to common stock, a few corporations may issue preferred stock. The most important priority an investor in preferred stock enjoys is receiving cash dividends before any cash dividends are paid to common stockholders.

LO12.2 A wealth of information is available to stock investors. A logical place to start the evaluation process is with the classification of different types of stock investments that range from very conservative to very speculative—see Exhibit 12–3. Today, many investors use the information available on the Internet to evaluate individual stocks. Information is also available from stock advisory services, the newspaper, the corporations that issue stocks, business and personal finance periodicals, and government publications.

LO12.3 Many analysts believe that a corporation's ability or inability to generate earnings in the future may be one of the most significant factors that account for an increase or decrease in a stock's price. Generally, higher earnings equate to higher stock prices, and lower earnings equate to lower stock prices. Investors can also calculate earnings per share and a price-earnings ratio to evaluate a stock investment. Whereas both earnings per share and price-earnings ratio are historical numbers based on what a corporation has already done, investors can obtain earnings estimates for most corporations. Other calculations that help evaluate stock investments include dividend yield, total return, beta, and book value. Stock prices are also affected by what another investor will pay for a share of stock.

LO12.4 A corporation may sell a new stock issue with the help of an investment banking firm. Once the stock has been sold in the primary market, it can be sold time and again in the secondary market. In the secondary market, investors purchase stock listed on a securities exchange or traded in the over-the-counter market. Securities transactions are made through a full-service brokerage firm, a discount brokerage firm, or an online brokerage firm. Whether you trade online or not, you must decide if you want to use a market, limit, or stop-loss order to buy or sell stock. Most brokerage firms charge a minimum commission for buying or selling stock. Additional commission charges are based on the number and value of the stock shares bought or sold and if you use a full-service or discount brokerage firm or trade online.

LO12.5 Purchased stock may be classified as either a long-term investment or a speculative investment. Long-term investors typically hold their investments for at least a year or longer; speculators (sometimes referred to as traders) usually sell their investments within a shorter time period. Traditional trading techniques long-term investors use include the buy-and-hold technique, dollar cost averaging, direct investment plans, and dividend reinvestment plans. More speculative techniques include buying stock on margin, selling short, and trading in options.

Key Terms

account executive 404

beta 401

book value 401

churning 404

common stock 388

direct investment
  plan 408

dividend 388

dividend reinvestment
  plan 408

dividend yield 400

dollar cost
  averaging 408

earnings per share 398

equity financing 388

initial public offering
  (IPO) 403

investment bank 403

limit order 406

margin 409

market order 406

Nasdaq 404

option 411

over-the-counter (OTC)
  market 403

preferred stock 391

price-earnings (PE)
  ratio 399

primary market 403

proxy 388

record date 389

secondary market 403

securities exchange 403

selling short 410

specialist 403

stock market
  bubble 402

stock split 390

stop-loss order 406

total return 400

Key Formulas

Page	Topic	Formula
398	Earnings per share	$\text{Earnings per share} = \dfrac{\text{Earnings}}{\text{Number of shares outstanding}}$
399	Price-earnings (PE) ratio	$\text{Price-earnings (PE) ratio} = \dfrac{\text{Price per share}}{\text{Earnings per share}}$
400	Dividend yield	$\text{Dividend yield} = \dfrac{\text{Annual dividend amount}}{\text{Current price per share}}$
400	Total return	$\text{Total return} = \text{Dividends} + \text{Capital gain}$
401	Volatility for a stock	$\text{Increase in overall market} \times \text{Beta for a specific stock}$
401	Book value	$\text{Book value} = \text{Assets} - \dfrac{\text{Liabilities}}{\text{Number of shares outstanding}}$

Discussion Questions

1. In your own words, describe how an investment in common stock could help you obtain your investment goals.   (LO12.1)
2. Assume you have $5,000 to invest and are trying to decide between two different companies. One company is a tobacco company that has increased sales, profits, and dividends over the last five years. The second company manufactures high-tech "green" products. The second company has only been in existence for three years and has seen a slow increase in sales and profits and pays no dividends. You like the second company because it is a green company that could help to sustain the planet, but you like the financials of the tobacco company. Which company would you choose?   (LO12.2)
3. Explain the relationship between earnings per share, projected earnings, and the price for a share of stock.   (LO12.3)

Copyright © 2016 by McGraw-Hill Education

4. What is the difference between the dividend yield and total return calculations that were described in this chapter? (LO12.3)
5. Prepare a list of questions you could use to interview an account executive about career opportunities in the field of finance and investments. (LO12.4)
6. Prepare a chart that describes the similarities and differences among the long-term and short-term investment strategies described in this chapter. (LO12.5)

Self-Test Problems

1. Four years ago, Ken Guessford purchased 200 shares of Mountain View Manufacturing. At the time, each share of Mountain View was selling for $30. He also paid a $24 commission when the shares were purchased. Now, four years later, he has decided it's time to sell his investment. The Mountain View share price when sold was $32.50. In addition, he paid a $36 commission to sell his shares. He also received total dividends of $1.80 per share over the four-year investment period.

   a. What is the total amount of dividends Mr. Guessford received over the four-year period?
   b. What was the total return for Mr. Guessford's investment?

2. Karen Newton is trying to decide between two different stock investments, and she asks for your help. Information about each investment is below.

Company	Price per Share	Annual Dividend	Earnings This Year	Projected Earnings Next Year	Number of Shares Outstanding
Jackson Utility Construction	$22	$0.30	$34 million	$39 million	20 million shares
West Coast Homes	$46	$0.52	$182 million	$142 million	130 million shares

   a. Calculate the dividend yield for each company.
   b. Calculate the earnings per share for each company.
   c. Based on this information, which company would you recommend?

Solutions

1. a. Total dividends = $1.80 per share dividends × 200 shares = $360.
   b. Dividends = $1.80 per share dividends × 200 shares = $360.
      Purchase price = $30 per share × 200 shares = $6,000 + $24 commission = $6,024.
      Selling price = $32.50 per share × 200 shares = $6,500 − $36 commission = $6,464.
      Capital gain = $6,464 selling price − $6,024 purchase price = $440.
      Total return = $360 dividends + $440 capital gain = $800.

2. a. The dividend yield for each company is

   Jackson: Dividend yield = $\dfrac{\$0.30 \text{ annual dividend}}{\$22 \text{ current price}}$

   $= 0.014 = 1.4$ percent

   West Coast: Dividend yield = $\dfrac{\$0.52 \text{ annual dividend}}{\$46 \text{ current price}}$

   $= 0.011 = 1.1$ percent

b. The earnings per share for each company are

Jackson: Earnings per share $= \dfrac{\$34,000,000 \text{ income}}{20,000,000 \text{ shares}}$

$= \$1.70$

West Coast: Earnings per share $= \dfrac{\$182,000,000 \text{ income}}{130,000,000 \text{ shares}}$

$= \$1.40$

c. On the surface, the financial amounts for West Coast Homes are impressive because they are larger than the amounts for Jackson Utility Construction. But as the calculations for dividend yield and earnings per share illustrate, Jackson Utility Construction may be the better investment. Jackson's dividend yield (1.4 percent) is higher than West Coast's dividend yield (1.1 percent). Also, the earnings per share for Jackson are higher ($1.70) when compared to the earnings per share for West Coast ($1.40). Before making your choice, look at the projected earnings for next year. Jackson's earnings are increasing; West Coast's earnings are projected to decline. Given just the above information, Jackson Utility Construction may be the better choice. What do you think?

Problems

1. Jamie and Peter Dawson own 220 shares of Duke Energy common stock. Duke Energy's quarterly dividend is $0.28 per share. What is the amount of the dividend check the Dawson couple will receive for this quarter?   (LO12.1)

2. During the four quarters for 2015, the Browns received two quarterly dividend payments of $0.18, one quarterly payment of $0.20, and one quarterly payment of $0.22. If they owned 300 shares of stock, what was their total dividend income for 2015?   (LO12.1)

3. Jim Johansen noticed that a corporation he is considering investing in is about to pay a quarterly dividend. The record date is Thursday, March 15. In order for Jim to receive this quarterly dividend, what is the last date that he could purchase stock in this corporation and receive this quarter's dividend payment?   (LO12.1)

4. Sarah and James Hernandez purchased 140 shares of Macy's stock at $57 a share. One year later, they sold the stock for $61 a share. They paid a broker an $8 commission when they purchased the stock and a $12 commission when they sold the stock. During the 12-month period the couple owned the stock, Macy's paid dividends that totaled $1.00. Calculate the Hernandezes' total return for this investment.   (LO12.1)

5. Wanda Sotheby purchased 120 shares of Home Depot stock at $82 a share. One year later, she sold the stock for $74 a share. She paid her broker a $34 commission when she purchased the stock and a $39 commission when she sold it. During the 12 months she owned the stock, she received $188 in dividends. Calculate Wanda's total return on this investment.   (LO12.1)

6. In September, the board of directors of Chaparral Steel approved a 2-for-1 stock split. After the split, how many shares of Chaparral Steel stock will an investor have if he or she owned 400 shares before the split?   (LO12.1)

7. Michelle Townsend owns stock in National Computers. Based on information in its annual report, National Computers reported after-tax earnings of $9,700,000 and has issued 7,000,000 shares of common stock. The stock is currently selling for $32 a share.   (LO12.3)

    a. Calculate the earnings per share for National Computers.
    b. Calculate the price-earnings (PE) ratio for National Computers.

8. Analysts that follow JPMorgan Chase, one of the nation's largest providers of financial services, estimate that the corporation's earnings per share will increase from $5.56 in the current year to $6.12 next year.   (LO12.3)

   a. What is the amount of the increase?
   b. What effect, if any, should this increase have on the value of the corporation's stock?

9. Currently, Boeing pays an annual dividend of $2.92. If the stock is selling for $128, what is the dividend yield?   (LO12.3)

10. Ford Motor Company has a 1.35 beta. If the overall stock market increases by 6 percent, how much will Ford change? (LO12.3)

11. Casper Energy Exploration reports that the corporation's assets are valued at $185,000,000, its liabilities are $80,000,000, and it has issued 6,000,000 shares of stock. What is the book value for a share of Casper stock?   (LO12.3)

12. For four years, Marty Campbell invested $4,000 each year in Harley-Davidson. The stock was selling for $36 in 2011, $45 in 2012, $52 in 2013, and $70 in 2014.   (LO12.5)

   a. What is Marty's total investment in Harley-Davidson?
   b. After four years, how many shares does Marty own?
   c. What is the average cost per share of Marty's investment?

13. Bob Orleans invested $3,000 and borrowed $3,000 to purchase shares in Verizon Communications. At the time of his investment, Verizon was selling for $45 a share.   (LO12.5)

   a. If Bob paid a $30 commission, how many shares could he buy if he used *only* his own money and did not use margin?
   b. If Bob paid a $60 commission, how many shares could he buy if he used his $3,000 and borrowed $3,000 on margin to buy Verizon stock?
   c. Assuming Bob did use margin, paid a $60 total commission to buy his Verizon stock and another $60 to sell his stock, and sold the stock for $52 a share, how much profit did he make on his Verizon stock investment?

14. After researching Valero Energy common stock, Sandra Pearson is convinced the stock is overpriced. She contacts her account executive and arranges to sell short 300 shares of Valero Energy. At the time of the sale, a share of common stock had a value of $56. Three months later, Valero Energy is selling for $47 a share, and Sandra instructs her broker to cover her short transaction. Total commissions to buy and sell the stock were $36. What is her profit for this short transaction?   (LO12.5)

 **To reinforce the content in this chapter, more problems are provided at connect.mheducation.com.**
|FINANCE

Case in Point

RESEARCH INFORMATION AVAILABLE FROM VALUE LINE

This chapter stressed the importance of evaluating potential investments. Now it's your turn to try your skill at evaluating a potential investment in the Walt Disney Company. Assume you could invest $10,000 in the common stock of this company. To help you evaluate this potential investment, carefully examine Exhibit 12–5, which reproduces the research report about Disney from Value Line. The report was published in February 2014.

Questions

1. Based on the research provided by Value Line, would you buy Disney stock? Justify your answer.

2. What other investment information would you need to evaluate Disney common stock? Where would you obtain this information?

3. On February 7, 2014, Disney stock was selling for $75 a share. Using the

Internet or a newspaper, determine the current price for a share of Disney. Based on this information, would your Disney investment have been profitable? (*Hint:* Disney's stock symbol is DIS.)

4. Assuming you purchased Disney stock on February 7, 2014, and based on your answer to question 3, how would you decide if you want to hold or sell your Disney stock? Explain your answer.

Continuing Case

INVESTING IN STOCKS

The triplets are now entering high school and Jamie Lee and Ross are comfortable with their financial and investment strategies. They budgeted throughout the years and are on track to reach their long-term investment goals of paying the triplets' college tuition and accumulating enough to purchase a beach house to enjoy when Jamie and Ross retire.

Recently, Ross inherited $50,000 from his uncle's estate. Ross would like to invest in stocks to supplement their retirement income goals.

Jamie Lee and Ross have been watching a technology company that has an upcoming initial public offering and several other stocks for well-established companies, but they are unsure which stocks to invest in and are also wondering if their choices will fit their moderate risk investment strategies. They want to make the best decisions they can to maximize chances they will benefit from positive investment returns.

Questions

1. What is the benefit to Jamie Lee and Ross of investing in a company's IPO? Will they be guaranteed a large return from this investment? At this life stage, would you recommend that Jamie Lee and Ross invest in an IPO? Why or why not?

2. Jamie Lee's father suggested that they purchase stock in a company that he has held shares in for decades. They want to take advantage of the stock tip, but Jamie Lee and Ross are trying to decide between purchasing the company's common stock and preferred stock. What are the advantages to each type of stock?

3. Currently, the economy is in the recovery stage. Referring to Exhibit 12–3, what types of stock would you suggest for Jamie and Ross to invest in considering their life stage and current moderate investment strategies? What characteristics are associated with the types of investments you suggested?

4. Suppose Jamie Lee and Ross are evaluating corporate stocks to add to their investment portfolio. Using "Your Personal Financial Plan" sheet 38, select a company from your own personal experiences, such as an automobile or technology company, and research the information needed to complete the worksheet.

   a. Do you suggest that Jamie Lee and Ross invest in this company? Provide support for your evaluation based on "Your Personal Financial Plan" sheet 38 research findings for that company.

   b. If they should invest in that company, how much of their $50,000 inheritance should they allocate toward the purchase of shares in that company?

   c. Regardless of your position on whether they should invest in your chosen company, if Jamie Lee and Ross went ahead and purchased shares of stock in that company, how many shares could they purchase with the $50,000?

   d. What would be the total transaction cost if they purchased the shares online? (List the source for your answer.)

"INVESTING IN STOCK IS NOT POSSIBLE. I'M BARELY ABLE TO PAY MY VARIOUS LIVING EXPENSES."

Directions Your Daily Spending Diary will help you manage your expenses to create a better overall spending plan. Once you know and try to control your spending, you will likely be able to have funds available for various types of investments. The Daily Spending Diary sheets are located in Appendix D at the end of the book and in Connect Finance.

Questions

1. What information from your daily spending records could help you achieve your financial goals?
2. Based on your observations of our society and the economy, what types of stocks might you consider for investing now or in the near future?

YOUR PERSONAL FINANCIAL PLAN

Name: _____ Date: _____

Evaluating Corporate Stocks

Purpose: To identify a corporate stock that might help you attain your investment goals.

Financial Planning Activities: No checklist can serve as a foolproof guide for choosing a common or preferred stock. However, the following questions will help you evaluate a potential stock investment. Use stock websites on the Internet and/or use library materials to answer these questions about a corporate stock that you believe could help you obtain your investment goals. This sheet is also available in an Excel spreadsheet format in Connect Finance.

Suggested Websites: finance.yahoo.com   www.marketwatch.com   money.msn.com

Category 1: The Basics

1. What is the corporation's name?

   _____

2. What are the corporation's website address and telephone number? _____

   _____

3. Have you read the latest annual report and quarterly report? ☐ Yes ☐ No

4. What information about the corporation is available on the Internet? _____

   _____

5. Where is the stock traded (NYSE or Nasdaq)?

   _____

6. What types of products or services does this firm provide? _____

7. Briefly describe the prospects for this company. (Include significant factors like product development, plans for expansion, plans for mergers, etc.) _____

Category 2: Dividend Income

8. Is the corporation currently paying dividends? If so, how much? _____

9. What is the dividend yield for this stock?

   _____

10. Have dividends increased or decreased over the past three years?_____

    _____

11. How does the dividend yield for this investment compare with other potential investments?

    _____

Category 3: Financial Performance

12. What are the firm's earnings per share for the last year? _____

13. Have the firm's earnings increased over the past three years? _____

14. What is the firm's current price-earnings ratio?

    _____

15. How does the firm's current price-earnings (PE) ratio compare with that of firms in the same industry? _____

16. Describe trends for the firm's price-earnings ratio over the past three years. Do these trends show improvement or decline in investment value? ____

    _____

17. What are the firm's projected earnings for the next year? _____

18. Have sales increased over the last five years?

    _____

19. What is the stock's current price?

    _____

20. What are the 52-week high and low for this stock? _____

21. Does your analysis indicate that this is a good stock to buy at this time?

    _____

22. Briefly describe any other information that you obtained from Mergent, Value Line, Standard & Poor's, or other sources of information.

A Word of Caution

When you use a checklist, there is always a danger of overlooking important relevant information. Quite simply, it is a place to start. If you need more information, *you* are responsible for obtaining it and for determining how it affects your potential investment.

Suggested App:
• Yahoo! Finance

What's Next for Your Personal Financial Plan?

• Identify additional factors that may affect your decision to invest in this corporation's stock.
• Develop a plan for monitoring an investment's value once a stock is purchased.

Investment Broker Comparison

Purpose: To compare the benefits and costs of different investment brokers.

Financial Planning Activities: Compare the services of an investment broker based on the factors listed below. This sheet is also available in an Excel spreadsheet format in Connect Finance.

Suggested Websites: www.brokerage-review.com   www.brokerstance.com
www.stockbrokers.com

	Broker Number 1	Broker Number 2
Broker's name		
Brokerage firm		
Address		
Phone		
Website		
Years of experience		
Education and training		
Areas of specialization		
Certifications and licenses held		
Employer's stock exchange and financial market affiliations		
Information services offered		
Minimum commission charge		
Commission on 100 shares of stock at $50 per share		
Fees for other investments: • Corporate bonds • Government bonds • Mutual funds		
Other fees: • Annual account fee • Inactivity fee • Other		

What's Next for Your Personal Financial Plan?

- Using the information you obtained, choose a brokerage firm that you feel will help you attain your investment goals.
- Access the website for the brokerage firm you have chosen and answer the questions on page 405 in your text.

13 Investing in Mutual Funds

3 Steps to Financial Literacy . . . Begin Investing in Mutual Funds

Learn about different types of funds.
Website: www.mfea.com

1

Research the services and fees offered by different brokerage firms.
App: Vanguard

2

Evaluate different funds that will help achieve your investment goals.
Website: finance.yahoo.com

3

For many investors, mutual funds have become the investment of choice. In fact, you can choose from almost 11,000 different funds. So how do you choose the right fund to help you attain your long-term investment goals? To help answer that question, read the material in this chapter. At the end of the chapter, "Your Personal Finance Dashboard," along with other end-of-chapter learning activities, will help you improve your ability to pick the right funds to develop a long-term investment program and achieve your financial goals.

CHAPTER 13 LEARNING OBJECTIVES

In this chapter, you will learn to:

LO13.1 Explain the characteristics of mutual fund investments.

LO13.2 Classify mutual funds by investment objective.

LO13.3 Evaluate mutual funds.

LO13.4 Describe how and why mutual funds are bought and sold.

YOUR PERSONAL FINANCIAL PLAN SHEETS

40. Evaluating Mutual Fund Investment Information
41. Mutual Fund Evaluation

If you ever thought about buying stocks or bonds but decided not to, your reasons were probably like most other people's: You didn't know enough to make a good decision, and you lacked enough money to diversify your investments among several choices. These same two reasons explain why people invest in mutual funds. A **mutual fund** pools the money of many investors—its shareholders—to invest in a variety of securities.[1] For a fee, a professional fund manager or team of managers that work for an investment company invest money from investors in stocks, bonds, money market securities, or some combination of these securities appropriate to a fund's investment objective.

Mutual funds are an excellent choice for many individuals. In many cases, they can also be used for retirement accounts, including traditional individual retirement accounts, Roth IRAs, and 401(k) and 403(b) retirement accounts.

An investment in mutual funds is based on the concept of opportunity costs, which we have discussed throughout this text. Simply put, you have to be willing to take some chances if you want to get larger returns on your investments. But a "real risk" is associated with investing in funds. The fact that fund investments can decrease in value does underscore the need to understand the risk associated with all investments, including mutual funds.

mutual fund Pools the money of many investors—its shareholders—to invest in a variety of securities.

LO13.1

Explain the characteristics of mutual fund investments.

ACTION ITEM

I understand the reasons investors invest in mutual funds.

☐ **Agree**   ☐ **Disagree**

Why Investors Purchase Mutual Funds

For many investors, the notion of investing their money in a mutual fund may be a new idea, but mutual funds have been around for a long time. Fund investing began in Europe in the late 1700s and became popular in the United States before the Great Depression in 1929. After the depression, government regulation increased, the number of funds grew, and the amount invested in funds continued to increase. New types of funds, including index funds, aggressive growth funds, and social responsibility (or green) funds, were created

[1]The Mutual Fund Education Alliance (www.mfea.com), accessed May 20, 2014.

to meet the needs of a larger and more demanding group of investors. During this same time period, the cost of investing in funds decreased while the popularity of fund investing increased. Experts often say that one man, John Bogle, was the driving force behind attempts to make fund investing affordable for the average American. When he introduced the Vanguard 500 Index Fund in 1976, he gave investors a low-cost way to invest in funds while providing investment diversification. Today, the Vanguard Group he founded is one of the largest fund companies that competes with other companies in the fund industry.

Despite the accusations of fraud and mutual fund scandals in the first part of the 21st century and poor fund performance and investor losses during the last economic crisis, mutual funds are still the investment of choice for many investors. The following statistics illustrate how important mutual fund investments are to both individuals and the nation's economy:

1. Over 96 million individuals own mutual funds in the United States.[2]
2. The number of funds grew from 361 in 1970 to almost 11,000 by 2013.[3]
3. The combined value of assets owned by investment companies in the United States totals $17 trillion.[4]

No doubt about it, the mutual fund industry is big business. And yet you may be wondering why so many people invest in mutual funds.

did you know?

Who owns mutual funds?

- 9% 65 years old and over
- 24% Less than 35 years old
- 12% 55 to 64 years old
- 23% 45 to 54 years old
- 32% 35 to 44 years old

SOURCE: The Investment Company Fact Book at www.ici.org, accessed May 20, 2014.

The Psychology of Investing in Funds

The major reasons investors purchase mutual funds are *professional management* and *diversification.* Most investment companies do everything possible to convince you that they can do a better job of picking securities than you can. Sometimes these claims are true, and sometimes they are just so much hot air. Still, investment companies do have professional fund managers with years of experience who devote large amounts of time to picking just the "right" securities for their funds' portfolios. *Be warned:* Even the best portfolio managers make mistakes. So you must be careful and evaluate a fund before investing your money.

The diversification mutual funds offer spells safety, because a loss incurred with one investment contained in a fund may be offset by gains from other investments in the fund. For example, consider the diversification provided in the portfolio of the Invesco Dividend Income Fund, shown in Exhibit 13–1. An investment in the $517 million Invesco Dividend Income Fund represents ownership in over 50 different companies included in the fund's investment portfolio. Investors enjoy diversification coupled with Invesco's stock-selection expertise. For beginning investors or investors without a great deal of money to invest, the diversification offered by funds is especially important because there is no other practical way to purchase the individual stocks issued by a large number of corporations. A fund like the Invesco Dividend Income Fund, on the other hand, can provide a practical way for investors to obtain diversification because the fund can use the pooled money of a large number of investors to purchase shares of many different companies.

[2]The Investment Company Institute (www.ici.org), accessed May 20, 2014.
[3]Ibid.
[4]Ibid.

Top Industries	% of Total Assets
Electric utilities	12.42
Multi-utilities	10.22
Packaged foods and meats	8.03
Pharmaceuticals	7.29
Integrated telecommunication services	6.94
Aerospace and defense	5.94
Integrated oil and gas	5.70
Tobacco	4.66
Regional banks	3.54
Semiconductors	3.36
Top Equity Holdings I	**% of Total Assets**
Lockheed Martin Corp.	4.21
Pepco Holdings Inc.	3.40
Kraft Foods Group Inc.	3.20
Total SA	2.87
Altria Group Inc.	2.81
Duke Energy Corp.	2.65
AGL Resources Inc.	2.55
General Mills Inc.	2.48
Federated Investors Inc.	2.48
Johnson & Johnson	2.43

Exhibit 13–1

Types of Securities Included in the Portfolio of the Invesco Dividend Income Fund

Holdings are subject to change and are not buy/sell recommendations.
SOURCE: Invesco (www.invescoaim.com), accessed May 20, 2014.

Characteristics of Funds

Today funds may be classified as closed-end funds, exchange-traded funds, or open-end funds.

CLOSED-END, EXCHANGE-TRADED, OR OPEN-END MUTUAL FUNDS

Approximately 600, or about 6 percent, of all mutual funds are closed-end funds offered by investment companies.[5] A **closed-end fund** is a mutual fund whose shares are issued by an investment company only when the fund is organized. As a result, only a certain number of shares are available to investors. After all the shares originally issued have been sold, an investor can purchase shares only from another investor who is willing to sell. Closed-end funds are actively managed by professional fund managers and shares are traded on the floors of stock exchanges or in the over-the-counter market. Like the prices of stocks, the prices of shares for closed-end funds are determined by the factors of supply and demand, by the value of stocks and other investments contained in the fund's portfolio, and by investor expectations.

closed-end fund A mutual fund whose shares are issued by an investment company only when the fund is organized.

[5]The Investment Company Institute (www.ici.org), accessed May 20, 2014.

exchange-traded fund (ETF) A fund that invests in the stocks or other securities contained in a specific stock or securities index, and whose shares are traded on a securities exchange or over the counter.

An **exchange-traded fund (ETF)** is a fund that invests in the stocks or other securities contained in a specific stock or securities index. While most investors think of an ETF as investing in the stocks contained in the Standard & Poor's 500 stock index, the Dow Jones Industrial Average, or the Nasdaq 100 Index, many different types of ETFs available today attempt to track all kinds of indexes, including:

- Midcap stocks.
- Small-cap stocks.
- Fixed-income securities.
- Stocks issued by companies in specific industries.
- Stocks issued by corporations in different countries.

Like a closed-end fund, shares of an exchange-traded fund are traded on a securities exchange or in the over-the-counter market. With both types of funds, an investor can purchase as little as one share of a fund. Also like a closed-end fund, prices for shares in an ETF are determined by supply and demand, the value of stocks and other investments contained in the fund's portfolio, and by investor expectations.

Although exchange-traded funds are similar to closed-end funds, there is an important difference. Most closed-end funds are actively managed, with portfolio managers making the selection of stocks and other securities contained in a closed-end fund. An exchange-traded fund, on the other hand, invests in the securities included in a specific index. Exchange-traded funds tend to mirror the performance of the index, moving up or down as the individual securities contained in the index move up or down. Therefore, there is less need for a portfolio manager to make investment decisions. Because of passive management, fees associated with owning shares are generally lower than those of both closed-end and open-end funds. In addition to lower fees, other advantages to investing in ETFs include:

- There is no minimum investment amount, because shares are traded on an exchange and not purchased from an investment company.
- Shares can be bought or sold through a brokerage firm any time during regular market hours at the current price.
- You can use limit orders and the more speculative techniques of selling short and buying on margin—all discussed in Chapter 12—to buy and sell ETF shares.

open-end fund A mutual fund whose shares are issued and redeemed by the investment company at the request of investors.

Although increasing in popularity, approximately 1,300, or about 12 percent of all funds, are exchange-traded funds.[6]

Approximately 9,000, or about 82 percent of all mutual funds, are open-end funds.[7] An **open-end fund** is a mutual fund whose shares are issued and redeemed by the investment company at the request of investors. Investors are free to buy and sell shares at the net asset value. The **net asset value (NAV)** per share is equal to the current market value of securities contained in the mutual fund's portfolio minus the mutual fund's liabilities divided by the number of shares outstanding.

net asset value (NAV) The current market value of the securities contained in the mutual fund's portfolio minus the mutual fund's liabilities divided by the number of shares outstanding.

[**EXAMPLE: Net Asset Value**

The investments contained in the New American Frontiers Mutual Fund have a current market value of $980 million. The fund also has liabilities that total $10 million. If this mutual fund has 40 million shares, the net asset value per share is $24.25, as shown below.

$$\text{Net asset value} = \frac{\text{Value of the fund's portfolio} - \text{Liabilities}}{\text{Number of shares outstanding}}$$

$$= \frac{\$980 \text{ million} - \$10 \text{ million}}{40 \text{ million shares}} = \$24.25 \text{ NAV per share}$$

]

[6]Ibid.
[7]Ibid.

For most open-end funds, the net asset value is calculated at the close of trading each day.

In addition to buying and selling shares on request, most open-end funds provide their investors with a wide variety of services, including payroll deduction programs, automatic reinvestment programs, automatic withdrawal programs, and the option to change shares in one fund to another fund within the same fund family—all topics discussed later in this chapter.

COSTS: LOAD FUNDS COMPARED TO NO-LOAD FUNDS

Before investing in mutual funds, you should compare the cost of this type of investment with the cost of other investment alternatives, such as stocks or bonds. With regard to cost, mutual funds are classified as load funds or no-load funds. A **load fund** (sometimes referred to as an *A fund*) is a mutual fund in which investors pay a commission every time they purchase shares. The commission, often referred to as the *sales charge,* may be as high as 8.5 percent of the purchase price for investments.

> **load fund** A mutual fund in which investors pay a commission (as high as 8.5 percent) every time they purchase shares.

EXAMPLE: Sales Charge Calculation

The Davis Opportunity mutual fund charges a sales load of 4.75 percent. If you invest $10,000, you must pay a $475 commission to purchase shares. After paying the commission, the amount available for investment is $9,525, as shown below.

Load charge = Dollar amount of investment × Load stated as a percentage

= $10,000 × 4.75 percent = $475

Amount available for investment = Investment amount − Load charge

= $10,000 − $475 = $9,525

Many exceptions exist, but the average load charge for mutual funds is between 3 and 5 percent. In fact, two specific exceptions should be noted. First, investment companies offering front-end load funds often waive or lower fees for shares purchased for retirement accounts. Second, load funds are often lower for investors who make large purchases.[8] The "stated" advantage of a load fund is that the fund's sales force (account executives, financial planners, or employees of brokerage divisions of banks and other financial institutions) will explain the mutual fund, help you determine which fund will help you achieve your financial objectives, and offer advice as to when shares of the fund should be bought or sold.

> **no-load fund** A mutual fund in which the individual investor pays no sales charge.

A **no-load fund** is a mutual fund in which the individual investor pays no sales charge. No-load funds don't charge commissions when you buy shares because they have no salespeople. If you want to buy shares of a no-load fund, you must make your own decisions and deal directly with the investment company. The usual means of contact is by telephone, the Internet, or mail. You can also purchase shares in a no-load fund from many discount brokers, including Charles Schwab, TD Ameritrade, and E*Trade.

As an investor, you must decide whether to invest in a load fund or a no-load fund. Some investment salespeople have claimed that load funds outperform no-load funds. But many financial analysts suggest there is generally no significant difference between mutual funds that charge commissions and

digi – know?

Where can I find out more information about mutual fund fees?

For more information about the different types of fees that mutual funds charge, you can use an Internet search engine like Google or Yahoo! and enter "mutual fund fees." You can also learn about mutual fund fees at the Securities and Exchange Commission website at www.sec.gov/answers/mffees.htm.

---

[8]The Investment Company Fact Book at www.ici.org, accessed May 20, 2014.

those that do not.[9] Since no-load funds offer the same investment opportunities load funds offer, you should investigate them further before deciding which type of mutual fund is best for you.

contingent deferred sales load A 1 to 5 percent charge that shareholders pay when they sell shares in a mutual fund.

Instead of charging investors a fee when they purchase shares in a mutual fund, some mutual funds charge a **contingent deferred sales load** (sometimes referred to as a *back-end load*, a *B fund*, or a *redemption fee*) when shares are sold. Typically, these fees range from 1 to 5 percent, depending on how long you own the mutual fund before making a withdrawal. For example, you may pay a 5 percent contingent deferred sales load if you withdraw money the first year after your initial investment. In most cases, this fee declines every year until it disappears if you own shares in the fund for more than five years.

EXAMPLE: Contingent Deferred Sales Load

Assume you withdraw $6,000 from B shares that you own in the Oppenheimer Capital Income Fund within a year of your purchase date. If you purchase shares with a contingent deferred sales load, you must pay a 5 percent fee for any withdrawals during the first year. Your fee is $300. After deducting the fee, you will receive $5,700, as shown below.

$$\text{Contingent deferred sales load} = \text{Amount of withdrawal} \times \text{Fee stated as a percentage}$$

$$= \$6,000 \times 5 \text{ percent} = \$300$$

$$\text{Amount you receive} = \text{Amount of withdrawal} - \text{Contingent deferred sales fee}$$

$$= \$6,000 - \$300 = \$5,700$$

COSTS: MANAGEMENT FEES AND OTHER CHARGES Mutual fund fees are important because they reduce your investment return and are a major factor to consider when choosing a fund. For example, the investment companies that sponsor funds charge management fees. This fee, which is disclosed in the fund's prospectus, is a fixed percentage of the fund's net asset value on a predetermined date. Today annual management fees range between 0.25 and 1.5 percent of the fund's net asset value. While fees vary considerably, the average is 0.5 to 1 percent of the fund's net asset value.

12b-1 fee A fee that an investment company levies to defray the costs of advertising and marketing a mutual fund.

The investment company may also levy a **12b-1 fee** (sometimes referred to as a *distribution fee*) to defray the costs of marketing a mutual fund, commissions paid to a broker who sold you shares in the fund, and shareholder service fees. Approved by the Securities and Exchange Commission, annual 12b-1 fees are calculated on the value of a fund's net assets and cannot exceed 1 percent of a fund's assets per year. *Note:* For a fund to be called a "no-load" fund, its 12b-1 fee must not exceed 0.25 percent of its assets.

Unlike the one-time sales load fees that mutual funds charge to purchase or sell shares, the 12b-1 fee is often an ongoing fee that is charged on an annual basis. Note that 12b-1 fees can cost you a lot of money over a period of years. Assuming there is no difference in performance offered by two different mutual funds, one of which charges a 12b-1 fee while the other doesn't, choose the latter fund. The 12b-1 fee is so lucrative for investment companies that a number of them have begun selling Class C shares that often charge a higher 12b-1 fee and no sales load or contingent deferred sales load to attract new investors. (*Note:* Some investment companies may charge a small contingent deferred sales load for Class C shares if withdrawals are made within a short time—usually one year.) When compared to Class A shares (commissions charged when shares are purchased) and Class B shares (commissions charged when withdrawals are made over the first five years),

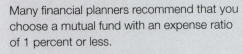

CAUTION!

Many financial planners recommend that you choose a mutual fund with an expense ratio of 1 percent or less.

[9]Bill Barker, "The Truth about Mutual Fund Loads," *The Motley Fool* (www.fool.com), accessed May 21, 2014.

Class C shares, with their ongoing, higher 12b-1 fees, may be more expensive over a long period of time.

Together, all the different management fees and fund operating costs are often referred to as an **expense ratio.** Since it is important to keep fees and costs as low as possible, you should examine a fund's expense ratio as one more fact to consider when evaluating a mutual fund.

The investment company's prospectus must provide all details relating to management fees, sales fees, 12b-1 fees, and other expenses. Exhibit 13–2 reproduces the summary of expenses (sometimes called a *fee table*) taken from the Davis Opportunity Fund. Notice that this fee table has two separate parts. The first part describes shareholder transaction expenses. For this fund, the maximum sales charge is 4.75 percent. The second part describes the fund's annual operating expenses. For this fund, the expense ratio is 0.98 percent for Class A shares.

By now, you are probably asking yourself, "Should I purchase Class A shares, Class B shares, or Class C shares?" There are no easy answers, but your professional financial advisor or broker can help you determine which class of shares of a particular fund best suits your financial needs. You can also do your own research to determine which fund is right for you. Factors to consider include whether you want to invest in a load fund or no-load fund, management fees, 12b-1 fees, and expense ratios. As you will see later in this chapter, a number of sources of information can help you evaluate investment decisions.

To reinforce the material on the costs of investing in funds, Exhibit 13–3 summarizes information for load charges, no-load charges, and Class A, Class B, and Class C shares. In addition, it reports typical management fees, contingent deferred sales loads, and 12b-1 charges.

expense ratio The amount that investors pay for all of a mutual fund's management fees and operating costs.

Exhibit 13–2 Summary of Expenses Paid to Invest in the Davis Opportunity Fund

	Class A Shares	Class B Shares	Class C Shares
SHAREHOLDER FEES (fees paid directly from your investment)			
Maximum sales charge (load) imposed on purchases (as a percentage of offering price)	4.75%	None	None
Maximum deferred sales charge (load) imposed on redemptions (as a percentage of the lesser of the net asset value of the shares redeemed or the total cost of such shares. Only applies to Class A shares if you buy shares valued at $1 million or more without a sales charge and sell the shares within one year of purchase)	0.50%	4.00%	1.00%
Redemption fee (as a percentage of total redemption proceeds)	None	None	None
ANNUAL FUND OPERATING EXPENSES (expenses that you pay each year as a percentage of the value of your investment)			
Management fees	0.55%	0.55%	0.55%
Distribution and/or service (12b-1) fees	0.22%	1.00%	1.00%
Other expenses	0.21%	0.40%	0.23%
Total annual fund operating expenses	0.98%	1.95%	1.78%

Expenses may vary in future years.

SOURCE: Excerpted from the Davis Opportunity Fund Prospectus (www.davisfunds.com), accessed May 1, 2014, Davis Funds, P.O. Box 8406, Boston, MA 02266.

Exhibit **13–3**

Typical Fees Associated with Mutual Fund Investments

Type of Fee or Charge	Customary Amount
Load fund	Up to 8.5 percent of the purchase.
No-load fund	No sales charge.
Contingent deferred sales load	1 to 5 percent of withdrawals, depending on how long you own shares in the fund before making a withdrawal.
Management fee	0.25 to 1.5 percent per year of the fund's net asset value.
12b-1 fee	Cannot exceed 1 percent of the fund's assets per year.
Expense ratio	The amount investors pay for all fees and operating costs.
Class A shares	Commission charge when shares are purchased.
Class B shares	Commission charge when money is withdrawn during the first five years.
Class C shares	No commission to buy or sell shares of a fund, but may have higher, ongoing 12b-1 fees.

PRACTICE QUIZ 13–1

1. Closed-end, exchange-traded, and open-end mutual funds are available today. Describe the differences between each type of fund.

2. What is the net asset value (NAV) for a mutual fund that has assets totaling $730 million, liabilities totaling $10 million, and 24 million shares outstanding?

3. In the table below, indicate the typical charges for each type of mutual fund.

Fee	Typical Charge
Load fund	
No-load fund	
Contingent deferred sales load	
Management fee	
12b-1 fee	

4. What is an expense ratio? Why is it important?

Apply Yourself!

Use the Internet or library research to find a fund you think will help you attain a long-term investment goal. Then determine the fund's load charge (if any), management fee, and expense ratio.

Classifications of Mutual Funds

The managers of mutual funds tailor their investment portfolios to the investment objectives of their customers. Usually a fund's objectives are plainly disclosed in its prospectus. For example, the objective of the Vanguard Mid-Cap Growth Fund is described as follows:

> This actively managed mid-capitalization option invests primarily in the stocks of mid-size domestic companies that the fund's investment managers believe have stronger earnings and revenue growth prospects than the average midcap company. Investors who are seeking exposure to the midcap arena of the U.S. stock market and who are willing to endure the volatility that can come from an investment in stocks may wish to consider this fund as an option for their portfolio.[10]

Although categorizing almost 11,000 funds may be helpful, note that different sources of investment information may use different categories for the same fund. In most cases, the name of the category gives a pretty good clue to the types of investments included within the category. The *major* fund categories are described as follows:

Stock Funds

- *Aggressive growth funds* seek rapid growth by purchasing stocks whose prices are expected to increase dramatically in a short period of time. Turnover within an aggressive growth fund is high because managers are buying and selling stocks of small growth companies. Investors in these funds experience wide price swings because of the underlying speculative nature of the stocks in the fund's portfolio.
- *Equity income funds* invest in stocks issued by companies with a long history of paying dividends. The major objective of these funds is to provide income to shareholders. These funds are attractive investment choices for conservative or retired investors.
- *Global stock funds* invest in stocks of companies throughout the world, including the United States.
- *Growth funds* invest in companies expecting higher-than-average revenue and earnings growth. While similar to aggressive growth funds, growth funds tend to invest in larger, well-established companies. As a result, the prices for shares in a growth fund are less volatile compared to aggressive growth funds.
- *Index funds* invest in the same companies included in an index like the Standard & Poor's 500 stock index, the Dow Jones Industrial Average, or the Nasdaq 100 Index. Since fund managers pick the stocks issued by the companies included in the index, an index fund should provide approximately the same performance as the index. Also, since index funds are cheaper to manage, they often have lower management fees and expense ratios.
- *International funds* invest in foreign stocks sold in securities markets throughout the world; thus, if the economy in one region or nation is in a slump, profits can still be earned in others. Unlike global funds, which invest in stocks issued by companies in both foreign nations and the United States, a true international fund invests outside the United States.

LO13.2

Classify mutual funds by investment objective.

ACTION ITEM

I can identify the types of mutual funds that will help me achieve my investment goals.

☐ **Yes**   ☐ **No**

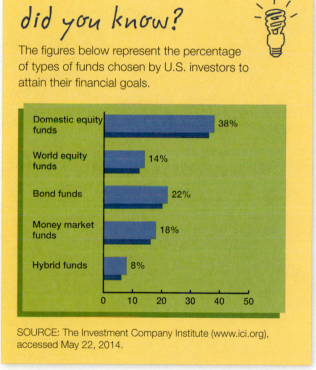

did you know?

The figures below represent the percentage of types of funds chosen by U.S. investors to attain their financial goals.

- Domestic equity funds — 38%
- World equity funds — 14%
- Bond funds — 22%
- Money market funds — 18%
- Hybrid funds — 8%

SOURCE: The Investment Company Institute (www.ici.org), accessed May 22, 2014.

---

[10]The Vanguard Group website at www.vanguard.com, accessed May 22, 2014.

did you know?

Socially responsible investing (SRI) is becoming more popular because ...

- Today there are almost 150 SRI funds.
- Often SRI funds outperform traditional funds.
- SRI funds help you align your invest-ments with your personal values.

For more information on socially responsi-ble and ethical investing, go to the US SIF website at www.ussif.org.

- *Large-cap funds* invest in the stocks of companies with total capitalization of $10 billion or more. Large-capitalization stocks are generally stable, well-established companies and are likely to have minimal fluctuation in their value.
- *Midcap funds* invest in companies with total capitalization of $2 billion to $10 billion whose stocks offer more security than small-cap funds and more growth potential than funds that invest in large corporations.
- *Regional funds* seek to invest in stock traded within one specific region of the world, such as the European region, the Latin American region, and the Pacific region.
- *Sector funds* invest in companies within the same industry. Examples of sectors include Health and Biotech, Science & Technology, and Natural Resources.
- *Small-cap funds* invest in smaller, lesser-known companies with a total capitalization of between $300 million and $2 billion. Because these companies are small and innovative, these funds offer higher growth potential. They are more speculative than funds that invest in larger, more established companies.
- *Socially responsible funds* avoid investing in companies that may cause harm to people, animals, and the environment. Typically, these funds do not invest in companies that produce tobacco, nuclear energy, or weapons or in companies that have a history of discrimination. These funds invest in companies that have a history of making ethical decisions, establishing efforts to reduce pollution, and other socially responsible activities.

Bond Funds

- *High-yield (junk) bond funds* invest in high-yield, high-risk corporate bonds.
- *Intermediate corporate bond funds* invest in investment-grade corporate debt with maturities between 5 and 10 years.
- *Intermediate U.S. government bond funds* invest in U.S. Treasury securities with maturities between 5 and 10 years.
- *Long-term corporate bond funds* invest in investment-grade corporate bond issues with maturities in excess of 10 years.
- *Long-term (U.S.) government bond funds* invest in U.S. Treasury securities with maturities in excess of 10 years.
- *Municipal bond funds* invest in municipal bonds that provide investors with tax-free interest income.
- *Short-term corporate bond funds* invest in investment-grade corporate bond issues with maturities that are less than 5 years.
- *Short-term (U.S.) government bond funds* invest in U.S. Treasury issues with maturities that are less than 5 years.
- *World bond funds* invest in bonds and other debt securities offered by foreign companies and governments.

Other Funds

- *Asset allocation funds* invest in different types of investments, including stocks, bonds, fixed-income securities, and money market instruments. These funds seek high total return by maintaining precise amounts within each type of asset.
- *Balanced funds* invest in both stocks and bonds with the primary objectives of conserving principal, providing income, and providing long-term growth. Often the percentage of stocks, bonds, and other securities is stated in the fund's prospectus.

- *Fund of funds* invest in shares of other mutual funds. The main advantage of a fund of funds is increased diversification and asset allocation, because this type of fund purchases shares in many different funds. Higher expenses and extra fees are common with this type of fund.
- *Lifecycle funds* (sometimes referred to as *lifestyle funds* or *target-date funds*) are popular with investors planning for retirement by a specific date. Typically, these funds initially invest in risk-oriented securities (stocks) and become increasingly conservative and income oriented (bonds and CDs) as the specified date approaches and investors are closer to retirement.
- *Money market funds* invest in certificates of deposit, government securities, and other safe and highly liquid investments.

A **family of funds** exists when one investment company manages a group of mutual funds. Each fund within the family has a different financial objective. For instance, one fund may be a long-term government bond fund and another a growth stock fund. Most investment companies offer exchange privileges that enable shareholders to switch among the mutual funds in a fund family. For example, if you own shares in the Franklin Biotechnology Discovery Fund, you may, at your discretion, switch to the Franklin Balance Sheet Investment Fund. Generally, investors may give instructions to switch from one fund to another within the same family in writing, over the telephone, or via the Internet. The family-of-funds concept allows shareholders to conveniently switch their investments among funds as different funds offer more potential, financial reward, or security. Charges for exchanges, if any, generally are small for each transaction. For funds that do charge, the fee may be as low as $5 per transaction.

family of funds A group of mutual funds managed by one investment company.

Choosing the Right Fund for a Retirement Account

Assume you have just secured a new job, and your new employer offers you the opportunity to participate in the company's 401(k) or 403(b) retirement plan. In this situation, you must weigh at least three considerations that can affect your financial future.

1. *Do you want to participate in the retirement account?* The answer to this question is a definite "yes" for two reasons. The reasons are simple: Employer-sponsored retirement accounts—as explained in the next chapter—provide a way to reduce the amount of current income tax that is withheld from your paycheck. So there are immediate tax savings. A second reason for participating in a retirement plan is because many employers will match your contributions. A common match would work like this: For every $1.00 the employee contributes, the employer contributes an additional $0.50. All monies—both the employee's and employer's contributions—are then invested in mutual funds that are selected by the employee.

2. *Which mutual funds do you want to invest in?* Most retirement plans allow you to choose the mutual funds for your plan from a number of different fund options. When making your choices keep in mind your long-term goals and the time value of money concept that was discussed in Chapter 1. The time value of money concept is especially important because the investments in your plan will grow because you (and your employer) continue to contribute money to your retirement account *and* quality investments should increase in value over a long period of time.

3. *What is your stage in life?* The actual choice of investments for your retirement account should be determined by your age, how long before you retire, and your tolerance for risk. Typically, younger workers choose more risk-oriented funds that have greater potential for growth over a long period of time. Older workers closer to retirement tend to choose more conservative funds with less risk.

 CAUTION!

Although some employers reduced or eliminated matching provisions during the recent economic crisis, some employers still match employee contributions. In fact, during a job interview you may want to ask about the employer's matching provisions for a 401(k) or 403(b) retirement account.

Employers Trim Their 401(k) Fees

Lower expenses and cheaper share classes are good news for workers

An Aon Hewitt survey found that more than 75% of employers had attempted to cut 401(k) expenses in the past two years. What's behind the trend? The Department of Labor's fee disclosure requirement shone a spotlight on fees for a lot of employers, and it has made more people aware of what they're paying for. A second motivation is employers' legal obligation to act in their employees' best interest, known as their fiduciary duty. Employers want to make sure they provide the best investments at the best price.

The survey also found a big increase in the number of plans that offer "institutional class" funds. Why? Employers can use their purchasing power to invest in funds used by professionals that are not broadly available to individual investors outside of 401(k) plans. Ultimately, the funds can provide better returns and lower fees.

More companies are charging a record-keeping fee instead of a fee based on a percentage of assets. How does that benefit employees? When employees are charged a flat rate of $50 a year, a typical participant with a starting

salary of $75,000 ends up with $200,000 more in retirement than he or she would have had if a yearly fee of as little as 0.25% of assets were imposed. A flat fee is a little more equitable, too. Whether a person has a balance of $100 or $100,000, he or she has access to the same technology, the same phone lines. Why should the employee who has more money pay more for those tools and resources?

Are employees who leave their jobs better off keeping their money in their former employer's 401(k), rather than rolling it into an IRA? That can be a good idea for a number of reasons. You have investment products that have lower fees. You also have the power of

fiduciary responsibility through an employer plan that you wouldn't have in a typical retail IRA. In an employer plan, there are people who have to monitor these funds to make sure that fees are competitive and returns are good.

What should employees do if they're dissatisfied with their 401(k)? Do a little legwork to make sure your employer is choosing the right funds. Plan administrators who are doing the right thing and have documented why they're choosing the funds on their menu have no reason to fear. But if they can't say for sure why they've chosen particular funds, then that makes for a difficult conversation.

Sandra Block

SOURCE: Reprinted by permission from *Kiplinger's Personal Finance.* Copyright © 2014. The Kiplinger Washington Editors, Inc.

1. What are the primary reasons why employers are attempting to reduce the fees that employees pay to participate in an employer-sponsored 401(k) retirement plan?

2. The survey conducted by Aon Hewitt found a big increase in the number of employer-sponsored plans that offer "institutional class" funds. Based on the information in this *Kiplinger* article, what are the advantages of shares in an institutional class fund for employers?

3. Assume you are an employee leaving your job. Should you keep your money in your former employer's employer-sponsored 401(k) retirement plan or roll it into an IRA? Explain your answer.

Regardless of the type of funds you choose for your retirement plan, it is important to evaluate each fund before making your choices. The information in the next section will help you choose the right funds. Once your choices are made, it is also important to continue to monitor each of your funds to determine if you are on the right track to achieve your financial objectives.

PRACTICE QUIZ 13-2

1. How important is the investment objective as stated in a mutual fund's prospectus?

2. Identify one mutual fund in each of the three categories (stocks, bonds, and other) and describe the characteristics of the fund you select and the type of investor who would invest in that type of fund.

General Fund Type	Fund Name	Characteristics of Fund	Typical Investor
Stock			
Bond			
Other			

3. How can choosing the right fund help you save for retirement?

Apply Yourself!

Using the information in this section, pick a type of mutual fund that you consider suitable for each of the following investors and justify your choice:

1. A 24-year-old single investor with a new job that pays $32,000 a year.

2. A single parent with two children who has just received a $400,000 inheritance, has no job, and has not worked outside the home for the past five years.

3. A husband and wife who are both in their mid-60s and retired.

How to Make a Decision to Buy or Sell Mutual Funds

LO13.3

Evaluate mutual funds.

ACTION ITEM

I know how to evaluate a mutual fund.

☐ **Yes** ☐ **No**

Often the decision to buy or sell shares in mutual funds is "too easy" because investors assume they do not need to evaluate these investments. Why question what the professional portfolio managers decide to do? Yet professionals do make mistakes. And, sometimes, economic and financial conditions beyond the control of a fund manager cause a fund's value to decrease. And yet you should realize that the responsibility for choosing the right mutual fund rests with *you*.

Fortunately, a lot of information is available to help you evaluate a specific mutual fund. To help you sort out all the research, statistics, and information about mutual funds and give you some direction as to what to do first, read the suggestions in the nearby "Personal Finance in Practice" box. Then answer one basic question: Do you want a managed fund or an index fund?

Mutual Funds: Getting Started

Here are some suggestions for beginning a mutual fund investment program.

1. *Perform a financial checkup.* Before investing, you should make sure your budget is balanced and you have established an emergency fund.

2. *Obtain the money you need to purchase mutual funds.* Although the amount will vary, $250 to $2,000 is usually required to open an account with a brokerage firm or an investment company.

3. *Determine your investment objectives.* Without investment objectives, you cannot know what you want to accomplish. For more information on the importance of objectives, review the material in Chapter 11.

4. *Find a fund with an objective that matches your objective.* Financial publications, professional advisory services, and personal finance magazines may help you identify funds with objectives that match your investment objectives.

5. *Evaluate, evaluate, and evaluate any mutual fund before buying or selling.* Possible sources of information include the Internet, professional advisory services, the fund's prospectus, the fund's annual report, financial publications, and newspapers—all sources described in the remainder of this section.

6. *Continue to evaluate your funds after your investment.* Evaluate your investments on a regular basis. If necessary, sell funds that no longer are helping you achieve your financial objectives or that you think will decrease in value.

Managed Funds versus Index Funds

Most mutual funds are managed funds. In other words, there is a professional fund manager (or team of managers) who chooses the securities that are contained in the fund. The fund manager also decides when to buy and sell securities in the fund. To help evaluate a fund, you may want to determine how well a fund manager manages during both good and bad economic times. The benchmark for a good fund manager is the ability to increase share value when the economy is good and retain that value when the economy is bad. For example, most funds increased in value in the years after the recent economic crisis. Many funds provided investors with a 10, 20, or 30 percent or higher annual return. And yet the question remains whether these same funds can retain their value when there is another economic crisis. One important consideration is how long the present fund manager has been managing the fund. If a fund has performed well under its present manager over a 5-year, 10-year, or longer period, there is a strong likelihood that it will continue to perform well under that manager in the future. On the other hand, if the fund has a new manager, his or her decisions may affect the performance of the fund. Managed funds may be open-end funds or closed-end funds.

CAUTION!
Don't forget the role of the fund manager in determining a fund's success.

Instead of investing in a managed fund, some investors choose to invest in an index fund. Why? The answer to that question is simple: Over many years, the majority of managed mutual funds fail to outperform the Standard & Poor's 500 stock index—a benchmark of stock market performance often reported on financial news programs. The exact statistics vary, depending on the year, but a common statistic often found in mutual fund research is that the Standard & Poor's 500 stock index outperforms 50 to 80 percent of all mutual funds.[11]

Because an index mutual fund is a mirror image of a specific index like the Standard & Poor's 500, the Nasdaq Composite, the Wilshire 5000 Total Market, or similar indexes, the dollar value of a share in an index fund also increases when the index increases. Unfortunately, the reverse is also true. If the index goes down, the value of a share in an index fund goes down. Index funds, sometimes called "passive" funds, have managers, but they simply buy the stocks or bonds or securities contained in the index.

[11]"Index Investing: Index Funds," *Investopedia* (www.investopedia.com), accessed May 26, 2014.

A second and very important reason why investors choose index funds is the lower expense ratio charged by these passively managed funds. As mentioned earlier in this chapter, the total fees charged by a mutual fund is called the expense ratio. If a fund's expense ratio is 1.25 percent, then the fund has to earn at least that amount on its investment holdings just to break even each year. With very few exceptions, typical expense ratios for an index fund are 0.50 percent or less. And while lower fees may not sound significant, don't be fooled. Over a long period of time, even a small difference can become huge. For example, assume two different investors each invest $10,000. One investor chooses an index fund that has annual expenses of 0.20 percent; the other chooses a managed fund that has annual expenses of 1.22 percent. Both funds earn 10 percent a year. After 35 years, the index fund is worth $263,683 while the managed fund is worth $190,203. That's a difference of $73,480. Thus, even though the two funds earned the same 10 percent a year, the difference in annual expenses made a substantial difference in the amount of money each investor had at the end of 35 years.[12] Index funds may be open-end funds, closed-end funds, or exchange-traded funds.

Should you choose a managed fund or an index fund? Good question. The answer depends on which managed fund you choose. If you pick a managed fund that has better performance than an index, then you made the right choice. If, on the other hand, the index (and the index fund) outperforms the managed fund—which happens as often as 50 to 80 percent of the time—an index fund is a better choice. With both investments, the key is how well you can research a specific investment alternative using the sources of information that are described in the remainder of this section.

The Internet

Many investors have found a wealth of information about mutual fund investments on the Internet. Basically, you can access information three ways. First, you can obtain current market values for mutual funds by using one of the Internet search engines, such as Yahoo! The Yahoo! Finance page (finance.yahoo.com) has a box where you can enter the symbol of the mutual fund you want to research. If you don't know the symbol, you can enter in the name of the mutual fund in the Quote Lookup box. The Yahoo! Finance website will respond with the correct symbol. In addition to current market values, you can obtain a price history for a mutual fund, a profile including information about current holdings, performance data, risk, and purchase information.

Second, most investment companies that sponsor mutual funds have a web page. To obtain information, all you have to do is access one of the Internet search engines and type in the name of the fund or enter the investment company's Internet address (URL) in your computer. Generally, statistical information about performance of individual funds, procedures for opening an account, promotional literature, and different investor services are provided. *Be warned:* Investment companies want you to become a shareholder. As a result, the websites for *some* investment companies read like a sales pitch. Read between the glowing descriptions and look at the facts before investing your money.

Finally, professional advisory services, covered in the next section, offer online research reports for mutual funds. A sample of the information available from the Morningstar website for the T. Rowe Price Value Fund is illustrated in Exhibit 13–4. Note that information about the fund symbol, Morningstar Risk Measures, and past growth record is provided. In many cases, more detailed information is provided by professional advisory services like Morningstar, Inc. (www.morningstar.com) and Lipper Analytical Services, Inc. (www.lipperweb.com) for a small fee for premium services. While the information available on the Internet is basically the same as that in the printed reports described later in this section, the ability to obtain up-to-date information quickly without having to wait for research materials to be mailed or to make a trip to the library is a real selling point.

[12]Bankrate.com, "Index Funds vs. Actively Managed Funds" (www.bankrate.com), accessed January 21, 2012.

Exhibit 13–4   Information about the T. Rowe Price Value Fund Available from the Morningstar Website

Information from T. Rowe Price Mutual Fund Center

T. Rowe Price Value   TRVLX

Fund Family Data   Add to Portfolio   Get E-mail Alerts   Print This Page   PDF Report   Data Definition   Data Question

Quote | Chart | Fund Analysis | Performance | Ratings & Risk | Management | Stewardship | Portfolio | Expense | Tax | Purchase | Filings

NAV	**NAV Day Change**	**TTM Yield** 1.10%	**Load** None	**Total Assets** $ 19.6 bil	**Expenses** 0.84%
$35.41	0.14 | 0.40%				
As of Fri 05/23/2014 | USD		**30-Day SEC Yield** --	**Category** Large Value		

Fee Level	**Turnover**	**Status**	**Min. Inv.**
Below Average	44%	Open	$ 2,500
Investment Style Large Value			

Growth of 10K TRVLX   More...

05/26/2004 - 05/25/2014   Zoom: 1M 3M YTD 1Y 3Y 5Y **10Y** Maximum
                                                        Custom

XNAS:TRVLX:23,610.39   Large Value:19,549.97   S&P 500 TR USD:21,023.14

Morningstar Risk Measures TRVLX   More...

		Low	Avg	High
Risk vs.Category* (1,068)	+Avg			
Return vs.Category* (1,068)	High			
*Overall Ranking		Low	Avg	High

Morningstar's Take TRVLX   **Access Premium with a free trial**

This fund has been upgraded to Bronze from Neutral.

Read full Analyst Report

Stewardship Grade Premium	**Morningstar Pillars**
	Process — Premium
	Performance — Premium
Role in Portfolio Premium	People — Premium
	Parent — Premium
	Price — Premium

Style Map TRVLX   More...

Giant
Large
Medium
Small
Micro

Deep Core Core Core High
Val   Val   Grw   Grw

Weighted Average of holdings

75% of fund's stock holdings

SOURCE: Morningstar, Inc. (www.morningstar.com), accessed May 26, 2014. Morningstar, Inc., 225 W. Wacker Drive, Chicago, IL 60606.

Professional Advisory Services

As pointed out in the last section, a number of subscription services provide detailed information on mutual funds. Lipper Analytical Services, Morningstar, Inc., and Value Line are three widely used sources of such information. Exhibit 13–5 illustrates the type of information provided by Morningstar, Inc., for the Oakmark Global Select I Fund. Although the Morningstar report is just one page long, it provides a wealth of information designed to

Exhibit 13–5   Mutual Fund Research Information for the Oakmark Global Select I Fund Provided by Morningstar, Inc.

Data through January 31, 2014

Oakmark Global Select I

Ticker	OAKWX
Status	Open
Yield	0.8%
Total Assets	$1,553 mil
Mstar Category	World Stock

Morningstar Analyst Rating 01-28-14

🛡 **Silver**

Morningstar Pillars

Process	⊕ Positive
Performance	⊕ Positive
People	⊕ Positive
Parent	⊕ Positive
Price	⊙ Neutral

Morningstar Analyst Rating

Morningstar evaluates mutual funds based on five key pillars, which its analysts believe lead to funds that are more likely to outperform over the long term on a risk-adjusted basis.

Analyst Rating Spectrum

🛡 Gold   🛡 Silver   🛡 Bronze   Neutral   Negative

Pillar Spectrum

⊕ Positive   ⊖ Negative   ⊙ Neutral

Performance 01-31-14

	1st Qtr	2nd Qtr	3rd Qtr	4th Qtr	Total
2009	-4.29	26.56	20.61	5.13	53.58
2010	6.41	-13.17	9.97	9.31	11.06
2011	5.15	2.15	-16.23	4.62	-5.87
2012	18.62	-8.74	3.28	10.87	23.95
2013	7.59	5.88	9.02	7.74	33.80

Trailing	Total Return%	+/- MSCI WexUS	+/- MSCI Ac Wrld ND	%Rank Cat	Growth of $10,000
3 Mo	0.99	4.53	1.95	31	10,099
6 Mo	5.64	0.16	-0.44	65	10,564
1 Yr	20.07	14.32	7.37	22	12,007
3 Yr Avg	12.91	9.72	5.22	7	14,395
5 Yr Avg	22.54	8.68	6.50	5	27,631
10 Yr Avg	—	—	—	—	—
15 Yr Avg	—	—	—	—	—

Tax Analysis	Tax-Adj Rtn%	%Rank Cat	Tax-Cost Rat	%Rank Cat
3 Yr (estimated)	12.42	6	0.44	40
5 Yr (estimated)	22.16	5	0.31	32
10 Yr (estimated)	—			

Potential Capital Gain Exposure: 15% of assets

Historical Profile

Return	High
Risk	Above Avg
Rating	★★★★★ Highest

94% 99% 97% 93% 96% 98% 94% 95%

15.5
12.5 **Growth of $10,000**
10.0 ▬ Investment Values of Fund
— Investment Values of MSCI WexUS
5.0

▼ Manager Change
▽ Partial Manager Change

Performance Quartile (within Category)

	2003	2004	2005	2006	2007	2008	2009	2010	2011	2012	2013	01-14	History
	—	—	—	10.78	10.20	6.53	9.99	11.07	10.42	12.65	16.51	15.87	NAV
	—	—	—	-1.16	-32.49	53.58	11.06	-5.87	23.95	33.80	-3.88	Total Return %
	—	—	—	-17.81	13.04	12.13	-0.09	7.84	7.12	18.51	0.66	+/-MSCI WexUS
	—	—	—	-12.82	9.70	18.95	-1.61	1.48	7.82	11.00	0.12	+/-MSCI Ac Wrld ND
	—	—	—	0.22	3.45	0.59	0.25	0.00	1.55	1.07	0.00	Income Return %
	—	—	—	-1.38	-35.94	52.99	10.81	-5.87	22.40	32.73	-3.88	Capital Return %
	—	—	—	96	11	8	66	33	3	11	62	Total Rtn % Rank Cat
	—	—	—	0.01	0.02	0.35	0.04	0.02	0.00	0.16	0.14	0.00	Income $
	—	—	—	0.00	0.44	0.00	0.00	0.00	0.00	0.10	0.27	0.00	Capital Gains $
	—	—	—		1.31	1.35	1.43	1.29	1.24	1.23	1.15		Expense Ratio %
	—	—	—		1.01	1.41	0.88	0.40	0.33	0.72	1.01	—	Income Ratio %
	—	—	—		33	62	41	50	49	36	36	—	Turnover Rate %
	—	—	—		293	198	299	363	443	630	1,476	1,553	Net Assets $mil

Investment Style
Equity
Stock %

Rating and Risk

Time Period	Load-Adj Return %	Morningstar Rtn vs Cat	Morningstar Risk vs Cat	Morningstar Risk-Adj Rating
1 Yr	20.07			
3 Yr	12.91	High	+Avg	★★★★★
5 Yr	22.54	High	+Avg	★★★★★
10 Yr	—			
Incept	8.70			

Other Measures	Standard Index MSCI WexUS	Best Fit Index MSCI World
Alpha	9.6	3.0
Beta	0.86	1.06
R-Squared	78	83
Standard Deviation	16.25	
Mean	12.91	
Sharpe Ratio	0.83	

Portfolio Analysis 12-31-13

Share change since 09-13 Total Stocks:20

Share change since 09-13	Sector	Country	% Assets
⊕ CNH Industrial NV	Industrl	Netherlands	5.59
⊕ Kering	Cnsmr Cyc	France	5.37
⊖ Daimler AG	Cnsmr Cyc	Germany	5.27
⊕ Diageo PLC	Cnsmr Def	U.K.	5.08
⊕ Canon, Inc.	Industrl	Japan	4.86
⊕ K hne & Nagel Internatio	Industrl	Switzerland	4.86
⊕ Credit Suisse Group	Finan Svs	Switzerland	4.81
⊖ Oracle Corporation	Technology	United States	4.72
⊕ Daiwa Securities Co., Lt	Finan Svs	Japan	4.72
⊕ Intel Corp	Technology	United States	4.66
⊕ Bank of America Corporat	Finan Svs	United States	4.62
⊕ JPMorgan Chase & Co	Finan Svs	United States	4.60
⊕ TE Connectivity Ltd	Technology	Switzerland	4.59
⊕ Directv	Comm Svs	United States	4.57
⊕ Liberty Interactive Corp	Technology	United States	4.53
⊕ American International G	Finan Svs	United States	4.53
⊕ Medtronic, Inc.	Hlth care	United States	4.52
⊕ Capital One Financial Co	Finan Svs	United States	4.50
⊕ FedEx Corporation	Industrl	United States	4.45
⊖ Adecco SA	Industrl	Switzerland	4.05

Current Investment Style

Value Blnd Growth

Market Cap	%
Giant	45.5
Large	49.8
Mid	4.8
Small	0.0
Micro	0.0
Avg $mil:	47,007

Value Measures		Rel Category
Price/Earnings	13.40	0.91
Price/Book	1.42	0.74
Price/Sales	1.46	1.12
Price/Cash Flow	4.42	0.62
Dividend Yield %	1.50	0.61

Growth Measures	%	Rel Category
Long-Term Erngs	11.38	1.01
Book Value	4.20	2.03
Sales	-11.05	NMF
Cash Flow	4.03	5.17
Historical Erngs	8.13	0.17

Composition - Net

	%		
Cash	5.1	Bonds	0.0
Stocks	94.9	Other	0.0
Foreign (% of Stock)	51.8		

Sector Weightings	% of Stocks	Rel MSCI WexUS	3 Year High Low
⤴ Cyclical	40.46	—	
🔷 BasicMat	0.00	—	— —
🔶 CnsmrCyc	11.20	—	22 11
🟠 FinanSvs	29.26	—	30 14
🏠 Real Est	0.00	—	— —
→ Sensitive	49.42		
📶 CommSrvs	4.81	—	6 5
🔋 Energy	0.00	—	5 4
⚙ Industrl	25.11	—	27 10
💻 Technlgy	19.50	—	33 18
→ Defensive	10.11		
🛒 CnsmrDef	5.35	—	11 4
➕ Hlthcare	4.76	—	5 4
💡 Utilities	0.00	—	— —

Regional Exposure	% Stock		
UK/W. Europe 42	N. America	48	
Japan 10	Latn America	0	
Asia X Japan 0	Other	0	

Country Exposure	% Stock		
United States 48	Netherlands	6	
Switzerland 19	France	6	
Japan 10			

Morningstar's Take by Shannon Zimmerman 01-28-14

This concentrated world-stock fund just missed the category's top decile last year, gaining nearly 34% and landing in the peer group's 11th percentile. With just 20 holdings and lopsided sector weights bearing little resemblance to the those of the MSCI World Index or the fund's average rival, managers Bill Nygren and David Herro delivered those results with an idiosyncratic portfolio. Its financials exposure nearly doubles the category norm, and it doesn't own any energy, materials, or utilities stocks.

That's par for the course, however, as is the fund's recent success. The fund launched in October 2006, and between November of that year and December 2013, its cumulative gain of 87% trumps the index by 51 percentage points and the average world-stock fund by 50 points. In that time frame's rolling three-year periods, the fund placed in the category's top quartile more than 82% of the time. And while the fund's standard deviation has been modestly higher than its typical peer's, it has staved off loss better and gained more in rising markets: Versus the category norm, its upside capture ratio is 113%; its downside is 97%. The fund has essentially matched the bogy during downturns, while enjoying 117% of its upside.

That risk/reward profile owes to a strategy focused on fundamentals, giving Nygren and Herro freedom to pursue value wherever they find it. Indeed, roughly 35% of assets are currently invested in stocks residing in the large-growth square of the Morningstar Style Box. Provided a company's share price implies a discount of at least 40% to estimated intrinsic value, it's a candidate for this fund's portfolio.

With just 20 names, and with assets split roughly 50/50 between domestic and foreign stocks, the fund is a focused best-ideas vehicle. And while its since-inception risk profile is attractive, volatility-averse investors may prefer Nygren and Herro's more expensive funds.

For those comfortable with its concentration and nontraditional approach to value investing, however, this fund warrants a close look. Over time, investors have been well compensated for its risks.

Address:	Harris Associates LP Chicago, IL 60602-3790 800-625-6275
Web Address:	www.oakmark.com
Inception:	10-02-06
Advisor:	Harris Associates L.P.
Subadvisor:	None
NTF Plans:	Fidelity Retail-NTF, CommonWealth NTF

Minimum Purchase:	$1000	Add: $100 IRA: $1000
Min Auto inv Plan:	$500	Add: $100
Sales Fees:	No-load	
Management Fee:	1.00% mx./0.85% mn.	
Actual Fees:	Mgt:0.96%	Dist: —
Expense Projections:	3Yr:$365	5Yr:$633 10Yr:$1398
Income Distribution:	Annually	

M⭐RNINGSTAR® Mutual Funds

SOURCE: *Morningstar Mutual Funds,* February 2014, Morningstar, Inc., 225 W. Wacker Drive, Chicago, IL 60606.

help you decide if this is the right fund for you. Notice that the information is divided into various sections. At the top, a small box entitled "Historical Profile" contains information about financial return, risk, and rating. Notice that this Oakmark fund is rated five stars, Morningstar's highest rating. The report also provides historical financial and statistical information toward the top of the page. The middle section of the report provides information about the fund's performance, risk, and portfolio analysis. In the last section at the very bottom, the "Morningstar's Take" section summarizes the analyst's research.

As you can see, the research information for this fund is pretty upbeat. However, other research firms like Lipper Analytical Services and Value Line, as well as Morningstar, Inc., will also tell you if a fund is a poor performer that offers poor investment potential.

In addition, various mutual fund newsletters provide financial information to subscribers for a fee. All of these sources are rather expensive, but their reports may be available from brokerage firms or libraries.

The Mutual Fund Prospectus and Annual Report

An investment company sponsoring a mutual fund must give potential investors a prospectus. You can also request a prospectus by mail, by calling a toll-free phone number, or by accessing the investment company website.

According to financial experts, the prospectus is usually the first piece of information investors receive, and they should read it completely before investing. Although it may look foreboding, a commonsense approach to reading a fund's prospectus can provide valuable insights. In addition to information about objectives and fees, the prospectus should provide the following:

- A statement describing the risk factor associated with the fund.
- A description of the fund's past performance.
- A statement describing the type of investments contained in the fund's portfolio.
- Information about dividends, distributions, and taxes.
- Information about the fund's management.
- Information on limitations or requirements, if any, the fund must honor when choosing investments.
- The process investors can use to buy or sell shares in the fund.
- A description of services provided to investors and fees for services, if any.
- Information about how often the fund's investment portfolio changes (sometimes referred to as its *turnover ratio*).

Finally, the prospectus provides information about how to open a mutual fund account with the investment company.

If you are a prospective investor, you can request an annual report by mail or by calling a toll-free telephone number, or you can view it on the Internet. Once you are a shareholder, the investment company will send you an annual report. A fund's annual report contains a letter from the president of the investment company, from the fund manager, or both. The annual report also contains detailed financial information about the fund's assets and liabilities, performance, statement of operations, and statement of changes in net assets. Next, the annual report includes a schedule of investments. Finally, the fund's annual report should include a letter from the fund's independent auditors that provides an opinion as to the accuracy of the fund's financial statements.

Financial Publications and Newspapers

Investment-oriented magazines like *Bloomberg Businessweek, Forbes, Kiplinger's Personal Finance,* and *Money* are excellent sources of information about mutual funds. Depending on the publication, coverage ranges from detailed articles that provide in-depth information to simple listings of which funds to buy or sell. And many investment-oriented magazines now provide information on the Internet about mutual funds. The material in Exhibit 13–6 was obtained from the Kiplinger website, and is a partial listing of 25 different funds that were recommended in the Kiplinger 2014 retirement guide. Information is provided about its choices for best funds and ETFs and includes:

- The fund name and symbol.
- The fund's one-year return.
- The fund's five-year return.
- The fund's expense ratio.
- A description of the fund.

In addition to mutual fund information in financial publications, a number of mutual fund guidebooks are available at your local bookstore or public library.

Although many newspapers have reduced or eliminated mutual fund coverage, many large metropolitan newspapers and *The Wall Street Journal* often provide news and

Exhibit 13–6 Information about Funds Recommended in the 2014 Kiplinger Retirement Guide

KIPLINGER 25 U.S. Stock Funds	1-Yr. Return	5-Yr. Return	Expense Ratio	Description
Akre Focus (AKREX)	33.5%	—	1.36%	Chuck Akre invests in high-quality firms run by smart executives.
Artisan Value (ARTLX)	18.6	22.5%	1.04	Large, out-of-favor, bargain-priced companies find a home here.
Baron Small Cap (BSCFX)	29.7	25.9	1.31	Fund favors undervalued, steady growers with a competitive edge.
Davenport Equity Opportunities (DEOPX)	26.5	—	1.01	Managers like growing midsize firms run by execs who act like owners.
Dodge & Cox Stock (DODGX)	32.9	25.9	0.52	Nine managers are value investors who go where others fear to tread.
Homestead Small Co Stock (HSCSX)	28.9	31.5	0.91	Seeks small, out-of-favor companies poised to turn around.
Mairs & Power Growth (MPGFX)	25.8	24.8	0.67	Managers look for attractively priced, growing large companies.
Fidelity New Millennium (FMILX)	34.2	27.5	0.87	Portfolio holds a mix of large and small, old and new companies.
T. Rowe Price Sm-Cap Value (PRSVX)	24.7	25.7	0.81	The manager prizes unloved and undervalued small companies.
Vanguard Dividend Growth (VDIGX)	23.3	20.4	0.29	Reliable companies with rising dividends offer growth and stability.
Vanguard Selected Value (VASVX)	33.1	26.2	0.43	Two separate management teams buy undervalued midsize firms.
Wells Fargo Advantage Discovery (STDIX)	36.1	29.1	1.28	The fund targets midsize firms with rapid profit growth.

SOURCE: Nellie S. Huang, "Three Plans to Help You Reach Your Goals," *Kiplinger Retirement Planning 2014,* the Kiplinger website (www.kiplinger.com), accessed May 25, 2014.

information about mutual funds. Typical coverage includes information about the name of the fund family and fund name, the current net asset value for a fund, net change, and year-to-date percentage of return. Much of this same information (along with more detailed information) is also available on the Internet.

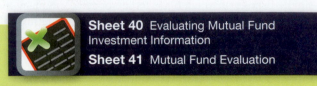

Sheet 40 Evaluating Mutual Fund Investment Information

Sheet 41 Mutual Fund Evaluation

PRACTICE QUIZ 13–3

1. In your own words, describe the difference between a managed fund and an index fund. Which one do you think could help you achieve your investment goals?

2. Describe how each of the following sources of investment information could help you evaluate a mutual fund investment.

Source of Information	Type of Information	How This Could Help
The Internet		
Professional advisory services		
Mutual fund prospectus		
Mutual fund annual report		
Financial publications		
Newspapers		

Apply Yourself!

Choose the Alger International Growth Fund (symbol ALGAX), the Gabelli Asset Fund (symbol GATAX), or the Calvert Long-Term Income Fund (symbol CLDAX) and use the Internet or library sources to report the type of fund, one-year return, net asset value, and Morningstar rating for the fund. *Hint:* You may want to use the Yahoo! Finance website at finance.yahoo.com or the MSN Money website at money.msn.com.

LO13.4

Describe how and why mutual funds are bought and sold.

ACTION ITEM

I am aware of the purchase and withdrawal options for a mutual fund.

☐ Yes ☐ No

The Mechanics of a Mutual Fund Transaction

For many investors, mutual funds have become the investment of choice. In fact, you probably either own shares or know someone who owns shares in a mutual fund—they're that popular! They may be part of a 401(k) or 403(b) retirement account, a SEP IRA, a Roth IRA, or a traditional IRA retirement account, all topics discussed in Chapter 14. They can also be owned outright in a taxable account by purchasing shares through a registered sales representative who works for a bank or brokerage firm or an investment company that sponsors a mutual fund. Although there are exceptions, most individuals invest in mutual funds to achieve long-term financial objectives. When you invest your money, you are counting on the time value of money concept to help build your nest egg. Remember that in Chapter 1 *time value of money* was defined as the increases in an amount of money as a result of interest earned. For example, saving or investing $2,000 instead of spending it today results in a future amount greater than $2,000. If the $2,000 is used to purchase shares in a fund, your shares can increase in value and you can also receive income from your investment that can be reinvested to purchase more shares. As you will see later in this section, it's easy to purchase shares in a mutual fund. For $250 to $2,000 or more, you can open an account and begin investing. And there are other advantages that encourage investors to purchase shares in funds. Unfortunately, there are also disadvantages. Exhibit 13–7 summarizes the advantages and disadvantages of fund investments.

One advantage of any investment is the opportunity to make money on the investment. In this section, we examine how you can make money by investing in funds. We consider how taxes affect your fund investments. Then we look at the options used to purchase shares in a fund. Finally, we examine the options used to withdraw money from a fund.

Return on Investment

As with other investments, the purpose of investing in a closed-end fund, exchange-traded fund, or open-end fund is to earn a financial return. Shareholders in such funds can receive a return in one of three ways. First, all three types of funds pay income dividends. **Income dividends** are the earnings a fund pays to shareholders from its dividend and interest income. *Note:* Many exchange-traded funds often pay dividends on a monthly or quarterly basis. Second, investors may receive capital gain distributions. **Capital gain distributions** are the payments made to a fund's shareholders that result from the sale of securities in the fund's portfolio. Both amounts generally are paid once a year. *Note:* The majority of exchange-traded funds don't usually pay end-of-the-year capital gain distributions. Third, as with stock and bond investments, you can buy shares in funds at a low price and then sell them after the price has increased. For example, assume you purchased shares in the Fidelity Stock Selector All Cap Fund at $31.00 per share and sold your shares two years later at $35.50 per share. In this case, you made $4.50 ($35.50 selling price minus $31.00 purchase price) per share. With this financial information and the dollar amounts for

income dividends The earnings a fund pays to shareholders from its dividend and interest income.

capital gain distributions The payments made to a fund's shareholders that result from the sale of securities in the fund's portfolio.

Advantages
• Diversification.
• Professional management.
• Ease of buying and selling shares.
• Multiple withdrawal options.
• Distribution or reinvestment of dividends and capital gain distributions.
• Switching privileges within the same fund family.
• Services that include toll-free telephone numbers, complete records of all transactions, and savings and checking accounts.

Disadvantages
• Purchase/withdrawal costs.
• Ongoing management fees and 12b-1 fees.
• Poor performance that may not match the Standard & Poor's 500 stock index or some other index.
• Inability to control when capital gain distributions occur and complicated tax reporting issues.
• Potential market risk associated with all investments.
• Some sales personnel are aggressive and/or unethical.

Exhibit 13–7

Advantages and Disadvantages of Investing in Mutual Funds

Figure It Out!

Calculating Total Return for Mutual Funds

In Chapter 12, we defined total return as a calculation that includes not only the yearly dollar amount of income but also any increase or decrease in market value. For mutual funds, you can use the following calculation to determine the dollar amount of total return:

> Income dividends
> + Capital gain distributions
> + Change in share price when sold
> Dollar amount of total return

For example, assume you purchased 100 shares of Majestic Growth Fund for $12.20 per share for a total investment of $1,220. During the next 12 months, you received income dividends of $0.20 a share and capital gain distributions of $0.30 a share. Also, assume you sold your investment at the end of 12 months for $13.40 a share. As illustrated below, the dollar amount of total return is $170:

Income dividends = 100 × $0.20 =	$ 20
Capital gain distributions = 100 × $0.30 =	+ 30
Change in share price = $13.40 − $12.20	
= $1.20 × 100 =	+ 120
Dollar amount of total return	$ 170

To calculate the percentage of total return, divide the dollar amount of total return by the original cost of your mutual fund investment. The percentage of total return for the above example is 13.9 percent, as follows:

$$\text{Percent of total return} = \frac{\text{Dollar amount of total return}}{\text{Original cost of your investment}}$$

$$= \frac{\$170}{\$1,220}$$

$$= 0.139 = 13.9\%$$

Now it's your turn. Use the following financial information for the Northeast Utility Fund to calculate the dollar amount of total return and percent of total return over a 12-month period.

Number of shares, 100

Purchase price, $14.00 a share

Income dividends, $0.30 a share

Capital gain distribution, $0.60 a share

Sale price, $15.25 a share

Calculation	Calculation Formula	Your Answer
Dollar amount of total return		
Percent of total return		

income dividends and capital gain distributions, you can calculate a total return for your mutual fund investment. Before completing this section, you may want to examine the actual procedure used to calculate the dollar amount of total return and percentage of total return in the nearby "Figure It Out!" box.

When shares in a fund are sold, the profit that results from an increase in value is referred to as a *capital gain.* Note the difference between a capital gain distribution and a capital gain. A capital gain distribution occurs when *the fund* distributes profits that result from *the fund* selling securities in the portfolio at a profit. On the other hand, a capital gain is the profit that results when *you* sell your shares in the mutual fund for more than you paid for them. Of course, if the price of a fund's shares goes down between the time of your purchase and the time of sale, you incur a capital loss.

Taxes and Mutual Funds

Taxes on reinvested income dividends, capital gain distributions, and profits from the sale of shares can be deferred if fund investments are held in your retirement account. Assuming all qualifications are met, you can even eliminate taxes on reinvested income, capital gain distributions, and profits from the sale of shares for funds held in a Roth individual retirement account. For mutual funds held in taxable accounts, income dividends, capital gain distributions, and financial gains and losses from the sale of funds are subject to taxation. At the end of each year, investment companies are required to send each shareholder a statement specifying how much he or she received in income dividends and capital gain distributions. Although investment companies may provide this information as part of their year-end statement, most funds also use IRS Form 1099 DIV. The following information provides general guidelines on how mutual fund transactions are taxed when held in a taxable account:

- Income dividends are reported on your federal tax return and are taxed as income.
- Capital gain distributions that result from the fund selling securities in the fund's portfolio at a profit are reported on your federal tax return. Capital gain distributions are taxed as long-term capital gains regardless of how long you own shares in the fund.[13]
- Capital gains or losses that result from your selling shares in a mutual fund are reported on your federal tax return. How long you hold the shares determines if your gains or losses are taxed as a short-term or long-term capital gain. (See Chapter 3 for more information on capital gains and capital losses, or visit the IRS website at www.irs.gov.)

did you know?

CHARACTERISTICS OF MUTUAL FUND OWNERS

56.7 million	The number of U.S. households that own mutual funds
92 percent	The percentage of shareholders who are saving for retirement
51 percent	The percentage of shareholders who are saving for emergencies
47 percent	The percentage of shareholders who own funds to reduce taxable income
25 percent	The percentage of shareholders who are saving for education

SOURCE: The Investment Company Institute (www.ici.org), accessed May 23, 2014.

Two specific problems develop with taxation of mutual funds. First, almost all investment companies allow you to reinvest income dividends and capital gain distributions from the fund to purchase additional shares instead of receiving cash. Even though you didn't receive cash because you chose to reinvest such distributions, they are still taxable and must be reported on your federal tax return as current income.

Second, when you purchase shares of stock, corporate bonds, or other investments, you decide when you sell. Thus, you can pick the tax year when you pay tax on capital gains or deduct capital losses. Mutual funds, on the other hand, buy and sell securities within the fund's portfolio on a regular basis during any 12-month period. At the end of the year, profits that result from the mutual fund's buying and selling activities are paid to shareholders in the form of capital gain distributions. Unlike the investments you manage, you have no control over when the mutual fund sells securities and when you will be taxed on capital gain distributions. Because capital gain distributions are taxable, one factor to consider when choosing a mutual fund is its turnover. For a mutual fund, the **turnover ratio** measures the percentage of a fund's holdings that have changed or "been replaced" during a 12-month period of time. Simply put, it is a measure of a fund's trading activity. *Caution:* A mutual fund with a high turnover ratio can result in higher income tax bills. A higher turnover ratio can also result in higher transaction costs and fund expenses.

turnover ratio A ratio that measures the percentage of a fund's holdings that have changed or "been replaced" during a 12-month period of time.

To ensure having all of the documentation you need for tax reporting purposes, it is essential that *you* keep accurate records. The same records will help you monitor the value of your fund investments and make more intelligent decisions with regard to buying and selling these investments.

Purchase Options

You can buy shares of a closed-end fund or exchange-traded fund through a stock exchange or in the over-the-counter market. You can purchase shares of an open-end, no-load fund by contacting the investment company that manages the fund. You can purchase shares of an open-end load fund through a salesperson who is authorized to sell them, or through an account executive of a brokerage firm or directly from the investment company that sponsors the fund.

[13]"Dividends and Other Distributions," Internal Revenue Service (www.irs.gov), accessed May 24, 2014.

You can also purchase both no-load and load funds from mutual fund supermarkets available through most brokerage firms. A mutual fund supermarket like Fidelity, Charles Schwab, or TD Ameritrade offers at least two advantages. First, instead of dealing with numerous investment companies that sponsor funds, you can make one toll-free phone call or use the Internet to obtain information, purchase shares, and sell shares in a large number of mutual funds. Second, you receive one statement from one brokerage firm instead of receiving a statement from each investment company or brokerage firm you deal with. One statement can be a real plus because it provides the information you need to monitor the value of your investments in one place and in the same format.

Because of the unique nature of open-end fund transactions, we will examine how investors buy and sell shares in this type of mutual fund. To purchase shares in an open-end mutual fund, you may use four options:

- Regular account transactions.
- Voluntary savings plans.
- Contractual savings plans.
- Reinvestment plans.

The most popular and least complicated method of purchasing shares in an open-end fund is through a regular account transaction. When you use a regular account transaction, you decide how much money you want to invest and when you want to invest, and then you simply buy as many shares as possible.

The chief advantage of the voluntary savings plan is that it allows you to make smaller purchases than the minimum purchases required by the regular account method described above. At the time of the initial purchase, you declare an intent to make regular minimum purchases of the fund's shares. Although there is no penalty for not making purchases, most investors feel an "obligation" to make purchases on a periodic basis, and, as pointed out throughout this text, small monthly investments are a great way to save for long-term objectives. For most voluntary savings plans, the minimum purchase ranges from $25 to $100 for each purchase after the initial investment. Funds try to make investing as easy as possible. Most offer payroll deduction plans, and many will deduct, upon proper shareholder authorization, a specified amount from a shareholder's bank account. Also, many investors can choose voluntary savings plans as a vehicle to invest money contributed to a 401(k), 403(b), or individual retirement account.

Not as popular as they once were, contractual savings plans (sometimes referred to as *periodic payment plans*) require you to make regular purchases over a specified period of time, usually 10 to 15 years. These plans are sometimes referred to as *front-end load plans* because almost all of the commissions are paid in the first few years of the contract period. Also, you may incur penalties if you do not fulfill the purchase requirements. For example, if you drop out of a contractual savings plan before completing the purchase requirements, you sacrifice the prepaid commissions. In some cases, contractual savings plans combine mutual fund shares and life insurance to make these plans more attractive. Many financial experts and government regulatory agencies are critical of contractual savings plans. As a result, the Securities and Exchange Commission and many states have imposed new rules on investment companies offering contractual savings plans.

reinvestment plan A service provided by an investment company in which shareholder income dividends and capital gain distributions are automatically reinvested to purchase additional shares of the fund.

You may also purchase shares in an open-end fund by using the fund's reinvestment plan. A **reinvestment plan** is a service provided by an investment company in which income dividends and capital gain distributions are automatically reinvested to purchase additional shares of the fund. Most reinvestment plans allow shareholders to use reinvested money to purchase shares without having to pay additional sales charges or commissions. *Reminder:* When your dividends or capital gain distributions are reinvested, you must still report these transactions as taxable income.

All four purchase options allow you to buy shares over a long period of time. As a result, you can use the principle of *dollar cost averaging,* which was explained in Chapter 12. Dollar cost averaging allows you to average many individual purchase prices over a long period of time. This method helps you avoid the problem of buying high and selling low. With dollar cost averaging, you can make money if you sell your fund shares at a price higher than their *average* purchase price.

Withdrawal Options

Because closed-end funds and exchange-traded funds are listed on stock exchanges or traded in the over-the-counter market, an investor may sell shares in such a fund to another investor. Shares in an open-end fund can be sold on any business day to the investment company that sponsors the fund. In this case, the shares are redeemed at their net asset value. All you have to do is give proper notification and the fund will send you a check. With some funds, you can even write checks to withdraw money from the fund.

In addition, most funds have provisions that allow investors with shares that have a minimum asset value (usually at least $5,000) to use four options to systematically withdraw money. First, you may withdraw a specified, fixed dollar amount each investment period until your fund has been exhausted. Normally, an investment period is three months.

A second option allows you to liquidate or "sell off" a certain number of shares each investment period. Since the net asset value of shares in a fund varies from one investment period to the next, the amount of money you receive will also vary.

A third option allows you to withdraw a fixed percentage of asset growth. If no asset growth occurs, no payment is made to you. Assuming you withdraw less than 100 percent of asset growth, your principal continues to grow.

EXAMPLE: Withdrawal Calculation

You arrange to receive 60 percent of the asset growth of your mutual fund investment. In one investment period, the asset growth amounts to $3,000. For that period, you will receive a check for $1,800, as shown below.

Amount you receive = Investment growth × Percentage of growth withdrawn

$$= \$3,000 \times 60 \text{ percent} = \$1,800$$

A final option allows you to withdraw all asset growth that results from income dividends and capital gain distributions earned by the fund during an investment period. Under this option, your principal remains untouched.

PRACTICE QUIZ 13–4

1. In your own words, describe the advantages and disadvantages of mutual fund investments.

2. In the table below indicate how each of the key terms affects a mutual fund investment and how each would be taxed.

Key Term	Type of Return on a Mutual Fund Investment	Type of Taxation
Income dividends		
Capital gain distributions		
Capital gains		

3. How would you purchase a closed-end fund? An exchange-traded fund?

4. What options can you use to purchase shares in or withdraw money from an open-end mutual fund?

Apply Yourself!

Use the Internet to obtain a prospectus for a specific mutual fund that you believe would be a quality long-term investment. Then describe the purchase and withdrawal options described in the fund's prospectus.

YOUR PERSONAL FINANCE DASHBOARD

SOME MONEY AVAILABLE

HAVEN'T STARTED SAVING

READY TO INVEST

$1000

$500 $1500

$0 $2000

HAVE YOU SAVED ENOUGH MONEY TO INVEST IN MUTUAL FUNDS?

Because of professional management and diversification, beginning investors often choose mutual funds. Still you must choose the right fund that will help you achieve your financial objectives. Then you must evaluate each fund alternative before investing your money.

YOUR SITUATION: Are you ready to invest in mutual funds? The first step is to save the money you need to begin investing. Typically most brokerage firms and investment companies require investors to have $250 to $2,000 to open an account. The second step is to evaluate each mutual fund alternative before investing your money.

POSSIBLE ACTIONS TO TAKE

✓ Reconsider the three steps required to begin investing in mutual funds that were described at the beginning of the chapter.

✓ Reconsider the suggestions for beginning a mutual fund investment program in the "Personal Finance in Practice" box in this chapter.

✓ Review the material in the section "How to Make a Decision to Buy or Sell Mutual Funds."

✓ Choose a specific fund and use the Internet or library research to complete "Your Personal Financial Plan" sheet 41 (Mutual Fund Evaluation) located at the end of this chapter.

Chapter Summary

LO13.1 The major reasons investors choose mutual funds are professional management and diversification. Mutual funds are also a convenient way to invest money—especially for retirement accounts. There are three types of funds: closed-end funds, exchange-traded funds, and open-end funds. A closed-end fund is a fund whose shares are issued only when the fund is organized. An exchange-traded fund (ETF) is a fund that invests in the stocks contained in a specific stock index or securities index. Both closed-end and exchange-traded funds are traded on a stock exchange or in the over-the-counter market. An open-end fund is a mutual fund whose shares are sold and redeemed by the investment company at the net asset value (NAV) at the request of investors.

Mutual funds can also be classified as A shares (commissions charged when shares are purchased), B shares (commissions charged when money is withdrawn during the first five years), and C shares (no commission to buy or sell shares, but often

higher, ongoing fees). Other possible fees include management fees and 12b-1 fees. Together all the different management fees and operating costs are referred to as an expense ratio.

LO13.2 The managers of funds tailor their investment portfolios to the investment objectives of their customers. The major fund categories are stock funds and bond funds. There are also funds that invest in a mix of different stocks, bonds, and other securities that include asset allocation funds, balanced funds, fund of funds, lifecycle funds, and money market funds. Today many investment companies use a family-of-funds concept, which allows shareholders to switch among funds as different funds offer more potential, financial reward, or security. It is also possible to participate in a retirement plan and choose different funds to obtain your financial objectives.

LO13.3 The responsibility for choosing the "right" mutual fund rests with you, the investor. Often, the first question investors must answer is whether they want a managed fund or an index fund. With a managed fund, a professional fund manager (or team of managers) chooses the securities that are contained in the fund. Some investors choose to invest in an index fund, because over many years, index funds have outperformed the majority of managed funds. To help evaluate different mutual funds, investors can use the information on the Internet, from professional advisory services, from the fund's prospectus and annual report, in financial publications, and in newspapers.

LO13.4 The advantages and disadvantages of mutual funds have made mutual funds the investment of choice for many investors. For $250 to $2,000 or more, you can open an account and begin investing. The shares of a closed-end fund or exchange-traded fund are bought and sold on organized stock exchanges or the over-the-counter market. The shares of an open-end fund may be purchased through a salesperson who is authorized to sell them, through an account executive of a brokerage firm, from a mutual fund supermarket, or from the investment company that sponsors the fund. The shares in an open-end fund can be sold to the investment company that sponsors the fund. Shareholders in mutual funds can receive a return in one of three ways: income dividends, capital gain distributions when the fund buys and sells securities in the fund's portfolio at a profit, and capital gains when the shareholder sells shares in the mutual fund at a higher price than the price paid. To ensure having all of the documentation you need for tax reporting purposes, it is essential that you keep accurate records. A number of purchase and withdrawal options are available for mutual fund investors.

Key Terms

capital gain distributions 443	expense ratio 429	no-load fund 427
closed-end fund 425	family of funds 433	open-end fund 426
contingent deferred sales load 428	income dividends 443	reinvestment plan 446
	load fund 427	turnover ratio 445
exchange-traded fund (ETF) 426	mutual fund 423	12b-1 fee 428
	net asset value (NAV) 426	

Key Formulas

Page	Topic	Formula
426	Net asset value	Net asset value $= \dfrac{\text{Value of the fund's portfolio} - \text{Liabilities}}{\text{Number of shares outstanding}}$
427	Load charge	Load charge = Dollar amount of investment $\times$ Load stated as a percentage
428	Contingent deferred sales load	Contingent deferred sales load = Amount of withdrawal $\times$ Fee stated as a percentage
		Amount you receive = Amount of withdrawal − Contingent deferred sales fee
444	Total return	Income dividends + Capital gain distributions + Change in share price when sold Dollar amount of total return
444	Percent of total return	Percent of total return $= \dfrac{\text{Dollar amount of total return}}{\text{Original cost of your investment}}$
447	Withdrawal calculation	Investment growth $\times$ Percentage of growth withdrawn

Discussion Questions

1. For many investors, mutual funds have become the investment of choice. In your own words, describe why investors purchase mutual funds. (LO13.1)
2. Describe the type of fees that you would pay to purchase a load fund. What annual fees would you typically pay for your mutual fund investment? (LO13.1)
3. Assume your employer offers you the opportunity to participate in the company's 401(k) retirement plan. (LO13.2)

   a. Would you participate in the company's retirement plan? Justify your answer.
   b. Assume you decide to participate in the employer-sponsored plan. What factors would you consider when choosing the funds for your retirement plan?

4. This chapter explored a number of different classifications or types of mutual funds. (LO13.2)

   a. Based on your age and current financial situation, which type of mutual fund seems appropriate for your investment needs? Explain your answer.
   b. As people get closer to retirement, their investment goals often change. Assume you are now 45 and have accumulated $110,000 in a retirement account. In this situation, what type of mutual funds would you choose? Why?
   c. Assume you are now 60 years of age and have accumulated $400,000 in a retirement account. Also assume you would like to retire when you are 65. What type of mutual funds would you choose to help you reach your investment goals? Why?

5. Choose either the Invesco Charter (symbol CHTRX) mutual fund or the Fidelity Fifty (symbol FFTYX) mutual fund. Then describe how each of the following sources of information could help you evaluate one of these funds. (LO13.3)

   a. The Internet.
   b. Professional advisory services.
   c. The fund's prospectus.
   d. The fund's annual report.
   e. Financial publications.
   f. Newspapers.

6. Visit the Yahoo! Finance website and evaluate one of the following mutual funds. To complete this activity, follow these steps: (LO13.3)

   a. Go to finance.yahoo.com.
   b. Choose one of the following three funds, enter its symbol, and click on the Quote Lookup button: Oppenheimer International Bond Fund (OIBAX), Janus Enterprise Fund (JAENX), or the Fidelity Select Biotechnology Portfolio (FBIOX).
   c. Print out the information for the mutual fund that you chose to evaluate.
   d. Based on the information included in this research report, would you invest in this fund? Explain your answer.

7. Obtain a mutual fund prospectus to determine the options you can use to purchase and redeem shares. (LO13.4)

   a. Which purchase option would appeal to you? Why?
   b. Assuming you are now of retirement age, which withdrawal option would appeal to you?

1. Three years ago, Mary Applegate's mutual fund portfolio was worth $410,000. Now, because of the recent economic crisis, the total value of her investment portfolio has decreased to $296,000. Even though she has lost a significant amount of money, she has not changed her investment holdings, which consist of either aggressive growth funds or growth funds.

   a. How much money has Ms. Applegate lost in the last three years?
   b. Given the above information, calculate the percentage of lost value.
   c. What actions would you take to get your investment back in shape if you were Mary Applegate?

2. Twelve months ago, Gene Peterson purchased 200 shares in the no-load Fidelity Growth Company Fund—a Morningstar five-star fund that seeks capital appreciation. His rationale for choosing this fund was that he wanted a fund that was highly rated. Each share in the fund cost $110. At the end of the year, he received dividends of $0.70 and a capital gain distribution of $8.12 a share. At the end of 12 months, the shares in the fund were selling for $118.

   a. How much did Mr. Peterson invest in this fund?
   b. At the end of 12 months, what is the total return for this fund?
   c. What is the percentage of total return?

Solutions

1. a. Dollar loss = $410,000 Value three years ago − $296,000 Current value

   = $114,000

   b. Percent of dollar loss = $114,000 ÷ $410,000 Value three years ago

   = 0.278 = 27.8 percent

   c. While Ms. Applegate has several options, any decision should be based on careful research and evaluation. First, she could do nothing. While she has lost a substantial portion of her investment portfolio ($114,000, or 27.8 percent), it may be time to hold on to her investments if she believes the economy is improving or the value of her shares will increase. Second, she could sell (or exchange) some or all of her shares in the aggressive growth or growth funds and move her money into more conservative money market or government bond funds, or even certificates of deposit. Finally, she could buy more shares if she believes the economy is beginning to improve. Because of depressed prices for quality funds, this may be a real buying opportunity. Deciding which option for Ms. Applegate to take may depend on the economic conditions at the time you answer this question.

2. a. Total investment = Price per share × Number of shares

   = $110 × 200 = $22,000

   b. Income dividends = $0.70 Dividend per share × 200 shares = $140
   Capital gain distribution = $8.12
   Capital gain distribution × 200 shares = $1,624
   Change in share value = $118 ending value − $110 beginning value = $8 a share gain
   Total increase in value = $8 gain per share × 200 shares = $1,600 gain

   Total return = $140 Income dividends + $1,624 Capital gain distribution
   + $1,600 Change in share value = $3,364

   c. Percent of dollar gain = $\dfrac{\$3,364 \text{ gain}}{\$22,000 \text{ investment}}$

   = 0.153 = 15.3 percent

Problems

1. The Western Capital Growth mutual fund has
   Total assets, $750,000,000
   Total liabilities, $7,200,000
   Total number of shares, 24,000,000
   What is the fund's net asset value (NAV)?   (LO13.1)

2. Jan Throng invested $31,000 in the Invesco Charter mutual fund. The fund charges a 5.50 percent commission when shares are purchased. Calculate the amount of commission Jan must pay.   (LO13.1)

3. As Bart Brownlee approached retirement, he decided the time had come to invest some of his nest egg in a conservative fund. He chose the Franklin Utilities Fund. If he invests $46,000 and the fund charges a 4.25 percent load when shares are purchased, what is the amount of commission that Bart must pay?   (LO13.1)

4. Mary Canfield purchased shares in the New Dimensions Global Growth Fund. This fund doesn't charge a front-end load, but it does charge a contingent deferred sales load of 4 percent for any withdrawals during the first five years. If Mary withdraws $7,500 during the second year, how much is the contingent deferred sales load?   (LO13.1)

5. The value of Mike Jackson's shares in the New Frontiers Technology Fund is $11,400. The management fee for this particular fund is 0.80 percent of the total asset value. Calculate the management fee Mike must pay this year.   (LO13.1)

6. Betty and James Holloway invested $71,000 in the Financial Vision Social Responsibility Fund. The management fee for this fund is 0.60 percent of the total asset value. Calculate the management fee the Holloways must pay.   (LO13.1)

7. As part of his 401(k) retirement plan at work, Ken Lowery invests 5 percent of his salary each month in the Capital Investments Lifecycle Fund. At the end of this year, Ken's 401(k) account has a dollar value of $36,400. If the fund charges a 12b-1 fee of 0.75 percent, what is the amount of the fee?   (LO13.1)

8. When Jill Thompson received a large settlement from an automobile accident, she chose to invest $146,000 in the Vanguard 500 Index Fund. This fund has an expense ratio of 0.17 percent. What is the amount of the fees that Jill will pay this year?   (LO13.1)

9. The Yamaha Aggressive Growth Fund has a 1.83 percent expense ratio.   (LO13.1)

   a. If you invest $55,000 in this fund, what is the dollar amount of fees that you would pay this year?
   b. Based on the information in this chapter and your own research, is this a low, average, or high expense ratio?

10. Jason Mathews purchased 300 shares of the Hodge & Mattox Energy Fund. Each share cost $14.15. Fifteen months later, he decided to sell his shares when the share value reached $17.10.   (LO13.4)

    a. What was the amount of his total investment?
    b. What was the total amount Mr. Mathews received when he sold his shares in the Hodge & Mattox fund?
    c. How much profit did he make on his investment?

11. Three years ago, James Matheson bought 200 shares of a mutual fund for $23 a share. During the three-year period, he received total income dividends of $0.92 per share. He also received total capital gain distributions of $0.80 per share. At the end of three years, he sold his shares for $29 a share. What was his total return for this investment?   (LO13.4)

12. Assume that one year ago, you bought 120 shares of a mutual fund for $33 a share, you received a $0.60 per-share capital gain distribution during the past 12 months, and the market value of the fund is now $38 a share.   (LO13.4)

    a. Calculate the total return for your $3,960 investment.
    b. Calculate the percentage of total return for your $3,960 investment.

13. Over a four-year period, LaKeisha Thompson purchased shares in the Oakmark I Fund. Using the following information, answer the questions that follow. You may want to review the concept of dollar cost averaging in Chapter 12 before completing this problem. (LO13.4)

Year	Investment Amount	Price per Share	Number of Shares*
February 2011	$1,500	$45.00	
February 2012	$1,500	$43.00	
February 2013	$1,500	$57.00	
February 2014	$1,500	$65.00	
*Carry your answer to two decimal places.			

  a. At the end of four years, what is the total amount invested?
  b. At the end of four years, what is the total number of shares purchased?
  c. At the end of four years, what is the average cost for each share?

14. During one three-month period, Matt Roundtop's mutual fund grew by $6,000. If he withdraws 35 percent of the growth, how much will he receive? (LO13.4)

 **CONNECT** **|FINANCE** To reinforce the content in this chapter, more problems are provided at connect.mheducation.com.

Case in Point

RESEARCH INFORMATION AVAILABLE FROM MORNINGSTAR

This chapter stressed the importance of evaluating potential investments. Now it is your turn to try your skill at evaluating a potential investment in the Oakmark Global Select I Fund. Assume you could invest $10,000 in shares of this fund. To help you evaluate this potential investment, carefully examine Exhibit 13–5, which reproduces the Morningstar research report for the Oakmark Global Select I Fund. The report was published February 2014.

Questions

1. Based on the research provided by Morningstar, would you buy shares in the Oakmark Global Select I Fund? Justify your answer.

2. What other investment information would you need to evaluate this fund? Where would you obtain this information?

3. On May 23, 2014, shares in the Oakmark Global Select I Fund were selling for $16.78 per share. Using the Internet or a newspaper, determine the current price for a share of this fund. Based on this information, would your investment have been profitable? (*Hint:* The symbol for this fund is OAKWX.)

4. Assuming you purchased shares in the Oakmark Global Select I Fund on May 23, 2014, and based on your answer to question 3, how would you decide if you want to hold or sell your shares? Explain your answer.

Continuing Case

INVESTING IN MUTUAL FUNDS

Jamie Lee and Ross did several weeks' worth of research trying to choose the right stock to invest in. After all, the $50,000 inheritance was a lot of money and they wanted to make the most informed investment choices they could. They discovered, by doing their homework, the various companies' stocks that they were looking to invest in did not seem like they were going to have the promising future that Jamie Lee and Ross were hoping for. They were aware that they were taking a chance with any investment instrument, but they were both nervous about "putting all of their eggs in one basket" and wanted to be more confident in making their investment choices. But how could they be more assured?

They decided to speak to their professional investment advisor, who suggested that investing in mutual funds may be the way to lessen the risk by joining a pool of other investors in a variety, or bundle, of securities chosen by the mutual fund manager. This way, Jamie Lee and Ross could lessen the pressure of choosing the right company, and minimize the chances of losing all of their investment money by diversifying their portfolio.

A mutual fund sounded like the sensible investment choice for them, but which mutual fund would best match their investment strategy? Jamie Lee and Ross are in their mid-40s and well on their way to reaching their long-term investment goals, as they committed to reaching their objectives early in their marriage. They set their sights on having the triplets graduate from college debt-free and saving enough to purchase a beach house when they retire. They are looking for a mutual fund that will provide investment income while maintaining the moderate risk investment path that they are on, as they have some time to go before retirement.

Current Financial Situation

Assets *(Jamie Lee and Ross combined):*

Checking account, $7,500

Savings account, $83,000 (including the $50,000 inheritance)

Emergency fund savings account, $45,000

House, $410,000

IRA balance, $78,000

Life insurance cash value, $110,000

Investments (stocks, bonds), $230,000

Cars, $18,500 *(Jamie Lee)* and $24,000 *(Ross)*

Liabilities *(Jamie Lee and Ross combined):*

Mortgage balance, $73,000

Student loan balance, $0

Credit card balance, $0

Car loans, $0

Income:

Jamie Lee, $45,000 gross income ($31,500 net income after taxes)

Ross, $135,000 gross income ($97,200 net income after taxes)

Monthly Expenses

Mortgage, $1,225

Property taxes, $500

Homeowner's insurance, $300

IRA contribution, $300

Utilities, $250

Food, $600

Gas/Maintenance, $275

Entertainment, $300

Life insurance, $375

Questions

1. It has been suggested by Jamie Lee and Ross's professional investment counselor that they perform a financial checkup as the first step in investing in mutual funds, even though they are investing $50,000 that was inherited from Ross's late uncle's estate. Is it a good time to invest the inheritance, or should Jamie Lee and Ross balance their budget first?

2. Jamie Lee and Ross have been reading quite a lot about stock funds while researching the classifications of mutual funds. At Jamie Lee and Ross's stage in life, what different types of stock funds would be recommended for them to invest their $50,000 inheritance in? Why?

3. The investment advisor recommended looking into managed funds, which could help remove from Jamie Lee and Ross the burden of decision making about when to buy and sell. But Ross was considering index funds, which have a lower management expense. Using your text as a guide, compare managed funds and index funds.

Managed Funds	Index Funds

Which fund would you recommend for Ross and Jamie Lee? Why?

4. Jamie Lee and Ross are ready to evaluate a mutual fund more closely. Choose a mutual fund that has been mentioned in your Chapter 13 text or one that has been recommended by a friend or family member, and complete "Your Personal Financial Plan" sheet 41. Would you recommend this mutual fund for Jamie Lee and Ross? Why or why not?

Spending Diary

"I MUST CHOOSE BETWEEN SPENDING MONEY ON SOMETHING NOW OR INVESTING FOR THE FUTURE."

Directions Monitoring your daily spending will allow you to better consider financial planning alternatives. You will have better information and the potential for better control if you use your spending information for making wiser choices. The Daily Spending Diary sheets are located in Appendix D at the end of the book and in Connect Finance.

Questions

1. Are there any spending items that you might consider revising to allow you to increase the amount you invest?
2. Based on your investment goals and the amount available to invest, what types of mutual funds would you consider?

Name: _____ Date: _____

Evaluating Mutual Fund Investment Information

Purpose: To identify and assess the value of various mutual fund investment information sources.

Financial Planning Activities: Obtain samples of several items of information that you might consider to guide you in your investment decisions. This sheet is also available in an Excel spreadsheet format in Connect Finance.

Suggested Websites: www.morningstar.com   www.kiplinger.com   www.mfea.com

Criteria Evaluation	Source 1	Source 2	Source 3
Information source			
Website			
Overview of information provided (main features)			
Cost, if any			
Ease of access			
Evaluation • Reliablility • Clarity • Value of information compared to cost			

What's Next for Your Personal Financial Plan?

- Talk with friends and relatives to determine what sources of information they use to evaluate mutual funds.
- Choose one source of information and describe how the information could help you attain your investment objectives.

Mutual Fund Evaluation

Purpose: No checklist can serve as a foolproof guide for choosing a mutual fund. However, the following questions will help you evaluate a potential investment in a specific fund.

Financial Planning Activities: Use mutual fund websites and/or library materials to answer these questions about a mutual fund that you believe could help you attain your investment objectives. This sheet is also available in an Excel spreadsheet format in Connect Finance.

Suggested Websites: www.morningstar.com   finance.yahoo.com   www.marketwatch.com

Category 1: Fund Characteristics

1. What is the fund's ticker symbol? What is the fund's name?
   _____

2. What is the fund's Morningstar rating?
   _____

3. What is the minimum investment?
   _____

4. Does the fund allow telephone or Internet exchanges? ☐ Yes ☐ No

5. Is there a fee for exchanges? ☐ Yes ☐ No

Category 2: Costs

6. Is there a front-end load charge? If so, how much is it? _____

7. Is there a contingent deferred sales load? If so, how much is it? _____

8. How much is the annual management fee?
   _____

9. Is there a 12b-1 fee? If so, how much is it?
   _____

10. What is the fund's expense ratio?
    _____

Category 3: Diversification

11. What is the fund's objective?
    _____

12. What types of securities does the fund's portfolio include?
    _____

13. How many different securities does the fund's portfolio include?
    _____

14. How many types of industries does the fund's portfolio include?
    _____

15. What are the fund's five largest holdings?
    _____

Category 4: Fund Performance

16. How long has the fund manager been with the fund?
    _____

17. How would you describe the fund's performance over the past 12 months?
    _____

18. How would you describe the fund's performance over the past five years?
    _____

19. How would you describe the fund's performance over the past 10 years?
    _____

20. What is the current net asset value for this fund?
    _____

21. What is the high net asset value for this fund over the last 12 months?
    _____

22. What is the low net asset value for this fund over the last 12 months?
    _____

23. What do the experts say about this fund?
    _____

Category 5: Conclusion

24. Based on the above information, do you think an investment in this fund will help you achieve your investment goals? ☐ Yes ☐ No

25. Explain your answer to question 24.

A Word of Caution

When you use a checklist, there is always a danger of overlooking important relevant information. This checklist is not a cure-all, but it does provide some very sound questions that you should answer before making a mutual fund investment decision. Quite simply, it is a place to start. If you need other information, *you* are responsible for obtaining it and for determining how it affects your potential investment.

Suggested App:
• Morningstar

What's Next for Your Personal Financial Plan?

- Identify additional factors that may affect your decision to invest in this fund.
- Develop a plan for monitoring an investment's value once a mutual fund(s) is purchased.

14 Starting Early: Retirement and Estate Planning

3 Steps to Financial Literacy . . . Planning to Live Off of Preretirement Earnings

1 Conduct a financial analysis of your situation. Review assets, housing, life insurance, retirement funds, and other investments. *App:* RetirePlan

2 Estimate the annual amount you will need to live comfortably during your retirement years. *App:* Retirement Income Calculator

3 Develop a plan to create a retirement fund with a future amount based on your result in Step 2. *Website:* money.cnn.com/retirement

For every 10 years you delay in starting to save for retirement, you will need to save three times as much each month to catch up. That's why, no matter how young you are, the sooner you begin saving for retirement, the better. Whether you are 18 or 58, take steps toward a more secure financial future. At the end of the chapter, "Your Personal Finance Dashboard" will provide additional information on planning your retirement income.

CHAPTER 14 LEARNING OBJECTIVES

In this chapter, you will learn to:

LO14.1 Analyze your current assets and liabilities for retirement and estimate your retirement living costs.

LO14.2 Determine your planned retirement income and develop a balanced budget based on your retirement income.

LO14.3 Analyze the personal and legal aspects of estate planning.

LO14.4 Distinguish among various types of wills and trusts.

YOUR PERSONAL FINANCIAL PLAN SHEETS

42. Retirement Plan Comparison
43. Forecasting Retirement Income
44. Estate Planning Activities
45. Will Planning
46. Trust Comparison

Planning for Retirement: Start Early

Your retirement years may seem a long way off right now. However, the fact is, it's never too early to start planning for retirement. Planning can help you cope with sudden changes that may occur in your life and give you a sense of control over your future.

A recent poll from Harris Interactive reported that 95 percent of people ages 55 to 64 years old plan to do at least some work after they retire. Another survey reported that future retirees expect to continue to learn and to pursue new hobbies and interests. Someday, when you retire, you too may desire an active life.

If you have not done any research on the subject of retirement, you may have some misconceptions about the "golden years." Here are some myths about retirement:

- You have plenty of time to start saving for retirement.
- Saving just a little bit won't help.
- You'll spend less money when you retire.
- Your retirement will only last about 15 years.
- You can depend on Social Security and a company pension plan to pay your basic living expenses.
- Your pension benefits will increase to keep pace with inflation.
- Your employer's health insurance plan and Medicare will cover all your medical expenses when you retire.

LO14.1

Analyze your current assets and liabilities for retirement and estimate your retirement living costs.

ACTION ITEM

I have plenty of time before I start saving for retirement.

☐ **True**   ☐ **False**

Some of these statements were once true but are no longer true today. You may live for many years after you retire. If you want your retirement to be a happy and comfortable time of your life, you'll need enough money to suit your lifestyle. You can't count on others to provide for you. That's why you need to start planning and saving as early as possible. It's never too late to start saving for retirement, but the sooner you start, the better off you'll be. (See Exhibit 14–1.)

Saving Smart for Retirement

Long-term financial security starts with a savings plan. If you save on a regular basis, you will have money to pay your bills, make major purchases, meet your living expenses during your retirement, and cope with emergencies. Here are a few tips on how to start saving early.

- Start now. Don't wait. Time is critical.
- Start small, if necessary. Money may be tight, but even small amounts can make a big difference given enough time; the right kind of investments; and tax-favored investments such as company retirement plans, IRAs, and SEPs.
- Use automatic deductions from your payroll or your checking account for deposit in mutual funds, IRAs, or other investments.
- Save regularly. Make saving for retirement a habit.
- Be realistic about investment returns. Never assume that a year or two of high market returns will continue indefinitely. The same goes for market declines.
- If you change jobs, keep your retirement account money in your former employer's plan or roll it over into your new employer's plan or an IRA.
- Don't dip into retirement savings unless it is absolutely necessary.

[

EXAMPLE: Starting Early

Suppose that you want to have at least $1 million when you retire at age 65. If you start saving for retirement at age 25, you can meet that goal by putting about $127 per month into investment funds that grow at a rate of about 11 percent each year. If you wait until you're 50, the monthly amount skyrockets to $2,244.

]

As you think about your retirement years, consider your long-range goals. What does retirement mean to you? Maybe it will simply be a time to stop working, sit back, and relax. Perhaps you imagine traveling the world, developing a hobby, or starting a second career. Where do you want to live after you retire? What type of lifestyle would you like to have? Once you've pondered these questions, your first step in retirement planning is to determine your current financial situation. That requires you to analyze your current assets and liabilities.

Conducting a Financial Analysis

As you learned in Chapter 2, an asset is any item of value that you own—cash, property, personal possessions, and investments—including cash in checking and savings accounts, a house, a car, a television, and so on. It also includes the current value of any stocks, bonds, and other investments that you may have as well as the current value of any life insurance and pension funds.

Your liabilities, on the other hand, are the debts you owe: the remaining balance on a mortgage or automobile loan, credit card balances, unpaid taxes, and so on. If you subtract

Exhibit 14–1 Tackling the Trade-Offs: Saving Now versus Saving Later—The Time Value of Money

Get an early start on your plan for retirement.

Age	Years	Contributions	Year-End Value	Age	Years	Contributions	Year-End Value
		SAVER ABE (THE EARLY SAVER)				SAVER BEN (THE LATE SAVER)	
25	1	$ 2,000	$ 2,188	25	1	$ 0	$ 0
26	2	2,000	4,580	26	2	0	0
27	3	2,000	7,198	27	3	0	0
28	4	2,000	10,061	28	4	0	0
29	5	2,000	13,192	29	5	0	0
30	6	2,000	16,617	30	6	0	0
31	7	2,000	20,363	31	7	0	0
32	8	2,000	24,461	32	8	0	0
33	9	2,000	28,944	33	9	0	0
34	10	2,000	33,846	34	10	0	0
35	11	0	37,021	35	11	2,000	2,188
36	12	0	40,494	36	12	2,000	4,580
37	13	0	44,293	37	13	2,000	7,198
38	14	0	48,448	38	14	2,000	10,061
39	15	0	52,992	39	15	2,000	13,192
40	16	0	57,963	40	16	2,000	16,617
41	17	0	63,401	41	17	2,000	20,363
42	18	0	69,348	42	18	2,000	24,461
43	19	0	75,854	43	19	2,000	28,944
44	20	0	82,969	44	20	2,000	33,846
45	21	0	90,752	45	21	2,000	39,209
46	22	0	99,265	46	22	2,000	45,075
47	23	0	108,577	47	23	2,000	51,490
48	24	0	118,763	48	24	2,000	58,508
49	25	0	129,903	49	25	2,000	66,184
50	26	0	142,089	50	26	2,000	74,580
51	27	0	155,418	51	27	2,000	83,764
52	28	0	169,997	52	28	2,000	93,809
53	29	0	185,944	53	29	2,000	104,797
54	30	0	203,387	54	30	2,000	116,815
55	31	0	222,466	55	31	2,000	129,961
56	32	0	243,335	56	32	2,000	144,340
57	33	0	266,162	57	33	2,000	160,068
58	34	0	291,129	58	34	2,000	177,271
59	35	0	318,439	59	35	2,000	196,088
60	36	0	348,311	60	36	2,000	216,670
61	37	0	380,985	61	37	2,000	239,182
62	38	0	416,724	62	38	2,000	263,807
63	39	0	455,816	63	39	2,000	290,741
64	40	0	498,574	64	40	2,000	320,202
65	41	0	545,344	65	41	2,000	352,427
		$20,000				$62,000	
Value at retirement*			$545,344	Value at retirement*			$352,427
Less total contributions			− 20,000	Less total contributions			− 62,000
Net earnings			$525,344	Net earnings			$290,427

*The table assumes a 9 percent fixed rate of return, compounded monthly, and no fluctuation of the principal. Distributions from an IRA are subject to ordinary income taxes when withdrawn and may be subject to other limitations under IRA rules.

SOURCE: *The Franklin Investor* (San Mateo, CA: Franklin Distributors Inc., January 1989).

Personal Finance in Practice

The Psychology of Planning for Retirement While You Are Still Young

Retirement probably seems vague and far off at this stage of your life. Besides, you have things to buy right now. Yet there are some crucial reasons to start preparing now for retirement.

- You'll have to pay for more of your own retirement than earlier generations. The sooner you get started, the better.

- You have one huge ally—time. Let's say that you put $1,000 into an IRA at the beginning of each year from age 20 through age 30 (11 years) and then never put in another dime. The account earns 7 percent annually. When you retire at age 65 you'll have $168,514 in the account. A friend doesn't start until age 30, but saves the same amount annually

for 35 years straight. Despite putting in three times as much money, your friend's account grows to only $147,913.

- You can start small and grow. Even setting aside a small portion of your paycheck each month will pay off in big dollars later.

- You can afford to invest more aggressively. You have years to overcome the inevitable ups and downs of the market.

- Developing the habit of saving for retirement is easier when you are young.

SOURCE: U.S. Department of Labor (www.dol.gov/ebsa), accessed May 29, 2014.

---

your liabilities from your assets, you get your net worth. Ideally, your net worth should increase each year as you move closer to retirement.

It's a good idea to review your assets on a regular basis. You may need to make adjustments in your saving, spending, and investments in order to stay on track. As you review your assets, consider the following factors: housing, life insurance, and other investments. Each will have an important effect on your retirement income.

HOUSING A house will probably be your most valuable asset. However, if you buy a home with a large mortgage that prevents you from saving, you put your ability to meet your retirement goal at risk. In that case you might consider buying a smaller, less expensive place to live. Remember that a smaller house is usually easier and cheaper to maintain. You can use the money you save to increase your retirement fund.

LIFE INSURANCE At some point in the future, you may buy life insurance to provide financial support for your children in case you die while they are still young. As you near retirement, though, your children will probably be self-sufficient. When that time comes, you might reduce your premium payments by decreasing your life insurance coverage. This would give you extra money to spend on living expenses or to invest for additional income.

OTHER INVESTMENTS When you review your assets, you'll also want to evaluate any other investments you have. When you originally chose these investments, you may have been more interested in making your money grow than in getting an early return from them. When you are ready to retire, however, you may want to use the income from those investments to help cover living expenses instead of reinvesting it.

Estimating Retirement Living Expenses

Next you should estimate how much money you'll need to live comfortably during your retirement years. (See the nearby "Personal Finance in Practice" box.) You can't predict

digi – know?

Kiplinger.com's retiree tax map (kiplinger.com/tools/retiree_map) is a state-by-state guide that can help determine the most tax-friendly states for you and your assets in retirement. You can sort the map by such categories as states that don't tax Social Security benefits and states that impose their own estate tax.

Your Retirement Housing

The place where you choose to live during retirement can have a significant impact on your financial needs. Use vacations in the years before you retire to explore areas you think you might enjoy. If you find a place you really like, go there at different times of the year. That way you'll know what the climate is like. Meet people who live in the area and learn about activities, transportation, and taxes.

ETHICAL AND PSYCHOLOGICAL ASPECTS OF MOVING

Consider the downside of moving to a new location. You may find yourself stuck in a place you really don't like after all. Moving can also be expensive and emotionally draining. You may miss your children, your grandchildren, and the friends and relatives you leave behind. Be realistic about what you'll have to give up as well as what you'll gain if you move after you retire.

AVOIDING RETIREMENT RELOCATION PITFALLS

Some retired people move to the location of their dreams and then discover that they've made a big mistake financially. Here are some tips from retirement specialists on how to uncover hidden taxes and other costs before you move to a new area:

- Contact the local chamber of commerce to get details on area property taxes and the local economy.
- Contact the state tax department to find out about income, sales, and inheritance taxes as well as special exemptions for retirees.
- Read the Sunday edition of the local newspaper of the city where you're thinking of moving.
- Check with local utility companies to get estimates on energy costs.
- Visit the area in different seasons, and talk to local residents about the various costs of living.
- Rent for a while instead of buying a home immediately.

What are your findings?

---

exactly how much money you'll need when you retire. You can, however, estimate what your basic needs will be. To do this, you'll have to think about your spending patterns and how your living situation will change when you retire. For instance, you probably will spend more money on recreation, health insurance, and medical care in retirement than you do now. At the same time, you may spend less on transportation and clothing. Your federal income taxes may be lower. Also, some income from various retirement plans may be taxed at a lower rate or not at all. As you consider your retirement living expenses, remember to plan for emergencies. Look at Exhibit 14–2 for an example of retirement spending patterns.

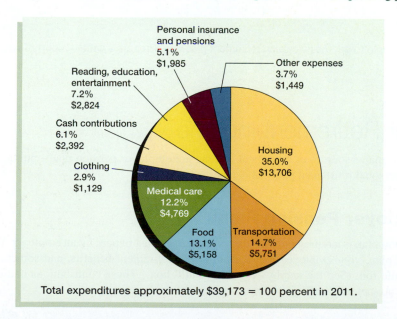

Personal insurance and pensions
5.1%
$1,985

Other expenses
3.7%
$1,449

Reading, education, entertainment
7.2%
$2,824

Cash contributions
6.1%
$2,392

Clothing
2.9%
$1,129

Medical care
12.2%
$4,769

Housing
35.0%
$13,706

Food
13.1%
$5,158

Transportation
14.7%
$5,751

Total expenditures approximately $39,173 = 100 percent in 2011.

Exhibit 14–2

How an "Average" Older (65 +) Household Spends Its Money

Retired families spend a greater share of their income for food, housing, and medical care than nonretired families.

SOURCE: U.S. Bureau of Labor Statistics, *Consumer Expenditure Survey,* September 2013 (www.bls.gov/cex/csxann11.pdf), accessed May 29, 2014.

Exhibit **14-3**

The Effects of Inflation
over Time: The Time
Value of Money

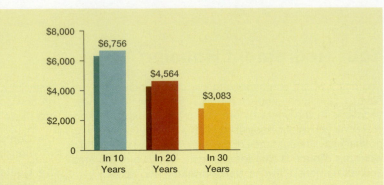

This chart shows you what $10,000 today will be worth in 10, 20, and 30 years assuming a fairly conservative 4 percent rate of inflation.

The prices of goods and services rarely remain the same for any significant period of time because of inflation. How much will $10,000 be worth in 30 years, assuming a 4 percent rate of inflation? What can you do to counteract the effects of inflation?

Don't forget to take inflation into account. Estimate high when calculating how much the prices of goods and services will rise by the time you retire (see Exhibit 14–3). Even a 3 percent rate of inflation will cause prices to double every 24 years.

PRACTICE QUIZ 14-1

1. What are the three assets you should review on a regular basis during retirement?

2. What expenses are likely to increase during retirement?

3. What expenses are likely to decrease during retirement?

Apply Yourself!

Survey friends, relatives, and other people to get their views on retirement planning. Prepare a written report of your findings.

LO14.2

Determine your planned retirement income and develop a balanced budget based on your retirement income.

Your Retirement Income

The four major sources of retirement income are employer pension plans, public pension plans, personal retirement plans, and annuities.

Employer Pension Plans

A pension plan is a retirement plan that is funded, at least in part, by an employer. With this type of plan, your employer contributes to your retirement benefits, and sometimes you contribute too. (See the nearby "Figure It Out!" box.) These contributions and earnings remain tax-deferred until you start to withdraw them in retirement.

Private employer pension plans vary. If the company you work for offers one, you should know when you become eligible to receive pension benefits. You'll also need to know what benefits you'll receive. Ask these questions during your interview with a prospective employer and start participating in the plan as soon as possible. Most employer plans are one of two basic types: defined-contribution plans or defined-benefit plans.

DEFINED-CONTRIBUTION PLAN

A **defined-contribution plan,** sometimes called an *individual account plan,* consists of an individual account for each employee to which the employer contributes a specific amount annually. This type of retirement plan does not guarantee any particular benefit. When you retire and become eligible for benefits, you simply receive the total amount of funds (including investment earnings) that have been placed in your account.

Several types of defined-contribution plans exist. With a money-purchase plan, your employer promises to set aside a certain amount of money for you each year. The amount is generally a percentage of your earnings. Under a stock bonus plan, your employer's contribution is used to buy stock in the company for you. The stock is usually held in a trust until you retire. Then you can either keep your shares or sell them. Under a profit-sharing plan, your employer's contribution depends on the company's profits.

In a **401(k) plan,** also known as a *salary-reduction plan,* you set aside a portion of your salary from each paycheck to be deducted from your gross pay and placed in a special account. Your employer will often match your contribution up to a specific dollar amount or percentage of your salary. For example, as one of the retirement benefits, McGraw-Hill Education (the publisher of your textbook) offers its employees a 401(k) savings plan. Under this plan, employees can contribute up to 25 percent of their pay with a maximum contribution limit of $17,500 in 2014. The company matches up to the first 6 percent of the employee's pretax contributions.

The funds in 401(k) plans are invested in stocks, bonds, and mutual funds. As a result, you can accumulate a significant amount of money in this type of account if you begin contributing to it early in your career. In addition, the money that accumulates in your 401(k) plan is tax-deferred, meaning that you don't have to pay taxes on it until you withdraw it.

If you're employed by a tax-exempt institution, such as a hospital or a nonprofit organization, the salary-reduction plan is called a Section 403(b) plan. As in a 401(k) plan, the funds in a 403(b) plan are tax-deferred. The amount that can be contributed annually to 401(k) and 403(b) plans is limited by law, as is the amount of annual contributions to money-purchase plans, stock bonus plans, and profit-sharing plans.

Employee contributions to a pension plan belong to you, the employee, regardless of the amount of time that you are with a particular employer. What happens to the contributions that the employer has made to your account if you change jobs and move to another company before you retire? One of the most important aspects of such plans is vesting. **Vesting** is the right to receive the employer's pension plan contributions that you've gained, even if you leave the company before retiring. After a certain number of years with the company, you will become *fully vested,* or entitled to receive 100 percent of the company's contributions to the plan on your behalf. Under some plans, vesting may occur in stages. For example, you might become eligible to receive 20 percent of your benefits after three years and gain another 20 percent each year until you are fully vested.

DEFINED-BENEFIT PLAN

A **defined-benefit plan** specifies the benefits you'll receive at retirement age, based on your total earnings and years on the job. The plan does not specify how much the employer must contribute each year. Instead your employer's contributions are based on how much money will be needed in the fund as each participant in the plan retires. If the fund is inadequate, the employer will have to make additional contributions.

ACTION ITEM

I'll need 70 to 90 percent of preretirement earnings to live comfortably during my retirement.

☐ **Yes**   ☐ **No**

defined-contribution plan A plan—profit sharing, money purchase, Keogh, or 401(k)—that provides an individual account for each participant; also called an *individual account plan.*

401(k) plan A plan under which employees can defer current taxation on a portion of their salary; also called a *salary-reduction plan.*

vesting An employee's right to at least a portion of the benefits accrued under an employer pension plan, even if the employee leaves the company before retiring.

defined-benefit plan A plan that specifies the benefits the employee will receive at the normal retirement age.

Saving for Retirement

Calculate how much you would have in 10 years if you saved $2,000 a year at an annual compound interest rate of 10 percent, with the company contributing $500 a year.

	Contributions	10% Interest	Total
Annual contribution of 10% of a $20,000 salary	$2,000.00		
Company annual contribution matching $0.50 of 5% of the salary	500.00		
1st Year			
2nd Year			
3rd Year			
4th Year			
5th Year			
6th Year			
7th Year			
8th Year			
9th Year			
10th Year			
Total			

CARRYING BENEFITS FROM ONE PLAN TO ANOTHER Some pension plans allow *portability,* which means that you can carry earned benefits from one pension plan to another when you change jobs. Workers are also protected by the Employee Retirement Income Security Act of 1974 (ERISA), which sets minimum standards for pension plans. Under this act the federal government insures part of the payments promised by defined-benefit plans.

Public Pension Plans

Another source of retirement income is Social Security, a public pension plan established by the U.S. government in 1935. The government agency that manages the program is called the Social Security Administration.

SOCIAL SECURITY Social Security is an important source of retirement income for most Americans. The program covers 97 percent of all workers, and almost one out of every six Americans currently collects some form of Social Security benefit. Social Security is actually a package of protection that provides benefits to retirees, survivors, and disabled persons. The package protects you and your family while you are working and after you retire. Nevertheless, you should not rely on Social Security to cover all of your retirement expenses. Social Security was never intended to provide 100 percent of your retirement income.

Who Is Eligible for Social Security Benefits?

The amount of retirement benefits you receive from Social Security is based on your earnings over the years. The more you work and the higher your earnings, the greater your benefits, up to a certain maximum amount.

The Social Security Administration provides you an annual history of your earnings and an estimate of your future monthly benefits. The statement includes an estimate, in today's dollars, of how much you will get each month from Social Security when you retire—at age 62, full retirement age, or 70—based on your earnings to date and your projected future earnings.

To qualify for retirement benefits you must earn a certain number of credits. These credits are based on the length of time you work and pay into the system through the Social Security tax, or contribution, on your earnings. You and your employer pay equal amounts of the Social Security tax. Your credits are calculated on a quarterly basis. The number of quarters you need depends on your year of birth. People born after 1928 need 40 quarters to qualify for benefits.

Certain dependents of a worker may receive benefits under the Social Security program. They include a wife or dependent husband aged 62 or older; unmarried children under 18 (or under 19 if they are full-time students no higher than grade 12); and unmarried, disabled children aged 18 or older. Widows or widowers can receive Social Security benefits earlier.

Social Security Retirement Benefits   Most people can begin collecting Social Security benefits at age 62. However, the monthly amount at age 62 will be less than it would be if the person waits until full retirement age. This reduction is permanent.

In the past, people could receive full retirement benefits at age 65. However, because of longer life expectancies, the full retirement age is being increased in gradual steps. For people born in 1960 and later, the full retirement age will be 67. If you postpone applying for benefits beyond your full retirement age, your monthly payments will increase slightly for each year you wait, but only up to age 70.

Social Security Information   For more information about Social Security, you can visit the Social Security website. It provides access to forms and publications and gives links to other valuable information. To learn more about the taxability of Social Security benefits, contact the Internal Revenue Service at 1-800-829-3676 and ask for Publication 554, *Social Security and Equivalent Railroad Retirement Benefits.*

CAUTION!

This chart shows the percentage of final earnings Social Security is estimated to replace. Will you have enough to make up the difference?

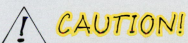

Your Retirement "Gap"

Preretirement Salary	Percent of Income Replaced by Social Security	The "Gap" You and Your Employer Must Fill
$20,000	45%	35%
30,000	40	40
40,000	33	47
60,000	25	55
$100,000	15	65

SOURCE: TIAA-CREF.

CAUTION!

Safeguard your Social Security card. You are limited to three replacement cards in a year and 10 during your lifetime.

did you know?

The estimated average monthly Social Security benefit payable to retirees in 2014 was $1,294.

OTHER PUBLIC PENSION PLANS Besides Social Security, the federal government provides several other special retirement plans for federal government workers and railroad employees. Employees covered under these plans are not covered by Social Security. The Veterans Administration provides pensions for survivors of people who died while in the armed forces. It also offers disability pensions for eligible veterans. Many state and local governments provide retirement plans for their employees as well.

Personal Retirement Plans

In addition to public and employer retirement plans, many people choose to set up personal retirement plans. Such plans are especially important to self-employed people and other workers who are not covered by employer pension plans. Among the most popular personal retirement plans are individual retirement accounts (IRAs) and Keogh accounts.

individual retirement account (IRA) A special account in which the employee sets aside a portion of his or her income; taxes are not paid on the principal or interest until money is withdrawn from the account.

INDIVIDUAL RETIREMENT ACCOUNTS An **individual retirement account (IRA)** is a special account in which the person sets aside a portion of income for retirement. Several types of IRAs are available:

- *Regular IRA:* A regular (traditional or classic) IRA lets you make annual contributions until age 70½. The contribution limit was $5,500 per year in 2014 and after ($6,500 if 50 or over). Depending on your tax filing status and income, the contribution may be fully or partially tax-deductible. The tax deductibility of a traditional IRA also depends on whether you belong to an employer-provided retirement plan. For example, in 2014, if you were covered by a retirement plan at work and you filed a joint return, then your tax-deductible contribution was reduced if your adjusted gross income was between $96,000 and $116,000.
- *Roth IRA:* Annual contributions to a Roth IRA are not tax-deductible, but the earnings accumulate tax-free. You may contribute the amounts discussed above if you're a single taxpayer with an adjusted gross income (AGI) of less than $129,000. For married couples the combined AGI must be less than $191,000. You can continue to make annual contributions to a Roth IRA even after age 70½. If you have a Roth IRA, you can withdraw money from the account tax-free and penalty-free after five years if you are at least 59½ years old or plan to use the money to help buy your first home. You may convert a regular IRA to a Roth IRA. Depending on your situation, one type of account may be better for you than the other.

CAUTION!

Withdrawals from a regular IRA prior to age 59½ may be subject to a 10 percent penalty. From a Roth IRA, contributions may be withdrawn at any age without penalty if the account has been open for five years.

- *Simplified Employee Pension (SEP) Plan:* A simplified employee pension (SEP) plan, also known as a SEP IRA, is an individual retirement account funded by an employer. Each employee sets up an IRA account at a bank or other financial institution. Then the employer makes an annual contribution of up to $50,000. The employee's contributions, which can vary from year to year, are fully tax-deductible, and earnings are tax-deferred. A business of any size, even the self-employed, can establish a SEP IRA. The SEP IRA is the simplest type of retirement plan if a person is self-employed.
- *Spousal IRA:* A spousal IRA lets you make contributions on behalf of your nonworking spouse if you file a joint tax return. The contributions are the same as for the traditional and Roth IRAs. As with a traditional IRA, this contribution may be fully or partially tax-deductible, depending on your income. This also depends on whether you belong to an employer-provided retirement plan.
- *Rollover IRA:* A rollover IRA is a traditional IRA that lets you roll over, or transfer, all or a portion of your taxable distribution from a retirement plan or other IRA.

You may move your money from plan to plan without paying taxes on it. To avoid taxes, however, you must follow certain rules about transferring the money from one plan to another. If you change jobs or retire before age 59½, a rollover IRA may be just what you need. It will let you avoid the penalty you would otherwise have to pay on early withdrawals.

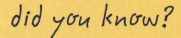

- *Education IRA:* An education IRA, also known as a Coverdell Education Savings Account, is a special IRA with certain restrictions. It allows individuals to contribute up to $2,000 per year toward the education of any child under age 18. The contributions are not tax-deductible. However, they do provide tax-free distributions for education expenses. Exhibit 14–4 summarizes the various types of IRA.

Whether or not you're covered by another type of pension plan, you can still make IRA contributions that are not tax-deductible. All of the income your IRA earns will compound tax-deferred, until you begin making withdrawals. Remember, the biggest benefit of an IRA lies in its tax-deferred earnings growth. The longer the money accumulates tax-deferred, the bigger the benefit.

IRA Withdrawals   When you retire, you can withdraw the money from your IRA by one of several methods. You can take out all of the money at one time, but the entire amount will be taxed as income. If you decide to withdraw the money from your IRA in

Type of IRA	IRA Features
Regular IRA	• Tax-deferred interest and earnings • Annual limit on individual contributions • Limited eligibility for tax-deductible contributions • Contributions do not reduce current taxes
Roth IRA	• Tax-deferred interest and earnings • Annual limit on individual contributions • Withdrawals are tax-free in specific cases • Contributions do not reduce current taxes
Simplified Employee Pension Plan (SEP IRA)	• "Pay yourself first" payroll reduction contributions • Pretax contributions • Tax-deferred interest and earnings
Spousal IRA	• Tax-deferred interest and earnings • Both working spouse and nonworking spouse can contribute up to the annual limit • Limited eligibility for tax-deductible contributions • Contributions do not reduce current taxes
Rollover IRA	• Traditional IRA that accepts rollovers of all or a portion of your taxable distribution from a retirement plan • You can roll over to a Roth IRA
Education IRA	• Tax-deferred interest and earnings • 10% early withdrawal penalty is waived when money is used for higher-education expenses • Annual limit on individual contributions • Contributions do not reduce current taxes

Exhibit 14–4

Various Types of IRA

IRAs can be a good way to save money for retirement. What are the features of the Education IRA?

"My Employer Now Offers a Roth Option in Our 401(k). Should I Invest in It?"

In a word, yes. Or at least consider investing a portion of your 401(k) contribution in the Roth. Contributions to a Roth 401(k) won't reduce your tax bill now. While pretax salary goes into a regular 401(k), aftertax money funds the Roth. But as with Roth IRAs, withdrawals from Roth 401(k)s are tax- and penalty-free as long as you've had the account for five years and are at least 59½ when you take the money out.

Because there are no income limits on Roth 401(k) contributions, these accounts provide a way for high earners to invest in a Roth without converting a traditional IRA. In 2014, you can contribute up to $17,500 to a Roth 401(k), a traditional 401(k) or a combination of the two. Workers 50 or older can contribute up to $23,000 annually. If you get matching funds from your employer, they go into a traditional pretax 401(k) account.

Consider the benefits. Younger workers stand to gain the most from investing in a Roth 401(k) because they will enjoy many years of tax-free growth.

But older workers can benefit, too. Consider this example from Fidelity Investments: Tom and Elaine, both 45, contribute $5,000 to their 401(k) plans. Tom contributes to a traditional 401(k) plan, while Elaine contributes to a Roth. They don't take withdrawals until they're 75. If their tax

rates and investment returns remain equal, Tom will end up with $27,404, after paying taxes on the withdrawal, while Elaine will have $38,061 tax-free (this example assumes a 7% annual rate of return and a 28% tax bracket). Even if Tom invested the $1,400 in tax savings he enjoyed by investing pretax money in the taxable account, he'd still lag Elaine by $2,616.

If you expect your tax bracket to decline when you retire, the Roth 401(k) loses some of its appeal, but it's still the superior option for many savers—even those who are close to retirement, says Stuart Ritter, financial planner for T. Rowe Price. If you take withdrawals from taxable and tax-deferred accounts and leave the money in the Roth for decades, tax-free earnings will continue to pile up.

If you plan to withdraw money from the Roth within ten years and you expect your tax bracket to drop significantly in retirement, then you might come out ahead with a traditional 401(k) plan, Ritter says. But you'd lose the flexibility to

take tax-free withdrawals for major expenses, such as home repairs or medical bills. And a large withdrawal from a tax-deferred account will increase your taxable income, which could affect everything from taxes on your Social Security benefits to the size of your Medicare premiums. Those worries disappear with a Roth because withdrawals are tax-free.

Although the rules require owners to take distributions from Roth 401(k)s starting at age 70½, you can get around that by simply rolling the Roth account tax-free into a Roth IRA.

Convert your 401(k)? The law now allows employees to convert funds from a traditional 401(k) plan to a Roth 401(k), if the plan allows it. About 50% of large employers offer a Roth 401(k), according to human resources consultant Aon Hewitt. Of those employers, 27% allow in-plan conversions, and an additional 16% expect to add that option this year.

You'll have to pay taxes in the year you convert, just as you would if you converted a traditional IRA to a Roth. Plus, a large conversion could bump you into a higher tax bracket. Note that unlike converting from a traditional IRA to a Roth, you can't change your mind and undo a 401(k) conversion to a Roth.

Sandra Block

1. What saving options are available for retirement accounts if you max out on your 401(k) or Roth IRA?

2. What might be an advantage of investing some of your savings in a taxable account?

3. What are the advantages and disadvantages of investing some of your savings in variable annuities?

installments, you will have to pay tax only on the amount that you withdraw. A final alternative would be to place the money that you withdraw in an annuity that guarantees payments over your lifetime. See the discussion of annuities later in this section for further information about this option.

KEOGH PLANS   A **Keogh plan,** also known as an *H.R. 10 plan* or a *self-employed retirement plan,* is a retirement plan specially designed for self-employed people and their employees. Keogh plans have limits on the amount of annual tax-deductible contributions as well as various other restrictions. Keogh plans can be complicated to administer, so you should get professional tax advice before using this type of personal retirement plan.

Keogh plan A plan in which tax-deductible contributions fund the retirement of self-employed people and their employees; also called an *H.R. 10 plan* or a *self-employed retirement plan.*

LIMITS ON PERSONAL RETIREMENT PLANS   With the exception of Roth IRAs, you cannot keep money in most tax-deferred retirement plans forever. When you retire, or by age 70½ at the latest, you must begin to receive "minimum lifetime distributions," withdrawals from the funds you accumulated in the plan. The amount of the distributions is based on your life expectancy at the time the distributions begin. If you don't withdraw the minimum distributions from a retirement account, the IRS will charge you a penalty.

Annuities

What do you do if you have funded your 401(k), 403(b), Keogh, and profit-sharing plans up to the allowable limits and you want to put away more money for retirement? The answer may be an annuity. You will recall from Chapter 10, an *annuity* is a contract purchased from an insurance company that provides for a sum of money to be paid to a person at regular intervals for a certain number of years or for life.

You might purchase an annuity with the money you receive from an IRA or company pension. You can simply buy an annuity to supplement the income you'll receive from either of these types of plans.

You can choose to purchase an annuity that has a single payment or installment payments. You will also need to decide whether you want the insurance company to send the income from your annuity to you immediately or begin sending it to you at a later date. The payments you receive from an annuity are taxed as ordinary income. However, the interest you earn from the annuity accumulates tax-free until payments begin.

Living on Your Retirement Income

As you plan for retirement, you'll estimate a budget or spending plan. When the time to retire arrives, however, you may find that your expenses are higher than you expected. If that's the case, you'll have some work to do.

First, you'll have to make sure that you're getting all the income to which you're entitled. Are there other programs or benefits for which you might qualify? You'll also need to think about any assets or valuables you might be able to convert to *cash* or sources of income.

You may have to confront the trade-off between spending and saving again. For example, perhaps you can use your skills and time instead of money. Instead of spending money on an expensive vacation, take advantage of free and low-cost recreation opportunities, such as public parks, museums, libraries, and fairs. Retirees often receive special discounts on movie tickets, meals, and more.

WORKING DURING RETIREMENT Some people decide to work part-time after they retire. Some even take new full-time jobs. Work can provide a person with a greater sense of usefulness, involvement, and self-worth. It may also be a good way to add to your retirement income.

DIPPING INTO YOUR NEST EGG When should you take money out of your savings during retirement? The answer depends on your financial circumstances, your age, and how much you want to leave to your heirs. (Your *heirs* are the people who will have the legal right to your assets when you die.) Your savings may be large enough to allow you to live comfortably on the interest alone. On the other hand, you may need to make regular withdrawals to help finance your retirement.

> **EXAMPLE: Dipping into Your Nest Egg**
>
> If you have $10,000 in savings that earns 5.5 percent interest, compounded quarterly, you could take out $68 every month for 20 years before reducing those savings to zero. If you have $40,000, you could withdraw $224 every month for 30 years.

If you dip into your retirement nest egg, you should consider one important question: How long will your savings last if you make regular withdrawals?

Whatever your situation is, once your nest egg is gone, it's gone. As shown in Exhibit 14–5, dipping into your nest egg is not wrong, but do so with caution.

Exhibit **14–5**

Dipping into Your Nest Egg

Starting Amount of Nest Egg	YOU CAN REDUCE YOUR NEST EGG TO ZERO BY WITHDRAWING THIS MUCH EACH MONTH FOR THE STATED NUMBER OF YEARS . . .					Or You Can Withdraw This Much Each Month and Leave Your Nest Egg Intact
	10 Years	**15 Years**	**20 Years**	**25 Years**	**30 Years**	
$ 10,000	$ 107	$ 81	$ 68	$ 61	$ 56	$ 46
15,000	161	121	102	91	84	69
20,000	215	162	136	121	112	92
25,000	269	202	170	152	140	115
30,000	322	243	204	182	168	138
40,000	430	323	272	243	224	184
50,000	537	404	340	304	281	230
60,000	645	485	408	364	337	276
80,000	859	647	544	486	449	368
100,000	1,074	808	680	607	561	460

NOTE: Based on an interest rate of 5.5 percent per year, compounded quarterly.

SOURCE: Select Committee on Aging, U.S. House of Representatives.

PRACTICE QUIZ 14-2

Sheet 42 Retirement Plan Comparison
Sheet 43 Forecasting Retirement Income

1. What are four major sources of retirement income?

2. What are the two basic types of employer pension plans?

3. What are the most popular personal retirement plans?

4. What is the major difference between a regular IRA and a Roth IRA?

5. What might you do if your expenses during retirement are higher than you expected?

Apply Yourself!

Read newspaper or magazine articles to determine what expenses are likely to increase and decrease during retirement. How might this information affect your retirement planning decisions?

Estate Planning

The Importance of Estate Planning

Many people think of estates as belonging only to the rich or elderly. The fact is, however, everyone has an estate. Simple defined, your **estate** consists of everything you own. During your working years your financial goal is to acquire and accumulate money for both your current and future needs. Many years from now, as you grow older, your point of view will change. Instead of working to acquire assets, you'll start to think about what will happen to your hard-earned wealth after you die. In most cases you'll want to pass that wealth along to your loved ones. That is where estate planning becomes important.

What Is Estate Planning?

Estate planning is the process of creating a detailed plan for managing your assets so that you can make the most of them while you're alive and ensure that they're distributed wisely after your death. It's not pleasant to think about your own death. However, it is a part of estate planning. Without a good estate plan, the assets you accumulate during your lifetime might be greatly reduced by various taxes when you die.

Estate planning is an essential part of both retirement planning and financial planning. It has two phases. First, you build your estate through savings, investments, and insurance.

Second, you ensure that your estate will be distributed as you wish at the time of your death. If you're married, your estate planning should take into account the needs of your spouse and children. If you are single, you still need to make sure that your financial affairs are in order for your beneficiaries. Your *beneficiary* is a person you've named to receive a portion of your estate after your death.

When you die, your surviving spouse, children, relatives, and friends will face a period of grief and loneliness. At the same time, one or more of these people will probably be responsible for settling your affairs. Make sure that important documents are accessible, understandable, and legally proper.

Legal Documents

An estate plan typically involves various legal documents, one of which is usually a will. When you die, the person who is responsible for handling your affairs will need access

LO14.3

Analyze the personal and legal aspects of estate planning.

ACTION ITEM

I believe estate planning is only for the rich and famous.

☐ **Agree**   ☐ **Disagree**

estate Everything one owns.

estate planning A definite plan for the administration and disposition of one's property during one's lifetime and at one's death.

to these and other important documents. The documents must be reviewed and verified before your survivors can receive the money and other assets to which they're entitled. If no one can find the necessary documents, your heirs may experience emotionally painful delays. They may even lose part of their inheritance. The important papers you need to collect and organize include:

- Birth certificates for you, your spouse, and your children.
- Marriage certificates and divorce papers.
- Legal name changes (especially important to protect adopted children).
- Military service records.
- Social Security documents.
- Veteran's documents.
- Insurance policies.
- Transfer records of joint bank accounts.
- Safe-deposit box records.
- Automobile registration.
- Titles to stock and bond certificates.

 Sheet 44 Estate Planning Activities

PRACTICE QUIZ 14–3

1. What is estate planning?

2. What are the two stages in planning your estate?

3. List some important documents you will need to collect and organize.

Apply Yourself!

Contact several lawyers in your area to find out how much they would charge to prepare a simple will. Are their fees about the same?

LO14.4

Distinguish among various types of wills and trusts.

ACTION ITEM

I can free myself from managing my assets by setting up a trust.

☐ Yes ☐ No

will The legal declaration of a person's mind as to the disposition of his or her property after death.

Legal Aspects of Estate Planning

Wills

One of the most important documents that every adult should have is a written will. A **will** is the legal document that specifies how you want your property to be distributed after your death. If you die **intestate**—without a valid will—your legal state of residence will step in and control the distribution of your estate without regard for any wishes you may have had.

You should avoid the possibility of dying intestate. The simplest way to do that is to make sure that you have a written will. By having an attorney help you draft your will, you may forestall many difficulties for your heirs. Legal fees for drafting a will vary with the size of your estate and your family situation. A standard will costs between $300 and $400. Make sure that you find an attorney who has experience with wills and estate planning.

Types of Wills

You have several options in preparing a will. The four basic types of wills are the simple will, the traditional marital share will, the exemption trust will, and the stated amount will. The differences among them can affect how your estate will be taxed.

SIMPLE WILL A simple will leaves everything to your spouse. Such a will is generally sufficient for people with small estates. However, if you have a large or complex estate, a simple will may not meet your objectives. It may also result in higher overall taxation, since everything you leave to your spouse will be taxed as part of his or her estate.

intestate Without a valid will.

TRADITIONAL MARITAL SHARE WILL The traditional marital share will leaves one-half of the adjusted gross estate (the total value of the estate minus debts and costs) to the spouse. The other half of the estate may go to children or other heirs. It can also be held in trust for the family. A **trust** is an arrangement by which a designated person, known as a *trustee,* manages assets for the benefit of someone else. A trust can provide a spouse with a lifelong income and would not be taxed at his or her death.

trust A legal arrangement through which one's assets are held by a trustee.

EXEMPTION TRUST WILL With an exemption trust will, all of your assets go to your spouse except for a certain amount, which goes into a trust. This amount, plus any interest it earns, can provide your spouse with lifelong income that will not be taxed. The tax-free aspect of this type of will may become important if your property value increases considerably after you die.

STATED AMOUNT WILL The stated amount will allows you to pass on to your spouse any amount that satisfies your family's financial goals. For tax purposes you could pass the exempted amount of $5.34 million (in 2014). However, you might decide to pass on a stated amount related to your family's future income needs or to the value of personal items.

WILLS AND PROBATE The type of will that is best for your particular needs depends on many factors, including the size of your estate, inflation, your age, and your objectives. No matter what type of will you choose, it's best to avoid probate. **Probate** is the legal procedure of proving a valid or invalid will. It's the process by which your estate is managed and distributed after your death, according to the provisions of your will. A special probate court generally validates wills and makes sure that your debts are paid. You should avoid probate because it's expensive, lengthy, and public. As you will read later, a living trust avoids probate and is also less expensive, quicker, and private.

probate The legal procedure of proving a valid or invalid will.

Formats of Wills

Wills may be either holographic or formal. A *holographic will* is a handwritten will that you prepare yourself. It should be written, dated, and signed entirely in your own handwriting. No printed or typed information should appear on its pages. Some states do not recognize holographic wills as legal.

A *formal will* is usually prepared with the help of an attorney. It may be typed, or it may be a preprinted form that you fill out. You must sign the will in front of two witnesses; neither person can be a beneficiary named in the will. The witnesses must then sign the will in front of you.

A *statutory will* is prepared on a preprinted form, available from lawyers, stationery stores, or Internet sites. Using preprinted forms to prepare your will presents serious risks. The form may include provisions that are not in the best interests of your heirs. Therefore, it is best to seek a lawyer's advice when you prepare your will.

Writing Your Will

Writing a will allows you to express exactly how you want your property to be distributed to your heirs. If you're married, you may think that all the property owned jointly by you and your spouse will automatically go to your spouse after your death. This is true of some assets, such as your house. Even so, writing a will is the only way to ensure that all of your property will end up where you want it.

executor Someone willing and able to perform the tasks involved in carrying out your will.

SELECTING AN EXECUTOR

An **executor** is someone who is willing and able to perform the tasks involved in carrying out your will. These tasks include preparing an inventory of your assets, collecting any money due, and paying off your debts. Your executor must also prepare and file all income and estate tax returns. In addition, he or she will be responsible for making decisions about selling or reinvesting assets to pay off debt and provide income for your family while the estate is being settled. Finally, your executor must distribute the estate and make a final accounting to your beneficiaries and to the probate court.

did you know?

Who can be an executor? Any U.S. citizen over 18 who has not been convicted of a felony can be named the executor of a will.

SELECTING A GUARDIAN

If you have children, your will should also name a guardian to care for them in the event that you and your spouse die at the same time and the children cannot care for themselves. A **guardian** is a person who accepts the responsibility of providing children with personal care after their parents' death and managing the parents' estate for the children until they reach a certain age.

guardian A person who assumes responsibility for providing children with personal care and managing the deceased's estate for them.

ALTERING OR REWRITING YOUR WILL

Sometimes you'll need to change the provisions of your will because of changes in your life or in the law. Once you've made a will, review it frequently so that it remains current. Here are some reasons to review your will:

- You've moved to a new state that has different laws.
- You've sold property that is mentioned in the will.
- The size and composition of your estate have changed.
- You've married, divorced, or remarried.
- Potential heirs have died, or new ones have been born.

Don't make any written changes on the pages of an existing will. Additions, deletions, or erasures on a will that has been signed and witnessed can invalidate the will. If you want to make only a few minor changes, adding a codicil may be the best choice. A **codicil** is a document that explains, adds, or deletes provisions in your existing will.

codicil A document that modifies provisions in an existing will.

A Living Will

At some point in your life you may become physically or mentally disabled and unable to act on your own behalf. If that happens, you'll need a living will. A **living will** is a document in which you state whether you want to be kept alive by artificial means if you become terminally ill and unable to make such a decision. Many states recognize living wills. Exhibit 14–6 is an example of a typical living will.

living will A document that enables an individual, while well, to express the intention that life be allowed to end if he or she becomes terminally ill.

To ensure the effectiveness of a living will, discuss your intention of preparing such a will with the people closest to you. You should also discuss this with your family doctor. Sign and date your document before two witnesses. Witnessing shows that you signed of your own free will.

Give copies of your living will to those closest to you, and have your family doctor place a copy in your medical file. Keep the original document readily accessible, and look it over periodically—preferably once a year—to be sure your wishes have remained unchanged. To verify your intent, redate and initial each subsequent endorsement.

Most lawyers will do the paperwork for a living will at no cost if they are already preparing your estate plan. You can also get the necessary forms from nonprofit advocacy groups. Partnership for Caring: America's Voices for the Dying is a national nonprofit organization that operates the only national crisis and information hotline dealing with end-of-life issues. It also provides living wills, medical powers of attorney, and similar documents geared to specific states. Working through end-of-life issues is difficult, but

Copyright © 2016 by McGraw-Hill Education

Exhibit **14–6**

A Living Will

Living Will Declaration

Declaration made this _____ day of _____ (month, year)

I, _____, being of sound mind, willfully and voluntarily make known my desire that my dying shall not be artificially prolonged under the circumstances set forth below, do hereby declare

If at any time I should have an incurable injury, disease, or illness regarded as a terminal condition by my physician and if my physician has determined that the application of life-sustaining procedures would serve only to artificially prolong the dying process and that my death will occur whether or not life-sustaining procedures are utilized, I direct that such procedures be withheld or withdrawn and that I be permitted to die with only the administration of medication or the performance of any medical procedure deemed necessary to provide me with comfort care.

In the absence of my ability to give directions regarding the use of such life-sustaining procedures, it is my intention that this declaration shall be honored by my family and physician as the final expression of my legal right to refuse medical or surgical treatment and accept the consequences from such refusal. I understand the full import of this declaration, and I am emotionally and mentally competent to make this declaration.

Signed _____

City, County, and State of Residence _____

The declarant has been personally known to me, and I believe him or her to be of sound mind.

Witness _____

Witness _____

Some people who become terminally ill cannot make decisions on their own behalf. What is the basic purpose of a living will?

it can help avoid forcing your family to make a decision in a hospital waiting room—or worse, having your last wishes ignored.

POWER OF ATTORNEY Related to the idea of a living will is power of attorney. A **power of attorney** is a legal document that authorizes someone to act on your behalf. If you become seriously ill or injured, you'll probably need someone to take care of your needs and personal affairs. This can be done through a power of attorney.

power of attorney A legal document authorizing someone to act on one's behalf.

LETTER OF LAST INSTRUCTION In addition to a traditional will, it is a good idea to prepare a letter of last instruction. This document is not legally binding, but it can provide your heirs with important information. It should contain your wishes for your funeral arrangements as well as the names of the people who are to be informed of your death.

Trusts

Basically, a trust is a legal arrangement that helps manage the assets of your estate for your benefit or that of your beneficiaries. The creator of the trust is called the *trustor,* or *grantor.* The *trustee* might be a person or institution, such as a bank, that administers the trust. A bank charges a small fee for its services in administering a trust. The fee is usually based on the value of the assets in the trust.

Individual circumstances determine whether establishing a trust makes sense. Some of the common reasons for setting up a trust are to:

- Reduce or otherwise provide payment of estate taxes.
- Avoid probate and transfer your assets immediately to your beneficiaries.
- Free yourself from managing your assets while you receive a regular income from the trust.
- Provide income for a surviving spouse or other beneficiary.
- Ensure that your property serves a desired purpose after your death.

Types of Trusts

There are many types of trusts, some of which are described in detail in this section. You'll need to choose the type of trust that's most appropriate for your particular situation. An estate attorney can advise you about the right type of trust for your personal and family needs.

All trusts are either revocable or irrevocable. A *revocable trust* is one in which you have the right to end the trust or change its terms during your lifetime. An *irrevocable trust* is one that cannot be changed or ended. Revocable trusts avoid the lengthy process of probate, but they do not protect assets from federal or state estate taxes. Irrevocable trusts avoid probate and help reduce estate taxes. However, by law you cannot remove any assets from an irrevocable trust, even if you need them at some later point in your life.

CREDIT-SHELTER TRUST A credit-shelter trust is one that enables the spouse of a deceased person to avoid paying federal taxes on a certain amount of assets left to him or her as part of an estate. Perhaps the most common estate planning trust, the credit-shelter trust has many other names: bypass trust, "residuary" trust, A/B trust, exemption equivalent trust, or family trust. It is designed to allow married couples, who can leave everything to each other tax-free, to take full advantage of the exemption that allows $5.34 million (in 2014) in every estate to pass free of federal estate taxes. The surviving spouse's estate in excess of $10.68 million (in 2014) faces estate tax of 40 percent.

DISCLAIMER TRUST A disclaimer trust is appropriate for couples who do not yet have enough assets to need a credit-shelter trust but may have in the future. With a disclaimer trust, the surviving spouse is left everything, but he or she has the right to disclaim, or deny, some portion of the estate. Anything that is disclaimed goes into a credit-shelter trust. This approach allows the surviving spouse to protect wealth from estate taxes.

LIVING TRUST A living trust, also known as an inter vivos trust, is a property management arrangement that goes into effect while you're alive. It allows you, as a trustor, to receive benefits during your lifetime. To set up a living trust, you simply transfer some of your assets to a trustee. Then you give the trustee instructions for managing the trust while you're alive and after your death. A living trust has several advantages:

- It ensures privacy. A will is a public record; a trust is not.
- The assets held in trust avoid probate at your death. This eliminates probate costs and delays.
- It enables you to review your trustee's performance and make changes if necessary.
- It can relieve you of management responsibilities.
- It's less likely than a will to create arguments between heirs upon your death.
- It can guide your family and doctors if you become terminally ill or unable to make your own decisions.

Read the nearby "Personal Finance in Practice" box, "The Psychology of Living Trust Offers," to make sure that living trust offers are trustworthy.

Setting up a living trust costs more than creating a will. However, depending on your particular circumstances, a living trust can be a good estate planning option.

TESTAMENTARY TRUST A testamentary trust is one established by your will that becomes effective upon your death. Such a trust can be valuable if your beneficiaries are inexperienced in financial matters. It may also be your best option if your estate taxes will be high. A testamentary trust provides many of the same advantages as a living trust.

Taxes and Estate Planning

Federal and state governments impose various types of taxes that you must consider in estate planning. The four major types of taxes are estate taxes, estate and trust federal income taxes, inheritance taxes, and gift taxes.

The Psychology of Living Trust Offers: Is It Ethical?

Misinformation and misunderstanding about estate taxes and the length or complexity of probate provide the perfect cover for unethical salespeople, who have created an industry out of older people's fears that their estates could be eaten up by costs or that distribution of their assets could be delayed for years. Some unethical businesses are advertising seminars on living trusts or sending postcards inviting consumers to call for in-home appointments to learn whether a living trust is right for them. In these cases, it's not uncommon for the salesperson to exaggerate the benefits or appropriateness of the living trust and claim—falsely—that locally licensed lawyers will prepare the documents.

Other businesses are advertising living trust "kits": consumers send money for these do-it-yourself products but receive nothing in return. Still other businesses are using estate planning services to gain access to consumers' financial information and to sell them other financial products, such as insurance annuities.

What's a consumer to do? It's true that, for some people, a living trust can be a useful and practical tool. But for others, it can be a waste of money and time. Because state laws and requirements vary, "cookie-cutter" approaches to estate planning aren't always the most efficient way to handle your affairs. Before you sign any papers to create a will, a living trust, or any other kind of trust:

- Explore all your options with an experienced and licensed estate planning attorney or financial advisor. Generally, state law requires that an attorney draft the trust.
- Avoid high-pressure sales tactics and high-speed sales pitches by anyone who is selling estate planning tools or arrangements.
- Avoid salespeople who give the impression that AARP is selling or endorsing their products. AARP does not endorse any living trust products.
- Do your homework. Get information about your local probate laws from the Clerk (or Registrar) of Wills.
- If you opt for a living trust, make sure it's properly funded—that is, that the property has been transferred from your name to the trust. If the transfers aren't done properly, the trust will be invalid and the state will determine who inherits your property and serves as guardian for your minor children.
- If someone tries to sell you a living trust, ask whether the seller is an attorney. Some states limit the sale of living trust services to attorneys.

ESTATE TAXES An estate tax is a federal tax collected on the value of a person's property at the time of his or her death. The tax is based on the fair market value of the deceased person's investments, property, and bank accounts, less an exempt amount of $5.34 million in 2014; this tax is due nine months after a death.

ESTATE AND TRUST FEDERAL INCOME TAXES In addition to the federal estate tax return, estates and certain trusts must file federal income tax returns with the Internal Revenue Service. Taxable income for estates and trusts is computed in the same manner as taxable income for individuals. Trusts and estates must pay quarterly estimated taxes.

INHERITANCE TAXES Your heirs might have to pay a tax for the right to acquire the property that they have inherited. An inheritance tax is a tax collected on the property left by a person in his or her will.

Only state governments impose inheritance taxes. Most states collect an inheritance tax, but state laws differ widely as to exemptions and rates of taxation. A reasonable average for state inheritance taxes would be 4 to 10 percent of whatever the heir receives.

GIFT TAXES Both the state and federal governments impose a gift tax, a tax collected on money or property valued at more than $14,000 (in 2014) given by one person to another in a single year. One way to reduce the tax liability of your estate is to reduce the size of the estate while you're alive by giving away portions of it as gifts. You're free to make such gifts to your spouse, children, or anyone else at any time. (Don't give away assets if you need them in your retirement!)

did you know?

Charitable gifts can be an important tool in estate planning. Giving to charity supports a cause and offers benefits such as reduced taxes and increased interest income. The National Philanthropic Trust is an independent public charity dedicated to increasing philanthropy in our society. For more information, visit www.nptrust.org.

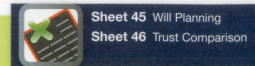
Sheet 45 Will Planning
Sheet 46 Trust Comparison

PRACTICE QUIZ 14–4

1. What is a will?

2. What are the four basic types of wills?

3. What are the responsibilities of an executor?

4. Why should you name a guardian?

5. What is the difference between a revocable and an irrevocable trust?

6. What are the four major types of trusts?

7. What are the four major types of taxes to consider in estate planning?

Apply Yourself!

Discuss with your attorney the possibility of establishing a trust as a means of managing your estate.

YOUR PERSONAL FINANCE DASHBOARD

PERCENT OF PRERETIREMENT EARNINGS

A dashboard is a tool used by organizations to monitor key performance indicators, such as delivery time, product defects, or customer complaints. As an individual, you can use a personal finance dashboard to assess your own financial situation.

You have several retirement savings opportunities available to you—from IRAs and SEPs to 401(k)s and 403(b)s. These options are especially important now that traditional pensions and other employer-funded retirement plans have become increasingly rare.

YOUR SITUATION: Have you figured out how much money you should save for retirement? Most financial advisors suggest that you will need 70 to 90 percent of preretirement earnings to live comfortably. Are you taking advantage of retirement savings programs at work, especially those where your employer matches contributions? Have you made sure that your investments are diversified?

POSSIBLE ACTIONS TO TAKE

 Reconsider your responses to the "Action Items" (in the text margin) in the chapter to determine actions you might take to improve your retirement and estate planning activities.

 Reevaluate your retirement and estate planning goals to make sure they reflect what is important to you and your family.

 Consider information from several sources when making retirement and estate planning decisions. Consult older friends and relatives, bankers, and tax advisors.

 Use future value and present value computations to help you achieve your retirement and estate planning goals. Calculators are available at www.dinkytown .net, www.moneychimp.com/calculator, and www .rbccentura.com/tools.

LO14.1 The difference between your assets and your liabilities is your net worth. Review your assets to ensure they are sufficient for retirement. Then estimate your living expenses. Some expenses are likely to decrease while others will increase.

LO14.2 Your possible sources of income during retirement include employer pension plans, public pension plans, personal retirement plans, and annuities. If your income approximates your expenses, you are in good shape; if not, determine additional income needs and sources.

LO14.3 The personal aspects of estate planning depend on whether you are single or married. Never having been married does not eliminate the need to organize your financial affairs. Every adult should have a written will. A will is a way to transfer your property according to your wishes after you die.

LO14.4 The four basic types of wills are the simple will, the traditional marital share will, the exemption trust will, and the stated amount will. Types of trusts include the credit-shelter trust, the disclaimer trust, the living trust, and the testamentary trust.

Federal and state governments impose various types of estate taxes; you can prepare a plan for paying these taxes.

codicil 476

defined-benefit plan 465

defined-contribution plan 465

estate 473

estate planning 473

executor 476

401(k) plan 465

guardian 476

individual retirement account (IRA) 468

intestate 474

Keogh plan 471

living will 476

power of attorney 477

probate 475

trust 475

vesting 465

will 474

1. How will your spending patterns change during your retirement years? Compare your spending patterns with those shown in Exhibit 14–2. (LO14.1)
2. Obtain Form SSA-7004 from your local Social Security office. Complete and mail the form to receive a personal earnings and benefits statement. Use the information in this statement to plan your retirement. (LO14.2)
3. Prepare a written report of personal information that would be helpful to you and your heirs. Be sure to include the location of family records, your military service file, and other important papers; medical records; bank accounts; charge accounts; location of your safe-deposit box; U.S. savings bonds, stocks, bonds, and other securities; property owned; life insurance; annuities; and Social Security information. (LO14.3)
4. Visit Metropolitan Life Insurance Company's web page at www.lifeadvice.com. Using this information, prepare a report on the following: (*a*) Who needs a will? (*b*) What are the elements of a will (naming a guardian, naming an executor, preparing a will, updating a will, estate taxes, where to keep your will, living will, etc.)? (*c*) How is this report helpful in preparing your own will? (LO14.3)
5. Make a list of the criteria you will use in deciding who will be the guardian of your minor children if you and your spouse die at the same time. (LO14.3)

1. Beverly Foster is planning for her retirement. She has determined that her car is worth $10,000, her home is worth $150,000, her personal belongings are worth $100,000, and her stocks and bonds are worth $300,000. She owes $50,000 on her home and $5,000 on her car. Calculate her net worth.

2. Calculate how much money an average older (65 +) household with an annual income of $39,173 spends on food each year. (*Hint:* Use Exhibit 14–2.)

3. On December 31, 2014, George gives $14,000 to his son and $14,000 to his son's wife. On January 1, 2015, George gives another $14,000 to his son and another $14,000 to his son's wife. George made no other gifts to his son or his son's wife in 2014 and 2015. What is the gift tax?

Solutions

1.

Assets		Liabilities	
Car	$ 10,000	Mortgage	$ 50,000
Home	$150,000	Car	5,000
Personal belongings	$100,000	Total liabilities	$ 55,000
Stocks and bonds	$300,000		
Total assets	$560,000		

Net worth = Assets − Liabilities

= $560,000 − $55,000 = $505,000

2. An average older household with an annual income of $39,173 spends about 13.1 percent of their income on food. Thus $39,173 × 13.1% = $5,158.

3. There is no gift tax in 2014 or in 2015 since George gifted $14,000 to his son and son's wife in each of the two years.

Problems

1. Shelly's assets include money in checking and saving accounts, investments in stocks and mutual funds, and personal property such as furniture, appliances, an automobile, a coin collection, and jewelry. Shelly calculates that her total assets are $165,200. Her current unpaid bills, including an auto loan, credit card balances, and taxes, total $21,300. Calculate Shelly's net worth.   (LO14.1)

2. Prepare your net worth statement using the Assets − Liabilities = Net worth equation.   (LO14.1)

3. Ted Riley owns a 2012 Lexus worth $40,000. He owns a home worth $275,000. He has a checking account with $800 in it and a savings account with $1,900 in it. He has a mutual fund worth $110,000. His personal assets are worth $90,000. He still owes $25,000 on his car and $150,000 on his home, and he has a balance on his credit card of $1,600. What is Ted's net worth?   (LO14.1)

4. Calculate approximately how much money an older (65+) household with an annual income of $45,000 spends on housing each year. (*Hint:* Use Exhibit 14–2.)   (LO14.1)

5. Using Exhibit 14–2, calculate approximately how much money the household from problem 4 spends on medical care.   (LO14.1)

6. Ruby is 25 and has a good job at a biotechnology company. She currently has $10,000 in an IRA, an important part of her retirement nest egg. She believes her IRA will grow at an annual rate of 8 percent, and she plans to leave it untouched until she retires at age 65. Ruby estimates that she will need $875,000 in her *total* retirement nest egg by the time she is 65 in order to have retirement income of $20,000 a year (she expects that Social Security will pay her an additional $15,000 a year).   (LO14.2)

a. How much will Ruby's IRA be worth when she needs to start withdrawing money from it when she retires? (*Hint:* Use Exhibit 1–A in the Chapter 1 Appendix.)

b. How much money will she have to accumulate in her company's 401(k) plan over the next 40 years in order to reach her retirement income goal?

7. Gene and Dixie, husband and wife (ages 35 and 32), both work. They have an adjusted gross income of $50,000 in 2014, and they are filing a joint income tax return. Both have employer-provided retirement plans at work. What is the maximum IRA contribution they can make? How much of that contribution is tax-deductible? (LO14.2)

8. You have $100,000 in your retirement fund that is earning 5.5 percent per year, compounded quarterly. How many dollars in withdrawals per month would reduce this nest egg to zero in 20 years? How many dollars per month can you withdraw for as long as you live and still leave this nest egg intact? (*Hint:* Use Exhibit 14–5.) (LO14.2)

Problems 9, 10, and 11 are based on the following scenario:

In 2014, Joshua gave $14,000 worth of Microsoft stock to his son. In 2015, the Microsoft shares are worth $23,000.

9. What was the gift tax in 2014? (LO14.4)

10. What is the total amount removed from Joshua's estate in 2015? (LO14.4)

11. What will be the gift tax in 2015? (LO14.4)

12. In 2014, you gave a $12,000 gift to a friend. What is the gift tax? (LO14.4)

Problems 13, 14, and 15 are based on the following scenario:

Barry and his wife Mary have accumulated over $3.5 million during their 50 years of marriage. They have three children and five grandchildren.

13. How much money can they gift to their children in 2014 without any gift tax liability? (LO14.4)

14. How much money can Barry and Mary gift to their grandchildren in 2014 without any gift tax liability? (LO14.4)

15. What is the total amount of estate removed from Barry and Mary's estate in 2014? (LO14.4)

16. The date of death for a widow was 2014. If the estate was valued at $7.5 million and the estate was taxed at 40 percent, what was the heir's tax liability? (LO14.4)

17. Joe and Rachael are both retired. Married for 55 years, they have amassed an estate worth $4.4 million. The couple has no trust or other type of tax-sheltered assets. If Joe or Rachael dies in 2014, how much federal estate tax would the surviving spouse have to pay, assuming that the estate is taxed at the 40 percent rate? (LO14.4)

 To reinforce the content in this chapter, more problems are provided at connect.mheducation.com.

Case in Point

PLANNING FOR RETIREMENT

Is a bad day fishing better than a good day at the office? Yes, according to a retired dad, Chuck. With his company pension, at least he didn't have to worry about money. In the good old days, if you had a decent job, you'd hang on to it, and then your company's pension combined with Social Security payments would be enough to live comfortably. Chuck's son, Rob, does not have a company pension and is not sure whether Social Security will even exist when he retires. So when it comes to retirement, the sooner you start saving, the better.

Take Maureen, a salesperson for a computer company, and Therese, an accountant for a lighting manufacturer. Both start their jobs at age 25. Maureen starts saving for retirement right away by investing $300 a month at 9 percent until age 65. But Therese does nothing until age 35. At 35 she begins investing the same $300 a month at 9 percent until age 65. What a shocking difference! Maureen has accumulated $1.4 million, while Therese has only $553,000 in her retirement fund. The moral? The sooner you start, the more you'll have for your retirement. Women especially need to start sooner, because they typically enter the workforce later, have lower salaries, and, ultimately, have lower pensions.

Laura Tarbox, owner and president of Tarbox Equity, explains how to determine your retirement needs and how your budget might change when you retire. Tarbox advises that the old rule of thumb—that you need 60 to 70 percent of preretirement income—is too low an estimate. She cautions that most people will want to spend very close to what they were spending before retiring. There are some expenses that might be lower, however, such as clothing for work, dry cleaning, and commuting expenses. Other expenses, though, such as insurance, travel, and recreation, may increase during retirement.

Questions

1. In the past, many workers chose to stay with their employers until retirement. What was the major reason for employees' loyalty?
2. How did Maureen amass $1.4 million for retirement, while Therese could accumulate only $553,000?
3. Why do women need to start early to save for retirement?
4. What expenses may increase or decrease during retirement?

Continuing Case

STARTING EARLY: RETIREMENT AND ESTATE PLANNING

Jamie Lee and Ross, now in their 50s, have plenty of time on their hands now that the triplets are away at college. They both realize that time has flown by; more than 24 years have passed since they married!

Looking back over the years, they realize that they have worked hard in their careers, Jamie Lee as the proprietor of a cupcake café and Ross, self-employed as a web page designer. They enjoyed raising their family and strived to be financially sound as they looked forward to a retirement that is just around the corner. They saved regularly and invested wisely over the years. They rebounded nicely from the recent economic crisis over the past few years, as they watched their investments closely and adjusted their strategies when they felt it necessary. They purchase vehicles with cash and do not carry credit card balances, choosing to use them for convenience only. The triplets are pursuing their master's degrees and have tuition covered through work-study programs at the university.

Jamie Lee and Ross are just a few short years from realizing their goals of retiring at 65 and purchasing the home at the beach!

Current Financial Situation

Assets (Jamie Lee and Ross combined):
Checking account, $5,500
Savings account, $53,000
Emergency fund savings account, $45,000
House, $475,000
IRA balance, $92,000
Life insurance cash value, $125,000
Investments (stocks, bonds), $750,000
Cars, $12,500 (*Jamie Lee*) and $16,000 (*Ross*)

Liabilities (Jamie Lee and Ross combined):
Mortgage balance, $43,000
Credit card balance, $0
Car loans, $0

Income:
Jamie Lee, $45,000 gross income ($31,500 net income after taxes)
Ross, $135,000 gross income ($97,200 net income after taxes)

Monthly Expenses
Mortgage, $1,225
Property taxes, $500
Homeowner's insurance, $300
IRA contribution, $300
Utilities, $250
Food, $600
Gas/Maintenance, $275
Entertainment, $300
Life insurance, $375

Questions

1. As Jamie Lee and Ross review their assets, can you tell them which will be valuable to them for income as retirement approaches?

2. Jamie Lee and Ross estimate that they will have $1 million in liquid assets to withdraw from at the start of their retirement. They plan to be in retirement for 30 years. Using Exhibit 14–5 how much do you think Jamie Lee and Ross can withdraw each month and still leave their next egg intact? How much can they withdraw each month that will reduce their nest egg to zero?

3. Jamie Lee and Ross have been hearing many stories recently about acquaintances who are passing away without leaving a will, which made Jamie Lee and Ross anxious to review their estate plan with an attorney. They do not want to think about eventually passing on, but they know it is an essential part to careful financial planning. It was suggested that they assemble all of their legal documents in a place where their heirs would be able to access them if necessary. What documents would you suggest that Jamie Lee and Ross make accessible?

4. Jamie Lee and Ross are now having the attorney draw up a will for each of them. What is the purpose of having a will? Do they need to have an attorney to draft a will? What type of will would you recommend they have, based on their marital/family status?

Spending Diary

"KEEPING TRACK OF MY DAILY SPENDING GETS ME TO START THINKING ABOUT SAVING AND INVESTING FOR RETIREMENT."

Directions The consistent use of a Daily Spending Diary can provide you with ongoing information that will help you manage your spending, saving, and investing activities. Taking time to reconsider your spending habits can result in achieving better satisfaction from your available finances. The Daily Spending Diary sheets are located in Appendix D at the end of the book and in Connect Finance.

Analysis Questions

1. What portion of your available finances involve saving or investing for long-term financial security?

2. What types of retirement and estate planning activities might you start to consider at this point of your life?

YOUR PERSONAL FINANCIAL PLAN

Name: _____   Date: _____

Retirement Plan Comparison

Purpose: To compare benefits and costs for different retirement plans: 401(k), 403(b), 457, IRA, Roth IRA, SEP IRA, etc.

Financial Planning Activities: Analyze advertisements and articles, and contact your employer and financial institutions to obtain the information requested below. This sheet is also available in an Excel spreadsheet format in Connect Finance.

Suggested Websites: www.lifenet.com   www.aarp.org   www.financialengines.com

Type of plan			
Name of financial institution or employer			
Address			
Phone			
Website			
Type of investments			
Minimum initial deposit			
Minimum additional deposits			
Employer contributions			
Current rate of return			
Service charges/fees			
Safety insured? By whom?			
Amount of coverage			
Payroll deduction available?			
Tax benefits			
Penalty for early withdrawal: • IRS penalty (10%) • Other penalties			
Other features or restrictions			

What's Next for Your Personal Financial Plan?

- Survey local businesses to determine the types of retirement plans available to employees.
- Talk to representatives of various financial institutions to obtain their suggestions for IRA investments.

Name: _____ **Date:** _____

Forecasting Retirement Income

Purpose: To determine the amount needed to save each year to have the necessary funds to cover retirement living costs.

Financial Planning Activities: Estimate the information requested below. This sheet is also available in an Excel spreadsheet format in Connect Finance.

Suggested Websites: www.ssa.gov   www.pensionplanners.com   www.choosetosave.org

Estimated annual retirement living expenses

Estimated annual living expenses
if you retired today $ _____

Future value for _____ years until retirement at
expected annual income of _____%(use future
value of $1, Exhibit 1–A of Chapter 1 Appendix)   × _____

**Projected annual retirement living expenses
adjusted for inflation** . . . . (A) $ _____

Estimated annual income at retirement

Social Security income $ _____

Company pension, personal retirement
account income $ _____

Investment and other income $ _____

Total retirement income . . . . (B) $ _____

Annual shortfall of income after retirement (subtract B from A) . . . . (C) _____

**Additional amount required to fund the income
shortfall at retirement**

Expected annual rate of return on funds
before retirement   _____

Expected years in retirement   _____

Expected annual rate of return on invested
funds after retirement   _____

Additional amount needed at retirement to fund the shortfall . . . . (D) $ _____

Future value factor of a series of deposits for _____ years until
retirement and an expected annual rate of return before retirement
of _____ % (use Exhibit 1–B of Chapter 1 Appendix) equals   (E) $ _____

**Annual deposit required to accumulate the amount needed
(D ÷ E)** . . . . $ _____

Suggested
App:
• RetirePlan

What's Next for Your Personal Financial Plan?

- Survey retired individuals or people close to retirement to obtain information on their main sources of retirement income.

- Make a list that suggests the best investment options for an individual retirement account.

Name: _____   Date: _____

Estate Planning Activities

Purpose: To develop a plan for estate planning and related financial activities.

Financial Planning Activities: Respond to the following questions as a basis for making and implementing an estate plan. This sheet is also available in an Excel spreadsheet format in Connect Finance.

Suggested Websites: www.nolo.com   www.brightline.com   www.law.cornell.edu

Are your financial records, including recent tax forms, insurance policies, and investment and housing documents, organized and easily accessible?	
Do you have a safe-deposit box? Where is it located? Where is the key?	
Location of life insurance policies. Name and address of insurance company and agent.	
Is your will current? Location of copies of your will. Name and address of your lawyer.	
Name and address of your executor.	
Do you have a listing of the current value of assets owned and liabilities outstanding?	
Have any funeral and burial arrangements been made?	
Have you created any trusts? Name and location of financial institution.	
Do you have any current information on gift and estate taxes?	
Have you prepared a letter of last instruction? Where is it located?	

Suggested App:
- ACTEC Wealth Advisor

What's Next for Your Personal Financial Plan?

- Talk to several individuals about the actions they have taken related to estate planning.
- Create a list of situations in which a will would need to be revised.

Name: _____ **Date:** _____

Will Planning

Purpose: To compare costs and features of various types of wills.

Financial Planning Activities: Obtain information for the various areas listed based on your current and future situation; contact attorneys regarding the cost of these wills. This sheet is also available in an Excel spreadsheet format in Connect Finance.

Suggested Websites: www.netplanning.com   www.estateplanninglinks.com   the.nnepa.com

Type of will	Features that would be appropriate for my current or future situation	Cost Attorney, address, phone

What's Next for Your Personal Financial Plan?

- Create a list of items that you believe would be desirable to include in a will.
- Obtain the cost of a will from a number of different sources.

Name: _____   **Date:** _____

Trust Comparison

Purpose: To identify features of different types of trusts.

Financial Planning Activities: Research features of various trusts to determine their value to your personal situation. This sheet is also available in an Excel spreadsheet format in Connect Finance.

Suggested Websites: www.brightline.com   www.lifenet.com

Type of trust	Benefits	Possible value for my situation

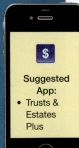

Suggested App:
• Trusts & Estates Plus

What's Next for Your Personal Financial Plan?

• Talk to legal and financial planning experts to contrast the cost and benefits of wills and trusts.
• Talk to one or more lawyers to obtain information about the type of trust recommended for your situation.

A Education Financing, Loans, and Scholarships

The desire to pursue higher education has grown steadily since the 1940s. According to the Census Bureau, in 1940 approximately 5 percent of the population held a bachelor's degree. Today, that percentage has grown to greater than 30 percent. The increase in demand for education has created an expansion in many areas, including the number of higher education institutions, the development of different types of degree programs, and specialization in occupations. All of these have contributed to the overall higher cost of a college education.

What is driving the increase in demand for education? Some of the main drivers appear to be higher projected salaries with additional education and reduced potential for unemployment. Numerous studies have shown a correlation between additional education and higher salaries. In addition, lower unemployment rates are correlated with higher education levels (see Exhibit A–1). However, along with additional education come the opportunity costs associated with it: lost wages while in school, and the associated tuition and living costs. Paying for these educational pursuits is the primary focus of this appendix.

Exhibit A–1   Education Pays

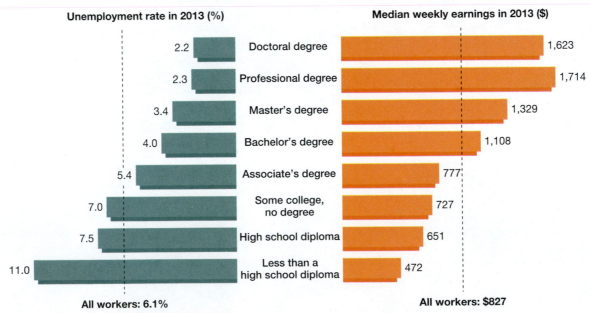

Education pays in lower unemployment rates and higher earnings

Unemployment rate in 2013 (%)		Median weekly earnings in 2013 ($)
2.2	Doctoral degree	1,623
2.3	Professional degree	1,714
3.4	Master's degree	1,329
4.0	Bachelor's degree	1,108
5.4	Associate's degree	777
7.0	Some college, no degree	727
7.5	High school diploma	651
11.0	Less than a high school diploma	472

All workers: 6.1%   All workers: $827

NOTE: Data are for persons age 25 and over. Earnings are for full-time wage and salary workers.
SOURCE: U.S. Bureau of Labor Statistics, accessed June 18, 2014.

Increasing Costs of Education

As college enrollments have swelled, increases in tuition, especially over the last decade, have been significant. Not only are there major increases in the numbers of traditional students coming straight from high school, but the number of those who are returning to school to "retool" and change careers has risen greatly as well. A common issue for many of these students is finding ways to pay for tuition, books, school fees, and living expenses while they pursue an education.

For some students, being accepted into their "dream college" can be a euphoric experience. The more earthbound question is how do you pay for the education? This question should clearly be asked before students apply to schools, but school endowments and additional assistance available frequently add to the challenge of determining the full costs until the college applications are accepted and the financial aid process begins.

The majority of students fund their education through a combination of loans, scholarships, grants, savings, and current earnings. Loans have specific repayment terms, but scholarships and grants do not need to be repaid and thus are sometimes referred to as "free money." Yet nothing in life is free, as the saying goes, and although there are no repayment requirements, you will have to put in some time and effort to find these scholarships. Information about scholarships will be provided later in this appendix.

> ### did you know?
>
> The average student loan balance in 2013 was $33,000, up from $15,000 in 2005.
>
> SOURCE: Federal Reserve Bank of New York, 2014 Q1, *Quarterly Report on Household Debt and Credit,* accessed June 18, 2014.

FAFSA (Free Application for Federal Student Aid)

The very first step to funding your education, whether with loans or certain grants, is completing and submitting the FAFSA (Free Application for Federal Student Aid) form. Most state and institutional aid programs require this form to be filed before they consider providing any type of funding. After the FAFSA has been processed, you will receive notification of your expected family contribution (EFC). For dependent students being claimed on their parents' tax return, the amount of parental income, assets, and college savings accounts will be important factors in determining the amount of the EFC. For an independent student, individual assets will also be carefully considered in determining eligibility for aid.

The schools that the student designates on the FAFSA will receive notification that the FAFSA has been processed. Once the admission application is accepted, the schools will take the FAFSA information and prepare a financial aid package. The goal is to evaluate each student's situation and provide the best possible selection of aid. In many cases, the aid package will not cover the full cost of attendance. In addition, the federal student aid may be reduced based on other aid that has been awarded (scholarships, state aid, etc.).

The financial aid package received from the school will often include a combination of grants, loans, and work-study options. The student will be sent an award letter with each portion designated (see Exhibit A–2). The family should carefully consider their ability to fund the expected family contribution and repay the loans offered in the aid package. These aid types will now be reviewed with the goal of understanding the repayment requirements and the terms of acceptance of each.

Scholarships

Scholarships do not have to be repaid. Scholarships awarded from organizations outside the school have to be reported on the FAFSA or to the financial aid office, if awarded later.

Exhibit A-2   Sample Financial Aid Award Package

Cost of Attendance		
Tuition and fees	$22,000	
Room and meals	8,000	
Books and personal	3,500	
Travel	700	
Total Cost of Attendance (1)	**$34,200**	
Expected Family Contribution		
Student	$ 2,000	
Parent	5,000	
Total Family Contribution (2)	**$ 7,000**	
Calculated Financial Need (1 + 2)	$27,200	
	Fall 20XX	**Spring 20XX**
Your college grant	$1,000	$1,000
Your college scholarship	$1,500	$1,500
Federal Perkins Loan	$2,000	$2,000
Federal Unsubsidized Stafford Loan	$5,500	$5,500
Parent PLUS Loan Option	$3,600	$3,600

Big-name scholarships (e.g., Coca-Cola and Prudential) receive an extraordinary number of applicants, but there are many other places to consider. Examples include rotary clubs, churches, professional associations, and local or regional businesses. Although the reward amounts may be smaller, they might add up to big dollars and some may have the benefit of being renewed in subsequent years. Special attention should be spent on knowing the deadlines for each scholarship. Carefully research the type of candidate they are interested in helping and tailor your information to show how you qualify, much like you would do with a résumé.

Grants

Grants also do not need to be repaid. They can be used to pay for education, training, books, tuition, or any school-related expenses. Students who have demonstrated financial need may receive grants. The most common type is the Federal Pell Grant, which offers a maximum of $5,645 for the 2014–15 academic year. The maximum amount can change each year and has increased significantly in the past few years. For the most up-to-date numbers, visit studentaid.ed.gov. The Pell Grant will only be disbursed for a maximum of 12 semesters. Another grant that is available is the Federal Supplemental Educational Opportunity Grant (FSEOG). It can be worth up to $4,000 annually. You must receive a Pell Grant to be eligible for the FSEOG. This grant is typically provided to students who have demonstrated exceptional financial need.

The Teacher Education Assistance for College and Higher Education (TEACH) Grant may also be available depending upon the types of courses taken and the student's future career. This grant provides up to $4,000 annually and requires a signed TEACH Grant agreement that the student will fulfill his or her teaching requirement within eight years of graduation or leaving school.

Another relatively new grant is the Iraq and Afghanistan Service Grant. These are available to students whose parents have died as a result of military service in Iraq or Afghanistan after 9/11. The grant offers a maximum of $5,317.44 for the 2014–15 academic year.

In addition to these federal grants, many states offer institutional grants that are distributed through the schools' financial aid offices. Certain colleges and schools also provide grants to women and minority groups, and for certain degree programs, to encourage enrollment.

Loans

Education loans are often a substantial part of the financial aid package. These types of loans have also become a significant part of outstanding consumer debt. The Federal Reserve Bank of New York and the U.S. Department of Education reported that the total amount of student loans distributed annually in recent years was $100 billion. Additionally, they have reported that total student loan balances outstanding are more than $1.11 trillion, an amount that is almost double the total amount owed on consumer credit cards.[1]

Federal education loans that are available today originate from the Direct Loan Program. Each college's financial aid office disburses the funds provided by the U.S. Department of Education. The interest rates and fees can change annually and are adjusted by the federal government. The current (2014–2015) range for interest rates for federal loans is between 4.66 percent and 7.21 percent.[2] Interest rates are expected to rise in the future. The rates are adjusted annually on July 1 for the coming academic year.

Education loans are typically divided into four main categories:

1. Stafford Loans

   a. Stafford Loans were initially called the Federal Guaranteed Student Loan Program. In 1988, the loans were renamed to honor U.S. Senator Robert Stafford, based on his work with higher education.

   b. Stafford Loans are the most frequently disbursed loan. They are typically disbursed directly from the financial aid office directly to the student. (*Note:* The Stafford Loan can also be disbursed through a private lender, which will be discussed later.)

   c. One key element to the Stafford Loan is how the interest accrues while the student is in school. In cases of extreme financial need, the federal government will pay the interest payments during the time that the student is in school and for certain grace periods. This type of loan is commonly referred to as a *subsidized loan.* Subsidized loans are no longer available for graduate or professional education programs.

   d. The more common Stafford Loan makes paying the interest the responsibility of the borrower while in school and during the grace period. This type of loan is commonly referred to as an *unsubsidized loan.* Two options exist for paying the interest: Pay the interest while still enrolled in school or have the interest added to the balance of the loan. The borrower must carefully calculate the cost of allowing this interest to be added to the loan. This process is commonly called *negative amortization* and occurs when the amount of the loan exceeds the original amount borrowed. This not only adds to the amount of the loan but can extend the time for repayment.

   e. The maximum amounts allowed for Stafford Loans vary considerably based on many factors, including the student's current year in school, type of schooling, cumulative amount of subsidized and unsubsidized loans, and dependency status. The federal website with the most up-to-date information is studentaid.ed.gov.

2. Perkins Loans

   a. Perkins Loans are named after Carl D. Perkins, a former member of the U.S. House of Representatives from Kentucky. Mr. Perkins was an advocate for higher education, as well as a strong supporter of education for underprivileged students.

---

[1] 2014 Q1, *Quarterly Report on Household Debt and Credit* (www.newyorkfed.org), accessed June 18, 2014.
[2] http://studentaid.ed.gov/types/loans/interest-rates.

    b. The Perkins Loan is typically provided to students who have demonstrated exceptional financial need. This program is administered by individual schools, which serve as the lender using money provided by the federal government. This type of loan is provided only in a subsidized form; it offers a very low interest rate, a long repayment schedule of 10 years, and a slightly longer grace period to begin repayment.

    c. Although each school's financial aid office will determine the amount each student receives, there are still annual and cumulative limits for this loan. Currently, the maximum Perkins Loan allowed for undergraduate students is $5,500 per academic year, with a cumulative maximum of $27,500. For graduate students, the annual maximum is $8,000, with a cumulative maximum of $60,000.

3. Parent Loans (PLUS loans), formerly known as the Parent Loan for Undergraduate Students

    a. There are times when parents of dependent children want to contribute financially to help with educational expenses. If they do not currently have funds to contribute, they may apply for a loan. After July 1, 2010, all new PLUS loans are provided by the government and can only be obtained by contacting the financial aid office of the school, not a private lender. Currently, there is no maximum amount; however, the parent may only borrow amounts not covered by the student's current financial aid package, up to the total cost of attending the school.

    b. For PLUS loans, the parent is responsible for repaying the loan. The parent's creditworthiness is a factor in determining whether the loan will be granted. If the parent does not qualify, the student may have the option of taking out additional unsubsidized Stafford Loans.

    c. One variant of the PLUS loan program is the Grad PLUS loan that allows graduate students to borrow for educational expenses.

    d. PLUS loans and Grad PLUS loans have higher interest rates than Stafford and Perkins Loans, so they should be considered very carefully.

4. Private Student Loans (also called Alternative Student Loans)

    a. Private student loans should also be considered very carefully. They tend to have higher interest rates than the government programs. In addition, the interest rates are commonly variable, which can make the payments more challenging to manage.

    b. The three most common reasons that borrowers choose private student loans are

        1. To fund additional education expenses above the limits that the other programs provide.

        2. There is no requirement for a FAFSA form to be completed. The loan is based upon the creditworthiness of the borrower.

        3. To provide additional flexibility to the borrower in terms of repayment or deferral while the student is in school.

In addition to traditional student loans, a new form of nontraditional lending has also begun to be used to fund education expenses. It is known as *social lending* or *peer-to-peer lending*. This newest form of student loan comes from the private sector. The basic premise is that borrowers can post relevant information and stories regarding why they need money, and prospective lenders or individuals can view the information and choose to fund these aspirations. A large majority of social lending has been in the form of short-term lending, covering periods of six months to three years. Student lending has been slow to catch on, primarily due to the time frame for repayment. Now, however, a few websites have started to offer longer repayment periods. Examples of social lending sites are www.greennote.com, www.prosper.com, and www.lendingclub.com.

Repaying Your Loans

Acquiring the funds to attend school is only the beginning of the financial aid process. The more lengthy part of the process is the repayment. Many of the different types of loans have differing *grace periods* before the first payment is due.

- Stafford Loans require repayment to begin six months after the student no longer attends school or has dropped below half-time enrollment.
- Perkins Loans require repayment to begin nine months after the student no longer attends school or has dropped below half-time enrollment.
- Federal PLUS loans, which are typically taken out by parents or graduate students, require repayment to begin 60 days after the loan is disbursed. The repayment can sometimes be deferred while the student is in school, but the interest will still accrue, much like an unsubsidized Stafford Loan.

Once repayment begins, federal borrowers have numerous options to consider regarding repaying the loan. The most common plans are as follows:

1} *Standard Repayment.* This is one of the most common repayment plans. A fixed monthly amount is paid for a repayment term not to exceed 10 years.

2} *Extended Repayment.* Students elect this option to lower the monthly payment amounts. The length of the repayment term is up to 25 years. One point to consider is the increase in the amount of total interest that will be paid over this time period.

3} *Graduated Repayment.* This repayment plan allows newly graduated students to make lower payments as they start their careers and then slowly increase the amount of the monthly payment over the life of the loan.

4} *Income-Contingent Repayment.* This repayment plan is designed to provide the borrower with some leniency in terms of the amount to be repaid. The monthly payments are recalculated annually, based on the most recent reported income as well as the total debt amount. The length of the repayment is up to 25 years. If the borrower follows through with the entire repayment plan, any remaining balance will be forgiven. One thing to keep in mind is that the forgiven amount will be considered taxable income to the borrower.

5} *Income-Sensitive Repayment.* This repayment plan is similar to the income-contingent repayment plan. The income-sensitive plan allows the borrower the option to set his or her monthly payment based on a percentage of gross monthly income. The length of this repayment is limited to 10 years.

6} *Income-Based Repayment (IBR).* This repayment plan is currently calculated as 15 percent of discretionary income. To calculate discretionary income, take your adjusted gross income (see Chapter 3) and subtract 150 percent of the poverty line for your state and family size. The plan provides a reduction to the previously discussed Income-Contingent and Income-Sensitive Repayment Plans. This program provides forgiveness beyond a 25-year time period, if all prior payments were timely. This newer repayment plan was included in the College Cost Reduction and Access Act of 2007.

7} *Pay-As-You-Earn (PAYE) Repayment.* This is the newest repayment option. The repayment amount is capped at 10 percent of discretionary income (see IBR Plan to calculate). This program provides forgiveness beyond a 20-year time period (10 years for those employed in public service), if all prior payments were timely. The plan does require proof of a partial financial hardship to qualify for the more favorable terms compared to the IBR Plan.

All seven plans are available for student loans, but only the first three plans are available for PLUS loans to parents.

 CAUTION!

Repayment plans based upon income will result in

1. Paying more interest than a standard repayment plan.
2. Providing income documentation each year to reassess your payments for the coming year.
3. Taxable income for any amount forgiven at the end of the repayment period.

Consolidation Loan

Another attractive repayment option for borrowers is the option to combine their student loans into one loan and thus have one convenient monthly payment. Just like the Extended Repayment Plan, this method will lower the total monthly payment amount and increase the length of the loan up to 30 years. Remember to carefully consider the increase in the amount of total interest that will be paid over this time period. Unless you are struggling to make the individual loan payment amounts, typically there is no advantage to consolidating loans other than ease of administration (i.e., one payment).

Private loans may have the option of refinancing to obtain a lower interest rate based on an improved credit situation for the borrower. However, in most cases, a federal consolidated loan does not offer this option.

Student Loan Default Statistics

The ease of obtaining money and the ever-increasing student loan balances that new graduates must begin to repay have created many challenges. These issues, combined with a significant number of graduates who are all vying for a smaller pool of available jobs, have created some very unfortunate side effects relating to students' abilities to repay loans. The percentage of student borrowers who are more than 90 days late on their student loan payments has increased significantly in the last decade (see Exhibit A–3).

Default rates on student loans have increased dramatically for students who have attended all types of higher education: public, private, and for-profit schools. Student loans will not typically be included in bankruptcy. There are no limitations on the number of years that the lender can seek repayment. For federal student loans, the government can garnish wages, take tax refunds, or take other federal benefits for which you might be eligible. Careful consideration should be given to the costs associated with repaying loans.

Exhibit A–3

Percentage of Balances 90+ Days Delinquent

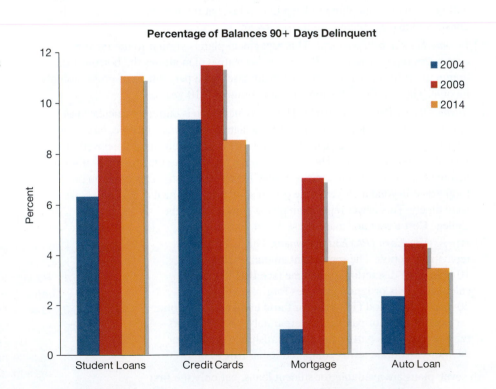

Percentage of Balances 90+ Days Delinquent

Loan Deferment

Loan deferments allow you to temporarily stop making payments on existing student loans. The most common reasons for the deferments are re-enrollment in school, demonstrated financial hardship, unemployment, and military deployment.

Loan Forgiveness

Loan forgiveness is the option to have all or a portion of your student loan forgiven (paid off on your behalf). The most common forgiveness options are for volunteer work and public or military service.

The Public Service Loan Forgiveness Program was established by the College Cost Reduction and Access Act of 2007. Under this program, full-time qualifying public service employees who make 120 qualifying loan payments on eligible federal Direct Loans will have the balance of their federal Direct Loans forgiven. Eligibility for the public service provision includes working for the government or for an organized nonprofit organization, service in the Peace Corps or AmeriCorps, or even working for a private organization that provides public service.

Many of these organizations also have specific programs to allow a portion of the loan to be canceled even sooner. For example,

- The Peace Corps provides partial cancellation of Perkins Loans (15 percent for each year of service, up to 70 percent in total).
- AmeriCorps volunteers who serve for 12 months can receive $4,725 to be used toward cancellation of their loan.
- Military service also offers a cancellation program. Students who enlist in the Army National Guard may be eligible for up to $10,000 of cancellation of student loans.
- In addition, there are a variety of other programs for teachers who serve in low-income areas, work with students with disabilities, or work in high-need schools. Law students can find loan forgiveness programs for serving with nonprofit or public interest organizations. Medical students may be eligible for loan forgiveness for performing certain medical research or working in low-income or remote areas. It is strongly advised that you review each program's requirements for eligibility, conditions of employment, and repayment to ensure that you are a good candidate for the program.

Loan Cancellation (Discharge)

In very special circumstances, student loans may be permanently canceled. The most common situations include:

- Death.
- Total and permanent disability.
- Fraud by the school (e.g., in the event of forged promissory notes, the school owes the lender a refund).
- Bankruptcy (very rare because the bankruptcy court would need to establish that repayment would create a significant hardship).

Work-Study Programs

Aside from loans, there are other ways to earn money to pay for educational expenses. The Federal Work-Study Program is available at many schools. It is commonly included as part of the financial aid package. Students who decline this option are expected to fund the amount from another source. Some students like the options that the program offers; they can work on campus without needing additional transportation, apply to a variety of positions that interest them, and get to know faculty and staff that they may want to work with on teaching or research assignments. Some students decline the option in favor of higher-paying jobs off-campus. You should consider very carefully the opportunity costs with this decision (fuel costs, commuting time, wardrobe needs, etc.).

Decision Making for Financial Aid

Navigating the process of financing an education can be very daunting and time consuming, but the rewards are very high. Finding the money for school and repaying the loans in a manner that works best for your personal situation can lead to long-term success, improved credit scores, higher salaries, and a lower potential for future unemployment. One excellent source for choosing a school and the financial aid package for your needs is the College Affordability and Transparency Center (collegecost.ed.gov). This is a one-stop website where you can evaluate a college based on net price, average student debt, state funding, graduation rates, and much more. It is very important for your financial future that you find the most affordable education that fits your budget, future career, and long-term financial goals.

B Developing a Career Search Strategy

"Only two days until the weekend." "Just 10 more minutes of sleep!" "Oh no!" " Excellent!" These are some common responses to "It's time to get up for work."

Have you ever wondered why some people find great satisfaction in their work while others only put in their time? As with other personal financial decisions, career selection and professional growth require planning. The average person changes jobs, or even careers, five or more times during a lifetime. Most likely you will reevaluate your choice of work on a regular basis.

The Career Planning Process

Career planning activities may be viewed using the following steps:

1} *Personal assessment*—to determine interests and values, and to identify talents and abilities.
2} *Employment market analysis*—to assess geographic, economic, technological, and social influences on employment opportunities.
3} *Application process*—in which you prepare a résumé and create a cover letter.
4} *Interview process*—in which you practice your interview skills, research the organization, and send a follow-up message to the organization.
5} *Employment acceptance*—when you assess the salary and other financial factors as well as the organizational environment of your potential employer.
6} *Career development and advancement*—in which you develop plans to enhance career success behaviors and build strong work relationships.

CAREER ACTIVITY 1

For each of the six steps of the career planning process, write: (*a*) a goal you have now or might have in the future and (*b*) an action you might take regarding this career planning area.

Using Career Information Sources to Identify Career Trends

While careers have dwindled in some sectors of our economy, opportunities in other sectors have grown. Service industries that are expected to have the greatest employment potential include computer technology, health care, business services, social and government services, sales and retailing, hospitality and food services, management and human resources, education, and financial services.

Many career information sources are available; these include:

1} *Career development offices* have information and services for career planning and assistance in creating a résumé and preparing for an interview.

did you know?

An *elevator speech* is a short, persuasive, focused summary of your experiences and skills used when networking and in other settings. This talk should be conversational (not forced), memorable, and sincere. The use of an engaging idea or question can help keep the conversation going.

2} *Online sources* are available to assist you with all aspects of career planning. Consider an Internet search to gather information about résumés, effective interviewing, or creating a career portfolio. Also available is the *Occupational Outlook Handbook* (www.bls.gov/ooh/), which provides detailed information on most careers.

3} *Informational interviews* are very effective for obtaining career information. A planned discussion with a person in a field of interest to you will help you learn about the job duties, required training, and the person's feelings about the career. Most people like to talk about their work experiences. Before the interview, plan to ask questions such as:

- How did you get your current position? Did other jobs lead to this one?
- In what ways do you find your work most satisfying? What are your main frustrations?
- What tasks and activities are required in your work?
- What are the most important qualifications for working in this field? What training and education are needed?
- What advice would you give a person who is considering this type of work?

CAREER ACTIVITY 2

Select a career information source. Prepare a brief summary of key ideas that could be valuable to you in the future.

Obtaining Employment Experience

Most people possess more career skills than they realize. Your involvement in school, community, and work activities provides a foundation for employment experiences. The following opportunities offer work-related training:

1} *Part-time employment* can provide experience and knowledge for a career field.

2} *Volunteer work* in community organizations or agencies can help you acquire skills, establish good work habits, and make contacts.

3} *Internships* allow you to gain experience needed to obtain employment in a field.

4} *Campus projects* offer work-related experiences to help you obtain career skills through campus organizations, course assignments, and research projects.

> ### did you know?
>
> Résumés often include vague words such as "competent," "creative," "flexible," "motivated," or "team player." Instead, give specific examples of your experiences and achievements to better communicate these capabilities.

CAREER ACTIVITY 3

Create a list of your work, volunteer, and school activities. Describe how each could apply to a future work situation.

Identifying Job Opportunities

Some of the most valuable sources of job information include:

1} *Job advertisements* in newspapers, professional periodicals, and online posting boards are a common source. However, most available jobs may not be advertised to the general public, so you need to also consider other job search activities.

2} *Career fairs,* on campus and at convention centers, allow you to contact several firms in a short time. At a career fair, you will be asked a couple of questions to determine if you qualify for a longer interview. Prepare for job fairs by being ready to quickly communicate your potential contributions to an organization. Knowing something about the organization will help distinguish you from other applicants.

3} *Employment agencies* match job hunters with employers. Often the hiring company pays the fee. Be wary when asked to pay a fee in advance. Government employment services may be contacted through your state employment service or state department of labor.

4} *Business contacts* advise people about careers. Friends, relatives, and others are potential business contacts. *Networking* is the process of making and using contacts to obtain and update career information.

5} *Job creation* involves developing a position that matches your skills with organizational needs. As you develop skills you enjoy, you may be able to create a demand for yourself.

6} *Other job search sources* include (*a*) visits to companies to make face-to-face contacts; (*b*) business directories and websites to obtain names of organizations that employ people with your qualifications; and (*c*) alumni who work in your field.

CAREER ACTIVITY 4

Using one or more of the sources of available jobs, select a position that you might apply for in the future. How well do your qualifications match those required for the job?

Developing a Résumé

Marketing yourself to prospective employers usually requires a résumé, or personal information sheet.

Résumé Elements

A résumé is a summary of your education, training, experience, and other qualifications with these main components:

1} *The personal data section* presents your name, address, telephone number, and e-mail address. Do not include your birth date, sex, height, and weight unless this information applies to a specific job qualification.

2} *A career objective* is designed to clearly focus you to a specific employment situation. Your career objective is usually omitted from the résumé and communicated in your cover letter. Also, consider a summary section with a synopsis of your main skills and capabilities.

3} *The education section* should include dates, schools attended, fields of study, and degrees earned.

4} *The experience section* lists organizations, dates of involvement, and responsibilities for previous employment, relevant school activities, and community service. Highlight computer skills, technical abilities, and other specific competencies. Use action verbs to connect your experience to the needs of the organization. Focus this information on results and accomplishments.

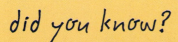
did you know?

A *combination résumé* blends the chronological and functional types. With this format, you first highlight skills and experience relevant to the position. This is followed by your employment history section, which reports specific experiences that match the requirements for the job.

5} *The related information section* may include honors, awards, and other activities related to your career field.

6} *The references section* lists people who can verify your skills. These individuals may be teachers, past employers, supervisors, or business colleagues. References are usually not included in a résumé; however, have this information available when requested.

Résumé Preparation

No exact formula exists; however, a résumé must be presented in a professional manner. Many candidates are disqualified by poor résumés. The use of bulleted items, bold type, and short sentences improves readability. Be sure to read your résumé on a phone or tablet since many hiring managers review applications on a mobile device. Limit your résumé to one page. Send a two-page résumé only if you have enough material to fill three pages; then use the most relevant information to prepare an impressive two-page presentation.

One key to successful résumé writing is the use of action words to demonstrate what you have accomplished or achieved. Examples of strong action words include:

- Achieved
- Administered
- Coordinated
- Created
- Designed
- Developed
- Directed
- Edited
- Facilitated
- Initiated
- Implemented
- Managed
- Monitored
- Organized
- Planned
- Produced
- Researched
- Supervised
- Trained
- Updated

Other words and phrases that commonly impress prospective employers include foreign language skills, computer experience, achievement, research experience, flexible, team projects, and overseas study or experience. Instead of just listing your ability to use various software packages (such as Excel or PowerPoint), describe how these tools were used to research information or to present findings for a specific project. For best results, seek assistance from counselors, the campus placement office, and friends to find errors and suggest improvements (see Exhibit B–1).

When preparing a résumé, consider using the STAR principle to communicate your experiences and achievements:

S	Situation, or the setting	*Example:* Fundraising coordinator for campus organization
T	Task, your duties	*Example:* Prepared a plan to raise funds for social service agency
A	Actions you took	*Example:* Administered a team that solicited donations on campus
R	Result, the outcome	*Example:* Resulted in donating over $2,000 to a homeless shelter

On your résumé, this experience could be presented in this manner:

- Coordinated fundraising campaign for campus organization to raise funds for social service agency, resulting in soliciting and donating over $2,000 to a homeless shelter.

The STAR principle is also useful when communicating your background in an interview.

Exhibit **B–1** Résumé Makeover

BEFORE:
CAREER OBJECTIVE
An entry-level position in medical or health care administration.

BEFORE:
Researched overdue accounts, created collection method for faster accounts receivable turnover, assisted in training billing clerks.

...also consider including relevant class experiences, such as:
• Coordinated team research project to identify health care opportunities in Asian markets.

BEFORE:
Newsletter editor, University of South Arkansas chapter of Financial Management Association, January–June 2016.

CHAD BOSTWICK
bostwc@unsoark.edu
Phone: (407)555-1239

SCHOOL ADDRESS
234B Weber Drive (Apt. 6)
Jasper, MO 54321

HOME ADDRESS
765 Cannon Lane
Benton, KS 67783

CAREER SUMMARY

Customer service specialist in health care industry. Effective training, technology capabilities. Qualified in team building and innovation development. Planned and implemented strategies to increase customer satisfaction by over 20 percent.

EDUCATION

Bachelor of Science in Business Administration and Health Care Marketing, University of South Arkansas, June 2016.

Associate of Arts, Medical Technician Assistant, Arrow Valley Community College, Arlington, Kansas, June 2014.

ORGANIZATIONAL EXPERIENCE

Patient account clerk, University Hospital, Jasper, Missouri, November 2014 – present
  • Researched accounts to reduce uncollectible amounts by 12 percent
  • Created collection method to improve accounts receivable turnover
  • Trained newly hired billing clerks in database applications
Sales data clerk, Jones Medical Supply Company, Benton, Kansas, January–August 2014
  • Maintained inventory records, processed customer records
  • Supervised quality control of entry-level data clerks

CAMPUS ACTIVITIES

Newsletter editor, University of South Arkansas chapter of Financial Management Association, January–June 2016
  • Managed editorial staff to research, design, and publish online newsletter
  • Researched and prepared news stories on financial industry trends
Tutor for business statistics and computer lab, 2014–2016
  • Coordinated review sessions for exams and homework assignments
  • Developed problems and case studies to supplement course materials

HONORS

College of Business Community Service Award, University of South Arkansas, June 2016
Arrow Valley Health Care Society Scholarship, June 2014

EXAMPLE: Your Social Résumé Strategy

Résumés have become online "living entities" through LinkedIn, Twitter, and other social media networks. Your interactions with hiring managers may include

- A LinkedIn profile highlighting career achievements and competencies to enhance your employment potential.
- Twitter use to communicate unique skills and a personal brand by linking prospective employers to your website.
- QR codes on your résumé or business card to link to a personal website, blog, or other online location communicating your career activities.
- Instagram and Pinterest postings of photos, videos, and other visuals to communicate career competencies, expertise, and achievements.
- Showing what others have to say about you. Recommendations on LinkedIn can provide a foundation for further discussion in the job application process.

CAREER ACTIVITY 5

Outline the main sections of a résumé that you might create for a job offer in the next couple of years. Conduct an Internet search to find a résumé format that you might use.

Résumé Submission

Traditionally, résumés have been mailed or hand delivered. When presenting a résumé in person, you have an opportunity to observe the company environment and make a positive impression about your career potential. Today, most résumés are submitted online.

Most résumé posting sites are free. Never pay a large fee; scam artists have set up phony websites with an online payment system to defraud people. Only post to sites with jobs in the geographic region of interest to you, and for which you qualify.

Résumés sent by e-mail should be addressed to a specific person with a subject line referencing the specific job. Your e-mail should include a cover letter to introduce yourself and to encourage the recipient to read your résumé. Properly format your résumé and include it in the body of the e-mail or attach it as a PDF.

Follow up with a call or e-mail to reinforce your qualifications and interest. Ask about how and when to follow up on your status in the job search process.

CAREER ACTIVITY 6

Go to a website that posts résumés. Obtain information on the process involved in posting your résumé online.

Creating a Cover Letter

A *cover letter*, designed to express your interest in a specific job, accompanies your résumé and consists of three main sections:

1} The *introductory paragraph* gets the reader's attention. Indicate your reason for writing by referring to the employment position. Communicate what you have to offer the organization. If applicable, mention the person who referred you.

2} The *development paragraphs* highlight aspects of your background that specifically qualify you for the position. At this point, elaborate on experiences and training. Connect your skills and competencies to specific organizational needs.

3} The *concluding paragraph* should request action. Ask for an interview to discuss your qualifications in detail. Include your contact information, such as telephone numbers and the times when available. Close your letter by summarizing your benefits to the organization.

Create a personalized cover letter for each position addressed to the appropriate person in the organization. A poorly prepared cover letter guarantees rejection (see Exhibit B–2).

In recent years, job applicants are increasingly using a *targeted application letter* instead of a résumé and cover letter. After researching a position and company, you can communicate how your specific skills and experiences will benefit the organization. Once again, your goal is to emphasize achievements and accomplishments so you will be invited for an interview.

did you know?

The Q letter (Q for *qualifications*) provides a side-by-side comparison of your experiences and abilities with the job requirements. The two coordinated lists allow you to be quickly rated as a viable candidate for the position.

Exhibit **B–2**

Sample Cover Letter

May 23, 2015
Ms. Hanna Cabral
Human Resources Director
Global Translation Services
3400 Superior Boulevard
Jamestown, NY 13456

Dear Ms. Cabral:

Experience in providing superb customer service for global organizations is the basis of my application for the client relations position. Brenda Kelly in your accounting department recommended that I contact you. An ability to connect with people from varied cultures along with my studies in international relations and global business provides a strong foundation for this position. In addition, I have taken several courses in international business along with an internship in the exporting department of an electronics company.

My previous work in cross-cultural environments provides your organization with a person who is able to:
• adapt to varied business settings and meet the diverse needs of clients.
• use language skills to handle customer relations with international customers.
• prepare cross-cultural marketing materials for current and potential clients.
• implement social media promotions using Facebook, Twitter, and YouTube.
• prepare content and develop features for the organization's website.
• effectively manage multiple projects to meet required deadlines.
• build relationships that cultivate trust and enhance organizational credibility.

In my past work, I developed an ability to create and implement a strategy for effectively using technology to manage a client database. Ongoing learning about technology is a high priority for me, which occurs in work environments, at professional conferences, and through observations of market trends.

As a result of my experiences and skills, detailed on my résumé, I believe I will make an important contribution to your organization. I look forward to discussing my qualification in greater detail. You may contact me at 555-963-4556 or at jhopkinsl@internet.com.

Sincerely,

Jerry Hopkins
5678 Collins Road
West Barrington, NY 14332
jhopkinsl@internet.com

CAREER ACTIVITY 7

Select a potential job. Create a cover letter for that position. Conduct an online search to obtain additional suggestions for effective cover letters.

Career Portfolios

In addition to a résumé, many job applicants prepare a *career portfolio.* This collection of documents and other items provides tangible evidence of your abilities and skills. A career portfolio may include the following items:

1} *Documentation*—a résumé, sample interview answers, a competency summary, and letters of recommendation.
2} *Creative works*—ads, product designs, packages, brand promotions, and video clips on a DVD, USB drive, or your personal website.
3} *Research project samples*—research findings, PowerPoint presentations, website designs, marketing plans, and photos of project activities.
4} *Employment accomplishments*—published articles, sales results data, financial charts, and news articles of community activities.

A career portfolio can present your abilities and experiences in a tangible manner. In addition, these materials will communicate your initiative and uniqueness. The cover page of your portfolio should connect your abilities to the needs of the organization.

A digital portfolio can be developed on a website with graphics and links. Be sure your home page is not cluttered and is organized to quickly find desired information.

[
EXAMPLE: Your Career Brand

Your professional image, or "brand," should

- Communicate unique skills, experiences, and competencies.
- Provide a vision of your potential contribution to an employer.
- Have a consistent message online, in print, and elsewhere.
- Involve ongoing actions that communicate your image, such as "collaborator" or "international expert."
]

CAREER ACTIVITY 8

List the various items (be specific) that you might include in your career portfolio.

The Job Interview

The interview phase is limited to candidates who possess the desired qualifications.

Preparing for the Interview

Prepare by obtaining additional information about the organization. The best sources include the library, the Internet, observations during company visits, analysis of company

EDUCATION AND TRAINING QUESTIONS
What education and training qualify you for this job?
Why are you interested in working for this company?
In addition to going to school, what activities have helped you expand your interests and knowledge?

WORK AND OTHER EXPERIENCE QUESTIONS
In what types of situations have you done your best work?
Describe the supervisors who motivated you most.
Which of your past accomplishments are you proud of?
Have you ever had to coordinate the activities of several people?
Describe some people whom you have found difficult to work with.
Describe a situation in which your determination helped you achieve a specific goal.

PERSONAL QUALITIES QUESTIONS
What are your major strengths?
What are your major weaknesses? What have you done to overcome your weaknesses?
What do you plan to be doing 5 or 10 years from now?
Which individuals have had the greatest influence on you?
What traits make a person successful?
How well do you communicate your ideas orally and in writing?
How would your teachers and your past employers describe you?

Exhibit **B–3**

Common Interview Questions

products, informal conversations with employees, and discussions with people knowledgeable about the company or industry. Research the company's operations, competitors, recent successes, planned expansion, and personnel policies to help you discuss your potential contributions to the company.

Another preinterview activity is preparing questions you will ask, such as:

- What do employees like most about your organization's working environment?
- What challenges are most often encountered by new employees?
- What training opportunities are available to employees who desire advancement?
- What qualities do your most successful employees possess?
- What actions of competitors are likely to affect the company in the near future?

Successful interviewing requires practice. Use a video or work with friends to develop confidence when interviewing. Organize ideas, speak clearly and calmly, and communicate enthusiasm. Prepare specific answers regarding your strengths. Campus organizations and career placement offices may offer opportunities for interview practice.

When interviewing, keep in mind that proper dress and grooming are vital. Dress more conservatively than current employees. A business suit is usually appropriate. Avoid trendy and casual styles, and don't wear too much jewelry.

Confirm the time and location of the interview. Take copies of your résumé, your reference list, and paper for notes. Arrive about 10 minutes earlier than your appointed time.

> ### did you know?
>
> Forbes.com reports that executive recruiters agree on the three true job interview questions: (1) Can you do the job? (to assess your strengths); (2) Will you love the job? (to assess your motivation); and (3) Can we tolerate working with you? (to assess your organizational fit).

EXAMPLE: Preparing for a Skype Interview

1. Prepare as you would for any other interview.
2. Test your computer connection in advance; avoid WiFi use.
3. Eliminate visual distractions that might be seen by the interviewer.
4. Locate the webcam at eye level to avoid distorted face angles.
5. Go online early to communicate punctuality and readiness.
6. Maintain eye contact with the webcam to project confidence and professionalism.
7. Tape notes and questions on a wall behind the camera to avoid looking down.

The Interview Process

Interviews may include situations or questions to determine how you react under pressure. Answer clearly in a controlled manner. Career counselors suggest having a "theme" for interview responses to focus your key qualifications. Throughout the interview come back to the central idea that communicates your potential contributions to the organization.

Behavioral interviewing, also called *competency-based interviewing,* is frequently used to evaluate an applicant's on-the-job potential. In these questions, you might be asked how you would handle various work situations. Behavioral interview questions typically begin with "Describe . . ." or "Tell me about . . ." to encourage interviewees to better explain their work style.

In *situational interviewing,* you are asked to participate in role-playing, similar to what may be encountered on the job. For example, you might be asked to resolve a complaint with a

> ### did you know?
>
> In *situational interviewing,* candidates for a sales position may be asked to interact with a potential customer. Prospective employees for Southwest Airlines participate in a "job audition." This starts the moment they apply, with extensive notes from the initial phone call. During the flight to the interview, gate agents, flight attendants, and other company employees are instructed to pay special attention to the candidate's behaviors. Thus, the candidate is being observed constantly in situations similar to the job setting. The process also includes giving a talk to a large group. Bored or distracted audience members are disqualified. This selection process has been shown to reduce employee turnover and increase customer satisfaction.

customer or negotiate with a supplier. This interview experience is used to evaluate your ability to work in various organizational environments.

Avoid talking too much, but answer each question completely, maintaining good eye contact. Stay calm during the interview. Remember, you are being asked questions about a subject about which you are the world's expert—YOU! Finally, thank the interviewer for the opportunity to discuss the job and your qualifications.

EXAMPLE: Asking for the Job

Near the conclusion of an interview, show your enthusiasm and desire for the position by asking for the job:

- "I believe my experiences would contribute to the continued success of your organization. Is there any additional information you need for making me an offer for the job?"
- "Based on my abilities in the area of _____, am I the appropriate fit for this position?"
- "This job is of great interest to me. What additional information would convince you that I'm the right person?"
- "Since my background and skills seem very appropriate for the position, what is the next step in the hiring process?"

After the Interview

Most interviewers conclude by telling you when you can expect to hear from them. While waiting, do two things. First, send a follow-up letter or e-mail within a day or two expressing your appreciation for the opportunity to interview. If you don't get the job, this thank-you letter can make a positive impression to improve your chances for future consideration.

Second, do a self-evaluation of your interview performance. Write down the areas to improve. Try to remember the questions you were asked that differed from your expected questions. Remember, the more interviews you have, the better you will present yourself and the better the chance of being offered a job.

CAREER ACTIVITY 9

Have someone ask you sample interview questions and then point out the strengths and weaknesses of your interview skills.

Job Offer Comparison

The financial aspects of a job should be assessed along with some organization factors.

1} *Salary and financial factors*—Your rate of pay will be affected by the type of work and your experience. The position may also include employee benefits. These include insurance, retirement plans, vacation time, and other special benefits for employees. Many organizations offer recreational facilities, discounts, and other advantages for workers.

2} *Organizational environment*—While the financial elements of a job are very important, also consider the working environment. Leadership style, dress code, and the social atmosphere should be investigated. Talk with

did you know?

The main factors college graduates consider when choosing an employer are enjoyment of the work, integrity of the organization, potential for advancement, benefits, and job location.

Exhibit **B–4** Updating Your Career Activities

While many career planning actions from the past are still valid, you should consider others to compete in a changing employment market.

When you want to . . .	Previously, people would . . .	Today, you can also . . .
Obtain career planning assistance.	Talk with others in career fields in which they were interested.	Acquire guidance from online contacts, videos, and webinars.
Develop potential career contacts.	Go to professional meetings, seminars, and community events.	Use social media, such as LinkedIn, to connect with professional contacts.
Follow up with networking contacts.	Talk by phone or send an e-mail.	Stay in contact on LinkedIn and through other social media networks.
Gain entry-level career experience.	Pursue part-time employment, volunteer work, and community service activities.	Participate in virtual volunteering, online communities, and online tutorials.
Identify employment opportunities.	Obtain leads from contacts, media, and positions in their current organization.	Connect through your online network to enhance other sources of employment.
Create a cover letter.	Highlight experiences related to the specific job or organizational needs.	Create a Q letter with bulleted items to communicate your specific experiences for a position.
Communicate your key skills on a résumé.	Include a career objective on their résumé.	Use a career profile or summary of skills and abilities.
Submit a résumé.	Mail or drop off at a company's office to make a personal contact.	Send by e-mail or post on a website.
Prepare for an interview.	Talk to others for interview tips; participate in mock interviews.	Create a video to have others critique your poise and professionalism.
Conduct company research.	Talk to people who have worked at the organization or who have done business with them.	Use Linkedin, Twitter, Facebook, and blogs to study the company and people who will interview you.
Participate in an interview.	Meet face to face.	Take part in a Skype interview or a video conference.
Follow up after an interview.	Send a handwritten note or e-mail to express appreciation and to reinforce their interest in the available position.	Send a work sample, evidence of your experience, such as a news article or report, or link to your e-portfolio.
Achieve career advancement training.	Participate in on-the-job training, professional seminars, graduate study.	Participate in webinars and online courses.
Develop and promote a personal brand.	Use business cards to communicate their organization and title.	Develop an online presence with a summary of unique experiences and competencies; use a personal website to convey your potential work contribution.

Your online presence can be a valuable asset for your career planning activities. Be sure to avoid actions that might present you in less than a professional manner. To communicate an appropriate online image, consider these actions:

- DO get connected on LinkedIn.com and other professional networking sites.
- DON'T put items online that create an inappropriate image; search your name to assess online presence.
- DO use keywords for capabilities and experiences expected in the industry in which you work.
- DON'T post your résumé online arbitrarily; select websites appropriate for your specific job search.
- DO regular follow-ups with online contacts; share current news and ideas on industry trends.
- DON'T join online groups in which you will not be an active participant.
- DO create a blog to enhance your online image and to communicate areas of expertise.

Additional career planning information is available at: www.jobhuntersbible.com   www.rileyguide.com   jobsearch.about.com college.monster.com   www.careerbuilder.com   www.monster.com   www.career-success-for-newbies.com   "Smart Career Planning" and "Career Planning Forum" on LinkedIn.com

(*NOTE*: about.me allows you to connect a personal website, blog, and social media sites in one location.)

people who have worked in the organization. Advancement potential might also be evaluated. Training programs may be available. These opportunities can be very beneficial for your long-term career success.

CAREER ACTIVITY 10

Prepare a list of factors that you would consider when accepting a job. Talk to other people about what they believe to be important when accepting a job.

Career Strategies in a Weak Job Market

In times of weak economic conditions, obtaining employment can be difficult. What actions would be useful to take when attempting to seek employment or maintain your current position? Consider the following:

- Acknowledge stress, anxiety, frustration, and fear. Eat properly and exercise to avoid health problems.
- Assess your financial situation. Determine sources of emergency funds to pay needed expenses. Cut unnecessary spending.
- Evaluate your current and future employment potential. Consider work and community experiences that you have which are not on your résumé.
- Maintain a focus with a positive outlook. Your ability to communicate confidence and competency will result in more job offers.
- Connect with others in professional and social settings.
- Consider part-time work, consulting, and volunteering to exercise your skills, develop new contacts, and expand your career potential.

An ability to obtain and maintain employment in difficult economic times will serve you in every type of job market. Exhibit B–4 provides suggestions for guidelines for updating your career activities based on recent market trends and technological developments.

C Consumer Agencies and Organizations

The following government agencies and private organizations can offer information and assistance on various financial planning and consumer purchasing topics when you want to:

- Research a financial or consumer topic.
- Obtain information for planning a purchase decision.
- Seek assistance to resolve a consumer problem.

Section 1 provides an overview of federal, state, and local agencies and other organizations you may contact for information related to various financial planning and consumer topics. Section 2 covers state consumer protection offices that can assist you in local matters.

Section 1

Most federal agencies may be contacted online; websites are noted below. In addition, consumer information from several federal government agencies may be accessed at www.usa.gov/topics/consumer.shtml.

Information on additional government agencies and private organizations available to assist you may be obtained in the *Consumer Action Handbook,* available at no charge at publications.usa.gov/USAPubs.php.

Exhibit C-1 Federal, State, and Local Agencies and Other Organizations

Topic Area	Federal Agency	State, Local Agency; Other Organizations
Advertising False advertising Product labeling Deceptive sales practices Warranties	Federal Trade Commission 1-877-FTC-HELP (www.ftc.gov)	State Consumer Protection Office c/o State Attorney General or Governor's Office National Fraud Information Center (www.fraud.org)
Air Travel Air safety Airport regulation Airline route	Federal Aviation Administration 1-800-FAA-SURE (www.faa.gov)	International Airline Passengers Association 1-800-527-5888 (www.iapa.com)
Appliances/Product Safety Potentially dangerous products Complaints against retailers, manufacturers	Consumer Product Safety Commission 1-800-638-CPSC (www.cpsc.gov)	Council of Better Business Bureaus 1-800-955-5100 (www.bbb.org)

Exhibit **C-1** (continued)

Topic Area	Federal Agency	State, Local Agency; Other Organizations

Automobiles
New cars
Used cars
Automobile repairs
Auto safety
	Federal Trade Commission
	1-877-FTC-HELP
	(www.ftc.gov)
	
	National Highway Traffic Safety
	  Administration
	1-800-424-9393
	(www.nhtsa.gov)
		National Automobile
		  Dealers Association
		1-800-252-6232
		(www.nada.org)
		
		Center for Auto Safety
		(202) 328-7700
		(www.autosafety.org)

Banking and Financial Institutions Checking accounts Savings accounts Deposit insurance Financial services	Federal Deposit Insurance Corporation 1-877-275-3342 (www.fdic.gov) Comptroller of the Currency (202) 447-1600 (www.occ.treas.gov) Federal Reserve Board (202) 452-3693 (www.federalreserve.gov) National Credit Union Administration (703) 518-6300 (www.ncua.gov)	State Banking Authority (www.usa.gov/topics/consumer/ banking.pdf) Credit Union National Association (608) 232-8256 (www.cuna.org) American Bankers Association (202) 663-5000 (www.aba.com) Treasury Direct U.S. Savings Bonds 1-800-US-BONDS (www.savingsbonds.gov)
Career Planning Job training Employment information	Coordinator of Consumer Affairs Department of Labor (202) 219-6060 (www.dol.gov)	State Department of Labor or State Employment Service
Consumer Credit Credit cards Deceptive credit advertising Truth-in-Lending Act Credit rights of women, minorities	Consumer Financial Protection Bureau (855) 411-2372 (www.consumerfinance.gov) Federal Trade Commission 1-877-FTC-HELP (www.ftc.gov)	Clearpoint Credit Counseling 1-800-251-2227 (www.cccsatl.org) National Foundation for Credit Counseling (301) 589-5600 (www.nfcc.org)
Environment Air, water pollution Toxic substances	Environmental Protection Agency 1-800-438-4318 (indoor air quality) 1-800-426-4791 (drinking water safety) (www.epa.gov)	Clean Water Action (202) 895-0420 (www.cleanwater.org)
Food Food grades Food additives Nutritional information	U.S. Department of Agriculture 1-800-424-9121 (www.usda.gov) Food and Drug Administration 1-888-463-6332 (www.fda.gov)	Center for Science in the Public Interest (202) 332-9110 (www.cspinet.org)

Exhibit C-1 (continued)

Topic Area	Federal Agency	State, Local Agency; Other Organizations
Funerals Cost disclosure Deceptive business practices	Federal Trade Commission 1-877-FTC-HELP (www.ftc.gov)	National Funeral Directors Association 1-800-228-6332 (www.nfda.org)
Housing and Real Estate Fair housing practices Mortgages Community development	Department of Housing and Urban Development 1-800-669-9777 (www.hud.gov)	National Association of Realtors 1-800-874-6500 (www.realtor.com) (www.move.com) National Association of Home Builders 1-800-368-5242 (www.nahb.com)
Insurance Policy conditions Premiums Types of coverage Consumer complaints	Federal Trade Commission 1-877-FTC-HELP (www.ftc.gov) National Flood Insurance Program 1-888-CALL-FLOOD (www.floodsmart.gov)	State Insurance Regulator American Council of Life Insurance (www.acli.com) Insurance Information Institute 1-800-331-9146 (www.iii.org)
Investments Stocks, bonds Mutual funds Commodities Investment brokers	Securities and Exchange Commission (202) 551-6551 (www.sec.gov) Commodity Futures Trading Commission (202) 418-5000 (www.cftc.gov)	Investment Company Institute (202) 293-7700 (www.ici.org) Financial Industry Regulatory Authority (301) 590-6500 (www.finra.org) National Futures Association 1-800-621-3570 (www.nfa.futures.org) Securities Investor Protection Corporation (202) 371-8300 (www.sipc.org)
Legal Matters Consumer complaints Arbitration	Department of Justice Office of Consumer Litigation (202) 514-2401 (www.justice.gov/civil/cpb/cpb_home.html)	American Arbitration Association (212) 484-4000 (www.adr.org) American Bar Association 1-800-285-2221 (www.abanet.org)
Internet/Mail Order Damaged products Deceptive business practices Illegal use of U.S. mail	Internet Crime Complaint Center (www.ic3.gov) U.S. Postal Service 1-800-ASK-USPS (www.usps.gov)	Direct Marketing Association (212) 768-7277 (thedma.org)

Topic Area	Federal Agency	State, Local Agency; Other Organizations
Medical Concerns Prescription medications Over-the-counter medications Medical devices Health care	Food and Drug Administration 1-888-463-6332 (www.fda.gov) Public Health Service 1-800-621-8335 (www.usphs.gov)	American Medical Association 1-800-336-4797 (www.ama-assn.org) Public Citizen Health Research Group (202) 588-1000 (www.citizen.org/hrg)
Retirement Old-age benefits Pension information Medicare	Social Security Administration 1-800-772-1213 (www.ssa.gov)	AARP (202) 434-2277 (www.aarp.org)
Taxes Tax information Audit procedures	Internal Revenue Service 1-800-829-1040 1-800-TAX-FORM (www.irs.gov)	Department of Revenue (in your state capital city) The Tax Foundation (202) 464-6200 (www.taxfoundation.org) National Association of Enrolled Agents 1-800-424-4339 (www.naea.org)
Telemarketing 900 numbers	Federal Communications Commission 1-888-225-5322 (www.fcc.gov)	National Consumers League (202) 835-3323 (www.nclnet.org)
Utilities Cable television Utility rates	Federal Communications Commission 1-988-225-5322 (www.fcc.gov)	State utility commission (in your state capital)

Section 2

State, county, and local consumer protection offices provide consumers with publications, online information, and complaint handling assistance. In addition, agencies regulating banking, insurance, securities, and utilities are available in each state; these may be located with an online search.

Consumer's Resource Handbook	publications.usa.gov/USAPubs.php
State consumer offices	National Association of Attorneys General (www.naag.org) or search "(*state*) consumer protection agency"
State departments of insurance	www.naic.org/state_web_map.htm
State tax departments	www.taxadmin.org/fta/link/ www.aicpa.org/yellow/yptsgus.htm

To save time, call or e-mail the office before sending in a complaint. Determine if the office handles the type of complaint you have or if complaint forms are available.

D Daily Spending Diary

Effective short-term money management and long-term financial security are dependent on spending less than you earn. The use of a Daily Spending Diary will provide information to better understand your spending patterns and to help you achieve desired financial goals.

The following sheets should be used to record *every cent* of your spending each day in the categories provided. You can indicate the use of a credit card with (CR). Or you can create your own format to monitor your spending. Various apps (see below) are also available for this purpose.

This experience will help you better understand your spending habits and identify desired changes you might want to make in your spending activities. Your comments should reflect what you have learned about your spending and can assist with changes you might want to make. Ask yourself, "What spending amounts can I reduce or eliminate?"

Many people who take on this task find it difficult at first, and may consider it a waste of time. However, nearly everyone who makes a serious effort to keep a Daily Spending Diary has found it beneficial. The process may seem tedious at first, but after a while recording this information becomes easier and faster. Most important, you will know where your money is going. Then you will be able to better decide if that is truly how you want to spend your available financial resources. A sincere effort with this activity will result in very beneficial information for monitoring and controlling your spending. At the end of each chapter, questions are provided to guide your daily spending related to the topic covered in the chapter.

Using a Daily Spending Diary can help to:

- Reveal hidden aspects of your spending habits so you can better save for the future.
- Create and achieve financial goals.
- Revise buying habits and reduce wasted spending.
- Control credit card purchases.
- Improve recordkeeping for measuring your financial progress and filing your taxes.
- Plan for major expenditures encountered during the year.
- Start an investment program with the money you save through controlled spending.

The following Daily Spending Diary sheets are also available in an Excel format in Connect Finance.

Various apps are available for you to monitor your daily spending; these include:

- Spending Tracker
- Track Every Coin
- Mint
- Level Money
- Spendee

Daily Spending Diary

Directions: Record *every cent* of your spending each day in the categories provided, or create your own format to monitor your spending. You can indicate the use of a credit card with (CR). Comments should reflect what you have learned about your spending patterns and desired changes you might want to make in your spending habits. (*Note:* As income is received, record in Date column.)

Month: _____   Amount available for spending: $_____   Amount to be saved: $_____

Date (Income)	Total Spending	Auto, Transportation	Housing, Utilities	Food (H) Home (A) Away	Health, Personal Care	Education	Recreation, Leisure	Donations, Gifts	Other (note item, amount)	Comments
Example	$83	$20 (gas) (CR)		$47 (H)		$2 (pen)	$4 (DVD rental)	$10 (church)		This takes time but it helps me control my spending.
1										
2										
3										
4										
5										
6										
7										
8										
9										
10										
11										
12										
13										
14										
Subtotal										

(continued)

Date (Income)	Total Spending	Auto, Transportation	Housing, Utilities	Food (H) Home (A) Away	Health, Personal Care	Education	Recreation, Leisure	Donations, Gifts	Other (note item, amount)	Comments
15										
16										
17										
18										
19										
20										
21										
22										
23										
24										
25										
26										
27										
28										
29										
30										
31										
Total										

Total Income $ _____

Total Spending $ _____

Difference (+/−) $ _____

Actions: amount to savings, areas for reduced spending, other actions . . .

Daily Spending Diary

Directions: Record *every cent* of your spending each day in the categories provided, or create your own format to monitor your spending. You can indicate the use of a credit card with (CR). Comments should reflect what you have learned about your spending patterns and desired changes you might want to make in your spending habits. (*Note:* As income is received, record in Date column.)

Month: _____ Amount available for spending: $ _____ Amount to be saved: $ _____

Date (Income)	Total Spending	Auto, Transportation	Housing, Utilities	Food (H) Home (A) Away	Health, Personal Care	Education	Recreation, Leisure	Donations, Gifts	Other (note item, amount)	Comments
1										
2										
3										
4										
5										
6										
7										
8										
9										
10										
11										
12										
13										
14										
Subtotal										

(continued)

Date (Income)	Total Spending	Auto, Transportation	Housing, Utilities	Food (H) Home (A) Away	Health, Personal Care	Education	Recreation, Leisure	Donations, Gifts	Other (note item, amount)	Comments
15										
16										
17										
18										
19										
20										
21										
22										
23										
24										
25										
26										
27										
28										
29										
30										
31										
Total										

Total Income $ _____

Total Spending $ _____

Difference (+/−) $ _____

Actions: amount to savings, areas for reduced spending, other actions . . .

Daily Spending Diary

Directions: Record *every cent* of your spending each day in the categories provided, or create your own format to monitor your spending. You can indicate the use of a credit card with (CR). Comments should reflect what you have learned about your spending patterns and desired changes you might want to make in your spending habits. (*Note:* As income is received, record in Date column.)

Month: _____   Amount available for spending: $ _____   Amount to be saved: $ _____

Date (Income)	Total Spending	Auto, Transportation	Housing, Utilities	Food (H) Home (A) Away	Health, Personal Care	Education	Recreation, Leisure	Donations, Gifts	Other (note item, amount)	Comments
1										
2										
3										
4										
5										
6										
7										
8										
9										
10										
11										
12										
13										
14										
Subtotal										

(continued)

Date (Income)	Total Spending	Auto, Transportation	Housing, Utilities	Food (H) Home (A) Away	Health, Personal Care	Education	Recreation, Leisure	Donations, Gifts	Other (note item, amount)	Comments
15										
16										
17										
18										
19										
20										
21										
22										
23										
24										
25										
26										
27										
28										
29										
30										
31										
Total										

Total Income
$ _____

Total Spending
$ _____

Difference (+/−)
$ _____

Actions: amount to savings, areas for reduced spending, other actions . . .

Daily Spending Diary

Directions: Record every cent of your spending each day in the categories provided, or create your own format to monitor your spending. You can indicate the use of a credit card with (CR). Comments should reflect what you have learned about your spending patterns and desired changes you might want to make in your spending habits. (*Note:* As income is received, record in Date column.)

Month: _____   Amount available for spending: $ _____   Amount to be saved: $ _____

Date (Income)	Total Spending	Auto, Transportation	Housing, Utilities	Food (H) Home (A) Away	Health, Personal Care	Education	Recreation, Leisure	Donations, Gifts	Other (note item, amount)	Comments
1										
2										
3										
4										
5										
6										
7										
8										
9										
10										
11										
12										
13										
14										
Subtotal										

(continued)

Date (Income)	Total Spending	Auto, Transportation	Housing, Utilities	Food (H) Home (A) Away	Health, Personal Care	Education	Recreation, Leisure	Donations, Gifts	Other (note item, amount)	Comments
15										
16										
17										
18										
19										
20										
21										
22										
23										
24										
25										
26										
27										
28										
29										
30										
31										
Total										

Total Income
$ _____

Total Spending
$ _____

Difference (+/−)
$ _____

Actions: amount to savings, areas for reduced spending, other actions . . .

Photo Credits

Index

A

Accelerated benefits, 331
Accidental death benefit, 330
Account executives, 404
Activity accounts, 125
Actual cash value (ACV), 262
Add-on interest method, 164
Adjustable-rate mortgages (ARMs), 232–233
Adjusted gross income (AGI)
  exemptions to, 80–81
  explanation of, 78
Adjustments to income, 86
Adoption tax credit, 83
Adult life cycle, 4
Affordable Care Act. *See* Patient Protection and Affordable Care Act of 2010
Age
  credit decisions and, 157
  investment risk and, 361
  life insurance and, 322
Aggressive growth funds, 431
Alternative minimum tax (AMT), 83
Alternative student loans, 496
AmeriCorps, 499
Amortization
  explanation of, 231
  negative, 233, 495
Annual Credit Report Request Form, 158
Annual percentage rate (APR), 161, 162, 164
Annual percentage yield (APY), 120, 121
Annual reports, 396, 440
Annuities. *See also* Life insurance
  costs of, 337–338
  deferred, 336–337
  explanation of, 336, 471
  fixed, 336, 340
  function of, 337, 339
  future value of, 34–35
  immediate, 336
  index, 337
  present value of, 36
  for retirement income, 471
  tax issues related to, 338, 340
  variable, 336, 337, 339
Appraisals, home, 227, 237
Asset allocation, 359–360
Asset allocation funds, 432
Asset management accounts, 109
Assets, 49, 50
Attorneys, for consumer complaint resolution, 206
Audits, Internal Revenue Service, 93–94
Auto brokers, 199–200
Automatic teller machines (ATMs), 109, 110, 167
Automobiles. *See* Motor vehicle insurance; Motor vehicles
Average tax rate, 81

B

Balanced funds, 432
Balance sheets, 48–51
Banking services, online and mobile, 109–110
Bank of America, 171
Bank reconciliation, 128, 130
Bankruptcy
  declaring personal, 173
  effects of, 176
  explanation of, 7–8
  federal legislation related to, 174–176
Bankruptcy Abuse Prevention and Consumer Protection Act of 2005, 175–176
Banks
  commercial, 112–113, 148
  investment, 403
  mutual savings, 113
  online and mobile, 109–110
Bank statements, 128
Basic health insurance coverage, 288. *See also* Health insurance
Behavioral interviewing, 510
Beneficiaries
  explanation of, 473
  on life insurance policies, 329
Beta, 401
Bill payment
  credit scores and, 159
  online, 124–125
Blank endorsement, 128
Bloomberg Businessweek, 110, 397, 441
Blue chip stocks, 393
Blue Cross, 295
Blue Shield, 295
Bodily injury liability, 264–265
Bond funds, 432
Bond indenture, 367
Bonds
  corporate, 367–371
  government, 365–367
  information sources for, 371–372, 374–375
  municipal, 366
  overview of, 364–365
  quotations for, 372
  ratings for, 372–374
  yield calculations for, 373–374
Book value, 401–402
Borrowing, 108. *See also* Consumer credit; Credit cards; Loans
Brand comparison, 190
Broad form, renter's insurance, 258–259
Brokerage firms
  explanation of, 113
  full-service, discount and online, 404–405
Budgets
  balancing, 350
  characteristics of successful, 59
  emergency fund for, 55
  explanation of, 54
  financial goals for, 54
  fixed expenses for, 55–56
  income estimates for, 55
  recording spending amounts for, 57–58
  review of, 58–59
  savings allocations for, 55
  selecting system for, 59
  steps to develop, 56
  variable expenses on, 57
Budget variance, 57
Bump-up CDs, 115
Business contacts, 504
Business failure risk, 357
Buy-and-hold technique, 407
Buy-downs, 233
Buyer agents, 227

C

Callable CDs, 118
Call feature, 368
Capacity, 152
Capital, 152
Capital gain distributions, 443–444
Capital gains
  on bonds, 366
  explanation of, 96
Capitalized cost, 198
Car-buying services, 199–200
Career fairs, 504
Career portfolios, 508
Careers
  financial planning and, 22
  trends in, 502–503
Career search
  cover letters and, 507–508
  employment experience and, 503
  identifying career trends and, 502–503
  identifying job opportunities and, 503–504
  job interviews and, 509–511
  job offer comparison and, 511, 513
  portfolio development and, 508

résumé development and, 504–507
steps in, 502, 512
in weak job market, 513
Car title loan companies, 114
Cash cards. *See* Debit cards
Cash flow
explanation of, 51–52
net, 53–54
Cash flow statements, 52–54
Cashier's checks, 127
Cash inflow, 51
Cash machines. *See* Automatic teller
machines (ATMs)
Cash outflows, 52, 53
Cash value, 327
Casualty losses, 79
Certificates of deposit (CDs)
explanation of, 115
management of, 118
tax-deferred fixed annuities vs., 340
types of, 115, 117–118
Certified checks, 127
Certified pre-owned (CPO) vehicles, 197
Chapter 7 bankruptcy, 174–176
Chapter 13 bankruptcy, 176
Character, 152
Charitable contributions, 79
Charles Schwab, 446
Check-cashing outlets (CCOs), 114
Checking accounts
evaluation of, 126–127
management of, 127–128
types of, 118, 125–126
Children, 96–97. *See also* Education
financing
Churning, 404
Claims, insurance, 254
Class-action suits, 206
Closed-end credit, 144
Closed-end funds, 425, 445–447
Closing, home purchase, 234–236
Closing costs, 234
Codicils, 476
Coinsurance, 288
Collateral, 153
College Affordability and Transparency
Center, 500
College Cost Reduction and Access Act
of 2007, 499
Collision insurance, 266
Commercial banks
function of, 112–113
as source of consumer credit, 148
Commission charges, stock transaction,
406–407
Commodity Futures Trading
Commission, 516
Common areas, 226
Common stocks
dividends from, 388–390
explanation of, 388

issuing rationale for, 388
purchasing rationale for, 388–391
Competency-based interviewing, 510
Compounding, 120, 121. *See also*
Future value
Comprehensive form, renter's
insurance, 259
Comprehensive physical damage
coverage, 266–267
Comptroller of the Currency, 515
Condominium fees, 226
Condominiums, 226
Consolidated Omnibus Budget
Reconciliation Act of 1986
(COBRA), 287
Consolidation loans, 498
Consumer Action Handbook, 514
Consumer complaints
related to credit issues, 169–171
steps to resolve, 203–206
Consumer credit. *See also* Debt
advantages of, 142–143
billing errors and disputes and, 166
closed-end, 144
complaints related to, 169–171
cost of, 160–165
credit cards and, 145–147 (*See also*
Credit cards)
disadvantages of, 143
ethical concerns related to, 353
explanation of, 141
identity theft and, 166–169
importance of, 141
loans and, 148–150 (*See also* Loans)
management of, 171–176
open-end, 145
sources of, 147–150
use and misuse of, 142
volume of, 144, 145
Consumer credit applications
affordability issues and, 151
cosigning in, 169
credit capacity rules and, 151
credit reports and, 153–155
credit scores and, 155–156
creditworthiness factors and, 157
denial of, 157, 159
five Cs of credit and, 151–153, 158
sample questions on, 156
Consumer Credit Counseling Service
(CCCS), 173
Consumer credit finance charges
add-on interest and, 164
inflation and, 164
lender risk vs. interest rate and,
162–163
minimum monthly payment
trap in, 165
open-ended credit and, 164
simple interest formula for, 163–164
term vs. interest costs and, 162

Consumer Credit Reporting Reform
Act, 170
Consumer debt. *See* Debt
Consumer finance companies, 148
Consumer Financial Protection Bureau
(CFPB), 171, 515
Consumer Leasing Act, 169
Consumer price index (CPI), 7
Consumer Product Safety Commission, 514
Consumer protection, for purchase
complaints, 206
Consumer purchases
complaints related to, 203–205
legal options related to, 205–207
motor vehicle, 195–203
online, 190, 191
research-based, 192–193
service contracts and, 192
strategies for, 189–192
tax considerations and, 95
warranties for, 191–192
Consumer Reports, 199
Contingency clause, 228
Contingent deferred sales load, 428
Conventional mortgages, 231. *See also*
Mortgages
Conversion term insurance, 327
Convertible bonds, 368
Cooperative housing, 226
Coordination of benefits (COB)
provision, 287
Coordinator of Consumer Affairs, 515
Copayments, 291
Corporate bonds. *See also* Bonds
explanation of, 367
functions of, 367–388
provisions for repayment of, 368–369
reasons to purchase, 369–371
transactions for, 370–371
types of, 368
Corporate earnings, 398–399
Correspondence audits, 94
Cosigning loans, 169
Cost-of-living protection, 331
Counteroffers, 227
Coverage, insurance, 250
Coverdell Education Savings Accounts,
97, 469
Cover letters, 507, 508
Credit. *See* Consumer credit; Loans
Credit bureaus, 153, 166
Credit Card Accountability
Responsibility and Disclosure Act
of 2009 (CARD Act), 170–171
Credit card companies, 113
Credit cards. *See also* Consumer credit;
Consumer credit applications
debit cards vs., 124, 147
debit management for, 350–351
finance charges for, 145–146
function of, 145

Credit file. *See* Credit reports
Credit life insurance, 329
Credit Repair: How to Help Yourself
(Federal Trade Commission), 160
Credit reports
availability of, 154
credit scores in, 155–157
function of, 153
information in, 153–155, 158
legal rights related to, 155
unfavorable data in, 155
Credit scores
determination of, 155–157
methods to improve, 158–160
methods to protect, 166
Credit-shelter trusts, 478
Credit unions, 113, 148
Current liabilities, 50
Current ratio, 51
Cyclical stocks, 393

D

Daily spending diary, 518–526
Dashboard, 23
Davis Opportunity Fund, 429
Debentures, 368
Debit cards
credit cards vs., 124, 147
explanation of, 110, 124
prepaid, 110, 125
Debt. *See also* Consumer credit;
Credit cards; Loans
bankruptcy declaration and, 173–176
collection practices for, 172–173
financial counseling services for,
173, 174
taxes and, 95
warning signs of problems with, 171–172
Debt-payments ratio, 51
Debt-payments-to-income ratio, 151
Debt ratio, 51
Debt-to-equity ratio, 151
Declining balance method, 164
Decreasing term insurance, 327
Deductibles
explanation of, 251
health insurance, 294
Deductible taxes, 79
Deeds, 234–235
Defective goods/services, 166
Defensive stocks, 393
Deferred annuities, 336–337
Deficit, 53, 57
Defined-benefit plans, 465
Defined-contribution plans, 465
Deflation, 7
Dental expense insurance, 289
Deposit institutions, 108, 112
Deposit insurance, 122–123
Deposit tickets, checking account, 128

Digital budgets, 59
Direct deposit, 62
Direct investment plans, 408–409
Disability income insurance
determining individual needs for, 307
explanation of, 285, 305–306
sources of, 306
trade-offs in, 306–307
Disclaimer trusts, 478
Discount brokerage firms, 404–405
Discounting. *See* Present value
Discretionary income, 53
Discrimination, in credit applications, 157
Distribution fees, 428
Diversification, mutual funds and, 424
Dividend reinvestment plans (DRIPs),
408–409
Dividends
common stock, 388–390
income, 443–444
policy, 325
Dividend yield, 400–401
Dollar cost averaging, 408, 446
Double indemnity, 330
Dread disease insurance, 289
Dual agents, 227
Duplexes, 225

E

Earned income, 78
Earnest money, 228
Earnings, higher education and, 492
Earnings per share, 398
Earthquake insurance, 257, 258
Economic conditions
career search and, 513
financial services and, 110
global, 4
Economics, 4
Edmund's New Car Prices, 199
Edmund's Used Car Prices, 199
Education
cost of, 493
demand for higher, 492
earnings and, 492
Education financing
Coverdell Education Savings
Accounts as, 97
decisions related to, 500
529 plans as, 97
401(k) plans as, 97–98
Free Application for Federal Student
Aid and, 493
grants and, 494–495
loans and, 495–499
sample award package for, 494
scholarships and, 493–494
work-study programs and, 499–500
Education IRAs, 469
EE savings bonds, 118–119

Electronic banking, 109–110
Electronic Deposit Insurance Estimator
(EDIE), 122
Electronic Fund Transfer Act, 170
Electronic payments, types of, 124–125
Emergency fund, 55, 352
Emergency road service coverage, 267
Employee Benefits Security
Administration (EBSA), 286
Employee Retirement Income Security
Act of 1974 (ERISA), 337, 466
Employer disability insurance, 306
Employer pension plans, 464–466
Employer self-funded health plans, 297
Employment agencies, 504
Endorsement, 128, 258
Endowment life insurance, 329
Environmental Protection Agency
(EPA), 515
Equal Credit Opportunity Act (ECOA),
157, 170
Equity financing, 388
Equity income funds, 431
Escrow accounts, 236
Estate, 473
Estate planning
explanation of, 473
legal documents and, 473–474
taxes and, 478–479
trusts and, 477–478
wills and, 474–477
Estate taxes, 479
Estimated payments, tax, 85
Ethical issues
in health care, 303, 310
in living trusts, 479
related to credit, 270, 353
E*Trade Bank, 109
Exchange-traded funds (ETFs), 426, 447
Exclusions, 78
Executors, 476
Exemptions, 80–81
Exemption trust wills, 475
Expense ratio, 429
Expense risk charge, 338
Expenses
budgeting for, 55–57
fixed, 53
health care, 80, 95
job-related, 80, 95
retirement, 462–464
variable, 53
Express warranties, 191
Extended repayment plans, 497
Extended warranties, 192

F

Face value, 367
Fair Credit and Charge Card Disclosure
Act, 169

Fair Credit Billing Act (FCBA) (1975), 166, 170
Fair Credit Reporting Act (FCRA) (1971), 154, 155, 170, 270
Fair Debt Collection Practices Act (FDCPA), 172–173
Family of funds, 433
Federal Aviation Administration (FAA), 514
Federal Communications Commission, 517
Federal Deposit Insurance Corp. (FDIC), 121, 122, 515
Federal Housing Authority (FHA), 232
Federal income taxes. *See also* Taxes
adjusted gross income and, 78
audits of, 93–94
choosing forms for, 85
common errors in filing, 93
computing taxes owed for, 81–83
deadlines and penalties for, 84
electronic filing of, 90
estimated payments on, 84
exemptions and, 80–81
filing procedure for, 85
filing status for, 85
Form 1040, 85–88
online filing of, 88–91
payment of, 83–84
planning strategies for, 95–98
preparation assistance for, 91–92
refunds of, 87–88
sources for assistance with filing, 91–92
steps to complete, 85–88
taxable income and, 78–80
tax-planner calendar for, 91
tax preparation services for, 92–93
tax preparation software for, 89
tax rate schedules for, 90
withholding, 83–84
Federal Pell Grant, 494
Federal Reserve Bank of New York, 495
Federal Reserve Board, 515
Federal Supplemental Educational Opportunity Grant (FSEOG), 494
Federal Trade Commission (FTC), 160, 166, 172, 514–516
Federal Work-Study Program, 499–500
Fee table, 429
FICO credit scores, 155–156
Fidelity Investments, 446
Field audits, 94
50-20-30 rule, 61
Finance charges, 160–161
Finance companies, 113
Financial aid. *See* Education financing
Financial aid websites, 493
Financial analysis, retirement planning and, 460–462
Financial documents table, 70
Financial goals

budgeting and, 54
guidelines for setting, 9, 10
intermediate, 9
long-term, 9
money management and, 60, 62
reference sheet for, 29
short-term, 9
SMART approach, 9, 54
types of, 9
Financial institutions
comparison of, 111–112
identifying problematic, 113–114
types of, 108, 112–113
Financial planning. *See* Personal financial planning
Financial plans, 3, 336. *See also* Personal financial plans
Financial ratios, 51
Financial records, 46, 47
Financial responsibility law, 264
Financial services
comparison of, 111–112
economic conditions and, 110
to manage daily money needs, 107–108
online and mobile banking as, 109–110
payment methods and, 124–128
prepaid debit cards as, 110
savings plans and, 115–123 (*See also* Savings plans)
types of, 108–109
Financial statements. *See* Personal financial statements
Financial supermarkets, 113
The Financial Times, 110
Financing
equity, 388
for home purchases, 229–236 (*See also* Mortgages)
for motor vehicles, 200–201
Fitch Ratings, 372
529 plans, 98
Fixed annuities, 336, 337, 340
Fixed expenses
on budgets, 55–56
explanation of, 53
Fixed-rate, fixed-payment mortgages, 231–232
Flat tax, 98
Flexible-rate mortgages, 232–233
Flexible spending accounts (FSAs), 95, 298, 299
Flood insurance, 257–258
Food and Drug Administration (FDA), 305, 515, 517
Forbes, 110, 397, 441
Foreign tax credit, 83
Formal wills, 475
Fortune, 110, 397
401(k) plans, 97, 434, 465, 470
403(b) plans, 465

Fraud
in health care costs, 310
identity theft as, 129
motor vehicle repair, 202
Free Application for Federal Student Aid (FAFSA), 493
Front-end load plans, 446
Frugality, 351
Full-service brokerage firms, 404–405
Full warranties, 191–192
Funds of funds, 433
Future value
explanation of, 11, 13
of series of deposits, 13–14
of series of equal amounts, 34–35
of single amount, 13, 33–34
Future value table, 12

G

General obligation bonds, 366
Gift cards, 125, 147
Gift taxes, 479
Global economy, influence of, 4, 6
Global stock funds, 431
Goals. *See* Financial goals
Government bonds, 365–367. *See also* Bonds
Government-guaranteed financing programs, 232
Grace period, 330, 497
Graduated repayment plans, 497
Grantors, 477
Grants, higher-education, 494–495
Gross income, 53
Group health insurance, 285–287. *See also* Health insurance
Group life insurance, 328
Growth funds, 431
Growth stocks, 393
Guaranteed insurability option, 331
Guardians, 476

H

Hazards, 250
Health care costs
bankruptcy and, 174
efforts to contain, 310–311
expenses related to, 80, 95
factors contributing to, 310
statistics related to, 308–310
Healthfinder, 304
Health information technology, 311
Health information websites, 304–305
Health insurance. *See also* Disability income insurance
basic coverage in, 288–289
COBRA and, 287
decisions in choice of, 294

Health insurance—*Cont.*
  deductibles and coinsurance
    provisions in, 294
  dental expenses and, 289
  dread disease policies and, 289
  explanation of, 285
  group, 285–287
  health maintenance organizations,
    296, 297
  hospital indemnity policies and, 289
  individual, 287
  internal limits vs. aggregate limits in, 294
  long-term care insurance and,
    289–292
  Medicaid, 300
  Medicare, 298–301
  Patient Protection and Affordable
    Care Act and, 300–305
  policy provisions, 291
  preferred provider organizations,
    296–297
  private, 295–298
  reimbursement vs. indemnity plans
    and, 293
  trade-offs in, 293–294
  vision care and, 289
Health Insurance Portability and
  Accountability Act of 1996
  (HIPAA), 285, 286
Health maintenance organizations
  (HMOs), 296, 297
Health reimbursement accounts (HRAs),
  298, 299
Health savings accounts (HSAs), 95,
  297–299
HH savings bonds, 119
Hidden inflation, 7
Highballing, 200
Higher education. *See* Education;
  Education financing
High-yield bond funds, 368, 432
Holographic wills, 475
Home equity conversion mortgages, 233
Home equity loans, 233
Home health care agencies, 297
Home inspections, 227, 228
Homeownership, taxes and, 95
Homeowner's insurance. *See also*
    Insurance
  choosing coverage amount for, 262
  cost factors of, 263–264
  coverage provided by, 255–257
  damage coverage in, 261
  discounts on, 263
  earthquakes and, 258
  floods and, 257–258, 261
  personal liability coverage in, 257
  personal property coverage in, 255–257
  selecting companies for, 263–264
  specialized coverage and, 257–258
  types of policies for, 259–260

Home purchases. *See also* Housing
  affordability of, 226
  down payments for, 229
  final steps in transactions for, 234–236
  financing for, 229–234 (*See also*
    Mortgages)
  location decisions for, 226–227
  price negotiation for, 227–228
  renting vs., 219, 221
Home sales
  home preparation for, 236–237
  by owner, 238
  by real estate agent, 238
  selling price determination for,
    237–238
Hospital expense insurance, 288
Hospital indemnity insurance, 289
Household inventory, 256, 257
Housing. *See also* Home purchases;
    Home sales
  lifestyle and, 219
  renting vs. buying decisions for,
    219–224
  retirement and, 462, 463
  types of, 225–226
H.R.10 (Keogh) plans. *See* Keogh plans
Hybrid cars, 197

I

I bonds, 119
Identity theft
  actions for suspected, 166–169
  explanation of, 129
Immediate annuities, 336
Implied warranties, 192, 236
Impulse buying, 189
Income. *See also* Retirement income
  adjusted gross, 78
  on budgets, 55, 58
  on cash flow statement, 53
  discretionary, 53
  earned, 78
  gross, 53
  investment, 78, 358
  from mutual fund dividends, 443–444
  passive, 78
  from stock dividends, 389–390
  taxable, 78–80
  tax-deferred, 78
  tax-equivalent, 95–96
  tax-exempt, 78
Income-based repayment (IBR) plans, 497
Income-contingent repayment plans, 497
Income-sensitive repayment plans, 497
Income stocks, 393
Incontestability clause, 329–330
Indemnity policies, 293
Index annuities, 337
Indexed CDs, 117
Index funds, 431, 436–437

Individual checking accounts, 127
Individual retirement accounts (IRAs),
  468–469, 471
Inflation
  cost of credit and, 164–165
  explanation of, 6
  financial planning and, 6–7
  hidden, 7
  retirement planning and, 464
  savings plans and, 120
Inflation risk, 356
Inheritance taxes, 479
Initial public offering (IPO), 403
Insolvency, 51
Insurable risk, 250
Insurance. *See also specific types of*
    insurance
  disability income, 305–307
  earthquake, 257, 258
  explanation of, 249–250
  flood, 257–258
  health, 285–305
  homeowner's, 255–264
  life, 321–340
  methods to lower cost of, 265
  motor vehicle, 264–271
  personal property, 255–256
  planning for, 251–253
  premiums for, 249, 250, 269–270, 285
  property and liability, 254–255
  renter's, 224, 258–259
  risk management methods and,
    250–252
  risk types and, 250, 252
  setting goals for, 251–252
  title, 234
  umbrella policies, 257
Insurance companies
  comparing rates offered by, 269–270
  explanation of, 249–250
  health insurance, 295
  life, 113, 148, 325–326, 332
  use of credit information by, 270
Insurance policies, 150, 249
Insured, 250
Insurers, 249, 250
Interest
  add-on, 164
  calculation of, 11–13
  deductible, 79
  simple, 163–164
  on U.S. Treasury securities, 365, 366
Interest-adjusted indexes, 334
Interest-earning checking accounts, 118,
  126, 127
Interest-only mortgages, 233
Interest rate risk, 356–357
Interest rates
  annual percentage rate, 161, 162, 164
  basics of, 11–13, 32–33
  on bonds, 365–366, 369

disclosure requirements related to, 157
financial planning and, 7
financial service decisions and, 111
lender risk vs., 162–163
mortgages and, 230–231
risk-based pricing and, 157
variable, 163
Intermediate corporate bond funds, 432
Intermediate financial goals, 9
Internal Revenue Service (IRS), 517
audits by, 93–94
estates and trust filings with, 479
Form 1099 DIV, 445
taxpayer assistance by, 91–92
International funds, 431
Internet
bond research on, 371–372
consumer purchasing on, 190, 191
mutual fund research on, 437, 438
protecting credit information on, 167, 169
stock research on, 392–394
Internet Crime Complaint Center, 516
Interviews
informational, 503
job, 509–511
Intestate, 474
Invesco Dividend Income Fund, 424, 425
Investment assets, on balance sheet, 50
Investment banks, 403
Investment decisions
numerical measures that influence, 398–401
stock, 392–401
Investment income, 78
Investment programs
getting money needed to start, 352–353
goals for, 349–350
performing financial checkup for, 350–352
seeking professional help for, 363
time value of money and, 353–355
your role in, 361–363
Investment risk
age factor and, 361
asset allocation and, 359–360
time factor and, 360–361
Investments. *See also specific types of investments*
age and, 361
asset allocation and, 359–360
in bonds, 364–374
for current income, 8
evaluating potential, 361
fear of, 262
growth of, 358
income from, 78, 358
keeping records of your, 363
liquidity of, 358
monitoring your, 362–363

in mutual funds (*See* Mutual funds)
reasons for, 8
risk factors in, 356–358
safety and risk of, 355–356
as source of income, 358
tax considerations related to, 95–97
tax-exempt, 95–96
time factor and, 360–361
Invoice price, 199
Iraq and Afghanistan Service Grant, 494
IRAs. *See* Individual retirement accounts (IRAs)
Irrevocable trusts, 478
Itemized deductions, 78–80

J

Job advertisements, 503
Job creation, 504
Job interviews, 509–511
Job-related expenses, 80, 95
Joint checking accounts, 127

K

Kelley Blue Book, 199
Keogh plans, 97, 471
Kiplinger's Personal Finance, 397, 441

L

Labeling, 190
Large-cap funds, 432
Large-cap stocks, 393
Leases, 222–223
Leasing, motor vehicle, 197–199
Legal aid society, 206
Legal documents, 473–474
Legal issues
for consumer credit, 155, 157, 160, 169–171
for consumer purchase complaints, 205–207
for motor vehicle insurance, 268
for rental properties, 222–223
for trusts, 477–478
for wills, 474–477
Levison, Clare K., 351
Liabilities
on balance sheet, 50
explanation of, 50, 254
Liability insurance, 254–255
Liability risks, 250
Lifecycle funds, 433
Life expectancy, 322
Life income option, 335
Life insurance. *See also* Annuities
comparison of types of, 328
credit, 329
determining need for, 322–323
endowment, 329

estimating your requirements for, 323–325
explanation of, 321
group, 328
guidelines to purchase, 332–335
life expectancy and, 322
policy provisions for, 329–331
purpose of, 321–322
retirement planning and, 462
riders to, 330–331
settlement options for, 334–335
switching, 335
term, 326–327
types of companies that sell, 325–326
whole life, 327–328
Life insurance agents, 332, 333
Life insurance companies, 113, 148, 325–326, 332
Limited installment payment option, 335
Limited payment policies, 327
Limited warranties, 191–192
Limit orders, stock, 406
Line of credit, home equity, 233
Lipper Analytical Services, 438
Liquid assets, 49
Liquid CDs, 117
Liquidity
investment, 358
savings plans and, 121
Liquidity ratio, 51
Living benefits, 331
Living trusts, 478, 479
Living wills, 476–477
Loan funds, 427–428
Loans. *See also* Mortgages
affordability of, 151
applying for, 151–157
cash advances as, 149, 150
cosigning, 169
cost of, 160–166
denial of, 157–160
expensive, 149
function of, 148
home equity, 149–150, 233
inexpensive, 149
length of term of, 162
management of, 171–176
medium-priced, 149
motor vehicle, 200–201
preapproval for, 200
problematic sources of, 113–114
secured, 163
student, 495–499
subsidized, 495
unsubsidized, 495
Location
homeowner's insurance costs and, 263
purchasing decisions based on, 189–190
Long-term capital gains, 96

Long-term care insurance (LTC)
  checklist for, 292
  explanation of, 289, 291
  method to deal with, 290
Long-term corporate bond funds, 432
Long-term financial goals, 9
Long-term government bond funds, 432
Long-term liabilities, 50
Lowballing, 200
Lump-sum payment option, 335

M

Major medical expense insurance,
  288–289
Managed funds, 436–437
Management fees, mutual fund, 428–430
Manufactured homes, 226
Margin, 409–410
Marginal tax rate, 81
Market orders, stock, 406
Market risk, 357–358
Maturity date, 367, 370
Mediation, for consumer purchasing
  issues, 205
Medicaid, 300
Medical/dental expenses, 78–79
Medical expense insurance, 285. *See
  also* Health insurance
Medical payments coverage, 257–258
Medicare, 298–301
Medigap (MedSup) insurance, 299
MedlinePlus, 304
Mental budgets, 59
Mergent, Inc., 372, 394
Micro cap stocks, 393
Midcap funds, 432
Midcap stocks, 393
Minimum monthly payment, 165
Misstatement of age provision, 330
Mobile commerce, 147
Mobile homes, 226, 259
Mobile payments, 125
Money
  managing daily needs for, 107
  tips for stretching your, 61
Money factor, 198
Money magazine, 397, 441
Money management
  budgeting and, 54–59 (*See also* Budgets)
  components of, 45–46
  explanation of, 45
  financial goal achievement and, 60, 62
  financial ratios and, 51
  personal financial statements and, 48–54
  recordkeeping for, 46–47
  savings techniques for, 62
  SWOT analysis and, 58
Money market accounts, 118
Money market funds, 113, 433
Money orders, 127

Moody's Investor Service, 372
Morningstar Inc., 437–439
Mortgage bonds, 368
Mortgage companies, 113
Mortgages
  adjustable-rate, 232–233
  applying for, 229
  buy-downs and, 233
  down payments for, 229
  explanation of, 229
  factors in obtaining, 229–230
  fixed-rate, fixed-payment, 231–232
  government-guaranteed, 232
  interest-only, 233
  interest rates and, 230–231
  legal protections related to, 157
  qualifying for, 229, 230
  refinancing, 234
  reverse, 233
  second, 233
  subprime, 229
  types of, 231–233
Motor vehicle insurance. *See also*
  Insurance
  bodily injury coverage in, 264–266
  comprehensive physical damage
    coverage in, 266–267
  cost of, 268–271
  financial responsibility laws and, 264
  medical payments coverage in,
    265–266
  no-fault, 267
  property damage coverage and,
    266–268
  rental reimbursement coverage in, 267
  towing/emergency road service
    coverage in, 267
  uninsured motorist protection
  in, 266
Motor vehicles
  buying vs. leasing, 197–199
  certified pre-owned, 197
  evaluation of alternatives for, 194,
    196–198
  hybrid, 197
  loans for, 200–201
  maintenance costs for, 201, 202
  new vs. used, 196–197
  operating costs for, 201
  postpurchase activities for, 201–202
  preshopping activities for, 195–196
  price negotiation for, 198–201
  repair fraud for, 202
  servicing sources for, 201–202
  warranties for, 192
Moving expenses, 80
MSN Money website, 399
Multiunit dwellings, 225
Multiyear level term insurance, 326
Municipal bond funds, 432
Municipal bonds, 366

Mutual fund investment decisions
  financial publications and newspapers
    for, 441–442
  Internet research for, 437, 438
  managed funds vs. index funds and,
    436–437
  overview of, 435
  professional advisory services for,
    438–440
  prospectus and annual reports for, 440
  for retirement accounts, 433–435
Mutual funds
  asset allocation, 432
  balanced, 432
  bond funds, 432
  closed-end, 425
  exchange-traded, 426
  explanation of, 423
  family of funds, 433
  fees associated with, 428–430
  fund of funds, 433
  lifecycle, 433
  load vs. no-load, 427–428
  money market, 433
  open-end, 426–427
  overview of, 423–424
  psychology of investing in, 424
  purchase options for, 445–446
  return on investment of, 443–444
  stock funds, 431–432
  tax considerations for, 444–445
  transaction mechanics for, 442–447
  withdrawal options for, 447
Mutual savings banks, 113

N

Nasdaq, 404
Nasdaq Composite Index, 436
National Association of Attorneys
  General, 517
National-brand products, 190
National Credit Union Administration
  (NCUA), 122, 515
National Flood Insurance Program,
  257–258, 516
National Guard, 499
National Highway Traffic Safety
  Administration, 515
National Insurance Consumer Helpline
  (NICH), 331
Negative amortization, 233, 495
Negative equity, 200
Negligence, 250
Net asset value (NAV), 426
Net cash flow, 53–54
Net pay, 53
Net worth, 50–51
Newspapers, as financial information
  source, 397
NIH Health Information Page, 304–305

No-fault insurance, 267
No-load funds, 427–428, 445
Non-deposit institutions, 108, 113
Nonforfeiture clause, 330
Nonparticipating (nonpar) policies, 325, 326

O

Occupational Outlook Handbook, 503
Office audits, 94
Online bill payments, 124–125
Online brokerage firms, 404–405
Online payments, 124–125
Open dating, 190
Open-end credit, 144, 145, 164
Open-end funds, 426–427, 445–446
Opportunity costs. *See also* Time value of money
  explanation of, 10–11
  financial, 11–15
  personal, 11
Options, stock, 411
Orman, Suze, 361
Overdraft protection, 127
Over-the-counter (OTC) market, 403–404

P

Parent Loans (PLUS loans), 496, 497
Participating (par) policies, 325, 326
Partnership for Caring: America's Voice for the Dying, 476
Passive income, 78
Patient Protection and Affordable Care Act of 2010
  enrollment statistics and, 302–303
  explanation of, 285, 300
  provisions of, 300–302
  shared responsibility and, 303–304
Pawnshops, 114
Pay-as-you-earn repayment (PAYE), 497
Payday loan companies, 114
Payment caps, 233
Payment methods
  checking accounts, 125–128
  electronic, 124–125
  evaluation of, 126–127
  function of, 108
  miscellaneous, 127
Payment schedule, motor vehicle leasing, 198
Payroll deduction, 62
Peace Corps, 499
Peer-to-peer lending, 496
Peer-to-peer payments, 125
Pell Grant, 494
Penny stocks, 393
Pensions. *See* Retirement
Peril, 250
Periodic payment plans, 446

Perkins, Carl D., 495
Perkins Loans, 495–497
Personal catastrophe policies, 257
Personal finance dashboard, 23
Personal finances
  data sheet for, 28
  goal-setting for, 29
  recordkeeping for, 46, 47
Personal financial planning
  activities related to, 7–8
  adult life cycle and, 4
  advantages of, 4
  career choice and, 22
  for couples, 21
  economic factors for, 4, 6–7
  explanation of, 3
  information sources for, 18
  life situation and, 3–5
  opportunity costs and time value of money, 10–15
  process for, 15–18
  taxes in, 75–98
  values and, 4
Personal financial plans
  annuities in, 336
  creating and implementing, 19–20
  health insurance in, 285
  life insurance in, 321–322
  property and liability insurance in, 254–255
  review and revision of, 20, 22
  steps to create, 15–18
Personal financial statements
  balance sheet, 48–51
  case flow statement, 51–54
  function of, 48
Personal identification number (PIN), 124
Personal money management. *See* Personal financial planning
Personal possessions, on balance sheet, 50
Personal property coverage, in homeowner's insurance, 255–256
Personal property floater, 257
Personal risks, 250
Physical budgets, 59
Physician expense insurance, 288
PLUS loans, 496, 497
Point-of-service (POS) plans, 296–297
Points, mortgages and, 231
Police reports, 167
Policies, insurance, 249, 250
Policy dividends, 325
Policyholders, 249, 250
Policy loan provisions, 330
Portability, 466
Power of attorney, 477
Prefabricated homes, 226
Preferred provider organizations (PPOs), 296–297
Preferred stock, 391–392

Premiums, insurance, 249, 250, 269–270, 285
Prepaid debit cards, 110, 125
Prepaid legal services, 206
Present value
  to determine loan payments, 37
  explanation of, 11, 14
  of series of deposits, 15
  of series of equal payments, 36
  of single amount, 14, 35
Present value table, 12
Price comparison, in consumer purchases, 190
Price-earnings (PE) ratio, 398–399
Price negotiation
  for home purchases, 227–228
  for motor vehicles, 198–201
Price-to-rent ratio, 224
Pricing
  comparison, 190
  risk-based, 157
  unit, 190
Primary market, for stocks, 403
Private-label products, 190
Private student loans, 496
Probate, 475
Projected earnings, 399
Promotional CDs, 118
Property damage liability, 266–268
Property risks, 250
Property taxes, 76, 237
Prospectus, mutual fund, 440
Proxy, 388
Public assistance, 157
Public Health Service, 517
Public pension plans, 466–468
Public Service Loan Forgiveness Program, 499
Purchase agreements, home, 227
Purchases. *See* Consumer purchases
Pure risk, 250

R

Rate caps, 233
Rate of return
  after-tax savings, 122
  explanation of, 120
Ratios, financial, 51
Real estate, 50. *See also* Housing
Real estate agents, 227, 238
Real Estate Settlement Procedures Act (RESPA), 235
Record date, 389–390
Recordkeeping
  daily spending diary, 518–526
  investment, 363
  legal documents, 473–474
  money management, 46–47
  system for financial, 46, 47
  tax, 81

Refinancing, home, 234
Regional funds, 432
Registered bonds, 369
Registered coupon bonds, 369
Regular checking accounts, 125
Regular IRAs, 468, 469
Reimbursement policies, 293
Reinvestment plans, 446
Renewable term insurance, 326
Rental housing. *See also* Housing
    activities related to, 220
    advantages of, 221–222
    buying vs., 219–220, 224
    cost of, 223
    disadvantages of, 222
    leasing arrangements for, 222–223
    selection of, 221
Rental reimbursement coverage, 267
Renter's insurance, 224, 258–259
Rent-to-own centers, 114
Replacement cost, 262
Replacement value, 262
Research
    for consumer purchases, 192–193
    for motor vehicle purchases, 195–196
Residual value, 198
Restrictive endorsement, 128
Résumés
    cover letters for, 507, 508
    elements of, 504–505
    preparation of, 505–506
    submission of, 507
Retirement. *See also* Estate planning
    conducting a financial analysis for,
        460–462
    housing costs during, 462, 463
    living expenses during, 462–464
    myths about, 459–460
    saving for, 460
    working during, 472
Retirement income
    allocation of, 463
    annuities for, 471
    employer pension plans for, 464–466
    individual retirement accounts for,
        468–469, 471
    living on your, 471–472
    part-time employment as, 472
    public pension plans for, 466–468
    use of savings as, 472
Retirement plans
    403(b) plans, 465
    defined-benefit, 465
    defined-contribution, 465
    individual, 468–469, 471
    Keogh plans as, 97, 471
    401(k) plans as, 97–98, 465, 470
    mutual funds selection for, 433–435
    Roth IRAs as, 97, 468, 469
    Social Security, 466–467
    traditional IRAs as, 97

Return-of-premium term insurance, 327
Return on investment, mutual fund,
    443–444
Revenue bonds, 366
Reverse mortgages, 233
Revocable trusts, 478
Riders, to life insurance policies,
    330–331
Rising-rate CDs, 115
Risk
    avoidance of, 250–251
    business failure, 357
    evaluation of, 18
    explanation of, 250
    inflation, 356
    insurable, 250
    interest rate, 356–357
    investment, 355–356, 359–363
    lender, 162–163
    liability, 250
    management of, 8, 250–252
    market, 357–358
    personal, 250
    reduction of, 251
    shifting of, 251
    speculative, 250
Risk-based pricing, disclosure issues
        related to, 157
The Road to Wealth (Orman), 361
Rollover IRAs, 468–469
Roth IRAs, 97, 468, 469
Roth 401(k), 470

S

Safe deposit boxes, 46, 47
Safety. *See* Risk
Salary-reduction plans. *See* 401(k) plans
Sales taxes, 75–76
Savers credit, 83
Saving
    budgeting for, 55
    calculating amounts for, 62
    function of, 108
    methods for, 116
    for retirement, 460
    selecting technique for, 62
Savings and loan associations (S&Ls),
    113, 148
Savings bonds, United States, 118–119
Savings plans
    certificates of deposit, 115, 117–118
    comparison of, 124–128
    deposit insurance and, 122–123
    evaluation of, 120–123
    interest-earning checking accounts, 118
    money market accounts/funds, 118
    online and mobile, 109–110
    rate of return on, 120, 122
    restrictions and fees for, 123
    U.S. savings bonds, 118–119

Savings ratio, 51
Scholarships, 493–494
Secondary market, for stocks, 403–404
Second mortgages, 233
Second-to-die life insurance, 331
Sector funds, 432
Secured loans, 163
Securities and Exchange Commission
        (SEC), 516
Securities exchange, 403
Security deposits, 223
Self-employment taxes, 96
Self-insurance, 251
Selling short, 410–412
Serial bonds, 368–369
Service contracts, 192
Set-price dealers, 199
Settlement costs, 234
Short-term capital gains, 96
Short-term corporate bond funds, 432
Short-term financial goals, 9
Short-term government bond funds, 432
Simple interest, 163–164
Simple interest formula, 163–164
Simple wills, 475
Simplified employee pension (SEP)
        plans, 468, 469
Single-family dwellings, 225
Sinking fund, 368
Situational interviewing, 510–511
Skimming, 167
Small-cap funds, 432
Small-cap stocks, 393
Small claims court, 205–207
SMART approach, 9, 54
Smart cards, 125, 147
Smartphones, 147
Social lending, 496
Socially responsible funds, 432
Social Security Administration,
        467, 517
Social Security benefits, 306, 466–467
Special endorsement, 128
Specialists, stock, 403
Speculative investments, 355
Speculative risk, 250
Speculators, 407
Spending
    keeping track of, 61
    review of, 58–59
Spending diary, 518–526
Spending plans. *See* Budgets
Spousal IRAs, 468, 469
Sprauve, Anthony, 155
Stafford, Robert, 495
Stafford Loans, 495, 497
Standard deduction, 78–80
Standard & Poor's Corporation, 372, 394
Standard & Poor's 500 stock index, 387,
        401, 436
Standard repayment plans, 497

Stated amount wills, 475
State taxes
    on estates, 478–479
    method to file, 88
Statutory wills, 475
Sticker price, 199
Stock advisory services, 394–395, 397
Stock funds, 431–432
Stockholders, voting rights of, 388
Stock investment decisions
    corporate earnings and, 398–399
    dividend yield and total return and,
        400–401
    informational websites for,
        393–394, 399
    information sources for, 392–397
    long-term strategies for, 407–409
    short-term strategies for, 409–411
Stock investment strategies
    buy-and-hold, 407
    buying on margin, 409–410
    direct investment and dividend
        reinvestment plans, 408–409
    dollar cost averaging, 408
    selling short, 410–411
    trading in options, 411
Stock life insurance companies,
        325–326
Stock market bubble, 402
Stocks
    common, 388–391
    factors influencing price of, 398–402
    initial public offering of, 403
    investment in, 387–388
    over-the-counter market for,
        403–404
    preferred, 391–392
    primary market for, 403
    psychology of investing in, 388–389
    rationale for investment in, 388–391
    secondary market for, 403–404
Stock splits, 390–391
Stock transactions
    brokerage firms for, 404
    commission charges for, 406, 407
    computerized, 405
    full-service, discount or online
        brokerage firms for, 404–405
    secondary markets for, 403–404
    types of, 405–406
Stop-loss orders, 306
Stop-loss provisions, 289
Stop-payment orders, 128
Store-brand products, 190
Stored-value cards, 125, 147
Straight life policies. *See* Whole life
    insurance
Student loans
    cancellation of, 499
    categories of, 495–496
    consolidation, 498

default rate on, 498
deferment of, 499
explanation of, 495
forgiveness of, 499
repayment of, 497
Sublets, 223
Subprime crisis, 229
Subsidized loans, 495
Suicide clause, 330
Summary plan description (SPD), 286
Surplus, 53, 57
Surrender charges, 337, 338
Survivorship life insurance, 331
SWOT analysis, 58

T

T. Rowe Price Value Fund, 437, 438
Take-home pay, 53
Target-date funds, 433
Targeted application letters, 507
Taxable equivalent yield, 366–367
Taxable income, 78–80
Tax audits, 93–94
Tax code, changes in, 98
Tax credits, 82, 83, 87
Tax deductions, 78–80, 82
Tax-deferred income, 78
Tax-equivalent income, 95–96
Taxes. *See also* Federal income taxes
    annuities and, 338, 340
    calculation of, 82–83
    consumer purchases and, 95
    deadlines and penalties for, 84
    deductible, 79
    on earnings, 76
    estate, 478–479
    flat, 98
    gift, 479
    inheritance, 479
    investment decisions and, 95–97
    making payments on, 83–84
    mutual funds and, 444–445
    planning strategies for, 95–98
    property, 76, 237
    recordkeeping for, 81
    retirement and education plans and,
        97–98
    sales, 75–76
    savings plans and, 121
    state and local, 79
    value-added, 98
    on wealth, 76
    when traveling, 77
Tax-exempt income, 78
Tax-planner calendar, 91
Tax preparation services, 92–93
Tax preparation software, 89
Tax rate, 81
Tax shelters, 78
TD Ameritrade, 446

Teacher Education Assistance for
    College and Higher Education
    (TEACH) Grant, 494
Temporary life insurance. *See* Term life
    insurance
Term life insurance, 326–327. *See also*
    Life insurance
Testamentary trusts, 478
Theft. *See* Identity theft
Theft losses, 79
Time value of money
    explanation of, 11
    future value and, 11
    future value of series of deposits and,
        13–14
    future value of series of equal
        amounts, 34–35
    future value of single amount and,
        13, 33–34
    insurance cost and, 335
    interest rates and, 11–13, 32–33
    investments and, 353–355
    methods to calculate, 11–14, 39
    present value and, 11
    present value of series of deposits
        and, 15
    present value of series of equal
        payments and, 36
    present value of single amount and,
        14, 35
    present value to determine loan
        payments and, 37
    replacement cost and, 262
    retirement savings and, 461
Time value of money table, 12
Title insurance, 234
Towing/emergency road service
    coverage, 267
Townhouses, 225
Trade-offs. *See* Opportunity costs
Traders, stock, 407
Traditional IRAs, 97
Traditional marital share wills, 475
Travel and entertainment (T&E)
    cards, 147
Traveler's checks, 127
Traveling, taxes and, 77
Treasury bills, 365, 366
Treasury bonds, 365, 366
Treasury Inflation-Protected Securities
    (TIPS), 365, 366
Treasury notes, 365, 366
Trustees, 367, 475, 477
Trustors, 477
Trusts
    explanation of, 109, 475
    reasons for, 477
    types of, 478
Truth in Lending Act, 164, 169
Turnover ratio, 445
12b-1 fees, 428–429

U

Umbrella policies, 257
Underwriting, 270
Uninsured motorist protection, 266
Unit pricing, 190
Universal life insurance, 328
Unsubsidized loans, 495
Upside-down equity, 200
U.S. Department of Agriculture, 515
U.S. Department of Education, 495
U.S. Department of Housing and Urban
    Development (HUD), 516
U.S. Department of Justice, 516
U.S. Department of Labor, 515
U.S. savings bonds, 118–119
U.S. Treasury securities, 365
Used motor vehicles. *See also* Motor
    vehicles
    comparison of, 196–197
    price negotiation for, 199
    warranties for, 192

V

Value-added tax (VAT), 98
Value Line, 394, 438
Value Line Investment Survey, 394, 395
Values, 4

Vanguard Mid-Cap Growth Fund, 431
VantageScore, 156
Variable annuities, 336, 337, 339
Variable expenses, 53
Variable interest rates, 163
Variable life policies, 327–328
Variable-rate mortgages, 232–233
Vesting, 465
Veterans Administration (VA), 232, 468
Vision care insurance, 289
Volunteer work, 503

W

Wage loss insurance, 267
Waiver of premium disability benefit,
    330
Walk-throughs, 234
The Wall Street Journal, 110, 397, 441
Warranties
    explanation of, 191–192
    implied, 192, 236
Warranty deeds, 234–235
Warranty of merchantability, 192
Warranty of title, 192
Websites
    for bond information, 372
    for financial aid information, 493
    for government agencies, 514–517

for health information, 304–305
    for stock information, 393–394, 399
Wellness programs, 286
Whole life insurance, 327–328
Wills
    aspects of writing, 475–476
    explanation of, 474
    formats of, 475
    living, 476–477
    probate and, 475
    types of, 474–475
Wilshire 5000 Total Market, 436
Witholding, tax, 84–85
Workers' compensation, 306
Work-study programs, 499–500
World bond funds, 432
Written budgets, 59

Y

Yahoo! Finance, 393–394, 437
Yield
    annual percentage, 120, 121
    bond, 370

Z

Zero-coupon CDs, 117
Zoning laws, 226–227